The Topography of Violence in the Greco-Roman World

The Topography of Violence in the Greco-Roman World

Werner Riess and Garrett G. Fagan, editors

University of Michigan Press
Ann Arbor

First paperback edition 2020

Published in the United States of America by the
University of Michigan Press
Manufactured in the United States of America
♾ Printed on acid-free paper

First published in paperback July 2020

A CIP catalog record for this book is available from the British Library.

Library of Congress Cataloging-in-Publication Data

Names: Riess, Werner, editor. | Fagan, Garrett G., 1963– editor.
Title: The topography of violence in the Greco-Roman world / Werner Riess and Garrett G. Fagan, editors.
Description: Ann Arbor : University of Michigan Press, 2016. | Includes bibliographical references and index.
Identifiers: LCCN 2016009981| ISBN 9780472119820 (hardback) | ISBN 9780472121830 (e-book)
Subjects: LCSH: Violence—Greece—History—To 1500. | Violence—Rome. | Civilization, Greco-Roman. | BISAC: HISTORY / Ancient / Rome. | HISTORY /
Ancient / Greece.
Classification: LCC HN10.G7 T67 2016 | DDC 306.0938—dc23
LC record available at http://lccn.loc.gov/2016009981

ISBN: 978-0-472-03844-2 (pbk. : alk. paper)

Contents

Introduction

Werner Riess

Academic research on violence has been burgeoning in recent years. Violence is an intrinsic part of every human society and is always culturally defined. But the highly heterogeneous forms of violence make the phenomenon elusive and hard to define. Despite sociologists' intensive research, they have not yet established a "sociology of violence." Since various disciplines in the humanities and natural sciences are preoccupied with the phenomenon, there is a multitude of divergent definitions of "violence." As a result, studies of violence, even within one area, are so diverse that we are far from a coherent picture of what violence signifies in specific cultural contexts.

One remedy to this situation might be sought in probing more deeply into the category of space. Historical studies have been overemphasizing time as a heuristic category for too long, if we think of the French school of the *Annales* and its focus on the *longue durée* of historical developments. But history unfolds not only in time but also in space, in specific places. In recent decades, cultural studies have been turning increasingly to the category of space, so that we have learned to speak of a spatial, a topographical, or even a topological turn.[1] The term *spatial turn* has prevailed in historical studies.[2] Especially in the study of historical *lieux de mémoire*, "spaces of remembrance," the term has been fruitfully applied. Important representatives of this trend are the studies of Aleida and Jan Assmann on the Holocaust and Ancient Egypt, respectively, and Karl Galinsky's study on Augustus.[3]

---

1. On terminology, cf. Döring and Thielmann 2009: 13.

2. Wagner (2010: 100) observes that the term *spatial turn* is used in historical and social studies, whereas *topographical turn* is frequently applied in literary, cultural, and media studies.

3. A. Assmann 2009, 2012; J. Assmann 2007; Galinsky 1996.

The notion of "spatial turn" comprises at least two basic approaches with different sets of questions.

On the one hand, space itself can be regarded as the object of study. The guiding questions in this regard are how spaces are architecturally shaped, marked, defined, and staged. Galinsky's work on the Forum of Augustus, for example, is situated within this domain. Spaces are understood as *lieux de mémoire* and researched accordingly.[4]

On the other hand, space can be conceived as a nonphysical, symbolic category, where, for example, gender-specific relations of power are observable.[5] The chapters of this volume are situated within this second domain. To define it more precisely, one has to take into account the close relationship between the history of the body and the history of social practices, a research field that Pierre Bourdieu has established in the second half of the past century.[6]

A space consists of material and symbolic components. Only human beings and, therefore, human societies construct the symbolic meaning of space, through bodies moving across a certain space and acting within it.[7] Thus, the history of the body (and its social practices) and the history of space condition each other. Only a somatic component turns an unspecified place into a specific space, which is characterized by a certain quality. As a consequence, bodies and societies construe spaces. Bourdieu and Henri Lefebvre speak of "social space," and the characteristics of a social space hinge on the rank of the human beings who move within this space, their sex and gender, their age, their hierarchical relationships, and, especially, what they do in these spaces—that is, the kind of social practice in which they engage.[8] It is especially this social practice that can be observed from outside; that is, the performative aspect of human behavior constructs space in the final analysis. Social practice, as a result, charges a place with a symbolic meaning and turns it into a space with significance. A building turns into a prison only if guards detain human beings there. The Agora in Athens is not the Agora until human beings gather there again and again for certain purposes and shape that area with architecture so that it meets these purposes well. Thus, we can say that space is a societal construction, which consists of the

4. Bachmann-Medick 2006: 313.

5. Piltz 2009: 79, 96.

6. Bourdieu 1972.

7. Löw 2001: 67; cf. also Levebvre 1991, for a Marxist perspective.

8. Bourdieu 1995. On the societal production of space, cf. Belina and Michel 2007; on "social space," Kessl et al. 2005.

relational position of human beings and social goods toward each other.[9] At the same time, this understanding of space is dynamic, a concept in constant action and flux, in contrast to an immobile and static place.[10]

Against this backdrop, we should wonder how violent actions affect a certain place, how they affect its nature, and to what purposes perpetrators of violence reshape, reuse, and abuse a space. According to Bourdieu's hierarchical theory of social space, the social relations of the actors within a certain space make for its characteristics. Whoever dominates another person or exerts violence against him or her is often physically and maybe also socially and economically superior and, thus, constructs the victim as weaker and inferior. It is in line with the material from the ancient world that, according to Bourdieu, space is to be understood as a field of forces, a "combat zone" in which the vying for power and keeping it take place.[11]

In this sociospatial thinking, there is a duplex social reality: an objective-hierarchical one and a personal-subjective one.[12] In the case of Athens, both components are clear. When metics kill the Athenian citizen Phrynichus in the Agora, they challenge an objective hierarchy and construct a new one from their personal-subjective perspective: although the metics are socially and politically inferior to the oligarch Phrynichus, they demonstrate that they are physically and, most of all (in their view), morally superior. Maybe more interesting, but difficult for us to grasp, is the personal-subjective aspect of actions by persons who were not direct agents: how did people who were not involved in the assassination view the Agora after Phrynichus had been slain there? How did the Athenians perceive the Acropolis, where Cylon's adherents had been murdered? More generally, how do the qualities of spaces change in the perception of contemporaries after escalations of violence? Modern equivalents are, for example, Tiananmen Square in Beijing after 1989 or Ground Zero in New York after September 11, 2001. It is for the following generations that these spaces become *lieux de mémoire*, where networks of experiences and histories from different periods crystallize. Broaching this topic brings us into the middle of the research agenda on cultures of remembrance, as previously mentioned, which is beyond the scope of this volume.

9. Werlen 2009; Bachmann-Medick 2006: 285; Löw 2001: 131, 212.

10. Schroer 2009: 142–43; Thrift 2009: 397–98; Löw 2001: 15, 273.

11. Cf. the focus of Foucault ([1967] 2002) on power relations and his theory of heterotopies, that is, spaces of crisis, deviation, and illusion. On Bourdieu's field of forces, cf. Schultheis 2004: 15.

12. Schultheis 2004: 24.

The goals of this book are more confined: this collection of essays seeks to explore some of the topographical and circumstantial aspects that helped define violence in antiquity. By addressing the (topographical) context of violence, the contributors focus on how Greeks and Romans charged violent acts with specific meanings on the basis of situation and space. The contributors' overarching thesis is that the manifold situational framings in which violence occurred crucially shaped ancient perceptions of it. Thus, topography is understood by us in a broad sense: not only the spatial but also the social, ethnical, gendered, political, and religious dimensions of violence will be considered. The differentiation between inside and outside, summarized by the Romans in the term *domi militaeque*, also serves as a guiding post to come closer to the symbolism of spaces and violence committed there.

To elucidate differences between Greek and Roman culture, the principle of comparison figures prominently in this volume. Each contributor deals with a decisive aspect of violence in the Greco-Roman world, such as assassinations, the battlefield, violence against slaves and women, and violent *symposia/cenae*. At the same time, the striving for symmetry and balance in the book will not gloss over crucial differences, that is, phenomena that are unique to one culture but not to the other, such as hubris on the Greek side or gladiators on the Roman.

Although the contributors come from diverse backgrounds in classical studies and different scholarly traditions and employ different methodologies, all contributions are firmly grounded in the relevant sources. No overarching theoretical model presses the complex evidence and highly diverse situations across time and cultures into one-size-fits-all categories. Rather, a coherent whole forms through the common endeavor to discern, more precisely than before, the circumstantial and topographical aspects of acts of violence in their specific historical and cultural contexts.

In this volume, the contributions are organized under Greek or Roman culture, respectively. To demonstrate their interconnectedness, however, the following synopsis juxtaposes those articles that thematically belong together. Thus, it will become clear why some aspects are treated in addition to the symmetric pairs—that is, in order to address cultural specifics in the Greek world as well as the Roman.

With his contribution, "Xenophon and the Muleteer: Hubris, Retaliation, and the Purposes of Shame," David D. Phillips sets the tone of the volume by shedding new light on a cultural specific of the Greek world, hubris. Whereas previous research on hubris has focused to a large extent on whether hubris, understood as the infliction of shame, requires a victim or arrogant attitude, Phillips widens the discussion by distinguishing between constructive and destructive shame. Only the latter constitutes hubris. The infliction of shame can be constructive indeed, if it has positive consequences for the aggrieved party or the community in the long run. This further refinement of an important concept of Greek law is a major advance in our understanding of hubris, insofar as it takes into consideration the vastly different circumstances under which violence was inflicted.

In "The Spartan *Krypteia*," Matthew Trundle treats a phenomenon that, like hubris, is culturally specific and does not have a counterpart in the Roman world. Trundle discusses the contradictory ancient sources and differing opinions of modern scholars. Whereas Plato paints a benign picture of the *krypteia* by describing it as an educational program to generate physically fit warriors, Plutarch represents it as a harsh institution through which members of the Spartan elites brutally suppressed the helots. How can these versions be reconciled? Trundle discusses the possible evolutions and functions of the *krypteia* and the different answers that have been formulated so far. According to the standard version, a tribal initiation rite of passage turned into a more standardized institution, with Spartan youths spreading terror among the helot population by hiding during the day and killing helots at night. This turning point is most commonly dated to the great helot revolt of the 460s BCE. Finally, the *krypteia* was integrated into the Spartan army. In the battle of Sellasia (222 BCE), we encounter it as a special military unit, responsible for reconnaissance. Some researchers, however, understand the *krypteia* very differently, contending that it originated in an innocuous rite of Sparta's educational program (the *agoge*) and only developed into a kind of guerilla warfare after the liberation of Messene (369 BCE). This version would explain Plato's mild image. For many reasons, Trundle adheres to the first view. The helot population outnumbered the Spartans many times over. The Spartans had to hold their serfs under tight control, but due to the lack of infrastructure and an administrative apparatus, Sparta's interventions could only be sporadic and random. To the Spartans, spreading terror seemed the ideal means to achieve this goal.

Whereas Trundle is concerned with the violence that Spartan youths perpetrated in secret, Werner Riess deals with violence in the Athenian public space. In "Where to Kill in Classical Athens: Assassinations, Executions, and the Athenian Public Space," he focuses on lethal violence in the city of Athens, including executions. In doing so, he makes an important observation: almost all public murders have considerable political significance; they are assassinations, whereas most privately committed homicides do not carry any political weight. This observation suggests that Athenians often deliberately chose a public venue to kill an enemy if they intended to convey a special meaning to an audience, the Athenian citizenry. Space thus becomes a political category. The democratic belief in the negotiability of the meaning of any political event required the citizens to go public with everything political, even political murder.

The meaning of assassinations in the Roman world, however, treated by Josiah Osgood in "The Topography of Roman Assassination, 133 BCE–222 CE," is structured differently from the Greek counterpart. As in the Greek world, the spatial setting of a Roman assassination contributed to its significance as a kind of criminal execution, expiatory sacrifice, or tyrannicide. However, the killing of Tiberius Gracchus became emblematic of Rome's politics in the last century of the republic. Political assemblies became standard venues for deadly violence. Its frequency was such that assassinations became a legitimate tool in pursuing one's own political agenda and, thus, part of Rome's political culture. In choosing to kill Caesar away from the public limelight of the comitia and *contiones*, within the Curia Pompei, the plotters distanced themselves from many earlier assassinations. Caesar's murder in the Senate House was a highly symbolic action due to its location: Caesar died on the steps of a statue of Pompey, his greatest enemy, whose defeat and death he had brought about with utmost ruthlessness. At the same time, the Ides of March links republican-style assassinations to imperial ones, where only one person was to be struck down and where major uproar was to be avoided. The killing of an emperor required a strong justification. The different versions of Caligula's murder offer various motives for the deed: revenge on a tyrant, execution of a criminal, and sacrifice to appease the gods. Most assassinations of emperors occurred in the palace, the center of power at Rome. By killing Vitellius on the Scalae Gemoniae, Flavian soldiers and the Roman mob staged a kind of execution—the "just" punishment of a tyrant—thus claiming legitimacy for their deed. When Elagabalus was killed in the Praetorian Camp, the shift of power had become obvious. The Praetorians no longer felt the need to justify their murder. During the third century CE, it was the army that made and killed emperors.

But not only prominent individuals were killed in the Roman world. In "Urban Violence: Street, Forum, Bath, Circus, and Theater," Garrett G. Fagan examines instances of casual "daily" violence in the city of Rome's public spaces and to what extent the location lent specific meaning to violent acts. The streets of Rome and other urban centers were notoriously unsafe, especially at night. Drunken brawls, organized street fights, bars, and prostitution in the back alleys contributed to the ill fame of quarters where the "mob" lived. This kind of violence was perceived as habitual by the upper classes that shaped our sources. Similar to the streets, Roman baths were considered places charged with the potential for violence. Often, they were overcrowded, visitors got drunk, and young and ambitious males resorted to fisticuffs. Theater performances, especially pantomimes, also bred violence, which is more frequently attested for the early and high empire than violence in the circus. Although the details are unclear to us, intense rivalry among the actors seems to have spilled over into the audience, where organized fan groups were interacting with "their" actors and were exhorted by them to use violence against the rival team. More spectacular and large-scale violence is attested for late antique circus games in the east of the empire. The fan culture of the so-called circus factions was brutal and tied into sociopolitical conditions. Hooligans had always existed yet were not as organized during the high empire as in late antiquity. The most famous instance was the Nika Riot in Constantinople (532 CE), in the course of which political discontent found its vent in the wake of circus games and led to the death of thousands of people and nearly to the collapse of Justinian's reign. The political impact of violence in public places was mostly visible in the civic center of late republican and early imperial Rome, such as the Forum Romanum, which always evinced a complex moral landscape, attracting people from all walks of life and from all over the known world. Due to the architectural arrangement of temples, holy shrines, and buildings of political and public character (the Curia Iulia, the basilicae, the Capitolium, etc.), violence committed in this urban context almost always carried political weight. The shift of political violence away from the Forum to the imperial palace and the Praetorian Camp tracks the trajectory of political power from republic to empire.

In daily life, many women in both Greek and Roman culture became victims of violence. Whereas Roman authors graphically describe violence against women, violence disappears in front of our eyes in the Attic orators whom Rosanna Omitowoju subjects to careful scrutiny in "The Crime That Dare Not Speak Its Name: Violence against Women in the Athenian Courts." Not only was rape a "silent crime," not being talked about, but all stories about violence against women are ultimately stories about men. We see this most clearly in cases where the violence is termed as hubris, a concept inextricably linked to the male sphere. Raping a woman, for example, was shocking not because of the plight of the woman but because of the dishonor imputed to the man under whose tutelage the woman stood. Women were not even victims of violence in the sense that the listener or reader of an Attic speech would feel pity with her. Even the agency of being a victim was denied to women and was implicitly a male role. The glimpse of violence we see perpetrated on Neaira's body works to her detriment because it does not arouse sympathy but, on the contrary, stigmatizes her as a noncitizen, a worthless woman. In the way Athenians committed violence against their women and especially in how they talked about it, we can discern strategies of very unequal power relations between men and women.

In "Violence against Women in Ancient Rome: Ideology versus Reality," Serena S. Witzke delineates the gendered spaces of violence to which women in Roman culture were subject. In doing so, she makes an important distinction: citizen women inhabited different worlds from noncitizen slaves as well as free prostitutes of low social status. In the mythohistorical narratives of Livy, violence against citizen women was of public concern and served the ideological purpose of state formation. The description of violence in these narratives is largely unrealistic. During the late republic, the citizen woman was protected by the law, at least in theory. Most marriages were now *sine manu*; that is, the wife stayed under the protection of her natal family. Her punishment had to be decided in court and happened in public. Hidden violence against citizen women was strongly discouraged and, if a husband maltreated his wife, could have easily resulted in divorce. Noncitizen slaves and free prostitutes, however, found themselves in a radically different situation. Slaves, especially female ones, were constantly exposed to physical and sexual violence. Their masters and other slaves could abuse them sexually as they pleased. Whereas the slaves were totally subject to the whim of men in their surroundings, the free prostitutes were slightly better off. In theory, they could choose their customers and control the sexual relationships. In reality, however, they had to endure the constant threat of violence. The elegists' poems about *meretrices*, purchasable women, speak for themselves. A customer could always become violent and abusive behind closed doors, where the *meretrix* had to offer her services. This violence was very real and generally happened in private. Unlike the citizen women's homes, the domestic space of prostitutes was not protected by the law, with the result that these women did not have recourse to Roman courts.

At the lowest echelon of society, both Greek and Roman, stood the slaves. In "Violence against Slaves in Classical Greece," Peter Hunt explores three topographies of violence in the Greek system of slaveholding: the role of violence in the system of social control, its place in the wider world of Greek thinking and values (i.e., the ideological level), and the physical topography of where violence was meted out against slaves. When talking about slaves in classical Greece, we should bear in mind that we predominantly refer to the situation in Athens, from which most of our evidence hails. Blows, hunger, chaining, and especially whipping coerced slaves into submission. The psychological consequences for the slaves are hard to assess, but it seems logical to posit that the fear of whipping already intimidated many slaves. The punishment of slaves was all the more efficacious if it happened in public, if other slaves witnessed the violent treatment and could spread the news of what happened in a particular household in the neighborhood. That violence was often on display is also true for evidentiary torture, without which the testimony of a slave was invalid in court, and for *apotumpanismos*, a slow and extremely painful method of crucifixion to which slaves and poor citizens were subject even on grounds of trifling charges. The public and performative aspect of violence was part and parcel of the Athenian thinking about hierarchies and power relationships in their cosmos. The dichotomy of slaves and citizens worked in binaries and was mapped onto bodies. Whereas the slave body was vulnerable and, thus, subject to torture and *apotumpanismos*, the citizen body was inviolable and exempt from torture. Although citizens could be executed by *apotumpanismos*, honorable Athenians normally had to drink hemlock in prison and were thus spared the shame of dying in public. In the symbolic value system of the Athenians, slaves were considered domesticated animals and equated with horses, which could be maltreated with the whip. Whipping, branding, and tattooing left scars and visibly marked the victims as distinct from the free. Like in Roman law, the moment of capturing a free person in war and thus enslaving him or her defined the defeated person as a lesser, if not worthless, human being. In the process of purchasing a slave, this initial moment was upheld as a fiction. The master literally bought into the scheme that the sale process was equal to winning the slave in war as booty. From this perspective, it is comprehensible that the Greek ideal of self-control and restraint—core values especially from the fourth century BCE on—could only provide the slave with spotty protection against violence. Nonexcessive violence was always tolerated, and masters could delegate the execution of corporal punishment to officials of the city, thus maintaining their own image as moderate slave owners. Although masters likely killed their own slaves only rarely, there was no legal procedure available to indict them for murder if they did, a clear and frightening signal to the slave population. Female slaves suffered differently: they were exposed to the hits of their female owners, under whose supervision they often worked in the household, as well as to rape and sexual abuse. They also were subject to evidentiary torture. Set against the whole panorama of violence in ancient Greece, we can say with confidence that slaves had to endure more violence than most other social groups and that only male citizens inhabited an "island" of safety from violence, at least in times of peace.

Unlike in the Greek case, our sources on slavery in the Roman world are more abundant, geographically more widespread, and more reliable. In "Violence and the Roman Slave," Noel Lenski demonstrates that violence not only lay at the heart of the slave-master relationship but also encompassed the slave's whole existence. Lenski reveals two basic contradictions in the Roman system of slavery. First, violence was mainly used against slaves, who were denied agency, and yet, at the same time, slaves committed violence and were thus endowed with or took for themselves some agency. Slaves perpetrated violence on behalf of their masters as bodyguards, hit men, or gladiators, especially in times when the state was weak, as during the late republic or the late empire, and when the masters were engaged in political fights. The violence of slaves against their masters is also amply attested, most of all in the uprisings and slave wars from the 130s BCE onward. There is also abundant evidence for slave suicide, cases where desperate men and women resorted to this last "freedom" to prevent being caught and enslaved or to flee an unbearable situation forever. A second contradiction concerns the "personlessness" of the slave. On the one hand, Roman law ascribes to the slaves the legal status of things or tools. On the other hand, the Romans were well aware of the human nature of this kind of property. Cicero, Pliny, and Seneca the Younger emphasize this aspect in their writings. Lenski sketches the diachrony of slavery on the level of the individual slave as well as on the state level. Slavery has its ideological roots in the moment of capture, where the vanquished was at the mercy of the victor. The ensuing existence as slave perpetuated this complete exposure to the whim of the master. In maintaining slaves, violence was an acknowledged social practice, taken for granted by the Romans as well as by all preceding and subsequent slaveholding societies. Its functions were manifold—suppression, breaking the slave's will, intimidation by the threat of violence, and sexual abuse, to name just a few. Under the empire, the Roman state gradually tried to limit excessive violence against slaves, so the middle to late republic can be regarded as the epochs during which the slaves were worst off in Roman history. The advent of Christianity set a new tone. Far from abolishing slavery, though, Constantine forbade the crucifixion and the tattooing of slaves and their deliberate murder. The idea that slaves were humans gradually won acceptance.

Leaving the civilian sphere behind, the massive violence perpetrated and suffered in Greek and Roman warfare needs to be addressed. In "The Greek Battlefield: Classical Sparta and the Spectacle of Hoplite Warfare," Ellen Millender zooms in on Sparta and explores battlefields as focal points of Spartan virtues and values. Paradoxically, concentration on the battle itself allows us to comprehend hoplite warfare more broadly than before, in its social, cultural, mental, and, especially, performative contexts. Millender interprets the battlefield as a stage, where Spartan virtues were on display and where the Spartans enacted their social codes and ideology. This martial ideology was inculcated into the boys from early childhood, in an educational program, the ultimate goals of which were to endure extreme hardship in order to display self-discipline and to obey elders and commanders. Although physical prowess and military bravery were immensely competitive, the fostering of a communal spirit led to a "cooperative sociability" that ensured the unmatched coherence and organization of the Spartan phalanx. Since the whole education process transpired in public, in front of adult men and under their auspices, this specific kind of cooperative sociability was performed as a spectacle, open for all to see. What the youngsters had learned at home could finally be demonstrated by them on the battlefield, where the Spartans engaged in the competition of obedience and outdoing their comrades in the phalanx by, at the same time, putting on a spectacle of egalitarianism, cooperation, and solidarity. The battlefield thus became the spatial performance of Spartan values that the "onlookers," other Greeks and barbarians alike, could admire and fear. But not only foes had to endure what must have been the terrifying sight of Spartan hoplites marching into battle calmly and orderly, as if in a religious procession ready to sacrifice victims. The primary audience who had already been part of the training was the many non-Spartiate soldiers who fought along with the Spartiates—the *perioeci*, some helots, allies, and mercenaries. The impressive spectacle of cohesion and superiority sent a powerful and symbolic message to these groups: resistance against the Spartiates' dominance was futile and doomed to failure from the outset. So the success of Spartan hoplite warfare lay partly in its performative nature, from the boyhood *agoge*, to practicing the art of war with non-Spartiate groups, to finally driving this message brutally home to the enemy on the battlefield.

In "The Roman Battlefield: Individual Exploits in Warfare of the Roman Republic," Graeme Ward also emphasizes the performative aspect of battle, the importance of being seen. The circumstances were crucial to how individual exploits were assessed by eyewitnesses and the community at large.

In general, an audience was required to validate special deeds as heroic acts. Out of the Roman military oath, Ward extracts three conditions under which a soldier was permitted to leave his ranks and avoid opprobrium for having abandoned his post in the well-honed machinery of a Roman fighting unit. A soldier could do so honorably in order to retrieve a weapon or military standard, to strike at an enemy, or to save a comrade. Whereas the first reason was unproblematic, the other two were only legitimate under special caveats. A positive assessment of leaving one's line by rushing forward into the heat of battle to kill an enemy hinged on the permission of the commander, the benefit to the legion, and a positive effect on the spectators; that is, it lay in the visibility of the deed. Saving a comrade or avenging him was indeed an example of outstanding *amicitia* and *pietas*, as long as it was connected to killing an enemy at the same time and in the same place. The rarely attested *devotio*, the self-sacrifice of a commander by consecrating himself to assure victory for Rome, was the epitome of the ideology of saving one's comrade. The dramatic effect of self-sacrifice was meant to spur on the warriors to win the battle and, thus, glory for Rome. The necessity of an audience is enshrined in this pinnacle of Roman military ideology. To ensure the visibility that was crucial to lend legitimacy and fame to bloody deeds, witnesses were required.

In "War as Theater, from Tacitus to Dexippus," David Potter continues the aspect of performativity and explores the relationship between battle narratives and visual representations of martial violence as evinced in paintings, monuments, and drama. He does so by comparing the concept of the theatrical in Tacitus, Cassius Dio, Herodian, and Dexippus. To what extent these four authors used visual media as sources for the literary space they created helps us better understand their respective historiographies. Tacitus, master of the visual, offers suggestive descriptions, replete with pictorial elements that dramatize whole scenes. At the same time, Tacitus is highly suspicious of theatricality: he portrays the people watching spectacles, thus distancing his readers from public entertainment. He deconstructs the theatricality of the world and of his own narrative, just because he is aware of the power and importance of spectacles. The Greek-speaking historians Cassius Dio, Herodian, and Dexippus each show different treatments of the literary art of *dramatike*. Cassius Dio, being a senator, is fully conversant with classical rhetorical education. He employs all the stylistic devices he could borrow from the long tradition of rhetorical battle narratives. Herodian, also based in Rome, writes from the perspective of a lower-rank outsider. Dio and Herodian both experienced and saw the mechanisms of empire in the capital as performed in great spectacles. As a consequence, spectacular and theatrical elements also inform the rhetoric of their war narratives. Their goal is to make the distant understandable by using verbal theatricality. Dexippus is far removed from this Roman "imperial" style. A native of Athens, he writes in a decidedly Thucydidean style, avoiding visualization, although he had actually seen battle, in contrast to his two Greek-writing colleagues. Not influenced by Latin or imperial historiography, he is imbued with a common literary culture that he shared with his Athenian, provincial but educated audience.

A peculiarity of the Roman world without which this volume would not be complete is gladiatorial combat, the upshot of theatrical fighting. In "Manipulating Space at the Roman Arena," Garrett G. Fagan sheds new light on the old question of why Romans enjoyed the bloody fighting and watching the dying in the arena. Focusing on the theatrical and artificial packaging of arena violence—manifested, for instance, in the strange costumes and gear the gladiators wore and wielded, their use of stage names, the rules and regulations that governed their fights and were enforced by umpires, and, above all, the stage sets and props deployed to enhance the spectacle—Fagan argues that people can enjoy watching violence as long as it is carried out according to thoroughly defined rules and in orchestrated settings. The packaging of violent sights, then as now, is crucial to the enjoyment of their consumption by spectators.

Violence even occurred as a focal point of social dining practice, between men and women, citizens and slaves, and high- and low-ranking members of society. Greek and Roman dining ideology found its echo in literary and visual sources, along with representations of violence during Greek *symposia* and Roman *cenae*. In "Violence at the *Symposion*," Oswyn Murray chooses as his point of departure the general assumption that the *symposion* normally stands for joyful feasting. Yet violence committed in the context of *symposia* is a recurrent theme throughout Greek literature. By surveying a broad spectrum of sources (e.g., the Homeric epics, archaic poetry, tragedy, and historiography), Murray is able to trace the link between dining and violence back to archaic times. Already at the beginning of what we perceive to be Greek history, drinking and war were inextricably intertwined in the realm of archaic feasts. By drinking alcohol together, the elite warriors bonded to prepare for war and relax from war. The warrior feast thus framed violent actions. Greeks had long been aware that alcohol releases inhibitions and, therefore, that the consumption of alcohol had to be ritualized on various levels. At a certain point, the drunken revelers had to leave the *andron*, the men's dining room, to release their pent-up feelings and to demonstrate, to themselves and others, their belonging together, which they did through the so-called *komos*, the uncontrolled and ideally frolicsome marching around of drunken revelers. As long as things remained peaceful, everything was fine, but the situation quite frequently escalated into what the Greeks called hubristic behavior. It comes as no surprise that the profanation of the Mysteries and the mutilation of the herms in 415 BCE had their origins in oligarchic *symposia*. Many myths provided prototypes for drunken hubris. Macedonian drinking habits, especially, oscillate between Greek norms and barbarian behavior (e.g., that of Philipp II and Alexander). The *symposion* thus became an interpretative room for the negotiation of Greekness and otherness.

In "Party Hard: Violence in the Context of Roman *Cenae*," John Donahue examines how Romans understood and represented the occurrence of violence in dining contexts. Latin epic and novel are the literary background against which Donahue assesses violent feastings. Vergil's *Aeneid* depicts several festive contexts in which violence does not happen but is recounted with the purpose of building up a Latin identity. The performances of these passages, which might have themselves occurred in dining contexts, thus became *lieux de mémoire* of literary violence foundational for the history of Rome. In contrast to epic, the Roman novel offers glimpses of "real" violence at the dinner table. In the *Satyrica* of Petronius, Trimalchio's violence against his slaves may be exaggerated and bizarre but can be regarded as emblematic for Roman social relations, especially with regard to slaves being at the whim of their masters. Commensality had always been a means of forging and maintaining social bonds. So, by necessity, the falling apart of these bonds is also reflected in atrocities committed at the dinner table. Donahue discerns three scenarios where violence overshadowed the common feasting: the problematic dinners of late republican dynasts, the *collegia* and taverns ordinary people frequented, and the table of the emperor. The triumvirs knew all about political violence and were not above inviting their rivals for dinner in order to eliminate them. Thus, they foreshadowed the political and dynastic murders that occurred in the context of imperial feasts. The *collegia* and taverns (*popinae*) were habitual hotbeds of violence, where brawls and fights were to be expected. The emperors, finally, staged the most sinister dinner parties Roman history had seen so far: some banquets were supposed to instill fear and intimidation into the guests and thus make the unrivaled position of the emperor abundantly clear. Prominent victims of dinner-table violence of the first century CE are the emperor Claudius and his son Britannicus. Connecting commensality, violence, and space, Donahue comes to the conclusion that "staging an event in a space that could be easily controlled contributes to the unleashing of violence."

Concerning the choice of topics, sources, and epochs considered herein, it is appropriate to note that this book is a work of ancient history, not literary criticism. Within the chapters, a great variety of source material, much of it literary, is analyzed, often in detail. Treatments of violence in literary genres such as epic, oratory, or tragedy warrant books in their own right. Hellenistic and late antique violence are not considered in this volume, for the simple reason that the Hellenistic era lacks detailed evidence for this topic. Excluding a well-trodden focus on battles and warfare, we lack the speeches, plays, and other material essential for investigating violence and topography in the classical age. On violence in late antiquity, two large books have been published recently.[13]

By considering many circumstances under which Greeks and Romans committed violence, we learn more about how contextual factors shaped the meaning and significance of violence in the imaginations of the ancients. These new perspectives on the role of situation and "topography" in Greek and Roman perceptions and understandings of violence will hopefully open up further avenues for research on the vexed question of how violence was defined in antiquity.

Works Cited

Assmann, A. 2009. *Erinnerungsräume: Formen und Wandlungen des kulturellen Gedächtnisses*. 4th ed. Munich.

Assmann, A. 2012. *Die Zukunft der Erinnerung und der Holocaust*. With Geoffrey Hartman. Constance.

Assmann, J. 2007. *Das kulturelle Gedächtnis: Schrift, Erinnerung und politische Identität in frühen Hochkulturen*. 6th ed. Munich.

Bachmann-Medick, D. 2006. *Cultural Turns: Neuorientierungen in den Kulturwissenschaften*. Reinbek.

Belina, B., and Michel, B., eds. 2007. *Raumproduktionen: Beiträge der Radical Geography; Eine Zwischenbilanz*. Münster.

Bourdieu, P. 1972. *Esquisse d'une théorie de la pratique précédé de trois études d'éthnologie kabyle*. Geneva.

Bourdieu, P. 1995. *Sozialer Raum und Klassen: Zwei Vorlesungen*. Frankfurt am Main.

Döring, J., and Thielmann, T. 2009. "Einleitung." In J. Döring and T. Thielmann,

13. Drake 2006; Shaw 2011.

eds., *Spatial Turn: Das Raumparadigma in den Kultur- und Sozialwissenschaften*, 7–45. 2nd ed. Bielefeld.

Drake, H., ed. 2006. *Violence in Late Antiquity: Perceptions and Practices*. Ashgate.

Foucault, M. (1967) 2002. "Andere Räume." In K. Barck et al., eds., *Aisthesis: Wahrnehmung heute oder Perspektiven einer anderen Ästhetik; Essais*, 34–46. 7th ed. Leipzig.

Galinsky, K. 1996. *Augustan Culture: An Interpretive Introduction*. Princeton.

Kessl, F., Reutlinger, C., Maurer, S., and Frey, O., eds. 2005. *Handbuch Sozialraum*. Wiesbaden.

Levebvre, H. 1991. *The Production of Space*. Oxford.

Löw, M. 2001. *Raumsoziologie*. Frankfurt am Main.

Piltz, E. 2009. "Trägheit des Raums: Fernand Braudel und die Spatial Stories der Geschichtswissenschaft." In J. Döring and T. Thielmann, eds., *Spatial Turn: Das Raumparadigma in den Kultur- und Sozialwissenschaften*, 75–102. 2nd ed. Bielefeld.

Schroer, M. 2009. "Bringing Space Back In: Zur Relevanz des Raums als soziologischer Kategorie." In J. Döring and T. Thielmann, eds., *Spatial Turn: Das Raumparadigma in den Kultur- und Sozialwissenschaften*, 125–48. 2nd ed. Bielefeld.

Schultheis, F. 2004. "Das Konzept des sozialen Raums: Eine zentrale Achse in Pierre Bourdieus Gesellschaftstheorie." In G. Mein and M. Rieger-Ladich, eds., *Soziale Räume und kulturelle Praktiken: Über den strategischen Gebrauch von Medien*, 15–26. Bielefeld.

Shaw, B. 2011. *Sacred Violence: African Christians and Sectarian Hatred in the Age of Augustine*. Cambridge.

Thrift, N. 2009. "Raum." In J. Döring and T. Thielmann, eds., *Spatial Turn: Das Raumparadigma in den Kultur- und Sozialwissenschaften*, 393–407. 2nd ed. Bielefeld.

Wagner, K. 2010. "Topographical Turn." In S. Günzel, ed., *Raum: Ein interdisziplinäres Handbuch*, 100–109. Stuttgart.

Werlen, B. 2009. "Körper, Raum und mediale Repräsentation." In J. Döring and T. Thielmann, eds., *Spatial Turn: Das Raumparadigma in den Kultur- und Sozialwissenschaften*, 365–92. 2nd ed. Bielefeld.

PART I

The Greek World

ONE

Xenophon and the Muleteer

Hubris, Retaliation, and the Purposes of Shame[1]

David D. Phillips

A Tale of Two Generals

During Operation Husky, the Allied invasion of Sicily (July 10–August 17, 1943), Lieutenant General George S. Patton Jr. of the United States Army conducted two visits to military hospitals that resulted in disaster. On August 3, at the 15th Evacuation Hospital, Patton confronted Private Charles H. Kuhl, who presented with the condition known at the time as "battle fatigue."[2] Patton hurled invective at Kuhl and ordered him to leave the hospital's receiving tent; when Kuhl did not immediately comply, Patton slapped him in the face with his gloves, pulled him to a standing position, and forced him outside with a kick to the buttocks. On August 10, in the receiving tent of the 93rd Evacuation Hospital, Patton came upon another patient with battle fatigue, Private Paul G. Bennett. Patton berated Bennett as a "goddamned coward" and a "yellow son of a bitch," ordered that he be denied admission, and told Bennett that he was to return to battle, although he deserved to be shot—which Patton

1. I wish to express my gratitude to the editors for their invitation to contribute to this volume, and to the participants at Colloquium Atticum II, held at the Universität Hamburg in June 2013, for their comments on a condensed version of this essay.

2. Other contemporary terms for this condition, known in modern diagnostic parlance as posttraumatic stress, were *combat fatigue* and *shell shock*, the latter popularized during the First World War.

threatened to do himself, drawing his sidearm. Interrupted by the arrival of the hospital's commanding officer, Patton reiterated his order to expel Bennett. He resumed his tirade at Bennett, slapped him in the face with an open hand, started to make his way outside, and then changed his mind, advanced on Bennett again, and dealt him a second, harder slap. The hospital commander moved to shield his patient, and Patton left to complete his inspection.

These slapping incidents ignited a scandal that might have ended the career of another officer, but General Dwight D. Eisenhower, Allied commander in chief in the Mediterranean theater of operations, decided that Patton's record of military successes made him indispensable. He did not relieve Patton of his command or subject him to a court-martial, though he sent him a letter warning him that no such behavior would be tolerated in the future and ordering him to apologize. (Soon thereafter, in September, Lieutenant General Omar N. Bradley would be selected over Patton for the command of American ground forces in Operation Overlord, which commenced with the D-day landings at Normandy on June 6, 1944.) Although Patton made a series of public acts of contrition and, at times, privately acknowledged the error of his actions, his prevailing and considered opinion maintained that his slapping of Kuhl and Bennett had been not only justified but intended as beneficial to the men he struck and to the Army as a whole. In his posthumously published memoir *War As I Knew It*, he advocates the use of verbal shaming by fellow soldiers against men displaying signs of incipient battle fatigue ("[t]he greatest weapon against the so-called 'battle fatigue' is ridicule"), in order to "prevent its spread, and also save the man who allows himself to malinger by this means from an after-life of humiliation and regret." Officers, however, need not limit themselves to shaming words. In his final chapter (titled "Earning My Pay"), which lists "episodes [that] stand out in my mind as occasions on which my personal intervention had some value," Patton includes his slapping of Kuhl: "I . . . slapped him across the face with my glove and told him to get up, join his unit, and make a man of himself, which he did. . . . I am convinced that my action in this case was entirely correct, and that, had other officers had the courage to do likewise, the shameful use of 'battle fatigue' as an excuse for cowardice would have been infinitely reduced."[3]

3. Patton (1947) 1995: 340, 367, 381–82. See also D'Este 1995: 533–63; Atkinson 2007: 147–49, 169–72, 293–97. Under the U.S. Articles of War (revised 1912–20; approved June 4, 1920), Patton could have been court-martialed under Article 95 (concerning conduct unbecoming an officer and a gentleman), Article 90 (concerning reproachful

As a lifelong student of military history and the art of command, with a particular interest in Greco-Roman antiquity, Patton had read, at least once, the account of another illustrious general, Xenophon, who actually did face a court-martial for striking soldiers (X. *An.* 5.8).[4] In Xenophon's retelling in the *Anabasis*, the mercenary corps known as the Ten Thousand Greeks, encamped at Cotyora by the shore of the Black Sea in the spring or summer of 400 BC, constitute a court, with a jury consisting of the company commanders (*lochagoi*), and resolve that their generals submit to a review of their conduct (5.7.34–5.8.1). After the court convicts and fines three other generals, several men (who are not identified by name or place of origin) come forward to accuse Xenophon. Alleging that he struck them (*phaskontes paiesthai hyp' autou*), they charge him with hubris (*hôs hybrizontos tên katêgorian epoiounto*, 5.8.1).[5] The first prosecutor to speak specifies that Xenophon beat him "where we were dying of cold and there was a huge amount of snow"—that is, in western Armenia during the previous winter (4.4–6); Xenophon concedes that "if during such a crisis I was committing hubris, I admit to being more hubristic than donkeys" (5.8.2–3).[6] "But tell me," he continues, "the reason that you were struck [*ek tinos eplêgês*]. Did I demand something from you and strike you when you refused to give it? Was I demanding something back from you? Was I fighting with you over a boy? Did I get drunk and abusive?" When the prosecutor replies in the negative, Xenophon next seeks to ascertain the prosecutor's role in the army; the answers reveal that, at least at the time of the alleged offense, the prosecutor was not serving as a hoplite or a peltast[7]

or provoking speeches or gestures), Article 93 (concerning various crimes, including assault with intent to do bodily harm), and/or Article 96 (a general article including "all disorders and neglects to the prejudice of good order and military discipline [and] all conduct of a nature to bring discredit upon the military service").

4. Patton's introduction to Xenophon occurred in his early childhood, when his maternal aunt read aloud to him from the *Anabasis*; he read the *Anabasis* on his own (presumably not for the first time, given his interests and his formal education at the Virginia Military Institute and the United States Military Academy) during the 1920s (D'Este 1995: 39, 317; Hanson 1999: 275).

5. The trial of Xenophon receives brief attention in Fisher 1992 (125–26), the most complete and valuable modern study of hubris. For other discussions, see Lendle 1995: 355–59; Couvenhes 2005: 452–53; Lee 2007: 101–3; Flower 2012: 146–47.

6. On the hubris of donkeys (to which anyone with sufficient experience riding one can attest), cf. Ar. *V.* 1304–10; Pi. *P.* 10.33–36; Hdt. 4.129 (for varying interpretations of the term here, see MacDowell 1976: 15; Fisher 1992: 120).

7. The present optatives (*hopliteuoi*, *peltazoi*) in Xenophon's indirect questions may represent imperfect indicatives in the original direct questions (*hôpliteues*, *epeltazes*; they are

but had been assigned by his tentmates to drive a mule, "although he was a free man [*eleutheros ôn*]" (5.8.4–5).

The details of the incident now emerge. One day, on the march, Xenophon commandeered the prosecutor and his mule to transport a grievously ill soldier, who was in danger of being abandoned to the enemy. To make way for the man, the prosecutor complains, Xenophon scattered his and his tentmates' baggage; Xenophon responds that he distributed the baggage among others and later collected it all and returned it to the prosecutor. Xenophon sent the prosecutor on ahead but later found him digging a grave for the man while he was still alive; when the prosecutor refused to carry the man further, Xenophon struck him (5.8.6–10). The prosecutor retorts that the man subsequently died nonetheless; Xenophon offers the rejoinder, "We are all going to die; should we all be buried alive on that account?"; whereupon those in attendance "shouted out that he had struck [the prosecutor] too few blows," acquitting their general by acclamation (5.8.11). When Xenophon then invites his other prosecutors to stand and explain why they were struck, they remain seated and silent, thus dropping their cases (5.8.12).

Not content with ad hoc vindication, Xenophon proceeds to harangue the assembled army in justification of his use of violence against insubordinate soldiers (5.8.13–22).

> Gentlemen, I admit that I have indeed struck men on account of their lack of discipline [*ataxias*]—those who were content to be saved by you while you were marching in order and fighting where required, while they themselves had abandoned their stations and were running ahead, wishing to seize plunder and take more than you. If we all did

taken as such by Rehdantz and Carnuth 1905 ad loc.), referring to the status of the muleteer at the time of the event in question ("Were you a hoplite/peltast?"), which would not necessarily be permanent. Greek, however, usually avoids confusion by retaining original imperfect indicatives in indirect discourse (Smyth 1956: § 2623b); therefore, Xenophon's original direct questions were probably present indicatives (*hopliteueis*, *peltazeis*), referring to a more or less permanent status ("Are you a hoplite/peltast?"), and the muleteer's negative answers indicate that he was an archer (see, e.g., 1.2.9, 3.4.17), javelineer (if these existed separately from the javelin-wielding peltasts: they appear to be identical at 4.3.27–28 but are distinguished, with reference to the Athenian democrats at Munychia, at *HG* 2.4.12), or slinger (a unit of some two hundred Rhodian slingers is constituted—along with some fifty cavalry, from whom we can confidently exclude the muleteer—at 3.3.16–20). Complicating the issue, though, is Xenophon's occasional use of the term "peltasts" to refer to all nonhoplite troops (e.g., 1.2.9 *ad fin.*, whereas earlier in the same section Thracian peltasts and Cretan archers are enumerated separately).

this, we would all be dead. [14] And also, when someone has shown weakness and refused to stand up, instead forsaking himself to the enemy, I have struck him and forced him to go forward. For during the intense cold, I myself on one occasion, while waiting for some men who were packing up their baggage, sat down for a considerable time and then realized that I could barely stand up and extend my legs. [15] So, having gained this personal experience, whenever I saw a man sitting down and slacking, I would drive him on: movement and manly persistence provided some warmth and fluidity, while sitting and resting, I saw, were conducive to freezing of the blood and rotting off of toes, which, as you know, many people suffered. [16] And, perhaps, when someone was lagging behind due to laziness and preventing both you in the front and us in the rear from proceeding, I struck him with my fist so that the enemy would not strike him with a spear. [17] As a result, these people, their lives saved, may now get satisfaction if they suffered any treatment from me in violation of justice [*para to dikaion*]; but if they had fallen into the hands of the enemy, however great their suffering, what satisfaction could they expect to receive?

[18] My argument . . . is simple. If I punished someone for his own good [*ei men ep' agathôi ekolasa tina*], I think I should submit to the same sort of judgment as parents do at the hands of their sons and teachers do at the hands of their students; doctors, too, burn and cut for the good [*ep' agathôi*; sc., of their patients]. [19] But if you believe that I commit these acts out of hubris [*ei de hybrei nomizete me tauta prattein*], bear in mind that now I have more confidence, thanks to the gods, than I did then, and I am bolder now than I was then, and I drink more wine, but all the same I don't hit anybody. . . . [21] You yourselves have cast judgment that I was right to hit them. You were standing there, holding swords, not votes, and you could have come to their aid if you wished. But, by Zeus, you neither came to their aid nor joined me in striking the one who was being disorderly.[8] [22] And so you actually gave the bad men among them license to commit hubris, by letting them be; I think that if you are willing to look, you will find that the same men who were the worst then are the most hubristic now.

8. The army had earlier (3.2.31–33) unanimously approved a motion, proposed by Xenophon, that any disobedient soldier was to be punished by any witnessing soldier in concert with the commanding officer.

After rounding off his reported speech with a case in point and a recommendation that the army remember his good services, Xenophon concludes the episode by noting that people stood and offered testimonials, with the result that "things turned out well" (5.8.23–26).

At the trial of Xenophon, as for Patton in the aftermath of the slapping incidents more than two millennia later, the immediate problem concerned the proper aims and enforcement of military discipline, and the proposed solution (accepted in Xenophon's case and rejected in Patton's) advocated the use of violence for the benefit, immediate and/or ultimate, of the individual on the receiving end and of the community of soldiers as a whole. But whereas the Patton affair occurred within a strictly defined military jurisdiction distinct in both formal and real terms from civilian life, to Xenophon and his fellow classical Greeks, the army *was* the state. This was true not just in the special case of the Ten Thousand—who operated (especially after reaching the relative safety of the Black Sea) as a mobile virtual polis, with an assembly of the army as a whole being competent to decide both internal and external policy and with a court of law instituted at Cotyora[9]—but in the hundreds of actual Greek poleis, where the identification of citizen and soldier was essentially complete for adult males, who were liable to military service until the age of sixty.[10] Accordingly, we should not be surprised if these citizen soldiers, who had to obey their generals on campaign but could call them to account upon returning home (if not earlier),[11] expected

9. See esp. Dillery 1995: 59–98 (including, in particular, the meetings and powers of the assembly of soldiers and the functions of the generals as chief executive magistrates and of the officer corps as a probouleutic council: pp. 78–79 *et alibi*); also, e.g., Hornblower 2004 (with comparison to other Greek armies from the *Iliad* to Alexander the Great and beyond); Perlman 1976–77: 278; Rehdantz 1888: 7 (on the terminology of assemblies and lawcourts employed in the *Anabasis*); contra Lee 2007: 9–11. Had the army accepted Xenophon's proposal to found a city on the Black Sea (5.6.15–34), it would have become a polis in fact.

10. See, e.g., Hanson 2009: 30–31, 89, 92. This is not to discount the military obligations of noncitizen residents of the polis (e.g., the metics at Athens or the *perioikoi* and helots at Sparta), the increasing importance of mercenaries in Greek warfare in the fourth century, or the fact that some citizens were excused from military service for reasons such as physical disability (e.g., Lys. 24; Plu. *Sol.* 31.3–4).

11. At Athens, in addition to failing to win reelection, a general might be prosecuted for various forms of misconduct at his end-of-term *euthynai* (review: e.g., D. 4.47; [Arist.] *Ath.* 59.1–2) or by *eisangelia* (impeachment) at any time (e.g., Hyp. 4.1–2, 7–8; on the frequency of *eisangeliai* against Athenian generals, see Hansen 1975; 1991: 212–18). At Sparta, the ephors could fine, depose, imprison, or remand for capital trial a serving general (X. *Lac.* 8.4); in his previous life as a Spartan general, Clearchus, one of the original generals

that the rights they enjoyed as against their fellows *militiae* would not differ radically from those they enjoyed *domi.*[12] Given the limited evidence at our disposal, these rights appear to have included—at least sometimes and perhaps frequently—protection against corporal punishment,[13] corresponding to domestic prohibitions against physical assault.[14]

These factors are specifically and informatively at play in Xenophon's trial

of the Ten Thousand, had violated an order of recall issued by the ephors and consequently had been tried and sentenced to death in absentia (so X. *An.* 2.6.2–4; D.S. 14.12.2–7 gives a much more detailed and lurid account of Clearchus' misbehavior). The trial of a Spartan general took place before the *gerousia* of the two kings and twenty-eight elders; when the defendant general was himself a king, his colleague remained on the jury, to which the five ephors were added (as perhaps in other cases): X. *Lac.* 10.2; Arist. *Pol.* 1270b28–29, 35–41; 1294b18–34; Plu. *Lyc.* 26.1–2; Paus. 3.5.2; de Ste Croix 1972: 131–38; MacDowell 1986: 123–50. On the trial of Leotychidas II, see below, n. 32. Returning Argive armies held trials for misconduct on campaign just outside and before entering the city walls of Argos (Th. 5.60.6; I see no warrant for the skepticism of Gomme, Andrewes, and Dover 1945–81: 4.86). Pritchett 1974: 4–33 includes a catalog of seventy trials of Greek (predominantly, but not exclusively, Athenian and Spartan) generals from the seventh century to 338.

12. The major (apparent) exception, the obligation to obey the orders of superior officers, differed only in specifics, not in kind, from the obligation to obey magistrates at home. Ordinary Spartiates, whether at home or abroad, stood in the same relation to the ephors as did their commanders (X. *Lac.* 8.4; above, n. 11); the ephors heard *ta peri tôn symbolaiôn dikaia* ("lawsuits concerning contracts," or perhaps "private lawsuits" generally: MacDowell 1986: 130–31) every day, even in the army on campaign (Plu. *Mor.* 221a–b = *Apophth. Lac.*, Eurycratidas).

13. In the fourth century, Athenian generals could confine, discharge, or fine men for insubordination ([Arist.] *Ath.* 61.2) but evidently could not beat them, as instances in which we would expect corporal punishment if it were allowed (e.g., Lys. 3.45; D. 54.3–5) appear to confirm the argument *e silentio*. In general, short of the death penalty for major offenses, explicit references to military corporal punishment, actual or threatened (see Pritchett 1974: 232–45; Couvenhes 2005), tend to involve Spartan officers' punishing non-Spartan subordinates, with drastically negative results. Plu. *Arist.* 23 (Byzantium, 478/7): Pausanias' corporal punishment of allied troops helps to motivate the defection of the Ionians to Athens. Th. 8.84 (Miletus, 411/10): Astyochus' merely raising his staff to threaten the Thurian commander Dorieus, who is supporting his sailors' demands for back pay, causes the sailors to attempt to stone him. X. *HG* 6.2.18–19 (Corcyra, 373/2): Mnasippus strikes one mercenary *lochagos* with his staff and another with the butt-spike of his spear for observing that withholding pay does not make for obedient troops; "as a result," Xenophon concludes, "they all marched out in poor spirits and hating him, which is least advantageous for battle"(!).

14. This was true at Athens under the laws governing the *dikê aikeias* (for battery) and the *graphê hybreôs* (for hubris): see below, pp. 27–37. Antipho 4 δ 7, plausibly a priori, posits as universal principle sanctions against the wrongful initiator of violence (and, more problematically, impunity of response thereto).

scene. Nowhere in his defense against the muleteer and only obliquely in his postacquittal oration—as in his opening admission (5.8.13), which assumes the right and responsibility to enforce discipline, and in his later comparison to parents and teachers (5.8.18)—does Xenophon assert that his superior rank per se grants him special privileges in the use of violence;[15] indeed, he criticizes those soldiers who failed to join him in punishing disorderly conduct.[16] Rather, the muleteer brings his accusation of hubris, and Xenophon responds, first specifically and then generally, in terms designed to resonate with their audience, not specifically or predominantly as members of an ad hoc military community with specially prevailing rules, but instead according to common and preexisting cultural standards. Against this decidedly Panhellenic background[17] and in light of the Panhellenic readership at which the *Anabasis* is aimed,[18] Xenophon's trial scene is a source of prime importance for the concept of hubris among the classical Greeks. Under Xenophon's *ep' agathôi* standard (5.8.18), justified violence, and in particular justified shaming violence, is distinguished from hubristic violence on the grounds of perceived benefit to the sufferer and/or to third parties arising from the purpose(s) of the shame provoked. In what follows, I argue that this standard applies across Greek literary genres and cultural practices and that, in this light and others, the prevailing Aristotelian definition of hubris requires modification.

15. Xenophon's personal opinion may well have differed. Hornblower (2004: 255) is doubtless correct to suggest that Xenophon's use of corporal punishment during the campaign of the Ten Thousand was intentional Laconizing (cf. n. 13); his immediate (partial) role model was Clearchus, who "was always harsh and rough, with the result that his soldiers were disposed toward him as students are toward their teacher" (!) (2.6.12; cf. 1.5.11–17, 2.3.11, 2.6.9–10).

16. X. *An.* 5.8.21. Insofar as the Ten Thousand were unaccustomed to commanders' striking troops, they will naturally have hesitated to do so themselves, specific empowerment (above, n. 8) notwithstanding.

17. Over half of the Ten Thousand were Arcadians and Achaeans, with the rest including men from Argos, Sparta, Elis, Sicyon, Megara, Athens, Boeotia, Locris, Aetolia, Acarnania, Ambracia, Dolopia, Thessaly, Olynthus, Amphipolis, Dardanus, Chios, Samos, Miletus, Rhodes, Crete, Syracuse, and Thurii. See Lee 2007: 9, 60–66.

18. Whether or not we accept that one of Xenophon's goals in writing the *Anabasis* was to promote Panhellenic action against Persia (e.g., Dillery 1995: 59–63; Cawkwell 2004: 59–67), it cannot be disputed that the work envisaged and won a broad Greek readership (note, e.g., Arr. *An.* 1.12.3, 2.7.8–9).

The Trial of Xenophon in Its Contemporary Legal Context: Hubris and Shame in the Athenian Courts (and Elsewhere)

Within only a few years of Xenophon's trial,[19] an unnamed Athenian who had been struck by one Lochites hired Isocrates to write his speech for the trial of his assailant by a private lawsuit for battery (*dikê aikeias*).[20] Anticipating Lochites' argument that the beating caused him no harm, the prosecutor deploys the language of hubris and shame. "If there had been no hubris involved in what happened," he explains, "I would never have come before you [the jury]; but as it is, I have come to exact punishment from him not for the physical damage [*tês allês blabês*] that resulted from his blows, but for the indignity [*aikias*, used here in the original sense of "unseemliness": *a-eik(e)ia*] and the dishonor [*atimias*], things at which free men should feel the greatest anger and for which they should obtain the greatest retribution" (Isoc. 20.5–6). Half a century later, in 349/8, Meidias punched Demosthenes in the face at the Greater Dionysia before a capacity crowd at the god's own theater; in a speech composed two years later for Meidias' trial, Demosthenes cites the case of Euaeon, who killed Boeotus at a dinner party on account of a single blow. "It wasn't the blow that caused [Euaeon's] anger," Demosthenes maintains, "but the dishonor [*atimia*]; it isn't being hit [*typtesthai*] that is so terrible for free men—terrible though it is—but being hit for the purpose of hubris [*eph' hybrei*]. The hitter might do many things . . . , some of which the victim could not even describe to another, with his bearing, his glance, his voice, when he hits to commit hubris, when he hits as an enemy, when he hits with his fist, when he hits [the victim] in the face" (D. 21.72).

In the cases of Lochites, Euaeon, and Demosthenes—who, less than a week after being punched, had recovered sufficiently to secure, in propria persona, a preliminary condemnation (*katacheirotonia*) of Meidias by the

19. Lochites was a minor during the reign of the Thirty (Isoc. 20.11), so the *terminus ante quem non* for his trial is 403/2; since he is still young (§ 21) and since the oligarchy is treated as a recent event, most modern commentators place the trial ca. 400 (Spatharas 2009: 60–62; Mirhady in Mirhady and Too 2000: 123; Blass [1887–98] 1979: 2.217, with n. 4; Mathieu and Brémond 1928: 37).

20. Despite the prevalence of the language of hubris in the speech, the presence of the formula for *aikeia* (below, p. 36) in the first sentence ("That Lochites beat [*etypte*] me, starting a fight without justification [*archôn cheirôn adikôn*], all those who were present have testified to you," § 1) and, in particular, the prospect of damages payable to the prosecutor (§§ 16–19; cf. [D.] 47.64) identify the lawsuit as a *dikê aikeias* rather than a *graphê hybreôs* (below, p. 32), in which any fine assessed was paid to the state (D. 21.45).

Athenian Assembly[21]—physical harm to the victim is comparatively minor, not only in the absolute sense, but specifically in relation to the mental attitude of the perpetrator (as in the *Meidias* passage) and/or the corresponding mental harm (shame, indignity, dishonor) suffered by the victim (as in the *Lochites* and *Meidias* passages), which aggravate the assault so as to constitute hubris. The observation holds even when physical harm to the victim is severe. In his speech prosecuting Conon for *aikeia* (D. 54, 355/341?),[22] which resounds with the language of hubris from beginning (its very first word is *hybristheis*) to end, Ariston describes in detail the course and results of the beating administered to him that forms the *casus litis* (§§ 7–12). His assailants—Conon, his son Ctesias, and the son of Andromenes—stripped him, tripped him, pushed him into the mud, and jumped on his prone body, inflicting a split lip, two black eyes, various other cuts and bruises, and internal damage to the chest and abdomen. At the end of the beating, Ariston could neither stand nor speak; bystanders carried him home, and he was placed under the care of a doctor. His condition deteriorated, and according to the doctor, only spontaneous (probably oral) discharging of blood at the height of his illness saved Ariston from death by (pulmonary?) suppuration.[23] Yet, in the narration of his assault, Ariston locates the gravamen of his accusation of hubris in the act that did him no physical harm

21. A special session of the Assembly convened in the Theater of Dionysus the day after the Pandia (i.e., 17 Elaphebolion?) was the mandatory venue for the initiation of the procedure known as *probolê* for offenses concerning the Greater Dionysia (10–15 Elaphebolion), with the possible exception of cases in which a fine—presumably of 500 drachmas or less ([D.] 47.43)—had been imposed by the Council of Five Hundred and immediately paid (D. 21.8, with MacDowell 1990: 227–29). The Assembly's *katacheirotonia* was only formally punitive; if Demosthenes wished to pursue actual sanctions, he had to bring the *probolê* to trial before a regular jury court (*dikastêrion*). D. 21 is ostensibly the speech that Demosthenes delivered at Meidias' trial by jury two years later (§ 13). Debate over whether the speech (or some version thereof) was actually delivered in court revolves around the interpretation of Aeschin. 3.52: Demosthenes "sold for thirty minae the hubris committed against him and the *katacheirotonia* that the Assembly rendered against Meidias in the Theater of Dionysus." This might mean that Demosthenes took a bribe from Meidias to drop his lawsuit (Plu. *Dem.* 12.3–6; [Plu.] *Mor.* (*Vit. X orat.*) 844d; *Suda* s.v. *Dêmosthenês*, δ 456 Adler) or that he prosecuted Meidias and secured a conviction but proposed a penalty of (only) thirty minae (as opposed to death or confiscation of all Meidias' property: D. 21.152): see MacDowell 1990: 23–28; Harris 2008: 84–86. On the language of hubris in D. 21, see Rowe 1993.

22. For the possible dates, see Carey and Reid 1985: 69.

23. On the symptoms, see Sandys and Paley 1910: 199; Carey and Reid 1985: 85, with references.

whatsoever but manifests *par excellence* Conon's state of mind. "Here," he declares, "is an indication of [Conon's] hubris [*ho de tês hybreôs esti tês toutou sêmeion*] and proof that the whole thing happened under his direction. . . . He crowed, imitating victorious roosters, and the others encouraged him to slap his sides with his elbows, as though they were wings" (§ 9).[24]

The same considerations, albeit with different conclusions, lie behind the case of Xenophon and the muleteer, as well as the other cases mentioned in Xenophon's postacquittal speech. Striking alone does not constitute hubris: Xenophon never disputes hitting the muleteer, and he goes on to volunteer instances of his hitting other soldiers. In all probability, Xenophon did not inflict severe injury either on the muleteer, whom he was trying to compel to carry a wounded man (and note the acclamation verdict, at *An.* 5.8.11, that Xenophon should have hit him more), or in the cases where he acted to save men from death at the hands of General Winter or hostile locals. Moreover, whereas Patton represented in his own person the sole immediate physical danger to the men he assaulted, Xenophon had the justification that temporary minor physical harm to an individual outweighed both severe and permanent harm (up to and including death) to that individual and widespread (and potentially equally severe and permanent) harm to the army as a whole: "If we all [broke ranks in pursuit of plunder], we would all be dead" (*An.* 5.8.13; cf. the observation at 5.8.16 that stragglers on the march hinder movement of the entire force under enemy pressure).

Where Xenophon's case (by implication) coincides with Patton's (by his own statement, above, p. 20), as well as with the cases of Lochites, Euaeon, Demosthenes, and Ariston, is in the emphasis on the intent of the actor and the mental effects on the sufferer. We are at Xenophon's mercy for our knowledge of his trial, so the explicit language of shaming is predictably absent (since such an admission, however qualified, would be against Xenophon's interests). Yet the centrality of mental factors remains evident. In the mouth of the muleteer, *eleutheros ôn* (*An.* 5.8.5, above, p. 22) is a pointed comment. Driving a mule, though an unquestionably vital function under the circumstances,[25] was characteristically (although not exclusively) slave

24. On the foregoing cases and on the Athenian *graphê hybreôs* (below, pp. 32–37), see Fisher 1976: 180–81; 1990; 1992: 36–85; MacDowell 1976; 1978: 129–32, 194–97, 256–57; 1990: esp. 18–23, 263–69; Cohen 1991: 176–80; 1995: 87–162; 2005: 215–22; Lipsius (1905–15) 1984: 420–35; Ruschenbusch 1965; Gagarin 1979; Murray 1990; Todd 1993: 268–71; van Wees 2011; Riess 2012: 57–82, 87–94, 96–99, 104–10, and esp. 115–31.

25. This is observed by Lee (2007: 101–3), who also notes that the assignment to drive the mule was given by the man's tentmates, not by a superior officer.

labor. Already inconvenienced (if not necessarily shamed) by this burdensome assignment, the muleteer was intercepted by Xenophon and ordered to unload the cargo that belonged to and was crucial to the survival of himself and his tentmates[26] and to replace it with a man on the verge of death who certainly did not belong to his tent and probably did not belong to his unit.[27] Finally, having been divested of his and his tentmates' property and sent forward with no secure knowledge that it would be returned,[28] the muleteer found himself on the receiving end of Xenophon's fists, submitting to a punishment that, regardless of his own conduct, was, for an adult Greek male, assuredly more the mark of slave status[29] than mule driving—a punishment that was thus, by definition and in the full sense of the word, humiliating.[30]

Xenophon himself, both in his defense against the muleteer and thereafter, focuses on issues of justification, desert, and benefit. In his first two questions to the muleteer, before he even recognizes the man and recalls the events in question, Xenophon assumes that he hit him and proceeds immediately to address circumstance and motive. His first question, regarding the location of the alleged offense (*An.* 5.8.2), goes to broad circumstance, and his reply to the muleteer's answer posits that hubris committed in such a dire situation would be particularly grave ("more hubristic than donkeys," 5.8.3). His next question (5.8.4) goes to specific circumstance and motive,

26. The muleteer's reported description of Xenophon's "throwing about" (*dierrhipsas*, 5.8.6) their baggage connotes a high-handed and disrespectful attitude.

27. This is indicated by the wounded man's proper forward position in the order of march, the muleteer's ensuing callous behavior, and Xenophon's silence on a matter that would be sure to prejudice his audience in his favor.

28. Cf. nn. 37 *ad fin.*, 65 on wrongful appropriation as hubris. The eventual return notwithstanding, assurances may or may not have been given, and any assurances given may have been reasonably disbelieved due to the situation of enemy pursuit.

29. Couvenhes 2005: 452.

30. D. 22.54–55: the most significant difference between free men and slaves is that the latter are liable to corporal punishment while the former are not; Androtion has committed hubris against both citizens and metics by "inflict[ing] his punishments upon their bodies, as though they were slaves [*eis ta sômata hôsper andrapodois*]." Cf. D. 21.180: during a procession, Ctesicles horsewhipped an enemy and "was deemed to strike out of hubris rather than intoxication [which, together with the procession,] he seized upon as the pretext for committing the offense of treating free men as slaves [*hôs doulois chrômenos tois eleutherois*]." Note the contrast between the assumptions in these passages and the terms of the Athenian hubris law (below, p. 32), which protected slaves and free people alike. On the (theoretical) inviolability of the citizen's body, see Fisher 1992: 59; Hunter 1994: 154–84; Allen 2000: 213–24; Riess 2012: 87–88.

opening with a blunt demand for the precipitating event (*ek tinos eplêgês*) and proceeding to list some typical situations of potential hubristic assault (refused demand for or recovery of property, erotic rivalry, and drunken violence).[31] He justifies his order to the muleteer both by his conduct after the fact (he returned the mule's original cargo whole and undamaged: 5.8.7) and on grounds of duress (with the enemy in pursuit, the wounded man would surely die if left behind: 5.8.8). Striking the muleteer, Xenophon's most egregious act from his victim's point of view, receives the fullest justification, as it occurred in response to the attempted live burial of a comrade (thus amounting to defense of another against imminent, not to mention grotesque, death); and Xenophon's rhetorical question (which precipitates the immediate and vocal vindication that ends his trial and cows his other would-be accusers into silence) "We are all going to die; should we all be buried alive on that account?" (5.8.11) cleverly (however unrealistically) casts his punishment of the muleteer as a defense of all against an almost hyperbolically repugnant act. The *ep' agathôi* standard, implied for third parties here, is openly posited, and extended to the actual sufferers of violence, in Xenophon's ensuing speech. The general, he argues, stands in relation to (in)subordinate soldiers as parents do to sons, as teachers do to students (see below, p. 47), and as doctors do to patients; and the hubristic infliction of physical harm is defined both negatively (in opposition to the same conduct performed *ep' agathôi*) and positively (by association with confidence/[over]boldness—*tharrô, thrasyteros*—and with intoxication; cf. 5.8.4 [*methyôn eparôinêsa?*] and n. 31) by the state of mind of the actor and the effects, intended and/or actual, on the sufferer (and others) (5.8.18–19).

The appearance of hubris, however ad hoc, as an offense at law among the Panhellenic Ten Thousand (above, n. 17) indicates that a critical mass of Greek poleis either recognized hubris as a term of substantive law or could do so without significant difficulty. The same conclusion is suggested by Hippodamus of Miletus' proposed division of all laws and the corresponding lawsuits into the categories of hubris, damage (*blabê*), and homicide (*thanatos*) (Arist. *Pol.* 1267b37–39) and by Aristotle's efforts at defining

31. Withholding property is frequently described as hubris in Attic oratory: see n. 37 *ad fin.* On erotic rivalry, in addition to the Pittalacus case (below, p. 35; the assault on Pittalacus took place after Timarchus transferred his affections from Pittalacus to Hegesander: Aeschin. 1.55–58), note, e.g., Lys. 3.5–7; D. 54.13–14 (below, p. 48–49, with n. 83). Drunkenness, depending on the needs of the speaker, might be held either to exacerbate or to mitigate a violent act and, accordingly, to support (e.g., D. 54.3, 7–8) or rebut (e.g., by implication at D. 21.180: above, n. 30) an allegation of hubris: see Riess 2012: 67–69.

hubris, especially in his *Rhetoric* (insofar as its target readership was not only Panhellenic but specifically concerned with winning lawsuits), but also in the *Nicomachean Ethics* (below, pp. 37–39). In fact, though, apart from Athens (and the Ten Thousand), we have relatively limited evidence for laws or lawsuits concerning hubris among the classical Greeks.[32] Moreover, whereas the trial of Xenophon presents a hubris lawsuit without a hubris law, the situation in Athens is nearly reversed: the law on hubris survives, but evidence for its application is thin and controversial. The Athenian hubris law (D. 21.47) provides that "if a person commits hubris against another, whether a child, a woman, or a man, free or slave, or does anything *paranomon*[33] to any of these," any adult male citizen may file a *graphê* (commonly translated "indictment" or "public lawsuit") with the *thesmothetai*, who, under normal circumstances, have thirty days to refer the lawsuit for trial. The penalty for a convicted defendant is assessable and unlimited, up to and including death, and in cases where the penalty is a fine and the victim is a free person, the offender is to be imprisoned pending its payment.[34]

Despite the latitude of the law's opening condition (which neither defines hubris nor restricts the law's scope to hubris: it encompasses as well "anything *paranomon*")[35] and although Athenian litigants accuse their opponents

32. Hdt. 6.85 (Sparta, ca. 490): in response to a complaint by Aeginetan ambassadors, the Spartans convene a court, which finds that the Aeginetans have been treated with extreme hubris by Leotychidas II (*dikastêrion synagagontes egnôsan perihybristhai Aiginêtas hypo Leutychideô*) and sentences him to extradition to Aegina in return for Aeginetan hostages being detained at Athens (see Fisher 2000: 105–6). The Spartan regent Pausanias may have stood trial for hubris (among other offenses) in 478/7 (Th. 1.95; Hdt. 8.3: *prophasin tên Pausanieô hybrin proischomenoi apeilonto tên hêgemoniên tous Lakedaimonious*, "alleging as their pretext the hubris of Pausanias, they [sc., the Athenians, the other non-Peloponnesian allies, or some combination of the two: Macan 1908: 1.2.361–62] divested the Spartans of their hegemony [over the Hellenic League]"; cf. Plu. *Cim.* 6; *Arist.* 23 (above, n. 13); D.S. 11.44.3–6; Nep. *Paus.* 2.6; Fisher 1992: 132 n. 308, 344, 381). *IG* XII 2.646, *a* 23–25 = Stauber 1996: no. 36 (Nasos, fourth century): Agesistratus is convicted of hubris and fined twenty-five gold staters. Cf. *PHalensis* 1 (*Dikaiomata*: Bechtel et al. 1913), col. IX, lines 210–13 (mid-third-century hubris law of Egyptian Alexandria), with Fisher 1992: 83–85; Hirata 2008. Note also that hubris could be alleged as a casus belli: e.g., Th. 1.38, 41, 68; X. *HG* 5.3.13; Fisher 1992: 136–42; 2000: 105–6, 110–11. On these cases, see Phillips 2014.

33. On the disputed meaning of this word ("unlawful" or "contrary to custom"), see Ruschenbusch 1965; MacDowell 1976: 26–27; Gagarin 1979: 233–34; Fisher 1992: 53–56; van Wees 2011.

34. On this law and the cases that follow, see the references in n. 24.

35. The law does restrict the cases it governs to those in which both the perpetrator and the victim are human beings (MacDowell 1976: 24; 1978: 130; Gagarin 1979:

of hubris as a matter of course, the most cautious reading of the sources yields only two unmistakable *graphai hybreôs*.

(1) Isaeus 8.41: in order to prevent the husband of one of his uterine half-sisters from pursuing a claim to her father's estate, Diocles of the deme Phlya "walled him up in his house and by a plot [*katoikodomêsas kai epibouleusas*] *êtimôse* him." As of the delivery (or at least the composition) of Isaeus 8 (383–363?),[36] a *graphê hybreôs* has been initiated against Diocles but has not yet come to trial; that trial eventuated is indicated by the survival of fragments of another speech by Isaeus, *Against Diocles for Hubris* (Is. fr. VIII Baiter-Sauppe).[37]

230; cf. below, pp. 39, 40, 42, with nn. 51, 58, 63). Moreover, cases in which the victim was an orphan, *epiklêros* (legitimate daughter of a man who died with no legitimate son), or widow who remained in her deceased husband's household claiming to be pregnant were subject to separate remedies ([D.] 43.75; cf. D. 37.33, 45–46: below, p. 36).

36. Wyse 1904: 588; Wevers 1969: 21.

37. Against the traditional interpretation of *êtimôse*—that by imprisoning his brother-in-law Diocles (somehow) procured his legal *atimia* (disfranchisement) (Wyse 1904: 621; Roussel 1922: 156; Forster 1927: 316; Michailidis-Nouaros 1939: 300–1; Fisher 1990: 125; 1992: 40–41; Carey 1995: 410 n. 12)—Avramović (2010) argues that the verb refers simply to shaming, with the victim becoming an object of general mockery. Depending on the duration of his confinement, he may have been incommoded after the manner described in the thirteenth-century Icelandic *Laxdœla saga* 47. Shortly after Christmas 1002, Kjartan Olafsson assembled sixty men and barricaded his cousin and foster brother Bolli Thorleiksson, Bolli's wife (Gudrun Osvifsdottir), and others inside their farmstead for three days, forcing them to excrete inside rather than going to the outhouse, which—the author takes pains to observe—was the custom of the time. The victims "thought it was a much bigger humiliation than if Kjartan had killed one or two of their men" (*þótti þetta miklu meiri svívirðing ok verri, en þótt Kjartan hefði drepit mann eða tvá fyrir þeim*). The result was a full-blown feud, and Kjartan would be killed in ambush a few days after Easter 1003 (*Laxdœla saga* 49, with Magnusson and Pálsson 1969: 21). Whatever the significance of *êtimôse*, observe that there is no mention of any direct physical injury to the victim, although Harp. s.v. *katôikodomêsen* (= Is. fr. VIII.6 Baiter-Sauppe) glosses the word as "shut [the victim] up in a house/room [*oikêma*] and tried to kill [*apekteinen*, conative] [him]" (by starvation? by hurling down roof tiles? by smoke?). This is certainly an abnormal case: Avramović (2010: 269–71) compares, inter alia, the barricading of Philocleon at the beginning of Ar. *V.* and the legend of the Athenian who punished his daughter for losing her virginity before marriage by walling her up in an empty house with a horse at Aeschin. 1.182; note, however, that Avramović's interpretation of the passage is incorrect—the purpose of the act was not the preservation of the girl's virginity but the infliction of her death by horse (cf. the more specific variant of the legend at Heraclides Lembus, *Epitome of the Ath. Pol.* 1, and see Fisher 2001: 331–34). What concerned Athenians was the vulnerability of their homes not to barricading but to breaking and entering, commonly by digging

(2) Demosthenes 45.3–5: upon returning to Athens from service as a trierarch in 368/7,[38] Apollodorus filed (but later dropped, in return for negotiated concessions) a *graphê hybreôs* against the freedman (now metic) Phormion for marrying Apollodorus' mother, Archippe. The grounds for the lawsuit consisted in the impropriety of the marriage and/or—since Apollodorus suggests (§ 84) that his younger brother Pasicles is Phormion's son and since Pasicles was born eight years before Archippe's first husband (and Apollodorus' father), Pasion, died—Phormion's seduction of Archippe during her marriage to Pasion.[39]

To these cases, we may add several possible instances of the *graphê hybreôs*.

(3) Lysias fragment 279 Carey (*Against Teisis*): Teisis invited Archippus into his house, then tied him to a column, whipped him, and confined him; the next day, Teisis had his slaves repeat the tying and whipping, and

---

through walls, *toichôrychia*, which rendered the actor liable to *apagôgê*, summary arrest (Ar. *Pl.* 565; X. *Mem.* 1.2.62; [D.] 35.47; [Arist.] *Ath.* 52.1); Diocles' victim evidently escaped by the reverse method, tunneling out of his house (Harp. s.v. *ekplintheusas* = Is. fr. VIII.4 Baiter-Sauppe). Apart from the special case of Diocles, actual or hypothetical bad actors in disputes concerning estates are described as committing hubris, or their victims as suffering hubris, at Lys. 32.10; Is. 2.15, 33; 3.46, 48; 4.11; 5.24; 6.48; 8.1, 45; D. 27.65, 68.

38. Sandys and Paley 1910: 62; Trevett 1992: 10, 33.

39. This case, too, is abnormal to some degree, as Apollodorus essentially confesses by way of explaining that he initiated a *graphê hybreôs* because private lawsuits (*dikai idiai*: see n. 40) were suspended owing to the war (with Thebes: Sandys and Paley 1910: 62–63). Since Apollodorus alleges that Phormion withheld the estate left to him by Pasion (§ 3) and that the will of Pasion adduced by Phormion—which marries Archippe to Phormion—is a forgery (§§ 6, 28–42), private lawsuits by which he might have proceeded include a *diadikasia* (for adjudication of the estate) and a *dikê blabês* (for damage, i.e., wrongfully inflicted financial loss). However, both improper marriage and seduction are elsewhere described as hubris. At [D.] 59.72, the term hubris (albeit with no hint of a *graphê hybreôs*) is applied to Stephanus' and Neaira's falsely representing Phano as a citizen in marrying her to Theogenes. A complicating factor in Apollodorus' case will have been the evident hypocrisy of his objecting to the remarriage of Archippe—whose first husband, Pasion, was a naturalized former slave—to another former slave. Seduction (*moicheia*) could be prosecuted by a *graphê hybreôs* (Hyp. 1.12: below, p. 36); for seduction as hubris, cf. Lys. 1.2–4: Eratosthenes commits "what all men consider the most terrible kind of hubris" by entering Euphiletus' house and sleeping with his wife. Other sexual offenses described as hubris include rape (seen as a particular vice of tyrants: e.g., Arist. *Pol.* 1314b23–25, with Hdt. 3.80; Fisher 1976: 183; for rape as justiciable under the *graphê hybreôs*, see Harris 1990: 373; 2004: 63–66; Cohen 1991: 178; Fisher 1992: 13; Carey 1995: 410) and the prostitution of citizen males, as involving hubris by the pimp, by the client, and against and/or by the prostitute: see Aeschin. 1, with Cohen 1991: 175–80; Fisher 1992: 109–10; 2001; 2005; in Aeschines' estimation (e.g., §§ 15, 87), all parties are at least aware of the shame inflicted on the prostitute, even if they do not specifically intend it. Fisher (1992: 42) notes the "highly unusual circumstances" of Apollodorus' *graphê hybreôs* but correctly warns against the assumption that the action was "patently absurd."

Archippus was only released thanks to the arrival and intercession of friends of Teisis. The resulting lawsuit was either a *graphê hybreôs* (D.H. *Dem.* 11 introduces the fragment as *diêgêsin tina . . . hybristikên*, "a narrative dealing with hubris") or a *dikê aikeias.*[40]

(4) Aeschines 1.58–64: Hegesander, Timarchus, and others broke into the house of the public slave[41] Pittalacus, destroyed property, killed his birds, and then tied him to a column and whipped him. The following day, Pittalacus, "taking their hubris hard, filed a lawsuit [*dikên*] against each of them [i.e., Hegesander and Timarchus]" (§ 62),[42] but the disputants subsequently referred the matter to private arbitration.

(5) Deinarchus 1.23: Athenian courts executed Menon for confining a citizen boy in his mill, Themistius "because he committed hubris against the female cithara player from Rhodes at the Eleusinia," and Euthymachus "because he put the girl from Olynthus in a brothel"; one or more of these cases may have been *graphai hybreôs.*[43] (For other possible cases, see Fisher 1990: 125–26, 133 with n. 29.)

40. The speaker who delivers the *Against Teisis* is not the victim Archippus and refers to the lawsuit with the word *dikê* (*Teisis ho pheugôn tên dikên*, "Teisis, the defendant in this *dikê*," § 1). Neither of these facts is dispositive as to the legal action. The speaker might be appearing as a *synêgoros* (supporting speaker, advocate) for Archippus in a *dikê aikeias* (which Archippus would have had to prosecute in propria persona) or might be either a *synêgoros* or (less probably) the prosecutor of record in a *graphê hybreôs*, in which case *dikên* at § 1 is used in the general sense of (any) "lawsuit" rather than in specific reference to the type of private lawsuit called *dikê*. On general versus specific *dikê*, see Phillips 2007: 95–96. On the identification of the lawsuit against Teisis, see Blass (1887–98) 1979: 1.623; Gernet and Bizos 1989: 2.241; Todd 2000: 347.

41. He was perhaps a freed metic by this point: see Fisher 2001: 190–91.

42. By the letter of the hubris law, the noncitizen Pittalacus could not bring a *graphê hybreôs* in his own name; accordingly, Fisher (2001: 199–200) tentatively identifies the action as a *dikê aikeias* but also raises the possibility of a *dikê blabês* (for damage to property: cf. n. 39 above) or a *dikê biaiôn* (for "acts of violence": cf. Lys. 23.12; Lys. frr. 31, 299–302 Carey; D. 21.44–45; Harp. s.v. *biaiôn*). Note, though, that if Pittalacus was a slave, he had no more legal right to bring a *dikê* than a *graphê*. Here, too, *dikên* might be used generally (cf. n. 40): given the Athenians' lack of legal professionalism and their tendency to interpret and enforce laws inconsistently and casuistically (note the influence of equity at, e.g., Isoc. 7.33; Arist. *EN* 1137a31–b38, esp. 1137b11–13; see generally Meyer-Laurin 1965, and, on the phenomenon of "legal insecurity," Lanni 2006: 115–48), we cannot eliminate the possibility that Pittalacus convinced the *thesmothetai* to admit a *graphê hybreôs*.

43. In Themistius' case, the action may have been *probolê* for "wrongdoing concerning the festival" (*adikein peri tên heortên*): for *probolê* arising from the Eleusinia (as arising from the Dionysia in the case of Meidias: above, p. 27), see D. 21.175, with MacDowell 1990 ad loc. Worthington (1992: 169) and Harris (2008: 79–81) incorrectly conflate *probolê* with the *graphê hybreôs*; for the distinction between the procedures, see D. 21.25–26, with MacDowell 1990: 16–17, 246–48.

Finally, we have litigants' assertions about acts for which a *graphê hybreôs* would potentially lie. Both the speaker of Isocrates 20 and Ariston (above, pp. 27–29), prosecuting *dikai aikeias* (private lawsuits for *aikeia*, simple battery, defined as *archein cheirôn adikôn*, "beginning unjust hands"—i.e., starting a fight without justification),[44] assert that their defendants have committed the more serious offense of hubris in order to prove *aikeia* a fortiori (see esp. D. 54.1, 8–9; Isoc. 20.1–6). Demosthenes asserts that Meidias' conduct meets the standard for both *aikeia* and hubris (e.g., D. 21.25, 28, 31–35), but since the conduct occurred during the Greater Dionysia—and thus Meidias committed hubris not just against Demosthenes but against the city and Dionysus—Demosthenes opted to proceed by *probolê* for "wrongdoing concerning the festival" (e.g., § 1). On the assumption that the actions brought against Teisis and initiated against Hegesander and Timarchus were not *graphai hybreôs*, we find a similar strategy at work in the speech against Teisis and in Aeschines' description of the Pittalacus affair. Binding and beating recur at [Demosthenes] 53.16: Nicostratus and Arethusius attempt to entrap Apollodorus by sending a citizen boy to pluck his roses, "so that if I caught him and bound or beat him in the belief that he was a slave, they could bring a *graphê hybreôs* against me."

Other passages assert the applicability of the *graphê hybreôs* to acts with a sexual element, whether patent or latent. At Hypereides 1.12, the speaker Lycophron, on trial for seducing the sister of the Olympic victor Dioxippus, criticizes the prosecution's choice to proceed by *eisangelia* (impeachment) rather than "*graphai* before the *thesmothetai* provided by the laws"; in all probability, the reference is to the *graphê hybreôs* as well as the *graphê moicheias* (for seduction).[45] A similar procedural objection occurs at Demosthenes 37.33, 45–46. At trials over contested mining rights, Pantaenetus first convicted Euergus and now accuses the speaker Nicobulus on charges including "going to his house in the country and intruding upon his *epiklêroi* and his mother." Maintaining that Pantaenetus should have filed an *eisangelia*[46] with

44. D. 23.50 quotes from a law the condition "if a person strikes [*typtêi*] another, *archôn cheirôn adikôn*"; that his source is the law governing *aikeia* (of which the quoted words presumably comprise the opening condition) is indicated by the fact that the speaker of [D.] 47 twice defines *aikeia* as *archein cheirôn adikôn* (§§ 40, 47; cf. §§ 7, 8, 15, 35, 39; Isoc. 20.1 [above, n. 20]). The phrase is at least as old as the legislation of Draco (*IG* I^3 104.33–35).

45. Phillips 2006: 383–84.

46. This would have been not an *eisangelia* for major offenses against the state, as in Hypereides 1, but an *eisangelia kakôseôs epiklêrou*, for maltreatment of an *epiklêros*: [Arist.] *Ath.* 56.6–7; [D.] 43.75.

the archon, Nicobulus observes that in one section of Pantaenetus' written statement of the charge (*enklêma*) "he charges me with many terrible things at the same time: *aikeia*, hubris, acts of violence (*biaiôn*: see above, n. 42), and offenses against *epiklêroi*," all subject to separate lawsuits. Aeschines 1.15 (see above, n. 39) specifically contends that hiring a boy prostitute constitutes grounds for a *graphê hybreôs*.

The Aristotelian Definition of Hubris and Its Problems

These cases of potential *graphai hybreôs* amply demonstrate a defining characteristic of Athenian law; namely, significant procedural flexibility whereby a given wrongful act might entitle the would-be prosecutor to choose from among multiple legal actions.[47] This flexibility, along with the absence (at least at Athens) of a substantive legal definition of hubris (above, p. 32), will have helped impel Aristotle to essay his own definition, which he intended to obtain not just in Athens or in the arena of law alone but among the Greeks generally and in all contexts.[48] Various (but mutually consistent) formulations of this definition are found in Aristotle's *Rhetoric* and *Nicomachean Ethics*.

> But seeing that people often admit having committed an act but do not admit either the title [of the act] or what the title concerns—for example, . . . [they admit] "taking" but not "stealing," or "striking first" [*pataxai proteron*] but not "committing hubris" [*hybrisai*] . . . , for these reasons, concerning these matters, too, it must be determined what is theft, what is hubris, . . . so that, whether we wish to demonstrate that such is the case or not, we are able to make clear our claim to right. All such cases are a dispute over whether a person is unjust and bad or not unjust: the depravity and the offense lies in the deliberate choice [of the actor] [*proairesei*],[49] and words such as

47. Osborne 1985, esp. 50–51; Gagarin 1979: 232–34; Carey 2004; Riess 2008: 58–61. See also, e.g., D. 22.25–27, on various remedies for theft and for impiety.

48. Fisher 1976: 179–80; 1992: 9; contra MacDowell 1976: 27–28; Cairns 1996: 6 n. 32.

49. *Proairesis* is a difficult word to translate. "Choice" alone (as at Ross 1925 *ad EN* 1149b34: see below) does not account sufficiently for the *pro-*; "intention" (Fisher 1992: 10) is too weak. As Cairns (1996: 3, with n. 18) observes, in the *Nicomachean* (and *Eudemian*) *Ethics*, "*prohairesis* follows deliberation . . . [but] not every action that is with

these indicate the deliberate choice as well [as the act]; for example, hubris and theft. For if a person struck, he did not in all cases commit hubris, but only if he did so for a reason; for example, [*hoion*] in order to dishonor his victim or give himself pleasure [*tou atimasai ekeinon ê autos hêsthênai*]. (*Rh.* 1373b38–1374a15)

There are three types of contempt: scorn, spite, and hubris. . . . A man who commits hubris also exhibits contempt, for hubris is doing and saying things that involve shame [*aischynê*] for the victim, not in order that anything accrue to the actor other than what happened, but so that he may feel pleasure; those who act in response [*hoi antipoiountes*] do not commit hubris but get vengeance [*timôrountai*].[50] The cause of pleasure for those who commit hubris is their belief that by doing [others] ill they themselves excel more. . . . Dishonor [*atimia*] is an element of hubris, and he who dishonors exhibits contempt. (*Rh.* 1378b14–30)

Those who are suffering, have suffered, or are about to suffer such things as lead to dishonor [*atimian*] and censure [*oneidê*] feel shame [*aischynontai*]. These are the things that deal with subservience of the person or of shameful [*aischrôn*] acts, and among them is to be the victim of hubris. (*Rh.* 1384a15–18)

Or if someone were to say that striking free men is hubris: for it is not so in all cases, but only when one starts a fight unjustly [*archêi cheirôn adikôn*]. (*Rh.* 1402a1–3)

Moreover, no one commits hubris in a state of pain [*lypoumenos*], and everyone who acts in anger [*orgêi*] acts in a state of pain, whereas one

---

prohairesis need follow *actual* deliberation" (emphasis in the original). I have accordingly adopted "deliberate choice" (as at Gagarin 1979: 231; cf. Cope and Sandys 1877: 1.239, "deliberate intention"), with the caveat that "deliberate" should not be pressed too hard: cf. the continuing use of the common-law definition of murder as requiring "malice aforethought" (e.g., California Penal Code § 187) despite the fact that some killings involving neither malice nor forethought qualify as murder (LaFave 2000: 653–55).

50. Cf. *EN* 1138a21–22: "he who, because he has suffered, does *the same* in response [***to auto*** *antipoiôn*] is not deemed to do wrong." For Aristotle, the distinction between *timôria* (vengeance) and *kolasis* (punishment) is that whereas the former occurs to satisfy the avenger, the latter occurs for the sake of the person punished (*Rh.* 1369b12–14; cf. *EN* 1104b16–18); but see n. 70 below.

> who commits hubris acts with pleasure. If, then, acts at which it is most right to feel anger are the more serious offenses, then so is the lack of self-control that arises from desire; for hubris does not subsist in anger [*ou gar estin en thymôi hybris*]. . . . [W]e do not call animals temperate [*sôphrona*] or incontinent [*akolasta*] except metaphorically [*kata metaphoran*] and if some one species of animals generally exceeds another in hubris, destructiveness, and omnivorousness: it has no [capacity of] deliberate choice [*proairesin*] or calculation [*logismon*], but it is an aberration from nature, as are the insane among human beings. (*EN* 1149b20–1150a1)[51]

As these passages[52] demonstrate, Aristotle is especially concerned with distinguishing hubris from other forms of physical assault, particularly *aikeia*: note the occurrence of the definitional phrase *archein cheirôn adikôn* (above, p. 36) at *Rhetoric* 1402a1–3 (cf. *pataxai proteron* at *Rh.* 1374a3). Owing to its clear correspondence with the descriptions of hubristic assaults in the Attic orators, the essence of Aristotle's distinction[53]—that hubris consists literally of adding insult to injury, requiring the intentional infliction of shame upon the victim (which brings pleasure to the perpetrator)[54]—has long been recognized as correct by the majority of commentators, at least

51. Significantly, the metaphor lies in the attribution of *sôphrosynê* and *akolasia* to animals, not in the application of the term hubris (unless we are to take Aristotle, improbably, as justifying one metaphor by the use of another: for Aristotle's principles of metaphor, see *Po.* 1457b6–33; *Rh.* 1405a3–b34; 1411a1–1412b33, esp. 1405a10–13). For the metaphor to be effective, the term hubris must apply to animals just as it does to humans (contra Fisher 1992: 18). That in human beings hubris lies in the *proairesis*, while animals possess no *proairesis* or *logismos*, points to the conclusion that human hubris is worse than animal hubris, in that the former involves fuller volition and therefore greater culpability: in this sense, animal hubris is "attenuated" (cf. Fisher 1976: 189).

52. See also (inter alia) the passages in n. 70 below; *EN* 1128b10–35 (on shame: *aidôs*, *aischynê*); 1149a25–b1 (*thymos*, *logos*, *timôria*, hubris); *Pol.* 1311a25–b36, including the characterization of hubris as *polymerous*, "diverse in its forms," at 1311a33, which echoes Pl. *Phdr.* 238a2–3: "hubris has many names, since it has many members and many forms" (*hybris de dê polyônymon—polymeles gar kai polymeres*).

53. This is true whether the distinction is drawn as against *aikeia* or otherwise: note especially the phrase "doing and saying things" at *Rh.* 1378b23–24.

54. This is reflected in the concise definitions in [Pl.] *Def.* 415e12 ("hubris is an injustice [*adikia*] leading to dishonor [*atimia*]"); Phot. *Lexicon* s.v. *hybris* = *Suda* s.v. *hybris*, υ 16 Adler ("Hubris: battery [*aikia*] accompanied by humiliation [*propêlakismou*] and spite [*epêreias*]; battery is blows [*plêgai*] alone").

with regard to acts justiciable under the Athenian *graphê hybreôs*.[55] Allowing for variation in mental states and capacities, it encompasses not only other forms of hubris committed by humans (and gods and bodies of water), who typically[56] are motivated by the pleasure of their own perceived self-aggrandizement and/or[57] the humiliation of their victims, but also hubris committed by animals and plants.[58]

55. E.g., Cope and Sandys 1877: 1.239–40, 2.17; Lipsius (1905–15) 1984: 424–26; Harrison 1968–71: 1.172 ("the necessary ingredient for *hybris* of intention to insult"); MacDowell 1976: 27; 1978: 129–32; Fisher 1990; Murray 1990; Cohen 1991: 178; 1995, esp. 143–62; 2005: 216; Todd 1993: 107, 270–71 (without explicitly citing Aristotle); Harris 2004: 63–65; Spatharas 2009: 31–38. Saunders (1991: 268–71) recognizes the Aristotelian definition but insists (unconvincingly) that the *graphê hybreôs* "applied to assaults on *weaker people*" (emphasis in the original). For various dissenting positions, see Gernet 1917: 183–97, esp. 195–96 (*graphê hybreôs* aimed at acts perpetrated against the community as a whole and particularly against its religious principles); Ruschenbusch 1965 (*graphê hybreôs* as a catchall procedure intended for the redress of all wrongs against the person); Gagarin 1979 (the *graphê hybreôs* "could apply to any attack against a person" but was intended for use in the case of severe, unprovoked physical assaults).

56. This is not always the case: note the qualifying *hoion*, "for example," at *Rh.* 1374a14.

57. Note the disjunctive *ê* (ibid.).

58. See esp. Fisher 1992. MacDowell (1976, esp. 28; cf. 1990: 18–23, 262–68) concurs, at least regarding cases that involve human victims. Emphasis may be laid on the state of mind either of the victim, as by Fisher, or of the perpetrator, as by MacDowell, who defines hubris as "having energy or power and misusing it self-indulgently" (1976: 22) and contends that hubris does not always have a victim (1976: 23), and so a fortiori the perpetrator need not intend to shame. My own position is that hubris does always have a victim, either expressed or implied (cf. Fisher 1992: 148) and whether intended by the perpetrator or not (cf. Cairns 1996: 10, "hubris may be a subjective attitude or disposition which can be construed as an implicit affront"; I would lay more stress than Cairns does on the requirement that hubris must involve an act in word, deed, or both). At Antipho 3 β 3, even though both prosecution and defense stipulate that the youth who threw the javelin intended no physical harm to the boy who was accidentally struck and killed, the speaker feels the need to absolve the thrower of hubris—that is, in this instance, negligence (Fisher 1976: 187) or, at most, recklessness; MacDowell's "larking about" (1976: 18) is closer than Gagarin's "'arrogance' [which] would indicate an intentional killing" (1997: 149)—and *akolasia* (cf. Arist. *EN* 1149b31–34); the grounds for rejecting these attributes are that the thrower was practicing the javelin properly. As to animals (in addition to the proverbially hubristic donkeys at X. *An.* 5.8.3: above, p. 21) and bodies of water (which, if not gods in their own right, enjoy special divine protection: n. 60 below), note Hdt. 1.189: one of the sacred white horses of Cyrus the Great acts with hubris in attempting to swim across the Gyndes River, and the river responds with hubris by drowning the horse (for various theories on why the horse is guilty of hubris, see Cairns 1996: 17 n. 69). Although the horse presumably did not intend to insult the Gyndes, its behavior was negligent, if not reckless (there is at least an implied reasonable-horse standard in the fact that no other horse charged into

Yet, upon close inspection, Aristotle's definition founders on specifics as to both the state of mind of the perpetrator and the shame suffered by the victim. With regard to the former, Aristotle insists that hubris may not be retaliatory, may not be committed in anger, and may not involve any benefit to the perpetrator other than that comprised in the act itself (*Rh.* 1378b14–30; *EN* 1149b20–1150a1; for the exclusion of anger, cf. *Rh.* 1380a35–36, 1385b29–31). These assertions are impeached by the overwhelming evidence of other sources. Xenophon stood accused of hubris (pp. 21–24) for an act that he obviously committed in anger, and he was acquitted not because he was angry but because he was justified; in fact, the reaction of the crowd at the trial (X. *An.* 5.8.12) suggests that he was not angry enough. Moreover, the presence of anger (among other emotions) can be assumed not only in Xenophon's other confessed uses of corporal punishment (*An.* 5.8.13–16) but also in the hypothetical cases he mentions at the beginning of his trial (*An.* 5.8.4). Retaliatory hubris is evident in the accusations against Conon, Meidias, and Teisis (pp. 27–29, 36), whose respective prosecutors all explicitly represent the instant offense as the culmination of an escalating quarrel;[59] in the hypothetical case in [Demosthenes] 53 (p. 36); and in the Gyndes' drowning of Cyrus the Great's horse (above, n. 58). Additional examples, from a variety of genres, include Xerxes' punishment of the Hellespont by whipping, verbal abuse, shackling, and (perhaps) branding, done in retaliation for the destruction of his first bridges (Hdt. 7.34–35);[60] Ajax's

the river), and the umbrage taken by the river is shown in Herodotus' expression of and Cyrus' fury at its agency (the river "snatched [the horse] up, pulled it under, and carried it off. Cyrus was greatly angry at the river for this act of hubris . . ."). Hubristic plants (Arist. *GA* 725b34–726a3; Thphr. *HP* 2.7.6) literally aggrandize themselves without regard for the needs of their owners (Michelini 1978, esp. 38–39).

59. D. 54.3–6; 21.78–101; Lys. fr. 279.1–3. See Cohen 1995: 87–142; Phillips 2008: 18–19, 21–22; MacDowell 1990: 2, 294–99.

60. Although no hubris-word appears in the passage, there is no question that we are meant to see Xerxes' acts as constituting hubris of a particularly spectacular and revolting kind (e.g., Fisher 1992: 377–78). Artabanus' warning against hubris (Hdt. 7.16α) foreshadows Xerxes' behavior, and Herodotus, both in his own words (7.35) and in those of Themistocles (8.109), applies to the punishment of the Hellespont the term *atasthalos* (reckless, wicked, outrageous), which is closely associated with hubris (e.g., 3.80; Hom. *Od.* 3.207, 17.588, 20.170; on the connection between *atasthalia* and hubris, see Fisher 1992, esp. 155–56, 166–78 [Homer], 377–81 [Herodotus]; on Xerxes' acts, cf. Cairns 1996: 14–15, 18; Fisher 1979: 37–38, 42–43). The insulting speech recited by the men doing the whipping may acknowledge the divinity of the Hellespont ("It is right that no man sacrifices to you, since you are a muddy, salty river"; contrast the sacrifices to the Strymon at Hdt. 7.113), as may Xerxes' casting of offerings into the Hellespont upon the successful comple-

hubris (in the form of binding, torturing, and killing, followed by mockery) against cattle, sheep, and dogs, which he mistakes for Odysseus, Agamemnon, Menelaus, and other commanders of the Greeks (S. *Aj.* 296–304, 1060–61; cf. 51–111, 233–44),[61] and Menelaus' resulting prohibition of his burial (1091–92);[62] Dionysus' revenge upon Pentheus for imprisoning him (E. *Ba.* 616–37), which the god himself describes as hubris (*kathybris' auton*, 616); and Prometheus' response to his punishment ("So must one commit hubris against those who commit hubris," A. *Pr.* 970).[63] In most (and arguably all) of these cases, moreover, the actors are not just retaliating but doing so in anger.[64]

tion of his second bridging attempt, if done in repentance for his earlier actions (7.54). Aeschylus (*Pers.* 745–50) has the ghost of Darius specify that the Hellespont belongs to Poseidon; as Alexander the Great crossed the Hellespont, he sacrificed to Poseidon and the Nereids and poured a libation into the water (Arr. *An.* 1.11.6). Cf. Stafford 2005: 198–202, on Persian hubris as displayed in the campaign of 490 that terminated at Marathon.

61. Note esp. v. 304, *hosên kat' autôn hybrin ekteisait' iôn* (in the immediate aftermath of his rampage, Tecmessa reports, Ajax gloated at "all of the hubris he had repaid them with in full as he went"). For various interpretations, see Blundell 1989: 70; Fisher 1992: 313–14.

62. Cairns (1996: 11–13), noting the "process of retaliatory hubris," correctly observes (contra Fisher 1992: 316, 318–29) that the ascription of hubris to Menelaus need not be limited to this specific act; but there are no good grounds for his doubting whether "the primary reference of [vv. 1091–92] is to non-burial": to Menelaus' prohibition, which includes the description of Ajax as "a blazing *hybristês* (perpetrator of hubris)" (v. 1088), the Coryphaeus responds, "Menelaus, do not lay a foundation of wise maxims and then yourself become a *hybristês en thanousin*." *En thanousin* is often translated "on the dead" (Jebb 1907: 165; Fisher 1992: 316; Cairns 1996: 12), but the preposition signifies not just "on" but also "in respect of, in the case of" (LSJ[9] s.v. *en* I.7): Menelaus' act would constitute hubris not only against Ajax but also against universal Greek burial custom and the gods who serve as its guardians and guarantors (cf. Lys. 2.7–8; S. *Ant.*, in which Creon's edict is clearly an act of hubris although nowhere labeled as such: Fisher 1992: 311). On hubris in the *Ajax*, see also Bacelar 2006.

63. Despite the apparent lacuna of at least one line immediately preceding (Griffith 1983: 258), Prometheus' statement, unless purely gnomic (cf. A. *A.* 763–66: "old hubris is wont to beget young hubris among evil men sooner or later"; Gorg. *Epitaphius* fr. 6 D-K: the dead were "*hybristai* to the *hybristai*"), must refer to his responding in kind to the hubris perpetrated against him not only by Hermes but also, since Hermes has just identified himself as Zeus' agent (v. 969), by Zeus, for ordaining his chaining (and by Zeus' subordinates, at least the enthusiastic Cratus [and Bia?], if not the reluctant Hephaestus, for executing it?), which Zeus will eventually exacerbate by sending an eagle to devour his liver every other day (vv. 1020–25; Cic. *Tusc.* 2.23–25 = A. fr. 193 Nauck) (cf. Fisher 1992: 248–50). See also *PHerc.* 1017, with Karamanolis 2005.

64. Note D. 21.41: even as Demosthenes contends that Meidias' premeditated hubris excludes a mitigating defense of anger, he acknowledges—against his own immediate

Arguably, though, the most blatant contradiction of Aristotle's exclusion of anger, retaliation, and ulterior benefit to the perpetrator lies in the example he himself cites immediately following *Rhetoric* 1378b14–30 (above, p. 38): "For that which is worthless has no honor/value [*timên*], either for good or for ill. This is why Achilles says in anger, '[Agamemnon] has dishonored [*êtimêsen*] me, for he took [*helôn*] and keeps my prize, having wrested it away [*apouras*] himself' [Hom. *Il.* 1.356] and 'as if I were some vagabond bereft of honor [*atimêton*]' [*Il.* 9.648 = 16.59], explaining that these are the reasons for his anger" (*Rh.* 1378b30–35). Aristotle presumably chose the seizure of Briseis because it was the best-known instance of hubris[65] in all of Greek literature; and on the surface, the incident complies with Aristotle's definition: it is an act of violence[66] intended for and successful at the shaming of Achilles. On matters of detail, however, *Iliad* 1 controverts Aristotle. Agamemnon, already roused to anger by Calchas' insistence that he return Chryseis ("Then rose up . . . Agamemnon, vexed; his heart, black all about, was greatly filled with fury, and his eyes were like blazing fire," 1.101–4), will not have had his mood improved by Achilles' calling him shameless, greedy, and dog-eyed (1.149, 159). Agamemnon explicitly justifies his act as one of retaliation: "Just as Phoebus Apollo takes Chryseis from me . . . , I shall carry

---

interests—that hubris and anger can coincide: "acts that a person is suddenly carried away to commit before thinking, even those done hubristically [*hybristikôs*], may be said to have been done in anger [*di' orgên*]."

65. It is explicitly condemned as such by Achilles, who is seconded by Athena: *Il.* 1.203, 214; cf. 9.368. On this episode, see Cantarella 1983; Fisher 1992: 151–54; Scheid 2005: 403–6; Cairns 2011. For wrongful appropriation (violent or otherwise) as hubris (Fisher 1976: 184; MacDowell 1976: 19), cf. Hom. *Il.* 13.620–39 (the Trojans' hubris includes their abduction of Helen and theft of property from Menelaus in defiance of Zeus Xeinios); *Od.* 1.224–29 (Athena calls the suitors *hybrizontes* for feasting on Odysseus' food in his palace: see Fisher 1976: 186–87; contra MacDowell 1976: 16); n. 28 above; p. 31, with n. 31; n. 37 *ad fin.*

66. On this point, the opinions of Homer and his characters are consistent and unmistakable. In Homer's own words: *Il.* 1.428–30: Thetis "left Achilles there, angered in his heart about the . . . woman whom they had wrested away [*apêurôn*] by force [*biêi*] against his will [*aekontos*]." Agamemnon, speaking before the fact: 1.137–39: "if the Achaeans do not give [me appropriate compensation], I shall myself come and take [*helômai*] your prize or Ajax's, or take and carry off [*axô helôn*] Odysseus'"; 1.323–25 (to Talthybius and Eurybates, even after Achilles has promised not to resist at 1.298–99): "Take by the hand and carry off [*cheiros halont' agemen*] fair-cheeked Briseis; and if he does not give her, I will take [*helômai*] her myself, coming with more men." Characters speaking after the fact and despite Achilles' failure to offer forcible resistance: 1.356 (above), *helôn . . . apouras* (Achilles), repeated by Thetis at 1.507 and by Thersites (!) at 2.240; cf. 9.106–11 (Nestor, answered by Agamemnon, esp. 9.131–32, and relayed by Odysseus, 9.273–74), 16.56–59 (Achilles).

off fair-cheeked Briseis, your prize, going myself to your hut" (1.182–85). The benefits Agamemnon expects are not limited to putting Achilles in his place and thereby diminishing Achilles' *timê*;[67] they also include immediate[68] material compensation for his own surrender of Chryseis and attendant loss of *timê* (1.118–20, 133–39), as well as the object lesson that the humiliation of Achilles will provide to the other Greeks ("and [so that] another man too may shrink from speaking as my equal and vying with me to my face," 1.186–87).[69] This closing comment, in which Agamemnon smugly reaffirms his superiority, is but one example demonstrating the falsity of Aristotle's refusal (at least in this instance)[70] to acknowledge that the perpetrator of hubris can (and frequently does) simultaneously feel anger at another and pleasure with himself.[71]

67. *Il.* 1.185–86: "so that you may know well how much greater I am than you"; Achilles' complaints in the lines quoted by Aristotle show that the loss of *timê* is absolute as well as relative.

68. Contrast the delayed and uncertain compensation proposed by Achilles at 1.127–29.

69. The additional benefit of Briseis' sexual services is not stated here but assumed, as we see in Agamemnon's oath of denial, proffered at *Il.* 9.132–34, 9.274–76, and 19.175–77 and finally sworn at 19.258–65: the repetition itself, including, in particular, the phrase "as is *themis* for men and women" (present with minor variations in the first three instances) testifies to the strength of the assumption. Other cases in which an act of hubris clearly involves expected and/or actual ulterior benefit include not only the broadly similar intended object lessons regarding resistance to authority inherent in the punishment of Prometheus and the proposed denial of burial to Ajax but also, e.g., Diocles' confinement of his brother-in-law, done to deter an inheritance claim (above, p. 33).

70. Cf. *EN* 1104b14–15: "every experience and every act is attended by pleasure and pain" (*panti de pathei kai pasêi praxei hepetai hêdonê kai lypê*); *EN* 1113b21–25, 1180a5–12: *kolasis* and *timôria* may coincide; *Rh.* 1378a30–b10: anger (*orgê*) is the desire for vengeance (*timôria*); it occurs with pain (*lypê*), but all anger is attended by the pleasure (*hêdonê*) that results from the hope of achieving vengeance. On the problems with Aristotle's theory of emotions, see Cairns 1993: 393–431; Leighton 1996; Cooper 1996; Frede 1996; Striker 1996; Fortenbaugh 2002, esp. 97–126; Dow 2011.

71. The combination is patent in Menelaus' speech at S. *Aj.* 1052–90; note esp. 1087–88: "before, [Ajax] was a blazing *hybristês*; but now it is my turn to think big [*meg' . . . phronô*]." Whether we are here meant to equate *mega phronein* with hubris (so, persuasively, Cairns 1996: 11–13; contra Fisher 1992: 315–16) has no bearing on the fact that Menelaus is clearly pleased with himself. In addition to the combination of anger and self-satisfaction evinced by or unproblematically ascribed to other persons acting in (assumed, if not actual) authority (such as Zeus and Xerxes; Xenophon may well have been pleased with himself when he struck the muleteer and other shirkers, but naturally he does not tell us so), consider, e.g., the case of Conon, who obviously enjoyed himself, as well as humiliating Ariston, by performing the rooster dance that, according to Ariston, provided the clearest sign of his hubris (above, p. 29). Fisher (1992: 17–18, 58) notes some of the Aristotelian

Hubris, Shame, and the *Ep' Agathôi* Standard: Acts, Perpetrators, Victims, and Third Parties

As the case of Agamemnon and Achilles illustrates, in defining hubris we must not limit our attentions to the state of mind (including motives, intentions, and expectations) of the perpetrator and the effects (intended, foreseen, or neglected, as well as actual) on the victim; equally important are the effects on third parties,[72] whose reactions and judgments are more informative than (but, in many cases, cannot be completely divorced from) the assertions of alleged perpetrators and victims, who naturally will respectively restrict and expand the concept of hubris. Greek literature and cultural practice abound with instances of violence involving a manifest intent to shame. In determining whether such acts constituted hubris, people made at least a tacit and sometimes an explicit distinction, not only generally, as to whether the act was merited, but specifically, as to the purposes, extent, and effects of the shame provoked. Shame varies not only in degree—involving minimal and/or fleeting to devastating and/or permanent impact on the sufferer—but also in type, where the scale ranges from almost absolutely[73] beneficial to absolutely harmful. Moreover, shame operates both (during and) after the fact, as a reaction felt by the sufferer (and, by extension, those associated with him, such as his family, friends, and fellow citizens), and (during and) before the fact, as a prospect that compels or deters conduct.[74] In brief, the greater the impact on the sufferer is as against his deserts (the latter including the extent to which the actor was specifically entitled to commit the act) and the less constructive the shame is for the sufferer and for third parties, the more hubristic the act is. With regard to hubris, to borrow the terminology of the Athenian *aikeia* law applied by Aristotle (above, p. 39), this was the principal calculus that determined whose *cheires* were *adikoi* and whose were *dikaiai*.

At one end of the spectrum lie acts that any reasonable person would characterize as extreme hubris. Pheidon of Argos, in Herodotus' estimation, "committed the greatest act of hubris of all the Greeks by expelling the Elean officials and presiding over the Olympic competition himself"

---

inconsistencies but does not fully pursue them.

72. Fisher 1990: 131; Rowe 1993: 400; Cohen 1995: 159 ("Hubris . . . required . . . the demonstration of intentionally insulting or degrading conduct *which fell within the categories acknowledged as such by the community*" [emphasis added]).

73. I include the qualifier "almost" because all shame involves harm to the victim.

74. Cairns 1993, esp. 13, 414–15; Dover 1994: 226–42.

(6.127.3). Apart from the disgruntled Eleans, Pheidon offended—without doing any bodily harm to—no less a personage than Zeus, king of the gods, guardian of justice, and honorand of the festival.[75] By definition, no human being, however highly placed or sorely provoked, is entitled to lash, vilify, and shackle (and perhaps brand) the Hellespont (p. 41); the shame inflicted is entirely destructive both for the victim and for third parties, insofar as the lesson they take is that treating a body of water in such a manner is permissible. The same combination of binding, whipping, and (presumed, if not attested) verbal abuse in the cases of Teisis (p. 34), Pittalacus (p. 35), and Ajax (p. 42) indicates that (at least in Athens) this constituted a paradigmatic form of consummate hubris also when inflicted upon a human victim.[76] The underlying assumption that the severity of the physical punishment and of the shame induced decisively outweighs any justification is borne out by the reactions not only of neutral third parties (in the cases of Teisis and Pittalacus)[77] but even of third parties friendly to the perpetrator (in the case of Teisis).[78]

---

75. Fisher 1992: 143.

76. Xerxes' explicit (and unmerited) assertion that he is the master (*despotês*, Hdt. 7.35) of the Hellespont is clearly implied in these cases (Fisher 1992: 39 n. 18, 52). Cf. Dover's (1994: 54; cf. 147) summary definition (at best only partial, as is commonly recognized: e.g., MacDowell 1976: 23–24; Fisher 1992: 48 n. 41) of hubris as "behaviour in which a citizen treats a fellow-citizen as if he were dealing with a slave or a foreigner" (cf. n. 30 above). A person might be entitled to inflict such treatment on his own slave by way of punishment or in order to produce evidence. Athenian law ordained that the testimony of slaves could be produced at trial only if it had been obtained under torture with the consent of the litigants (e.g., D. 37.39–44). For private evidentiary torture at the discretion of the owner, see Antipho 1.20 (simultaneously evidentiary and punitive); [D.] 48.16–18. This right might extend to some degree as to the slave of another ([D.] 53.16 [above, p. 36]: the presumption is that if the boy caught plucking Apollodorus' roses were a slave, Apollodorus could bind and beat him). But that the right does not extend absolutely to all citizens as to all slaves is established by the Athenian hubris law's explicit protection of slaves (above, p. 32) and is illustrated in practice by the Pittalacus case. For the torture of a confined person as hubris, cf. X. *An.* 2.6.29; 3.1.13, 29.

77. Lys. fr. 279.6: after Archippus' release, he was conveyed on a litter to the Deigma, where "onlookers not only were angry at the perpetrators but even denounced the city for not publicly and immediately punishing [them]." Aeschin. 1.60–61: the morning after the assault upon him, Pittalacus "went unclothed into the Agora and sat down at the altar of the Mother of the Gods; when a crowd came running up, as is wont to happen, Hegesander and Timarchus, afraid that their disgusting behavior would be announced to the entire city," enlisted the help of friends and together convinced Pittalacus to get up and leave the Agora.

78. Lys. fr. 279.5–6: Teisis, after both rounds of whipping and with Archippus still tied

At the opposite end of the spectrum lie acts that, though violent and committed with a manifest intent that includes asserting the dominance of the actor and shaming the sufferer, carry an inherent and strongly preponderant presumption against hubris. Xenophon's cavalier comparison of his own use of violence with those of parents and teachers (X. *An.* 5.8.18, above, p. 23; cf. his description of Clearchus, esp. *An.* 2.6.12, above, n. 15) is telling. Athenians were prohibited by law from beating their parents[79] but were expected to beat their sons (e.g., Ar. *Nu.* 1410–34; cf. *V.* 1297–98; Arist. *EN* 1149b8–13). Teachers regularly beat their students (note the proverbial *ho mê dareis anthrôpos ou paideuetai*, "the person who is not thrashed is not educated": Men. *Mon.* 422; cf., e.g., Ar. *Nu.* 492–97).[80] The licit and pervasive use of corrective shaming violence also characterized Greek athletics. Athletes who committed fouls, such as false starts in races (Hdt. 8.59), punching a fallen opponent or clinching in boxing, and biting or gouging in the pancration (the only two prohibited moves in that event: Philostr. *Im.* 2.6; cf. Ar. *Av.* 442–43; Ar. *Pax* 898–99), were flogged on the spot by supervising officials.[81] In all these cases, the act is presumed to occur in retaliation for wrongdoing; the actor has implicit or explicit standing ex officio for his conduct as against the sufferer; and the shame provoked, while destructive to the sufferer in the short term, is presumed to be constructive for the sufferer in the longer

to the column, summons Antimachus and falsely informs him that Archippus broke into his house drunk and verbally abused him, Antimachus, and their wives. Antimachus summons witnesses and asks Teisis how he got in; when Teisis replies that he was invited, Antimachus and his witnesses urge the immediate untying of Archippus, "considering what had happened to be terrible," and deliver Archippus to his brothers.

79. An Athenian child who beat his parent was liable to an *eisangelia kakôseôs goneôn* (for maltreatment of parents: e.g., [Arist.] *Ath.* 56.6; Lys. 13.91), in which the penalty was disfranchisement (*atimia*: e.g., And. 1.74; Aeschin. 1.28–32; [Arist.] *Ath.* 55.3). Falsely accusing a person of beating his parent constituted grounds for a *dikê kakêgorias* (for defamation: Lys. 10.8).

80. Note also the use of whipping as the standard punishment, designed to inflict and inculcate shame (X. *Lac.* 2.1–11), in the simultaneously pedagogical and military Spartan *agôgê*, of which Xenophon clearly approved, even if he did not (as implied at D.L. 2.54) send both of his sons through it.

81. Poliakoff 1987: 27–28, 54, 80; Crowther and Frass 1998 (including comparison with pedagogical and military flogging); Miller 2004, esp. figs. 90, 98, 102, 152; Potter 2011: 60–61. Cf. the (extraordinary) case of Lichas of Sparta at the Olympiad of 420 (Th. 5.50; X. *HG* 3.2.21; Paus. 6.2.2). A late sixth-century law of the Olympic Games (*SEG* 48.541; on Olympic laws, cf. Paus. 6.24.3) prescribes the penalty of flogging, except on the head, for a wrestler who breaks an opponent's finger. X. *Lac.* 8.4 (above, n. 11) compares the Spartan ephors' powers of summary punishment to those of tyrants and athletic officials.

term, as well as immediately and indefinitely constructive for third parties, as deterring similar (and, by extension, other) bad acts. The standard is not only objective (is the punisher entitled to act; does the punishment fit the offense?) but subjective (what are the understood motives and intentions of the punisher and the expected consequences of the punishment?). The same applies, Xenophon argues (however tendentiously: above, pp. 24–26 with n. 13), to the general. The determining factor lies in the intent of the actor and the expected consequences for the sufferer and for third parties. Striking a person for his own good (in the extreme case, in order to save his life) and for the good of others (punishing violations of military discipline deters not just the offenders but their comrades from acts that endanger all) is explicitly contrasted with striking a person out of hubris.

A definition of hubris that combines the Aristotelian and Xenophontic models—retaining Aristotle's characteristic elements of self-aggrandizement and shame but eliminating his rejection of anger, retaliation, and ulterior benefit to the perpetrator, while applying Xenophon's test of benefit to the sufferer and others—makes sense not only of those cases in which the standing of the actor and/or the sufferer raises a clear ex hypothesi prejudice either for or against hubris but also of those cases in which such prejudice is complicated, contested, or absent. Not a few Athenians might have thought that Demosthenes deserved a good punch in the face under other circumstances (p. 27); but Meidias chose the worst possible time and circumstances to deliver one. Insofar as, at the moment of the assault, Demosthenes represented his tribe, the sovereign Athenian demos, and the god,[82] the insult inflicted by Meidias increases in severity, is diverted from Demosthenes himself (who might otherwise be fair game) onto entities that are never legitimate targets, and accordingly loses any claim to justification on the grounds of benefit, resulting instead in positive and unqualified harm for all third parties concerned. Hence, whereas Xenophon won acquittal at Cotyora for an act of violence deemed reasonable and appropriate in its scope, target, motives, and intended and actual results, Demosthenes secured a formal condemnation of Meidias by the Athenian Assembly and perhaps a punitive verdict in court two years later (above, pp. 27–28 with n. 21). Ariston (above, p. 28) is aware that his jurors may conclude that he deserved a beating if they believe any or all of the arguments anticipated from the defense—namely, that the fight was a typical instance of wealthy young men scuffling over *hetairai* and, as such, does not merit the attention of the law; that it

82. See esp. D. 21.18, 32–35, 61, 126–27.

involved only Ariston and Conon's son Ctesias and was initiated by Ariston, thereby entitling Ctesias to defend himself; and that Ariston is exaggerating the extent of his injuries.[83] But as Ariston relates the event at Demosthenes 54.8–9, the fight was three (including Conon) against one, the hubris started when Ariston was already decloaked and prone in the mud, and it culminated after the beating was over, when Conon did his rooster dance.[84] The prime indicator of Conon's hubris thus occurs at the moment of greatest humiliation to Ariston, least practical purpose for his attackers (whose victim is already down and motionless), and least constructive effect on anyone else. Confinement and (additional) physical violence inflicted by one Athenian on another (or even on a slave, unless done by or with the consent of his owner) was, as we have seen (p. 46),[85] so far beyond the pale of licit behavior that it constituted a stereotypical form of hubris.

The *Moichos* and the Radish: Topographies of Hubris and Shame

There was, however, one notorious exception. Athenian law offered up to seven potential remedies to the man who caught a seducer (*moichos*) in the act with his wife, mother, sister, daughter, or concubine kept for the procreation of free children.[86] The captor might bring one of four actions at law—

83. D. 54.13–14, 31. That Conon will portray Ariston and his brothers as "violent drunks [*paroinous*] and *hybristai*" (§ 14; cf. X. *An.* 5.8.4, p. 21 above) surely indicates that he will identify Ariston as the aggressor in the fight. The caution evinced by Carey and Reid (1985: 70, 87) is unwarranted; since *aikeia* was, by definition, *archein cheirôn adikôn* (above, p. 36), any *aikeia* defendant capable of doing so will have argued that it was not he but his prosecutor who *êrxe*.

84. Cf. Harris 2004: 65: "When Ariston tries to prove that he suffered *hybris* at the hands of Conon, he lays stress on his opponent's behavior after striking him."

85. Citizen perpetrator and victim: Teisis and Archippus (p. 34); Apollodorus and a citizen boy (hypothetical, p. 36); by analogy (i.e., with a functional equivalence of status between perpetrator and victim), Ajax and the animals he mistakes for Odysseus et al. (p. 42). Compare the cases in which postconfinement violence is not specified (but may have been known or presumed): Diocles and his brother-in-law (p. 33); Menon and a citizen boy (p. 35). A fortiori, with human perpetrator and divine victim: Xerxes and the Hellespont (p. 41). Citizen perpetrators and slave victim: Timarchus et al. and Pittalacus (p. 35).

86. Kapparis 1995; 1996; 1999: 302–7; Schmitz 1997; Cohen 1991: 98–132; Cantarella 2005; Phillips 2006: 381–85.

(1) *graphê hybreôs*, (2) *graphê moicheias*, (3) *apagôgê*, or (4) *eisangelia*[87]—or inflict punishment on his own authority, either (5) killing the *moichos* on the spot[88] or detaining him (6) for ransom and/or (7) for physical abuse. According to his own narrative (Lys. 1.24–29), Euphiletus, accompanied by witnesses, caught Eratosthenes in bed with his wife, knocked him down, tied his hands behind his back, and asked why Eratosthenes was committing hubris against his house (cf. n. 39); Eratosthenes confessed and begged Euphiletus to exact ransom, but Euphiletus refused and killed him. In the famous case narrated in Apollodorus' *Against Neaira*, Stephanus entrapped Epaenetus of Andros into committing (apparent) *moicheia* with Neaira's daughter Phano, apprehended Epaenetus in the act, and, asserting his right as Phano's (alleged) father, confined Epaenetus until he agreed to pay thirty minae and posted two sureties ([D.] 59.64–65).[89]

A captor who elected not to kill a *moichos* may have been permitted by law "to do with him whatever he wishes," perhaps with the proviso that he not use a dagger.[90] Certainly he was entitled by custom (if not by law) to punish the *moichos* by extraordinary measures, including the forcible insertion of a large radish into the *moichos*' anus and the tearing out of his genital and/or buttock hair with the aid of heated ash.[91] These punishments and

87. *Graphê hybreôs*: above, p. 36. *Graphê moicheias* (for seduction): Hyp. 1.12; [D.] 59.87; [Arist.] *Ath.* 59.3–4. *Apagôgê* (summary arrest whereby the accused was haled before the Eleven, executed if he confessed, and brought to trial before a *dikastêrion* if he maintained his innocence): Aeschin. 1.90–91; [Arist.] *Ath.* 52.1. *Eisangelia* (impeachment): Hyp. 1, with Lyc. frr. X–XI Conomis.

88. D. 23.53; Plu. *Sol.* 23.1; cf. Lys. 1 (see below and n. 90).

89. Apollodorus maintains that Stephanus had used the same scheme before, with his alleged wife Neaira as the bait: [D.] 59.41.

90. Lys. 1.49: the laws "command that if a person catches a *moichos*, he may do with him whatever he wishes [*ean tis moichon labêi, ho ti an oun boulêtai chrêsthai*]." Kapparis (1995: 114–16; cf. Carey 1995: 413) takes this to be the paraphrase of a law on *moicheia* (cf. the similar legal provision for the female party to *moicheia* who violates her ban on wearing jewelry or attending public religious rites: see below) and tentatively imports from the law governing the *graphê adikôs heirchthênai hôs moichon* (see below) the proviso "without a dagger" (*aneu encheiridiou*). But it is equally possible that Euphiletus is referring to the law of Draco that permitted the killing of a *moichos* caught in the act (D. 23.53: above, n. 88), which he cites at § 30, and perhaps also to a law on *apagôgê* cited at § 28 (on the disputed identification of this law, see Cohen 1991: 120–22; Schmitz 1997: 56–69; Todd 2007: 124–25).

91. Ar. *Nu.* 1083–84, with schol. *ad* 1083; *Pl.* 168, with schol.; *Th.* 536–38; *Suda* s.v. *ô Lakiadai* (a deme famous for its radishes), ω 62 Adler; Kapparis 1996; 1999: 302–3;

possibly others like them[92] were not only painful but manifestly humiliating and talionic: for his violative act of seducing a woman, the *moichos* was himself violated as a woman.[93] The female party to *moicheia*, if subsequently caught wearing jewelry or attending public religious rites, was subject by law to "whatever she suffers, except death," at the hands of anyone who caught her.[94] Violent and/or shaming punishments for both *moichoi* and their paramours were not restricted to Athens. The Great Code of Gortyn (*IC* IV 72, col. 2, vv. 20–36) provides that if a *moichos* caught in the act and detained is not ransomed within five days of the announcement of capture to the *moichos*' relatives (or, if he is a slave, to his owner), "it shall be in the power of his captors to do with him whatever they wish" (*epi tois elonsi êmên krêththai opâi ka leiônti*, vv. 34–36). In various parts of the Greek world, the *moichos*, the female party, or both might be publicly paraded on a donkey, a punishment talionic in its symbolism (cf. X. *An.* 5.8.3, p. 21, with *moicheia* as hubris: p. 36; n. 39).[95]

Schmitz 1997: 91–107. Owing to the licit status of such practices, we may safely assume, a fortiori, that the captor was allowed to beat the *moichos* (cf. Kapparis 1996: 66; Forsdyke 2008: 24).

92. According to the *Suda* (n. 91 above), in the absence of radishes, Athenians used ax handles. Whether a scorpion fish (*skorpios*) could substitute for the radish (as may be indicated by Pl. Com. fr. 189.22 Kassel-Austin [= Ath. 5d]; cf. Catull. 15.17–19; Juv. 10.317) is debated (pro, e.g., Schmitz 1997: 100; contra, Kapparis 1996: 67–70). The statement at Ar. *Ach.* 849 that Cratinus "always has his hair cut *moichos*-style, with a single blade [i.e., with a razor (schol. vet. ad loc.) rather than with scissors]" (*aei kekarmenos moichon miai machairai*) may mean (1) that Cratinus' head resembles the depilated nether regions of a *moichos*, (2) that *moichoi* might have their scalps as well as their genitals and/or buttocks depilated by their captors, or (3) that (voluntarily) wearing one's hair as Cratinus does (presumably very short) was characteristic of *moichoi* (in which case *moichos* would be a derogatory name for the hairstyle [schol. Triclin. ad loc.]; we might compare the modern American slang "wife-beater" for a white sleeveless undershirt). See Sommerstein 1992: 199; Schmitz 1997: 93–101.

93. He was violated by penetration and/or by depilation, which was characteristic of women and especially of *hetairai*: Kapparis 1995: 112; 1996: 74–76; 1999: 303; Schmitz 1997: 95–99; Forsdyke 2008: 19–20.

94. [D.] 59.86–87; Aeschin. 1.183, which gives as examples of punishment tearing the woman's clothes, stripping her of her jewelry, and hitting her; adds the proviso that the woman may not be maimed; and highlights the shaming function of the punishment ("dishonoring [*atimôn*] [her] and making her life not worth living"). On the interpretation of these sources see, e.g., Schmitz 1997: 89–91; Kapparis 1999: 354–60; Fisher 2001: 334–38.

95. Plu. *Mor.* 291f (*Quaest. Graec.* 2) (Aeolian Cyme); Nicolaus of Damascus, *FGrHist* 90 F 103(l) (Pisidia); Schmitt-Pantel 1981. On the foregoing and for other punishments

At Athens, the nonlethal self-help punishments for *moichoi* were sufficiently unique and characteristic that the speaker of Isaeus 8, again describing the infamous Diocles of Phlya (p. 33), could state without elaboration that he "was caught as a *moichos* and suffered what befits people who commit such acts";[96] the sequel, "but even so has not desisted from the practice," shows that punishment was meant simultaneously to shame and to deter (the lack of effect on Diocles notwithstanding). In a similar but somewhat more explicit vein, Xenophon's Socrates (X. *Mem.* 2.1.5) summarizes the risks incurred by the *moichos* who enters his paramour's quarters as "suffering what the law threatens, and being ambushed, caught, and *subjected to hubris* [*lêphthenta hybristhênai*]."[97] Given the presence of such harmful and shameful (*kakôn te kai aischrôn*) threats and the availability of risk-free satisfaction of erotic desires, he concludes that the *moichos* must be possessed (*kakodaimonôntos*). The rightful punishment of the female party is likewise described as hubris in the *Against Neaira*: "the law made it so that, except in the case of death, she might not obtain satisfaction anywhere *for any hubris committed against her* [*talla hybristheisan*]" ([D.] 59.86). While it might be objected that Xenophon's Socrates passes no overt judgment on the punishment described, and thus in his mouth *hybristhênai* might be—as it almost always is—a term of condemnation, this cannot be true of Apollodorus in the *Against Neaira*: since the law is ex hypothesi just and right, we have here an unequivocal instance of hubris that is not only retaliatory but morally positive.[98]

But what if the detained man was innocent? Remedies for this eventuality were available both at Gortyn (*IC* IV 72, col. 2, vv. 36–45: if the detainee maintains that he has been taken by treachery, his captor and a variable

---

outside Athens, see Cole 1984: 108–11; Kapparis 1996: 74; Schmitz 1997: 107–15; Forsdyke 2008: 3–4, 12–16.

96. Is. 8.44. A supporting deposition, which does not survive, was read out at the close of the oration (§ 46). See Carey 1992: 108–9; Kapparis 1996: 66–67; Schmitz 1997: 102.

97. Cf. *Suda* s.v. *ô Lakiadai*, ω 62 Adler (above, nn. 91, 92): the Athenians used radishes *in committing hubris* (*enhybrizontes*) against captured *moichoi*. The proverbial status of the utterance "*ô Lakiadai*" (whence its inclusion in the *Suda*) seems itself to argue for the canonical status of the radish in this context (Schmitz 1997: 100).

98. Cf. Fisher 1976: 184; 1992: 96; contra MacDowell 1976: 21. "*Hybristai* to the *hybristai*" (above, n. 63), of the honored dead in a funeral oration (Gorgianic though it is), is intended as praise. If the connotations of hubris were universally and absolutely negative, Xenophon would not include *Hybris* in his list of recommended names for hunting dogs (*Cyn.* 7.5, discussed by Rawlings 2011).

number of others must swear an oath to the contrary) and at Athens, for which we return to the case of Epaenetus of Andros. After posting sureties and being released by Stephanus, Epaenetus filed with the *thesmothetai* a *graphê adikôs heirchthênai hôs moichon* ("for wrongfully having been detained as a *moichos*"). The law governing this procedure permitted the detainee[99] to prosecute his captor. If the prosecution prevailed at trial, the detainee was released from liability (and, if necessary, from detention), and his sureties were released from their obligation. "However," Apollodorus informs us, "if [the detainee] is found to be a *moichos*, the law commands that his sureties hand him over to his captor, and that there in the court, without using a dagger, the captor do with him whatever he wishes, since he is a *moichos*" ([D.] 59.66).

In the event, Epaenetus' case never went to trial. He admitted having sex with Phano but maintained that Stephanus lacked the standing to detain him, since Stephanus was not Phano's father; and he proffered a law forbidding the seizure of a man as a *moichos* in the company of a known prostitute,[100] alleging that Stephanus' house was a brothel. Arbitration by Epaenetus' sureties resulted in a settlement whereby Epaenetus dropped his lawsuit, his sureties were released from their obligation, and Epaenetus contributed one thousand drachmas to Phano's dowry ([D.] 59.67–71). Because this only known instance of the *graphê adikôs heirchthênai hôs moichon* was not carried to completion, we must resort to conjecture as to the specific results of a trial by this procedure. The victorious captor turned defendant could treat the *moichos* any way he wished, without using a dagger. In all probability, this meant that he could enact—or reenact—the nonlethal punishments he was entitled to use within the confines of his house, including binding, beating, and radishing.[101] In this way, otherwise private humiliating violence would be inflicted on the public stage, with the witnessing crowd performing a function at once exacerbating (with the shame incurred

99. Or, presumably, any adult male citizen acting on his behalf: the procedure was a *graphê*, and in cases where sureties did not immediately volunteer, initiating legal action might at least temporarily (see below) convince the captor to spare the radish.

100. Cf. Lys. 10.18–19; Plu. *Sol.* 23.1.

101. The prohibition of an edged weapon is presumably meant to prevent guaranteed bloodshed (as opposed to the incidental bloodshed caused by a blunt instrument) and the attendant ritual pollution of the court. For various interpretations, see Harris 1990: 374; Cohen 1991: 115–18; Kapparis 1995: 114–15; 1996; 1999: 302, 309; Schmitz 1997: 76; Allen 2000: 214; Forsdyke 2008: 18–19.

by the *moichos* increasing as a function of the number of witnesses)[102] and moderating (by ensuring that punishment did not exceed licit bounds).[103] The vindicated detainee, however, received (by Apollodorus' account of the law) only release from his debt to (and, if it had continued up to trial, detention by) his captor. There must also have been punitive measures available against the wrongful detainer, or else there will have been no legal deterrent to his behavior: any Athenian with a wife, mother, sister, daughter, or concubine could detain any man he wished in hopes of successful extortion, and if he lost an ensuing *graphê*, he would face only embarrassment and ill repute. MacDowell hypothesized that "the penalty for wrongful confinement was presumably assessed by the jury [sc., in the *graphê adikôs heirchthênai hôs moichon*] in each case."[104] However, as Apollodorus mentions nothing of the sort, it is more probable that a new action had to be brought. It will have been presumed that the detainee, during his confinement, had suffered treatment so heinous that even had it met Xenophon's *ep' agathôi* standard, it might nonetheless merit the name of hubris. Therefore, for the redress of such treatment that failed the *ep' agathôi* test, the natural choice of action—provided that the detainee was willing further to publicize (and thereby aggravate) his shame (however unmerited)—will have been the *graphê hybreôs*.[105]

Works Cited

Allen, D. 2000. *The World of Prometheus: The Politics of Punishing in Democratic Athens.* Princeton.

Atkinson, R. 2007. *The Day of Battle: The War in Sicily and Italy, 1943–1944*. New York.

Avramović, S. 2010. "Katoikodomeō in Isaeus, VIII 41: Imprisonment, Hybris, and Atimia in Athenian Law." *ZSS* 127: 261–74.

Bacelar, A. 2006. "As medidas de um conceito: Ocorrências de *hýbris* no *Ájax* de Sófocles." *Classica* (Brazil) 19: 234–44.

102. Cf., e.g., Meidias' assault on Demosthenes in the Theater of Dionysus, Agamemnon's humiliation of Achilles before the whole Achaean host, and the punishment of athletes at public games.

103. This may have occurred in the case of Xenophon and the muleteer (and others) but did not occur in the cases of Archippus (until his rescue by Teisis' friends) and Pittalacus. See Fisher 1992: 49; Carey 1995: 414; Forsdyke 2008: 16–18; Riess 2012: 51–65.

104. MacDowell 1978: 126.

105. Carey 1992: 119 (comparing the *graphê hybreôs* against Diocles); Kapparis 1999: 309: alternatives include a *dikê aikeias* (plausible) or a *dikê heirgmou* ("for detention," from MacDowell 1978: 126, but poorly attested).

Bechtel, F., et al. 1913. *Dikaiomata: Auszüge aus alexandrinischen Gesetzen und Verordnungen in einem Papyrus des philologischen Seminars der Universität Halle (Pap. Hal. 1)*. Berlin.

Blass, F. (1887–98) 1979. *Die attische Beredsamkeit.* Repr., 3 vols. in 4, Hildesheim.

Blundell, M. 1989. *Helping Friends and Harming Enemies: A Study in Sophocles and Greek Ethics.* Cambridge.

Cairns, D. 1993. *Aidōs: The Psychology and Ethics of Honour and Shame in Ancient Greek Literature.* Oxford.

Cairns, D. 1996. "*Hybris*, Dishonour, and Thinking Big." *JHS* 116: 1–32.

Cairns, D. 2011. "Ransom and Revenge in the *Iliad*." In S. Lambert, ed., *Sociable Man: Essays on Ancient Greek Social Behaviour in Honour of Nick Fisher*, 87–116. Swansea.

Cantarella, E. 1983. "Spunti di riflessione critica su *hybris* e *timê* in Omero." In P. Dimakis, ed., *Symposion 1979: Vorträge zur griechischen und hellenistischen Rechtsgeschichte*, 85–96. Cologne.

Cantarella, E. 2005. "Gender, Sexuality, and Law." In M. Gagarin and D. Cohen, eds., *The Cambridge Companion to Ancient Greek Law*, 236–53. Cambridge.

Carey, C. 1992. *Greek Orators*. Vol. 6, *Apollodoros, "Against Neaira": [Demosthenes] 59.* Warminster.

Carey, C. 1995. "Rape and Adultery in Athenian Law." *CQ* 45: 407–17.

Carey, C. 2004. "Offence and Procedure in Athenian Law." In E. Harris and L. Rubinstein, eds., *The Law and the Courts in Ancient Greece*, 111–36. London.

Carey, C., and Reid, R. 1985. *Demosthenes: Selected Private Speeches.* Cambridge.

Cawkwell, G. 2004. "When, How, and Why Did Xenophon Write the *Anabasis*?" In R. Lane Fox, ed., *The Long March: Xenophon and the Ten Thousand*, 47–67. New Haven.

Cohen, D. 1991. *Law, Sexuality, and Society: The Enforcement of Morals in Classical Athens.* Cambridge.

Cohen, D. 1995. *Law, Violence, and Community in Classical Athens.* Cambridge.

Cohen, D. 2005. "Crime, Punishment, and the Rule of Law in Classical Athens." In M. Gagarin and D. Cohen, eds., *The Cambridge Companion to Ancient Greek Law*, 211–35. Cambridge.

Cole, S. 1984. "Greek Sanctions against Sexual Assault." *CP* 79: 97–113.

Cooper, J. 1996. "An Aristotelian Theory of the Emotions." In A. Rorty, ed., *Essays on Aristotle's "Rhetoric,"* 238–57. Berkeley.

Cope, E., and Sandys, J. 1877. *The "Rhetoric" of Aristotle.* 3 vols., Cambridge.

Couvenhes, J.-C. 2005. "*De disciplina Graecorum*: Les relations de violence entre les chefs militaires grecs et leurs soldats." In J.-M. Bertrand, ed., *La violence dans les mondes grec et romain*, 431–54. Paris.

Crowther, N., and Frass, M. 1998. "Flogging as a Punishment in the Ancient Games." *Nikephoros* 11: 51–82.

D'Este, C. 1995. *Patton: A Genius for War.* New York.

de Ste Croix, G. 1972. *The Origins of the Peloponnesian War.* London.

Dillery, J. 1995. *Xenophon and the History of His Times.* London.

Dover, K. 1994. *Greek Popular Morality in the Time of Plato and Aristotle.* Rev. ed. Indianapolis.

Dow, J. 2011. "Aristotle's Theory of the Emotions: Emotions as Pleasures and Pains." In

M. Pakaluk and G. Pearson, eds., *Moral Psychology and Human Action in Aristotle*, 47–74. Oxford.

Fisher, N. 1976. "*Hybris* and Dishonour: I." *Greece and Rome* 23: 177–93.

Fisher, N. 1979. "*Hybris* and Dishonour: II." *Greece and Rome* 26: 32–47.

Fisher, N. 1990. "The Law of *Hubris* in Athens." In P. Cartledge, P. Millett, and S. Todd, eds., *Nomos: Essays in Athenian Law, Politics, and Society*, 123–38. Cambridge.

Fisher, N. 1992. Hybris*: A Study in the Values of Honour and Shame in Ancient Greece.* Warminster.

Fisher, N. 2000. "*Hybris,* Revenge, and *Stasis* in the Greek City-States." In H. van Wees, ed., *War and Violence in Ancient Greece*, 83–123. London.

Fisher, N. 2001. *Aeschines, "Against Timarchos."* Oxford.

Fisher, N. 2005. "Body-Abuse: The Rhetoric of *Hybris* in Aeschines' *Against Timarchos*." In J.-M. Bertrand, ed., *La violence dans les mondes grec et romain*, 67–89. Paris.

Flower, M. 2012. *Xenophon's "Anabasis," or "The Expedition of Cyrus."* Oxford.

Forsdyke, S. 2008. "Street Theatre and Popular Justice in Ancient Greece: Shaming, Stoning, and Starving Offenders Inside and Outside the Courts." *Past and Present* 201: 3–50.

Forster, E. 1927. *Isaeus*. Cambridge, MA.

Fortenbaugh, W. 2002. *Aristotle on Emotion.* 2nd ed. London.

Frede, D. 1996. "Mixed Feelings in Aristotle's *Rhetoric*." In A. Rorty, ed., *Essays on Aristotle's "Rhetoric,"* 258–85. Berkeley.

Gagarin, M. 1979. "The Athenian Law against *Hybris*." In G. Bowersock et al., eds., *Arktouros: Hellenic Studies Presented to Bernard M. W. Knox on the Occasion of His 65th Birthday*, 229–36. Berlin.

Gagarin, M. 1997. *Antiphon: The Speeches*. Cambridge.

Gernet, L. 1917. *Recherches sur le développement de la pensée juridique et morale en Grèce.* Paris.

Gernet, L., and Bizos, M. 1989. *Lysias: Discours*. 2 vols., Paris.

Gomme, A., Andrewes, A., and Dover, K. 1945–81. *A Historical Commentary on Thucydides*. 5 vols., Oxford.

Griffith, M. 1983. *Aeschylus, "Prometheus Bound."* Cambridge.

Hansen, M. 1975. Eisangelia*: The Sovereignty of the People's Court in Athens in the Fourth Century B.C. and the Impeachment of Generals and Politicians*. Odense.

Hansen, M. 1991. *The Athenian Democracy in the Age of Demosthenes*. Oxford.

Hanson, V. 1999. *The Soul of Battle*. New York.

Hanson, V. 2009. *The Western Way of War: Infantry Battle in Classical Greece*. With an introduction by J. Keegan and a new preface by the author. Berkeley.

Harris, E. 1990. "Did the Athenians Regard Seduction as a Worse Crime than Rape?" *CQ* 40: 370–77.

Harris, E. 2004. "Did Rape Exist in Classical Athens? Further Reflections on the Laws about Sexual Violence." *Dike* 7: 41–83.

Harris, E. 2008. *Demosthenes, Speeches 20–22*. Austin.

Harrison, A. 1968–71. *The Law of Athens*. 2 vols., Oxford.

Hirata, A. 2008. "Die Generalklausel zur Hybris in den alexandrinischen Dikaiomata." *ZSS* 125: 675–81.

Hornblower, S. 2004. "'This Was Decided' (*Edoxe Tauta*): The Army as *Polis* in Xenophon's *Anabasis*—and Elsewhere." In R. Lane Fox, ed., *The Long March: Xenophon and the Ten Thousand*, 243–63. New Haven.

Hunter, V. 1994. *Policing Athens: Social Control in the Attic Lawsuits, 420–320 B.C.* Princeton.

Jebb, R. 1907. *Sophocles: The Plays and Fragments*. Part 7, *The "Ajax."* Cambridge.

Kapparis, K. 1995. "When Were the Athenian Adultery Laws Introduced?" *RIDA*, 3rd ser., 42: 97–122.

Kapparis, K. 1996. "Humiliating the Adulterer: The Law and the Practice in Classical Athens." *RIDA*, 3rd ser., 43: 63–77.

Kapparis, K. 1999. *Apollodoros, "Against Neaira" [D. 59]*. Berlin.

Karamanolis, G. 2005. "Philodemus, *Peri Hybreôs*? (*PHerc.* 1017): New Readings and the Philodemean Conception of *Hybris*." *Cronache Ercolanesi* 35: 103–10.

LaFave, W. 2000. *Criminal Law*. 3rd ed. St. Paul.

Lanni, A. 2006. *Law and Justice in the Courts of Classical Athens*. Cambridge.

Lee, J. 2007. *A Greek Army on the March: Soldiers and Survival in Xenophon's "Anabasis."* Cambridge.

Leighton, S. 1996. "Aristotle and the Emotions." In A. Rorty, ed., *Essays on Aristotle's "Rhetoric,"* 206–37. Berkeley.

Lendle, O. 1995. *Kommentar zu Xenophons Anabasis (Bücher 1–7)*. Darmstadt.

Lipsius, J. (1905–15) 1984. *Das attische Recht und Rechtsverfahren*. Repr., Hildesheim.

Macan, R. 1908. *Herodotus: The Seventh, Eighth, and Ninth Books*. 2 vols. in 3. London.

MacDowell, D. 1976. "*Hybris* in Athens." *Greece and Rome* 23: 14–31.

MacDowell, D. 1978. *The Law in Classical Athens*. Ithaca, NY.

MacDowell, D. 1986. *Spartan Law*. Edinburgh.

MacDowell, D. 1990. *Demosthenes, "Against Meidias" (Oration 21)*. Oxford.

Magnusson, M., and Pálsson, H. 1969. *Laxdæla Saga*. London.

Mathieu, G., and Brémond, E. 1928. *Isocrate: Discours*. Vol. 1. Paris.

Meyer-Laurin, H. 1965. *Gesetz und Billigkeit im attischen Prozess*. Weimar.

Michailidis-Nouaros, M. 1939. *Isaiou logoi*. Athens.

Michelini, A. 1978. "*Hybris* and Plants." *HSCP* 82: 35–44.

Miller, S. 2004. *Ancient Greek Athletics*. New Haven.

Mirhady, D., and Too, Y. 2000. *Isocrates I*. Austin.

Murray, O. 1990. "The Solonian Law of *Hubris*." In P. Cartledge, P. Millett, and S. Todd, eds., *Nomos: Essays in Athenian Law, Politics, and Society*, 139–45. Cambridge.

Osborne, R. 1985. "Law in Action in Classical Athens." *JHS* 105: 40–58.

Patton, G. (1947) 1995. *War as I Knew It*. Repr., with a new introduction by R. Atkinson, Boston.

Perlman, S. 1976–77. "The Ten Thousand: A Chapter in the Military, Social, and Economic History of the Fourth Century." *Rivista storica dell' antichità* 6–7: 241–84.

Phillips, D. 2006. "Why Was Lycophron Prosecuted by *Eisangelia*?" *GRBS* 46: 375–94.

Phillips, D. 2007. "*Trauma ek pronoias* in Athenian Law." *JHS* 127: 74–105.

Phillips, D. 2008. *Avengers of Blood: Homicide in Athenian Law and Custom from Draco to Demosthenes*. Stuttgart.

Phillips, D. 2014. "Hubris and the Unity of Greek Law." In M. Gagarin and A. Lanni, eds., *Symposion 2013: Vorträge zur griechischen und hellenistischen Rechtsgeschichte (Cambridge MA, 26.–29. August 2013)*. Vienna, 75–97.

Poliakoff, M. 1987. *Combat Sports in the Ancient World: Competition, Violence, and Culture*. New Haven.

Potter, D. 2011. *The Victor's Crown: A History of Ancient Sport from Homer to Byzantium*. London.

Pritchett, W. 1974. *The Greek State at War*. Part 2. Berkeley.

Rawlings, L. 2011. "A Dog Called *Hybris*." In S. Lambert, ed., *Sociable Man: Essays on Ancient Greek Social Behaviour in Honour of Nick Fisher*, 145–59. Swansea.

Rehdantz, C. 1888. *Xenophons Anabasis*. Vol. 1. 6th ed., rev. O. Carnuth. Berlin.

Rehdantz, C., and Carnuth, O. 1905. *Xenophons Anabasis*. Vol. 2. 6th ed., rev. W. Nitsche. Berlin.

Riess, W. 2008. "Private Violence and State Control: The Prosecution of Homicide and Its Symbolic Meanings in Fourth-Century BC Athens." In C. Brélaz and P. Ducrey, eds., *Sécurité collective et ordre public dans les sociétés anciennes*, 49–94. Geneva.

Riess, W. 2012. *Performing Interpersonal Violence: Court, Curse, and Comedy in Fourth-Century BCE Athens*. Berlin.

Ross, W., ed. 1925. *The Works of Aristotle*. Vol. 9. Oxford.

Roussel, P. 1922. *Isée: Discours*. Paris.

Rowe, G. 1993. "The Many Facets of *Hybris* in Demosthenes' *Against Meidias*." *AJP* 114: 397–406.

Ruschenbusch, E. 1965. "*Hybreôs graphê*: Ein Fremdkörper im athenischen Recht des 4. Jahrhunderts v. Chr." *ZSS* 82: 302–9.

Sandys, J., and Paley, F. 1910. *Demosthenes: Select Private Orations*. Part 2. 4th ed. Cambridge.

Saunders, T. 1991. *Plato's Penal Code: Tradition, Controversy, and Reform in Greek Penology*. Oxford.

Scheid, E. 2005. "Remarques sur les fondements de la vengeance en Grèce archaïque et classique." In J.-M. Bertrand, ed., *La violence dans les mondes grec et romain*, 395–410. Paris.

Schmitt-Pantel, P. 1981. "L'âne, l'adultère et la cité." In J. Le Goff and J.-C. Schmitt, eds., *Le charivari*, 117–22. Paris.

Schmitz, W. 1997. "Der nomos moicheias—Das athenische Gesetz über den Ehebruch." *ZSS* 114: 45–140.

Smyth, H. 1956. *Greek Grammar*. Rev. G. Messing. Cambridge, MA.

Sommerstein, A. 1992. *The Comedies of Aristophanes*. Vol. 1, *Acharnians*. Warminster.

Spatharas, D. 2009. *Isokratês: Kata Lochitou*. Athens.

Stafford, E. 2005. "*Nemesis*, *Hybris*, and Violence." In J.-M. Bertrand, ed., *La violence dans les mondes grec et romain*, 195–212. Paris.

Stauber, J. 1996. *Die Bucht von Adramytteion*. Bonn.

Striker, G. 1996. "Emotions in Context: Aristotle's Treatment of the Passions in the *Rhetoric* and His Moral Psychology." In A. Rorty, ed., *Essays on Aristotle's "Rhetoric,"* 286–302. Berkeley.

Todd, S. 1993. *The Shape of Athenian Law*. Oxford.

Todd, S. 2000. *Lysias*. Austin.
Todd, S. 2007. *A Commentary on Lysias, Speeches 1–11*. Oxford.
Trevett, J. 1992. *Apollodoros the Son of Pasion*. Oxford.
van Wees, H. 2011. "The 'Law of *Hybris*' and Solon's Reform of Justice." In S. Lambert, ed., *Sociable Man: Essays on Ancient Greek Social Behaviour in Honour of Nick Fisher*, 117–44. Swansea.
Wevers, R. 1969. *Isaeus: Chronology, Prosopography, and Social History*. The Hague.
Worthington, I. 1992. *A Historical Commentary on Dinarchus: Rhetoric and Conspiracy in Later Fourth-Century Athens*. Ann Arbor.
Wyse, W. 1904. *The Speeches of Isaeus*. Cambridge.

TWO

The Spartan *Krypteia*

Matthew Trundle

Violence permeated the topography of antiquity, from organized warfare to everyday social encounters. It made slaves of some and masters of others and enforced this social order. The threat of violence and fear of reprisal were essential components in maintaining unequal relationships of exploitation and subservience between the slave and free person. What follows examines the relationship between secrecy and violence from the perspective of Spartan society, specifically the role that the *krypteia* played as an institution that promoted, inspired, and enacted violence as a means of power and control, primarily over the helots, but also over other threats to the authority of the Spartiatae within the classical Spartan state. Unsurprisingly, little is known of the *krypteia*. This chapter presents what we do know in the context of Spartan political practice and sociopolitical apparatuses, alongside many of the leading theories regarding the nature of the *krypteia* and its purpose. The discussion aims to paint the *krypteia* in the context of a closed and hierarchical society, in which personal connections and private relationships, secrecy at every level, and spatial considerations like isolation and rural separation added to the threat of violence and, thus, combined to empower the elite and maintain a complex and inequitable system of exploitation and power.

Only Plutarch (who himself cites Aristotle as a source), Plato, and the obscure Heracleides Lembos refer explicitly to the *krypteia*. None of these authors are Spartans, and almost certainly none knew of the institution first-hand. They appear not to understand—or, if they did know, not to reveal—its real meaning or purpose, though perhaps they did. The secretive and allusive *krypteia* thus remained, as its name suggests, just that, a secret thing. As a result, the ancient authors present an allusive and occasionally contradictory image of this institution. Our earliest source, Plato (*Lg.* 633b), has a Spartan named Megillus describe to a Cretan and Athenian the way in which Spartan training made the *Spartiatae* strong and tough. He noted the *krypteia* among a variety of training methods that included contests and beatings. Members of the *krypteia* went barefoot in the winter, slept in the open, and went through the countryside without attendants. The implication here is both a time of hiding and a secretive institution. Interestingly, there is no mention here of killing or even threatening helots.

Plutarch (*Lyc.* 28.1–6) describes the *krypteia* in more detail. According to him, Aristotle attributed the *krypteia* to the great lawgiver Lycurgus, an attribution Plutarch doubts on account of the institution's brutality and the civil-minded nature of Lycurgus. Plutarch then relates that the ephors, from time to time (*dia chronou*), sent youths to live wild, hiding by day and killing helots that they found outside at night. Sometimes they killed the strongest helots as these worked in the fields. Plutarch (*Lyc.* 28.6) suggests that, rather than the result of Lycurgus' reforms, the *krypteia* emerged in the wake of the great helot revolt of the 460s BC. In support of the brutality of the Spartan regime of the fifth century BC toward braver helots, he cites Thucydides' account (Th. 4.80) of the disappearance of two thousand helots who volunteered to fight for the Spartan cause in return for their freedom, though it is here important to note that Thucydides makes no mention of the *krypteia* itself or its involvement in this incident.[1] He also notes Aristotle's report that the Spartans annually declared war on the helots to justify such atrocities (Plu. *Lyc.* 28.4; Heracleides 373.10; *FHG* 2). This surely reflects Plutarch's statements on the activities of the *krypteia*, hiding by day, killing helots by night, adding the statement that they do this even in his own day, most likely the second century AD, and that they kill as many as seems appropriate. The last explicit notice to the *krypteia* in a historical context comes also from Plutarch. In his biography of Cleomenes (28), following Phylarchus (*FGrH* 2a 81F59, line 28), the *krypteia* appears in the Spartan army as a unit responsible for reconnaissance in the third century BC and is present on the battlefield at Sellasia in 222 BC. Kennell (2009: 174) has suggested that this unit emerged as a result of the reforms of the later Cleomenes, and he links its emergence to the decline of the Spartan training system known as the *agoge*, of which the earlier *krypteia* had once been a part. Cleomenes thus reconstituted it, but only as a "special operations" unit within the Spartan army.

1. See D. Harvey 2004: 199–218.

Other events are often associated with the activities of the *krypteia*. In his history of the Messenian War, Myron of Priene (see Athenaeus 14.657d) reports that the Spartans degraded the helots in every way, stipulating a shameful dress code (which included the dogskin cap) and a set number of beatings a year regardless of fault, so that they would not forget their servile status (*douleuein*). Significantly, if any helots appeared more vigorous and well fed than a slave ought, they killed them and punished their Spartan overseer. This last statement appears closely allied with stories of the *krypteia* killing brave helots randomly.

Xenophon's (*HG* 3.3.5–11) account of the failed coup of Cinadon mentions young men available to the senior guard commander for state service. Cinadon came from a social group inferior to that of the Spartiatae. Xenophon describes him as one of the Hypomeiones (often simply translated as "Inferiors"), though he was clearly neither helot nor *perioikos*. In 399 or 398 BC, a conspiracy against the elite Spartan system formed around this man. The ephors discovered the plot and acted secretly and quickly. They ordered the Hippagretae (the commanders of the royal bodyguard) and chosen young men to arrest Cinadon. Michell (1952: 164) thought that the commander and those young men involved in Cinadon's arrest came from within the *krypteia*.[2] The secretive way in which the ephors established Cinadon's guilt and affected his arrest certainly lends itself neatly to the use of a secretive body of youths. The whole affair illustrates well the suspicious, closed, and cloak-and-dagger nature of Spartan political life. Finally, our later sources note the *phouaxir*, or "fox time," and the famous Roman-era flagellation of Spartan boys at the altar of Artemis Orthia as they attempted to steal cheese (Plu. *Lyc.* 16.13–14; Justin 3.3.6). Some have suggested that the *krypteia* played the role of the guardians of the cheese, with whips, though clearly such a role would not really fit Plutarch's or Plato's *krypteia* at all.[3]

Analysis of our sources reveals distinct differences that emerge over time regarding the nature of the *krypteia*. Plato's *krypteia* appears to be part of the process, called the agoge, used to create physically fit warriors from among

2. Michell (1952: 164) writes, "The only conclusion to which we can arrive is that service in the crypteia was a part of the training of Spartan youths, who were used by the ephors at their discretion, and that sometimes the removal of undesirable people was carried out through its agency. We are not expressly told so, but it is reasonable to suppose that the arrest of Cinadon was carried out by members of the crypteia."

3. Ducat 1999: 43–66, esp. 50. For the association of rituals like cheese stealing with the *krypteia*, see Michell 1952: 164. See also T. Meier 1939: 336; Levy 1988; M. Meier 1998: 151–83; Kennell 1995: 71.

the whole Spartan citizen body. This would fit with a *krypteia* established by Lycurgus, as Aristotle (cited in Plutarch) suggests, as part of a state program to create a warrior caste of *Spartiatae*. This view permeated throughout antiquity: Pompeius Trogus says that every Spartan served in it or was liable for service within it until the age of thirty (see Justin 3.3). Plutarch's *krypteia* demonstrates a more deliberate policy aimed at the suppression of the helots. In Plutarch's account only the most quick-witted of the young men went out in secret, and those only went from time to time, which suggests that the *krypteia* formed an elite group from within the already elite group of aspiring *Spartiatae*. Finally, by the third century and the battle of Sellasia, this elite group formed, no doubt in time of war, a special military unit in the Spartan battle line.

The existence of a secret group like the *krypteia* fits well with Sparta's reputation for secrecy.[4] Thucydides (5.68) comments in a frustrated tone about the difficulty of attaining information about Sparta and its institutions. The Athenians viewed such secrecy with suspicion (Th. 2.39.1).[5] Democratic Athenians embraced transparency and so abhorred institutional secrecy. The reason is no doubt connected closely to the private and secretive nature of tyranny and oligarchy. Democracy fostered openness, public debate, public voting, and public prosecution of those suspected of treason or conspiracy. Oligarchies governed behind closed doors and, unlike democracy, murdered opponents secretly and without trial. Private dining clubs called *hetaeriae* nurtured oligarchic thinking in Athens. They lay at the heart of the coup of 411 BC and illustrate well the kind of in-house, untransparent societies against which democracy toiled. Thucydides (8.66) connected the oligarchy of 411 with secrecy, random murders, beatings, and the threat of violence. Those who were not members of the oligarchic group and the so-called Five Thousand, whose names remained unpublished, remained silent and passive out of fear that any around them were members of the new in-group (Th. 8.92.5). Secrecy and the threat of violence, therefore, went hand in hand. It is

4. See, e.g., Ephraim 1999: 125, for the conspiracy of silence as typical at Sparta. For surveys of views of this self-reinforcing nature of Spartan secrecy and its effects both inside and outside of Laconia, see Millender 2001: 121–64; Detienne 1988: 56–64, esp. 58; Thomas 1992: 132, 144. For connections between Sparta's lack of written public inscriptions and the supposed secrecy of the oligarchic government, see F. Harvey 1966: 599; Cartledge 1978a: 35–37; Boring 1979: 7–8, 35; Detienne 1988: 58; Ducat 2006: 281–331; Thomas 1992: 144.

5. For further discussion, see Hesk 2000: 23–40, under the telling subtitle "Honest Hoplites and Tricky Spartans."

not surprising that the Athenians connected secrecy with random, extralegal violence supporting anti-Democratic politics. Jon Hesk (2000: 32–34) identified the *krypteia* as one of many features that outsiders saw as a deceitful aspect of Spartan society.

Scholars have long studied this singularly Spartan institution. None have fully unraveled its mysteries. George Grote described the *krypteia* as a police force spying in the countryside in harsh conditions and killing any "formidable" helots that they found.[6] Fittingly, the meaning of such a secret institution remains, as its name suggests, hidden. Even a survey of modern authors' translations of the term *krypteia* produces uncertainty.[7] Most translate it as "secret society" (e.g., Murray 1980: 179), though some suggest "secret service" or even "secret police" (Michell 1952: 81), while others describe it temporally, as the "time of hiding" (Tigerstedt 1965). Most splendidly of all, with a modernizing twist, Paul Cartledge offers up three different translations (implicitly descriptions) for the *krypteia*, all in the same book:[8] at one moment, the *krypteia* represents Sparta's "Special Ops Brigade" (32); at others, it is the "Secret Operations Executive" (70) or the "Secret Service Brigade" (236).[9] All these translations demonstrate the power of words, in and of themselves, as commentary. No doubt, each translation embodies something of the nature of the ancient institution. The name *krypteia* itself belies its secretive qualities, and all these translations at least embody secrecy. Some modern authors, perhaps wisely, do not attempt a translation at all, letting the Greek speak for itself.

Comments made by W. Den Boer sum up neatly the extreme views that an earlier generation of scholars held regarding the *krypteia*.

> Messenian power was thoroughly destroyed in Tyrtaeus' time. Evidently the vigilance of the Crypteia was adequate. The Spartans too must have taken this control seriously. I fail to understand why some modern scholars connect the duties and methods of the Crypteia with education. True, this control was considered as a suitable military exercise and a fitting pastime especially for young Spartans. But anyone who compares these journeys to helot farms with camping expeditions by modern boy-scouts cannot have read the sources well,

6. Grote 1849: 509–11.

7. See Levy 1988: 245–52, aptly titled "La kryptie et ses contradictions."

8. Cartledge 2003b.

9. Cartledge 2003b, 32, 70, 236, respectively; on 236, he also notes "the helot hunting *crypteia*."

> nor can he have realized that a secret state police is the same everywhere and in all ages. The Crypteia was one of the most revolting manifestations of the military state, preventing the Messenians for two centuries from organizing resistance.[10]

The targets of Den Boer's critique are the works of K. M. T. Chrimes and H. Michell.[11] Both embraced Plato's benign representation of the *krypteia*, as opposed to that found in Plutarch, with which I began this chapter. In his magisterial study of Agesilaus and fourth-century Sparta, Paul Cartledge (1987: 30) perceptively sees the *krypteia* as "soft" in one version (Plato) and "hard" in the other (Plutarch). Some scholars see it as integral to the management of the Spartan state. Figueira (2003: 222) describes the *krypteia* as "an important administrative mechanism over Messenia," especially "given the primitive character of the governmental apparatus," while Ephraim (1999: 124) likens it to a "pseudo-archaic institution" for "policing and terrorising the helots."

Perhaps we can trace the development of the institution over time. John Fine (1980: 164) sensibly thought that the *krypteia* changed and was perhaps at one time both an elite unit and a rite of passage. It is attractive to think of it in this way, transforming from an initiation rite of manhood, through a more formal means of suppressing the helots, until it ultimately became absorbed into the army of Sparta as a distinct unit of the younger men available for reconnaissance and dangerous or arduous duties. There are plenty of examples of the younger men of ancient armies, especially Peloponnesian armies, taking on hazardous or special missions detached from the main force.[12] Cartledge (1987: 32) is worth quoting with regard to this transformation of the *krypteia* over time.

> [The *krypteia*] represents a re-institutionalisation and re-adaptation of an existing initiation rite for it to serve not necessarily a social, but also a police function. If Sparta may under certain circumstances properly be described as a police state, the *krypteia* offered the appropriate kind of paramilitary training for those who were destined to be the superintendents and chief constables of this society.

10. Den Boer 1956: 162–77, 168.

11. Chrimes 1949: 375; Michell 1952: 33, 84, 162–64, 179.

12. E.g., in Spartan armies (X. *HG* 6.5.31) and in Xenophon's *Anabasis* (3.4.15), those under younger hoplites usually less than thirty years old are often called on for tasks that involve stealth, speed, or agility.

Importantly, dominating scholarship on the institution is a detailed analysis of the *krypteia* as a rite of passage with similarities to tribal practices in Africa, Australia, and North America, by Henri Jeanmaire (1913: 121–50).[13] According to that analysis, the *krypteia* represented the final ritual in the transformative process between boyhood and manhood for the *Spartiatae*. Elite boys of a certain age removed themselves from society for a short period of time and returned to become men within the group. In this respect, we can identify similarities with a coming-of-age ritual in Dorian Crete, in which boys disappeared into the wilderness, were abducted by adult men before their return, and were then ritually reintegrated into the community (see Str. 10.4). Vidal-Naquet's *Le Chasseur Noir* develops the idea further.[14] The *kryptoi* and the *Spartiatae* represent two extremes of the same continuum. On the one hand are the boys, naked outsiders who are not yet citizens, roaming in the countryside by night and in winter; on the other are the men, well-armed citizens and absolute insiders of the city, fighting by day in the summer heat. Vidal-Naquet argued that the helots assumed the role of animals hunted at night and that the *krypteia* resembled a night hunt. The young Spartans ("les chasseurs noirs") appear like lone wolves in the wild.[15] Ducat (1974: 1451–64) takes it all one step further. For him, the murder of helots was a "magical rite, a symbolic representation intended to reaffirm the norm that Helots were not and could not become Spartans," and, thus, an extreme enforcement of the social hierarchy.[16] Recently, Kennell (2009: 173) argued that the *krypteia* came from the age-group of *Spartiatae* called the *hebontes*, essentially those *Spartiatae* under the age of thirty. This would place the *krypteia* slightly beyond the age-group of boys coming of age and into the group of young adults who had achieved Spartiate status.

Assuming Jeanmaire's analysis has currency, the *krypteia* must have played a critical role in the life of every single Spartan citizen, as a specific moment in the Spartan *agoge*. This may well be an exaggeration, and Aristotle rejected the possibility that every *Spartiatae* underwent at least this part of the ritual; he limited it to only a few of the Spartiate elites. But if Jeanmaire is right and every Spartiatês needed to kill a helot, the result would indeed be carnage on a great scale. Scholars have naturally challenged the notion that every single

13. See, once again, Ducat 2006, for an excellent related discussion.

14. Vidal-Naquet 1986.

15. Jeanmaire 1939: 550–69; Vidal-Naquet 1986: 112–14; Burkert 1983: 84–93; Epstein 1995: 58–73.

16. Ducat 1974: 1451–64; see also Cartledge 1979.

Spartiatês killed a helot in order to achieve his full status.[17] But the rite of passage may well have evolved away from Helot murder or at least from the killing of Messenians (as many of the Helots in fact were) and, thus, from its origins in the days of the ancient Messenian wars. Among certain ancient tribes, killing an enemy was the means of achieving full tribal status. This would explain the relationship between the two phenomena and would perhaps explain the almost contradictory images that Plato and Plutarch provide of the *krypteia* as a rite of passage (even if only for some *Spartiatae)* and a formal oppression of the helot group. Thus, such tribal origins became formalized in the fifth century, associated with helot suppression and perhaps the great revolt of ca. 465. Redfield (1977–78: 155) envisages something along these lines. He suggests that the Spartans modeled helotage on the experiences of colonial encounters overseas in which local populations became serfs to dominant Greek colonists. He then states,

> In the Spartan version, further, the solidarity characteristic of the founding generation was institutionalised by a myth which froze the moment of initial conquest into permanence and a quasi-ritual which re-enacted it. In these terms we can, I think, understand the perpetual war declared annually by the ephors on the helots (see Aristotle fragment 538 Rose) and the hunting of the helots by the krypteia as an element of ephebic training. The Spartans were perpetually conquering their subjects; the helots were perpetually surrendering. In the Greek tradition freedom is the privilege of the victor and slavery the burden of the vanquished; in this sense at Sparta it was true that "the free man is most free and the slave most a slave" (Critias fragment 37 Diels).[18]

Many Greek states recognized a transitional phase between boyhood and manhood. The Athenian *ephebeia* formalized the integration of Athenian youths into the army with two years of training and military service.[19] Significantly, the second year saw the *ephebes* as border guards on the periphery of the state. Thucydides (1.105.4, 2.13.6–7) has the youngest Athenians

17. Michell (1952: 162) optimistically doubts that every young Spartan "took a course in murder as part of his regular training." He cites Plutarch's statement "from time to time" as referring only to "extraordinary occasions."

18. Redfield 1977–78: 146–61.

19. See Burckhardt 1996: 26–74; Vidal-Naquet 1968: 49–64; Reinmouth 1952: 34–50; Hesk 2000: 86–89.

on guard duty at the city walls and border forts in the fifth century, while patrols (*peripoloi*) oversaw Piraeus and might launch ambushes (Th. 4.67.2). Significantly, recent research has demonstrated that not every single Athenian became an *ephebos*.[20] Thus, joining the *ephebeia* was not a prerequisite of citizenship. Similarly, the Macedonian elite alone entered into royal service.[21] These "pages" served for two years before entering the elite companion cavalry. In the case of the *krypteia*, this could explain Plutarch's reference to those boys whose wits were sharpest. In other words, they represented an elite group. Recent work on Sparta reveals its complex hierarchies even within the supposed group of equals, the *homoioi*.[22] Vidal-Naquet (1986: 148) is worth quoting at length in regard to the evolution and nature of the *krypteia*.

> It is probable that, once they became adults and full warriors, it was the *kryptoi* who composed the elite formation of the three hundred "cavalrymen" concerned above all with police duties. In other words, it is impossible to detach the *krypteia* from the practical part it played in Spartiate society, a role that must have been developed for the most part from the eighth century, the date of the conquest of Messenia; that is to maintain in every way possible a repressive regime faced with the endemic rebellions of the subject population of Messenia and of Laconia itself. The *kryptos*, like the ephebe of Athenian myth, is a guileful hunter—but he hunts helots. The temporary wildness of the *krypteia* is an utterly socialised, even political, wildness: it functions directly to maintain the political and social order.[23]

Jacqueline Christien (2006: 176) and Vincent Azoulay (2006: 504–31) have recently argued for a reversed development of the *krypteia*.[24] They maintain that rather than emerging from a primitive rite of passage from the Messenian Wars and, thus, away from helot killing, the *krypteia* developed

20. Pritchard (2003: 329), basing his figures on Hansen's (1985: 12, 47–50, 67–68), argues that about 500 of 990 eighteen-year-olds became ephebes in any given year in later classical Athens.

21. Hammond 1990: 261–90, esp. 266.

22. See, e.g., Hodkinson 1999.

23. Vidal-Naquet 1986: 148.

24. See also Whitby 1994: 87–126; at 104, Whitby observes that the liberation of the helots was a highly topical subject in the fourth century and thus influenced the writings of Plato and Aristotle, who then viewed Spartan institutions with a good deal of hindsight.

into a guerrilla group and away from a more innocent rite of the *agoge*. Noting that the *krypteia* goes unmentioned by authors like Thucydides and Xenophon and that only later fourth-century writers refer to it, they consider the *krypteia* to have developed as a result of the liberation of Messenia in 369 BC. Azoulay points to the Isocratic speech *Archidamus* (see esp. 6.74–76), in which the Spartan king outlines his plan for a guerrilla war of attrition and surprise throughout the countryside of the Peloponnese in order to reconquer Messenia. Christien and Azoulay suggest that this very unhoplite and almost un-Spartan way of war provided the context for the helot-killing *krypteia* and explains why the benign image of the *krypteia* existed first (in Plato), why Plutarch was skeptical of the institution's original violent purpose, and, naturally, why earlier sources appear not to know of its existence. Birgalias (2002: 249–66) lends support to this view, in thinking that the annual declaration of war on the helots dates to this Messenian period of postliberation. At first, this creative and original explanation appears attractive (especially to explain the absence of the *krypteia* in our earlier sources).

We might add to this an episode in the Peloponnesian War that lends weight to Spartan ignorance of guerrilla wars and tactics. In 425/4 BC, the Athenians established some of the Messenians from Naupactos at Pylos. These Messenians raided the Peloponnese, liberating helots and generally making a nuisance of themselves. Thucydides (4.41.3) tells us that the Spartans were ignorant (*amatheis*) until this time (*en to prin chrono*) of such raiding (*lesteias*) and this kind of warfare (*tou toioutou polemou*). He implies that they could not successfully prohibit or parry the attacks of these incursions. Hoplite armies were not particularly designed for this kind of warfare, but surely this would have been exactly the kind of military action suited to the *krypteia* and that outlined in the *Archidamus*, if *Spartiatae* had undergone their wilderness initiation.

As we have seen, however, it appears that the *krypteia* may well have existed prior to 369. Michael Vickers (1995: 354) identifies an obscure reference to the *krypteia* (alongside other Spartan customs) in Aristophanes' *Birds* (line 841), produced in 414 BC, in which the speaker refers to concealing fire, accustoming eyes to darkness, and running to give messages, all of which are Spartan practices. Thus, to Vickers at least, the *krypteia* likely existed in some form in the later fifth century. If it did, what form did it take?

To emphasize the relationship between the *krypteia*, education, and *rites de passage* without referring to the helots sanitizes the institution's nature. As we have seen, this occurs partly due to the Platonic view of the *krypteia*. Thus, many modern researchers have rejected the idea that the *krypteia* serendipitously and deliberately killed helots. Many years ago, Girard (1898: 31–38) first suggested that Spartan youths were *melleirens*, about eighteen to twenty years old, and thus in a transition phase between boyhood and manhood. He follows Plato (*Lg.* 6.760) regarding the *agronomoi*, who, when ordered by the ephors of Sparta, busied themselves, as Michell (1952: 163) disparagingly remarks, "like boy scouts" in rural parts of the country. Michell (164) sensibly rejects the notion that such Spartan elite youths would have done any such toil or manual labor. Rightly, I think, he suggests that such work "would have been utterly alien to the warrior caste." Despite his assertion of an aristocratic ethos for this warrior caste, Michell still embraces a benign view of the *krypteia*. He follows a standard line of argument, suggesting that Plutarch exaggerated the deeds of the *krypteia* (33), that the declaration of war was an archaic ritual that became meaningless (81), and, finally, that the idea that "the youths were sent out to commit murder indiscriminately is so monstrous as to be incredible" (164). Richard Talbert's (1989: 22–40) important study of what might be termed the economic symbiosis of *Spartiatae* and helots also depicts a *krypteia* intent more on initiation than on keeping down the helot population. He even concludes that any "widespread provocation of the [helot] class [would] seem senseless," and he argues, in general, for a relatively peaceful interaction between helot and Spartiate until the Theban victory at Leuctra in 371 and the subsequent invasion of 369 BC (Talbert 1989: 22–40, esp. 34).[25] Such optimistic views of the *krypteia* (and, implicitly, of Spartan policy toward the helots) have enjoyed some resurgence recently. Christien (2006: 176) thought it "absurd" that the *Spartiatae* would kill members of its own workforce on whom they relied so heavily. In a similar vein, Birgalias (2002: 249–66) thought that such murder would have been "catastrophic to the *homoioi*," while Luraghi (2002: 227–48), despite his recognition of the violence implicit in ancient power relationships, thought, following Alcock's work on the location of dwellings in the Peloponnese (2002: 185–99, esp. 190–98; see also Ducat 2006), that helot villages, rather than simply isolated helot homesteads, made it unlikely that the helots were separated by the terror of the *krypteia*.

But let us consider the realities inherent in controlling the large serf population of the southern Peloponnese. Helots outnumbered *Spartiatae* many times over. They lived across a large territorial area that the Spartans could not hope to control without a degree of sophisticated organization and coercion by fear and threat rather than constant pressure and occupation. Plenty

25. For a response to Talbert's arguments, see Cartledge 1991: 379–81.

of evidence suggests a latent hostility between helots and *Spartiatae*. The helots had been disenfranchised through war and violence. Thucydides (4.83.3) stated that most Spartan institutions aimed at their own security with regard to the helot presence. When the region had been hit by a large earthquake in the 460s BC, the helots revolted, and Spartan power must have been quite literally rocked. Helots deserted in numbers in the 420s, willingly supported Cinadon in the 390s, and finally overthrew the Spartans wholesale in the 360s. Even Xenophon's rose-tinted image of Sparta reveals that the helots and others lower down the Spartan socioeconomic tree would have eaten the Spartans raw if they could have (X. *HG* 3.3.6). Against this view, we know that helots campaigned with the Spartan army, and there is no evidence of dissent on campaign. But to leave too many helots behind while a large number of *Spartiatae* ventured abroad invited revolt at home, and we know from more modern contexts that the presence of "colonials" serving in the armies of their imperial masters need not imply mutual affection.[26] Even if the Laconian helots displayed some loyalty to their Spartan masters, the regionally distinct Messenians can have harbored few such feelings. Outsiders recognized the plight of the helots, burdened with tariffs and servitude. Theopompus (*FHG* 115 fr. 13) noted that the helot ethnos occupied a totally raw and bitter position. Even the oligarchic Athenian Critias (fr. 37 Diels) noted that "the free man is most free and the slave most a slave" at Sparta. The Messenians, if not their Laconian siblings, revolted when given the opportunity, such as after the great earthquake in the 460s. That the Messenians established their own state in the wake of Spartan defeats against Thebes in the 370s and 360s is surely evidence that Messenian identity survived centuries of oppression. Aristotle (*Pol.* II a 1269a29 ff.) lists the helots among the weaknesses of Sparta's state, as they waited for the opportunity to attack the Spartans and overthrow their rule (1269a37–38).

Many modern scholars have thus recognized the tension between the *Spartiatae* and helots. Jean Ducat (1974; 1990: 105–27) has shown that violence and dishonor were a central aspect of the relationship between them. Oliva (1971: 48) claimed a "fundamental conflict between the two groups at the opposite poles of Spartan society," while de Ste Croix (2002: 193) more emphatically noted that "the basic relationship between the Spartiates and at any rate the Messenian helots . . . was one of fear and hatred on both sides." Importantly, Devereux (1965: 18–44) highlights the psychological impact of

26. For references and discussion, see Pritchett 1971: 49–51; van Wees 2004: 45; Cartledge 1979: 356; Talbert 1989: 23–26, esp. nn. 9–28.

Spartan power over their helot subjects and the atmosphere of terror that must have pervaded the Spartan state.

The sources note that the *krypteia* moved about secretly in the countryside, almost as if they spied on the helots. Plutarch's last historical notice of the *krypteia* fulfilling the role of a reconnaissance force in the army of Cleomenes III suggests as much (*Cleom.* 28). As they spied, they also identified stronger members of the helot group for elimination and enforced a curfew. Such espionage provided the Spartans with important intelligence about their subjects. Ancient Greek states understood the importance of such local knowledge. The Athenians employed *episkopoi* (literally, "overseers": see *M&L* 276; *ATL* 3.144; Ar. *Av.* 1021) to keep an eye on subject island states in conjunction with local friendly elites (*proxenoi*). Intriguingly, a reference to *kruptê archê* used by the Athenians in their subject states appears in the fifth part of the *Anecdota Graeca*, under the *lekseis rêtorikai*, a tenth-century Byzantine compilation found in Coslinianus (345).[27] Unfortunately, such a "secret command" has no parallel in the Athenian Empire anywhere else in the contemporary or even ancient sources. Perhaps it shared some association with the Spartan *krypteia* and its function as a means of spying on subjects who were removed geographically from the overseeing agency.

Spying alone, however, did not make the *krypteia* the most sinister of institutions. The violence inherent in its legacy requires a final word. The Spartans were not averse to crimes of violence even against those not of the helot group, like the apparently brutal suppression of the Cinadon conspiracy. Cartledge (2003b: 22–23, esp. n. 30) points out several instances in which the Spartans killed seemingly innocent or, at best, neutral free Greeks. He cites Sparta's murder of neutral traders, along with Athenian and allied traders of Athens caught sailing around the Peloponnese (Th. 2.67.3), the two hundred Plataeans executed when their city fell (Th. 3.68.2), and the murder of all free men found in Hysiae after its capture (Th. 5.83.2). The callous murder of two thousand helots simply because they appeared brave and almost to spite (if not because of) their willingness to fight for the Spartan state shows even more clearly the Spartiate willingness to purge any potential threat to its authority. Cartledge (1979: 176) notes Spartan cruelty and identified an important passage in Herodotus (4.146) in which the early Spartans performed official killings by night. This report immediately alludes to secrecy and naturally, therefore, to the *krypteia*. We might once again note Vickers' reference to nighttime activity and to the secrecy of the

27. See Tolkiehn 1925: 2460, 2478; Bekker 1814: 273; Losada 1972: 112.

potential Spartans of Aristophanes' *Birds*. Spartans acted in secret, and the threat of violence must have played a significant role to cower the vast numbers of non-*Spartiatae* across the southern Peloponnese into acquiescence. There can be no doubt that the Spartans did commit murders in secret. Isocrates (12.181) stated that, among Greeks, the Spartans alone "deny the wickedness of all homicide." This was of course a reference to the guilt-absolving declaration of war made against the helots to justify their killings. Spartan policy fostered fear, and fear fostered control.

The violence inherent in the idea of the *krypteia*—its menace, secrecy, and randomness—provided the *Spartiatae* with a perfect mechanism for managing a widely dispersed group of subordinates across the landscape of the southern Peloponnese. It is easy to envisage the power of this threat. Even if not true, rumors of a group of men who were constantly alert to plots or even idle talk of revolution and from whom attack might come at any time, as well as stories of the murders of unarmed and vulnerable helots working in the fields or out wandering at night, would play on the minds of even the bravest helots, if not with regard to their own safety, then concerning that of their families and friends. Parallels with the Gestapo, the NKVD, or the Stasi come to mind. A handful of secret police can terrorize a community of hundreds of thousands due to rumors of brutalities and due to widespread fear of their secrecy.

Despite all the denial of some modern commentators regarding the extreme activities of the *krypteia*, there can be little doubt that ancient elites exploited the weak and maintained their power without pity. The helots were owned communally; the loss of one or two did not affect any single Spartan master economically. The murder of a few helots, especially a few who appeared as potential leaders of their group, would be worth its cost in gold to maintain the social order among the many. In the topography of violence, the *krypteia* played its role well to maintain the balance of power within the Spartan state.

Works Cited

Alcock, S. 2002. "A Simple Case of Exploitation." In P. Cartledge, L. Foxhall, and E. Cohen, eds., *Money, Labour, and Land: New Approaches to the Economics of Ancient Greece*, 185–99. London.

Azoulay, V. 2006. "L'Archidamos d'Isocrate: Une politique de l'espace et du temps." *REG* 119: 504–31.

Bekker, I. 1814. *Anecdota Graecae*. Berlin.

Birgalias, N. 2002. "Helotage and Spartan Social Organisation." In A. Powell and S. Hodkinson, eds., *Sparta: Beyond the Mirage*, 249–66. Swansea.

Den Boer, W. 1956. "Political Propaganda in Greek Chronology." *Historia* 5: 162–77.

Boring, T. 1979. *Literacy in Ancient Sparta*. Leiden.

Burckhardt, L. 1996. *Söldner und Bürger als Soldaten für Athen: Aspekte der politischen und militärischen Rolle athenischer Bürger im Kriegswesen des 4. Jahrhunderts v. Chr.* Stuttgart.

Burkert, W. 1983. *Homo Necans: The Anthropology of Ancient Greek Sacrificial Ritual and Myth*. Trans. Peter Bing. Berkeley.

Cartledge, P. 1979. *Sparta and Lakonia: A Regional History, 1300–362*. London.

Cartledge, P. 1987. *Agesilaos and the Crisis of Sparta*. Baltimore.

Cartledge, P. 1991. "Richard Talbert's View of the Spartan-Helot Struggle: A Reply." *Historia* 40: 379–81.

Cartledge, P. 2003a. "Raising Hell? The Helot Mirage—a Personal Re-view." In N. Luraghi and S. Alcock, eds., *Helots and Their Masters in Laconia and Messenia: Histories, Ideologies, Structures*, 12–30. Cambridge, MA.

Cartledge, P. 2003b. *The Spartans: The World of the Warrior-Heroes of Ancient Greece, from Utopia to Crisis and Collapse*. Virginia.

Chrimes, K. 1949. *Ancient Sparta*. Manchester.

Christien, J. 2006. "The Lacedaemonian State: Fortifications, Frontiers, and Historical Problems." In S. Hodkinson and A. Powell, eds., *Sparta and War*, 163–84. Swansea.

de Ste Croix, G. 2002. "The Helot Threat." In M. Whitby, ed., *Sparta*, 190–95. Edinburgh,. Originally published in *The Origins of the Peloponnesian War*. London, 1972.

Detienne, M. 2010. "L'espace de la publicité: Ses opérateurs intellectuels dans la cité." In M. Detienne, ed., *Les Savoirs de l'écriture en Grèce Anciennne*, 29–81. 2nd ed. Lille.

Detienne, M., and Vernant, J.-P. 1989. *Cunning Intelligence in Greek Culture and Society*. Chicago.

Devereux, G. 1965. "La Psychanalyse et l'Histoire: Une application à l'histoire de Sparte." *Annales* 20: 18–44.

Ducat, J. 1974. "Le mépris des Hilotes." *Annales* 29: 1451–64.

Ducat, J. 1997. "La cryptie en question." In P. Brulé and J. Oulhen, eds., *Esclavage, guerre, économie en Grèce ancienne: Hommage à Yvon Garland*, 43–74. Rennes.

Ducat, J. 1999. "Perspectives on Spartan Education in the Classical Period." In S. Hodkinson and A. Powell, eds., *Sparta: New Perspectives*, 43–66. Swansea.

Ducat, J. 2006. *Spartan Education: Youth and Society in the Classical Period*. Trans. E. Stafford, P.-J. Shaw, and A. Powell. Swansea.

Ephraim, D. 1999. "Sparta, Kosmos of Silence." In S. Hodkinson and A. Powell, eds., *Sparta: New Perspectives*, 117–46. Swansea.

Epstein, S. 1995. "Longus' Werewolves." *CPh* 90: 58–73.

Figueira, T. 2003. "The Demography of the Helots." In N. Luraghi and S. Alcock, eds., *Helots and Their Masters in Laconia and Messenia: Histories, Ideologies, Structures*, 193–239. Cambridge, MA.

Fine, J. 1983. *The Greeks: A Critical History*. Cambridge, MA.

Girard, P. 1898. "Un texte inédit sur la *cryptie* des Lacédémoniens." *REG* 11: 31–38.
Grote, G. 1849. *History of Greece*. Vol. 2. London.
Hansen, M. 1985. *Demography and Democracy*. Herning.
Harvey, D. 2004. "The Clandestine Massacre of the Helots (Thucydides 4.80)." In T. Figueira, ed., *Spartan Society*, 199–218. Swansea.
Harvey, F. 1966. "Literacy in the Athenian Democracy." *REG* 79: 585–635.
Hesk, J. 2000. *Deception and Democracy in Classical Athens*. Cambridge.
Hodkinson, S. 1999. *Property and Wealth in Classical Sparta*. Swansea.
Hodkinson, S. 2006. "Was Classical Sparta a Military Society?" In S. Hodkinson and A. Powell, eds., *Sparta and War*, 111–62. Swansea.
Jeanmaire, H. 1913. "La cryptie lacédémonienne." *REG* 14: 121–50.
Jeanmaire, H. 1939. *Couroi et Courètes: Essai sur l'éducation spartiate et sur les rites d'adolescence dans l'antiquite hellenique*. Lille.
Kennell, N. 1995. *The Gymnasium of Virtue*. Chapel Hill.
Kennell, N. 2009. *Spartans: A New History*. Oxford.
Levy, E. 1988. "La kryptie et ses contradictions." *Ktema* 13: 245–52.
Losada L. 1972. *The Fifth Column in the Peloponnesian War*. Leiden.
Luraghi, N. 2002. "Helotic Slavery Reconsidered." In S. Hodkinson and A. Powell, eds., *Sparta: Beyond the Mirage*, 227–48. Swansea.
Luraghi, N. 2009. "The Helots: Comparative Approaches, Ancient and Modern." In S. Hodkinson and A. Powell, eds., *Sparta: Comparative Approaches*, 261–304. Swansea.
Meier, M. 1998. *Aristokraten und Damoden: Untersuchungen zur inneren Entwicklung Spartas im 7. Jarhundert v. Chr. und zur politischen Funktion der Dichtung des Tyrtaios*. Stuttgart.
Meier, T. 1939. *Wesen der spartanischen Staatsordnung: Nach ihren lebensgesetzlichen und bodenrechtlichen Voraussetzungen*. Leipzig.
Michell, H. 1952. *Sparta*. Cambridge.
Millender, E. 2001. "Spartan Literacy Revisited." *Classical Antiquity* 20 (2001), 121–64.
Murray, O. 1980. *Early Greece*. London.
Oliva, P. 1971. *Sparta and Her Social Problems*. Prague.
Pierart, M. 1974. *Platon et la cité grecque*. Brussels.
Pritchard, D. 2003. "Athletics, Education, and Participation in Classical Athens." In D. Phillips and D. Pritchard, eds., *Sport and Festival in the Ancient Greek World*, 293–350. Swansea.
Pritchett, W. 1971. *The Greek State at War*. Vol. 1. Los Angeles.
Redfield, J. 1977–78. "The Women of Sparta." *CJ* 73: 146–61.
Reinmouth, O. 1952. "The Genesis of the Athenian Ephebia." *TAPhA* 83: 34–50.
Talbert, R. 1989. "The Role of the Helots in the Class Struggle at Sparta." *Historia* 38: 22–40.
Thomas, R. 1992. *Literacy and Orality in Ancient Greece*. Cambridge.
Tolkiehn, J. 1925. "Lexikographie." *RE* 12: 2460, 2478.
van Wees, H. 2004. *Greek Warfare: Myths and Realities*. London.
Vickers M. 1995. "Alcibiades at Sparta: Aristophanes' *Birds*." *CQ* 45: 339–54.

Vidal-Naquet, P. 1968. "The Black Hunter and the Origin of the Athenian Ephebia." *PCPhS* 194: 49–64.

Vidal-Naquet, P. 1986. *The Black Hunter: Forms of Thought and Forms of Society in the Greek World.* Trans. A. Szegedy-Maszak. Baltimore.

Wachsmuth, W. 1844. *Alterthumskunde: Hellenische Alterthumskunde aus dem Gesichtspunkte des Staats.* 2nd ed. 2 vols. Halle.

Whitby, M. 1994. "Two Shadows: Images of Spartans and Helots." In S. Hodkinson and A. Powell, eds., *The Shadow of Sparta*, 87–126. London.

THREE

Where to Kill in Classical Athens

Assassinations, Executions, and the Athenian Public Space[1]

Werner Riess

This essay examines the spatial and topographical dimension of lethal violence among citizens in classical Athens. I here omit mythological narratives, such as the stories about King Codrus or Theseus or the Amazons; the focus of this study is on historically attested cases of violence. (The example of King Hippomenes, who brutally exerts his paternalistic right of coercion by locking up his daughter in a barn with a stallion after she loses her virginity, is pseudohistoric. It appears first in table 2 in the appendix, though it goes without a number there.) With a few exceptions, we are concerned here primarily with killings and executions of Athenians and occasionally with those of metics and foreigners whom we know by name. Therefore, summary executions are not included, nor are executions of individuals whose names we do not know.[2] Killings and executions of Athenian citizens outside Athens (e.g., the killing of Alcibiades)[3] are likewise excluded, even if they

---

1. I thank Michael Zerjadtke for helping me visualize the six semantic fields as represented in table 1, and I thank my student helpers Sebastian Bündgens, Tobias Nowitzki, and Jan Seehusen for providing me with much of the secondary literature and working with me on the vast amount of literature on the spatial turn.

2. In the aftermath of the profanation of the Eleusinian Mysteries and the mutilation of the herms, many people whose names we do not know were denounced and executed (cf. Graf 2000; Furley 1996; Lehmann 1987; Osborne 1985; Th. 6.27–29, 53, 60–61; And. 1; Lys. 6).

3. Nemeth 2006: 144–45.

were perpetrated by Athenians. The focus of this discussion is very much on the topography of Athens. It is obvious that more people than those mentioned in table 2 lost their lives during the turmoils of 411 and 404/3 BCE, but the sources mostly speak only of summary executions ordered by the oligarchs. I trust that some prominent cases shall suffice in this context, in the hope that they can be considered paradigmatic for others. The same situation applies to the turbulent time after the battle of Chaeronea, for which Lysicles and Phocion may stand as representative of other victims.

Previous studies of interpersonal violence in Athens have been predominantly concerned with the frequency of outbreaks of violence,[4] its role in triggering stasis,[5] or whether Athenian violence can be explained by "Mediterranean" models of anthropology,[6] where the rules of honor, shame, and revenge hold uncontested sway. This essay sheds light on the symbolic side of violence as it was constructed via its spatial dimension. I here argue that the performance of a killing in a specific public place charged the act with political significance that went well beyond ordinary homicide. Since many Greeks had a clear understanding of the semantics of political assassination,[7] many Athenians deliberately chose the place in which to kill an enemy so as to convey a specific message to their fellow citizens. Concomitantly, executions are to be seen against this backdrop: it made a big difference whether someone was sentenced to death by drinking hemlock[8] or by the public and therefore ignominious method of *apotumpanismos*, a kind of bloodless crucifixion.[9]

An examination of all historically attested homicides and executions in Athens down to the end of the fourth century BCE reveals quite obvious divisions into six heuristic fields (see table 1 in the appendix).[10] First, political assassinations were almost exclusively committed in public spaces (field

4. Herman 1994.

5. Gehrke 1985.

6. So argues Cohen (1995), sharply criticized by Harris (2007) and Herman (e.g., 1998; 2006: 268).

7. Cf. Riess 2006: 85–86 (summary).

8. Drinking hemlock was a last concession to political opponents, who were still respected as citizens and were granted a death outside the public limelight if they could afford the expensive poison. Cf. Barkan 1936: 73–78; Cantarella 1991: 106–16, emphasizing that *apotumpanismos* (bloodless crucifixion) did not become obsolete after the introduction of hemlock by the end of the fifth century (contra Barkan 1936: 81–82).

9. Barkan 1936: 63–72; Cantarella 1991: 41–46.

10. The numbers in the fields in table 1 correspond to the case numbers in table 2. They represent the cases.

1). By assassination, I mean the planned and sudden killing of high-ranking individuals whom we often know by name. For a homicide to qualify as an assassination, there must also be political implications. Second, privately motivated homicides were almost exclusively perpetrated outside the public limelight (field 6). In between, there are cases that evince a political background but are without an explicit call to action (fields 2 and 5). In very rare cases (fields 3 and 4), privately motivated homicides were committed in public (field 3), or highly political crimes were committed outside the city center (field 4). As we will see, these are abnormal cases, and patterns are recognizable. We could say that since the killers in many cases carefully chose a location appropriate to their deed, the place of killing can be a clue to the killers' motives that are not mentioned or are only hinted at in our sources. The three basic motives are a public call to action, as in the case of a tyrannicide; a political act without a public call to action; and a private quarrel. We will see that these motives can serve as heuristic categories and, indeed, often account for the location chosen, which means that by looking more closely at the spatial dimension of homicides, we might be able to discern better the underlying motives of the assassins. What follows is a chronological overview of all those Athenian nonfictional homicide cases and executions for which the location is attested or probable.

Overview of Cases

No. 1: Our first account is legendary but not fictional. During the so-called Cylonian affair, possibly in 632 BCE, the aristocrat Cylon occupied the Acropolis with his followers, perhaps to establish a tyranny in Athens. In response, the Athenians laid siege to the Acropolis. Cylon escaped, but his men, cunningly lured out of the temple of Athena with the promise that they would get away scot-free, were slain outside the building, although some of them had taken refuge at altars.[11] The archon Megacles, who had ordered the killings, incurred *miasma* (pollution),[12] as did his whole family

11. To what extent these events contributed to Draco's proceedings of blood vengeance is a matter of debate. Whereas Phillips (2008: 35–49) and Gagarin (1981: 20–21) doubt a direct connection, Schmitz (2001: 35–36) takes it for granted. Ruschenbusch (1960: 147) is more skeptical.

12. According to Welwei (1992: 133–37), the Cylonian affair was not just an inner-aristocratic struggle. Megacles acted in his function as archon; that is, the polis, with its magistrates, tried to thwart Cylon's grip on power. It is possible that the situation got out of

for generations to come. Athens even had to be purified by the Cretan specialist for ritual cleansing, Epimenides.[13] The problem was not the killing per se of would-be tyrants,[14] which would later be regarded as legitimate,[15] nor was it the killing of men in public—perhaps Cylon's men were intentionally slain in public so as to be perceived as tyrants. The problem that incurred pollution (*miasma*) was the use of deception and the act of killing these men on sacred ground.[16]

No. 2: Sometime between the death of Peisistratus in 528 and the killing of Hipparchus in 514, Peisistratus' sons had Cimon, the father of Miltiades (who was later victorious at the battle of Marathon), killed near the Prytaneion. Cimon, who was a public figure as a prominent aristocrat, was trapped in an ambush at night. That he was murdered in the heart of the city is appropriate to his social position. This killing makes it abundantly clear that not even an aristocrat was safe in the urban and political center of the town. Cimon's murder was an act of terror, designed to express clearly the power of the Peisistratids over even the most prominent aristocratic families. This assassination was probably intended to bolster the position of the Peisistratids through an extreme act of intimidation.

No. 3: In 514 BCE, Hipparchus was killed by Harmodius and Aristogeiton near the temple of the daughters of Leo, while arranging the Panathenaic procession.[17] The Leocoricum may have been situated right at the northern edge of the Agora, close to the Altar of the Twelve Gods. This location is not pure accident, although it is true that Harmodius and Aristogeiton were frightened and felt the need to strike immediately because their plot had been betrayed. But it is worth considering that the tyrannicides had

---

control and that Megacles was not able to prevent his men from committing the atrocities on the Acropolis.

13. Parker 1983: 16–17, 142, 204, 206, 209–210, 211, 259, 270; Moulinier 1952: 46–47.

14. Cf. Rosivach 1988, on the tyrant as an ideological figure in fifth-century literature (esp. 44). Rosivach sketches the interpretive shift of the term from meaning a sole ruler to its capacity, finally, to denote "any civic villain" (56), "an all-purpose symbol of villainous rule" (56), and "the negation of good government" (57). On the image of the tyrant during the fourth century, cf. Mossé 1969: 133–45.

15. Cf. Maffi 2005, on Greek legislation on tyrannicide, with a focus on the Solonian regulation, the decree of Eucrates, and the law of Ilion.

16. Gagarin 1981: 20.

17. Cf. Welwei 1992: 255 (with older literature). Taylor (1981) traces the literary and iconographic representation of the tyrant slayers from the fifth century BCE through late antiquity, with an emphasis on the fifth century.

originally intended to kill Hippias at the Ceramicus. Though Harmodius and Aristogeiton might simply have found it easier to approach the tyrant during a civic festival and surely killed for personal reasons, it is intriguing to see how the Athenians understood the public killing. At least in the later democratic tradition, Harmodius and Aristogeiton's action was perceived as tyrannicide and a public call to action. The actual, private character of the killing fell into oblivion because of the spectacular location. A semantic reinterpretation of historical events is clearly recognizable in this case; I speak of an "interpretive shift." Other assassinations inside and outside of Athens adhered to the same spatial model. For a killing to qualify as tyrannicide, it had to take place, it seems, in public.

No. 4: When the Persian envoy Murychides came to Salamis in 479 BCE to report to the Athenians Mardonius' offer, which was in fact an order to surrender, one of the members of the Boulê (Council), Lycidas, thought that it might be beneficial for the Athenians to accept Murychides' offer and propose it, with approval, to the people of Athens. His uttering this opinion enraged the members of the Council and the people gathering outside, to such an extent that they stoned Lycidas to death. When news of this incident spread to Athens, some Athenian women followed the example of the men on Salamis by gathering at Lycidas' house and stoning his wife and children to death.[18] Obviously, Lycidas and his family were regarded as traitors; their cruel death was supposed to be a warning to all those who would ever again show sympathies to the Persians. Although the stoning was not perpetrated in the civic center of the city, the deed was highly political in meaning.

No. 5: Ephialtes was assassinated in secret in 461 BCE if he was assassinated at all. If he was indeed killed, he was probably not slain in a private quarrel, although we cannot rule out this possibility. The *Athenaion politeia* and Plutarch, in his *Life of Pericles*, clearly link Ephialtes' assassination to political motives. His aristocratic or oligarchic enemies hated him for his democratic reforms, most notably his curtailment of the Areopagus' prerogatives and his unflagging endeavor to bring to justice those who had done harm to the Athenian people.[19] Aristotle and Plutarch even claim to know

---

18. Stoning as a capital punishment seems to have been reserved for traitors and was never used again in classical Athens (Barkan 1936: 41–53; cf. Cantarella 1991: 73–87). The stoning of Alcibiades of Phlegous is contested in its historicity (X. *HG* 1.2.12–13). If the tradition is authentic, it happened in the eastern Mediterranean and has no bearing on the topography of violence in the city of Athens. Cf. Bleckmann 1998: 459–460. On stoning as a punishment of treason, cf. Rosivach 1987.

19. Cf. Welwei 1992: 193–194; 1999: 91–95; Wallace (1985) 1989: 83–87. Hall (1990)

that the assassin was Aristodicus of Tanagra. We can only guess why the hit man would choose not to kill Ephialtes in public. Perhaps Ephialtes' opponents did not want to make a public statement, given the strong democratic sentiments among the Athenian population, or perhaps Ephialtes' popularity deterred them from daring to attack him in the open. For these reasons, they may have opted for quietly removing their hated opponent. Also, they could not make Ephialtes correspond to the image of a tyrant. If Aristodicus was from Tanagra, he was a metic or even a foreigner, maybe a proxy, a hit man who committed a murder commissioned by aristocrats. The real plotters could remain in the background, and it was simply easier to get rid of Ephialtes during the night than during the day. Pragmatic reasons suggested this procedure. In this case, the killing beyond the public gaze does not suggest an absence of political motives. But the fact that Ephialtes' death could be understood in nonpolitical terms[20] supports my contention that most political murders that were supposed to convey a symbolic message were staged publicly. In the case of Ephialtes, the sending of such a message was to be avoided at all costs.

No. 6: In the wake of rendering his account (*euthynai*) in court, Paches, a successful commander who had taken Lesbos for the Athenians at the beginning of the Peloponnesian War, was subjected to an accusation by Cleon for a reason unknown to us (427 BCE). To express his despair and the groundlessness of the accusation against him, Paches killed himself with his sword in plain view of all attendants in the courtroom, a spectacular gesture and powerful display of emotions that was probably also supposed to reveal the flaws of the Athenian political and juridical system.

No. 7: Sometime between 420 and 411, a stepson brought charges of homicide against his stepmother for having poisoned his father twenty years before.[21] She had used a slave girl of her husband's friend to prepare and give an alleged love potion to both men. The husband's friend died on the spot; the plaintiff's father died some twenty days later, after severe illness. Before

aptly differentiates between a purge that Ephialtes undertook to free the honorable council of unworthy members and the new functions that he entrusted to the Areopagus. This theory explains, on the one hand, the hatred of Ephialtes in some aristocratic circles and, on the other, the testimony of Aeschylus' *Eumenides* in which the Areopagus is presented as a bulwark of democracy. In fact, from Ephialtes' time on, the Areopagus became a central organ of the democratic constitution, and it was the Thirty Tyrants that curtailed that council's right in order to boost their oligarchic agenda.

20. Stockton (1982: 227–228) suggests that Ephialtes died naturally, exactly because his death was not public.

21. On this case and Antiphon's strategy, cf. Gagarin 2002: 146–52.

passing away, the victim made a dying injunction, ordering his son, who was then a small child, to take revenge on his behalf once he grew up. Apart from the fact that the two men died, we do not know anything about this case. It is not even clear that the potion was supposed to kill the men. Both men died indoors, the plaintiff's father probably in his bedchamber. Thus, if it was a homicide, it was a typical, privately motivated homicide taking place outside the public sphere.

No. 8: Sometime before 417, Alcibiades used violence against his wife, Hipparete, a depressing detail from a failed Athenian marriage. Hipparete had been endowed with a generous dowry, but Alcibiades continued his flamboyant lifestyle in Athens' leading circles and constantly invited friends and prostitutes to lavish feasts. The honorable Hipparete, who hailed from a good family background, was no longer willing to accept her husband's behavior and filed for divorce with the archon basileus. She must have done so with the support of her family, because she would have had to return permanently to her home (*oikos*) if the divorce was to go through as planned (she already lived with her brother Callias by the time of the divorce filing). Alcibiades must have been informed beforehand about his wife's action on her own authority, gathered a posse of friends (obviously to constitute a kind of audience), and dragged Hipparete across the Agora back to his home.[22] This narrative sounds topical: in Greek mythology, victors drag the vanquished by their hair in order to demonstrate their superiority and humiliate the defeated.[23] But it is possible that Alcibiades intended to express his dominance over his wife with exactly this dramatic gesture, an interesting insight into Greek gender relations and the values of an overly self-confident Athenian head of a household, or *kurios* (see Omitowoju in this volume). It was not enough for Alcibiades to go to the archon on his own and drag his wife away; it was important to him that he was seen, that his interference in the filing of the divorce took on a performative character. With this staging of his prerogatives as a husband and *kurios*, Alcibiades also made clear his contempt for Athenian institutions, for the archon basileus, and for Athenian laws, which entitled a wife to file a divorce in cases of a husband's egregious misbehavior. That Alcibiades did not heed these

22. Alcibiades thus thwarted his wife's plans. In case of a divorce, he would have had to return the enormous dowry (Rhodes 2011: 19).

23. E.g., gods pull Gigantes by their hair to demonstrate their victory over them. See F. Vian and M. Moore, "Gigantes," *LIMC* IV 2, 1988, e.g., nos. 24 (p. 112), 60 (p. 115), 322 (p. 144). Cf. Riess 2012: 85 n. 283 (with more mythological sources).

democratic norms is in line with what we know about him from other sources. Two weeks later, Hipparete died under mysterious circumstances. It is possible that she died of an illness, but her death's close temporal proximity to her attempt at filing a divorce should make us suspicious. It is likely that Alcibiades maltreated her at home to such an extent that she died of the consequences. This brutality against one's own wife was not intended for the eyes of the public. It is telling that we do not hear of any kind of reaction on the part of Hipparete's family, who obviously had supported her divorce plans and who should have filed charges for homicide, even on the grounds of mere suspicion. Alcibiades' influence and social power must have seemed insuperable. Hipparete's family could not or did not want to challenge him, clear evidence for us that ancient Athens did not adhere to the "rule of law" in the modern sense. There was no state-organized independent prosecution that could have initiated investigations. Filing a lawsuit almost always lay with private persons and, thus, also hinged on social factors. Whoever was intimidated or felt that he could not win did not dare turn to the courts. In this system, the certainty of legal protection against personal injury could not exist, and Alcibiades knew that he had nothing to fear.

No. 9: In 419/18, a rich and politically active Athenian citizen served as *chorêgos* (choral director) and had boys practice in his house. In his absence, one of the boys, Diodotus, drank a potion and died in front of all the other trainees. Although all parties agreed that Diodotus' death was accidental, his brother nevertheless brought charges of unintentional homicide against the *chorêgos*. It may well have been that the death of the chorus boy was a pure accident, but his relatives were able to frame it in terms of unintentional or negligent homicide, because they alleged that the *chorêgos* had not done everything possible to guarantee the safety of the children. If homicide was involved—the speaker gives us no hint of who the killers could have been—the perpetrators obviously aimed for semipublicity. Because the death happened in front of many people, the weakness of the *chorêgos* was blatantly clear. Everyone could see that he was not able to protect the boys who trained on his behalf in order to embellish his *chorêgeia* (choregic performance). His lack of power and agency was fully revealed, and his social standing and political status were thus undermined. If he could not take care of young boys, he was even less suited to serve as *chorêgos* for the city. The death of the boy in a "private" context publicly dramatized the *chorêgos*' lack of power, whether he or someone else was responsible for the boy's death. This dramatization probably damaged the reputation of the *chorêgos* in the long term, even in the case of his acquittal.[24]

No. 10: In the wake of the mutilation of the herms and the profanation of the Eleusinian Mysteries on the eve of the Sicilian expedition (415 BCE), the Athenians, worked up into a religious frenzy, went on a witch hunt to chase down the culprits, convicted many of the alleged perpetrators, and executed them and confiscated their property. Some of the accused fled into exile before being caught or before being sentenced; some, like Andocides, denounced others and thus managed to save their own lives. Thanks to Andocides' speech on the Mysteries and the so-called Attic *stelai* that list the names of the convicted together with their confiscated property, which the *poletai* (public sellers) had to sell,[25] we know the names of more than fifty upper-class persons who may have been involved in the scandal. Not all of the people listed in table 2 were actually executed. Many escaped punishment. Those who were forced to die probably drank hemlock in prison.

No. 11: In preparation for the coup d'état of the Four Hundred in 411 BCE, oligarchically minded youths killed the popular leader of the democrats, Androcles. They did so secretly. Here again we discern the pattern that murder by stealth for political reasons was intended to spread terror, in a way

24. Cf. Riess 2012: 55–56; Gagarin 2002: 139–46; Wilson 2000: 116–20 (on this particular case). Heitsch (1984: 90–109) places a special emphasis on agency.

25. *IG* I³ 421–30. Cf. the first and fundamental analysis by Pritchett (1953; on the prosopography on the *stelai*, see 230–32). Pritchett (1956) and Amyx (1958) tackle economic questions by examining the confiscated goods and products as mentioned on the *stelai*. Lewis (1966), on the basis of Pritchett, deals with matters of accounting and finance. Lehmann (1987) contextualizes the scandal of 415 within the stream of events leading from the ostracism of Hyperbolus (417 BCE) to the oligarchic coup of 411. He notes (55) the considerable overlap between the mutilators of the herms and those profaning the Mysteries. The degree of this overlap is contested and broaches the difficult question whether or not the two impious actions constituted one act of sacrilege or have to be considered separately. In contrast to Lehmann, Osborne (1985), who elucidates the full political significance of the herms and their mutilation, especially with regard to Athenian individual and collective identity, comes to the conclusion that both acts have to be seen separately, because they differ considerably in meaning (66–67). To him, "the overlap between those named in connection with the mutilation and those named in connection with the profanation is limited" (73 n. 97). Furley (1996: 41–48) carefully distinguishes different source traditions. Whereas Andocides and Thucydides regarded the two sacrilegious acts as separate, the Attic *stelai* suggest that the Athenian public lumped the two impieties together. The later literary tradition followed popular sentiments.

similar to the killing of Cimon by the Peisistratids. As with Ephialtes, the oligarchs killed in secret.

Once the Four Hundred were in power, albeit only for a short period of time, they executed some people whose names we do not know,[26] but their rule can in no way be compared to the terror regime of the Thirty seven years later.[27]

No. 12: In 411 BCE, Phrynichus, one of the staunchly oligarchic leaders of the Four Hundred, was assassinated in the Agora near the Bouleutêrion (Council Hall).[28] The killers, two metics, Thrasybulus from Calydon and Apollodorus of Megara, could have chosen (like the killers of Ephialtes) to remove Phrynichus secretly. According to Thucydides, they took a great risk indeed by going public. The oligarchic regime of the Four Hundred was still in power, so the assassins were right to escape immediately after the deed. They clearly intended to send a call for action to the Athenian citizens or at least to the moderate oligarchs, and this assassination indeed triggered the downfall of the Four Hundred.[29] After the overthrow of the oligarchy, the assassins publicly claimed responsibility for the assassination. They correctly assessed Athenian sentiments: although the assassins were charged with murder by Phrynichus' relatives or friends and even spent some time in prison, the Athenians left the killers unharmed. Instead, they declared Phrynichus a traitor and regarded his killers as tyrant slayers who were to be honored for the rest of their lives.[30] This case is a typical example of a politically motivated assassination in public.

26. Th. 8.70.2. Flach (1977) subjects the partially contradictory reports of Thucydides and Aristotle's *Athenaion politeia* about the events of 411 to careful scrutiny. Both accounts have to be read together. While Aristotle emphasizes the role of the legal measures that the Four Hundred took to mask their coup d'état, Thucydides exposes the oligarchs' true intentions, though, in so doing, he condenses the sequence of events.

27. Lehmann (1997: 40–54) compares the oligarchic coup d'états of 411 and 404/3.

28. Grossi (1984) dwells on the differences between the reports of Thucydides (49–53), Lysias (69–73), and Lycurgus (73–80).

29. The assassins were clearly hired hit men from abroad. The commissioners of the deed were probably not democrats but moderate oligarchs (e.g., in the entourage of Theramenes) who were opposed to the radical wing represented by Phrynichus. Cf. Heftner 2001: 265–70 (with older literature and a discussion of the somewhat contradictory sources).

30. Brodersen, Günther, and Schmitt 1992: 140 = *IG* I³ 102 = Dittenberger (1883) 1915: 108 = Tod 1946: 86 = Meiggs and Lewis (1969) 1988: 85. Similar to Harmodius and Aristogeiton, Phrynichus' murderers, who were not necessarily supporters of the democracy, were interpreted as such by the populace. According to the honorary inscription, Thrasybulus was the main perpetrator; hence his rewards outshine those of Apollodorus and the other accomplices of the deed.

No. 13: In 411 or 410 BCE, after the restoration of the democracy, the orator and sophist Antiphon of Rhamnus was accused by Theramenes and Andron of having cooperated with the oligarchs of 411.[31] Despite his rhetorical talent, Antiphon could not save himself. He was sentenced to death and was executed, probably in prison. Theramenes was not far away from Antiphon's oligarchic thinking. By taking Antiphon to court, he emphasized his support for the renewed democracy. Research has shown, time and again, that prosecuting someone was considered a kind of revenge, an indirect form of exerting violence, which was—potentially—no less harmful than direct violence.[32] Violence that was issued by the courts was democratically legitimized through the judges' sentence, a fact that worked to Theramenes' advantage in the tense atmosphere after the failed coup.

No. 14: Although the rule of the Four Hundred was more moderate than the subsequent regime of the Thirty, there were also scores to settle between enemies after the restoration of the democracy. Aristarchus, a staunch conservative, member of the Four Hundred, and friend and posthumous defender of Phrynichus, betrayed the frontier fortress of Oenoe to the Thebans after

31. The debate between those scholars who think Antiphon the Sophist and Antiphon of Rhamnus were one and the same person (unitarians) and those who assume two different persons (separatists) is ongoing. E.g., Pendrick (1987) pleads for the latter view, whereas Gagarin (2002, esp. 7, 170–71) convincingly shows that writing sophistic literature and being a logographer did not exclude each other.

32. Athenians pursued enmity against one another in many venues, also in the political realm, that is, by means of legal proceedings. Scheid (2005: 410) notes, "L'idée de la vengeance reste associée à l'idée de la justice. La relation verticale, qui met face à face l'accusé et la cité, à travers les manquements aux lois de la cité dont il s'est rendu coupable, n'efface pas la relation horizontale que les contraintes de la vengeance instaurent entre l'aggresseur et la victime, en exigeant de cette dernière qu'elle réagisse pour restaurer un équilibre qui a été endommagé à ses dépens." Rhodes (1998: 161) writes that "politically active men who are personal enemies are likely to move in different political circles, and they are likely to pursue their enmity through prosecutions both on private and on public matters." As Fisher (1998: 92) explains, Athenians took revenge and could flaunt their manliness by going to court: "prevailing civic values encouraged those who felt insulted and wronged to have recourse to the courts and the arbitration procedures, and to believe that thereby revenge was achieved, and honour and manhood could be satisfied." Herman (e.g., 1995, 2000), however, claims that Athenians gave up the ideology of revenge by transferring their quarrels to the law courts. His studies in the 1990s led up to his magisterial study of 2006, in which he presents a highly idealized picture of classical Athens, in which cooperative behavior prevailed among citizens who preferred compromises over escalation (277). Due to the verbal restraint in the speeches, he comes to the conclusion that "the people of democratic Athens seem overall to have been of an unusually mild temper" (201).

the downfall of the oligarchy.[33] He was executed as a traitor between 411 and 406, and his corpse was buried outside of Attica.

No. 15: In the famous Arginusae trial, we know the names of the accused *stratêgoi* (commanders) who allegedly neglected to rescue shipwrecked sailors and hoplites after the naval battle.[34] The summary trial before the Assembly of the People was irregular,[35] for every *stratêgos* should have had the right to plead in an individual trial. Some pointed to this procedural mistake, most of all Socrates.[36] But the Assembly of the People insisted on its democratic prerogative to function as a law court and, in general, to decide all matters on its own authority. In a highly dramatic and political trial, the *stratêgoi* were sentenced to death on shaky juridical grounds.[37] A more direct and brutal action against high-ranking representatives of the Attic democracy, in which all democratic institutions were still fully functioning, would not have been possible. To spare the *stratêgoi* public humiliation, they were probably executed in prison.

No. 16: In 404 BCE, under the terror regime of the Thirty, Theramenes,[38]

---

33. Th. 8.98.

34. Theramenes was one of the accusers. Sordi (1981) elucidates his aims in doing so and anchors them in his political agenda.

35. So argues Nemeth (1984: 51, 57), who examines the prosopography of plaintiffs and accused alike. According to him (57), four groups were vying for power in Athens at the end of the fifth century: staunch oligarchs around Antiphon and Critias, moderate oligarchs around Theramenes, Alcibiades' friends and followers, and radical democrats led by demagogues.

36. Hatzfeld (1940: 170–71) relativizes the role of Socrates. He was not the only one to oppose the irregular procedure. Even if he turned out to be the only one remaining to hold on to his view, it was of no consequence for the further sequence of events. The vote of one *prytanis* (leading council member) was not enough to stop the Assembly of the People from further pursuing its rage against the generals. Xenophon, for the understandable reason of making his hero appear in an even brighter light, overemphasizes Socrates' role during this trial.

37. In contrast to, e.g., Nemeth 1984, Mehl (1982, with older literature on the topic) claims that according to the worldview of the populace at the end of the fifth century, the trial was not irregular. The reason for the accusation—that the generals neglected to rescue the shipwrecked and dead for the sake of their burial—was valid. Bleckmann (1998: 509–39) argues for a balanced view of things. According to him (537), Xenophon has exaggerated the "terroristic traits of the trial." Burckhardt (2000: 143) provides a similar argument.

38. Pesely (1983) engages in an in-depth source criticism investigating the bias of Thucydides, Lysias, Xenophon, and others toward or against Theramenes. A comparison to Thrasybulus is presented by McCoy (1970), who claims that both men had much in common and can be considered political moderates until their ways parted under the Thirty, when Theramenes joined the oligarchs and when Thrasybulus organized the democratic re-

by order of his colleague Critias, was torn away from the altar in the Bouleutêrion, spectacularly dragged across the Agora, and put into jail, where he was forced to drink hemlock.[39] The radical oligarch Critias thus eliminated his more moderate rival Theramenes. A public killing or execution would have rendered Theramenes a hero, a martyr figure.[40] The Thirty Tyrants might have preferred a secret removal in order to mask their intentions, but it was too late for that. By clinging to the altar in the Bouleutêrion, Theramenes had already gone public himself. The best the Thirty could do in this charged situation was to remove him from public sight and force him to drink hemlock in the *desmotêrion* (prison), which corresponded with the normal practice of executing Athenian citizens.

No. 17: What happened to Theramenes (no. 16) happened to many other people under the tyranny of the Thirty.[41] Allegedly, twenty-five hundred people were executed by the Thirty, fifteen hundred of whom were Athenian citizens.[42] The innocent Leon of Salamis,[43] whom Socrates was supposed to

---

sistance against them. On Theramenes' potential political "programs" and his opportunistic versatility, cf. Bleckmann 1998: 339–57. On Thrasybulus as distinct from Theramenes in his political views, cf. Krentz 1982: 70. Buck (1998: 47, 121–23) vehemently argues against the view of Thrasybulus as a political moderate and claims instead that he was a steadfast supporter of democracy throughout his life. On Theramenes' end in particular, cf. Adeleye 1976; Hatzfeld 1938.

39. On the idea that the revolution consumes its own children, cf. von Ungern-Sternberg 2000; Lehmann 1997: 52.

40. According to Usher (1968: 128, 132–133), because Critias circulated his speech against Theramenes to convince people of his view of things, Xenophon, our main source for this event, had access to a complete copy of that speech and could integrate it in condensed form into his narrative. Xenophon's knowledge of Theramenes' speech, however, is probably based on an eyewitness account from a member of the Boulê (Council) of the Thirty (Usher 1968: 128, 133–35). On the evolution of the Theramenes myth, with special consideration of the Michigan papyrus, cf. Andrewes 1970; Harding 1974; Engels 1993.

41. On the emergence of the Thirty and the value of Aristotle's testimony in *Ath.* 34.2–3, cf. McCoy 1975a, 132, 145; Lehmann 1972.

42. Nemeth 2006: 141; Loening 1987: 84 n. 70 (with discussion of the sources). Wolpert 2006 focuses on the role of violence as an intrinsic part of the Thirty's system of ruling Athens.

43. To resolve the vexed prosopographical question of how to identify the general Leon who was *stratêgos* (commander) in 412/11 and 406/05 (Th. 8.23–24, 54–55, 73; X. *HG* 1.5.16, 6.16), "Leon who signed both the Peace of Nicias and the fifty-year pact between Athens and Sparta in 421" (McCoy 1975b: 187; Th. 5.19.2, 24), and Leon of Salamis, McCoy (1975b) equates all three. If Leon of Salamis was only identical with one of the other two, he was still an outstanding and well-known man who had been of much use

arrest, may stand for many who died under the Thirty or in the immediate aftermath of the political turmoil. Socrates refused to follow the Thirty's order and thus dared to put up passive resistance. It goes without saying that Leon of Salamis was executed nevertheless. Some members of the Thirty wielded an excessive amount of power and were successful at persuading their colleagues to sentence certain people to death: Satyrus and Chremon, for example, had Calliades (no. 27), Cleophon (no. 28), and Strombichides (no. 29) executed.[44] Informers played an important role under the rule of the Thirty: Agoratus, Aischylides, Aristodemus from Bate, Batrachus, Hagnodorus from Amphitrope, and Menestratus collaborated with the oligarchs and brought many people to death.[45]

Nos. 18–29: These people were all executed by the Thirty and are considered as a group in this context.

Nos. 30–40: In his speech against Agoratus (Lys. 13),[46] Lysias mentions a certain Menestratus who, acting as an informer for the Thirty, denounced democratic leaders who were then executed (no. 30). After the downfall of the Thirty, Menestratus was executed (no. 38) by the aggravated form of *apotumpanismos* (bloodless crucifixion). One of the most evil figures under the Thirty was Agoratus, who was of low social birth and gained some merit by participating in the assassination of Phrynichus. The Thirty let him live only because he promised to collaborate and denounce people. He was responsible for many people's deaths (nos. 31–34). His most famous victim, according to Lysias, was the democrat Dionysodorus (no. 34). After the tyranny of the Thirty, Dionysodorus's brother, Dionysius, brought Agoratus to trial and demanded his execution by *apotumpanismos* (no. 39), by analogy with Menestratus' execution. We do not know whether or not Agoratus was sentenced. The tyrants' victim that Lysias describes in the greatest detail, however, is his own brother Polemarchus (no. 35), a metic, like Aristophanes from Cholleis (no. 33).

The Thirty staged and masked their murders as a kind of lawful execution. We could call them judicial murder. The Athenians, especially supporters of the democracy, felt the same. The Thirty did not rely on the traditional law courts, where jurors selected by lot applied the law in legal proceedings that were open for all to observe. Rather, the Thirty organized mock trials,

---

to his native city. McCoy suggests that to involve Socrates in his arrest and murder might demonstrate that the Thirty were "diabolical in their scheming" (197).

44. On the victims of the Thirty, cf., summarily, Krentz 1982: 60, 79–83.

45. Nemeth 2006: 129–32.

46. On the structure of the speech, cf. Bearzot 1997: 77–79.

issuing death sentences in camera, that is, within the Boulê (Council), which was dependent on the junta of the Thirty. The trauma of the Thirty Tyrants haunted the Athenians during the fourth century and made them recognize that a functioning legal system was the cornerstone of their democracy.[47] The Thirty were smart enough to see that their victims had to die indoors so as not to arouse anger and protests. Dying in prison by order of a governing body, however illegitimate this body was, did not suggest personal quarrels or greed, at least not on the surface.

Under the restored democracy, Menestratus, as mentioned above, was deliberately executed in public via *apotumpanismos*, the Athenian form of crucifixion (no. 38). Compared to drinking hemlock, dying through *apotumpanismos* was a more severe form of execution. Tied onto a wooden plank (the *tumpanon*), the delinquent died a slow and painful death over the course of several days. Under normal circumstances, this kind of execution was reserved for real malefactors, the so-called *kakourgoi*. With the use of *apotumpanismos*, Menestratus was turned into such a *kakourgos*. The underlying assumption might have been that on the grounds of his well-known denunciations against democrats, Menestratus could be regarded as a murderer who was caught in the act (*ep'autophoro*).[48] Or the assumption might have been that he had caused illegitimate executions and, thus, was a suspected murderer who could not appear any longer in public venues such as law courts, because he seemed to be polluted. Maybe Menestratus breached the stringent rules of *atimia* (dishonor, loss of civic status) this way.[49] By breaking the *atimia* regulations, one could also become a *kakourgos* liable for the humiliating punishment of *apotumpanismos*.

By analogy with Menestratus, Dionysius, the plaintiff in no. 39, pleaded for *apotumpanismos* as the correct form of execution for Agoratus, in order to take revenge on behalf of his brother and brother-in-law Dionysodorus

47. Arist. *Ath.* 41.2. Cf. *Pol.* 1275a22–33 (= 3.1.4–5), 1275b15–21 (= 3.1.8).

48. If the *ep'autophoro* clause was really applied, its semantic meaning must have been considerably expanded to "unambiguous guilt, manifestly, clearly" (Volonaki 2000: 168).

49. If Menstratus was accused of polluting holy places by his attendance, he was probably subjected to an *apagôgê phonou* (dragging away on grounds of homicide) and was thus not protected by the amnesty. So argue Volonaki (2000: 166) and MacDowell ([1963] 1966: 137–38), contra Hansen (1976: 104), who thinks that the *apagôgê kakourgôn* (dragging away of a malefactor) was applied. Evjen (1970: 413–414) lists the advantages for the prosecution to file an *apagôgê* instead of a *dikê phonou*, the regular procedure to indict someone for homicide. Most of all, the accused was imprisoned right away and had little chance to prepare his defense. He was also barred from going into voluntary exile before the sentence. Thus, in the case of a conviction, he was immediately executed.

(no. 34).[50] The executions of Agoratus and Menestratus had clear political implications, albeit without any call to action. By their public execution, they were stigmatized as murderers commissioned by the Thirty Tyrants. As a result, the democratic demos (people, populace) could see that some kind of revenge was fulfilled.

Allegedly, the Thirty also killed ten, thirty, or sixty metics, presumably in prison.[51] We know two of them by name, Aristophanes from Cholleis (no. 33) and Polemarchus (no. 35). In addition, we know the names of two foreigners who were killed by the tyrants (nos. 36–37).

I will deal with Lysias' famous first speech, in defense of Euphiletus (no. 40), in this essay's conclusion, as a counterproof to the thesis proposed here.

Nos. 41–42: The trial of Socrates in 399 BCE is so well known that it does not warrant detailed treatment here.[52] It may be interesting to note that the Athenians recognized their judicial error shortly afterward and executed Socrates' accusers Meletus and Lycon without a proper sentence (no. 42).[53] Socrates would certainly not have approved of this breach of constitutional principles of the Athenian democracy. Once more, it becomes clear that the Athenians did not understand Socrates, even in their revenge on his behalf.

Nos. 43–46, 48–49, 51–53, and 64: These political trials, mainly against *stratêgoi* (commanders), were initiated via the procedural forms of *eisangelia* (a form of bringing public charges) or *graphê paranomon* (action for improper legislation)[54] or in the context of the generals' having to lay open their accounts (*euthunai*). As reasons for the accusations, bribery, embezzlement, treason, defeat, or any kind of misconduct in office could be brought forward by political enemies. Accusations against commanders for trifling charges were among the standard methods employed by many politicians of the fifth and fourth centuries BCE to vie for prestige and power. That the true reason for these often deadly struggles lies in the fierce competition of

50. The plaintiffs of Agoratus used the same legal strategy as those of Menestratus in order to circumvent the amnesty. The case of Menestratus is thus a precedent for that of Agoratus. Cf. Riess 2007: 68–71, on both cases, with a detailed focus on the legal intricacies.

51. Lys. 12.6–7 (10); X. *HG* 2.3.21 (30); D.S. 14.5.6 (60).

52. Scholz (2000, with older literature on the trial of Socrates) argues against the view that the trial of Socrates was a judicial scandal. Scholz maintains that the jurors applied valid laws and judged to the best of their knowledge (171).

53. Allegedly, Anytus was exiled and stoned to death in Heracleia Pontus on the order of the Athenians.

54. G. Thür, s.v., in Brill's New Pauly online, accessed February 25, 2015, http://referenceworks.brillonline.com/search?s.q=graphe+paranomon&s.f.s2_parent=s.f.book.brill-s-new-pauly&search-go=Search.

the politically active members of the Athenian upper classes is obvious from the fact that all of them basically pursued the same policy in the Aegean Sea and toward their allies: that is, working to the benefit of Athens and strengthening its strategic and economic position.[55] It is striking for us to observe colleagues who supported each other abroad on behalf of Athens but launched trials against their peers at home, often trying to have them executed. Since the majority of jurors was fickle and could be swayed by the power of oratory, the outcome of a trial was always uncertain. As a result, serving as *stratêgos* (commander) was a risky undertaking, not least because of the peculiarities of the Athenian court system, which lacked legal certainty and served as an arena for potentially deadly contests between the powerful. The list in table 2 contains only those cases where executions actually took place. There were many more cases in which the accused was acquitted, was fined, or went into exile before the sentence was meted out.[56]

No. 47: Before the King's Peace, the Athenians suffered from a shortage of grain due to ongoing war. Some grain dealers, metics, took advantage of the opportunity, hoarded grain, and thus manipulated the price. The public outrage was such that they were almost lynched. A member of the Council intervened and launched a regular trial through *eisangelia*. For those who were convicted, the death penalty was looming. We do not know the outcome of the trial, but it is significant that even grain dealers could be accused through *eisangelia*, a procedure whose application was originally confined to traitors and underperforming commanders.

No. 50: Sometime between 371 and 366, the farmer Thydippus killed his own brother Euthycrates in a private quarrel over a piece of land. This homicide took place in public, on an open field. Some fellow demesmen of the brothers witnessed the scene while tilling their fields. It is likely that this homicide happened on the spur of the moment, in the heat of the argument; otherwise, Thydippus might have tried to kill his brother in a more remote place.

55. Funke 1980: 150–61.

56. Treating these cases in detail is beyond the scope of this contribution. Cf. the lists in Hansen 1975 (69–120) and Hamel 1998 (140–57). Still useful on political trials are Dombrowski 1934 and Mossé 1974. Strauss (1986: 172–173) describes the atmosphere that reigned in Athens during the first half of the fourth century: weakened by their disastrous defeat in the Peloponnesian War, the Athenians saw themselves engaged soon afterward in the Corinthian War. From 378/7 on, they ventured to build up a new naval empire, the Second Athenian League. Strauss summarizes the trials against generals and comes to the conclusion that politicians "considered vengeance not merely acceptable, but a moral obligation" (172).

No. 54: Stephanus accuses his longtime enemy Apollodorus of having killed a woman from Aphidna. We do not know more about this case; it may have been a false accusation to frame Apollodorus for murder.

Nos. 55–56: Sometime before 348 BCE, a certain Euaeon suffered a slight from his drinking mate Boeotus. He felt so offended that he could not restrain himself and killed the offender. He was then condemned by a single vote, on the grounds that he had exercised exaggerated revenge.[57] Demosthenes explains the meaning of the almost split vote. While many judges felt that Euaeon was right in retaliating even at the risk of killing the aggressor, a slight majority of judges had qualms not about the revenge but about its extreme form. This homicide happened semipublicly, in the context of a *symposion* (dining feast), and can be regarded as a private quarrel and a crime of passion. In this context, Demosthenes tells us about another brawl that occurred at a private party and resulted in a homicide. The passage is vexed; it is actually not clear whether Euthynus killed Sophilus or vice versa (no. 56).

No. 57: Around 350, the trierarch Theophemus and his friend Euergus killed a woman who was formerly a slave of the speaker of Pseudo-Demosthenes 47. In an attempt to seize property from the speaker, they went to his farm and started carrying off things. On this occasion, the old woman, who was the plaintiff's nurse, wanted to prevent the intruders from taking a pitcher. She hid it under her garment and would not hand it over to the aggressors.[58] In the ensuing fisticuffs, they treated the woman with such cruelty that she died six days later. We do not know how public this incident on the plaintiff's farm was, but we can assume that it happened without many witnesses.

No. 58: This case is transmitted within Demosthenes' famous speech *Against Meidias* (D. 21).[59] Although Nicodemus of Aphidna was not killed in public, the mutilation of his corpse in 348 BCE was spectacular: he was found with his eyes put out and his tongue cut off, which suggests a political

57. McHardy (2008) offers a nuanced picture of the motives that lay behind revenge in Greek culture. Complex decision-making processes almost always preceded any revenge actions, and men were more likely to retaliate violently in response to an attack on their women, wealth, or social status than in response to the killing of a relative (summarizing 119–120).

58. Cf. Riess 2012: 44, 51, 73–74, 78–79, 81–82, 88, 90–91, 107, 134, 390, on the legal ramifications of this case.

59. Dreyer (2000, with older literature on this topic) comes to the conclusion that Demosthenes never delivered the speech.

motive. Contemporaries suspected that Demosthenes was involved in the affair. Nicodemus was a friend of Meidias, who was an archenemy of Demosthenes. The signal character of the mutilation is in need of explanation. Why was a less drastic killing of Nicodemus not enough for his killer(s)? Private hatred can not be excluded, but the fact that Demosthenes' opponents tried to involve him in the affair again and again should make us suspicious. It suggests, at least, underlying political motives. The case shows a tendency to fall into field 4 in table 1, with the implication of a political message to be transmitted through the mutilation, or even into field 1, if Nicodemus' corpse was found in a prominent place. Nicodemus' case is thus ambivalent, which explains our difficulties in attributing it to one of the heuristic fields.

No. 59: After being disenfranchised in 346/5, a certain Antiphon committed high treason by promising Philip II of Macedon that he would burn down the dockyards of Athens. At first, thanks to the help of Aeschines, Antiphon was released by the Assembly. But on the initiative of Demosthenes, the Areopagus investigated the case again and transferred it back to the Assembly, which sentenced Antiphon to death. He was tortured on the rack and executed around 344 BCE, probably in public, which demonstrates that he was no longer regarded as a citizen.

No. 60: Around the middle of the fourth century, Demosthenes had the priestess Theoris of Lemnos executed on grounds of a *graphê asebeias* (public charge of impiety).[60] According to Plutarch, he accused her, most of all, of teaching slaves how to deceive. We do not know the background of this story but may assume that it was not of private nature.

No. 61: In passing, we learn that the Athenians had executed an alleged witch named Nino sometime before the trial of Theoris (no. 60). The case remains obscure for us.[61] If Nino, like Theoris, came from outside Athens, she was not a "citizen" woman and might have been executed in public.

No. 62: The next case shows that Demosthenes was able personally to lay hands on people. A certain Anaxinus of Oreos claimed to have been sent to Athens by Olympias, the Macedonian queen, in order to buy some goods. Demosthenes, however, was firmly convinced that he had recognized a spy of Philip. By means of *eisangelia* (a form of bringing public charges), he brought Anaxinus in front of the Assembly of the People and had a decree passed that if he should be convicted, Anaxinus would be executed. The case went to court, Demosthenes tortured Anaxinus personally, and Anaxinus

60. Collins (2001: esp. 477, 492–493) explains that Theoris was probably accused not of magic but of poisoning people. Another charge could have been that of impiety, *asebeia*.

61. On both cases, cf. Collins 2001.

confessed his guilt and was executed. We do not know the form of execution, but it is possible that it happened in public, in analogy to the traitor Antiphon (no. 59).

No. 63: In the aftermath of the defeat at Chaeronea, the Areopagite Autolycus brought his wife and children out of the country. Lycurgus considered this behavior treason and brought an *eisangelia* charge against the member of the Areopagus. Autolycus was convicted and executed, presumably forced to drink hemlock in prison.

No. 65: An Athenian merchant borrowed money from several lenders but provided one and the same sample of goods as a security, thereby breaching maritime contracts. One or more of the creditors realized what was going on and accused the *emporos* (merchant) through *eisangelia*, because he damaged not only them but Athens as a whole, in its capacity as a leading trading post. The unknown debtor was convicted and executed. The case is decidedly private, but by using the procedure of *eisangelia*, the accusers charged the case with public relevance, showing an interpretive shift from field 6 in table 1 to field 5.

Nos. 66–67: A major judicial error of early Hellenistic times that the Athenians regretted shortly afterward is the execution of the obviously innocent Phocion in 318 BCE. He was accused of having betrayed the Piraeus to Nicanor. Compared to trials in earlier times, this lawsuit was irregular.[62] Metics, slaves, foreigners, and women gathered in the theater, no longer in a *dikastêrion* (law court). Phocion was hardly heard, was booed down by the masses, and was sentenced to death by drinking hemlock together with some of his comrades. Shortly afterward, like in the case of Socrates, the Athenians regretted their error, buried Phocion's remains (which had been cast beyond the Attic border) in a state funeral, and erected a bronze statue in his honor. Also like in the trial of Socrates, the Athenians gave a sentence of death to the plaintiff, Phocion's accuser Hagnonides (no. 67).

Conclusion

In sum, in Athens (and in the Greek world generally speaking), the spatial dimension of homicide seems to have been a significant factor and potentially a political category. The evidence suggests that politically motivated

62. Tritle (1988: 140) emphasizes the irregularity of the trial before the Assembly of the People and the similarities to the trial of the Arginusae generals in 406 BCE. Cf. Lehmann 1997: 32–40, on Phocion's successful and long-standing career as a *stratêgos* (commander).

homicides, which were intended to convey a symbolic message, were rare and almost exclusively carried out in public. The same result can be stated in a different way: most public murders had considerable political significance; they are assassinations, whereas most privately committed homicides do not carry any political weight. The findings are too numerous and too significant to be mere coincidences of preservation in the historical record. It seems that everything political—even political murder—had to take place in the political centers of the city, the Agora and the Acropolis, to gain political relevance. Since the democratic polis insisted that all politics should be open to the public gaze (today we would speak of transparency),[63] a homicide could be charged with symbolic significance only through its location in the civic heart of the city or through the creation of an audience. This requirement of going public with everything political, even political murder, in tandem with the unflagging belief in the negotiability of the meaning of any political event, provided citizens with the chance of representing a homicide as tyrannicide or political necessity under certain circumstances.

The semantic visualization in table 1 reveals patterns: it not only represents well the tendency of our sources to focus on political violence (field 5), whereas privately motivated homicides (fields 3 and 6) are rather neglected, but it may also be indicative of contemporary reality: genuine assassinations (nos. 2 and 12) were extremely rare at Athens and always a matter of interpretation. The murder of Cylon's men (no. 1, in field 2) was perceived as a sacrilege not only because it happened on sacred ground within the urban center of the polis but also because it was perceived as a senseless deed by many contemporaries. The Alcmeonid perpetrators probably tried to represent their action differently, as the legitimate assassination of a would-be tyrant and his followers, which conveyed a symbolic message, but they did not prevail with their view of things. Applying our heuristic model, we could say that they failed with their interpretive shift from field 2 to field 1. It is interesting to note that the only case of a privately motivated homicide that happened in public, the killing of Hipparchus by Harmodius and Aristogeiton (no. 3, in field 3), could be categorized soon after the deed as an eminently political action and the rightful assassination of a tyrant (indicating a strong tendency toward field 1). Subsequently, the murderers were praised as tyrant slayers, and the interpretive shift from a private to a political action became one of the legendary foundation stories of Athenian

63. Cf. Riess 2006: 69–76, 85–86, on assassinations in hoplite poleis.

democracy.[64] This interpretive shift was also possible thanks to the location of the assassination: this means that the location where the deed occurred charged it immediately with political meaning. Field 4 is almost a *contradictio in adiecto*. The one and only case we know of, the stoning of Lycidas and his family, is highly irregular. Our sources focus on field 5, political trials. Most frequently, political opponents were killed outside the public limelight, in prison so as not to convey any kind of message; oligarchs in particular killed their democratic rivals in secret due to the basically democratic power structures in Athens (Ephialtes, Androcles). Supporters of the democracy never killed their oligarchic enemies in public. The most elegant solution was always to have enemies executed by court sentence. This manner of execution was employed for political as well as private motives (fields 5 and 6), because these spheres overlapped in the Athenian sociopolitical environment.

The Thirty staged mock trials behind closed doors. Because these trials were in camera, conducted by the new Boulê (Council) of the Thirty and not by the regular law courts, the Athenians of later times regarded these sentences as illegitimate, judicial murders. It is interesting to note that the secret removal of Ephialtes (no. 5) could be understood by modern researchers as privately motivated (showing a tendency toward field 6) and that the murder of Nicodemus of Aphidna (no. 58) was interpreted by Meidias as a political assassination (showing a tendency toward field 1) due to the spectacular mutilation of the corpse, a performative aspect that offset the fact that Nicodemus was probably not killed in public.

The number of privately motivated homicides (field 6), which almost always happened in a private or even secret context, must have been much higher. But such homicides are understandably not represented by the kinds of evidence we have, since our sources mostly focus on political and military history.

Chronologically, we observe a clear sequence, from the violent *staseis* (outbreaks of violence characteristic of civil war) of archaic times, to ostracism, and on to the formation of a complicated court system, which Athenian competitors for power and prestige regarded as a venue for political as well as personal fights and, especially, for enacting revenge. The assessment of the Athenian legal system is beyond the scope of this contribution. Suffice it to say that two aspects were particularly problematic: the lack of a separa-

64. The "tale of Harmodius and Aristogeiton" is characterized as a foundation story by McGlew (1993: 157–158).

tion of politics and justice as well as the fact that personal and political feuds, which were often indistinguishable anyway, were carried out in the public arena of the courts.

Instead of a more formal conclusion, I would like to present a test case that, I hope, will further corroborate my thesis. Let us return to no. 40 (Lysias 1). By calling on a posse of friends, the Athenian farmer and cuckolded husband Euphiletus deliberately established a semipublic atmosphere that helped to stage the purely private revenge killing (field 6) of the adulterer Eratosthenes as a justifiable homicide, even tyrannicide (shift to field 1). Eratosthenes had penetrated Euphiletus' house and wife just as the Thirty Tyrants had penetrated citizens' homes.[65] According to Euphiletus' far-fetched analogy, this homicide was the lawful execution of a would-be tyrant, as ordained by the city's laws. Both slaying a tyrant and executions require a public context. Visibility and the ability to witness homicide, it seems, were crucial in constructing and assessing its inherent symbolic qualities. Euphiletus followed these cultural parameters. Instead of removing Eratosthenes quietly, which would have been typical of a private quarrel, Euphiletus sought to establish a public event. In doing so, he meant to express that he had nothing to hide and that he did not have to feel ashamed of his deed, because, in killing the "tyrant" Eratosthenes, he acted not only on his own account but on behalf of and in the interest of the whole polis. We do not know whether the judges followed this bold interpretive shift and acquitted Euphiletus.

In general, we can say that, according to the killers' plans, wishes, and specific motives, the semantic categories of homicide as formed by locations could be combined and transformed so as to convey complex symbolic messages to an audience. This observation partly explains the manifold variations we encounter in the analysis of the spatial dimension of lethal violence in Athens. The category of space—namely, in the dichotomy public versus private—decisively contributed and still contributes to the construction and understanding of the symbolic meaning of lethal violence at Athens.

---

65. Perotti (1989–90) doubts the historicity of the speech, which he regards as a school speech. The plot is too good to be true, there are speaking names, and the grand political metaphor is clearly recognizable: Euphiletos (democracy) is married to a woman (polis), whose honor a tyrant (Eratosthenes) besmirches. Porter (1997: 447–448) emphasizes the similarity of the speech to the tradition of comic adultery tales. To him, Lysias 1 is a "display piece." As far as I know, despite these skeptical voices, the authenticity of the speech is not generally questioned.

Works Cited

Adeleye, G. 1976. "Theramenes: The End of a Controversial Career." *Mus. Afr.* 5: 6–19.

Amyx, D. 1958. "The Attic Stelai." Part 3. *Hesperia* 27: 163–310.

Andrewes, A. 1970. "Lysias and the Theramenes Papyrus." *ZPE* 6: 35–38.

Avery, H. 1959. *Prosopographical Studies in the Oligarchy of the Four Hundred.* Ann Arbor.

Barkan, I. 1936. *Capital Punishment in Ancient Athens.* Chicago.

Bearzot, C. 1997. *Lizia e la tradizione su Teramene: Commento storico alle orazioni XII et XIII del corpus Lysiacum.* Milan.

Bleckmann, B. 1998. *Athens Weg in die Niederlage: Die letzten Jahre des Peloponnesischen Krieges.* Stuttgart.

Borg. B. 2006. "Gefährliche Bilder? Gewalt und Leidenschaft in der archaischen und klassischen Kunst." In B. Seidensticker and M. Vöhler, eds., *Gewalt und Ästhetik: Zur Gewalt und ihrer Darstellung in der griechischen Klassik,* 223–257. Berlin.

Brodersen, K., Günther, W., and Schmitt, H. 1992. *Historische Griechische Inschriften in Übersetzung.* Vol. 1, *Die archaische und klassische Zeit.* Darmstadt.

Buck, R. 1998. *Thrasybulus and the Athenian Democracy: The Life of an Athenian Statesman.* Stuttgart..

Burckhardt, L. 2000. "Eine Demokratie wohl, aber kein Rechtsstaat? Der Arginusenprozeß des Jahres 406 v. Chr." In L. Burckhardt and J. von Ungern-Sternberg, eds., *Große Prozesse im antiken Athen,* 128–43, 273–74. Munich.

Cantarella, E. 1991. *I supplizi capitali in Grecia e a Roma.* Milan.

Cohen, D. 1995. *Law, Violence, and Community in Classical Athens.* Cambridge.

Collins, D. 2001. "Theoris of Lemnos and the Criminalization of Magic in Fourth-Century Athens." *CQ* 51: 477–93.

Dittenberger, W. (1883) 1915. *Sylloge inscriptionum graecarum.* 3rd ed. Vol. 1. Leipzig.

Dombrowski, H. 1934. "Die politischen Prozesse in Athen vom Archontat des Eukleides bis zum Ausgang des Bundesgenossenkrieges." Phd Diss., Greifswald University.

Dover, K. 1970. "Excursus on the Herms and the Mysteries." In A. Gomme, ed., *A Historical Commentary on Thucydides,* vol. 4, *Books V(25)–VII,* 264–88. Oxford.

Dreyer, B. 2000. "Der Tod des Nikodemos von Aphidnai und die Meidias-Rede des Demosthenes." *AHB* 14: 56–63.

Engels, J. 1993. "Der Michigan-Papyrus über Theramenes und die Ausbildung des Theramenes-Mythos." *ZPE* 99: 125–55.

Evjen, H. 1970. "*Apagoge* and Athenian Homicide Procedure." *RHD* 38: 403–15.

Fisher, N. 1998. "Violence, Masculinity, and the Law in Classical Athens." In L. Foxhall and J. Salmon, eds., *When Men Were Men: Masculinity, Power, and Identity in Classical Antiquity,* 68–97. London.

Flach, D. 1977. "Der oligarchische Staatsstreich in Athen vom Jahre 411." *Chiron* 7: 9–33.

Funke, P. 1980. *Homonoia und Arche: Athen und die griechische Staatenwelt vom Ende des Peloponnesischen Krieges bis zum Königsfrieden (404/3–387/6 v. Chr.).* Wiesbaden.

Furley, W. 1996. *Andokides and the Herms: A Study of Crisis in Fifth-Century Athenian Religion.* London.

Gagarin, M. 1981. *Drakon and Early Athenian Homicide Law*. New Haven, CT.
Gagarin, M. 2002. *Antiphon the Athenian: Oratory, Law, and Justice in the Age of the Sophists*. Austin, TX.
Gehrke, H.-J. 1985. *Stasis: Untersuchungen zu den inneren Kriegen in den griechischen Staaten des 5. und 4. Jhs. v. Chr.* Munich.
Gehrke, H.-J. 1987. "Die Griechen und die Rache: Ein Versuch in historischer Psychologie." *Saeculum* 38: 121–49.
Graf, F. 2000. "Der Myterienprozeß." In J. von Ungern -Sternberg and L. Burckhardt, eds., *Große Prozesse im antiken Athen*, 114–27. Munich.
Grossi, G. 1984. *Frinico: Tra propaganda democratica e giudizio tucidideo*. Rome.
Hall, L. 1990. "Ephialtes, the Areopagus, and the Thirty." *CQ* 40: 319–28.
Hamel, D. 1998. *Athenian Generals: Military Authority in the Classical Period*. Leiden.
Hansen, M. 1975. Eisangelia*: The Sovereignty of the People's Court in Athens in the Fourth Century B.C. and the Impeachment of Generals and Politicians*. Odense.
Hansen, M. 1976. Apagoge, Endeixis, *and* Ephegesis *against* Kakourgoi, Atimoi, *and* Pheugontes*: A Study in the Athenian Administration of Justice in the Fourth-Century BC*. Odense.
Harding, P. 1974. "The Theramenes Myth." *Phoenix* 28: 101–11.
Harris, E. 2007. "Feuding or the Rule of Law? The Nature of Litigation in Classical Athens; An Essay in Legal Sociology." In R. Wallace and M. Gagarin, eds., *Symposion 2001: Vorträge zur griechischen und hellenistischen Rechtsgeschichte*, 159–76. Vienna.
Hatzfeld, J. 1938. "La fin du régime de Théramène." *REA* 40: 113–24.
Hatzfeld, J. 1940. "Socrate au procès des Arginuses." *REA* 42: 165–71.
Heftner, H. 2001. *Der oligarchische Umsturz des Jahres 411 v. Chr. und die Herrschaft der Vierhundert in Athen: Quellenkritische und historische Untersuchungen*. Frankfurt am Main.
Heitsch, E. 1984. *Antiphon aus Rhamnus*. Wiesbaden.
Herman, G. 1994. "How Violent Was Athenian Society?" In R. Osborne and S. Hornblower, eds., *Ritual, Finance, Politics: Athenian Democratic Accounts Presented to David Lewis*, 99–117. Oxford.
Herman, G. 1995. "Honour, Revenge, and the State in Fourth-Century Athens." In W. Eder, ed., *Die athenische Demokratie im 4. Jh. v. Chr. Vollendung oder Verfall einer Verfassungsform?*, 43–66. Stuttgart.
Herman G. 1996. "Ancient Athens and the Values of Mediterranean Society." *Mediterranean Historical Review* 11: 5–36.
Herman, G. 1998. Review of D. Cohen, *Law, Violence, and Community in Classical Athens*. *Gnomon* 70: 605–15.
Herman, G. 2000. "Athenian Beliefs about Revenge: Problems and Methods." *PCPhS* 46: 7–27.
Herman, G. 2006. *Morality and Behaviour in Democratic Athens: A Social History*. Cambridge.
Hunter, V. 1994. *Policing Athens: Social Control in the Attic Lawsuits, 420–320 BC*. Princeton.
Krentz, P. 1982. *The Thirty at Athens*. Ithaca.
Lehmann, G. 1972. "Die revolutionäre Machtergreifung der 'Dreißig' und die sta-

atliche Teilung Attikas (404–401/0 v. Chr.)." In R. Stiehl and G. Lehmann, eds., *Antike und Universalgeschichte: Festschrift H. E. Stier*, 201–33. Münster.

Lehmann, G. 1987. "Überlegungen zur Krise der attischen Demokratie im Peloponnesischen Krieg." *ZPE* 69: 33–73.

Lehmann, G. 1997. *Oligarchische Herrschaft im klassischen Athen: Zu den Krisen und Katastrophen der attischen Demokratie im 5. und 4. Jh. v. Chr.* Opladen.

Lewis, D. 1966. "After the Profanation of the Mysteries." In A. Andrewes, ed., *Ancient Society and Institutions: Studies Presented to Victor Ehrenberg*, 177–91. Oxford.

Loening, T. 1987. *The Reconciliation Agreement of 403/2 BC in Athens.* Stuttgart.

MacDowell, D. (1963) 1966. *Athenian Homicide Law in the Age of the Orators.* 2nd ed. Manchester. Repr., 1999.

Maidment, K. 1941. *Minor Attic Orators.* Vol. 1. Cambridge, MA.

Maffi, A. 2005. "De la loi de Solon à la loi d'Ilion ou comment défendre la democratie." In J.-M. Bertrand, ed., *La violence dans les mondes grec et romain: Actes du colloque international (Paris, 2–4 mai 2002)*, 137–61. Paris.

McCoy, W. 1971. *Theramenes, Thrasybulos, and the Athenian Moderates.* Ann Arbor.

McCoy, W. 1975a. "Aristotle's *Athenaion politeia* and the Establishment of the Thirty Tyrants." *YCS* 24: 131–45.

McCoy, W. 1975b. "The Identity of Leon." *AJPh* 96: 187–99.

McGlew, J. 1993. *Tyranny and Political Culture in Ancient Greece.* Ithaca.

McHardy, F. 2008. *Revenge in Athenian Culture.* London.

Mehl, A. 1982. "Für eine neue Bewertung eines Justizskandals: Der Arginusenprozeß und seine Überlieferung vor dem Hintergrund von Recht und Weltanschauung im Athen des ausgehenden 5. Jhs. v. Chr." *ZRG* 99: 32–80.

Meiggs, R., and Lewis, D. (1969) 1988. *A Selection of Greek Historical Inscriptions to the End of the Fifth Century BC.* Rev. ed. Oxford.

Mossé, C. 1969. *La tyrannie dans la Grèce antique.* Paris.

Mossé, C. 1974. "Die politischen Prozesse und die Krise der athenischen Demokratie." In E. Welskopf, ed., *Hellenische Poleis: Krise—Wandlung—Wirkung*, 1.160–87. Berlin.

Moulinier, L. 1952. *Le pur et l'impur dans la pensée des Grecs.* Paris.

Nemeth, G. 1984. "Der Arginusen-Prozeß: Die Geschichte eines politischen Justizmords." *Klio* 66: 51–57.

Nemeth, G. 2006. *Kritias und die Dreißig Tyrannen: Untersuchungen zur Politik und Prosopographie der Führungselite in Athen 404/403 v. Chr.* Stuttgart.

Osborne, R. 1985. "The Erection and Mutilation of the Hermai." *PCPhS* 211: 47–73.

Parker, R. 1983. *Miasma: Pollution and Purification in Early Greek Religion.* Oxford.

Pendrick, G. 1987. "Once Again Antiphon the Sophist and Antiphon of Rhamnus." *Hermes* 115: 46–60.

Perotti, P. 1989–90. "La I Orazione di Lisia fu mai pronunciata?" *Sandalion* 12–13: 43–48.

Pesely, G. 1983. *Theramenes and Athenian Politics: A Study in the Manipulation of History.* Berkeley.

Phillips, D. 2008. *Avengers of Blood: Homicide in Athenian Law and Custom from Draco to Demosthenes.* Stuttgart.

Porter, J. 1997. "Adultery by the Book: Lysias 1 (*On the Murder of Eratosthenes*) and Comic *Diegesis*." *EMC* 40: 421–53. Reprinted in E. Carawan, ed., *Oxford Readings in the Attic Orators* (Oxford, 2007): 60–88.

Pritchett, W. 1953. "The Attic Stelai." Part 1. *Hesperia* 22: 225–99.

Pritchett, W. 1956. "The Attic Stelai." Part 2. *Hesperia* 25: 178–317.

Rhodes, P. 1998. "Enmity in Fourth-Century Athens." In P. Cartledge, P. Millett, and S. von Reden, eds., *Kosmos: Essays in Order, Conflict, and Community in Classical Athens*, 144–61. Cambridge.

Rhodes, P. 2011. *Alcibiades*. Barnsley.

Riess, W. 2006. "How Tyrants and Dynasts Die: The Semantics of Political Assassination in Fourth-Century Greece." In G. Urso, ed., *Terror et Pavor: Violenza, intimidazione, clandestinità nel mondo antico*, 65–88. Cividale del Friuli.

Riess, W. 2007. "Private Violence and State Control: The Prosecution of Homicide and Its Symbolic Meanings in Fourth-Century BC Athens." In C. Brélaz and P. Ducrey, eds., *Sécurité collective et ordre public dans les sociétés anciennes*, 49–101. *Entretiens de la Fondation Hardt 54*. Vandœuvres.

Riess, W. 2012. *Performing Interpersonal Violence: Court, Curse, and Comedy in Fourth-Century BCE Athens*. Berlin.

Roisman, J. 2005. *The Rhetoric of Manhood: Masculinity in the Attic Orators*. Berkeley – Los Angeles – London.

Rosivach, V. 1987. "Execution by Stoning in Athens." *CSCA* 18: 232–48.

Rosivach, V. 1988. "The Tyrant in Athenian Democracy." *QU* 30 (59): 43–57.

Rubinstein, L. 2005. "Differentiated Rhetorical Strategies in the Athenian Courts." In M. Gagarin and D. Cohen, eds., *The Cambridge Companion to Ancient Greek Law*, 129–145. Cambridge.

Ruschenbusch, E. 1960. "Phonos: Zum Recht Drakons und seiner Bedeutung für das Werden des athenischen Staates." *Historia* 9: 129–54.

Scheid, E. 2005. "Remarques sur les fondements de la vengeance en Grèce archaique et classique." In J.-M. Bertrand, ed., *La violence dans les mondes grec et romain: Actes du colloque international (Paris, 2–4 mai 2002)*, 395–410. Paris.

Schmitz, W. 2001. "Drakonische Strafen: Die Revision der Gesetze Drakons durch Solon und die Blutrache in Athen." *Klio* 83: 7–38.

Scholz, P. 2000. "Der Prozeß gegen Sokrates: Ein Sündenfall der athenischen Demokratie?" In J. von Ungern-Sternberg and L. Burckhardt, eds., *Große Prozesse im antiken Athen*, 157–73. Munich.

Sordi, M. 1981. "Teramene e il processo delle Arginuse." *Aevum* 55: 3–12.

Stockton, D. 1982. "The Death of Ephialtes." *CQ*, n.s., 32: 227–28.

Strauss, B. 1986. *Athens after the Peloponnesian War: Class, Faction, and Policy, 403–386 BC*. London.

Taylor, M. 1991. *The Tyrant Slayers: The Heroic Image in Fifth Century B.C. Athenian Art and Politics*. 2nd ed. Salem, NH.

Tod, M. 1946. *A Selection of Greek Historical Inscriptions: To the End of the Fifth Century*. Vol. 1. 2nd ed. Oxford.

Tritle, L. 1988. *Phocion the Good*. London.

Ungern-Sternberg, J. von. 2000. "'Die Revolution frißt ihre eigenen Kinder': Kritias vs. Theramenes." In J. von Ungern-Sternberg and L. Burckhardt, eds., *Große Prozesse im antiken Athen*, 144–56, 275–76. Munich.

Usher, S. 1968. "Xenophon, Critias and Theramenes." *JHS* 88: 128–35.

Volonaki, E. 2000. "'Apagoge' in Homicide Cases." *Dike* 3: 147–76.

Wallace, R. (1985) 1989. *The Areopagos Council, to 307 BC*. Baltimore.

Welwei, K.-W. 1992. *Athen: Vom neolithischen Siedlungsplatz zur archaischen Großpolis*. Darmstadt.

Welwei, K.-W. 1999. *Das klassische Athen: Demokratie und Machtpolitik im 5. und 4. Jahrhundert*. Darmstadt.

Wilson, P. 2000. *The Athenian Institution of the* Khoregia*: The Chorus, the City, and the Stage*. Cambridge.

Wolpert, A. 2006. "The Violence of the Thirty Tyrants." In S. Lewis, ed., *Ancient Tyranny*, 213–23. Edinburgh.

Appendix

Table 1. Heuristic fields of historically attested homicides and executions in Athens to the end of the fourth century BCE

		Motive		
		political with public call to action or communication of symbolic message	political without public call to action, sometimes communication of symbolic message	“private”
Location	urban centers (Acropolis, Agora etc.)	1 assassination 2, 12	2 1 (perceived as sacrilege), 6 (suicide)	3 “privately” motivated homicide 3 (tendency to field 1)
	outside of centers (house, field, farm etc.)	4 4	5 assassination in secret / secret removal of enemy / judicial murder / lawful execution 5 (tendency to field 6), 10, 11, 13–39, 41–49, 51–53, 58? (tendency to field 4 or even field 1), 59–64, 66–67	6 “privately” motivated homicide / secret removal of enemy / judicial murder / lawful execution 7–9, 40 (staged as belonging to field 1), 50, 54–57, 65 (staged as belonging to field 5)

Table 2. Killings and executions of mostly known individuals at locations in Athens until ca. 318 BCE

Case No.	Date	Sources	Plaintiff[a]	Murderer	Victim	Location and other pertinent information
0	?	Aeschin. 1.182; D.S. 8.22; Heraclid. Lemb. *Epit. Ath. pol.* 1		King Hippomenes	daughter Leimone	barn
1	632?	Hdt. 5.70–71; Th. 1.126; Plu. *Sol.* 12; Arist. *Ath.* 1; Heraclid. Pont. *Ath. pol.* fr. 4		Megacles and his men	Cylon's men	outside Acropolis
2	528–514	Hdt. 6.103		on order of Peisistratus' sons	Cimon, father of Miltiades	near Prytaneion, ambush, at night
3	514	Th. 1.20, 6.54–60; Hdt. 5.55–62, 6.123; Arist. *Ath.* 18.2–6; D.S. 9.1.4; 10.17; Heraclid. Pont. *Ath. pol.* fr. 6; Max. Tyr. *Diss.* 24.2; Paus. *Attica* 1.8.5, 1.23.1; Justin *Hist. phil.* 2.9		Harmodius, Aristogeiton	Hipparchus	Leocoreion, during Panathenaia
4	479	Hdt. 9.5; Lycurg. 1.122; D. 18.204		members of Boulê (Council), Athenian women	Lycidas and his wife and children	outside Boulê (Salamis), outside house of Lycidas in Athens
5	461	Arist. *Ath.* 25.4–5; Plu. *Per.* 10.7–8; D.S. 11.77.6; Antiphon 5.68		Aristodicus of Tanagra? (case never resolved)	Ephialtes	at night (Diod.)
6	427	Plu. *Arist.* 26.5; *Nic.* 6.1			Paches	suicide in front of jurors
7	420–411	Antiphon 1	son of victim	stepmother of plaintiff	father of plaintiff	at home
8	before 417	Ps.-And. 4.14; Plu. *Alc.* 8.4; indirect Lys. 14.42; Antiph. fr. 67 (Thalheim and Blass)		Alcibiades	Hipparete	at home
9	419/18	Antiphon 6	Philocrates, brother of victim	*chorêgos*? (choral director)	Diodotus, member of a choir	at home

10	415/14	And. 1.12–13, 15–18, 35, 52–53, 65, 67; Attic *stelai* (Pritchett 1953: 231–232)	informers are Andromachus, Teucrus, Agariste, Lydus, Andocides	accusation of mutilation of the herms and profanation of the Mysteries	Acumenus, Adeimantus, Alcibiades, Alcibiades of Phegus, Alcisthenes, Andromachus (slave), Antidorus, Antiphon, Archebiades, Archidamus, Archippus, Aristomenes, Autocrator, Axiochus, Cephisodorus, Chaeredemus, Charippus, Charmides, Diacritus, Diogenes, Diognetus, Eryximachus, Euctemon, Euphiletus, Eurydamas, Eurymachus, Glaucippus, Gniphonides, Hephaestodorus, Hicesius (slave), Isonomus, Leogoras, Lysistratus, Meletus, Menstratus, Nicides, Oionias, Panaetius, Pantacles, Phaedrus, Pherecles, Philocrates, Platon, Polyeuctus, Polystratus, Polytion, Smindyrides, Teisarchus, Telenicus, Teucrus, Theodorus, Timanthes, Diocleides (false informer: And. 1.37–69; Thu. 6.60.2–4; Plu. *Alc.* 20–21)	*desmôtêrion*? (prison)
11	411	Th. 8.65		oligarchic youths, gangs	Androcles, popular leader of democrats	in secret
12	411/10	Th. 8.90–92; Lys. 13.70–76; Lycurg. 1.112–15. Cf. Lys. 7.4, 20.9–12, 25.9; Plu. *Alc.* 25; Brodersen, Günther, and Schmitt 1992: 140 (= *IG* I³ 102 = Dittenberger [1883] 1915: 108 = Tod 1946: 86 = Meiggs and Lewis [1969] 1988: 85)	Phrynichus' relatives/friends	Thrasybulus from Calydon (killer), Apollodorus from Megara (Lys., Lyc.), or one of the *peripoloi* and a man from Argos (Th.)	Phrynichus	in Agora, near Bouleutêrion (Council Hall), during the day (Th.) or at night at the fountain close to the willows (Lyc.)
13	411/10	Lys. 12.67; Th. 8.68; 8.90; Antiph. fr. 1–6 (Blass), fr. III 1 (Gernet), fr. B 1 (Maidment); Krateros, *FGrHist* 342 F 5 (= Plu. *Mor.* 833d–834b)	Theramenes, Andron, Apolexis		Antiphon of Rhamnus, Archeptolemus of Agryle	*desmôtêrion*?
14	411–406	X. *HG* 1.7.28; Lycurg. 1.115			Aristarchus, former member of the Four Hundred (defendant of Phrynichus)	*desmôtêrion*?

15	406	X. *HG* 1.7; 2.3.32, 35; X. *Mem.* 1.1.18; D.S. 13.101–3; Val. Max. *Mem.* 3.8.3	Theramenes, Archedemus, Callixenus, Lycis-cus, Timokrates, Menekles, Diomedon Cholargeus, (Thrasybulus) (trial of the Arginusai)	Pericles the Younger, Diomedon, Lysias, Aristo-crates, Thrasyllus, Erasinides	*desmôtêrion?*
16	404/3	X. *HG* 2.3.23–56; D.S. 14.4.5–14.5.4; Arist. *Ath.* 28.5; 36–37; Th. 8.68; Lys. 12.77–78; Justin *Hist. phil.* 5.9	Critias	Theramenes	*desmôtêrion*
17	404/3	X. *Mem.* 4.4.3; X. *HG* 2.3.39; Pl. *Ep.* 7.324e–325c; Pl. *Ap.* 32c–d; Andoc. 1.94	the Thirty, espe-cially Meletus	Leon from Salamis	execution without trial, *desmôtêrion?*
18	404/3	X. *HG* 2.4.21		Cleocritus	*desmôtêrion*
19	404/3	Lys. 13.38, 63; 18.5		Eucrates	*desmôtêrion*
20	404/3	Arist. *Ath.* 38.2		Demaretus, victim of the Ten	*desmôtêrion*
21	404/3	Lys. 10.4, 10.27, 11.2, 11.9		father of Pantaleon	*desmôtêrion*
22	404/3	X. *HG* 2.3.40; Plu. *Mor.* 833A (= *FGrHist* 115 F 120)		Antiphon, son of Lysonides	*desmôtêrion*
23	404/3	D.S. 14.5.7; X. *Symp.* 1.2; Plu. *Lys.* 15; *SEG* 34.380; Athen. 187–188, 216d		Autolycus	*desmôtêrion*
24	404/3	Plu. *Vit. X orat.* 841b	Aristodemus of Bate	Lycurgus, son of Lycomedes, Butades	*desmôtêrion*
25	404/3	X. *HG* 2.3.39; Lys. 18.6, 19.47; D.S. 14.5.5; Plu. *Mor.* 998b; Pl. *R.* 327c; *Lach.* 200d; X. *Symp.* 4.6; Arist. *Rh.* 1413a		Niceratus, son of Nicias, Kydantides	*desmôtêrion*
26	404/3	Hieron. *Adv. Iovin.* 1.41 (307)		Pheidon and his daughters	unclear, suicide
27	404/3	Lys. 30.14	Satyrus and Chremon among the Thirty	Calliades	*desmôtêrion*

28	404	X. *HG* 1.7.35; Lys. 13.12, 30.10–14	Satyrus and Chremon among the Thirty, also Theramenes		Cleophon	*desmôtêrion*
29	404/3	Lys. 13.30.14	Satyrus and Chremon among the Thirty		Strombichides	*desmôtêrion*
30	404/3	Lys. 13.55–57	Menestratus		leader of democrats	*desmôtêrion*
31	404/3	Lys. 13.23, 13.30	Agoratus		Nicias	*desmôtêrion*
32	404/3	Lys. 13.23, 13.30	Agoratus		Nicomenes	*desmôtêrion*
33	404/3	Lys. 13.58–59	Agoratus		Aristophanes from Cholleis, metic	*desmôtêrion*
34	404/3	Lys. 13.13, esp. 40–41, 56–57, 86–87	Agoratus		democrat and taxiarch Dionysodorus	*desmôtêrion* (sentenced to death without trial)
35	404/3 or after 401/0 (Loening 1987: 70)	Lys. 12	Lysias, brother of victim	Eratosthenes	brother of plaintiff, Polemarchus, metic	*desmôtêrion*
36	404/3	Lys. 13.54			Hippias from Thasos, foreigner	*desmôtêrion*
37	404/3	Lys. 13.54			Xenophon from Kurion, foreigner	*desmôtêrion*
38	400/399	Lys. 13.55–57			Menestratus	*apotumpanismos* outside city walls?
39	400–398	Lys. 13.13, esp. 40–41, 56–57, 86–87	Dionysodorus' brother Dionysius and brother-in-law of Dionysodorus		Agoratus	*apotumpanismos* outside city walls?
40	400–380	Lys. 1	Eratosthenes' relatives	Euphiletus	Eratosthenes	at home
41	399	e.g., Pl. *Ap*, 23e, 36a; X. *Mem.* 1.1, 4.8.2; D.S. 14.37; D.L. 2.40–43	Anytus, Meletus, Lycon		Socrates	*desmôtêrion*
42	399	D.S. 14.37.7; D.L. 2.43; Themist. *Or.* 20.239c			Anytus (allegedly stoned in Heracleia Pontos), Meletus, Lycon	executed without sentence, *desmôtêrion*?

43	393/2	D. 19.191; Lys. 14.38	Conon of Anaphlystus		Adeimantus of Skambonidai	*desmôtêrion*?
44	391 or after 387/6	Lys. 19.7			generals Nicophemus and his son Aristophanes	*apagôgê*, put to death without trial (Cyprus?)
45	389	D.S. 14.94.4, 14.99.4–5; D. 19.180; Lys. 28.3–5, 29.2			general Ergocles	*desmôtêrion*?
46	388/7	D. 19.180			general Dionysius	sentenced to death or fined
47	386	Lys. 22.1–5, 13; D. 24.136			grain dealers	?
48	379/8	X. *HG* 5.4.19			general, name unknown; another sentenced to death in absentia	*desmôtêrion*?
49	373	D. 49.10	Callistratus of Aphidna, Iphicrates of Rhamnous		Antimachus, treasurer of Timotheus	*desmôtêrion*?
50	371–366	Is. 9.16–19		Thydippus, brother of victim	Euthycrates	in a field
51	367	D. 19.31; X. *HG* 7.1.38	Leon		envoy Timagoras	*desmôtêrion*?
52	363/2	Arist. *Rh*, 1380b12–13; Aeschin. 2.30			general Callisthenes	*desmôtêrion*?
53	361	Hyp. 3.1; Lycurg. 1.93			general Callistratus of Aphidna after seeking refuge at altar of the Twelve Gods	*desmôtêrion*?
54	after 349	Ps.-D. 59.9–10	Stephanus	Apollodorus	woman from Aphidna, maybe one of Stephanus' slaves; may be a false accusation	outside Athens
55	prior to 348	D. 21.72–75	Boiotus' relatives	Euaion	Boiotus	*deipnon* (meal) and *synodos* (gathering) in unknown context
56	prior to 348	D. 21.71	n/a	Euthynus	Sophilus	Samos, *synousia* (gathering) in unknown context
57	ca. 350	Ps.-D. 47.58–73	speaker of Ps.-D. 47	Theophemus and Euergus	wet nurse of speaker, former slave	on a farm

58	348	D. 21.104–22 with scholia 21.102, 104, 116, 205; Aeschin. 1.171–72, 2.148, 2.166 with scholia; Din. 1.30–31, 1.47; Idomeneus in Athen. *Deipn.* 13.592; *FGrHist* 338 F 12, ap. *Athen.* 592–93	1. Meidias 2. Nicodemus' relatives	Aristarchus	Nicodemus from Aphidna	?
59	ca. 344	D. 18.132–33; Din. 1.63; Plu. *Dem.* 14.5	Demosthenes		Antiphon	tortured on rack, then executed in public?
60	ca. 344	Ps.-D. 25.77–80; Plu. *Dem.* 14; Philochorus, *FGrHist* 328 F 60	Demosthenes		Theoris of Lemnos	in public?
61	ca. 344	D. 19.281			Nino	in public?
62	343–340	Aeschin. 3.223–224; D. 18.137	Demosthenes		Anaxinus of Oreos	in public?
63	338	Lycurg. fr. 3 (frr. 13–17); Lycurg. 1.53; Ps.-Plut. 843d	Lycurgus		Autolycus	*desmôtêrion*
64	338/37	D.S. 16.88.1–2	Lycurgus		Lysicles	*desmôtêrion*?
65	327	D. 34.50–51			Athenian *emporos*, for breach of maritime contracts	?
66	318	Corn. Nep. *Phoc.* 4.1–2; D.S. 18.65.6–18.67.5; Plu. *Phoc.* 33–37	Hagnonides, Demophilus, Epicurus		Phocion, Nicoles, Thudippus, Hegemon, Pythocles	*desmôtêrion*
67	after 317	Plu. *Phoc.* 38			Hagnonides	*desmôtêrion*?

[1]The meaning of the category "plaintiff" here is twofold. On the one hand, it can designate the plaintiff who accused someone of murder. In this case, the plaintiff was a relative or, in rare cases, the friend of a victim. On the other hand, the term *plaintiff* could stand for an accusation made with the intent to have someone killed. In this sense, the term has a highly aggressive undertone, almost synonymous with the term *murderer*. In Athens, capital charges were legal means of fighting against an opponent (Gehrke 1987: 140, 143; Hunter 1994: 128–29; Fisher 1998: 81, 92; Cohen 1995: 23, 33, 72, 83, 87, 104, 138–39; Roisman 2005: 177; Rubinstein 2005: 138 n. 20; Scheid 2005: 402–3; Borg 2006: 234–35; contra Herman [1994; 1996: 22; 1998: 610–11; 2000], who thinks that vengeance and litigation are incompatible). As a result, executions can be considered an indirect form of lethal violence initiated by a plaintiff (Riess 2012: 228–30, 391–92).

Table 3. Unclear Cases

Case No.	Date	Sources	Plaintiff	Murderer	Victim	Location and other pertinent information
1	389–343	Is. 8.41		Diocles	brother-in-law	unclear, Diocles never sentenced
2	355	Plu. Dem.. 22.2	Androtion	Diodorus	Diodorus' father	unclear, *graphê asebeias* against Diodorus' uncle Euctemon
3	Ca. 350	Ps.-D. 58.28–29	Theocrines does not prosecute Demochares	Demochares and others	Theocrines' brother	unclear, financial compensation

FOUR

The Crime That Dare Not Speak Its Name

Violence against Women in the Athenian Courts

Rosanna Omitowoju

Was classical Athens a violent place to live? How could we ever answer a question like that with any degree of certainty? As with many aspects of (Athenian) cultural history, there is a long and distinguished record of trying to explore the answers to such a question:[1] many of these are sophisticated, informative and highly attractive in their desire to piece together something of "what it was really like," but any claim to reliability is ultimately spurious. This essay is going to claim that we just cannot know about the reality in the end but that we can, on the way to saying that, make various interesting claims about the ideology that might at least partially vivify any of the realities we could posit for the classical city.

I am here going to be looking at a number of speeches by Attic orators, including some close readings of a number of specific passages. My interest is in how violence, most specifically violence against women, enters this discourse. I shall talk about "the world created by the orators," in a number of ways. I will partly address it in rather metaphorical terms, when I argue that certain texts offer us "silences" about violence against women or when I use the language of drama for "scenes" and "characters' from court speeches;

1. See, e.g., Cohen 1995: 115–18; Rhodes 1998: 144–69; Fisher 1998: 68–97; Herman 2006: 402–14; Llewellyn-Jones 2011: 231–66.

but I also want to think about oratory in relation to "reality." I have a strong sense that what the extant court speeches offer us is not the real but the "real" world, that is, a world that is not self-consciously fictive, mythic, or heroic. This world is heavily constructed, has as many genre constraints as the worlds created in any other group of texts, and mostly bears a totally unprovable relationship to what absolutely happened. However (and this is crucial, in my view), it is a world that is referencing reality in a very specific way. So its characters represent "real" and sometimes real people (often even named individuals), and the personae that are created for them are constructed to be believable, persuasive portraits of how a contemporary Athenian would, should, and maybe even did act. Thus, what we find in these texts may not be a provable actuality, but it is "real."

My focus is going to be on violence against women, but I would like to start by thinking briefly about male-on-male violence. Many of the extant speeches deal with cases that are about male violence with male victims, either explicitly or in some significant way.[2] What sort of world do they portray? Some scholars are eager to claim that it is a world in which violence is infrequent and in which reciprocity and cooperation are to the fore,[3] and I have much sympathy with such claims. Certainly, it is a convincing way of dealing with the long *narrationes* detailing the many violent, unlawful, or uncooperative acts to which the speaker has resisted responding or with the prevalence of rhetoric invoking the collective and endorsing civic acts of violence (punishment) at the expense of individual ones. However, I think that this view ultimately downplays the effects of concepts that are significantly alien to our modern, Western, middle-class, liberal zeitgeist: we see classical Athens as prioritizing reciprocity and cooperation because for humans to interact in this way makes more rational sense to us.

This is not to say that I would argue for entirely the opposite view. My Athens is not an exclusively violent, macho, honor-obsessed world, thinly masking the enthusiasm for blood feud with the occasional nod toward the possibility of law, though there are convincing arguments on this side too.[4] My argument is that for any reality we could imagine (and we can only imagine it), all we can do is try to plot an ideological line between opposing strategies (revenge versus forgiveness, individual action versus collective sanction, concerns of personal or familial honor versus the "rule of law") and

2. See, e.g., D. 21.54; Lys. 1.3.

3. E.g., Herman 2006: 402ff.

4. See Fisher 1998: 68–97; Llewellyn-Jones 2011: 231–66, esp. 233–42.

see that any individual moment of interaction will sit somewhere on that line. It is impossible to tell exactly where: even the preponderance of positions on that line is something we can only conjecture.

With that said, let us look briefly at some examples of male-on-male violence: *Against Meidias* and *Against Conon* can be useful exemplars here. These two speeches are both by Demosthenes yet show some significant and useful differences. One was delivered in court, one very likely not. One involves Demosthenes in propria persona; in the other, the speaker is a man called Ariston. One is a suit for assault, the other a *probole*[5] procedure for an offense at a religious festival. One involves an attack so (allegedly) severe in nature as to have brought the victim almost to death's door; the other involves blows that even the speaker acknowledges to have been harmful in ways more symbolic than physical.

How do these speeches frame my real focus on women as victims of violence? Firstly, there is a noticeable straightforwardness about their descriptions of violence. Even Demosthenes—accusing Meidias (whose physical blows were arguably more significant in terms of symbolic violence than actual bodily harm) of the more amorphous, politically and emotionally charged hubris and *aselgeia*[6]—says quite clearly,

> προὐβαλόμην ἀδικεῖν τοῦτον περὶ τὴν ἑορτήν,οὐ μόνον πληγὰς ὑπ' αὐτοῦ λαβὼν τοῖς Διονυσίοις, ἀλλὰ καὶ ἄλλα πολλὰ καὶ βίαια παθὼν παρὰ πᾶσαν τὴν χορηγίαν.[7]
>
> [I brought a charge against this man for wrongdoing concerning the festival, not only because I had received blows from him at the Dionysia, but because I had suffered many other acts of violence throughout my whole *choregia*.]

Compare the description of Conon's attack on Ariston:

> Κόνων δ' οὑτοσὶ καὶ ὁ υἱὸς αὐτοῦ καὶ ὁ Ἀνδρομένους υἱὸς ἐμοὶ προσπεσόντες τὸ μὲν πρῶτον ἐξέδυσαν,εἶθ' ὑποσκελίσαντες καὶ ῥάξαντες εἰς τὸν βόρβορον οὕτω διέθηκαν ἐναλλόμενοι καὶ ὑβρίζοντες, ὥστε τὸ μὲν χεῖλος διακόψαι, τοὺς δ' ὀφθαλμοὺς

5. On this procedure, see Todd 1993: 121.

6. D. 21.1.

7. D. 21.1–2.

> συγκλεῖσαι· οὕτω δὲ κακῶς ἔχοντα κατέλιπον, ὥστε μήτ' ἀναστῆναι μήτε φθέγξασθαι δύνασθαι.[8]
>
> [This man Conon and his son and the son of Andromenes fell upon me and first of all they stripped me, then, taking my legs out from under me and pushing me in the mud, they leaped on me and beat me to such an extent that my lip was split and my eyes closed up. They left me in such a bad way that I could neither get up nor speak.]

Ariston later claims to have suffered internal hemorrhaging that nearly killed him (D. 54.11–12). The point is that men have bodies that can be talked about in these clear terms, whose wounds can be discussed and (metaphorically at least) held up to show.

With this potential for talk about the male victim and the wounds he receives, there is a wide range of vocabulary available for such descriptions, from a number of registers. Looking no further than these two speeches, there are the politically charged term *hubris* (used repeatedly), emotive terms such as *aselgeia* (wanton outrage / brutality) and *paroinia* (drunken violence), and a whole range of largely practical descriptive terms for beating and striking (*plesso* and the cognate noun *plege*, *paio*, *enallomai*,[9] the pretty plain and no-nonsense *tupto*), plus the quasi-legal *aikeia* (assault).[10] What I am saying here (in contrast to the situation when I go on to discuss women) is that there is a possible discourse of male-on-male violence in the courts because men are rhetorically viable as both perpetrators and victims of violence. They enter the oratorical record as both: less often, perhaps, does a speaker tell the story of his own violence (Lysias 1 is unusual here), but speakers and their friends figure frequently in the speeches as the victims of violent abuse.

Even as victims of violence, however, men are still agents. They are owners of physical property (land, money, possessions), masters of animate property (women, children, slaves),[11] and, perhaps most important of all in our

8. D. 54.8–9.

9. "Leap upon" does not necessarily have to mean violence. In other contexts, it can refer to dancing.

10. For *aikeia* as a legal term, see Todd 1993: 269–71, 360.

11. Undoubtedly, these form three difference categories, and chattel slaves most clearly fit the category of "animate property": however, the status of all three and particularly of women and slaves as perpetual minors, under the *kureia* of a male, with all of the legal and personal restrictions that brings (again, different but overlapping for all three categories), means that we can see them all, at least generally, in these terms. For a longer and more careful discussion, see Todd 1993: 207–10, 212–15, 184–92.

record, possessors of the political capital of citizenship and the moral authority to exercise it. This last identity is perhaps particularly telling; undoubtedly skewed by the nature of our record, its survival, and its reflexive civic and legal concerns, the citizen victim becomes of particular interest and focus.[12] The male characters in the narratives that our speeches represent are all actors in their own stories, in a variety of individual ways. As well as this, though, as speakers in a case, either as plaintiffs seeking justice or as defendants exculpating themselves, men are structurally agents in a system that recognizes male wrongdoing, male victimhood, and the speech acts by which they are represented to the judgment of the (male) jury. One of the main arguments of this essay is that this level of agency, either actually or conceptually, is never available for women.[13]

Cherchez la Femme

The preceding summary of male-on-male violence in our sources leaves us with a large gap when we turn to the issue of women as the victims of violence. In my book on rape, I argued that I found it difficult to imagine a prosecution for rape realistically forming the basis of a legal case[14]—or, at the very least, the sort of legal case that our extant speeches represent, with their high-profile rhetoric and personal posturing. Issues surrounding sexual respectability, the virtual embargo on the naming of respectable women in court,[15] and the exclusion of women from all areas of civic speech create a convincing argument that rape was a "silent crime" as far as the formal courts and their proceedings were concerned. Informal channels for dispute settlement, such as arbitration, might be a different matter, of course.[16]

If this is true, though, for sexual violence against women, with all the taboos we might expect that to bring with it (especially for a highly sex-segregated society such as classical Athens), does it have to hold that it is the same for all forms of violence? If, as we have seen, it is acceptable for a man

12. For a particularly explicit version of this, see D. 21.79.

13. For women's inability to access law, see Omitowoju 2002: 121–22; Todd 1993: 201–2.

14. Omitowoju 2002: 122–33.

15. See Schaps 1977; Todd 1993: 201.

16. On arbitration, see MacDowell 1978: 203–6; Isager and Hansen 1975: 107–8; Todd 1993: 123–24; Hunter 1994: 55–67.

to take on the role of being a personal victim of violence in the courts,[17] could we not expect that the role of prosecutor in the case of a violent attack on a man's wife or daughter would be just as acceptable?

The evidence from our extant speeches would seem to give that question a pretty strong negative answer, which I will spend the rest of this chapter examining. I am not claiming that the issue of violence against women never enters the record through discussion in legal speeches or in Attic oratory more generally. Rather, I am arguing that whenever it does appear, the ensuing discussion or the points that a speaker wants us to draw from it always direct our attention elsewhere. It is therefore vital that we work out what we can do with these moments of redirection or, at their most extreme, the gaps and silences that the subject of such violence seems to elicit. I would like to qualify my position in three ways. First, I am aware that I am entering exactly the space of the imaginary (how could filling in the gaps in our record be anything else?) that I referred to in my introduction. I have no qualms about this, but I want to be explicit about what I am doing. Second, as I have already said (though in a less explicit way), to work on a basis that the corpus of Attic oratory in some straightforward way equates to "Athenian law" is to labor under a serious misapprehension. We have a fascinating, frustrating body of texts that have survived for us for specific reasons, usually the personal or the literary.[18] Inasmuch as they allow a reflection on "Athenian law" (which they, of course, but probably no more than on other things), it is a tangential, personal, selective, and arbitrary one. In a way, this situation itself is highly revealing: with very little written law, *hoi nomoi*, as a concept, are really only instantiated in a particular individual's presentation and interpretation of them. They comprise a legal system without precedent.[19] So when I claim that violent acts committed against women are treated often in our speeches with a resounding, if not total, silence, I do not mean that this is the sole response or even the sole legal response to them in the real world of Athens. But I do mean that I think there are good and interesting reasons, which are worth exploring, as to why violent acts against women are not a viable subject for the kind of edited rhetoric that

17. Herman (2006) would even claim that putting up with a whole series of violent and abusive acts without retaliation is a highly acceptable role. I am not so convinced.

18. On the survival of oratorical texts, see Worthington 1994: 244–63.

19. Although one does occasionally see a speaker attempting to establish some sort of sense of precedent (e.g., D. 21.71–72), this is always in reference to acts and their punishments, never in relation to interpretations of the law. On "precedent," see Lanni 2004: 159–71.

we have. Put another way, while not claiming that semiformal (or even occasionally formal) legal redress for acts of violence committed against women was impossible, I do not even momentarily imagine that a whole sheaf of high-profile, legal speeches concerning such acts has somehow been lost to us. At least some of that silence, I believe, echoes from the ancient world: in what follows, I am going to try and examine the nature of the silence and offer some speculations about its origins.

Cherchez l'Homme?

As I have argued, legal stories are stories about men. I have divided my attempts here to explore and explicate the nature of the silence surrounding violence against women into five separate sections that draw out and focus on different strands, but they are also significantly interlinked. This first section argues that any narratives that involve women and violence against them end up really being about men. Nowhere is this more pointed than in the story of hubris. Much has been written about hubris,[20] particularly about its relationship to key notions of egalitarian citizenship and the inviolability of the citizen's body. I and others have argued that assaults on women[21]—sexual or otherwise—could very well be thought of as hubris. But the rub is that acts of hubris infringe on the citizen's body, honor, and rights, and because women were not and could not be Athenian citizens,[22] the story of hubris is always one about men.

Although not a case about violence toward a woman, Lysias 1 can perhaps be instructive here. This is a defense speech by a man, Euphiletos, who is defending himself on a charge of murder on the grounds that his act of homicide, performed on a man whom he caught in intercourse with his wife, is justified. There is no suggestion that the act of sex has been nonconsensual: indeed, as I have argued elsewhere, much is made out of the wife's collusion.[23] It is key for us that the act of sex in which Eratosthenes has engaged is represented by Euphiletos as a criminal act, at least implicitly. Moreover, this crime, which Euphiletos glosses more than once as an act of hubris, is figured as being against Euphiletos himself, the agent and speaker in this case: Euphiletos does not represent himself as acting to avenge an

20. See, in particular, Fisher 1992 a full-scope monograph on hubris.

21. Fisher 1992: 41.

22. On the contested category of the citizeness, see Omitowoju 2002: 22–26.

23. Omitowoju 2002: 91–93.

act of hubris committed against his wife. While there is no suggestion, as I have said, that this act of sex employed violence, it is also the case (contra to what Euphiletos claims explicitly but speciously at 1.32–34) that female consent to sex in no way marks the distinction between the levels of criminality of an act of sex with the wife of another citizen: consequently, this pattern of illicit sex being figured as hubris against the woman's husband, as *kurios*, would seem to hold just as true for violent (sexual) attacks. The potential for such acts to be called hubris is exactly what allows their female victim to disappear: although an act of violence might have been perpetrated on the body of a woman or child, to discuss it as hubris takes it into the political realm of relations between men. In the context of such discussions, within either a forensic or political oratorical context, violence against a woman becomes hubris between men, because hubris is fundamentally an act between males.[24]

In the Demosthenic speech *On the Treaty with Alexander*, where Demosthenes is waxing lyrical about why the Athenians should not enter the treaty and should instead prefer to snatch up weapons and defend their liberty, he says that not to do so would be worse than being slaves, because

> τοὺς δὲ τυραννουμένους ἀκρίτους ἔστιν ὁρᾶν ἀπολλυμένους ἅμα καὶ ὑβριζομένους εἰς παῖδας καὶ γυναῖκας.[25]
>
> [those subject to tyranny can be seen to be put to death without trial at the same time as having hubris committed against them in relation to their children and wives.]

The passive masculine participle and the preposition *eis* (which I have translated here as "in relation to") in this passage make it clear that whatever these acts are, parallel to execution without trial, these (presumably but not necessarily) violent acts against women and children can, in this political context, only be described as acts of hubris against men. Acts performed on the bodies of their women and children equate to hubris carried out against them, which freeborn men should not endure.

In two of Isocrates' speeches—which are again political oratory, not

24. I mean here that hubris is very much associated with its rhetorical nature—i.e., no explicit act equates to hubris. Things are hubris because you describe them as such in the courts, and you can only really describe male acts and behavior (either as plaintiff or defendant) in a legal speech.

25. [D.] 17.3.

forensic—violence against women is alluded to but is firmly part of a discussion about male relations between a ruler and his subjects.

> Εἰδὼς γὰρ ἅπαντας ἀνθρώπους περὶ πλείστου ποιουμένους τοὺς παῖδας τοὺς αὑτῶν καὶ τὰς γυναῖκας, καὶ μάλιστ' ὀργιζομένους τοῖς εἰς ταῦτ' ἐξαμαρτάνουσιν, καὶ τὴν ὕβριν τὴν περὶ ταῦτα μεγίστων κακῶν αἰτίαν γιγνομένην, καὶ πολλοὺς ἤδη καὶ τῶν ἰδιωτῶν καὶ τῶν δυναστευσάντων διὰ ταύτην ἀπολομένους, οὕτως ἔφυγον τὰς αἰτίας ταύτας ὥστ' ἐξ οὗ τὴν βασιλείαν ἔλαβον, οὐδενὶ φανήσομαι σώματι πεπλησιακὼς πλὴν τῆς ἐμαυτοῦ γυναικός.[26]
>
> [Since I know that all men care most about their children and wives and get most angry at people who commit crimes against them and that the hubris committed in this regard is responsible for the greatest ills . . . , I avoided such causes so much that from the time that I took on the kingship, I was seen to have physical relations with no one other than my own wife.]

Of their opponents, Isocrates says,

> Φυγὰς δὲ καὶ στάσεις καὶ νόμων συγχύσεις καὶ πολιτειῶν μεταβολὰς, ἔτι δὲ παίδων ὕβρεις καὶ γυναικῶν αἰσχύνας καὶ χρημάτων ἁρπαγὰς τίς ἂν δύναιτο διεξελθεῖν;[27]
>
> [Who would be able to tell in full their periods of exile, their factionalism, their game playing with the laws, their subversions of constitutions, and, even more, their outraging of children, shaming of women, and snatching of money?]

Both these examples—one explicitly using the term *hubris* in relation to women and one not—share the sense that what matters in these acts is the effect, personal and political, that these acts of violence might have on men, as well as what they can tell us about men who have power. The fact of violence against women is explicitly mentioned, but it is part of a political debate about how men can and should act toward other men and how such acts should be regarded. Female victims of bodily violence are brought

26. Isoc. 3.36.
27. Isoc. 4.114.

before our eyes (along with a list of other issues), but in this political context, the point is a comment on the behavior and moral valuation of men.

Symbols and Taboos

In the previous section, I argued that one of the cloaks of silence that is spread over female victims is a silence filled with talk. It is talk about the male partner, father, or master of a woman whose rights and personal integrity as a *kurios* have been infringed by violent acts against a woman under his guardianship. A second strand in my story of silence is represented in Lysias 3, a defense speech against a prosecution for wounding with intent to kill.

The dispute has started because the plaintiff and defendant have been rivals for the love of a Plataean boy. The plaintiff started the violence (our speaker alleges), both at the beginning of the dispute and in the incident in question. Thus, this speech is quite clearly about violence between two men, and its mention of any physical aggression toward women is explicitly incidental. But is there even any violence toward women in this speech?

Here is the relevant section:

> πυθόμενος γὰρ ὅτι τὸ μειράκιον ἦν παρ' ἐμοί, ἐλθὼν ἐπὶ τὴν οἰκίαν τὴν ἐμὴν νύκτωρ μεθύων, ἐκκόψας τὰς θύρας εἰσῆλθεν εἰς τὴν γυναικωνῖτιν, ἔνδον οὐσῶν τῆς τε ἀδελφῆς τῆς ἐμῆς καὶ τῶν ἀδελφιδῶν, αἳ οὕτω κοσμίως βεβιώκασιν ὥστε καὶ ὑπὸ τῶν οἰκείων ὁρώμεναι αἰσχύνεσθαι. οὗτος τοίνυν εἰς τοῦτο ἦλθεν ὕβρεως ὥστ' οὐ πρότερον ἠθέλησεν ἀπελθεῖν, πρὶν αὐτὸν ἡγούμενοι δεινὰ ποιεῖν οἱ παραγενόμενοι καὶ οἱ μετ' αὐτοῦ ἐλθόντες, ἐπὶ παῖδας κόρας καὶ ὀρφανὰς εἰσιόντα, ἐξήλασαν βίᾳ.[28]
>
> [Thinking that the boy was with me, he came to my house, at night and already drunk, and after breaking down the doors, he entered the women's quarters, although my sister and nieces were in there, females who lived so modestly that they felt shame even to be seen by their male family members. But this man came to such a point of hubris that he refused to leave until the people who happened to be there and those who had come with him, thinking that he was acting outrageously by bursting in upon orphaned young girls, dragged him off by force.]

28. Lys. 3.6–7.

Is this passage describing violence? Old-fashioned books often cite it in lists of (sexualized) assaults on women, because of the reference to hubris. Some modern treatments are more cautious, perhaps seeing a paternalistic and sexist reflex in the assumption that any unlawful access to women—who should, of course, be secluded—is tantamount to sexual assault. But have those old-fashioned accounts somehow got nearer the mark?

It is perfectly possible that this episode might have included no actual personal or sexual violence directed at these women, but what if we are supposed to infer it (as those older accounts seem to do), because it is just not possible to describe it explicitly in such a context? Is talking about the physical actuality of assault on women's bodies so taboo—almost as if they have no bodies or as if there is no language for their parts—that only symbolic violence can be discussed? Violence against one aspect of a man's property, his house, may be a more possible subject than violence against his animate property, in the shape of the women of his household. The speaker describes the wounds he himself receives in great detail. There is even a significant amount about the wounds his opponent's crony has received (8–9), not to mention a multiplicity of actual physical trauma suffered by a cast of incidental male characters (14, 16, 18). But when it comes to the speaker's nearest and dearest, the doors of the women's quarters are as close as it can come—either in actuality, which is shocking enough for a society that regarded preservation of female seclusion as one of its chief concerns, or because talk of women's bodies is as taboo as mentioning their names.

Disappearing Acts I

There is one woman who does get talked about in our sources, Neaira in Apollodoros' prosecution speech. The speech is introduced as a prosecution of Neaira herself, and although Neaira is a vitally important player, it is obvious, even by the second sentence, that the source of the enmity and the real target of the prosecution (and, in addition, the person to whom all the summonses are delivered)[29] is Stephanos, the man with whom Neaira allegedly has been living as wife. The central crux of the allegation is that Neaira is a foreigner (*xene*) but has been living with Stephanos in marriage; both her foreign status and the nature of the relationship of cohabitation are key. The story starts with Neaira's origins as a child prostitute, slave to a madam in a Corinthian brothel (18–23). Her meteoric career from that

29. See Carey 1992: 23 n. 18.

point—out of the brothel, off the streets, into a stable relationship as a *pallake* and then freedom as a *hetaira*, and, finally, into the sort of relationship that could masquerade as marriage—is an absolutely fascinating document of social history about women's lives. Contrary to what we have found for all the Athenian women we have so far encountered, including citizens' wives or female relatives, Neaira is a woman who is named and visible, whose self and body are available for comment. Indeed, this is the point: the very fact that she is (repeatedly) named and viewed with such clarity is itself a subtle but intrinsic part of the argument that she cannot possibly be a legitimate citizen wife.

Is this, then, a speech in which violence toward women is narrated? There certainly are moments when we approach closer to that than in any other speech, once in relation to an unknown woman, which I will come back to, but also quite extensively in relation to the eponymous heroine (or villain) herself. All these moments center on a particular and particularly important relationship between Neaira and a man called Phrynion and culminate in a triangular episode that involves Stephanos as well. There is a wealth of interesting material for us here, and in many ways, the final episode is encapsulates the hub of the prosecution's case. But, as I shall show, despite all the talk that takes place about the violence carried out by Phrynion on Neaira, there is a certain quite extreme form of silence too. The violence in this speech constantly comes on stage only to perform its own disappearing act.

Phrynion arrives on the scene at a key point in Neaira's career. She has already managed to get herself out of the brothel run by Nikarete, as a result of being bought by two men and kept (in her own household) as a slave and *hetaira* of them both (29). But "when they planned to marry, they announced to her that they did not want to see her, who had been their *hetaira*, in Corinth working as a prostitute or under the control of a pimp, but they would be perfectly happy to get less money for her than they had paid out and to see her getting a lucky break for herself" (30). This is the moment when Phrynion is brought to our attention, because he is one of the former lovers to whom Neaira appeals. She has already collected funds from several of the others and has, in addition, her own savings, but she throws herself on Phrynion's mercy, asking him to take what she already has and make up the difference to the amount that she needs, which is twenty minas. He agrees and pays the money, and she is freed.

Phrynion takes Neaira with him to Athens, but all there does not go as she has planned.

> Ἀφικόμενος τοίνυν δεῦρο ἔχων αὐτὴν ἀσελγῶς καὶ προπετῶς ἐχρῆτο αὐτῇ, καὶ ἐπὶ τὰ δεῖπνα ἔχων αὐτὴν πανταχοῖ πορεύετο ὅπου πίνοι, ἐκώμαζέ τ' ἀεὶ μετ' αὐτοῦ, συνῆν τ' ἐμφανῶς ὁπότε βουληθείη πανταχοῦ, φιλοτιμίαν τὴν ἐξουσίαν πρὸς τοὺς ὁρῶντας ποιούμενος.[30]
>
> [After his arrival here with her, he treated her brutally and violently[31] and took her everywhere with him to dinner, wherever he was drinking, and he always partied with her and had sex/intercourse with[32] her openly in public whenever he wanted, showing off his power to do so to those who were watching.]

Does this passage describe a violent act? Phrynion's behavior certainly seems to be something Neaira dislikes and resents, so it can hardly be consensual, although we should note that the adverbs *aselgos* and *propetos*, which I have provocatively translated as "brutally" and "violently," cover the whole range of this episode—the going to dinners and partying as well as the inappropriately public sex. It is not impossible to imagine all of these actions going on accompanied by some sort of physical violence, but I think it is probably more realistic to think of such actions as the result of a level of constraint that is not necessarily physically violent.[33] In other words, due to a variety of pressures—emotional, social, moral, and perhaps sometimes physical—Neaira feels forced to go along with behavior she resents and dislikes. That there is something undoubtedly unpleasant—abusive—in this behavior is even validated by the speaker himself. In a striking summary of the situation, the speaker says that Neaira was abused (*proupelakizeto* at 35 literally means splattered with mud, and again here we have the adverb *aselgos*), though by adding that she was not loved as she expected (*hos oieto*) and that Phrynion did not provide her with everything she wanted, the

---

30. [D.] 59.33.

31. *Aselgos* can mean "licentiously," "wantonly," or "brutally (LSJ); *propetos*, "precipitately," "recklessly," or "violently" (LSJ). Both adverbs can connote violence or not.

32. *Suneimi*, literally "be with," is a curiously proper word for this context: it can mean "live with" or "be married to" but also "to have (sexual) relations with."

33. Of course, for us, consent must be unforced for it to have true legal status, and consent that is obtained under duress does not count as consent. Actions do not have to be physically violent to be abusive (e.g., rape), but this essay is about violence, so I am trying to think about the presence and especially the narration of explicit violence as a specific subset of abusive behavior.

speaker at least implies that this assessment is both from her perspective and part of a whole range of treatment that she takes exception to, rather than a description of a particular (violent?) act. In the extract above, as I said, I have provocatively translated the two adverbs that describe his treatment of her as meaning "brutally" and "violently," but the range that those adverbs can cover stretches as far as meaning "licentiously" and "recklessly," definitions that give us a far less clear picture of anything we could designate as physically violent, though, especially since we have an account of Neaira's response, it would not change its consensual status.

Thus, even for the visible Neaira, whose body, person, and experiences can be commented on, any explicit reference to physical violence keeps disappearing. Clearly something not nice[34] has gone on here, but the words themselves, available for translation as adverbs of violence, keep suggesting other, less overtly brutal translations for themselves. There may be a perpetrator here, but there is no clear victim of violence with whom we can legitimately sympathize or on whose behalf we are supposed to feel a sense of outrage. In fact, if anything—and explicitly, since this is a prosecution speech against Neaira—her vulnerability to the possibly violent, possibly "merely" inappropriate and degrading treatment that Phrynion has meted out becomes a way of commenting negatively on Neaira, that is, negatively on her chance of having or maintaining the status of a legitimate citizen(ness) and/or legitimate wife. For Neaira in this speech, there is no "being a victim of violence," if being such a victim means being the object of sympathy or sympathetic outrage; for her, merely the possibility of "being a victim" of violence equates to "being of nonrespectable status" and, consequently, "being guilty as charged."

This is a good example of my argument in this essay that violence against women is hidden and unseen as far as the formal record of legal speeches is concerned. If we continue a little further with Neaira's story, we can see another, complementary formulation of this disappearing act. Something unpleasant, abusive, possibly violent has occurred to Neaira, and even her opponent here acknowledges that, though arguably for his own ends. So how does she react? She does not respond with a legal proceeding—how could she?—but instead runs off and, like injured, legally disenfranchised (and practical) women the world over, takes with her what she can ("packing up things from the house and whatever clothes and gold she had had from

34. I have deliberately used this exceptionally weak and neutral adjective in an attempt not to insert my own interpretation of what Neaira has experienced.

him for her personal adornment and two slave girls, Thratta and Kokkaline," 59.36). She goes to Megara, but since economic and social conditions there are difficult, she does not manage to make enough money from prostitution there to meet the expenses of her household.[35] After three years of this struggle,[36] she meets Stephanos, an Athenian temporarily visiting Megara. They take up together, and Neaira tells him of Phrynion's treatment of her, using (in Apollodoros' account) the emotive term *hubris*. She also gives him all the material goods she has brought from Phrynion's house, asks to be taken to Athens with Stephanos, and makes him her *prostates*,[37]

> φοβουμένη δὲ τὸν Φρυνίωνα διὰ τὸ ἠδικηκέναι μὲν αὐτή, ἐκεῖνον δὲ ὀργίλως ἔχειν αὐτῇ, σοβαρὸν δὲ καὶ ὀλίγωρον εἰδυῖα αὐτοῦ τὸν τρόπον ὄντα.[38]

> [because she was afraid of Phrynion, since she had done him wrong and he was angry with her and she knew his arrogant and scornful manner.]

That Stephanos understands this as protecting her from any violence on Phrynion's part is immediate (in Apollodoros' narration).

> ἐπάρας δὲ αὐτὴν οὗτος ἐν τοῖς Μεγάροις τῷ λόγῳ καὶ φυσήσας, ὡς κλαύσοιτο ὁ Φρυνίων εἰ ἅψοιτο αὐτῆς, αὐτὸς δὲ γυναῖκα αὐτὴν ἕξων, τούς τε παῖδας τοὺς ὄντας αὐτῇ τότε εἰσάξων εἰς τοὺς φράτερας ὡς αὑτοῦ ὄντας καὶ πολίτας ποιήσων, ἀδικήσει δὲ οὐδεὶς ἀνθρώπων.[39]

> [He [Stephanos] built up her confidence in Megara and boasted that Phrynion would regret it if he laid hands on her and that he himself would take her as his wife and introduce her current children to the *phratry* as if they were his own and get citizenship for them. No one would wrong her.]

---

35. Again, this nod in the direction of Neaira's autonomy is a point about her lack of respectable status: no respectable woman runs a household without a *kurios*, and Neaira herself is eager enough to find a protective male.

36. For the timeline on this, see Carey 1992.

37. For the role of the *prostates*, see Todd 1993: 197–99.

38. [D.] 59.37.

39. [D.] 59.38.

When Phrynion realizes that Neaira is living with Stephanos in Athens, Stephanos has to put his promises into action. Phrynion takes a group of young men with him to Stephanos' house and tries to take Neaira. The verb here is the rather neutral *ago*, "lead," but the accompaniment of the young men—especially with their youth stressed—suggests at least the potential of violence.[40] There may be no actual violence here, but there is an underlying aggression and, at the very least, a perceived threat of force, perhaps mostly acutely in Stephanos' words to Neaira: *haptomai* means "touch" or "lay hands on" and can certainly mean violence. The verb I have translated as "regret" actually means "would weep / cry out in pain." It can be used symbolically, but even its symbolism is redolent of the bodily hurt and humiliation experienced by the loser in a physical set-to. However, we might expect the idea of violence to be most sharply figured in the words (allegedly, of course) of a man who is offering protection and showing off to a woman to whom he is sexually attracted.

Why do I think this scene is important? Again, leaving aside the fascination of a document that gives us (however doctored) such a window into the "real"[41] world of classical Athens, there lies here some of the heart of the argument I am making. To begin with, even visible—culpably visible—Neaira can still not really be seen as a victim of violence. What violence there is slips away constantly in front of our eyes, the words that might show it to us either never being quite unequivocal enough or being subtly but surely marked as Neaira's own or Stephanos' opinion or point of view as she tries to persuade him to take her under his wing. Secondly, what violence the speech's audience can infer works negatively for Neaira's case here and carries no suggestion on anyone's part (including, allegedly, on the part of Neaira herself) that it could or should ever form the basis of a legal prosecution. Instead, Neaira can only "sort it herself," in the time-honored tradition of running away, with the parting shot of stealing as much of Phrynion's property as she (and presumably the maidservants) can carry. For Neaira at least, being the victim of nonconsensual action does not and could not mean becoming the plaintiff in a suit about violence or having one brought on her behalf.

40. See Carey 1992: 107.

41. As I discussed briefly in my introduction, what I mean by "real" here is that the world created in the Attic orators is not self-consciously fictional. Although carefully constructed and bearing no provable relationship to actuality, events and characters in court speech need to persuade by their credibility as real occurrences and individuals.

The only other action we are shown Neaira taking in response to her unwanted and unwelcome treatment at Phrynion's hand is to swap his protection for the protection of another man, Stephanos. Although three years have elapsed since the harsh treatment and her flight from Phrynion, the speaker represents them as directly related. Stephanos' response (or alleged response) links them too and is also incredibly revealing and useful for us: his offer of (quasi) marriage is synonymous with the offer of protection in general and from Phrynion's violence in particular: Phrynion will not be able to lay hands on her, and no one will wrong her. As we might expect, perhaps, in a radically sex-segregated society in which women are perpetual legal minors and in which the bodies and persons of at least respectable women are ideally invisible from public sight, the offer of marriage—even when reprehensively or illegally made—is simultaneously an offer to interpose the male's body between a woman and any violent action. What I mean here, is that violence against a woman is again disappearing before our eyes in this example, because involvement in violence, either as a perpetrator but also as a victim or potential victim, is only visible or legally viable as a male role.

Stephanos' response to Phrynion's attempt to remove Neaira from Stephanos' house is to "assert her freedom according to the law,"[42] a move that Phrynion counters by forcing Stephanos to post bail (*katenguesen*, 40) for her before the polemarch.[43] He does bail her out, and they continue to live as before: Stephanos, Neaira, and the children of the household are supported on her earnings from prostitution, with the (alleged) addition of related scams.[44] Phrynion then brings a case against Stephanos, because Stephanos "had asserted her freedom and had received the things she had brought with her" from Phrynion. However, their case does not go to court, because their friends persuade them to go to arbitration.

The denouement of the Phrynion episode comes, interestingly, in a moment of arbitration that slips and slides between validation and invalidation of Neaira's position, but there is no reference, either in the speaker's preamble[45] or in the quoted terms of the arbitration, to the treatment Neaira had received at Phrynion's hands. The terms validate her freedom

42. The Greek is *aphairomenou*. Cf. Carey 1992: 45, for a quite technical legal translation.

43. On the polemarch, slaves, *aphaeresis*, etc., see Todd 1993, s.vv.

44. See, e.g., the Epainetos episode at [D.] 59.41–44.

45. The preamble actually contains a lot of information not contained/evidenced in the terms as they are subsequently quoted.

("that she is to be a free woman and *kuria* of herself"[46]) but invalidate her removal of Phrynion's property ("she should give back all the things she took from Phrynion when she left," 46), while validating her right to some personal property resulting from her relationship with Phrynion (she must give everything back "except the clothes, gold/jewelry and maidservants that had been bought for the woman herself," 46). Perhaps, for us, the most interesting clause comes at the end of the speakers' review—and it is the only one actually validated by the quoted terms for the settlement, for what that is worth: Neaira was to "live with"[47] each of them, both Stephanos and Phrynion, day for day (or for the same number of days in every month), unless they reach some other agreement.[48] In a way, it is hard to say what this stipulation validates or invalidates. But it certainly does not validate Neaira's right to consort with or even have sex with the man or men of her choice. It does not validate her right to refuse to have anything to do with a man who has abused her, possibly violently, and from whom she has already run away once.

Disappearing Acts II

In the previous section, I argued that any explicitly marked out physical violence with Neaira as its victim becomes invisible and keeps slipping away as an interesting, possible or legally viable subject for discussion. I argued that this happens for the following reasons: because the vocabulary used does not reference physical violence clearly enough; because Neaira as a victim is not an interesting or possible subject (in a speech that is a prosecution of her anyway); because the extent to which the speaker acknowledges her vulnerability to being such a victim is used to mark her status and character negatively, not as a victim who requires our sympathy; and because there was no suggestion that the abuse perpetrated against her could or should ever form the basis of a legal case. In this section, I want to look at quite a different way in which violence against women disappears. There are several moments in our speeches where such violence is referred to, even quite clearly. In some

46. Elsewhere, however, the assumption, at least implicitly, is that Stephanos is her *kurios*.

47. The verb is again *suneimi*, which was used for sexual relations when describing Phrynion's behavior.

48. This detail appears first in the speaker's version and then in the quotation of terms: it is one of the comparatively few details that does appear in both.

cases, it even appears to have led to legal action. However, as I shall go on to demonstrate, these moments no more make the subject clearly discussable than do any other of the examples I have foregrounded.

One important factor in this demonstration is the fact that the examples I am looking at in this section are in a very different position in their respective speeches. In the Neaira prosecution, the woman in question was the explicit plaintiff and, at the very least, an important central character in the narrative of the case, even if her partner, Stephanos, was the speaker's real enemy. The incidents I am about to discuss are all episodes related in passing. Indeed, that is my point: violence against women simply does not appear as the central issue of a case, and where it does appear, it is explicitly—and also implicitly—relegated to the margins. Again, it disappears.

The cases of Themistos and Euthymachus offer two examples.

> Θεμίστιον δὲ τὸν Ἀφιδναῖον, διότι τὴν Ῥοδίαν κιθαρίστριαν ὕβρισεν Ἐλευσινίοις, θανάτῳ ἐζημιώσατε, Εὐθύμαχον δέ, διότι τὴν Ὀλυνθίαν παιδίσκην ἔστησεν ἐπ' οἰκήματος.
>
> [You punished Themistos from Aphidna with death because he committed hubris against the Rhodian lyre player at the Eleusinia, and Euthymachus because he put the Olynthian girl in an *oikema*.[49]]

Both girls in these cases are unnamed, and both are foreigners. Both incidents are referred to in passing and with no more than a single clause in the Greek: neither the events nor the prosecutions or punishments—nor their connection—are attested by witness or any other testimony (cf. the witnesses brought to certain events and to the terms of arbitration in the Neaira story). In the case of the lyre player, the offense is most likely based on the blasphemy of the event occurring at a festival (cf. D. 21). The second example is perhaps even clearer. The speaker claims that Meidias has been collecting instances of people who have been assaulted, to try and lessen the sense of the seriousness of the attack he has perpetrated. In his account of this list, the speaker mentions

> καὶ τὸν θεσμοθέτην ὃς ἔναγχος ἐπλήγη τὴν αὐλητρίδ' ἀφαιρούμενος, καὶ τοιούτους τινάς.[50]

49. *Oikema* can mean "house," "storeroom," "prison," or "brothel": it is usually translated as "brothel" (see, e.g., Worthington 1999: 53, on Din. 1.23).

50. D. 21.36.

> [the thesmothete who just recently was struck as he removed/rescued the flute girl and several similar situations.]

A whole array of recognizable elements feature here: a brief clause, no name, no explicit reference to violence against the body of a woman (instead, we have to infer it), and an incident used not to draw attention to a female victim but to make a point about a male who is quite unrelated to the incident.

The prosecution of Neaira contains a similar reference. In Theomnestos' opening preamble, he describes how one of the episodes that developed the enmity between Apollodoros and Stephanos was Stephanos' false accusation that Apollodoros had struck and killed a woman while pursuing a runaway slave in Aphidna. All the same factors are present: the en passant comment, lack of names, occurrence overseas, and foreigner as victim. However, another act of disappearance is at play here.

> ἐξελεγχθεὶς δ' ἐπιορκῶν καὶ ψευδῆ αἰτίαν ἐπιφέρων, καὶ καταφανὴς γενόμενος μεμισθωμένος ὑπὸ Κηφισοφῶντος καὶ Ἀπολλοφάνους ὥστ' ἐξελάσαι Ἀπολλόδωρον ἢ ἀτιμῶσαι ἀργύριον εἰληφώς, ὀλίγας ψήφους μεταλαβὼν ἐκ πεντακοσίων ἀπῆλθεν ἐπιωρκηκὼς καὶ δόξας πονηρὸς εἶναι.[51]

> [He was proved to have been lying on oath and bringing a false charge and was openly revealed to have been in the pay of Cephisophon and Apollophanes in order to get Apollodoros exiled or disenfranchised for money: he got few votes for his five hundred drachmas and left the court a perjurer seen to be base.]

That we have, of course, no proof other than Theomnestos' assertion for this really does not matter for my argument, which is, after all, not about a "real reality"—what actually happened—but about how it enters our record. Here, arguments between men always supersede actions toward a woman, and the whole point of the inclusion of the episode is to pass comment on Stephanos' probity.[52] Violence against a woman appears briefly here only to disappear almost immediately in a puff of smoke.

---

51. D. 59.10.

52. See also the allegations at D. 19.196–98 that Aischines violently mistreated an Olynthian woman, as well as the refutation at Aischines 2.154–55, including the counteraccusation that it was a false charge brought for pay.

It's All Ancient History Anyway

My narrow concern in this essay has been to discuss how the topic of violence against women enters the specific rhetorical space of Athenian oratory. Quite often, however, I have used the language of drama to highlight what I want to say, often to illustrate my sense of the way in which characters here, although necessarily and crucially realistic, are playing roles that the logographer has written for them. Since my focus has been on oratory, I have not addressed the issue of violence against women in drama (despite my use of dramatic metaphors), partly due to lack of space, but also because characters in drama offer us a very different window onto the streets and *oikoi* of classical Athens, a view peopled by figures who are not real, "real," or, in certain senses, realistic. For the end of the classical period, Menander might offer us something that approaches the realistic,[53] though the picture there is interestingly consonant with the picture from oratory. Tragedy might be thought to offer us a different perspective, in that violence, including that against women, and the dramatic crises that violence engenders are staples of tragic plots. However, the scenarios we find there are marked as noncontemporary by their location within mythic stories and are highly stylized. It is true that they give us a world in which there is some discussion of violence against women—though it is worth noting that it is usually confined to female suicide, ritual sacrifice of virgins, or, in the case of Clytemnestra, intrafamilial revenge killing—but my view is that tragedy no more raises the possibility of a realistic account of violence against realistic women than does oratory.

Where does this leave us? I have made the claim before that if we want to look for accounts of violence against women where women are accepted as victims, where what they have suffered is described and both writer and audience are expected to feel sympathy and outrage, we have to go to a different genre. I made the claim before for rape,[54] but I stick by it here for violence of a more general nature against women. Where we do get this sort of story—though there are still caveats, which I shall come to—is in historical narratives that detail wars and the sacking of cities in particular[55] and in histories and treatises dealing with issues connected to tyranny.[56] In

53. For an account of the treatment of rape in Menander, see Omitowoju 2002: 137–229.

54. Omitowoju 2002: 33–34.

55. See, e.g., D. 23.56, 141; Isoc. 9.10; Hyp. 6.20, 36; Th. 8.86.3; Din. 1.19.6; Arist. *EN* 1115a23.

56. See, e.g., D. 17.3; Lys. 12.98; Isoc. 3.36, 4.114; Th. 9.74.3; Arist. *Ath.* 1314b24, 1315a15–28.

both of these situations, the abuse of women—violent or otherwise—does not function as an intrapolis comment about them, their status, or the status of the men to whom they are connected. Unlike the courts, where "real" people pass comments on other's rights to certain privileges and reputations, narratives of war and tyranny show entire groups of citizens at the mercy of hostile groups or powerful individuals. The comments that such actions and narratives contain are no longer political in the narrow sense: nobody's status in the internal game of citizenship is affected more than anyone else's by the behavior of tyrants or one's opponents in a war.

It is still true that these stories of war and tyranny are stories about men—their actions, shortcomings, views, and experiences. Here again, women only enter these narratives as en passant exempla of what men suffer. There is a crucial difference, however: in these stories, women and men share in the suffering of man's inhumanity to man, and women are not somehow tainted and penned by their femininity into marginalized positions that are impossible to mention or with which it is impossible to sympathize. Clearly, the law courts and legal cases—or, more important, the record of them that has survived for us via the extant Attic orators—is not the place to showcase women in any real way. The court cases that we have are like scenes from plays or from stories, where "real" people act out roles that require their audiences (the audience of jurors in the actual case, the reading audience of the edited pieces of rhetoric, even their later audiences who come to them as students of ancient history) to believe in them as if they are real. From this play of political posturing, women are largely excluded: men shield them, bar them, or occasionally display them (under duress or as an act of hostility) as is necessary to allow the men to play the best and most convincing roles as civic-minded figures worthy of respect, belief, and power in the democratic city. Besides this, the story of violence against women never really gets a space on the stage.

Works Cited

Carey, C. 1992. *Apollodoros, "Against Neaira": [Demosthenes] 59*. Warminster.

Cohen, D. 1995. *Law, Violence, and Community in Classical Athens*. Cambridge.

Fisher N. 1992. Hybris*: A Study in the Values of Honour and Shame in Ancient Greece*. Warminster.

Fisher, N. 1998 "Violence, Masculinity, and the Law in Classical Athens." In L. Foxhall and J. Salmon, eds., *When Men Were Men: Masculinity, Power, and Identity in Classical Antiquity*, 68–97. London.

Herman G. 2006. *Morality and Behaviour in Democratic Athens*. Cambridge.

Hunter, V. 1994. *Policing Athens: Social Control in the Attic Lawsuits, 420–320 B.C.* Princeton.

Isager, S., and Hansen, M. 1975. *Aspects of Athenian Society in the Fourth Century BC: A Historical Introduction to and Commentary on the* Paragraphe *Speeches and the Speech "Against Dionysiodoros" in the "Corpus Demosthenicum."* Odense.

Lanni, A. 2004. "Arguing from 'Precedent': Modern Perspectives on Athenian Practice." In E. Harris and L. Rubenstein, eds., *The Law and the Courts in Ancient Greece*, 159–71. London.

Llewellyn-Jones, L. 2011 "Domestic Abuse and Violence against Women in Ancient Greece." In S. Lambert, ed., *Sociable Man: Essays on Ancient Greek Social Behaviour, in Honour of Nick Fisher*, 231–66. Swansea.

MacDowell, D. 1978. *The Law in Classical Athens*. London.

Omitowoju, R. 2002. *Rape and the Politics of Consent in Classical Athens*. Cambridge.

Rhodes, P. 1998. "Enmity in Fourth Century Athens." In P. Cartledge, P. Millett, and S. von Reden, eds., *Kosmos: Essays in Order, Conflict, and Community in Classical Athens*, 144–61. Cambridge.

Schaps, D. 1977. "The Woman Least Mentioned: Etiquette and Women's Names." *CQ* 27: 323–30.

Todd, S. 1993. *The Shape of Athenian Law*. Oxford.

Worthington, I. 1994. "The Canon of the Ten Attic Orators." In I. Worthington, ed., *Persuasion: Greek Rhetoric in Action*, 244–63. London.

Worthington, I. 1999. *Greek Orators*. Vol. 2, *Dinarchus and Hyperides*. Warminster.

FIVE

Violence against Slaves in Classical Greece

Peter Hunt

Violence against slaves was ubiquitous in and crucial to the institution of slavery in ancient Greece. Force was often used to compel the obedience of individual slaves, but the most effective violence was public and spectacular, designed to frighten many slaves rather than simply to punish a few. Violence against slaves also served to define the roles of slaves, citizens, and masters within typical Greek worldviews. Nevertheless, its use was not uncontested but, rather, ran contrary to some ideals of natural rule and individual self-control. Unfortunately, these contradictions and complications probably did not have a great effect on the actual treatment of slaves.

Thus, violence against slaves needs to be understood in three types of contexts, within three topographies: first, within a system of social control of slaves—not always successful—the many tools of which included actual violence and the threat of violence;[1] second, within a wider system of Greek thinking and values; and, third, within the physical topography of Greek houses, farms, and cities, which affected who witnessed violence and how they reacted. This chapter will first consider violence against slaves as a method of social control and will then examine its place within wider Greek systems of thinking and values, but the two contexts were frequently and deeply intertwined in practice and cannot be rigidly separated or analyzed in isolation. The physical topography of violence against slaves will play a role in both of these explorations.

1. Cf. Bradley 1987, on the social control of Roman slaves.

Methodological issues will complicate this inquiry. First and most obvious, although all slaves were theoretically subject to harsh violence at their master's discretion, we cannot expect that all types of slaves suffered to the same extent: mine and mill slaves probably experienced violence in more harsh and frequent forms than did slave bankers or estate managers.[2] The personalities of the individual master and slave also played an independent and important role. Another issue is that the vast majority of our evidence comes from Athens. We may complain about how little evidence we have for Athenian slavery—and, of course, evidence from the slave's perspective is miniscule—but that small amount is greater by a couple of orders of magnitude than what we know about slavery in Corinth, for example. Chattel slavery was probably roughly similar in different Greek cities.[3] We do not have the evidence to assert this with much certainty, and aspects of the ideology of slavery—for example, the theoretical dichotomy between the bodily vulnerability of the slaves and the inviolability of the citizen—may have been different in an oligarchy in which not all free natives were full citizens. The possibility of change over time is also hard to judge. Some aspects of slavery are likely to have varied little over the centuries: a mill was still a mill, and the tasks and treatment of a house slave may not have changed much. But, for example, the ratio of slave to free went up and down over time as did the proportion of first-generation slaves; one imagines that these variations influenced masters' use of violence. In this chapter, I will continue to refer to "Greek slavery," but the reader should realize that this usually means classical Athenian slavery and (probably, more or less, I hope) slavery in other Greek cities and times.

Even more troublesome and resistant to easy solution is the issue of distinguishing literary, comic, or otherwise unrealistic stories from everyday practices. Does the prevalence of beating or threats of beating in comedy merely take advantage of the comic potential of an everyday occurrence? Or was it amusing to have a rare and serious occurrence, the beating of an intimate house slave, treated lightly? Or did the display of anger against slaves serve as a sign of full manhood?[4] The complications are not only literary. Some slaveholders may have tried to play down their own use of violence,

---

2. Cf. Fenoaltea 1984, on supervision, "pain incentives," and rewards of different types of slave workers.

3. States with a serf-like underclass, such as Sparta or Thessaly, are in a different category. On the helots, see Trundle's contribution to this volume.

4. Konstan 2013: 150. For the methodology of understanding Greek comic slaves, see Tordoff 2013.

out of embarrassment at their lack of self-control or their inability to manage their slaves. Others may have exaggerated and publicized their violence, to intimidate their slaves or to impress peers with their severity. These methodological issues are crucial, since one of the most important questions we would like to answer is whether masters managed to leverage a few dramatic displays of violence or whether the exploitation of slaves required constant violence. Notwithstanding these difficulties and complications, let us march bravely on in hopes that we will find clarity, rather than the devil, in the details.

Violence as Social Control

Fortunately for the historian, evidence of violence against slaves in Greece is hard to miss. Virtually every genre of ancient literature—and even epigraphy—attests to such violence.[5] For example, in the comedies of both Aristophanes and Menander, slaves are often threatened with or actually receive beatings at the hands of their masters for a variety of offenses—that is, offenses in the master's eyes, of course.[6] The frequency of whipping is implied in the use of the expression *mastigias*, "whipping boy," for a bad slave.[7] An apparent exception proves the rule: at the beginning of Aristophanes' *Clouds*, Strepsiades complains that, on account of the war—which made running away easier[8]—he cannot even beat his slaves.[9] The implication is that he normally could beat his slaves and that such punishment would be his first course of action if he found them oversleeping—as they are when the play begins.

A passage from Xenophon's *Memorabilia* sums up some of a master's options in dealing with recalcitrant slaves.

> But now let us see how masters treat such slaves. Don't they discipline their lust by starving them? stop their stealing by locking up what-

5. For a detailed treatment, see Klees 1998: 176–217.

6. The references collected in Hunter 1992: 284–85 include the following: Ar. *Av.* 1325–36; *Nu.* 56–59; *Lys.* 1215–23; *V.* 1292–1307; Men. *Sam.* 307, 322–25, 679; *Epit.* 564–66; *Pk.* 268–78; *Her.* 1–10. Cf. Dover 1993: 50; Riess 2012: 268–69.

7. Hunter 1992: 280 cites Aristophanes (*Eq.* 1228; *Ra.* 501) and Menander (*Epit.* 1113; *Sam.* 324; *Kol.* 125). For all genres, see Kamen 2010: 96 n. 8.

8. Hunt 1998: 106–14.

9. Ar. *Nu.* 6–7.

> ever they might get their hands on? prevent their escape by chaining them? and beat the laziness out of them with whips? What do *you* do when you discover a servant like that in your own house?
>
> I use every kind of punishment until I force them to slave.[10]

Xenophon anticipates no objections to the use of violence against slaves, seemingly a normal and accepted practice. But how frequent was it? Debates about the frequency of whipping in the antebellum American South, a vastly better-documented period, show how hard it is to come by even basic statistics—not to mention differences between individual masters.[11] We will never be able to show that one particular type of Greek slave suffered violence on average once every week or once every month. Indeed, I know no sure way of ruling out more extreme possibilities, ranging from once a day to once a year. In addition, although we can be sure that slaves witnessed violence as well as suffered it, we are on no firmer ground when it comes to quantifying the role of violence as a spectacle of the master's power. We can say that violence played a role in all depictions of slave life and, no doubt, in the lived reality itself, but it would be sour grapes to deny that we would understand ancient slavery better if we could gauge the frequency of violence more precisely.

The preceding passage from the *Memorabilia* also reminds us that blows constitute just one type of coercion that masters exercised over their slaves' bodies. Hunger, too, was considered one of a master's weapons—even if the connection between hunger and "lust" is not obvious to us.[12] Chaining slaves was a punishment as well as a way to prevent slaves from running away or fighting back.[13] Slaves were probably locked up in stone towers during the night in many rural areas.[14] Sale to a mill was an extreme threat that could be used to break a slave's will to resist, since the treatment of mill slaves was

10. X. *Mem.* 2.1.16–17, trans. Marchant 2013, modified. See also [And.] 4.17; Arist. *Rh.* 1380a16–19; D. 18.129; [D.] 53.8; Lys. 1.18; X. *Oec.* 3.4.

11. See Sutch 1975: 339–44, against Fogel and Engerman 1974, on whipping in the American South. Cf. Dew 1994: 108: "Not surprisingly, there is no indication that Weaver ever whipped one of his slave forge workers at any time during his forty years in the Valley."

12. "Lust" is a translation of the Greek *lagneia.* Although one can imagine various ways in which this would be objectionable to a master (cf. X. *Oec.* 9.5), Xenophon gives no hint that allows us to be more specific. A slave in Menander expresses the converse: too much food could make a slave apt to fall in love (Men. *Her.* 16–17).

13. Klees 1998: 185–86.

14. Papadopoulous and Morris 2005.

harsh and their work hard.[15] For slaves who had established families, the threat of separating families by sale was terrifying. It seems even to have raised occasional moral objections, although our evidence admittedly consists of only one passage: a speaker in a legal case claims that even slave traders, a greedy and immoral lot, were nevertheless not so cruel as to separate slave families, specifically mothers and children.[16] The pseudo-Aristotelian *Oeconomica* evinces what is probably a more common and calculating view, when it advises allowing slaves to have children, who would be like hostages for their parents' good behavior.[17]

The context of the *Memorabilia* passage requires that Xenophon's Socrates focus on the negative reinforcements that masters use to get their slaves to do what they want. But preemptive measures such as not buying too many slaves from the same place—who could speak to each other in a language not understood by the master—also played a role in the control of slaves.[18] Positive incentives were important as well: for example, in the *Oeconomicus*, Xenophon discusses the management of slaves and stresses rewarding good slaves as much as punishing the bad.[19] The topography of controlling slaves encompassed more than violent acts.

Violence itself worked most directly on an individual level. After a slave had been beaten or deprived of food for an insubordinate remark, for pilfering, or for delaying before carrying out an order, he or she was less likely to repeat that offense.[20] Although this use of violence to control slaves is simple, direct, and obvious, that does not mean that it was not effective. Nor should we underestimate the consequences, both physical and psychological, that violence had on individual slaves. For example, an Athenian litigant could show the scars from the shackles he wore after he was enslaved in war years

15. Lys. 1.18; Men. *Her.* 3; cf. D. 45.33. For a vivid description from a later period, see Apul. *Met.* 9.11. Threatening to sell a slave to the mines ought to have been equally effective.

16. Hyp. *Against Timandros*, in Jones 2008; Jones notes that this concern for slave families, well attested in Roman sources, is only mentioned here in surviving Greek evidence.

17. [Arist.] *Oec.* 1344b17–18; cf. X. *Oec.* 9.5. Cf. also Scott 1990: 24: "A cruel paradox of slavery, for example, is that it is in the interest of slave mothers, whose overriding wish is to keep their children safe and by their side, to train them in the routines of conformity."

18. Pl. *Lg.* 6.777c–d; [Arist.] *Oec.* 1344b18–19.

19. E.g., X. *Oec.* 5.15–16, 12.6–7, 12.15, 13.6–12, 14.6–10, 21.10. See Hunt, forthcoming.

20. At least that was the goal, although some individuals may have become contrary and obstinate after punishment.

earlier.[21] In a world without antibiotics, some slaves probably died as the result of infection or other complications of harsh punishment.[22]

The psychological impact of violence was also profound. Theophrastus characterizes the "tactless man" in one vignette: "He stands watching while a slave is being whipped and announces that a slave of his own once hanged himself after such a beating."[23] Theophrastus' interest is tactlessness, but this story dramatizes the feeling of powerlessness and humiliation that must have accompanied the pain of corporal punishment. A passage from Plato confirms what we might have guessed from New World slave narratives: among the horrors of slavery, which can make it a worse fate than death, is that slaves cannot come to the defense of those for whom they care.[24] For slaves to watch a family member or even a friend being harshly whipped must have been a devastating experience.

Indeed, violence was more effective as a tool of social control if other slaves saw, heard, or learned about it. For example, in the antebellum American South, it is possible to quantify the number of whippings per slaves—though only for some plantations and during some periods. Richard Sutch estimates that at least sixty out of eighty-eight slaves on Barrow's plantation were whipped at least once over a two-year period; on average, each slave older than eleven was whipped once each year.[25] Nevertheless, he points out that the punitive system's success depended mainly on the fear of whipping, a fear exacerbated by the fact that whippings were publicly administered in the slave quarters.[26] We do not possess ancient parallels to the statistics for the Barrow plantation, but it is almost certain that other slaves within Greek households, generally smaller than Southern plantations, witnessed acts of violence. It also requires little imagination to picture slaves in a household talking to each other about who had suffered beatings—or worse—and why. There is no direct evidence of masters making the punishment of slaves within the house into a spectacle, but Ischomachus announces to his slaves that he follows the laws of Draco and Solon, which, he believes, require

21. [D.] 53.8.

22. Roman laws against killing slaves made exceptions for slaves who died inadvertently as the result of punishment (*Cod. Theod.* 9.12.1, in Wiedemann 1981: 174). Cf. Pl. *Euthyphr.* 4c–d.

23. Thphr. *Char.* 12.12–14, trans. Diggle 2004.

24. Pl. *Grg.* 483b.

25. Sutch 1975: 341–42.

26. Sutch 1975: 342.

the death penalty for theft.[27] This suggests the display of both violence—perhaps the execution of a slave guilty of no more than pilfering—and the threat of violence.

Knowledge of violence against slaves might spread beyond the individual household. Most obvious, if less spectacular, was the fact that slaves talked with each other and were, indeed, notorious as gossips.[28] If master A had tied up and brutally whipped Manes for drinking his wine, the deed might quickly be known among the slaves of masters B, C, and D, whose own practices vis-à-vis the larder and wine jars might well be influenced by the knowledge of what had happened to Manes down the street.

Violence could be public in a more direct sense also.[29] In comedy, masters beat slaves, and slaves expressed their fears of punishment in front of other slave characters as well as the audience, which, in some periods, included slaves.[30] Turning from dramatic to real and legal violence, slaves who committed crimes were often executed in brutal and public ways. Like traitors or those subject to summary justice, slaves suffered execution by *apotumpanismos*, in which a convict would be hung from a board by his or her hands, feet, and neck until he or she died.[31] Stephen Todd argues that *apotumpanismos* was "a theatrical performance, and in a specifically public theater."[32] This was certainly the case when a slave killed his or her master: an epitaph of such a slain master states of his killer, "My fellow citizens crucified him alive, prey to animals and birds."[33] This epitaph publicized the punishment, but the process itself was likely a public and lengthy one, as the slave expired over the course of several painful days, no doubt an object of morbid curiosity to the local townspeople and slaves.[34] A passage in Antiphon implies

27. X. *Oec.* 14.4–5 (cf. X. *Mem.* 1.2.62), with Pomeroy 1994: 320–21. In other respects, Ischomachus is portrayed as a master of unusual sympathy for his slaves (Pomeroy 1994: 65–67).

28. Ar. *Ra.* 750–53; Thphr. *Char.* 8.4; cf. Hdt. 2.113.3. See also Hunter 1994: 80–83 and Forsdyke 2012: 37–89 on slave knowledge and communication.

29. Although the beating of slaves in comedy was certainly public and although slaves could be in the audience, the main purpose of such beating was probably not the intimidation of slaves but, rather, the amusement of the citizen audience. On slaves in comedy, see Sommerstein 2009; Akrigg and Tordoff 2013. On violence in comedy, see Riess 2012: 235–378.

30. Tordoff 2013: 39–40.

31. Bonner and Smith 1930–38: 2.280.

32. Todd 2000: 48.

33. Andreau and Descat 2011: 141.

34. Cf. Pl. *R.* 4.439e–440a, with Adam 1902, ad loc., for historical and topographic information about the *barathron*, a pit into which condemned criminals were thrown as

that if a slave murdered his or her master, all the slaves in the household were liable to be killed if the perpetrator was not discovered.[35] This was not quite Rome's infamous *Senatus Consultum Silanianum*, but it tended in the same direction.[36] Punishment of slaves in such a case was collective and brutal; innocence counted for less than making a display of violent power. Finally, when slaves were tortured for legal evidence—a topic to which I will return—the procedure took place in a public place and attracted a crowd.[37] All of these practices meant that slaves were reminded of their vulnerability and of the power of their masters, which was backed by the state and its resources.

Violence as a Symbolic System

I turn now to the second topography of violence against slaves: the role that violence played within symbolic or ideological systems, rather than its function of intimidation and social control.[38] This involves a change in focus, from the topography of masters' attempts to control the behavior of their slaves—whether slaves complied with or resisted such control—to the place of violence within the discourse of masters. I will not be arguing that violence ever convinced slaves that they were like animals, unmanly, inferior, and intrinsically different from the free, a thesis almost certainly false and certainly unknowable.[39] Rather, the ways masters conceived of and deployed violence against slaves reinforced their own perceptions of slaves and their place in the world.

For example, the violent displays that I have already discussed not only

---

another means of execution. We only hear of free men suffering this fate, but our evidence is skimpy and inconclusive.

35. Antiph. 5.69; Gagarin (1997a: 209) is perplexed about the legal ground for such a mass execution. It is also not clear whether this passage implies revenge by the dead master's family or executions by the state.

36. See Lenski's contribution to this volume.

37. Hunter (1992: 283) cites [D.] 47.12 (the Heliaia) and Isoc. 17.15 (the temple of Hephaistos).

38. Scholars who adopt this methodology invoke various social and cultural theories, but Geertz (1973a, 1973b, 1973c) provides lucid and seminal statements of this basic approach.

39. See Scott 1985 and, especially, 1990, for a detailed and persuasive rebuttal of theories that emphasize ideology's ability to win over the oppressed; cf. Abercrombie, Hill, and Turner 1980; *pace* Cox 2002 on slaves subject to violence in Menander.

sowed fear but also reinforced negative stereotypes about slaves.[40] Though some slaves may have handled their suffering stoically, most must have screamed, cried, and begged for mercy—especially if the punishment was particularly intense. With compelling illogic, this behavior was taken to show that slaves were truly inferior and unmanly, since the master was doing the whipping without flinching. Xenophon provides an example of this attitude, when he claims that by attacking the enemy unexpectedly and with vigor, "you will see right soon that just like a lot of slaves caught in an attempt to run away, some of them will beg for mercy, others will try to escape, others will not even have the presence of mind to do either."[41] For Xenophon, slaves are at their most despicable when they are expecting to be punished for running away.

The precise application of violence also repays exploration. In comedy, masters sometimes tied up and whipped slaves or just hit them. They could also delegate the task of whipping to other slaves. The delegation of violence may have helped masters reconcile the ideal of self-control—to which I shall return—with the violence necessary to the system of slavery. The application of violence was even less personal when slaves broke the law and were punished by the "public whip," or *mastix demosios*.[42] Slaves could also be handed over to the Eleven in Athens, for execution on the master's initiative, a way that masters could distance themselves from lethal violence committed on their behalf.[43] We do not know whether Greek masters could, on their own initiative and for their own reasons, request to pay for the professional, public punishment of their slaves, as was the case in Roman Italy.[44]

The tools of violence were also significant. In comedy, slaves are beaten by leather straps, sticks, and other objects—not to mention being drowned in a lake, burned with a lamp, or simply hit.[45] The whip, or *mastix*, is most often mentioned, and a slave can be described contemptuously as a *mastigias*, a "whipping boy."[46] A famous story in Herodotus confirms that the

40. See Hunt 1998: 160–64, on the stereotype of slaves as cowardly.

41. X. *Cyr.* 4.2.21, trans. Miller 1987; see X. *Cyr.* 1.4.13, on the punishment of runaway slaves. Cf. Plu. *Alex.* 49.6, for a comment attributed to Alexander the Great during the torture of Philotas.

42. Hunter 1992: 281, citing the parallel of *IG* II^2 380.40–42.

43. See n. 99.

44. See *L'année Épigraphique* 1971, 88 II.8–10, with Bodel 1994.

45. E.g., Ar. *V.* 449–51 (tied to olive tree then whipped), 1296 (stick); *Lys.* 1217–18 (burning with a lamp), where the joke is described as hackneyed (cf. Men. *Per.* 1–12); Men. *Epit.* 1073–74 (drowning). See Kamen 2010: 96 nn. 9–11.

46. See Klees 1998: 178; Kamen 2010: 96 nn. 7–8.

whip was the symbol of slavery par excellence: the very sight of their masters advancing with horsewhips reduced obstinately rebellious Scythian slaves to subservience to their Persian masters, something regular warfare had failed to do.[47] Of the wide variety of possible ways to physically punish slaves, the Greeks settled on one that equated slaves with draft animals and especially horses. Like everything horsy, this choice probably had aristocratic connotations.[48] The ideal slaveholder would be like a master of horses. On the other side, the animalization of slaves has been explored more on the Roman than on the Greek side,[49] but the notion that inflicting violence on slaves put them in the same category as domesticated animals finds support in the common Greek word for slaves, *andrapodon*, "man-footed creature," a word parallel in form to *tetrapous* (*-podos*) a common expression for livestock.[50] In addition, various Greek authors take the control of animals as a model for rule over slaves, even when they eventually decide to emphasize the different approaches likely to be successful in the two cases.[51] This particular way of situating slaves within a hierarchical world order obviously served the ideological function of naturalizing slavery.[52]

The whip not only evoked the mastery of horses; it also marked the slave permanently with scars.[53] Similarly, branding and tattooing, two other common punishments, were designed to leave permanent and visible signs, often on the face of a slave.[54] These practices served to punish slaves, most obviously with pain; they also discouraged running away, by preventing fugitives from passing themselves off as free. They may also have had a symbolic attraction for masters: the permanent marking of slaves served to set them apart from the free and intact. It may even have suggested an intrinsic distinction; indeed, Aristotle claims that branding was heritable.[55] Slaves seem to have been aware of the significance of their tattoos, and many attempted

47. Hdt. 4.3–4, with Hunt 1998: 51–52. To be precise, it was the sons of the original slaves who remembered their hereditary inferiority when faced with the whip.

48. This is not to deny the practical advantages of whipping, which is, after all, a painful and dramatic punishment that does not incapacitate a slave for work.

49. Bradley 2000.

50. Harvey 1988: 42; cf. Robertson 2008: 91–92.

51. E.g., Pl. *R.* 8.563b–c; X. *Oec.* 12.19–20, 13.6–9.

52. E.g., Arist. *Pol.* 1.1254b9–25.

53. Kamen 2010: 97. Kamen's thorough treatment includes both Greek and Roman cases.

54. Kamen 2010: 98–99.

55. DuBois 2003: 107–9, with Arist. *GA* 721b32.

to disguise or remove these permanent marks of their shame.[56]

A person's original enslavement was often a violent process, and classical Greek texts emphasize this violence. At first blush, this seems puzzling. Some Greeks found slavery repugnant, as an institution based on violence.[57] Conversely, effective and fair masters were supposed to have obedient slaves against whom they did not generally have to take harsh measures.[58] Probably stronger, however, was the view that violence was an ancient and natural basis for social discriminations.[59] Superiority in war was a crucial type of superiority, often indicating divine support; thus, victory or defeat in war was a mark of a man's basic worth.[60] For this reason, Plato advises that any members of the guardian class captured in war be left to their fate of slavery.[61] Modern historians typically contrast violent with ideological supports of oppressive institutions, but in ancient Greece, an emphasis on the violent origins of slavery was also an ideological claim. It assimilated the purchase of foreign slaves by Athenian citizens—whose military experience and prowess might be more, less, or none depending on the individual and the era—with the idealized capture of slaves by the strong right arms of Homeric heroes.[62] An additional ideological gain derived from the representation of slaves as products of war: the more slaves were considered foreign and the more their treatment was assimilated to warfare, the more natural did violence against them seem.[63]

Page duBois and Virginia Hunter argue that the vulnerability of the body of a slave to violence and the emphatic inviolability of the body of the male citizen were crucial to the construction of the opposing categories of slave

56. Kamen 2010: 104–7.

57. Most famous for this view are the "anonymous opponents of Aristotle" in Arist. *Pol.* 1.1253b19–22; cf. Arist. *Pol.* 1.1255a7–10. See Cambiano 1987.

58. X. *Oec.* 3.4. I know of no parallels to Artemesia's claim to Xerxes that good men typically have bad slaves (Hdt. 8.68c).

59. E.g., Heraclitus DK22b53, DK22b80.

60. Hunt 1998: 146–58, 198–202.

61. Pl. *R.* 5.468a. See also *Ap.* 39a; Th. 4.40; X. *HG* 4.5.14; And. 3.30. Conversely, the enslavement of women does not reflect on their worth. See Hunt 1998; 2011: 26, 36–37. Cf. Hall 1997: 93, 111.

62. This is not to say that this was the only ideology naturalizing slavery. Reference to "bought barbarians" also implies contempt for non-Greeks, which made their enslavement less problematic than the enslavement of Greeks. See Hunt 2011: 36–38.

63. See Rosivach 1999. The Spartans even declared war on their own helots each year, so that Spartans could kill them without incurring ritual pollution (Plu. *Lyc.* 28.4). See Trundle's contribution to the present volume.

and male citizen.[64] That slaves were subject to corporal punishment is obvious. Although free criminals caught in the act might be summarily executed by the slow and brutal process of *apotumpanismos*, Athenians were otherwise solicitous of the bodies of even the poorest citizen: the beating of another citizen with the intention to humiliate him risked the capital charge of hubris. Torture was not used on citizens; indeed, the method of execution most in line with Athenian ideals was the bloodless self-administration of poison hemlock.[65] This contrast with slaves is also explicit in several inscribed laws, in which slave offenders receive fifty blows of the whip in place of the fifty-drachma fine a citizen would owe.[66] Most explicitly, several court speeches by Demosthenes spell out the role of violence in determining the categories of male citizen and slave. For example, Demosthenes argues,

> Indeed, if you wish to examine the difference between a free man and a slave, you will find this the greatest distinction: the bodies of slaves are subject to punishment for all their crimes, but free men can keep theirs safe from harm even in the worst disasters. In general, it is right to punish the latter by taking their property. But he [my opponent] did the opposite: he inflicted punishment on their bodies as if they were slaves.[67]

This symbolic approach to violence against slaves, which emphasizes its function in defining the categories of slave and citizen, seems vulnerable to an obvious objection: in most cases, the practical goal of punishing and intimidating slaves seems to provide a full enough explanation of the use of force against them. In response, advocates of a symbolic interpretation of violence against slaves can point to one odd practice: what Michael Gagarin calls the "evidentiary" torture of slaves in the Athenian legal system, usually by whipping or breaking on the wheel.[68] This apparently pointless practice has become exhibit A for the thesis that violence against slaves served the

64. DuBois 1991: 62–64; Hunter 1992; 1994: 54–84

65. See Todd 2000, on Athenian methods of execution. See also Riess' contribution to the present volume.

66. Fisher 2001: 284, on Aeschin. 1.139.

67. D. 22.55, trans. Harris 2008. See Hunter 1992: 278. See also D. 10.27 (cf. 4.10), 24.166–67. Insofar as he misrepresents the actual situation—citizens could, on occasion, suffer corporal punishment—Demosthenes' categorization represents an ideological attempt to clarify and simplify a more complex social situation.

68. Gagarin 1996: 2.

function of marking off social boundaries, that it was a matter of the topography of Athenian values more than that of social control. Before we can investigate this claim, we need to discuss the various uses of torture against slaves, to distinguish the particular anomaly of evidentiary torture.

Slaves who committed egregious crimes could be tortured and killed.[69] In addition, torture was a standard investigatory technique used with slaves, an apparently unobjectionable way to make them tell the truth.[70] These two classes of torture are certainly brutal and violent, but they find many parallels throughout history. Unusual is evidentiary torture, *basanos*, the requirement that, when slaves give evidence of any sort in court, they do so under torture.[71] Slaves were privy to a great deal of information about their masters, so court speeches often make or respond to a challenge to interrogate slaves under torture. That we never hear of a case when a slave was actually tortured has attracted scholarly attention and controversy.[72] Nevertheless, our texts uniformly discuss evidentiary torture as if it took place occasionally—though apparently rarely, for a variety of reasons. Demosthenes describes a failed attempt to torture a slave.

> For the arbitration took place in the Heliaea, where those serving as arbitrators for the Oeneid and Erechtheid tribes hold their sessions; and when challenges of this sort are given and when a party brings his slave in person and delivers him up for examination by torture, hosts of people stand forth to hear what is said.[73]

The point of this spectacle cannot have been the straightforward one of punishing a slave's insubordination or crime and publicizing this punishment. In the case of evidentiary torture, slaves suffered violence simply for being at the wrong place at the wrong time. Indeed, the more intimate, trusted, and loyal a slave was, the more likely he or she was to be in possession of information relevant to a legal case and, thus, to be tortured. This provides strong support for the interpretation of judicial torture not in terms of intimidation of slaves—for it is too indiscriminate—but in

69. E.g., Antiph. 1.20.

70. D. 48.16–18. See also Charito 3.9.7, 4.2.10.

71. Trials about commercial issues in the maritime courts seem not to have made distinctions of status. Thus, slaves could testify directly, without torture. See Cohen 1973: 69–74; 1992: 96–98.

72. E.g., Mirhady 1996, 2000; Thür 1996, 2006; Gagarin 1996; Klees 1998: 393–409.

73. D. 47.12. Cf. Andoc. 1.64–5; Isoc. 17.15; D. 29.12.

terms of the confirmation of the categories of free and slave, as Hunter and duBois have argued.

But our analysis of this issue is not yet quite done: another interpretation in terms of the control of slaves must at least complement the ideological one. Athens was somewhat unusual in that slaves were allowed to testify against their masters at all. In many other slave societies, such testimony was not allowed except in rare cases such as treason or sacrilege.[74] The Athenian practice could have given slaves too much power over their masters, especially since the Athenians had a reputation for being litigious. In particular, the wealthy, who were most likely both to have many slaves and to engage in legal disputes, might often have ended up dependent on their slaves' goodwill.

Hunter emphasizes the power that slaves could attain by virtue of their knowledge of their master's personal life and their role in spreading gossip (or not) in a society in which reputation was a central concern.[75] One can easily go too far in this direction, since people must often have dismissed the gossip of disgruntled slaves.[76] If we ought rarely to deny agency to the weak, historians must be even more suspicious of any scheme that denies agency to the powerful—in this case, the slave masters, who held almost all the cards.[77] If not only a man's reputation but his property or life depended on the knowledge and testimony of slaves, slaves' power would have been magnified even beyond the picture Hunter paints. One Athenian litigant, for example, claims that it would have been an appalling reversal for him to have committed a crime in front of his slaves and thus been subjected to them.

> I would surely become the most wretched of human beings, if for the rest of my life I was to have my own attendants no longer as my slaves but as my masters, because they would share my guilty knowledge of this event—so that even if they committed the greatest offences towards me, it would not be possible for me to exact any punishment from them, because I would know full well that it was in their hands both to get revenge on me and to gain their own freedom by denouncing me.[78]

74. Hunter 1994: 70–71.

75. Hunter 1992; 1994: 81, 89. See also Forsdyke 2012: 37–89.

76. Thphr. *Char.* 8.4 has the "rumour monger" (Diggle 2004) cite a slave as his source of information.

77. See Johnson 2003 for a critique of the exaggeration of slave agency.

78. Lys. 7.16, trans. Todd 2007; cf. Lys. 5.3. Admittedly, it is in the speaker's interest to exaggerate the power and immunity that this state of affairs would give his slaves.

In this case, the crime was sacrilege, the cutting down of a sacred olive. In such cases, slaves could become informants (*mēnutai*) against their masters on their own initiative and might even win their freedom.[79] But for most masters involved in most types of legal disputes, the power that slaves might gain through their knowledge of their masters' lives and the threat to testify against them was effectively countered by the requirement of evidentiary torture. Should a slave say, "You better treat me well, Master, or I'll tell *X* to the court," the master could decisively reply, "Yes, you'll really show me—while your arms and legs are being pulled from their sockets?"[80]

Limits on Violence

The interpretations of slave torture in terms of the topography of Athenian conceptual categories and as a way to intimidate slaves are not mutually exclusive. They also both attribute a function to violence against slaves. But some violence and perhaps much must have been dysfunctional. Torture on the wheel might permanently cripple a valuable slave and render him or her useless. More generally, slaveholders might hit slaves while in a fit of temper, while drunk, or out of sadism. The powerlessness of slaves and their ubiquity made it inevitable that frustrations of all sorts were taken out on them physically. Slaveholders must often have done this despite, rather than because of, the likely consequences. In some cases, this violence made things worse for the master as well as the slave, such as if a valuable and hardworking slave became obstinate and violent after being beaten and ended up sold at a loss to a mill.[81]

Slaveholders do not always act in their own best interests, so Greek intellectuals occasionally recommend self-control rather than violence against slaves. When Xenophon advises prospective military officers never to make important decisions in anger, he adds that one should not even beat a slave in anger, "for masters in anger have often suffered greater harm than they have inflicted."[82] Plato insists that a just man would use only the minimum

79. Klees 1998: 376. In some periods, though, false accusations were penalized with death (McDowell 1978: 181–83).

80. Cf. Todd 2007: 388–89: "Athenian law encouraged slaves to spy on their masters only in very restricted circumstances [religious offenses]."

81. That this unprofitability might eventually bring trouble for the slave, too, does not make the violence any less dysfunctional.

82. X. *HG* 5.3.7; cf. Hdt. 1.137; D.L. 3.38–39.

violence necessary with his slaves.[83] These passages evince the more general Greek ideals of self-control and restraint. This advice and the way it is couched imply that many people did beat slaves in anger—or worse.[84] In Chariton's *Callirhoe*, Chaereas, who struck his wife in a jealous fit, is described as usually being so gentle that he would not even strike a slave in anger.[85] The implication is that only a particularly gentle person would refrain from striking a slave.

It would be excessively cynical to claim that the ideal of self-control, an important element in the topography of Greek thinking and values, never influenced the treatment and, thus, the social control of slaves. It was not, however, the only strain in Greek thinking about violence and slavery. In his detailed analysis of violence in curse tablets, forensic speeches, and comedy, Werner Riess argues that an ideal of self-control and restraint and an older ideal emphasizing defense of honor and revenge "coexisted side by side in uneasy tension, overlapping and at times clashing."[86] DuBois even views the open display of anger as a way that male citizens showed their superiority to slaves.[87] Finally, the ideal of restraint was not necessarily offended by violence against slaves: "non-excessive violence against subordinates was a suitable means of maintaining the social and political order of Athens" and barely counted as violence at all.[88] I have already noted that masters could delegate the actual violent acts to others. Thus, the ideal of restraint provided inconsistent protection at best.

At first glance, some laws appear to have guarded slaves from excessive violence. Most strikingly, the law against hubris, meaning outrageous or contemptuous treatment, specifically included slaves in its protection. Demosthenes even claimed that many people had actually been tried for hubris against slaves—almost certainly not against their own slaves.[89] It is not clear whether the hubris consisted of the humiliation of a slave—since one passage suggests that its goal was to discourage arrogant behavior in general[90]—or the insult that somebody else's harsh treatment of the slave

83. Pl. *Lg.* 6.777d–e.

84. Cf. Riess 2012: 137.

85. Charito 1.14.7.

86. Riess 2012: 135.

87. DuBois 2003: 206–17; see also Konstan 2013: 150.

88. Riess 2012: 385.

89. D. 21.46–50. See also Aeschin. 1.15–17; Hyp. fr. 120 Jensen, in Athen. 6.267a.

90. See Fisher 1992: 58–59. On the nature of hubris, see Phillips' contribution to the present volume.

could imply toward the master's honor. Masters might conceivably bring a charge of hubris to assert their rights and dignity, to protect their slaves, or to harass their enemies. Nevertheless, a couple of passages make it clear that masters did not always consider their slaves worth defending in court, even when others had abused them.[91]

Concern for slaves' mistreatment by others makes sense insofar as masters were seen as property owners, but several texts regard it as a uniquely Athenian practice that would strike other Greeks as eccentric.[92] The class superiority of the free over slaves—which might permit any free citizen to strike any slave—was in tension with individual ownership of slaves, according to which an injury done to a slave affected the master's interest and even his honor. Athens seems to have put more emphasis on the latter; that this attracted comment suggests that other states tended toward the former view.[93] But even the Athenian law was worthless against the violence that most threatened and harmed slaves, violence at the hands of their own masters. It is doubtful that anybody ever took a master, even an enemy, to court for the violent abuse and punishment of his own slaves: such practices were simply part of slavery. And, except in some commercial lawsuits, slaves had no legal standing to bring suits on their own.[94] It is hardly even worth invoking class solidarity among the free to explain this. Given that slavery was legal, the violence of the institution was also.

If somebody other than his or her owner killed a slave, the owner could bring a charge of murder.[95] The master's pecuniary loss and his legal standing as the slave's *kurios* (master or guardian) ensured that he was legally capable of bringing murder charges and may even have been expected to do so.[96] Furthermore, murder always seemed to incur religious pollution, regardless of the victim's status: in one court speech, we hear that a man who has killed his own slave purifies himself and tries to avoid places proscribed by the law.[97] Some passages imply that it was not only polluting but also illegal for

91. Fisher 1992: 40, on [D.] 53.16. Cf. Ar. *Ach.* 271–76; D. 54.4–5.

92. [X.] *Ath.* 1.10–11; cf. Pl. *R.* 8.563b.

93. The most conspicuous example is Sparta, where fathers were in command of all children and where Spartiates could use each other's helots if necessary (X. *Lac.* 6.1–3).

94. Morrow 1937: 224; MacDowell 1990: 262; Cohen 1992: 97.

95. Isoc. 18.52–54. The murder of slaves, as of foreigners, was tried at the Palladium, along with other killings considered less important than the murder of a citizen, as well as unintentional homicide or making a plan that led to a death (Arist. *Ath.* 57.3, with Rhodes 1992: 643).

96. [D.] 47.68–70; cf. Antiph. 5.48.

97. Antiph. 6.4. See the reservations at Eck 2012: 251. See also Isoc. 12.181; Pl. *Lg.* 9.865c–d, 9.868a; Eck 2012: 317–18.

a master to murder a slave.[98] The proper course of action if a master thought a slave deserved to die was to hand him or her over to the Eleven for execution.[99] If a master failed to do this and simply killed his slave, he was liable to a charge of murder. But the main legal process for murder, the *dike phonou*, was designed to be brought by a member of the victim's family or his or her *kurios*.[100] Since slaves had no recognized family, only their masters could prosecute their killers, an arrangement unlikely to provide justice if a master himself was the murderer. Thus, no legal procedure was likely to be available against masters who had killed their slaves.[101] Still, such murders were probably not very common. If nothing else, it was expensive to kill one's slave, and except for the cruel and angry master, recourse to the Eleven was a sufficient and convenient way to do it. But every population has its cruel and angry men, so I have no doubt that there were occasions when a master murdered one of his slaves himself. In particular, masters could do away with slaves behind closed doors at home or on their farms, an option especially attractive to those whose grounds for violence were too insubstantial or disreputable for the publicity that going before the Eleven would involve. That such murders were probably almost never punished must have sent to all the slaves in Athens a chilling signal of their defenselessness.[102]

Slaves did have a customary right to seek sanctuary from intolerable treatment in a public place. We know that the Theseion at Athens was a slave sanctuary whither slaves could flee and not be seized.[103] Of course, no slave society is likely to set up a system whereby people can escape their enslavement simply by alleging bad treatment and making it to a centrally located sanctuary. At Athens, if the slave could prove intolerable abuse, he was sold to another master: hence the process is described as fleeing "to seek a sale."[104] But who would buy a slave who had caused his master trouble by alleging

98. E. *Hec.* 291–92, with Morrow 1937: 225.

99. Edwards and Usher 1985: 101, on Antiph. 5.48.

100. Morrow 1937: 224. This view is upheld by Tulin (1996, esp. 21–54, on [D.] 47), against Gagarin (1979) and MacDowell (1963: 11–22). Cf. Gagarin 1997b; Helmis 2003: 92–97. Most recently, Phillips (2008: 110–31, 239) argues that nonkin could proceed against a murderer by *apogoge*, but this possibility was often ignored, and there remained the presumption that only kin can prosecute.

101. Tulin 1996: 106 n. 264, in agreement with MacDowell (1963: 21) and Gagarin (1979: 306). Pl. *Lg.* 9.865c–d and 9.868a specifies religious purification as the only penalty for a man who has killed his slave.

102. Cf. Jacobs 1987: 48.

103. See Christensen 1984.

104. Ar. fr. 567 Kock; Eupolis fr. 225 Kock. Cf. E. *Supp.* 268; Hdt. 2.113.

ill treatment and seeking sanctuary?[105] The most likely buyers were probably those slaveholders whose operations were based on brute violence and physical constraint, such as mill or mine operators. If it were determined that a slave had not suffered abuse, he went back to his owner, who was likely to be in an angry mood. As if that were not bad enough, the people who decided the slave's case were never slaves and were often slaveholders, likely to take a narrow view of what constituted abuse.

Slaves could not always get to sanctuaries and may have considered them a bad option. In several cases, we hear of a slave seeking intervention by third parties.[106] The most intriguing of these cases is a letter written on a sheet of lead, which was unearthed in the Athenian Agora. It is by a slave, Lesis, who asks his mother and a certain Xenocles to come to his rescue.

> Lesis is sending (a letter) to Xenocles and to his mother by no means to overlook that he is perishing in the foundry but to come to his masters and find something better for him. For I have been handed over to a man thoroughly wicked; I am perishing from being whipped; I am tied up; I am treated like dirt—more and more.[107]

We have no idea whether this appeal was successful; indeed, one scholar suspects that the letter was thrown out rather than delivered.[108] It does, however, hint at the complex social relations that may have occasionally allowed slaves to protect themselves. One of several possible scenarios that could explain this letter's plea runs as follows: Lesis' mother is a slave or ex-slave, for her son is a slave; she is the mistress of Xenocles, for a mistress might have more influence than a slave; Xenocles is an Athenian citizen, for more help might be expected from a citizen than from a *metic* or a slave; Xenocles knows Lesis' masters, which explains why he might be able to intercede; Lesis has been rented out to a foundry, which explains why his masters and the "man thoroughly wicked" are different. Regardless of the scenario, the hoped-for intercession in this case would have had no basis in law, since there were no legal grounds for intervention in the mistreatment of a slave.

105. Cf. the Roman case, as explained by Watson (1987: 121, on *Dig.* 21.1.19.1): "But it was standard practice in buying a slave to demand a guarantee that he had not fled to a statue."

106. *Life of Aesop* 58; D. 19.196–98; cf. Aeschin. 2.4.153–58.

107. Translation in Jordan 2000: 95. I accept the arguments of Harris (2004) and Harvey (2007) to the effect that Lesis was a slave.

108. Jordan 2000: 95.

The letter's success would simply depend on the relationships among all these individuals.

Gender and Violence

The treatment of male slaves by male masters dominates our evidence and has, so far, been the main focus of this chapter. But there were women who commanded or were slaves. At a time when expectations of men and women were so different, all relationships, including violent ones involving slaves, were influenced by the gender of the participants. Accordingly, to a significant extent, violence against women slaves needs to be understood within topographies—physical topographies and topographies of social control and of thought and value—that are different from those of male slaves. The treatment here will be brief, not because the topic is unimportant, but because our evidence for women slaves is scantier than our already poor evidence for slaves in general.

Women slaves usually did different sorts of work than men: for example, women slaves dominated prostitution and weaving.[109] In the latter case especially, this meant that slave women worked indoors and often under the supervision of other women. Free women's right to own property in Athens was severely limited, since they were subject to the tutelage first of their natal family and then of their husbands.[110] Nevertheless, some did command slaves, so I shall refer loosely to women masters. Indeed, Xenophon's Ischomachus describes the supervision of the slaves inside the house as one of the main duties of his wife.[111] Such women could inflict violence on slaves or order that it be inflicted—as men sometimes did.[112] The objects of their violence were usually those domestic slaves who served them directly. In literary sources, the violence or anger of women slaveholders is often directed at slave women who attract their husband's affections or sexual desire.[113] This explanation for violence was probably just the reason with the greatest literary appeal. One imagines that women slave masters usually beat slaves to intimidate them and to enforce obedience, just as men did. Likewise, just as a male slaveholder might hit a slave out of anger, so might a woman. To take

109. For weaving, cf. Rosivach 1989.

110. Ste. Croix 1970.

111. X. *Oec.* 7.35.

112. Aesop. 50, 61; cf. D. 19.197.

113. Cf. Charito 2.1.8–9, 2.5.5; Men. *Pk.* F. 333; A. *A.* 1438–47.

an example from a later period of Greek history, the doctor Galen describes the injuries that patients (masters) suffered from hitting their slaves and relates that his own mother, when in a rage, would sometimes bite her handmaidens.[114]

Women slaves were vulnerable to coerced sex, which seems to have been considered a matter of poor taste if the master were married, though it was not a particularly serious offense in any case.[115] Accordingly, Hunter notes of female slaves in Aristophanes, "Aristophanes does not depict female slaves as lazy, impudent, or clever: they have no significant roles. Instead they are discussed mainly as the object of men's amorous advances."[116] Women were also particularly vulnerable to threats against their families—for example, that a child might be sold away from his or her mother. Such threats might work against fathers, but the mother's bond was considered to be closer; in the absence of formal marriages among slaves, the maternal bond was the only one acknowledged at all.

Hunter raises the question of whether female slaves suffered as much violence as their male counterparts.[117] It is almost impossible to determine whether this was the case and, if we grant that it was, why it was. There was certainly no hard and fast rule that offered any protection to women slaves. One master threatened a woman with sale to a mill.[118] Another slave woman was tortured and killed for her role (apparently unintentional) in the death of her master.[119] Chariton's "gentle" character Chaereas, whom we have met before, tortures the slave women of his household in an investigation.[120] Female slaves were offered or demanded for evidentiary torture, just as males were.[121] Women slaves in comedy can suffer physical punishment, as can male slaves.[122] When an enslaved Olynthian woman was humiliated, stripped, and barely escaped whipping in the presence of Athenian envoys to Macedonia, the incident became notorious, not because women slaves

---

114. Gal. *Anim. Pass.* 1.4, 1.8, in Bradley 1994: 28–29. Cf. also Juvenal's harridan maltreating her maids out of sexual frustration at Juv. 6.475–93.

115. Thphr. *Char.* 4.7; Lys. 1.12; Men. *Mis.* A8–12. Characters in Aristophanes often either attempt or bring up sex with slave women (*Ach.* 271–76; *V.* 1341–42; *Av.* 1254–56; *Th.* 1172–99; Mactoux 1999). Cf. Men. *Sik.* 370–74. For sexual violence against slave women in Homer's *Odyssey*, see Gualerzi 2005.

116. Hunter 1994: 172.

117. Hunter 1994: 172–73.

118. Lys. 1.18.

119. Antiph. 1.20.

120. Chariton 1.5.1–2.

121. E.g., D. 29.25; [D.] 47.6, 59.120.

122. Men. *Dys.* 195–96, 205; *Epit.* 1073–74.

should not be treated violently, but because Olynthus had been an Athenian ally.[123] Of course, none of this evidence provides any basis for a quantitative judgment. It does not rule out the possibility that there was some tendency for women to suffer less violence. For example, in the American South, women slaves could be savagely whipped and punished,[124] but the records of the previously mentioned Barrow plantation show that women were whipped half as often as men.[125] Furthermore, Southern authorities punished women slaves less harshly than men for the same crimes.[126]

Is there any reason to suspect such a pattern in classical Athens? Was there anything like the modern injunction "Never hit a woman," which might have led to different treatment of men and women? The evidence on this score is extremely sparse and somewhat contradictory.[127] On the one hand, men were expected to be protectors of women and of their households.[128] Moreover, masters were not in competition with women as with their peers; they may not have regarded female slaves as potential threats. Thus, these motivations for violence were lacking. On the other hand, citizen males were in command of their women and households, and to their way of thinking, such command could require violence. Indeed, Lloyd Llewellyn-Jones argues persuasively that while ideal husbands should be able to convince their wives to obey them, the use of physical force was not condemned so long as it was not considered excessive.[129] The position of slave women was likely to be even more precarious than that of citizen wives.[130] Ariana Traill points out that Plutarch draws this contrast explicitly: "*hubris* and *paroinia* (alcohol-fueled violence) are acceptable with *hetairai* and slave girls but not with wives."[131]

---

123. D. 19.196–98; Aeschin. 2.4.153–58; Hunt 2010: 149–50.

124. See, e.g., Douglass 1987: 58–59, 61–63.

125. Paquette 1998: 255.

126. Paquette 1998: 257.

127. See Omitowoju's contribution to this volume.

128. Hunt 2010: 143–50.

129. See Llewellyn-Jones 2011: 253, endorsing the view of Nick Fisher. Llewellyn-Jones adduces the following passages: Hom. *Il.* 1.560–89, 15.12–23; Sem. fr. 7.12–20; E. *Melanipp. Capt.* fr. 497; Ar. *Lys.* 160–66, 507–20; *Nu.* 1443–46; Plu. *Alc.* 8.4; Charito 1.4.12–1.5.1. I do not find his interpretation of the red-figure *chous*, with which he begins, as convincing as the rest of his argument.

130. Riess 2012: 44–45.

131. Traill 2008: 147, on Plu. *Mor.* 140b3–12. Cf. Men. *Pk.* 1016–19. If Plutarch's attitude differs from classical ones, it is likely to be in his emphasis on the rights of wives, rather than in any harsher treatment of slave women.

Conclusion

This essay's focus on violence against slaves in Athens has resulted in a bleak picture. Such violence was common, and the threat of violence was deliberately kept prominent. The use of violence against slaves was not just a pragmatic necessity but was embedded in the ways Greeks understood their world. The ideal of restraint from violence, a growing strain in classical Athenian thinking, barely applied to slaves, while law and custom provided only minimal protection. Violence and the threat of violence were central to the relationship between masters and slaves and must have blighted the lives of many slaves throughout Greek antiquity. This way of looking at things, however, carries the risk of viewing the world of slaves as exceptional in their vulnerability to violence. Slaves probably did suffer more violence than other classes, but a man's use of violence to discipline his children or women was unexceptionable. Thieves caught in the act could face slow and painful deaths. Even ancient religion was violent: gods could be angry and cruel and were conciliated with blood sacrifice. To conclude with a topographic metaphor, it might be more accurate to view the male citizens alone as inhabiting an island where they were largely shielded from open violence—at least in peacetime.

Works Cited

Abercrombie, N., Hill, S., and Turner, B. 1980. *The Dominant Ideology Thesis.* Boston.

Adam, J., ed. 1902. *The "Republic" of Plato.* 2 vols. Cambridge.

Akrigg, B., and Tordoff, R., eds. 2013. *Slaves and Slavery in Ancient Greek Comic Drama.* Cambridge.

Andreau, J., and Descat, R. 2011. *The Slave in Greece and Rome.* Trans. Marion Leopold. Madison.

Bodel, J. 1994. *Graveyards and Groves: A Study of the Lex Lucerina.* Cambridge.

Bonner, R., and Smith, G. 1930–38. *The Administration of Justice from Homer to Aristotle.* 2 vols. Chicago.

Bradley, K. 1987. *Slaves and Masters in the Roman Empire: A Study in Social Control.* Oxford.

Bradley, K. 1994. *Slavery and Society at Rome.* Cambridge.

Bradley, K. 2000. "Animalizing the Slave: The Truth of Fiction." *JRS* 90: 110–25.

Cambiano, G. 1987. "Aristotle and the Anonymous Opponents of Slavery." In M. Finley, ed., *Classical Slavery,* 28–52. Totowa.

Cohen, E. 1973. *Ancient Athenian Maritime Courts.* Princeton.

Cohen, E. 1992. *Athenian Economy and Society: A Banking Perspective.* Princeton.

Cox, C. 2002. "Assuming the Master's Values: The Slave's Response to Punishment and Neglect in Menander." *Mouseion,* 3rd ser., 2: 23–38.

Dew, C. 1994. *Bond of Iron: Master and Slave at Buffalo Forge*. New York.

Diggle, J., ed. 2004. *Theophrastus: Characters*. Cambridge.

Douglass, Frederick. 1987. *My Bondage and My Freedom*. Ed. W. Andrews. Urbana.

Dover, K. 1993. *Aristophanes, "Frogs."* Oxford.

duBois, P. 1991. *Torture and Truth*. London.

duBois, P. 2003. *Slaves and Other Objects*. Chicago.

Eck, B. 2012. *La mort rouge: homicide, guerre et souillure en Grèce ancienne. Collection d'Études anciennes. Série greque*, 145. Paris.

Edwards, M., and Usher, S., eds. 1985. *Greek Orators*. Vol. 1, *Antiphon and Lysias*. Warminster.

Fenoaltea, S. 1984. "Slavery and Supervision in Comparative Perspective: A Model." *Journal of Economic History* 44: 635–68.

Fisher, N. 1992. Hybris*: A Study in the Values of Honour and Shame in Ancient Greece*. Warminster.

Fisher, N., ed. 2001. *Aeschines, "Against Timarchos."* Oxford.

Fogel, R., and Engerman, S. 1974. *Time on the Cross*. Boston.

Forsdyke, S. 2008. *Slaves Tell Tales, and Other Episodes in the Politics of Popular Culture in Ancient Greece*. Princeton.

Gagarin, M. 1979. "The Prosecution of Homicide in Athens." *GRBS* 19: 301–23.

Gagarin, M. 1996. "The Torture of Slaves in Athenian law." *CPh* 91: 1–18.

Gagarin, M., ed. 1997a. *Antiphon: The Speeches*. Cambridge.

Gagarin, M. 1997b. Review of Alexander Tulin, *Dike Phonou*. *BMCR* 97.4.17.

Geertz, C. 1973a. "Ethos, World View, and the Interpretation of Sacred Symbols." In *The Interpretation of Cultures*, 126–41. New York.

Geertz, C. 1973b. "Ideology as a Cultural System." In *The Interpretation of Cultures*, 193–233. New York.

Geertz, C. 1973c. "Thick Description: Towards an Interpretive Theory of Culture." In *The Interpretation of Cultures*, 3–30. New York.

Gualerzi, S. 2005. "Praised Slaves, Forgiven Slaves, and Punished Slaves in Odysseus' Palace." In V. Anastasiadis and P. Doukellis, eds., *Esclavage antique et discriminations socio-culturelles: Actes du XXVIIIe Colloque International du Groupement international de recherche sur l'esclavage antique (Mytilène, 5–7 décembre 2003)*, 17–32. Berne.

Hall, E. 1997. "The Sociology of Athenian Tragedy." In P. Easterling, ed., *The Cambridge Companion to Greek Tragedy*, 93–126. Cambridge.

Harris, E. 2004. "Notes on a lead letter from the Athenian agora." *HSCP* 102: 157-70.

Harris, E., trans. 2008. Demosthenes, Speeches, 20–22. Austin.

Harsh, P. 1955. "The Intriguing Slave in Greek Comedy." *TAPhA* 86: 135–42.

Harvey, F. 1988. "Herodotus and the Man-Footed Creature." In L. Archer, ed., *Slavery and Other Forms of Unfree Labour*, 42–52. London.

Harvey, F. 2007. "'Help! I'm Dying Here': A Letter from a Slave." *ZPE* 163: 49–50.

Hopkins, K., and Roscoe, P. 1977. "Between Slavery and Freedom: On Freeing Slaves at Delphi." In *Conquerors and Slaves*, 134–71. Cambridge.

Hunt, P. 1998. *Slaves, Warfare, and Ideology in the Greek Historians*. Cambridge.

Hunt, P. 2010. *War, Peace, and Alliance in Demosthenes' Athens*. Cambridge.

Hunt, P. 2011. "Slaves in Greek Literary Culture." In K. Bradley and P. Cartledge, eds.,

The Cambridge World History of Slavery, vol. 1, *The Ancient Near East and Mediterranean World to AD 500*, 22–47. Cambridge.

Hunt, P. Forthcoming. "Slaves as Active Subjects: Individual Strategies." In S. Hodkinson, M. Kleijwegt, and K. Vlassopoulos, eds., *The Oxford Handbook of Greek and Roman Slaveries*. Oxford.

Hunter, V. 1992. "Constructing the Body of the Citizen: Corporal Punishment in Classical Athens." *Echos du Monde Classique / Classical Views*, n.s., 11: 271–91.

Hunter, V. 1994. *Policing Athens: Social Control in the Attic Lawsuits, 420–320 BC*. Princeton.

Jacobs, H. 1987. *Incidents in the Life of a Slave Girl, Written by Herself*. Ed. J. Yellin. Cambridge.

Johnson, W. 2003. "On Agency." *Journal of Social History* 37 (1): 113–24.

Jones, C. 2008. "Hyperides and the Sale of Slave Families." *ZPE* 164: 19–20.

Jordan, D. 2000. "A Personal Letter Found in the Athenian Agora." *Hesperia* 69: 91–103.

Kamen, D. 2010. "A Corpus of Inscriptions: Representing Slave Marks in Antiquity." *Memoirs of the American Academy in Rome* 60: 95–110.

Klees, H. 1998. *Sklavenleben im Klassischen Griechenland*. Stuttgart.

Konstan, D. 2013. "Menander's Slaves: The Banality of Violence." In B. Akrigg and R. Tordoff, eds., *Slaves and Slavery in Ancient Greek Comic Drama*, 144–58. Cambridge.

Llewellyn-Jones, L. 2011. "Domestic Abuse and Violence against Women in Ancient Greece." In S. Lambert, ed., *Sociable Man: Essays on Ancient Greek Social Behavior in Honour of Nick Fisher*, 231–66. Swansea.

MacDowell, D. 1963. *Athenian Homicide Law in the Age of the Orators*. Manchester.

MacDowell, D. 1978. *The Law in Classical Athens*. London.

MacDowell, D., ed. 1990. *Demosthenes, "Against Meidias" (Oration 21)*. Oxford.

Mactoux, M. 1999. "Esclaves-femmes dans le corpus d'Aristophane." In F. Reduzzi Merola and A. Storchi Marino, eds., *Femmes-esclaves: Modèles d'interprétation anthropologique, économique, juridique; Atti del XXI Colloquio Internazionale Girea*, 21–46. Naples.

McCarthy, K. 2000. *Slaves, Masters, and the Art of Authority in Plautine Comedy*. Princeton.

Marchant, E., trans. 2013. *Xenophon: Memorabilia. Oeconomicus. Symposium. Apology*. Loeb Classical Library 168. Revised by Jeffrey Henderson. Cambridge.

Miller, N., trans. 1987. *Menander: Plays and Fragments*. Harmondsworth.

Mirhady, D. 1996. "Torture and Rhetoric in Athens." *JHS* 116: 119–31.

Mirhady, D. 2000. "The Athenian Rationale for Torture." In V. Hunter and J. Edmondson, eds., *Law and Social Status in Classical Athens*, 53–74. Oxford.

Morrow, G. 1937. "The Murder of Slaves in Attic Law." *CPh* 32: 210–27.

Papadopoulous, J., and Morris, S. 2005. "Greek Towers and Slaves: An Archaeology of Exploitation." *AJA* 109: 155–225.

Paquette, R. 1998. "Discipline and Punishment." In P. Finkelman and J. Miller, eds., *Macmillan Encyclopedia of World Slavery*, 252–57. New York.

Parker, H. 1989. "Crucially Funny, or Tranio on the Couch: The *Servus Callidus* and Jokes about Torture." *TAPhA* 119: 233–46.

Phillips, D. 2008. *Avengers of Blood: Homicide in Athenian Law and Custom from Draco to Demosthenes*. Stuttgart.
Pomeroy, S. 1994. *Xenophon, "Oeconomicus": A Social and Historical Commentary*. Oxford.
Rhodes, P. 1992. *A Commentary on the Aristotelian "Athenaion politeia."* Oxford.
Riess, W. 2012. *Performing Interpersonal Violence: Court, Curse, and Comedy in Fourth-Century BCE Athens*. Berlin.
Robertson, B. 2008. "The Slave Names of *IG* I³ 1032 and the Ideology of Slavery at Athens." In C. Cooper, ed., *Epigraphy and the Greek Historian*, 79–116. Toronto.
Rosivach, V. 1989. "*Talasiourgoi* and *Paidia* in *IG* 2² 1553—78: A Note on Athenian Social History." *Historia* 38: 365–70.
Rosivach, V. 1999. "Enslaving *Barbaroi* and the Athenian Ideology of Slavery." *Historia* 48: 129–57.
Scott, J. 1985. *Weapons of the Weak: Everyday Forms of Peasant Resistance*. New Haven.
Scott, J. 1990. *Domination and the Arts of Resistance: Hidden Transcripts*. New Haven.
Sommerstein, A. 2009. "Slave and Citizen in Aristophanic Comedy." In *Talking about Laughter, and Other Studies in Greek Comedy*, 136–54. Oxford.
Ste. Croix, G. de. 1970. "Some Observations of the Property Rights of Athenian Women." *CR*, n.s., 20: 273–78.
Sutch, R. 1975. "The Treatment Received by American Slaves: A Critical Review of the Evidence Presented in *Time on the Cross*." *EEH* 12 (4): 335–438.
Thür, G. 1996. "Reply to D. Mirhady: Torture and Rhetoric in Athens." *JHS* 116: 132–34.
Thür, G. 2006. "Neues zur Basanos." In R. Gamauf, ed., *Festschrift für Herbert Hausmaniger zum 70. Geburtstag*, 287–91. Vienna.
Todd, S. 2000. "How to Execute People in Fourth-Century Athens." In V. Hunter and J. Edmundson, eds., *Law and Social Status in Classical Athens*, 31–49. Oxford.
Todd, S., ed. 2007. *A Commentary on Lysias, Speeches 1–11*. Oxford.
Tordoff, R. 2013. "Introduction: Slaves and Slavery in Ancient Greek Comedy." In B. Akrigg and R. Tordoff, eds., *Slaves and Slavery in Ancient Greek Comic Drama*, 1–62. Cambridge.
Traill, A. 2008. *Women and the Comic Plot in Menander*. Cambridge.
Tulin, A. 1996. *Dike Phonou: The Right of Prosecution and Attic Homicide Procedure*. Stuttgart.
Watson, A. 1987. *Roman Slave Law*. Baltimore.
Wiedemann, T., ed. 1981. *Greek and Roman Slavery*. London.
Worthington, I. 1992. *A Historical Commentary on Dinarchus: Rhetoric and Conspiracy in Later Fourth-Century Athens*. Ann Arbor.
Zweig, B. 1992. "The Mute Nude Female Characters in Aristophanes' Plays." In A. Richlin, ed., *Pornography and Representation in Greece and Rome*, 73–89. Oxford.

SIX

The Greek Battlefield

Classical Sparta and the Spectacle of Hoplite Warfare

Ellen Millender

While violence may have pervaded the social, political, and cultural landscapes of ancient Greece, it found its fullest expression in the warfare that was such a fundamental and constant feature of the Greek way of life. Warfare, it must be said, occurred in a multitude of forms, reflecting, among other things, the diverse nature and number of Greek communities, the nature of individual disputes, the exigencies of topography, and the varying agendas of the combatants. As the ancient historians demonstrate, the Greeks settled their differences in a variety of ways, from sieges, naval encounters, and pitched battles, to agricultural devastation, night raids, and guerrilla warfare.[1]

Despite the tremendously variegated nature of Greek interstate violence, hoplite battle has received the lion's share of attention from both ancient authors and modern scholars. In reality, hoplite battles occurred with relative infrequency during the fifth and fourth centuries, the period under discussion in this essay.[2] Hoplite tactics, moreover, did not develop evenly

1. On the range of hostilities recorded by the ancient sources, see Hanson 2000a: 201–32.

2. Hanson (2000a: 214–19) argues that over the course of the fifth century, the Greeks became increasingly unwilling to settle disputes by hoplite battles. According to van Wees (2004: 116–17), agricultural devastation and other asymmetrical forms of warfare were at least as common as pitched battles and far more common than the most ritualized kind of set battles, even before this period. Cf. Wheeler and Strauss 2007: 215.

throughout the Greek world and did not arise at all in certain regions, for reasons of terrain or because of the lack of requisite social, political, and economic structures.[3] Nevertheless, several ancient sources, including Polybius (13.3.1–8), provide idealized treatments of pitched infantry battle as the standard method of resolving disputes in the Greek world.[4] Building on such ancient accounts, a number of modern studies of ancient warfare have tended to treat hoplite warfare as the dominant form of warfare between the eighth and fifth centuries BCE among agrarian communities governed by broad oligarchies of farmers and mostly situated in the plains of the central and southern mainland of Greece.[5]

Given the hoplite battle's position as the gold standard of Greek warfare and its correspondingly rich evidentiary base, it is the natural starting point for a study of the Greek battlefield as the locus classicus of violence in the broadest sense. Scholars have approached this particular brand of Greek violence from a variety of vantage points—from more traditional considerations of the mechanics, progression, and constitutive elements of the hoplite encounter, to more recent examinations of the psychological and cultural factors at play when two phalanxes met on the battlefield. Among the latter studies, one that has proved particularly provocative is Jon Lendon's investigation of the evolution of Greek and Roman military tactics. Lendon argues for the influence of Homeric epic on the development of Greek battle tactics and identifies the hoplite phalanx as a method of warfare that evolved from "epic" martial contests to constitute a site of competition between both individuals and contending cities.[6] Lendon's study demonstrates the benefits that come from a fuller understanding of the cultural context of Greek warfare. Nevertheless, its treatment of primordial competitiveness and reverence for epic tradition as the main cultural values that affected the practice of hoplite warfare belies the complex relationship that this form of warfare enjoyed with other core Greek institutions, structures, and values, especially the ideal of civic cooperation, as we shall see below.[7]

---

3. Hanson 2000a: 211. See also van Wees 2004: 47–52.

4. Cf. Hdt. 7.9β; D. 9.48. See Hanson 2000a: 206–7; van Wees 2004: 115–17.

5. See, e.g., Hanson 2000a: 211, 218.

6. Lendon 2005: 39–77, esp. 50–55, 61–65.

7. Lendon 2005: 44–45, 402–3. Lendon (45) admits that "hoplites cooperated in fact, and their need to rely on one another in battle was clearly understood." Nevertheless, he insists that "the ethos that lay underneath this cooperation was only superficially cooperative, for those who fought in the seemingly unheroic phalanx conceived of what they were doing in Homeric terms."

In the study that follows, I will take a broader look at hoplite warfare, as a communally embedded form of violence that enjoyed a particularly dynamic and reciprocal relationship with the communities that practiced it. More specifically, I will explore the performative nature of hoplite warfare and its function as an effective instrument of political action that responded to changing ideological and political needs.[8] To elucidate these dimensions of hoplite warfare, I have focused my analysis on ancient Sparta, aptly described by Paul Cartledge as the "*doyenne* of developed hoplite warfare" for nearly two centuries before its defeat at Leuctra in 371.[9] One might argue, of course, that Sparta was atypical in its military professionalization. The vagaries of Greek warfare, however, argue against a typology of the hoplite state; and, in many respects, Spartan military practices differed from those of other states in degree rather than in kind.[10] More important, much of the evidence that we possess for hoplite tactics and organization comes from accounts of battles that the Spartans fought against a variety of opponents in the late fifth and early fourth centuries.

Through a careful analysis of this relatively abundant body of evidence, I will argue that the battlefield was not merely the site of competition for the Spartans but also a veritable stage on which they at once enacted, defended, and displayed the grand spectacle of Sparta. Indeed, as we shall see, the battlefield was the ideal topos for the ostentatious performance of the ideology, social codes, and relations of power that organized the Spartan body politic and that structured Sparta's interactions with its subjects, neighbors, allies, and enemies. While the Spartans may have forged a particularly strong bond between their system of values and their practice of hoplite tactics, this study should help to illuminate those links between military organization, core societal structures, and ideology that surely existed not only at Sparta but also—albeit to varying degrees—in other Greek poleis.[11]

8. Both my terminology here and my reading of hoplite warfare builds on the claims of Cartledge (2001a: 153–54; cf. 1977: 12) concerning the impossibility of disassociating war from the society that practices it.

9. Cartledge 1977: 11; cf. Lazenby 1985: 40.

10. On the factors that made Sparta an atypical hoplite state, see Cartledge 1977: 27; 2001a: 165; Hodkinson 2006, esp. 133–34. Cf. Hanson 2000a: 211–12. For the view that Spartan military practices were consonant in many respects with those of other poleis, see Hodkinson 2006: 129; Humble 2006: 225.

11. As Raaflaub (1999: 138) notes, hoplite warfare "was only possible because the values and behavior codes involved were shared widely and reinforced regularly at interstate festivals and by the ethics promoted by the Panhellenic sanctuaries."

Hoplite Warfare: A "Crash" Course

Almost every aspect of hoplite warfare has, perhaps fittingly, constituted a scholarly battlefield, with much ink spilled on a host of issues, from the course of its development[12] to the nature of the *ōthismos*, the hoplite "shove" traditionally viewed as something akin to a scrum in a game of rugby.[13] The following necessarily basic overview of hoplite warfare tries to chart a middle course through such minefields in order to provide a fuller context for an examination of the Spartans' particular approach to hoplite organization, ethics, and tactics. Not all hoplite battles, of course, followed the game plan set out below; but, as Victor Hanson has shown, the hoplite encounter generally displayed a certain degree of regularity.[14]

The average hoplite was an amateur whose economic responsibilities limited the time he could devote to training or to prolonged campaigns.[15] This soldier, moreover, generally equipped himself with the standard panoply that consisted of helmet, corselet, greaves, spear and sword, and, finally, the big circular shield.[16] Thus protected and equipped, the hoplite was ready to answer his state's call to arms and would face battle that typically occurred during the summer, in daylight, and—whenever possible—on flat plains conducive to the massing and marching of heavily armed columns of men.[17] On the field, the hoplite would take his place with his fellow soldiers in a

12. While scholars like Schwartz (2009: 22, 103–46) have argued for relative consistency in hoplite weapons and tactics from ca. 750 to 338, others have posited a slow and steady evolution in Greek infantry tactics throughout the archaic and classical periods. See esp. van Wees 2000; 2004: 152, 166–84, 196.

13. For the traditional view of the *ōthismos* as a shoving match, see Pritchett 1985: 65–73; Hanson 2000b: 68–69, 152–59, 169–78; Luginbill 1994: 51–61; Lazenby 1991. Others have argued that hand-to-hand combat played an important role in the hoplite battle and that the phalanx was, accordingly, relatively open and fluid. See, e.g., Cawkwell 1978: 150–53; 1989; Krentz 1985b; 1994; Goldsworthy 1997; van Wees 2000: 131–32; 2004: 152, 172–91. Even though Schwartz (2009: 13–18, 183–200) views the *ōthismos* as a mass shove, he believes (199–200) that it probably occurred simultaneously with hand-to-hand combat with weapons.

14. Hanson 2000b: 185.

15. On the amateur nature of hoplite battle, see Hanson 2000b: 27–39.

16. See Hanson 1991; 2000b: 55–88; Anderson 1991; Schwartz 2009: 25–101.

17. As Hanson (2000a: 207) points out, hoplites later may have occasionally fought at sea as marines, in sieges, and on uneven ground, but "it was recognized that in these theaters they were not the decisive combatants, and that whole wars were decided only when two phalanxes of hoplite infantrymen met each other in daylight on level plains." On hoplites' activities beyond the phalanx, see Rawlings 2000.

phalanx, which could vary in size, length, and depth, though formations were normally at least eight ranks deep. While there is continued debate concerning the intervals between hoplites, Adrian Goldsworthy has cogently argued that hoplites likely began battle about three feet apart—a distance that would have provided them with a feeling of security from their comrades' proximity—and then inevitably spread further apart later, during the advance and charge.[18] The best hoplites would have been positioned in the front lines, where they would encounter the brunt of the action. Brave and experienced men also would have been stationed at the rear, where they would help to prevent panic, flight, and the dissolution of the phalanx. The best and most experienced men, moreover, were usually stationed on the right flank, the most dangerous and thus most honorable of positions, since it was the unshielded side of the phalanx.[19]

Thus arrayed, the phalanx would take the field, usually during the morning. The soldiers might then spend several hours in preparation—listening to the general's harangue, dressing their lines, and attending to the sacrifices and other rites that preceded battle—before advancing to meet the enemy, over distances ranging from a few hundred yards to more than a mile.[20] As it advanced, the phalanx had to maintain a fairly straight line and cohesion until it came closer to the enemy. At this point, it was normal for all except the Spartans to break into a run over the last hundred yards or so, likely as a result of nervous tension and the wish to get through the battle as quickly as possible.[21]

While scholars disagree on many aspects of the main battle that ensued, it generally seems to have proceeded as follows: (1) a charge; (2) a collision; (3) a combination of hand-to-hand combat with weapons and the shoving of shields against enemy shields, as individuals in the front lines tried to unbalance, topple, and kill their opponents, while those behind them simul-

18. Goldsworthy 1997: 16–17. For the more traditional view of the densely packed phalanx, with intervals of approximately three feet between hoplites, see Pritchett 1971: 144–54; Schwartz 2009: 157–67. For the view that the phalanx was far more open, with hoplites operating with intervals of at least six feet, see Krentz 1985b: 53–54; 1994: 46–47; Cawkwell 1989: 382–83; van Wees 2000: 128–30; 2004: 168–69, 185–87.

19. On the placement of soldiers, see Schwartz 2009: 172–73.

20. On the sacrifices and other religious rites that preceded battle, see Jameson 1991; Parker 2000. On the distances between armies, see Pritchett 1974: 157–60. As Hanson (2000b: 136–37) notes, phalanxes rarely failed to advance to meet the enemy.

21. On the run and the Spartans' exceptional slow advance into battle, see Hanson 2000b: 141–51. On the nervous tension at this point in the battle, see Hanson 2000b: 96–104, 135–51; Goldsworthy 1997: 11.

taneously offered support and prevented flight; (4) a "push," as the phalanx's collective efforts finally broke the enemy's formation; and (5) the eventual rout of the enemy.[22] Success depended on the phalanx's ability to preserve its formation—and thus on the ability of its individual soldiers to keep in step and maintain their position as much as possible—as it drove back the enemy's front ranks and opened a path through the opposing phalanx. When an entire army broke formation, the battle was over, since the difficulties involved in restoring the tight order of the classical phalanx made it highly unusual for both defeated and victorious troops to rally and charge again. The victorious troops typically would next engage in pursuit of the enemy, which could be long and heated—though not for the Spartans, who tended to keep their pursuits short, likely out of an interest in maintaining cohesion (cf. Th. 5.73.4).[23] Battle formally came to an end when the defeated side sent a herald requesting a truce for the return of its dead. The entire encounter, of which the actual battle may have been the shortest of several phases, might have ended quickly or lasted until dusk.[24]

Spartan Ideology, the Upbringing, and the Spectacle of Cooperative Sociability

As I have pointed out above, such set-piece battles were relatively rare during the classical period, even for the Spartans, who regularly engaged in other forms of conflict resolution and were renowned practitioners of the guile that so often figured in Greek warfare.[25] Particularly infamous was the series of ruses that enabled the Agiad king Cleomenes I and his army to kill approximately six thousand Argives in the battle of Sepeia and the massacre that followed it in 494 (Hdt. 6.76–80; cf. 7.148.2). The same kinds of tricks came into play in the sneak attack on the Athenian fleet at Aegospotami

22. I have based this reconstruction of the main battle, particularly my understanding of the responsibilities of both the individuals in the front lines and the men in the rear ranks, on Goldsworthy 1997. On the front ranks' use of shields to unbalance their enemies, see also Krentz 1985b: 56; 1994: 48–49; van Wees 2000: 131; 2004: 190. On the final "push," see van Wees 2000: 132; 2004: 190–91.

23. For examples of long pursuits, see Hdt. 6.113.2; Th. 1.62.6, 2.79.6; X. *HG* 2.4.6. See Schwartz 2009: 214.

24. On the duration of battles, see Pritchett 1985: 46–51; Schwartz 2009: 201–25. For the likely brevity of the actual battle, see Schwartz 2009: 211–15.

25. On the role that deception played in Greek warfare, see Krentz 2000.

in 405 executed by the Spartan admiral Lysander, who is credited with the saying, "Where the lion's skin will not reach, one must sew on the skin of a fox" (Plu. *Lys.* 7.4).[26]

The Spartans, however, demonstrated an unusual degree of adherence to and skill in hoplite tactics. Their supremacy in the set-piece battle down to 371 is perhaps not surprising when one remembers that eligibility for hoplite service was extended to all Spartan citizens between the ages of twenty and sixty, not just to the wealthiest thirty to fifty percent of citizens as typical in other poleis. Furthermore, Sparta's citizens were not only liable for military service throughout most of their adult lives but also were available for training year-round, thanks to the agricultural labor provided by their helots. The citizens of other poleis, as we have seen above, had far fewer opportunities to train, because of their need to supply their own subsistence (cf. Th. 1.141.3–4).[27]

As Xenophon makes clear in his *Constitution of the Lacedaemonians*, the Spartans also approached hoplite warfare with an unparalleled attention to detail that gave them an edge over their opponents (12.7). Among those practices that merit Xenophon's attention are the Spartans' highly organized levy of specified age-classes of infantry, cavalry, and even handicraftsmen (11.2); their centrally organized baggage train (11.2, 13.4); and their systematization of the military uniform, which included a red cloak and a bronze shield (11.3; cf. 13.8). In addition, Xenophon follows Thucydides in his emphasis on the Spartans' uniquely stratified system of military units and the corresponding hierarchical chain of command, which facilitated communication among the ranks and ensured that each man understood his place and responsibilities (11.4–10; cf. Th. 5.66.3–4). This organization, which gave the Spartans an unusual degree of control over the progress of the phalanx, allowed them to meet enemy attacks from the front, back, or either side (11.8–10). It also enabled the Spartans to execute difficult maneuvers, such as the "forward bend" (*epikampē*), the "countermarch" (*exeligmos*), and the

26. All translations are my own unless noted otherwise. Cf. X. *Ages.* 1.17; *HG* 3.1.8; Pl. *R.* 547d–8a; Plu. *Mor.* 238f. On the Spartans' expertise in guile, see Powell 1989: 178–79; Krentz 2000: 183–99; Lendon 2005: 82–83, 85–89; Ruzé 2006. We should remember, however, that treachery was a key component of fifth-century Athenian constructions of Spartan character. See Bradford 1994; Millender 1996: 182–83, 185–208, 320–27; Hesk 2000: 26–40, 64–84.

27. See nn. 10 and 15.

"back wheel" (*anastrophē*).[28] Equally striking, according to Xenophon, was the disciplined regimen that the soldiers followed while on campaign (12.5–7) and the Spartans' systematic performance of sacrifices throughout their expeditions (13.2–5).[29] When one adds the Spartans' careful delegation of responsibilities for everything from the king's commissariat to the allocation of booty (13.1, 11), it is no wonder that Xenophon viewed the Spartans as the only professional practitioners of the craft of war (τεχνίτας τῶν πολιμικῶν) amid a sea of amateurs (13.5).[30]

Xenophon may be a problematic source, given his reputed laconism, but his description of the Spartans' expertise accords with other ancient depictions of the Spartans as far more focused on military preparation and training than their fellow Greeks. Thucydides, for example, has the Athenian leader Pericles provide a hostile portrait of the Spartans as a people excessively preoccupied with military training (2.38–41.1; cf. 4.33.2). Aristotle later depicts Spartan education as wholly oriented toward war, while Isocrates has the Spartan prince Archidamus compare the Spartans' *politeia* to a military camp.[31]

We should obviously be wary of such tendentious treatments of Spartan militarism, since they are only part of a much more complex ancient portrait of Sparta's approach to war.[32] The ancient sources, however, make it clear that all Spartan males, with the exception of the hereditary kings (cf. Plu. *Ages.* 1.1, 3), received a rigorous upbringing that not only socialized them into all aspects of adult citizen life but also prepared them for the warfare that was

28. Cf. X. *HG* 4.2.20, 4.3.18, 6.5.18–19. See Lazenby 1991: 103–4; cf. 1985: 26–30. See also Goldsworthy 1997: 8–9. On the organization of the Spartan army, see Lazenby 1985: esp. 5–19, 41–62, 68–70, 76–77, 80; van Wees 2004: 243–49; Hawkins 2011.

29. On the Spartans' meticulous attention to the religious observances connected with war, see van Wees 2004: 119–20.

30. See also Hdt. 7.102–4; Plu. *Pel.* 23.3. On the professional nature of Spartan military practice, see Hodkinson 2006: 129–30. For a less positive reading of Xenophon's treatment of Spartan military practices, see Humble 2006: esp. 227–29. Humble argues that Xenophon's praise of the Spartan system includes a critique of its conservatism and inadaptability.

31. Arist. *Pol.* 1271b2–6, 1324b7–9, 1333b5–23, 1338b25–38; Isoc. 6.81. Cf. Pl. *Lg.* 666e–667a, 688a; *La.* 182e–183a; Isoc. 11.17–18; 12.202, 216–17. On ancient treatments of Sparta as unusually oriented toward warfare, see Ducat 2006a: 35–67, 139–46. See also Hodkinson 2006: 115–29.

32. Cf. Hodkinson 2006. For the more traditional view that Sparta was almost like an armed camp, see, e.g., Hooker 1980: 135; Cartledge 2001a: 165.

such a central part of their lives.[33] At the age of seven (cf. Plu. *Lyc.* 16.4), the Spartan male was taken from his home, housed in barracks away from his family, organized in a group with others of his age-class, and launched into a comprehensive state-organized system of education and initiation rites that would last until he was thirty years old.[34]

Our fullest sources on this process of enculturation, Xenophon's *Constitution of the Lacedaemonians* and Plutarch's *Life of Lycurgus*, suggest that the first part of the training emphasized practice to endure the physical hardships that a boy would later face as a hoplite soldier—especially fatigue, hunger, and cold.[35] As he advanced in his education, the Spartan boy became subject to an increasingly demanding regimen of physical exercise under the vigilant eyes of his elders, who, according to Plutarch, encouraged him to contend with his age-mates in order to assess his character.[36] At the age of twenty or twenty-one, the now young adult Spartiate, or *hēbōn* (X. *Lac.* 4.1), would be elected to one of Sparta's common messes, or *syssitia*, and thereby became a full-fledged citizen warrior.[37] His education continued, however, and was now marked by intense rivalry, since this was the age-group from which the Spartans selected the three hundred *hippeis* (X. *Lac.* 4.2–6), an elite force of infantry that, among other things, served as a royal bodyguard during battle.[38]

At the same time that the educational system encouraged competition, it continued to check personal ambitions and desires. Indeed, the enculturation process fostered a sense of collective enterprise and communal responsibility through the age-class system, the close ties that the Spartan male forged with his messmates and in his pederastic relationships, and, finally, his enforced cohabitation with his age-mates until the age of thirty,

---

33. Cf. Cartledge 1977: 17. On the exception of the royal heirs, see Cartledge 1987: 23–24, 32, 104. On the multiple functions of the upbringing, see Ducat 2006a, esp. 139–222. While Hodkinson (2006: 139–40) rightly notes both the important ritualistic elements of the upbringing and the absence of evidence for specialized military training, he perhaps too strongly downplays the military aspect of the Spartan educational system.

34. On the structure and organization of this comprehensive system of public education, see Ducat 2006a: 69–117.

35. Cf. X. *Lac.* 2.1–6; Plu. *Lyc.* 16.6–7, 17.3–5.

36. See Plu. *Lyc.* 16.5; cf. 17.1; X. *Lac.* 3.2.

37. On the *hēbōntes*' participation in battle and, thus, necessary membership in Sparta's *syssitia*, see X. *Lac.* 4.7; *HG* 2.4.32, 3.4.23, 4.5.14. See also Cartledge 1977: 16–17; Ducat 2006a: 101, 104–5.

38. On this rivalry, see Ducat 2006a: 102–3. On the *hippeis*, see Figueira 2006.

even if he was married (cf. Plu. *Lyc.* 15.3–5).[39] Perhaps even more important was the expectation that, throughout this process, the young Spartan male would internalize respect for and obedience to all of the members of the community—including older boys—who were put in command of his education.[40] As Noreen Humble has shown, Xenophon views obedience as the most important military and civic virtue inculcated by the upbringing, and he repeatedly emphasizes the constant supervision and threats of punishment that enforced such obedience.[41]

The upbringing, in sum, made Spartan boys physically fit for the rigors of war, simultaneously promoted competition among them and socialized them to be part of a pack, and instilled in them those character traits deemed essential for success in hoplite warfare: self-discipline, respect for authority, and, most important, obedience. Some scholars, following in the footsteps of ancient authors like Plato (*Lg.* 633a–c, 666e) and Isocrates (6.81), argue that Sparta's educational system—along with the very social structure and political system that it supported—was inextricably linked with its military organization.[42] This school of thought, in fact, views Spartan institutions and practices as militarily oriented in origin, designed primarily to maintain control over the subjugated helot populations of Laconia and Messenia.[43]

Whether or not one ascribes to this view of Sparta's development and the link between Sparta's military organization and suppression of the helots, the Spartans' extensive military training and acquisition of military experience through the actual practice of hoplite warfare would have well prepared them to respond to any security threats, including those posed by the helots.

39. Cartledge 1977: 16–17. Ducat (2006a: 104, 109) questions Plutarch's account of the ban on cohabitation with one's wife until the age of thirty. On the pederastic relationships, see X. *Lac.* 2.12–14; Plu. *Lyc.* 17.1, 18.4. See also Cartledge 2001b; Ducat 2006a, esp. 91–93, 107–8, 164–69, 196–201. Ducat (164–69) argues that these relationships were an institutionalized element of the educational system and created another link between boys and the larger community.

40. Cf. X. *Lac.* 2.2, 10–11; 6.1–2; Plu. *Lyc.* 16.5-6, 17.1–3.

41. Humble 2006. See X. *Lac.* 2.2, 8, 10–11, 14; 3.2–3; 4.3–6; 5.2; 6.1–2; 8. Cf. X. *HG* 7.1.8. On the Spartans' emphasis on the inculcation of obedience, see also Ducat 2006a: 164; Lendon 2005: 75–76. See, however, Millender 2002, for the argument that a number of fifth- and fourth-century works provide a negative treatment of Spartan obedience as artificial, fragile, and reliant on external discipline—in contrast with the internalized lawfulness that Athens' democracy engendered in its citizens.

42. See, e.g., Lazenby 1985: 63–80; Ducat 1999; Cartledge 2001a: 165.

43. Cf. Ste. Croix 1972: 89–94; Finley 1986: 177; Hooker 1980: 135, 141; Cartledge 1977: 27; 1987: 160–79; 2001a: 165; 2002: 134–35. Hodkinson (2006) questions this traditional view of Spartan society.

It is also easy to see how well the Lacedaemonians' educational practices and philosophy—especially their promotion of communality, rigorous discipline, and valuation of obedience—mapped onto hoplite organization, tactics, and ethics in general. Together, these foundational elements of Spartan society would have promoted the cohesion that was essential to any hoplite phalanx and that, according to Xenophon, allowed the Spartans to execute difficult maneuvers with ease (*Lac.* 11.8–10).[44]

Both the training for and performance of hoplite warfare, however, enjoyed a reciprocal relationship with core Spartan institutions, practices, and ideology, especially the intertwined values of egalitarianism and cooperation that some scholars have associated with the development of hoplite warfare in Sparta and the other poleis that practiced hoplite tactics. There is, of course, continued debate on the issue of the "hoplite revolution" and the link that scholars have long posited between the development of hoplite warfare and the rise of more broadly based and egalitarian citizen communities in archaic Greece.[45] Even if one downplays this relationship between hoplite warfare and Greek constitutional developments, both the Spartans' educational system and their performance of hoplite battle itself would have bolstered the ideology of the *Homoioi* ("peers") and the communal solidarity that underpinned the Spartan *politeia,* which emerged from the mid-seventh-century "Lycurgan" reforms.[46] As Stephen Hodkinson has noted, several classical sources attribute this "deep-rooted ethic of co-operative sociability" to "the willing collaboration of the elite in establishing the uniformity and discipline of Spartan life" (cf. Th. 1.6.4; X. *Lac.* 8.1–2).[47] The resulting civic *homonoia* (concord) between the classes, which shaped

44. See n. 28. Cf. Lazenby 1985: 4.

45. For the traditional view of the relationship between Greek constitutional developments and hoplite tactics, see, e.g., Cartledge 1977: 18–24; 2001a. For doubts concerning this relationship, see Salmon 1977: 93–101; Raaflaub 1997; 1999: 129–41; van Wees 2002: 61–82. However, van Wees (2004: 196, 233–35) argues for a similar link between sociopolitical change and the development of the "classical" phalanx in the late sixth and early fifth centuries.

46. Raaflaub (1999: 137) argues that the phalanx generally bolstered the values of solidarity and discipline. For a contrary view, see Lendon (2005: 403), who argues that "if the phalanx plays a political role in Greece, it is not in the incubation of a middling, cooperative ethos, it is in the diffusion of aristocratic ideals downward in society."

47. Hodkinson 2006: 128–29, at 128; cf. 2005: 258–63. While Hodkinson (128) views this ethic as non-military in nature, I argue that it underlay Spartan military organization and forged bonds between the Spartans' military practices and social relations.

Sparta's constitutional and social arrangements,[48] helped to curtail the internal conflict that apparently plagued early Sparta. It also ushered in Sparta's famed *eunomia*, which Cartledge has aptly defined as "orderly obedience to the agreed rules" (cf. Hdt. 1.65; Th. 1.18–19; Plu. *Lyc.* 2.3, 3.5, 5–13).[49]

Granted, the "Lycurgan" reforms never entailed a true leveling of Spartan society. The ideology that had developed in tandem with these reforms and that promoted uniformity and the prioritization of collective interests over private ones in its creation of the *Homoioi* ultimately proved incapable of quashing the aristocratic values of wealth and birth and the profound influence that patronage exercised on all levels of Spartan society.[50] The educational system, which was marked by continuous competition among the boys, also contributed to the creation of a Spartan elite.[51] Nevertheless, the key elements of the educational process were essentially the same for all Spartiate males besides the royal heirs, such as the one garment allotted per year to the boys and the severely restricted diet (X. *Lac.* 2.4–6; cf. Plu. *Lyc.* 16.4-7, 17.3–5). Equally egalitarian was the ability of all citizens both to punish the boys for misconduct and to order them to do whatever the citizens deemed good (X. *Lac.* 2.10–11).[52]

Most important, this educational system occurred under the gaze of the entire society and thereby "functioned like a continuously recurring *spectacle*—one of many offered by the city to its citizens."[53] In this case, the spectacle was one of cooperative sociability, witnessed over and over again by the many members of the community who supervised the educational process (cf. X. *Lac.* 4.1–2). Indeed, as both Xenophon and Plutarch make clear, the enculturation of future soldier-citizens was subject to intense surveillance beyond that of the ephors (X. *Lac.* 4.3–6; cf. 3.3) and the elite "warden" (*paidonomos*) and his "staff" of youths of varying age who oversaw the educa-

48. Cf. esp. X. *Lac.* 5.3, 6.3–4; Arist. *Pol.* 1263a26–40, 1270b21–26, 1294b19–29.

49. Cartledge 2001a: 162.

50. See esp. Hodkinson 1983; 2000.

51. On the important role that competition played in Spartan education and the educational system's aim to create a Spartan elite, see Hodkinson 1983: 248–49; Cartledge 1987: 27–29; Ducat 2006a: 171–75, 217–18.

52. On the egalitarian nature of the educational system, see Ducat 2006a: 169–71. Ducat argues (170–71) that a boy's education also had a private component and that it was this aspect of the education that was highly variable, since it was dependent on the individual family's status and means.

53. Ducat 2006a: 161–62. Powell (1989) persuasively argues that the Spartans were masterful manipulators of visual images.

tion of the boys (X. *Lac.* 2.2; 11; cf. Plu. *Lyc.* 16.5, 17.1–2, 18.3). Other participants included the boys' relations (X. *Lac.* 3.3), lovers (Plu. *Lyc.* 18.4), and even any citizen who happened to be on the scene (X. *Lac.* 2.10; cf. 4.6).[54]

The Battlefield as Spectacle: The Spatial Performance of Spartan Social Codes and Values

Several accounts of hoplite battles suggest that the Spartan hoplite phalanx that took the field would have provided an even more striking spectacle of egalitarianism and cooperation, both for the Lacedaemonians themselves and for their opponents. The ancient sources do not provide a clear picture of the Spartans' allocation of arms and armor. They do, however, suggest that all Spartans took the field garbed in the same basic costume (regardless of rank, wealth, or political status) and equipped with arms and armor supplied by the state from a civic arsenal—most important, the famous bronze shields emblazoned with lambdas.[55] All Spartan hoplites sported short cloaks that were dyed red, perhaps because of the color's magical properties or ability to disguise bloodstains.[56] An equally important element of the Spartan war costume was the famous long hair that served as a marker of adulthood and inclusion into the ranks of the *Homoioi*. It was thought to inspire terror in the enemy, and the Spartans would thus comb their hair in preparation for battle.[57] This uniformity in Spartan military gear may help to explain the Eurypontid king Agesilaus II's ability to groom his phalanx to look like a "solid mass of bronze and scarlet" when it met the enemy on the plain of Coronea in 394 (*Ages.* 2.7).[58]

Thus arrayed, the Spartan phalanx would demonstrate cooperative sociability at work, as Plutarch makes clear in his account of the Spartans' advance into battle (*Lyc.* 22.3; cf. *Mor.* 238b): "It was a sight at once awesome and terrifying as the Spartans marched in step to the pipe, creating no gap in

54. Cf. X. *Lac.* 6.1–2; Plu. *Lyc.* 17.1. See Ducat 2006a: 159–64.

55. For these shields, see Eup. 359 Kock; X. *Lac.* 11.3. Cf. X. *HG* 4.4.10. Here, again, Sparta may have departed from the norm in its central distribution of arms and armor from a civic arsenal. See Cartledge 1977: 27 and n. 110; 2001a: 165.

56. For the red cloaks, see Ar. *Lys.* 1138–41; X. *Lac.* 11.3; Plu. *Mor.* 238d, f.

57. For the famous long hair, see Hdt. 7.208.3, 209.3; X. *Lac.* 11.3, 13.8; Arist. *Rh.* 1367a27–31; Plu. *Lyc.* 22.1. Cf. Hdt. 1.82.8; Plu. *Lys.* 1; *Mor.* 189e, 228f, 230b. See also Cartledge 1977: 15; David 1992: 15–16.

58. See n. 102.

their line of battle nor suffering any disturbance in their hearts, but calmly and cheerfully approaching the confrontation in time to the music." While Plutarch is a late source, his account accords with Thucydides' description of the Spartans' advance against the Argives and their allies at the battle of Mantinea in 418. After encouraging one another man to man, singing war songs possibly inspired by Tyrtaeus' poetry (cf. Ath. 14.630f), and calling on their comrades to remember what they knew as brave men, the troops advanced slowly and to the music of the many flute players stationed among them, not for religious reasons, but in order that they might "proceed evenly by keeping in step and not break their formation, as large armies tend to do during their advance" (5.69.2–70). The Spartans' ability to function as one organism and to maintain the integrity of the phalanx was particularly on display at the battle of Nemea in 394. According to Xenophon, the Spartan troops halted to perform a sacrifice a mere two hundred yards from their opponents before they charged, wheeling their right wing inward in order to encircle the Athenians.[59] Marching past the routed Athenians, the Spartans—whose lines remained intact—next charged the Argives, Corinthians, and Thebans who were returning from their pursuit of the Spartans' defeated allies. The Spartans struck these enemies on their unprotected right sides (*HG* 4.2.19–22).

The exiled Eurypontid king Demaratus, in Herodotus' account of his dialogue with the Persian king Xerxes before the battle of Thermopylae in 480, suggests that it was both solidarity and steadfastness that made the Spartans such superb soldiers (7.104.4–5):

> So it is with the Lacedaemonians: fighting singly, they are no worse than any other men, but fighting together, they are the best soldiers among all men. For although free, they are not free in every respect. Law is master over them, and they fear it far more than your subjects fear you. Whatever this master commands, they do; and its command is always the same: never to retreat in battle, however great the odds, but always to remain at their posts and either conquer or die.[60]

Of course, Herodotus' portrait of the Spartan phalanx is idealized, both here and in his later description of the Lacedaemonians' refusal to give ground

59. Cf. Goldsworthy 1997: 9.

60. On Demaratus' praise for Spartan solidarity, see van Wees 2004: 180. For a more negative reading of Demaratus' praise as another testament to the Spartans' dependence on external discipline, see Millender 2002, 33–36.

during the battle of Thermopylae in 480 (7.225.3). Moreover, as Hans van Wees has pointed out, no Spartan army stood its ground to the death after that last heroic stand at Thermopylae, including Pausanias' army at Plataea in 479. Although the Spartans ultimately proved victorious at Plataea, Herodotus portrays Pausanias and his forces as irresolute, fearful, and disobedient to the *nomos* that, according to Demaratus, commanded them to remain at their posts (9.46–58). The infamous surrender of the Spartan force on Sphacteria in 425 particularly dispelled the belief that the Spartans would remain in position and fight to the bitter end (Th. 4.38).[61]

Thucydides, however, claims that the Sphacteria episode caused much surprise among the Greeks, who had believed that no form of compulsion could induce the Spartans to surrender their arms rather than fight to the death (Th. 4.40). He and other sources also suggest that both the insistence on keeping one's place in the line and the preference of death to surrender were key elements of the Spartan military code, whether or not the Lacedaemonians could always translate these ideals into practice on the field.[62] Most important is the oath—part of the oath sworn at Plataea (Tod II, 204, ll. 25–28)—that the Spartans took not to desert their officers and to remain on the battlefield unless their commanders led them away.[63]

Herodotus provides an example of almost absurd adherence to this principle in his treatment of the Spartan regimental commander Amompharetus. According to Herodotus, Amompharetus refused to change position even though the order for this shift came from his superiors, because he believed that it entailed a shameful withdrawal from the enemy (9.53–57.1). Thucydides likewise has the Spartan general Brasidas, in his critique of the Illyrians' approach to war, emphasize the importance of holding one's position and maintaining battle order (4.126.5). Xenophon later records Spartiates fighting to the bitter end in his accounts of the death of Anaxibius in Asia Minor in 389 (*HG* 4.8.38–39) and that of Mnassipus at Corcyra in 371 (*HG* 6.2.22–23).[64] As we have seen above, Xenophon's description of the complex maneuvers executed by the Spartan forces at the battle of Nemea in 394 and the preservation of their phalanx's integrity even after their victory provides a particularly vivid picture of the Spartans' commitment to the maintenance of their formation (*HG* 4.2.19–22).

---

61. Van Wees 2004: 193. Cf. Lazenby 1985: 83, 122. On the Spartans' fear and repeated changes in position in the run up to the battle of Plataea, see Millender 2002: 42–45.

62. Cf. Lendon 2005: 72–77.

63. On this oath, see van Wees 2004: 98, 243–44.

64. See Humble 2006: 227.

According to Lendon, it was the Spartans' superiority in military obedience that enabled them to excel in what he deems a contest in "passive courage"—the holding of one's position—waged at once by individual hoplites, the larger phalanxes that comprised them, and the poleis that deployed them. He even goes so far as to argue that for the Spartans obedience constituted yet another site of competition: "The Spartans made a contest of obedience to authority. . . . At Sparta obedience was a contest in excellence: it was this competitiveness that made the Spartans the most obedient of the Greeks."[65] The Lacedaemonians' obedience was indeed legendary; it was especially on display in the epitaph over the Spartan dead at Thermopylae (Hdt. 7.228.2): "O Stranger, go tell the Lacedaemonians that we lie here, obedient to their commands."

While Lendon sees this epitaph as another testimony to the Spartans' competition in obedience—with the dead outdoing their live compatriots, obedience was neither an end in itself nor simply another locus of that primordial competitiveness that he links to all Greek military developments.[66] Rather, obedience in Sparta functioned as a means to a very important end—the cooperative sociability that promoted cohesion on the field and socio-political stability at home. Xenophon, in fact, positions obedience at the very center of the Spartan *politeia.* For him, obedience defined the relationship of the Spartans to the "Lycurgan" laws (*Lac.* 1.2, 8.1). These laws, in turn, promoted a sense of collective responsibility and a common—albeit fictional—way of life (*Lac.* 5.1) through the privileging of civic over family and other personal ties, the mandated sharing of certain possessions in specified situations, restrictions on the making and possession of money, and the creation of common educational and social experiences.[67] As Xenophon makes clear, it was obedience to the laws that especially contributed to the cooperative sociability at the heart of Spartan *eunomia* (*Lac.* 8), which may explain why disobedience to the laws was considered not only unlawful but even impious (*Lac.* 8.5).[68]

Xenophon does not specify the penalties that would be meted out to those who violated these laws. He provides a detailed discussion, however,

65. Lendon 2005: 45–77, at 76.

66. Lendon 2005: 76.

67. On the promotion of civic over personal ties, see X. *Lac.* 1.6–10, 2.2, 3.3, 5.2, 5.5–7, 6.1–2. On the sharing of servants and certain possessions, see X. *Lac.* 6.3–4. On the restrictions on economic activity, see X. *Lac.* 7. On the common educational and social experiences, see X. *Lac.* 2–5. See also n. 47.

68. See n. 49.

of the punishments that awaited those Spartans deemed guilty of cowardice, or *kakia;* and he thus signals the Spartans' particular valuation of obedience in the military sphere.[69] According to Xenophon, the Spartans were conditioned to prefer death to the disgraceful life that awaited the coward, or *kakos* (*Lac.* 9.1–2, 6). The long list of dishonors he provides explains why the coward's fate was so ignominious (*Lac.* 9.3–5). The coward was, first and foremost, excluded from participation in the *syssition* and the gymnasium, two key loci of Spartan socio-political activity, as well as communal athletic and cultural events. In addition, the coward was constantly forced to defer to other citizens—even his juniors, was not allowed to contract marriages for himself or for his female relatives, and was forbidden both to walk about looking cheerful and to imitate honorable men, on pain of being beaten by his betters.

Tyrtaeus earlier had noted the evils that afflicted such cowards—whom he deems "tremblers," or *tresantes* (fr. 11.14–16 West), as did Herodotus in his account of the abuse and dishonor that the Spartan Aristodemus suffered at home as a result of his survival of the battle of Thermopylae (7.229–31). Aristodemus managed to avoid battle either because of ophthalmia or because of delaying tactics. No Spartan, accordingly, would light a fire for him or converse with him, and he endured the shame of being called "Aristodemus the Trembler" (7.231). While another survivor, Pantites, dealt with the dishonor that he met at home by hanging himself (Hdt. 7.232), Aristodemus tried to expiate his shame by hurling himself against the enemy at Plataea in 479 (9.71.2–4).[70]

In his account of the Spartans who surrendered at Sphacteria in 425, Thucydides claims that the authorities initially left these men in possession of their civic rights but then deprived them of their right to hold office or to buy or sell anything (5.34.2). The later restoration of these men to their former status (5.34.2) probably reflects the Spartans' growing anxieties about *oliganthrōpia*—that is, their shrinking pool of manpower—rather than a lessening of the disgrace that cowardice entailed.[71] Plutarch suggests that the

69. For Xenophon's emphasis on punishments for cowardice, see Humble 2006: 225–26. On the Spartans' punishment of cowardice, see esp. Ducat 2006b.

70. On Aristodemus, see Ducat 2005; 2006b: 34–38.

71. See Lazenby 1985: 122–23; Ducat 2006b: 47. On Spartan *oliganthrōpia*, see esp. Figueira 1986; Cartledge 2002: 263–72. As Ducat (2006b: 32–33) notes, there were probably several factors behind the Spartans' seeming change in policy toward the survivors of Sphacteria and Leuctra, including the difficulties and political dangers involved in the socio-political exclusion of hundreds of Spartiates. Cf. Ducat 2006b: 38–49. Ducat, how-

same demographic concerns, together with fear of a possible revolution, led to Agesilaus II's temporary suspension in 371 of the sanctions meted to cowards in the case of the runaways from Leuctra (*Ages.* 30.2–4; cf. *Mor.* 191c, 214b). Nevertheless, it appears that the Spartans at this time still considered *tresantes* to be worthy of a variety of serious political and social penalties (*Ages.* 30.3):

> In fact, not only are these people excluded from holding any office, but it is considered improper to give a spouse to one of them, or to receive one through him. Anyone who encounters them is free to strike them if he so chooses. They have to resign themselves to going about in coarse and dirty clothing, to wearing patched and dull-coloured mantles, to shave only part of the beard, leaving the rest to grow.[72]

We may not trust every detail provided by our sources, but the picture that emerges about the Spartans' penalties for cowardice is striking in several regards.[73] First, the punishments did not take place while the troops were still in the field; rather, they constituted a comprehensive form of public shaming that took place at home and before the eyes of the entire community.[74] Second, all Spartans were expected to participate in the punishment of cowardice, whether through the Assembly's debate and vote on the punishment of those deemed guilty of this offense,[75] the active social and physical humiliation of the "trembler," or the more passive shunning of the coward on the street, in the gymnasium, and in the *syssition.* Particularly key are the gymnasium and the *syssition* as sites of social exclusion, given the fundamen-

---

ever, seems to go too far in his hypothesis (33; cf. 42) that the sanction imposed on the Spartiates captured on Sphacteria was "pretty much a formality."

72. For this translation, see Ducat 2006b: 6.

73. One may question elements of both Xenophon's and Plutarch's accounts of the punishments for cowardice. Nevertheless, the relative abundance and range of evidence on this aspect of Spartan society argues against the possibility, raised by Ducat (2006: 49), that the "trembler"—as presented by Xenophon (*Lac.* 9)—was simply another element of the Spartan mirage, an ideological screen designed to hide the Spartans' incapacity to make their citizens respect the "Lycurgan" laws.

74. As Forsdyke (2008) points out, public humiliation performed before and with the active participation of the entire community served as an extra-legal form of punishment elsewhere in the Greek world, including classical Athens.

75. On the Assembly's role in the punishment of cowardice at Sparta, see Ducat 2006b: 33–44, 46.

tal role that these communal institutions played in both the enculturation of Sparta's soldier-citizens and the promotion of the cooperative sociability that bound the *Homoioi* together. The punishment of cowardice in battle, accordingly, constituted yet another public spectacle provided by Sparta for its citizens, for cowardice itself constituted a communal offense. Indeed, in his praise of the "Lycurgan" system's cultivation of public virtue, Xenophon treats cowardice as a crime against the entire polis and thus deserving of particularly heavy penalties (*Lac.* 10.6).[76]

By "cowardice," Xenophon and the other authors mentioned above surely do not mean fear of battle.[77] Consider, for example, Pantites, who, according to Herodotus, missed the battle of Thermopylae because he had been sent to Thessaly with a message (7.232). His later disgrace and suicide only make sense if we understand his cowardice as a failure to support his fellow hoplites in battle. This same concern with not letting one's team down may explain the Spartan Eurytus' insistence on being led into the thick of the battle at Thermopylae despite the inflammation of the eyes that he suffered along with the aforementioned Aristodemus (Hdt. 7.229).[78]

The Spartans' valuation of group solidarity becomes clear in their refusal to award public honor to Aristodemus as one of the most distinguished fighters at Plataea, despite Herodotus' belief that this Spartiate had shown great courage and despite the Spartans' admission that he had performed great deeds (9.71.2–4). As Herodotus makes clear, the Spartans faulted Aristodemus' selfishness, manifested in his primary concern to retrieve his lost honor. In his desire to die before the eyes of his comrades rather than among them, Aristodemus abandoned his place in the line (9.71.3: ἐκλείποντα τὴν τάξιν), thereby endangering his fellow hoplites, particularly the man to his left.[79] What ultimately mattered was the solidarity of the team, that is, the

76. See Humble 2006: 226.

77. Ducat (2006b: 10) notes that "it is not easy to arrive at an abstract definition of cowardice; it is an entirely relative notion and one that depends very largely on circumstances." He argues (16) that flight, the abandonment of one's shield, capitulation, the desertion of one's post, and the abandonment of the king were actions that constituted or aggravated the crime of "cowardice."

78. Lazenby (1991: 106–7) argues that the same ethic may account for the suicide of the lone Spartan survivor from the "Battle of Champions" (Hdt. 1.82.8).

79. Lazenby 1985: 56; 1991: 103. Cf. Ducat 2006b: 37; Schwartz 2009: 139. Van Wees (2004: 182, 297 n. 53) less persuasively argues that the Spartans regarded such charging ahead of one's comrades as acceptable and that they refused to reward Aristodemus because he had been suicidal rather than truly brave. Cf. Cawkwell 1989: 388. See also Lendon's claim (2005: 51) that the Spartans punished Aristodemus for failing "in the hoplites' competition in passive courage." While Lendon rightly notes the Spartans' concern with hold-

phalanx, which depended on individual Spartiates' commitment to their positions and to their fellow hoplites.

Tyrtaeus reflects this cooperative ethic in his exhortation to Sparta's young warriors "to fight remaining in place beside one another" (fr. 10.15 West: μάχεσθε παρ' ἀλλήλοισι μένοντες) and in his claim that the soldier who speaks encouraging words to the man beside whom he is stationed is the man "who proves himself good in war" (fr. 12.19–20 West).[80] Most explicit, perhaps, is Tyrtaeus' description of the benefits that come from adherence to this social code and the dangers entailed by its violation (fr. 11.11–14 West):

> Those who remain in place beside each other dare
> to advance into the fray and the van,
> die in lesser numbers, and save the army behind them;
> but when men flee in fear, all valor is lost.

Two centuries later, Thucydides' Brasidas likewise emphasizes the importance of teamwork in his aforementioned critique of his Illyrian enemies, whose way of fighting, with every man his own master, gives each a good excuse to save his own skin (4.126.5).[81]

The cohesion of the troops on the field would have reflected and, more important, bolstered the communal sensibility of the Spartiates at home, which became increasingly undermined by the structural changes that Spartan society experienced throughout the classical period, especially during and following the Peloponnesian War. Particularly pernicious were the increasing valuation and concentration of wealth as well as the growing competition for foreign commands and other important posts. Both trends exacerbated the inherent social, economic, and political fractures in Spartan society that the mid-seventh-century "Lycurgan" settlement had helped to temper. The greater play given to personal ambitions and desires, together with the increasing opportunities to realize them, undermined solidarity within the citizen body and thus threatened to pull apart the very fabric of Sparta's socio-political order.[82]

The successful performance of hoplite battle not only had tremendous

---

ing one's position (51, 72), he ignores Herodotus' focus on Aristodemus' selfishness, the primary reason why he abandoned his rank.

80. Lazenby 1991: 106–7; cf. 1985: 4.

81. Lendon (2005: 53), however, sees in Brasidas' speech another testament to the competitive nature of hoplite warfare.

82. On the various developments that eventually contributed to the breakdown of the solidarity of the Spartan citizen body, see Hodkinson 1993.

potential to counter threats to the ideology of the *Homoioi*. Victory in pitched battle could also demonstrate tangible political results, such as the reinforcement of the hereditary dyarchy that stood at the head of Sparta's socio-political order and that faced numerous challenges during the classical period.[83] Hoplite warfare's function as a political stabilizer becomes particularly clear in Thucydides' account of the troubled reign of the Eurypontid king Agis II, who incurred tremendous unpopularity because of his conclusion of a four-month truce with Argos in 418. Particularly noteworthy is Thucydides' focus on the unilateral nature of Agis' action (5.60.1–2). This assault on the Spartans' valued communal sensibility, compounded by the Argive coalition's capture of Orchomenus, led the enraged Spartans to threaten to pull down his house and to fine him ten thousand drachmae (5.63.2). In the end, the Spartans punished the Eurypontid king by passing an unprecedented law that stipulated the election of ten citizens to act as advisers to Agis. Without their authority, Agis was not empowered to lead an army out of the city—a serious diminishment of this king's hereditary role as military leader (5.63.4).[84]

In his account of the battle of Mantinea in 418, Thucydides suggests that Agis believed that he could atone for his errors with success on the battlefield (5.63.3) and perhaps too actively courted a pitched battle with Argos and its allies (5.65.2). When the two sides finally met on the field, Agis' planned rehabilitation almost came to naught. His decision to move certain regiments to the left to make his line level with that of the Mantineans met with disobedience from his polemarchs—perhaps another sign of his loss of authority—and created a hole, through which the enemy poured and overwhelmed the Spartan forces on the left wing. However, the rest of the Spartan army, especially the center where Agis was stationed, routed the opposing forces, precipitated the collapse of the entire Argive line, and later came to the rescue of the defeated left wing (5.71–73).[85] The Spartans' overwhelming victory at Mantinea, which Thucydides describes as the greatest battle that had taken place for a very long time among the Hellenes (5.74.1), revitalized Agis' reputation and the status of the dyarchy as a whole. After commanding the Spartans' fortification of Decelea from 413 to 404 and their expedition against Elis in 402, Agis II died and, according to Xenophon,

83. On the instability of the kingship during the fifth century, see Powell 2010; Millender, forthcoming.

84. On the kings' military prerogatives and powers, see Millender, forthcoming.

85. On this battle, see Lazenby 1985: 125–34; Schwartz 2009: 259–60.

received a burial that was far more splendid than that accorded to mere mortals (*HG* 3.3.1).[86]

The Other Audiences of the Spartan Hoplite Spectacle

One possible argument against this reading of hoplite warfare's intertwined relationship with Sparta's cooperative ideology and socio-political structure lies in the Spartans' increasing reliance on non-Spartiate soldiers during the classical period, thanks in large part to the *oliganthrōpia* that plagued Sparta.[87] In fact, it was not uncommon for Spartiates to find themselves outnumbered by soldiers who either lacked full political rights—that is, *hypomeiones* ("inferiors"), *perioeci*, and *neodamōdeis* (manumitted helots)—or possessed no political rights at all—that is, helots, mercenaries, and allies.[88] In the late fifth century and increasingly over the course of the fourth, we even find Spartan forces that comprised only one or a few Spartiates leading motley collections of non-Spartiates.[89] The Spartans, however, generally employed such heterogeneous forces, especially mercenary forces, for remote expeditions rather than for pitched battles on the Greek mainland.[90] Given their declining citizen numbers, it is not surprising that the Spartans were loath to commit their own troops to extended and risky campaigns abroad.

Nevertheless, the Spartans routinely deployed non-Spartiates for hoplite warfare as well, particularly the *perioeci*, the free inhabitants of the towns in Laconia and Messenia, apart from Sparta and Amyclae, who enjoyed local self-governance, lacked Spartan citizen rights, and occupied a position of dependence on Sparta. These "neighbors," in fact, typically contributed a disproportionately high number of hoplites to Spartan armies—as high as

86. On Agis at Decelea, see esp. Th. 7.19.1, 27.4; 8.3, 5, 70.2–71; X. *HG* 1.1.33–35; 2.2.7, 11–13; 2.3.3. On his command against the Eleans, see esp. X. *HG* 3.2.23–29.

87. On the demographic crisis, see n. 71. For its effect on Sparta's changing military organization, see Cawkwell 1983: 385–94; Cartledge 1987: 37–43. For the view that Sparta's increasing military reliance on non-Spartiates resulted from other factors, see van Wees 2004: 84–85.

88. Lazenby (1985: 16–20) and Hawkins (2011) argue that *hypomeiones* played an increasingly important role in Spartan armies as Spartan citizen numbers declined.

89. See, e.g., Brasidas' force in Thrace in 424 (Th. 4.80.5), Gylippus' force in Sicily in 413 (Th. 7.58.3), Clearchus' force in Byzantium in 408 (X. *HG* 1.3.15), and Thibron's force in Asia in 399 (X. *HG* 3.1.4–5). See also van Wees 2004: 45, 83–84; Millender 2006.

90. See van Wees 2004: 84–85; Millender 2006.

seventy percent of the Lacedaemonian forces that faced the Persians at Thermopylae in 480 and the Thebans at Leuctra in 371.[91] Although the *perioeci* and Spartiates who faced the Persians appear to have been brigaded in separate units, many scholars believe that the *perioeci* began to serve in the same units as the Spartiates at some point between the Persian and Peloponnesian Wars.[92] The evidence on this change, however, is unclear. We also lack information regarding the training and integration of the *perioecic* hoplites, who enjoyed no share in Sparta's educational system or the public messes that lay at the heart of Sparta's military organization.[93]

The helots, too, already figured in Spartan hoplite warfare during the Persian Wars, though it is unclear whether they served as light-armed troops or as attendants.[94] In 424 the Spartans enrolled seven hundred helots as hoplites for Brasidas' Thracian expedition (Th. 4.80.5). Thucydides later records forces of helots serving in the Spartans' campaigns in the Peloponnese in 418 (5.57.1, 64.2), but he provides no details about their numbers or the nature of their deployment.[95] At some point between 424 and 421, the Spartans also created the new force of *neodamōdeis* (Th. 5.34.1), who continued to figure in Spartan campaigns down to 370/69 (cf. X. *HG* 6.5.24).[96] In 413 the Spartans sent a force of six hundred hoplites specially selected from among both the helots and the *neodamōdeis* to fight in Sicily under a Spartiate commander (Th. 7.19.3, 58.3). Mercenaries also figured more frequently in Spartan armies in the late fifth and fourth centuries and participated in key battles, such as that at Coronea in 394 (X. *HG* 4.3.15–17; *Ages.* 2.10–11).[97] Last, but certainly not least, the Spartans' allies in the Peloponnesian League shouldered an increasingly disproportionate burden of the Spartans' hegemonic agenda. In

91. See van Wees 2004: 84, 275 nn. 28–29.

92. For the *perioeci*'s participation in the Persian Wars, see Hdt. 9.28, 49.3, 53–56, 61–65. See van Wees (2004: 83–84, 275 nn. 25–26), who points out (275 n. 26) that the only evidence on the separate brigades of Spartiates and *perioeci* is Herodotus' reference to a Spartiate formation within the body of the Lacedaemonian troops at Plataea (9.29.1). On the later brigading of *perioeci* and Spartan citizens in the same units, see Cartledge 1977: 17 and n. 52; 1987: 40–43; 2002: 154, 218–20; van Wees 2004, 84.

93. For challenges to the traditional view that the *perioeci* were brigaded in the same units as the Spartiates, see Lazenby 1985: 14–16; Hawkins 2011.

94. See Hdt. 7.229; 8.25.1; 9.10.1, 28.2, 29.1, 85.2. For the view that helots served as light-armed soldiers in early battles, including Thermopylae and Plataea, see Hunt 1997; 1998: 31–39; van Wees 2004: 61, 181–82. For a contrary view, see Schwartz 2009: 139–40.

95. Cf. Th. 4.8.9, 80.2–3. See Hunt 1998: 56–62.

96. On the helots' and *neodamōdeis*' service in the Spartan army, see Talbert 1989: 23–27; Hunt 1997; 1998.

97. See Millender 2006.

382, however, they successfully petitioned to convert their military obligations to the league from contingents of soldiers to cash payments (X. *HG* 5.2.21–22).[98]

While this reliance on non-Spartiate soldiers constituted—as Cartledge remarks—"a serious breach in the principle of the citizen militia," the Spartans were certainly not unusual in this regard.[99] More important, the inclusion of non-Spartiates in the Lacedaemonian phalanx would not necessarily have compromised the hoplite encounter's ability to bolster Spartan social relations and the ethic of cooperative sociability that underpinned them, especially if—contrary to the theory of the integration of the *perioeci* mentioned above[100]—the Spartans maintained a strict separation between core Spartiate units and the regiments of non-Spartiates that supported them. Cameron Hawkins has argued that the Spartans addressed their declining citizen numbers by incorporating into their units not *perioeci* but rather *hypomeiones*—those Spartans demoted from full Spartiate citizen status—because of their access to formal Spartan military training and continued commitment to the ideology of the *Homoioi.* The preserved distinction between Spartan and *perioecic* units, according to Hawkins, would have helped both "to ensure the ongoing accommodation of the *perioikoi* to their position of political dependence on Sparta" and to legitimate the Spartans' "monopolization of political privileges within the Lakedaimonian state."[101]

Even if the *perioeci* were brigaded in the same units as full Spartan citizens, their participation in Sparta's hoplite encounters, along with the other groups of non-citizens listed above, does not appear to have undermined the Spartans' ability to put a strikingly cohesive hoplite force into the field—a force that may have appeared cohesive even in terms of equipment and costume.[102] Peter Hunt has attributed the Spartans' ability to incorporate outsiders into their army to their unusual practice of stationing "an officer as the front rank man in each file."[103] Both this custom and the likelihood that the Spartans subjected their non-Spartiate comrades to regular and intense

98. On this change in the organization of the Peloponnesian League, see Millender 2006: 248–49, 261 nn. 69–70 (for bibliography).

99. Cartledge 1987: 40. See van Wees 2004: 45, 85; Hunt 1998.

100. See n. 92.

101. Hawkins 2011: 408, 413; cf. 414, 425–26. See also Lazenby 1985: 14–20.

102. As Cawkwell (1983: 398 and n. 47) notes, none of our extant evidence on the hair and dress of these soldiers suggests differences between Spartiates and non-Spartiates. Particularly suggestive here is Thucydides' inability to figure out the exact number of Spartiates captured on Sphacteria (4.38.5).

103. Hunt 1998: 37; cf. 173. See also Anderson 1970: 73.

training may account for the success of mixed forces such as the Lacedaemonian army that fought at Mantinea in 418 (Th. 5.67.1).[104] Agis II's last-minute—and nearly disastrous—decision to shift his line to the left demonstrates his confidence in his troops' cohesion and ability to perform such a complicated maneuver (Th. 5.71.2–3).[105] The Spartans' capacity to promote such a degree of cooperation and cohesion in its increasingly variegated hoplite forces would have provided a particularly powerful display of Spartan military superiority for the non-Spartan constituencies that witnessed and participated in hoplite encounters. Through their intense instruction, their observation of the Spartans' "professional" practice of the craft of war (cf. X. *Lac.* 13.5) on both the training grounds and the battlefield, and their front-row seats—so to speak—at the exhibition of the Lacedaemonians' defeat of their opponents, these groups became yet another audience of the grandiose spectacle of Spartan values and virtues.

Indeed, the Spartans' successful performance of hoplite warfare would have conveyed a number of symbolic and powerful messages to these non-citizen groups. The *perioeci*, for example, would have gained intimate knowledge of Spartan military organization, tactics, and ethics, whether or not they were brigaded in the same units as the Spartiates. Their close collaboration with the Spartiates on the field may account for their continued willingness to support Spartan hegemony in the southern Peloponnese and to acquiesce to Sparta's political control.[106]

For the helots, the display of the Spartan phalanx at work would have provided a strong reminder of the obedience, discipline, and cohesion that made the Spartans at once formidable masters and superlative soldiers. More important, those helots who witnessed the technical superiority of the Spartan army would have received a warning against seeking military support from other Greek states. The involvement of helots in Spartan warfare thus could have served as one of the mechanisms—the most famous being the *crypteia*—by which the Spartans maintained control over their subjugated

104. On the likelihood that non-Spartiates in the Lacedaemonian army received far more training than other Greek hoplites, see Cawkwell 1983: 397–98.

105. Cawkwell (1983: 398) argues that "the manoeuvre ordered by Agis at Mantinea during the advance into action . . . was only conceivable if all parts of his army were well trained in it." On the battle of Mantinea and what it reveals about Spartan military organization, see Singor 2002. See also Lazenby 1985: 125–34.

106. See esp. Hawkins 2011, cited above at n. 101. On the *perioecic* communities' collaboration in their dependency on Sparta, see Hall 2000: 87. See also Ducat 2010, esp. 201–3.

helot population.[107] The helots' participation in Lacedaemonian hoplite armies may, however, provide evidence of the interdependence that scholars like Hodkinson have viewed as a key feature of Spartan-helot relations, especially if they fought alongside their Spartiate masters as early as the Persian Wars.[108] While such cooperation on the field may have resulted from fear, self-interest, or the promise of rewards, it may also signal at least some helots' willingness to buy into Spartan domination.[109]

The Spartans, moreover, could exploit their successful performance of hoplite tactics to reaffirm their superior position vis-à-vis their allies in the Peloponnesian League, as we see in Thucydides' account of the battle of Mantinea in 418. Sparta's decision to make peace with Athens in 421 greatly angered a number of its allies, who refused to accept the treaty (5.17.2, 22.1, 25.1, 30, 35.3). The threat to Spartan hegemony in the Peloponnese became quite serious, as state after state began to distrust Sparta and to consider alliance with Argos (5.27–30). Ultimately, several of Sparta's allies entered into alliance with Argos, most significantly, Mantinea, Elis, and Corinth. Thucydides makes it clear that the Boeotians and Megarians considered this alliance as well (5.29–32, 36–38). The Argives, Mantineans, and Eleans also later concluded a treaty with the Athenians in 420 (5.43.3–48.1).[110] Thucydides claims that it was the fear of further revolts and instability in the region that led the Spartans to initiate a set battle with the Argives and their allies in midsummer 418. The political importance that the Spartans ascribed to this battle is clear in their decision to take the field against Argos with their full force, helots included (5.57.1).

This battle, however, never took place, thanks to the aforementioned truce that Agis II unilaterally concluded with the Argives (5.60.1). Fortunately both for a now very unpopular Agis and for the Spartans who were eager for battle, another chance to reclaim Spartan preeminence in the Peloponnese came later that summer at Mantinea, where the Spartan vic-

107. On the *crypteia*, see Trundle's contribution to this volume. On the Spartans' mechanisms for containing the helots, see Millender 2016. For the traditional view of the Spartan-helot relationship as a tense class struggle, see Cartledge 1987: 160–79; 1991; 2001c: 146–52; 2002: 138–53. See also Ducat 1974; 1990: 105–27. For a contrary view, see Talbert 1989.

108. Hodkinson 2000: 113–49. For the theory that helots played this role in Sparta's armies as early as the Persian Wars, see Hunt 1997; 1998: 31–39; cf. 116–20.

109. The Spartans' creation of the *neodamōdeis* also may have contributed to social stability by providing ambitious helots with an opportunity for advancement. See Cawkwell 1983: 392–93.

110. On these various diplomatic maneuverings, see Cartledge 2002: 214–16.

tory over the Argive coalition provided a powerful lesson about the dangers entailed by disloyalty to the Lacedaemonians (5.66–74).[111] This message was particularly loud and clear for the Mantineans who were arrayed on the enemy's right wing, opposite the Spartans (5.67.2). The Mantineans, along with their allies and the one thousand picked Argives, were initially successful. Later, however, the Spartans' sound defeat of the rest of the Argive force, the Argives' allies, and the Athenians highlighted the foolishness of the Mantineans' decision to throw their lot in with the Spartans' Argive and Athenian enemies.

More significantly, the Mantineans paid for their disaffection from Lacedaemon at the conclusion of the battle, when the victorious Spartans under Agis allowed the privileged Argive one thousand to escape but killed many of the fleeing Mantineans and the Argive democrats (5.73–74).[112] It is not coincidental that Sparta concluded a peace treaty and alliance with a newly pro-Spartan Argos during the following winter. The Mantineans, now isolated, likewise came to terms with the Lacedaemonians (5.76–81). As the Mantineans and other Greeks learned, Sparta was still the greatest land power in Hellas, no matter how much battering its reputation had sustained during the first half of the Peloponnesian War (5.75.3):

> By this one action they did away with the blame leveled against them by the Hellenes at this time, whether for cowardice because of the disaster on the island or for other examples of indecision and slowness. For it now seemed that although they had been worsted by fortune, they were still the same men in spirit.

The rich dividends of this battle help to explain why the Spartans, as the Athenian Alcibiades later declared, were willing to stake their all on the issue of one day's fighting at Mantinea (Th. 6.16.6)—and later, in 394, at Nemea and Coronea. Indeed, as the battle of Mantinea demonstrated, hoplite warfare proved to be an efficient way to destroy the enemy in the field and to put an end to the political aspirations of the opposing state(s).[113] This ritualized

111. Cartledge (1987: 46) rightly notes that "a combination of overconfident or incompetent generalship, insubordination, and perhaps some loss of morale had nearly brought disaster." However, the victory still demonstrated the superior military training and discipline of the Lacedaemonian force, which were even more evident at Nemea in 394.

112. For the view that the Spartans purposely spared the one thousand aristocratic Argives, who shared their oligarchic outlook, see Hanson 1999: 207; Ruzé 2006: 270–71.

113. Cf. Hanson 2000a: 222. See Lazenby 1985: 134.

and agonistic encounter, however, also provided a far more immediate display of the victor's military superiority than the many other forms of warfare practiced at this time. Among the Greeks, the Spartans especially grasped and exploited the performative nature of hoplite warfare, as we can see in their slow and rhythmic advance at Mantinea (Th. 5.69.2–70) and in their dramatic sacrifice of a goat to Artemis Agrotera when they were less than a stade away from their enemies at the battle of Nemea (X. *HG* 4.2.20).[114] In his account of the Lacedaemonians' military expertise, Xenophon reveals his appreciation for their attention to the sensory aspects of battle (*Lac.* 13.8):

> When the enemy is near enough to see, a she-goat is sacrificed, and custom ordains that all the flute players present are to play and that every Lacedaemonian is to wear a wreath. An order is also given to polish arms. It is also the privilege of the young men to enter battle with their hair groomed . . . and with a joyful, distinguished appearance.[115]

As van Wees has noted, the slow march, when combined with the hymns, flute players, and garlands, "could not fail to remind onlookers of a religious procession" and "was an all the more unnerving sight because it suggested that they [i.e., the Spartans] saw themselves as serenely advancing to the ritual slaughter of their enemies."[116] Perhaps even more unnerving was the display of discipline and cohesion that the Spartans likewise provided in their orderly and slow advance to battle.[117]

Apparently, the Spartans' very shields were enough to terrify their enemies, even if we do not credit the Athenian comic poet Eupolis' claim that Cleon took off at the mere sight of the lambdas that these shields displayed (359 Kock). According to Xenophon, the Argive force that bravely attacked the dismounted Spartan cavalrymen at Corinth in 392 only did so because the Spartans had borrowed the Sicyonians' sigma-bearing shields (*HG* 4.4.10). Even those Athenians who eventually defeated the Spartans on Sphacteria in 425 were at first filled with dread at the idea of attacking the "terrible" (δεινούς)—if heavily outnumbered—Spartans (Th. 4.34.1).[118] A

114. Cf. Powell 1989: 179–80.

115. Plutarch similarly highlights the performative nature of the Spartans' preparations for battle and only adds that the pipers were ordered to play Castor's song (*Lyc.* 22.2–3).

116. Van Wees 2004: 187.

117. Cf. Wheeler and Strauss 2007: 209, 215.

118. Compare the emotions of the Thebans who initially occupied the left wing of the force defeated by Sparta at Nemea in 394 (X. *HG* 4.2.18).

number of enemies did not even wait for the onslaught but actually gave way as soon as the Spartans charged, such as the Argives and their allies, who fled and even trampled one another to death in their haste to escape from Agis II and his forces at Mantinea in 418 (Th. 5.72.4).[119] By ending certain battles before the forces even engaged, this primal fear of the Lacedaemonian phalanx contributed to the Spartans' unparalleled success in hoplite encounters between their ill-considered expedition against Tegea ca. 550 (cf. Hdt. 1.66) and their loss at Leuctra in 371.[120] As John Lazenby has concluded, Leuctra proved decisive precisely because this battle "put an end to the myth of Spartan invincibility."[121]

Conclusion

As this study has shown, hoplite organization, ethics, and tactics enjoyed a mutually reinforcing relationship with core Spartan socio-political structures and performed key ideological roles for the Spartans that had wide-ranging ramifications for both domestic and foreign policy. The spectacle of cohesion and military superiority that the Spartan performance of hoplite tactics displayed bolstered at once the cooperative sociability that structured the Spartan *politeia*, the Spartiates' superior position vis-à-vis the *perioeci* and the helots, and Sparta's hegemonic status in the Peloponnese.

The battlefield, moreover, provided the Spartans with a stage on which they could orchestrate a mythic Sparta—a mirage that helped to obscure the various internal problems that undermined Sparta's socio-political order at home and hegemonic status abroad in the late fifth and early fourth centuries. Indeed, Sparta's understanding of the benefits provided by hoplite tactics and its ability to exploit them allowed this city-state to maintain its facade of stability and strength even as its chronic *oliganthrōpia* transformed the "*doyenne* of developed hoplite warfare" into a second-rate power.[122] Hoplite warfare's performativity and ideological multivalency may thus help to account for the Spartans' adherence to this highly ritualized form of violence during the fifth and early fourth centuries, as their fellow Greeks increas-

119. See also X. *HG* 4.3.17, 7.1.31.

120. On other Greeks' fear of the Spartans, see Lazenby 1985: 3; 1991: 104–5.

121. Lazenby 1985: 162.

122. See n. 9. As Lazenby (1985: 162) notes, "Sparta's position in Greece had long rested on what amounted to a gigantic bluff, since her man-power resources, in terms of actual citizen-soldiers, had never really been sufficient to sustain that position."

ingly turned to more asymmetrical forms of warfare and to the greater incorporation of light-armed forces and cavalry.[123]

Works Cited

Anderson, J. K. 1970. *Military Theory and Practice in the Age of Xenophon*. Berkeley.

Anderson, J. K. 1991. "Hoplite Weapons and Offensive Arms." In V. Hanson, ed., *Hoplites: The Classical Greek Battle Experience*, 15–37. London.

Bradford, A. S. 1994. "The Duplicitious Spartan." In A. Powell and S. Hodkinson, eds., *The Shadow of Sparta*, 59–85. London.

Cartledge, P. A. 1977. "Hoplites and Heroes: Sparta's Contribution to the Technique of Ancient Warfare." *JHS* 97: 11–27. Reprinted in German translation, with addendum, in K. Christ, ed., *Sparta*, 387–425, 470. Darmstadt, 1986.

Cartledge, P. A. 1987. *Agesilaos and the Crisis of Sparta*. London.

Cartledge, P. A. 1991. "Richard Talbert's Revision of the Spartan-Helot Struggle: A Reply." *Historia* 40: 379–81.

Cartledge, P. A. 2001a. "The Birth of the Hoplite: Sparta's Contribution to Early Greek Military Organization." In *Spartan Reflections*, 153–66, 225–28. Berkeley.

Cartledge, P. A. 2001b. "The Politics of Spartan Pederasty." In *Spartan Reflections*, 91–105, 206–11. Berkeley.

Cartledge, P. A. 2001c. "Rebels and *Sambos* in Classical Greece: A Comparative View." In *Spartan Reflections*, 127–52, 220–25. Berkeley.

Cartledge, P. A. 2002. *Sparta and Lakonia: A Regional History 1300–362 B.C.* 2nd ed. New York.

Cawkwell, G. L. 1978. *Philip of Macedon*. London.

Cawkwell, G. L. 1983. "The Decline of Sparta." *CQ* 33: 385–400.

Cawkwell, G. L. 1989. "Orthodoxy and Hoplites." *CQ* 39: 375–89.

David, E. 1992. "Sparta's Social Hair." *Eranos* 90: 11–21.

Ducat, J. 1974. "Le mépris des Hilotes." *Annales (ESC)* 29: 1451–64.

Ducat, J. 1990. *Les Hilotes*. Paris.

Ducat, J. 1999. "La société spartiate et la guerre." In F. Prost, ed., *Armées et sociétiés de la Grèce classique: Aspects sociaux et politiques de la guerre aux Ve et IVe s. au. J.-C.*, 35–50. Paris.

Ducat, J. 2005. "Aristodémos le trembleur." *Ktema* 30: 205–16.

Ducat, J. 2006a. *Spartan Education*. Trans. E. Stafford, P.-J. Shaw, and A. Powell. Swansea.

Ducat, J. 2006b. "The Spartan 'Tremblers.'" In S. Hodkinson and A. Powell, eds., *Sparta & War*, 1–55. Swansea.

123. On the Spartans' military conservatism and Xenophon's treatment of this weakness in the Spartan system, see Humble 2006: 227–29. See also Cawkwell 1983: 398–400; Lazenby 1985: 38–40. While the Spartans made use of cavalry, light-armed soldiers, and mercenaries, they adapted to changes in Greek warfare more slowly than many of their opponents, especially the Athenians. See Millender 2006.

Ducat, J. 2010. "The Ghost of the Lakedaimonian State." In A. Powell and S. Hodkinson, eds., *Sparta: The Body Politic*, 183–210. Swansea.

Figueira, T. J. 1986. "Population Patterns in Late Archaic and Classical Sparta." *TAPA* 116: 165–213.

Figueira, T. J. 2006. "The Spartan *Hippeis*." In S. Hodkinson and A. Powell, eds., *Sparta & War*, 57–84. Swansea.

Finley, M. I. 1986. "Sparta." In *The Use and Abuse of History*, 161–78. 2nd ed. London.

Forsdyke, S. 2008. "Street Theatre and Popular Justice in Ancient Greece: Shaming, Stoning and Starving Offenders Inside and Outside the Courts." *Past and Present* 201: 3–50.

Garlan, Y. 1975. *War in the Ancient World: A Social History*. London.

Goldsworthy, A. K. 1997. "The *Othismos*, Myths and Heresies: The Nature of Hoplite Battle." *War in History* 4: 1–26.

Hall, J. M. 2000. "Sparta, Lakedaimon and the Nature of Perioikic Dependency." In P. Flensted-Jensen, ed., *Further Studies in the Ancient Greek Polis*, 73–89. Stuttgart.

Hanson, V. D. 1991. "Hoplite Technology in Phalanx Battle." In V. Hanson, ed., *Hoplites: The Classical Greek Battle Experience*, 63–84. London.

Hanson, V. D. 1999. "Hoplite Obliteration: The Case of the Town of Thespiae." In J. Carman and A. Harding, eds., *Ancient Warfare: Archaeological Perspectives*, 203–17. Gloucestershire.

Hanson, V. D. 2000a. "Hoplite Battle as Ancient Greek Warfare: When, Where, and Why?" In H. van Wees, ed., *War and Violence in Ancient Greece*, 201–32. Swansea.

Hanson, V. D. 2000b. *The Western Way of War: Infantry Battle in Classical Greece*. 2nd ed. Berkeley.

Hawkins, C. 2011. "Spartans and *Perioikoi*: The Organization and Ideology of the Lakedaimonian Army in the Fourth Century B.C.E." *GRBS* 51: 401–34.

Hesk, J. 2000. *Deception and Democracy in Classical Athens*. Cambridge.

Hodkinson, S. 1983. "Social Order and the Conflict of Values in Classical Sparta." *Chiron* 13: 239–81.

Hodkinson, S. 1993. "Warfare, Wealth, and the Crisis of Spartiate Society." In J. Rich and G. Shipley, eds., *War and Society in the Greek World*, 146–76. London.

Hodkinson, S. 2000. *Property and Wealth in Classical Sparta*. London.

Hodkinson, S. 2005. "The Imaginary Spartan *Politeia*." In M. Hansen, ed., *The Imaginary Polis*, 222–81. Acts of the Copenhagen Polis Centre 7. Copenhagen.

Hodkinson, S. 2006. "Was Classical Sparta a Military Society?" In S. Hodkinson and A. Powell, eds., *Sparta & War*, 111–62. Swansea.

Hooker, J. T. 1980. *The Ancient Spartans*. London.

Humble, N. 1997. "Xenophon's View of Sparta: A Study of the *Anabasis, Hellenica,* and *Respublica Lacedaemoniorum*." PhD diss., McMaster University.

Humble, N. 2004. "The Author, Date, and Purpose of Chapter 14 of the *Lakedaimonion Politeia*." In C. Tuplin, ed., *Xenophon and His World*, 215–28. Stuttgart.

Humble, N. 2006. "Why the Spartans Fight So Well . . . Even in Disorder—Xenophon's View." In S. Hodkinson and A. Powell, eds., *Sparta & War*, 219–33. Swansea.

Humble, N. Forthcoming. "True History: Xenophon's *Agesilaos* and the Encomiastic Genre." In A. Powell and N. Richer, eds., *Xenophon & Sparta*. Swansea.

Hunt, P. 1997. "Helots at the Battle of Plataea." *Historia* 46: 129–44.

Hunt, P. 1998. *Slaves, Warfare, and Ideology in the Greek Historians.* Cambridge.

Jameson, M. H. 1991. "Sacrifice Before Battle." In V. Hanson, ed., *Hoplites: The Classical Greek Battle Experience*, 87–109. London.

Kennell, N. M. 1995. *The Gymnasium of Virtue: Education and Culture in Ancient Sparta.* Chapel Hill.

Kock, T. 1880–88. *Comicorum Atticorum Fragmenta.* 3 vols. Leipzig.

Krentz, P. 1985a. "Casualties in Hoplite Battles." *GRBS* 26: 13–20.

Krentz, P. 1985b. "The Nature of Hoplite Battles." *ClAnt* 4: 50–61.

Krentz, P. 1994. "Continuing the *Othismos* on *Othismos*." *AHB* 8: 45–49.

Krentz, P. 2000. "Deception in Archaic and Classical Greek Warfare." In H. van Wees, ed., *War and Violence in Ancient Greece*, 167–200. Swansea.

Lazenby, J. F. 1985. *The Spartan Army.* Warminster.

Lazenby, J. F. 1991. "The Killing Zone." In V. Hanson, ed., *Hoplites: The Classical Greek Battle Experience*, 87–109. London.

Lendon, J. E. 2005. *Soldiers and Ghosts: A History of Battle in Classical Antiquity.* New Haven.

Luginbill, R. D. 1994. "*Othismos*: The Importance of the Mass-Shove in Hoplite Warfare." *Phoenix* 48: 51–61.

Millender, E. G. 1996. "'The Teacher of Hellas': Athenian Democratic Ideology and the 'Barbarization' of Sparta in Fifth-Century Greek Thought." PhD diss., University of Pennsylvania.

Millender, E. G. 2002. "Νόμος Δεσπότης: Spartan Obedience and Athenian Lawfulness in Fifth-Century Thought." In V. Gorman and E. Robinson, eds., *Oikistes: Studies in Constitutions, Colonies, and Military Power in the Ancient World, Offered in Honor of A. J. Graham*, 33–59. Leiden.

Millender, E. G. 2006. "The Politics of Spartan Mercenary Service." In S. Hodkinson and A. Powell, eds., *Sparta & War*, 235–66. Swansea.

Millender, E. G. 2016. "Spartan State Terror: Violence, Humiliation, and the Reinforcement of Social Boundaries in Classical Sparta." In T. Howe and L. L. Brice, eds., *Brill's Companion to Insurgency and Terrorism in the Ancient Mediterranean.* Vol. 1, 117–50. Leiden.

Millender, E. G. Forthcoming. "Kingship: The History, Power, and Prerogatives of the Spartans' 'Divine' Dyarchy." In A. Powell, ed., *A Companion to Sparta.* Malden, MA.

Parker, R. 2000. "Sacrifice and Battle." In H. van Wees, ed., *War and Violence in Ancient Greece*, 299–314. Swansea.

Powell, A. 1989. "Mendacity and the Spartans' Use of the Visual." In A. Powell, ed., *Classical Sparta: Techniques Behind Her Success*, 173–92. London.

Powell, A. 2010. "Divination, Royalty and Insecurity in Classical Sparta." In A. Powell and S. Hodkinson, eds., *Sparta: The Body Politic*, 85–135. Swansea.

Pritchett, W. K. 1971–91. *The Greek State at War.* 5 vols. Berkeley.

Raaflaub, K. A. 1997. "Soldiers, Citizens, and the Evolution of the Early Greek *Polis*." In L. Mitchell and P. J. Rhodes, eds., *The Development of the* Polis *in Archaic Greece*, 49–59. London.

Raaflaub, K. A. 1999. "Archaic and Classical Greece." In K. Raaflaub and N. Rosenstein, eds., *War and Society in the Ancient and Medieval Worlds: Asia, the Mediterranean, Europe, and Mesoamerica*, 129–61. Cambridge, MA.

Rawlings, L. 2000. "Alternative Agonies: Hoplite Martial and Combat Experiences Beyond the Phalanx." In H. van Wees, ed., *War and Violence in Ancient Greece*, 233–59. Swansea.

Rusch, S. M. 2011. *Sparta at War: Strategy, Tactics, and Campaigns, 550–362 BC*. London.

Ruzé, F. 2006. "Spartans and the Use of Treachery among Their Enemies." In S. Hodkinson and A. Powell, eds., *Sparta & War*, 267–85. Swansea.

Salmon, J. B. 1977. "Political Hoplites?" *JHS* 97: 84–101.

Schwartz, A. 2009. *Reinstating the Hoplite: Arms, Armour, and Phalanx Fighting in Archaic and Classical Greece*. Stuttgart.

Singor, H. W. 2002. "The Spartan Army at Mantinea and Its Organisation in the Fifth Century B.C." In W. Jongman and M. Kleijwegt, eds., *After the Past: Essays in Ancient History in Honour of H. W. Pleket*, 235–84. Leiden.

Ste. Croix, G. E. M. de. 1972. *The Origins of the Peloponnesian War*. London.

Talbert, R. 1989. "The Role of the Helots in the Class Struggle at Sparta." *Historia* 38: 22–40.

Tod, M. N. 1948. *A Selection of Greek Historical Inscriptions* II. *From 403 to 323 BC*. Oxford.

van Wees, H. 2000. "The Development of the Hoplite Phalanx: Iconography and Reality in the Seventh Century." In H. van Wees, ed., *War and Violence in Ancient Greece*, 125–66. Swansea.

van Wees, H. 2002. "Tyrants, Oligarchs, and Citizen Militias." In A. Chaniotis and P. Ducrey, eds., *Army and Power in the Ancient World*, 61–82. Stuttgart.

van Wees, H. 2004. *Greek Warfare: Myths and Realities*. London.

West, M. L. 1992. *Iambi et Elegi Graeci ante Alexandrum Cantati* II. 2nd ed. Oxford.

Wheeler, E., and B. Strauss. 2007. "Battle." In P. Sabin, H. van Wees, and M. Whitby, eds., *The Cambridge History of Greek and Roman Warfare*, 1.223–47. Cambridge.

SEVEN

Violence at the *Symposion*

Oswyn Murray

The *symposion* is normally conceived of as a place of fellowship and conviviality, of *euphrosynē*; yet violence or *hybris* was never far away. There seem to be two reasons for this: the first derives from the origins of the *symposion* in the warrior fraternities of early Greece. The first class to emerge in Greece was a class of warriors, whose status was expressed in the group feast, carried out in an enclosed space and apart from the community. The members recognized equality within the banquet, but they sought to foster a sense of separateness and a group loyalty in preparation for the dangers of war. Homer describes the original setting of this distinctive type of feasting.

> Eumaeus, this must surely be the fine house of Odysseus: it would be easy to recognise and pick out even among many. There are buildings upon buildings, and the court is well fenced with a wall and cornice, and the double gates are well protected: no man could force it. And I see that many men are feasting within, for the smell of fat is there, and the lyre sounds, which the gods have made as companion to the feast.[1]

The leader feasted his warriors in the great hall (*megaron*) and, through this entertainment, established his right to call on their support.

The relationship between warfare and the feast remained close in archaic Greece. Elegiac poetry began as the poetry of a warrior group, performed at their common feasts. In Sparta, the ritual of group feasting was institutional-

1. Hom. *Od.* 17.264–71.

ized to create a new citizen army: all male citizens belonged to *syssitia*, where they ate and drank daily in groups that also formed the basis of the fighting formation. Elsewhere, in warfare and politics, organizations of groups of companions (*hetairoi*) who "drank together" in the *symposion* were a characteristic survival of the aristocratic age into the world of the classical polis. Alcohol is, of course, a drug, but it differs from all other types of drug in being socially useful, because it releases inhibitions at the same time as creating bonds between the participants. Thus, in western history, unlike in the Islamic world, alcohol has generally been accepted as the basis for all military activity: it has always puzzled me why it took so long for the armies of the bottle to overcome the armies of the crescent.

The male drinking group was both a preparation for war and a relaxation from war; the bonding process that is an essential aspect of all military training took place here in all Greek city-states of the archaic age.[2] In his formulation of the ideal *symposion*, Xenophanes, who queries so many aspects of archaic culture, from religion to sport, deplores the ancestral military themes in sympotic entertainment.

> Praise the man who reveals his worth while drinking and has memory and a song for virtue; do not recite the battles of Titans and Giants or Centaurs, the quarrels of old or their violent factions: there is no good in these, but it is always right to have respect for the gods.[3]

There evolved, however, a new style of poetry, military elegy, composed in the hortative mode and using the second-person plural, to incite the warrior group to courage and to exhort them, while at their leisure in the drinking group, to prepare themselves for battle.[4] The military atmosphere was always present at the *symposion*, and in halls hung with weapons, it was directly conducive to outbreaks of violence.

The second reason for the presence of violence in the *symposion* is the physiological effect of alcohol on the emotions, in the release of inhibitions as a result of indulging in the pleasures of Dionysus, a god both benign and terrifying. The encyclopedist of ancient feasting customs, Athenaeus of Naucratis, writing in the early third century AD, devotes a special section of his work (2.35–38) to the dangers of the *symposion*: "from the condition

2. Murray 1983, 1991.
3. Xenoph. fr. 13
4. Bowie 1990.

produced by drunkenness they liken Dionysus to a bull or a leopard, because those who have drunk too much are inclined to violence" (38e).

The ritualization inherent in the *symposion* is therefore more than the normal human tendency to intensify pleasures through complicating them: it is a defense against the dangers of violence inherent in alcohol consumption. The *symposion* is ordered by a rhythm both temporal and quantitative. Initially, the symposiarch determines the exact ratio of water to wine in accordance with the intention of the *symposion*. Greeks do not drink unmixed wine, because it leads to violence and madness; it is left to the gods and heroes, to barbarians, and to slaves and citizen women, who (excluded from the *symposion*) are reduced to stealing wine from the storeroom. There is a timetable of consumption in the properly ritualized style of drinking, which is created by the rhythm of the filling and emptying of the *kratēr*. For Panyassis, *hybris* is provoked by the third *kratēr* (F 17–18 Bernabé); the comic poet Eubulus specifies a whole range of disruptive behavior that begins with the fourth *kratēr* and ends in the tenth.

> Three *kratērs* only do I mix for the temperate—one to health, which they empty first, the second to love and pleasure, the third to sleep. When this is drunk up, wise guests go home. The fourth *kratēr* is ours no longer, but belongs to *hybris*, the fifth to uproar, the sixth to the *kōmos*, the seventh to black eyes. The eighth is the policeman's, the ninth belongs to vomiting, and the tenth to madness and hurling the furniture.[5]

Thus the filling and mixing of the *kratēr* imparted a rhythm to the social ritual, and each *kratēr* had its special character. The standard *kratēr* holds approximately fourteen liters;[6] for a seven-couch session, with two drinkers to a couch, each filling therefore represents one liter per participant, of wine and water mixed according to the prescription of the president. Greek wine was made from grapes, sweet and naturally fermented: since it retained some sugar content, the alcohol must have killed off the yeast before it had

5. Eub. F 93 in Ath. 2.36b.

6. This is based on my own measurements of the capacity of *kratērs*, where I identified two common sizes of approximately seven and fourteen liters. Until recently, professional archaeologists have shown a total lack of interest in the most important feature of the liquid containers they study, their capacity. But see now Tsingarida 2009: 129–33; Lynch 2011: app. II.

converted all the sugar. The wine's alcoholic strength was probably close to the maximum achievable without distillation, 17 to 18 percent. When the liquid was diluted two or three to one, the resulting alcoholic content will have fallen within the range of modern Western beers; it was clearly drunk in similar quantities. It is not surprising, then, that Eubulus' wise guest goes home after six pints. Greek wine was not a sophisticated drink sipped in small glasses: it needed a sieve to remove the skins and stalks floating on the surface, and it did not keep for more than a year, as containers (wineskins and unglazed amphorae) were porous and easily contaminated.[7] There were no vintages, merely places of origin (Pramnian, Samian, Chian, and so on), doubtless related to different types of grape or different modes of cultivation and fermentation in different areas. It was the Romans who invented the idea of aging and vintage years and the conception of old wine as a luxury.

The notion that drunkenness leads to lack of control is, of course, only partially true: drunken violence in all societies is highly ritualized, from the carnivals of medieval Europe and the peasant *kermesse* of the Netherlands to knife fights in Glasgow streets and the racial violence of closing time in modern urban cultures. Uncontrolled violence as a result of alcohol seldom occurs, and each society has its ritualized forms of release of tension. One way of reducing the threat of violence in the *symposion* was to externalize it: an important part of the ritual of the *symposion* was the drunken revel (*kōmos*) at the end, when the participants left the *andrōn* (men's room) and paraded singing and dancing through the streets, assaulting passersby and damaging property in a spirit of self-licensed carnival under the influence of Dionysus, god of wine. This activity also had its functional aspect. The main disadvantage of the *symposion* as a form of social behavior was that it took place in private: for it to have significance as a public lifestyle, it was necessary for the group to display its identity outside the walls of the *andrōn*, in the public streets. Such demonstrations were as much part of the ritual of public display by the aristocracy as were the great public funerals; like funerals, these demonstrations could take on political significance and be subject to control by the law of the wider community. The importance of the *kōmos* is shown by the many representations of it on sympotic pottery. The limits of tolerance of this type of behavior is illustrated by the portrayal of the activities of Philokleon in Aristophanes' *Wasps*: once the old man has learned how

7. As far as I know, the only Western winemaker who has genuinely reproduced the ancient process of fermentation is Josko Gravner of Friuli, basing his process on the traditional wine of northern Georgia fermented in an amphora (*qvevri*): see his excellent video at www.gravner.it. I tasted his wine at a conference in California in 2012; it was highly oxidated and resembled a light sherry.

to behave at a *symposion*, he adopts its customs wholeheartedly and returns home with an abducted flute girl in tow, pursued by outraged citizens claiming damages for assault and destruction of their property (1325–1449).

Drunken *hybris* was therefore often treated as a special case in law. Under the laws of Solon at Athens, most crimes against the person were prosecuted by the aggrieved individual, in the procedure known as *dikē*. But *hybris* was taken more seriously and defined as an offense against public order, for which anyone could bring a prosecution under the procedure of a written *graphē*. Various features of the law suggest that the activities that resulted in *hybris* were originally conceived of as belonging specifically within a sympotic context. The offense is described not in terms of actual physical damage but as derogation from the *timē* of another. "If a man has committed violence this is not always *hybris*, but only if he has struck with a purpose, such as in order to cause dishonour or for his own pleasure," says Aristotle (*Rh.* 1.1374a13–15), who characterises the offense as one most likely to be committed by the young and wealthy (2.1378b23–26). Moreover, *hybris* could be committed against women as well as men, slave as well as freeborn. It is difficult to imagine how one could attack the *timē* of a slave except in a sympotic context, by, for instance, molesting the naked slave boy who poured the wine, as Sophokles is represented as doing (Ion of Chios ap. Ath. 13.603e), or engaging in sexual intercourse with the hired flute girls and female entertainers or the *hetaira* of another participant, as is alleged as part of the evidence against Neaira ([Dem.] *In Neaeram*). The Solonian law thus appears to belong within that category of Greek laws that prescribe double penalties for drunken offenses, as at Mytilene.[8]

The social dimension of misbehavior in aristocratic drinking was always mistrusted by the polis, for the *symposion* was a private world apart from family and polis, at least in its developed form; it was therefore an ideal place to locate conspiracies and revolutionary activities. Tyrants were warned to fear *symposia* and were portrayed as regretting their loss of the conviviality of sympotic friendship. Our sources often discuss action (conspiracy, murder, etc.) actually taking place within a convivial context; the most famous historical example is the scandal of the profanation of the Mysteries and the mutilation of the herms that caused a witch hunt in democratic Athens in 415 BC and led to the fatal split between the demos and their traditional class of leaders. The oligarchic conspiracies of late fifth-century Athens rested on a *pistis* developed in the *symposion* and reinforced by violence.[9]

8. Murray 1990; Ampolo 1984.

9. Calhoun 1913; Murray 1990a.

This abnormal activity reflects the more formal activity of religious *thiasoi* and *orgeōnes*, private or semipublic associations for the worship of individual gods. Such associations had always existed, of course, and were already recognized in the Solonian law. In the classical age, they proliferated, together with the worship of minor heroes and foreign deities. The central act of such groups was the communal meal involving *deipnon* and *symposion*. Aristotle, who describes the purpose of these groups as "honouring the gods and providing relaxation and pleasure to themselves," classifies them as associations undertaken for the sake of pleasure (*EN* 8.1160a). The archetype of these heroic cults is the cult of Herakles, who operated as the prototype of transgressive behavior at the *symposion*.

The mighty drinker and mighty eater Herakles challenges symposiasts to excess, and the myths that are told about him reflect the consequences of this excess; bad behavior and drunken violence needed their heroic prototype.[10] One of the earliest scenes of the reclining *symposion*, on a famous Corinthian *kratēr* in the Louvre, represents Herakles at the palace of Euryt(i)os; the mythological narrative involving Herakles' murder of the sons of Eurytos, the destruction of his palace, and the abduction of his daughter Iole is surely present, even if these events are not explicitly depicted. The presentations of the boorish or badly behaved sympotic Herakles are central elements in Sophocles *Trachiniae*, the prosatyric Euripides' *Alcestis*, and Aristophanes' *Frogs*. The theme is inverted in the satyr play *Omphale* by the well-known sympotic author and dramatist Ion of Chios, where Herakles is presented as disrupting the luxurious feasting of Omphale by his excessive greed. Presumably, the play involved the transvestism of Herakles and Omphale, as they exchanged clothes and activities while he served as her slave and lover (Ath. 10.411c; *TGrF* 19 F 29). The myths of Herakles at the *symposion* are narratives of violence and seem to lie behind both the artistic and the literary evidence. In such portrayals, the sympotic Herakles presents a challenge and a warning, a sort of heroic Sardanapallus, just as, in a later age, the drunken Alexander the Great was both a heroic figure and a warning.

It is therefore perhaps no surprise that the ultimate form of violence, "murder in the *symposion*," is a prominent theme in sympotic literature and even in life. The theme of violence at the feast was a major topic of ancient mythology, from the marriage feast of Peirithous and Hippodameia and the subsequent battle of the lapiths and centaurs, to the cannibalistic feast of Thyestes that began the curse on the house of Atreus. Violence in a

10. On Herakles as glutton, see Ath. 10.411–12.

feasting context is a common theme in Athenian tragedy; leaving aside the subsequent ramifications of the Thyestes myth, the banquet scene in which Creusa seeks to poison her son Ion in Euripides' *Ion* has been extensively analyzed by Pauline Schmitt Pantel as an image of the *symposion*, and it can be paralleled in Euripides' *Cyclops* and other tragic scenes.[11] The earliest of these literary representations is the climax of the *Odyssey*, where, in the final banquet, the hero-poet, instead of offering sympotic entertainment, strings his bow "as a poet strings his lyre," then proceeds to shoot the suitors one by one, in a context that was perceived as sympotic by at least later Greeks.[12]

To the Greeks of the classical period, murder at the *symposion* was more closely connected with the image of foreign feasting.[13] This is what makes the high incidence of violence in the tradition about Macedonian *symposia* so problematic. It is sometimes held that Macedonian drinking culture may have preserved features of an earlier, more heroic style of drinking—notably, the practice of refusing the right to recline at *symposia* to young men until they had killed a wild boar,[14] as well as, perhaps, the trumpet bugle that called symposiasts to the feast.[15] Modern writers often assert that it was Macedonian practice to drink their wine neat,[16] which is thought to contribute to the wilder excesses of the Macedonian feast. It is true that, in a highly polemical passage, Polybius attacks Theopompus for accusing Philip of *akratoposia*;[17] but I can find no ancient evidence to support a more general claim. The drinking contest in unmixed wine indulged in by Alexander's court on the death of Calanus was an Indian custom undertaken in honor of the Indian philosopher, and it allegedly led to several deaths from alcohol poisoning; the implication is clearly that Macedonians (unlike Indians) were not used to unmixed wine.[18] Other references concern the drinking of multiple *proposeis*, and toasts were traditionally offered in unmixed wine.[19] Ath-

11. Schmitt Pantel 1992: part II, chap. IV.

12. Murray 2008.

13. Hobden 2013: 70–100.

14. Ath. 1.18a (from Hegesander) says that the thirty-five-year-old Cassander sat beside his father and could not recline because he had not achieved this feat.

15. On the bugle, see Ath. 12.538d and Ael. *VH* 8.7, both from Chares *FGH* 125 F 4, describing Alexander's marriage feast at Opus and, thus, perhaps a special ritual for the occasion. Other early Hellenistic lavish Macedonian *symposia* are described in the *deipnetikai epistolai* exchanged by Hippolochus and Lynceus of Samos (e.g., Ath. 4.128).

16. E.g., Borza 1983: 47–49.

17. Plb. 8.9.4 = *FGH* F 27.

18. Ath. 437a = Ael. *VH* 2.41 (Chares *FGH* 125 F 19); Plu. *Alex.* 70.

19. The whole question of *proposeis* and unmixed wine is discussed at length in Ath. 10.

enaeus makes no mention of the Macedonians in his list of hard-drinking societies (442b–443c), and it is highly unlikely that ancient sources would have overlooked such an opportunity to portray the Macedonians as uncivilized barbarians. Nevertheless, despite revealing the adoption of many Greek sympotic practices, the stories about Macedonian royal *symposia* are more highly colored and more violent than other traditions, and a whole literature of Macedonian excess evolved.

The earliest of these Macedonian stories reveals the tension between innate violence and sympotic rituals. Herodotus describes a notorious event conceived of as taking place at the court of Macedon shortly before the Persian Wars. Seven high-ranking Persian ambassadors had arrived to demand earth and water from the Macedonian king Amyntas and were entertained by him at a magnificent feast. When the feasting was over, the Persians said that it was their custom to invite their wives and mistresses to come as *paredroi*. The king replied that this was by no means the Macedonian custom, "which keeps men and women separate," but that he would comply with their request, since the Persians were the Macedonians' masters. The women entered and sat in a row opposite the guests, but the Persians complained that it was painful simply to look at them from afar. So the women were moved over and sat by the guests, whereupon the drunken Persians began to fondle them. Amyntas was too frightened to protest, but his son Alexander was incensed and persuaded his father to retire and leave the proceedings to him. Amyntas agreed, warning his son against doing anything rash. Alexander then offered the women to the guests but asked that they be allowed to retire to bathe themselves first. The women left for their quarters, and Alexander dressed an equal number of smooth-cheeked young men in women's clothes, armed them with daggers, and sent them in with the words "Persians you have enjoyed a perfect feast: we have provided you with everything we could; and now finally we give you freely our mothers and daughters, so that you may understand how much you are honoured by us, and report to the king who sent you how well a Greek, the lord of Macedonia, has received you at board and bed." When the Persians began to molest the young men, the guests were all stabbed. Despite many searches by the Persians, no trace of them or their servants and baggage train could be found. Instead, the leader of the search party was bought off by Alexander with a large sum of money and the gift of his own sister Gygaea (Hdt. 5.16–21).

This story is constructed around the customs of the Greek *symposion*. The seven Persians recline on seven couches (a standard sympotic number), they feast at a *deipnon* and proceed to get drunk afterward, and they demand female company in the guise of *hetairai*, as was normal in *symposia*. However, Greek sympotic customs are here contrasted with alleged Persian customs, in that Greek women of the family are normally excluded from the *andrōn*: the womenfolk are imagined as being treated as if they were slave *hetairai*. Every detail of the story is thus modeled on the rituals of the Greek *symposion*. It is also embedded in a section of Herodotus designed to show that the Macedonians are true Greeks entitled to compete in the Olympic Games and to suggest that the future king Alexander had always secretly supported the Greeks during the Persian invasion. It is, then, clearly a fiction modeled on Greek practices, designed to serve a particular political purpose in relation to the claims of the Macedonian monarchy during the fifth century.[20] The only independently verifiable element in the story appears to be the rather damaging reference to the marriage of Alexander's sister to a Persian noble, which suggests, of course, that the Macedonian elite was firmly on the side of the Persians from the start of their expansion into northern Greece. But this circumstantial detail also suggests that the whole section of the Herodotean account is derived from Macedonian royal circles.

The appearance of the Greek *symposion* in Macedon at this relatively early date is not implausible, as is shown by the amazing eighth-century sympotic finds at Methoni Pierias, on the mouth of the Strymon.[21] But it is an intrinsic part of the presentation of the Macedonians as truly Greek, and the story therefore acquires multidimensional significance precisely because it corresponds in so many ways to the self-image of the Greeks. This fictional story was so attractive to later generations that it inspired the remodeling of a real historical event. Xenophon describes how the Theban exiles plotted to kill the pro-Spartan polemarchs during the celebrations of the festival of Aphrodite in 379 BC. He gives two versions of the event. According to one, the seven conspirators were introduced into the city and presented to the polemarchs at a celebratory *symposion* as respectable Theban women with their maids; they asked for the other slaves to be sent away, lay down beside the polemarchs, and stabbed them to death. Because of illness, one polemarch was dining with his wife at his home, where, under the guise of an urgent message, the conspirators gained access and killed him as well (X. *HG* 5.4.1–7). This retelling of a historical event is clearly modeled by Xenophon or his source on the Herodotean account; Xenophon also gives an alternative, equally "sympotic" account of the event, in which the conspira-

20. Fearn 2007.

21. Besios, Tziphopoulos, and Kotsonas 2012.

tors burst into the *symposion* disguised as reveling komasts. Both versions reflect different aspects of an event that is told in a far more detailed and accurate form by Plutarch.[22] The theme of political murder in the *symposion* later developed into a common motif: similar stories are told of the Messenians and the Spartans (Paus. 4.4.3) and of the Athenians and Megarians (Plu. *Sol.* 8; Polyaen. 1.20).

The practices of the Macedonian court reveal a basic problem about their *symposia*: in a monarchic society, it is hard to maintain the equality of participation that is intrinsic to a well-ordered *symposion*. Aristotle comments on this feature in his discussion of the impossibility of true friendship between unequals.[23] Despite his admiration of Philip II, Theopompus seems to have built a large part of his characterization of the new forces in history around royal drinking excesses and tells a number of stories about Philip's aggressive and uncivilized behavior at drinking parties.[24] Philip was widely criticized for his drunken behavior after the battle of Chaeronea.[25] At his wedding feast, he had to be restrained from killing his son Alexander when the latter threw a cup at Attalus.[26] That son, Alexander the Great, carried on the same tradition, and his biography and early death have indeed been told as a story of alcohol abuse.[27] Despite the evidence of a hard-drinking culture, the only episode in Alexander's career that led to an actual death at a *symposion* was his notorious drunken killing of Black Cleitus,[28] and the king's excessive display of remorse perhaps suggests that murder was not regarded as part of a normal Macedonian *symposion*. But the tension between violence and the *symposion* remained a powerful force in stories about the behavior of kings at *symposia* in the Hellenistic period and led to a moralizing tradition of the conflict between royal anger and philosophical *parrhēsia*.[29]

Greek moderation is often asserted as a contrast with the otherness of foreign cultures. Ctesias' accounts of royal murders at the Persian court are inventions on the theme of the Persian other, and every Greek knew that Persian conviviality was different from Greek.[30] Philip's drinking habits were

22. Plu. *Pel.* 7–12; *de genio Socratis*, *Moralia* 575–98.
23. Arist. *EN* 1150b.
24. Flower 1994: esp. 107–10; see *FGH* 115 F 224–25 = Ath. 166–67, 260–61.
25. F 236; Diod. 16.87; Plu. *Dem.* 20.3.
26. Plu. *Alex.* 9.6–11.
27. O'Brien 1992.
28. Arr. 4.8–9; Curt. 8.1–2; Plu. *Alex.* 50–51.
29. Murray 1996; Scarpat 1964.
30. Hobden 2013, 182–85.

regarded as typical of his lack of Greek culture, and Alexander the Great's drunken rages could perhaps be placed within a Macedonian style of drinking, which purports to be Greek but was recognised as somewhat different. Still, it is hard to resist the conclusion that the Greeks were well aware of the close relationship between extremes of violent behavior and alcohol, as well as of the need to employ ritualization as a means of controlling alcohol consumption.

Works Cited

Ampolo, C. 1984. "Il Lusso nelle società arcaiche." *Opus* 3: 469–76.

Besios, M., Tziphopoulos, G., and Kotsonas, A. 2012. *Methōnē Pierias I: Epigraphes, charagmata kai emporika symbola stē geōmetrikē kai archaïkē keramikē apo to 'Hypogeio' tēs Methōnēs Pierias stē Makedonia*. Thessaloniki.

Borza, E. 1983. "The Symposium at Alexander's Court." In *Ancient Macedonia*, vol. 3, *Papers Read at the Fourth International Symposium Held in Thessaloniki, September 21–25, 1983*, 45–55. Thessaloniki.

Bowie, E. 1990. "*Miles Ludens*? The Problem of Martial Exhortation in Early Greek Elegy." In O. Murray, ed., Sympotica*: A Symposium on the* Symposion*; Records of the 1st Symposium on the Greek* Symposion*, Balliol College, 4–8 September 1984*, 221–29. Oxford.

Calhoun, G.1913. *Athenian Clubs in Politics and Litigation*. Austin, TX.

Fearn, D. 2007. "Narrating Ambiguity: Murder and Macedonian Allegiance (5.17–22)." In E. Irwin and E. Greenwood, eds., *Reading Herodotus: A Study of the* Logoi *in Book 5 of Herodotus' "Histories,"* 98–127. Cambridge.

Flower, M. 1994. *Theopompus of Chios: History and Rhetoric in the Fourth Century BC*. Oxford.

Hobden, F. 2013. *The* Symposion *in Ancient Greek Society and Thought*. Cambridge.

Lynch, K. 2011. *The Symposium in Context: Pottery from a Late Archaic House near the Classical Athenian Agora*. Princeton.

Murray, O. 1983. "*Symposion* and *Männerbund*." In P. Oliva, ed., *Concilium Eirene XVI: Proceedings of the 16. International Eirene Conference, Prague, 31.8.–4.9.1982*, 47–52. Prague.

Murray, O. 1990a. "The Affair of the Mysteries: Democracy and the Drinking Group." In O. Murray, ed., Sympotica*: A Symposium on the* Symposion*; Records of the 1st Symposium on the Greek* Symposion*, Balliol College, 4–8 September 1984*, 149–61. Oxford.

Murray, O. 1990b. "The Solonian Law of *Hubris*." In P. Cartledge, P. Millett, and S. Todd, eds., Nomos*: Essays in Athenian Law, Politics, and Society*, 139–45. Cambridge.

Murray, O. 1991. "War and the Symposium." In W. Slater, ed., *Dining in a Classical Context*, 83–103. Ann Arbor.

Murray, O. 1996. "Hellenistic Royal Symposia." In P. Bilde, T. Engberg-Pedersen, L. Hannestad, and J. Zahle, eds., *Aspects of Hellenistic Kingship*, 15–27. Aarhus.

Murray, O. 2008. "The *Odyssey* as Performance Poetry." In M. Revermann and P. Wilson, eds., *Performance, Iconography, Reception: Studies in Honour of Oliver Taplin*, 161–76. Oxford.

O'Brien, J. 1992. *Alexander the Great: The Invisible Enemy*. London.

Scarpat, G. 1964. *Parrhesia: Storia del termine e delle sue traduzioni in latino*. Brescia.

Schmitt Pantel, P. 1992. *La Cité au banquet: Histoire des repas publics dans les cités grecques*. Rome.

Tsingarida, A., ed. 2009. *Shapes and Uses of Greek Vases (7th–4th Centuries B.C.): Proceedings of the Symposium Held at the Université libre de Bruxelles 27–29 April 2006*. Brussels.

PART 2

The Roman World

EIGHT

The Topography of Roman Assassination, 133 BCE–222 CE

Josiah Osgood

Assassination—the murder of a politically important individual—is a familiar feature of Roman history in the late republican and imperial periods. A precedent was set with the killing of the tribune Tiberius Gracchus and his supporters in 133 BCE, another with the attack on his brother about a decade later. After a further spate of murders in 101–100 BCE, assassination, in various forms, was regularly used by the ruling class of Rome in their struggles against one another, and it increasingly became interconnected with major episodes of civil war. Despite the establishment of peace under Augustus, a number of emperors, beginning with Caligula, were successfully assassinated; the threat of assassination was more constant still; and emperors themselves, in cooperation with the Senate, regularly took the lives of individual senators or courtiers perceived to be hostile, sometimes with no or little trial. Typically, it was members of the court, such as imperial freedmen or the emperor's own relatives, along with the emperor's Praetorian Guard, who succeeded in assassination plots. (This was to change in the third century CE, when, in a dangerous spiral, armies began killing emperors and putting forth new ones.)

As explained by Greg Woolf, author of the principal study of Roman assassination in the early empire, it was no accident that "death usually came from within the claustrophobic world of the imperial court."[1] Palace officials

1. Woolf 2006: 114. Meijer 2004 gives brief synopses of each emperor's death. I am indebted to the editors of the present volume and to Andrew Meshnick for helpful advice on the arguments in this essay and their presentation.

and Praetorians had best access to the emperor (the firearms and explosives of more recent assassinations were not available to Romans, of course); at the same time, the influence and power of these individuals depended most directly on the emperor.[2] Thus, the palace or, later, the Praetorian Camp was where emperors generally were killed.[3] Still, the setting of some imperial assassinations was chosen not only for practicality but also in an effort to attach a specific meaning to the act of violence. Even if the place was predetermined, circumstances of the killing and, very crucially, the disposal of the corpse, might be adjusted to assimilate the action to a criminal execution, an expiatory sacrifice, or an act of tyrannicide harking back to the heroes of archaic Greece and Rome. New legends themselves might form around imperial assassinations, aimed to discredit particular emperors rather than the imperial system as a whole.

The principate, in other words, was able to endure for several centuries despite assassinations. The same cannot be said of the republic, in which assassination increasingly struck at core principles, including the peaceful rotation of annually elected magistrates and the protection of a citizen's life from summary judgment by those same magistrates. In this earlier period, the venues and, really, the whole context of political murder were quite different, not least because, as a recent study has boldly put it, "murder was not a crime."[4] Throughout Rome's republican history, there was no criminal legislation against murder as such (rather, families were to handle avenging the loss of their members). Certainly, some acts of violence were criminalized, but the murder of a politician was not necessarily viewed automatically as an act in defiance of the state, as imperial assassinations as well as assassinations in more recent times have occasionally been. Indeed, sometimes quite the opposite view was held, fueled, as we shall see, by a (constantly evolving) set of historical and religious traditions that sanctioned certain acts of violence. Also relevant here was the Greek tradition of heroic tyrannicides—above all, the Athenians Harmodius and Aristogeiton.[5] The late republic is marked by a sometimes lively debate on the ethics of political murder. By the imperial period, murder was a crime, and the emperor was also protected by the law

2. Jardine 2005 explores the first assassination of a head of state by means of a gun and its ramifications. Ford 1985 gives a survey of political murder from antiquity to the twentieth century.

3. For the palace, cf. Woolf 2006: 118–21.

4. See Gaughan 2010; Gaughan's discussion of assassination at pp. 109–25 has been especially useful and informs much of this paragraph.

5. For one interesting discussion, see Ober 2003.

of *maiestas*. At the same time, as noted above, the tradition of assassination was now established in Rome and could be appealed to for some kind of legitimacy.

Assassination in ancient Rome is a vast topic that, familiar as many assassinations within Roman history are, has not been thoroughly researched as a whole. Woolf's short book is focused on the most famous assassination, Julius Caesar's, and its later resonances in the imperial era and beyond; it is well complemented by several chapters in Peter Wiseman's *Remembering the Roman People* that examine the background to the Ides of March (including the ethical debate), along with the work of Andrew Lintott, François Hinard, Judy Gaughan, and others on violence, crime, and punishment in the republican period.[6] Also to be singled out is a paper by John Scheid on "la mort du tyran," highlighting similarities in accounts of several imperial deaths.[7] My aim here, in keeping with this volume as a whole, is to build on this work and use case studies to explore the significance of the setting of Roman assassinations (I use the term *setting* in a broad sense here, referring to not just venue but a whole variety of circumstances.) In the republican period, we shall see, a particular setting sometimes helped to inspire murder, even to make it seem entirely legitimate. The same was true in the principate. Of course, for some of these later, imperial assassinations, it is hard, for reasons suggested above, to be sure that our sources are not perpetuating tendentious memories of the event, rather than objective accounts. Inevitably, some of what we are dealing with is a political and cultural discourse of assassination, rather than hard fact.

My discussion shall begin with the origins of assassination in the second century BCE, with special attention paid to their locations. I shall then turn to the best-attested of all of Rome's political murders, the assassination of Julius Caesar. Looking back to earlier murders, it also served as an inspiration for later imperial assassinations; it was a bridge between two different political cultures.[8] In a final section, I look at the murders of several emperors, highlighting how the setting of the crime endowed it with particular meanings.

6. Woolf 2006; Wiseman 2009: 176–234; Lintott 1968; Hinard 1984, 1987; Gaughan 2010; *Du châtiment dans la cité* 1984; Linderski 2007: 277–81 (with helpful bibliographic references).

7. Scheid 1984.

8. Cf. Woolf 2006: 93: "The Ides of March are a bottleneck in Roman history."

Republican Origins: 133–100 BCE

In hindsight, we can see that Rome's culture of assassination had a precise starting point. In the summer of 133 BCE, after removing his tribunician colleague Octavius from office by controversial means, Tiberius Gracchus began to fear for his own future and decided to stand again for tribune, an action that struck his critics as king-like.[9] As voting began, his candidacy was called into question, and the election was eventually postponed. By the next morning, Tiberius' followers had seized the area where voting took place—the Area Capitolina, a large enclosed space in front of the mighty Temple of Jupiter Optimus Maximus, which incorporated other temples, shrines, and altars; numerous statues of the gods as well as of famous Romans, including the kings and the first consul, Brutus; and bronze tablets with treaties and laws.[10] Tiberius' hope was to control the outcome of the voting assembly, and he initially prevailed, driving out his opponents, including fellow tribunes. Reports of what was happening spread, along with rumors, and at a Senate meeting at the Temple of Fides nearby, the *pontifex maximus*, P. Scipio Nasica, urged the presiding consul, Scaevola, to take action to protect the res publica and put down the "king."[11] Scaevola resisted, for (as he said) he was not willing to execute a citizen without trial. Nasica then summoned a citizen army—invoking a procedure used when Rome was under sudden threat.[12] In the face of this force, the Gracchans offered little resistance, fled, and were slaughtered, including Tiberius himself, who was killed by the statues of the kings, according to Appian (*BC* 1.16). The bodies of Tiberius and his supporters were thrown into the Tiber.

Clearly, Tiberius' seizure of the Area Capitolina helped to precipitate his murder, but the significance of the murder's setting ran deeper than that. After Nasica's actions at the Senate meeting but before the actual attack on Tiberius, Nasica briefly ran to the Temple of Jupiter Optimus Maximus

9. Sources for major events in this section of this essay are conveniently found in Broughton 1951–52 (here 1.493–94). For recent work I have consulted on the death of Tiberius Gracchus, see Lintott 1994: 68–73; Fiori 1996: 407–24; Linderski 2007: 88–114 (reprinting Linderski 2002 with addenda); Badian 2004; Clark 2007; Mackay 2009: 46–52; Wiseman 2009: 177–87; Gaughan 2010: 110–17. Linderski, in particular, reviews the extensive earlier discussion, and I owe a great debt to his thorough study.

10. For the details, see *LTUR* s.v. *area Capitolina*.

11. Plutarch (*Ti. Gracch.* 19.3) writes that Nasica called Tiberius a *tyrannos*; in Latin, Nasica is likelier to have spoken of *regnum*. On the incorporation of the Greek word into Roman discourse, see Wiseman 2009: 183–84.

12. See Linderski 1995: 147–53 (reprinting Linderski 1984).

(where Tiberius would have been presiding over the election) and covered his head with the edge of his striped toga. In a brilliant analysis of this gesture—already a puzzle for Appian (*BC* 1.16)—Jerzy Linderski has suggested that this veiling of the head was a part of the rite of *consecratio*, by which an individual was "abandoned to the gods to be destroyed by their wrath—which guided a human hand."[13] As Scipio Nasica saw it, Tiberius was forfeit to Jupiter in particular (Linderski explains) because Tiberius had attempted to establish tyranny (*regnum*)—in violation of a law thought to have been passed with the establishment of the republic—and had injured sacrosanct tribunes of the plebs.[14] Nasica's quick trip to the temple and his veiling can thus be seen as a response to Tiberius' (perceived) impiety to Jupiter and desecration of Jupiter's sanctuary. The two men were fighting over sacred space. There were religious overtones to the disposal of the corpses into the Tiber too: this was the fate of *monstra*, including parricides.[15]

The end result was that one could argue that Nasica's actions were perfectly legitimate, and although he did leave Rome under a cloud, he was not found guilty of any crime (murder, recall, was not a crime per se). As Scipio Aemilianus said at a stormy public meeting several years later, there was a basis for maintaining that Tiberius was killed justly (*iure caesus*), a formula drawn from the Twelve Tables that would be used again in similar contexts in later years.[16] At the same time, the consul Scaevola's insistence that he could not execute a citizen was also defensible, for the ancient law of appeal held that no magistrate could execute or even flog a citizen within the sacred boundary of Rome; a death sentence could only be issued by a convoked session of the Assembly of the People.[17] Scaevola may well have judged, too, that Nasica's demand for action would set a dangerous precedent, which it did. Appian famously wrote, "No sword was ever carried into theAssembly, nor was there civil bloodshed, until Tiberius Gracchus . . . was the first to be killed in internal disturbance [*stasis*] and with him many others, crowded together on the Capitol around the temple, were slain. And the disturbances

13. Linderski 2007: 104.

14. Linderski 2007: 113. For the law forfeiting the head of would-be kings to Jupiter, see Liv. 2.8.2; Plu. *Publ.* 12.1. Wiseman (2009: 185–87) doubts Linderski's interpretation but offers no explanation for Nasica's veiling. In his study of the *homo sacer*, Fiori (1996: 407–24) has argued that Tiberius was killed on grounds of *adfectatio regni*, but he omits analysis of the gesture on which Linderski focuses.

15. Linderski 2007: 106.

16. For Scipio, see Cic. *Mil.* 8; *De orat.* 2.106; Vell. 2.4.4. For the formula in other contexts, see Cic. *Phil.* 13.2; Liv. 4.15.1; Suet. *Jul.* 76.1.

17. See, e.g., Liv. 2.8; Plu. *Publ.* 10–11. For one discussion, see Lintott 1972.

did not end with this abominable deed" (*BC* 1.2).[18] In time, the sacred basis for Nasica's actions came to be downplayed, while murder came to be seen as an easier way to settle difficult political quarrels, even if it still had to be justified on some grounds.[19]

It was no accident that one of the first actions of Tiberius' younger brother Gaius in his first tribunate a decade later was to affirm, by law, that no citizen should be sentenced to death without the people's authority (e.g., through a court set up only by senators).[20] Gaius' much more elaborate program for reform followed, and it created enough opposition to defeat him in his attempt to win reelection in 122 BCE. His opponents, including the consul Opimius, then hoped to overturn all his legislation, and a session of the Assembly of the People was called, again on the Capitol, to strike down one of the measures: Gaius arrived with his (armed) supporters, a man was killed, and everyone ran off the hill. That night, Opimius, not Gaius, seized control of the Capitol and also the Forum—the two venues where the Assembly of the People could vote on legislation. As in 133 BCE, efforts to control the Capitol were leading to murder. Shut out from there, the Gracchans now seized the Aventine Hill, a site that they could fortify and that was symbolically appealing because of its association with the secessions of the plebs in Rome's early history. To counterattack, Opimius, a holder of imperium (unlike Scipio Nasica) and, thus, directly subject to the law of appeal, had the Senate pass a vague decree that the consuls "should see to it that the res publica not be harmed."[21] Under cover of this decree, Opimius launched an assault on the Gracchans, at the end of which three thousand were dead, some killed in street fighting, others executed after being cast into prison.

Opimius was put on trial by a tribune before the Assembly of the People, on the grounds of taking citizens' lives without the people's approval. Since the trial would have occurred in their meeting place either in the Forum or on the Capitol, it can be seen as an effort to reclaim that space in the ongoing tug-of-war between Gracchans and anti-Gracchans. But Opimius was

18. For similar language elsewhere, see, e.g., Plut. *Ti. Gracch.* 20.1. (My translations throughout are usually based on those in the Loeb Classical Library series.)

19. Fiori (1996: 425–61) and Várhelyi (2011) argue, from different perspectives, that the sacral nature of Tiberius' murder continued to be one strand of ongoing debate on assassination—but only one strand, I would emphasize.

20. Cic. *Rab. perd.* 12; Plu. *CG* 4.1–2.

21. Broughton 1951: 220. See Lintott 1999: 89–93, for a helpful overview. See also Lintott 1968: 149–74.

acquitted, and so there was some kind of recognition of the new type of Senate decree, sometimes referred to as the *senatus consultum ultimum*.[22] Still, its legality was dubious, and it took twenty-one years for it to be invoked again, in the midst of yet more bloodshed. The year 100 BCE was the last of the stormy career of Appuleius Saturninus, a politician relied on by Gaius Marius in 103 BCE to pass legislation on behalf of the latter's veterans.[23] This only happened after Saturninus' tribunician colleague Baebius, who had imposed his veto, was driven off in a hail of stones thrown by Saturninus' supporters. Even worse were events in 101 BCE: a competitor of Saturninus in the tribunician elections, Nunnius, was seized in the voting assembly itself (most likely in the Field of Mars) and then killed nearby, only for Saturninus to be elected the following day.[24] Both electoral and legislative assemblies were on their way to becoming established venues for violence, especially when politicians did not attain their desired results.

In 100 BCE itself, Saturninus passed further legislation, bringing Marius' armed veterans into the Assembly; gaining yet another tribunician term himself that year, he also aimed to help his associate Servilius Glaucia pass straight from a praetorship into the consulship. The first step was to assassinate, at elections on the Field of Mars, Glaucia's opponent Memmius, which they did (inspired by the earlier elimination of Nunnius); the second was to seize the Capitol, as Tiberius Gracchus and then Opimius had, to pass a law authorizing Glaucia's candidacy.[25] For only the second time, the *senatus consultum ultimum* was passed, and Marius felt that he had no choice but to move against the sacrosanct tribune. Arms were distributed, and a militia was formed. Saturninus' supporters were cleared from the Forum and took refuge on the Capitol, and there Marius besieged them. Saturninus and Glaucia surrendered, with Marius promising protection: Saturninus and his supporters, though not Glaucia, were detained in the Senate House. But it was to no avail. Inside the Senate House, they were stoned to death by a mob, while Glaucia had his neck broken. Precisely who was responsible for these murders is unclear. One may wonder, though, if detention in the Senate House helped inspire the deed, for Saturninus, though a senator himself,

---

22. Liv. *Perioch.* 61; Cic. *Orat.* 2.106, 132–35, 165, 169. On the *senatus consultum ultimum*, see the sources cited in n. 21 above.

23. Broughton 1951: 575–76. For discussions I have consulted, see Badian 1984; Beness 1991; Lintott 1994: 92–103; Mackay 2009: 106–17; Gaughan 2010: 121–24.

24. By this time, electoral meetings of the Assembly of the People typically took place on the Field of Mars, not on the Capitol: see Taylor 1966: 47–58.

25. See esp. Badian 1984: 106–21.

had offended a great many senators through his actions. To kill him there was to reassert senatorial authority.

Saturninus was clearly an heir to the Gracchi; among his other schemes was an attempt to pass off a man named L. Equitius as a son of Tiberius Gracchus and to have Equitius elected tribune. Saturninus' use of violence, while arguably more extreme than what had happened before, can be seen as "a reasoned reaction to the defeat of the Gracchi by force";[26] that is, his violence gained legitimacy, in his eyes and that of his supporters, by precedents set earlier, such as both Tiberius Gracchus' and Opimius' seizure of the Capitoline and the deaths of the Gracchans in 133 and 121 BCE. At the same time, the consul Marius' fulfillment of the *senatus consultum ultimum* without challenge meant that the Senate itself was now above the law and could effectively authorize the execution of magistrates. Without anyone exactly intending it, the republic was slipping away.

Two consequences followed the events of 100 BCE. The first was that assassination—the sudden murder of politically important individuals—had now become a definite part of Rome's political culture, even if it was not named as such. Fuller justifications were worked out for it in years to come.[27] A clear example was the way in which the stories of the deaths of three would-be kings from the early annals of Rome—Spurius Cassius, Spurius Maelius, and Marcus Manlius—were retold to underscore the acceptability of killing those allegedly aiming for kingship.[28] (Maelius was especially important to Caesar's assassin Marcus Brutus, because, according to tradition, an ancestor on Brutus' mother's side, Servilius Ahala, had killed Maelius.)[29] In demanding action against Catiline in 63 BCE, Cicero can appeal to the story of this triad, along with the killings of the Gracchi, Saturninus, and Glaucia; and before that year was out, Cicero, as consul, would preside over the execution of five citizens without trial, under cover of the *senatus consultum ultimum*.[30] Greek conceptions of tyrannicide became folded into the Roman discourse of aspiring to *regnum*, and it was probably in the last century BCE that a copy of the famous statue group in Athens

26. Lintott 1994: 103.

27. Lintott 1968: 52–66 remains a very helpful discussion.

28. For some recent discussions that are in general agreement on late republican reworking of these stories, see Chassignet 2001; Smith 2006; Flower 2006: 44–51; Wiseman 2009: 183; Lowrie 2010.

29. As moneyer ca. 54 BCE, Brutus issued coins with Ahala on the obverse (*RRC* 433.2); a family tree displayed at one of his villas showed descent from Ahala (Cic. *Att.* 13.40.1).

30. For Cicero's appeal, see Cic. *Catil.* 1.3–6.

of the archaic tyrannicides Harmodius and Aristogeiton went up on the Capitol—perhaps likening, implicitly, Tiberius Gracchus to a tyrant.[31]

The other significance of 100 BCE was that, as has occurred so often in history, the violence of this year directly inspired yet worse violence, spreading beyond the fractious assemblies in which it had its origins and further eroding the Roman republic.[32] In the words, once more, of Appian, summing up the fall of Saturninus, "Neither freedom, nor democracy, nor laws, nor reputation, nor office were any longer of any help to anybody, since even the office of tribune, . . . though sacred and inviolable, committed such awful deeds *and* suffered them" (*BC* 1.33, emphasis mine). Appian can prove his point by immediately recounting that a former tribune put on trial (probably in 98 BCE) was lynched before his hearing. Within the same decade followed the assassination of another tribune, Livius Drusus, at his house, directly precipitating the Social War. In 88 BCE, just as the Social War was winding down, the tribune Sulpicius Rufus built up a force of armed gangs and had a law passed to transfer command in the war against Mithridates from Sulla to Marius; Sulla was not in Rome to attempt to block Sulpicius in the Assembly, so he simply took the army he had commanded during the Social War and marched on the city, killing Sulpicius and overturning the tribune's law.[33] From this unfolded a full civil war between Marius, Sulla, and others, by the end of which (81 BCE), as Harriet Flower has remarked, "violence was deliberately open and advertised."[34] This violence included assassination, especially in the form of proscription, through which high-ranking Romans were decapitated, with their heads displayed at the rostra in the Forum, a grim inversion of the splendid funerals staged there by the nobility.[35]

31. On the Greek tyrannicides, see, e.g., Cic. *Mil.* 79–80; *Att.* 14.21.3. On the copy of the statue group, see Stewart 1990: 135–36; Coarelli 1969 (avowedly speculative).

32. The role of violence in devastating the traditions of the res publica is briefly but powerfully argued by Flower (2010: 80–96) and developed at length in the narrative of Mackay 2009. Lintott (1968: 175–208), by contrast, aims to bring out continuities in the years before and after 133 BCE, with violence as symptomatic of even larger problems—legal, constitutional, and so forth. His own useful appendix ("Acts of Violence in Rome," 209–20) shows, though, that the generation of 133–100 BCE was a watershed.

33. Broughton 1952: 39–42.

34. Flower 2010: 95.

35. See esp. Hinard 1984. Sulla would be emulated in 43 by the triumvirs, who used spectacular violence to help establish a new form of government, the triumvirate: see Osgood 2006: 62–81.

The Ides of March

By the time of Caesar's assassination in 44 BC, there was a long history of political violence and murder in Rome. This helped to inspire the assassins and also prompted them to think about how to set their deed in a way that would enhance both its immediate reception and later memory of it. This was a more carefully planned murder than any that came before.[36] We are told that there were more than sixty conspirators, who met initially in smaller groups to discuss possible venues for their crime. Access to Caesar was, of course, a necessity. The earliest extant account of the plotting, that of Nicolaus of Damascus, indicates that three possibilities were considered: while Caesar was walking along the Via Sacra (near his house), at elections over which Caesar was presiding, or at gladiatorial games (*Vit. Aug.* 81). Suetonius also mentions the first two, along with a third possibility, perhaps related to Nicolaus' third: "at the entrance to the theater" (*Jul.* 80.4). Assassinations on the Field of Mars, where elections occurred, had succeeded before, as we saw, in 100 BCE, but their memory was hardly glorious. It was also risky, far riskier than in Saturninus' day, because even if Caesar had dismissed his bodyguard, he would have numerous friends (some of them likely armed) to come to his aid at the comitia. For the same reason, the other options mentioned were also fraught with peril.

Thus, when it was announced that Caesar would be in attendance at a meeting of the Senate on the Ides of March, to be held in the Curia, or meeting room, that was part of the portico of Pompey's large theater complex, the conspirators "without hesitation gave that time and place the preference," as Suetonius puts it (*Jul.* 80.4). The practical advantages, as the ancient sources make clear, were many. While nonsenatorial conspirators could not participate, the senators would easily be able to reach Caesar and crowd around him, sitting in isolation in his curule chair. They could smuggle weapons in easily, and he would have little protection. Additionally, it was possible to assemble gladiators nearby in the portico, should a serious fray ensue.

But it was not just that the conspirators had a better chance of successfully murdering Caesar on that occasion; to commit their deed in the Curia Pompei offered, as Nicholas Horsfall puts it, "an important symbolic

36. The principal ancient sources are Nic. Dam. *Vit. Caes.* 81–97; Suet. *Jul.* 80–88; Plu. *Caes.* 62–67; *Brut.* 14–18; App. *BC* 2.111–20; D.C. 44.13–20. Modern accounts that I have consulted are Gelzer 1968: 324–29; Horsfall 1974; Woolf 2006; Ramsey 2008; Lintott 2009; Wiseman 2009: 211–21; Pelling 2011: 459–91.

advantage."[37] This hall contained a statue of Pompey, dedicated by the people of Rome.[38] For those who still had sympathy for Pompey or those who simply likened that man's final defeat by Caesar to their own subjection, this statue could help steel them to act: some accounts even maintained, according to Plutarch (*Caes.* 66.2; *Brut.* 17.1), that the Epicurean Cassius looked at the statue before the attack and called on Pompey for help. Pompey, as Plutarch also puts it (*Caes.* 66.7; *Brut.* 14.3), could be seen to be presiding over revenge upon his enemy, whose body was (it seems) dragged by the assassins to the base of the statue, which it drenched with blood. By playing up this sense of poetic justice, Plutarch endows the Ides of March with a "cosmic dimension,"[39] but that dimension is already present (in different form) in Nicolaus' account and also had to have been in the conspirators' minds on some level. By murdering Caesar in the Curia Pompei, with Pompey (or his statue) looking on, Caesar's murderers forever linked the dictator's end to his own earlier ruthlessness and his destruction of the res publica that Pompey could be thought to have died trying to defend. That the conspirators had effectively exploited this setting is suggested by its subsequent fate: within a couple of years, the Curia was walled up, and the statue was removed to a marble arch outside the theater.[40] Pompey was not to preside over any more revenge on Caesar's successors.

To kill Caesar at a meeting of the Senate offered the conspirators a second symbolic advantage, or so at least they thought. With the murder underway, the conspirators could involve other senators and remind them of their lost freedom: this was a tyrant, an aspirant to kingship, being killed, and at the founding of the res publica (at least according to later tradition), Romans had sworn an oath never to be ruled by a king again (this was why Brutus' ancestor Ahala could be hailed as a savior of the res publica for his murder of Sp. Maelius).[41] In the event, the senators looking on fled in panic, and things ceased to go as planned or hoped. Not to be deterred, the assassins ran out of the Curia toward the Forum, brandishing their unsheathed daggers

37. Horsfall 1974: 194.

38. On the statue, see esp. Cic. *Div.* 2.23; Nic. Dam. *Vit. Caes.* 83, 90; Suet. *Aug.* 31.5; Plu. *Caes.* 66.1, 7; *Brut.* 14.2; D.C. 49.52.1. Woolf 2006: 1–3 briefly describes the theater complex, while Packer 2010 incorporates the results of recent work on the site.

39. Pelling 2011: 479.

40. Suet. *Jul.* 88; *Aug.* 31.5; D.C. 47.19.1.

41. According to Appian (*BC* 2.119), the assassins recalled this oath in their exhortation to the people immediately following the murder. For the oath, see Livy 2.1.9; Plu. *Publ.* 2. This oath is to be distinguished from the law forfeiting tyrants to Jupiter (see n. 14 above).

and shouting for freedom; the gesture echoed, quite possibly consciously, the pose of the Harmodius and Aristogeiton statue group.[42] It may also have evoked the pose of another statue on the Capitol, that of Lucius Brutus, who expelled Rome's last king.[43] But the people, equally terrified, also were not terribly receptive to their would-be liberators, who then fled to the Capitol—a practical action as well as a suggestion that Jupiter was on their side. These symbolic actions were not enough: for the people, along with soldiers and veterans of Caesar in Rome at the time, loyalty to the slain man was overwhelming. When the Senate convened to discuss Rome's future, rewards were initially proposed for the assassins, as if they were indeed Greek tyrannicides; but the consul Antony, sensing the political advantage of stoking the people's anger, blocked those and made arrangements for a funeral for Caesar that proved literally incendiary and sowed the seeds for the assassins' departure from Rome and subsequent condemnation.[44] It was no accident that the Senate voted to give the Ides of March the horrific sobriquet Parricidium, the Day of Parricide.[45]

Suetonius (*Jul.* 82.4) remarks that the conspirators had intended to drag Caesar's body into the Tiber, as well as confiscate his property and revoke his decrees.[46] Both Gracchi brothers and their followers were thrown into the Tiber as a form of disgrace, intended to accompany the deceased into the afterlife; disposal of their bodies also ensured that no funerary monument would be erected to serve as a locus to inspire their living supporters.[47] Certainly, from the view of hindsight, one could argue that abuse and disposal of Caesar's corpse might have helped the assassins in their quest to discredit Caesar by the manner in which they perpetrated their violence; leaving the body to his supporters was, on some level, a political miscalculation. Still, through the setting of the assassination itself, they succeeded not only in

42. On the gesture of the assassins, see, e.g., Nic. Dam. *Vit. Caes.* 91, 94; Plu. *Caes.* 67.3; App. *BC* 2.119. On the Athenian statue group and the copy in Rome, see n. 31 above; Wiseman 2009: 190. Appian (*BC* 2.119) adds the detail that "one of them [the assassins] bore a cap on the end of a spear as a symbol of freedom"—perhaps a later embroidery inspired by the cap of freedom that was shown on coins issued by Brutus after the Ides of March (*RRC* 508.3, a type noted by D.C. 47.25.3).

43. See Plutarch's description of Brutus' statue at *Brut.* 1.1.

44. On the proposal of rewards for the assassins, see Suet. *Tib.* 4.1 (*praemiis tyrannicidarum*); App. *BC* 2.121.

45. See esp. Suet. *Jul.* 88.

46. Cf. App. *BC* 2.134; D.C. 44.35.1.

47. For helpful remarks on this form of punishment, see Hinard 1987: 119–21; Beness 2000: 1–2; Barry 2008: 228–29.

murdering Caesar—their paramount goal—but also in suggesting that this was not (solely) a power play but the well-deserved fate of Caesar himself, seemingly with divine sanction. Not only would a murder committed as Caesar was walking on the Via Sacra have been harder to pull off; it would have had less emotional import. It would not have been nearly so much of an assertion of traditional Roman freedom as murder in the Senate House, followed by the parade of brandished daggers.

Some Later Imperial Examples

After Caesar's murder, no assassination would take place again at a meeting of the Senate, in large part because emperors made it impossible for senators to bring weapons in; while Praetorians sometimes did enter, they had other, better opportunities.[48] Senators could be and were searched upon entering the imperial palace, too, and emperors were protected in public venues by their Praetorian Guard as well as other forces.[49] It is not surprising, then, that despite widespread opposition to Caligula on the part of senators, it was a fearless Praetorian officer, Cassius Chaerea, who made assassination possible.[50] Repeatedly mocked by Caligula, Chaerea was eager to defend his personal honor, but he also knew that Caligula's rule was failing, making the Praetorians' own prospects less certain. Enlisting support from others, including, especially, fellow officers in the guard, Chaerea needed to find the right opportunity, "so that his resort to violence would not be in vain but fulfill his plans," as writes Josephus (*AJ* 19.27), who gives an illuminating, though not entirely unproblematic, account of the plot.[51]

As was already true in 44 BC with Caesar, murder of an emperor had to be planned most carefully—we are a world away from the more spontaneous violence of 133–100 BCE. A murder at the Circus, Chaerea concluded, was too risky. Other opportunities rejected were Caligula's visits to the Capitol, his appearances on top of the Basilica Julia to distribute largesse to the peo-

48. Talbert 1984: 154–62.

49. On searches, see esp. Suet. *Ves.* 12; D.C. 60.3.3. For the emperor's protection in general, see Millar 1977: 61–66.

50. For the principal ancient sources, see J. *AJ* 19.1–273 (with Wiseman 1991); Suet. *Cal.* 56–60 (with Hurley 1993); D.C. 59.29.30. For modern accounts that I have consulted (in addition to Wiseman 1991 and Hurley 1993), see Barrett 1989: 154–71; Winterling 2011: 154–71.

51. See the works cited in the previous note.

ple, and "the performance of the mysteries he had established" (*AJ* 19.71–2). Instead, Chaerea and his colleagues fixed on the Palatine Games, established by Livia in 14 CE in honor of the divine Augustus. On this occasion, a temporary wooden theater was erected in front of the imperial property on the Palatine.[52] The initial plan, according to Josephus, was to kill Caligula as he entered the theater, "when many thousands of people would be crowded in a small space . . . and his guards would not have the chance to come to his aid even if any of them should want to" (*AJ* 19.76). That proved impossible, and as the games dragged on, Chaerea worried that he would never have a chance. Finally it came, on the last day of the games, when Caligula left the theater sometime after midday to enter the palace complex to inspect a choir of boys; entering a quiet passage, Caligula was caught and killed.

While assassinating Caligula at games in honor of his venerable predecessor, Augustus, certainly added some solemnity to the event, it would be hard to maintain that the ultimate venue was not determined by practical considerations along with chance. An isolated section of the palace allowed the assassins access to the emperor, while also affording protection for themselves.[53] Yet the main authorities of the assassination, Suetonius along with Josephus, still attribute special significance to the manner of the violent act (if not the venue itself). According to Josephus, Chaerea presented himself to Caligula, asking for the password, and when Caligula gave it mockingly (as he had before), Chaerea did not hesitate; "he heaped abuse on Gaius and, drawing his sword, struck a strong blow" (*AJ* 19.105). Then the others joined in. In this version, Chaerea's action is depicted as not simply murder but just retribution on a man who has dishonored all those around him.

Josephus was aware of another version of the death, however, according to which "it was Chaerea's deliberate plan not to finish Gaius off with a single blow but to extract a greater revenge by inflicting many wounds" (*AJ* 19.106). Josephus (perhaps rightly) considers this unlikely, but this version, or something like it, is one of two referred to by Suetonius (*Gai.* 58.2). According to his biography, some maintained that as Caligula was talking to the choir of boys, Chaerea came up to him from behind and gashed his neck, crying out "Strike!" (*hoc age!*), before Chaerea's colleague stabbed Caligula in the breast. As Donna Hurley explains, this description assimilates the murder to a sacrifice, in which the victim was first struck from its blind side; "*[h]oc age* was the affirmative answer to the formulaic question

52. See esp. J. *AJ* 19.75, with Wiseman 1991: 55.

53. Hurley 1993: 208.

with which a sacrifice began: *agone?* = 'Do I proceed?'."[54] But because execution also was assimilated with sacrifice and because *hoc age* was a phrase used in executions, there is also a hint here of execution: through the means of his death, Caligula is being assimilated to a criminal. A second version mentioned by Suetonius has Caligula give the watchword "Jupiter" and has Chaerea respond, "Receive the watchword as fulfilled!" (*accipe ratum!*), before striking his jaw. The implication here is that Jupiter is having his revenge on Caligula, a god whom, according to Suetonius (*Gai.* 22.4), Caligula had challenged for preeminence.[55]

Patently not all of these versions can be true, and perhaps none of them is. Unlike the assassination of Caesar, which was witnessed by many—and which has a reasonable chance of being more or less accurately reported by the contemporary Nicolaus—Caligula's murder had few onlookers. The different versions reported do point to a desire to represent Caligula's assassination after his death as well deserved: this was not wanton murder but revenge on a tyrant, execution of a criminal, a quasi sacrifice to appease the gods, especially Jupiter.[56] Such an understanding satisfied not only those disgruntled with Caligula's rule but also subsequent emperors, beginning with Caligula's immediate successor, Claudius, who nevertheless saw to it that Chaerea was executed. In the immediate aftermath of the murder, the Senate contemplated voting honors to Chaerea and his colleagues (in the Greek tradition of honoring tyrannicides), but the honors were never passed.[57] Then, the day after Caligula was assassinated, Chaerea rashly called for Claudius' head, after the Praetorians had declared for the latter, and Chaerea was killed.[58] Still, his murder of Caligula was allowed to remain, at least tacitly, a tyrannicide, justifiable on the grounds of what its victim had done, just as Caligula's memory was unofficially but effectively condemned.[59]

A desire to cloak the murder of a ruling emperor as something else is evident in the widely witnessed and surely better-attested assassination of Vitel-

54. Hurley 1993: 210; the following point on execution is also owed to this discussion. Note that Dio Cassius, as epitomized by John of Antioch (59.30.1a) also describes the murder of Caligula in sacrificial terms.

55. Hurley 1993: 211.

56. In his epitome of Cassius Dio (59.29.7), Xiphilinus claims that the assassins of Caligula ate flesh. It seems likely that this is a significantly later invention, given that there is no trace of it before.

57. J. *AJ* 19.182–89.

58. J. *AJ* 19.258, 267–70; Suet. *Cl.* 11.1; D.C. 60.3.4.

59. On the latter point, see Flower 2006: 148–59.

lius in 69 CE.[60] As the Flavian army advanced on Rome, Vitellius initially tried to abdicate but then decided to resist Vespasian's brother, Sabinus, who was driven to the Capitol with his supporters and executed (while the great temple of Jupiter was also burned down). Vitellius' forces were defeated with the arrival of the Flavian army, who hunted the emperor down, finding him in the otherwise abandoned palace. They could easily have killed him on the spot. Instead, in the words of Suetonius,

> with his hands bound behind his back, a noose put around his neck, and his clothes torn, he was dragged half-naked into the Forum, amid great abuse and mockery, for the whole course of the Sacred Way. His head was held back by his hair, as is customary for convicted criminals, and his chin was raised up by the point of a sword, so that he would have to let his face be seen and could not look down. (*Vit.* 17)

Tacitus and Dio supply similar accounts. All agree, too, that Vitellius was finally brought to the Scalae Gemoniae, the Stairs of Wailing, on the eastern side of the Capitoline Hill, climbing between the state prison and the Temple of Concord (though Dio has a brief intermediary stop at the prison). On the stairs, Vitellius was repeatedly stabbed and was killed, then his body was dragged to the Tiber on a hook (this last according to Suetonius at *Vit.* 17.2).

For all the giddy violence of Vitellius' murderers—a mob of Flavian soldiers and city dwellers—there is a clear logic to their actions. They were inflicting on him something very close to a standard form of Roman execution, employed especially against traitors.[61] When a traitor was condemned, he was removed to the prison and killed, then his corpse was exposed on the Scalae Gemoniae. Exposure of traitors' bodies went back to republican days, but the use of the Scalae Gemoniae was almost certainly an imperial development, especially conspicuous in 31 CE, when Tiberius' Praetorian prefect Sejanus, condemned by a letter of the emperor, was taken to the prison, forced to keep his head exposed, and abused as he went; executed in the prison, he was thrown onto the Stairs of Wailing; his corpse was abused and then thrown into the Tiber.[62] As William Barry observes in his important study of the Scalae Gemoniae, there are some differences between this procedure and what happened to Vitellius; in particular, Vitellius was killed

60. For the principal ancient sources, see Suet. *Vit.* 15–17; Tac. *Hist.* 3.83–85; D.C. 64.20–21. Barry 2008 contains an outstanding analysis, to which I am indebted.

61. Barry 2008: 240–46.

62. D.C. 58.11.1–5 is the main source, supplemented by Ehrenberg and Jones 1955: 42.

on the Stairs of Wailing, and his body was mutilated before death.[63] The angry mob with soldiers was only imitating a civic ritual, not carrying it out precisely. Their doing so was an attempt, on some level, to legitimize their actions—to suggest that they, too, were executing an enemy of the state, a usurper like Sejanus.[64]

It must be noticed, though, that Flavius Sabinus himself had been dispatched in a similar fashion just days before.[65] Placed in chains and brought to Vitellius, he was heckled by a crowd, demanding his execution. Vitellius had no choice, Tacitus writes, and Sabinus was hacked to death, his head cut off and his decapitated body dragged to the Stairs of Wailing. While Vitellius' murder could, for some, have been revenge for the death of Sabinus, it was, like the earlier crime, also an assertion of power by inhabitants of Rome, whose violence was given direction by the Flavian soldiers. In this year of civil war across the Roman Empire, as well as in the city of Rome itself, this assassination was just one strand in a larger tapestry of violence. Still, it hardly suited Vespasian and the Flavian dynasty as a whole to rehabilitate the memory of Vitellius. For them, Vitellius' violent end, like Caligula's, was best understood in popular memory as the punishment of a usurping tyrant, rather than some kind of political attack on the principate as a whole or even outright murder; Vitellius would, posthumously, be turned into a tyrant, as was Domitian after his assassination in the palace and then Commodus after his (192 CE).[66]

Something of a parallel exists between the assassination of Vitellius and the final emperor to be considered, briefly, here, the notorious Elagabalus.[67] The contemporary historians Cassius Dio and Herodian give a similar account of this emperor's last moments, one that may be preferred to that

---

63. For this and the following points, see Barry 2008: 241–45.

64. A contrast can be made with the earlier death of Galba, in 69 AD. Soldiers supporting Otho found him in the Forum; dispersing the crowd he was hoping to address, they slew him after he fell out of his litter by the Lacus Curtius, then they mutilated his corpse. At least as described by our sources (see esp. Plu. *Galb.* 16–17; Suet. *Gal.* 18–20; Tac. *Hist.* 1.39–44; D.C. 63.5–6)—in general more sympathetic to Galba than Vitellius, since Galba was not the Flavians' opponent—the soldiers' actions did not evoke a civic ritual and brought discredit on themselves, not Galba.

65. See esp. Tac. *Hist.* 3.74.

66. Domitian is omitted in this essay because he is treated in detail by Woolf (2006: 100–114). On the memory of Vitellius, Levick 1999: 71–73 is a good starting point. For Commodus, see, e.g., Potter 2004: 85–93.

67. The principal ancient sources are Hdn. 5.8; D.C. 80.29–21; HA *Heliogab.* 13–17.7. Icks 2011: 41–43 gives a discussion.

in the later *Historia Augusta*.[68] Losing favor, especially because of his religious practices and policies, Elagabalus, they write, was forced to adopt his cousin (the future emperor Alexander Severus) but then came to blows with him; both were forced to appear in the Praetorian Camp (with Alexander being made, Herodian writes, to appear at the shrine of Mars within the camp—an affirmation of the traditional state religion that Elagabalus had neglected).[69] But for one reason or another, the Praetorians grew impatient with Elagabalus and proceeded to murder him, along with his influential mother, Soaemias, and his retinue. Elagabalus' body was dragged through the streets, mutilated, and thrown into a sewer and then into the Tiber.

The murder of Elagabalus in the Praetorian Camp, even if a spontaneous action, was an assertion of the Praetorians' own power. It was becoming routine to create emperors there, and the logical corollary was that emperors could be destroyed there. The Praetorians had murdered Pertinax in 193 in the palace and taken his head to the camp; they backed the murder (again in the palace) of the successor of Pertinax and rival of Septimius Severus, Didius Julianus; and Praetorians were involved in the murder of Caracalla, which took place while he was on campaign in the east, traveling from Edessa to Carrhae.[70] We are now in the period of Roman history where the army or armies were fully a player in politics, as had been true intermittently before (chiefly in 68–70 CE); assassination and usurpation was to be the norm in the third century and common in the fourth as well.[71] Also prominent in the Severan period itself and afterward was application of extreme sanctions against the memory of vanquished foes—carried out more systematically than before, by the soldiers themselves. Thus, it makes sense that not only was Elagabalus' corpse abused, as Vitellius' was, but the abuse was well publicized.[72] After his death, among the many nicknames by which he was known, he was dubbed *Tiberinus*, *Tractaticius* (or *Tractatitius*), and *Impurus*.[73] Here, in fact, we see the distance Romans had passed between the

68. Here I concur with Icks 2011: 43.

69. Whittaker 1970: 70–71.

70. For the details, see, e.g., Meijer 2004: 66–76; Potter 2004: 96–101, 144–46.

71. Potter 2004: 125–72 is helpful on the "army in politics"; Campbell 1984: 365–414 surveys the question in wider context. To be noted in the years immediately following Elagabalus' death are the assassinations of the Praetorian prefect Ulpian by members of the guard and of Flavius Heracleo, governor of Mesopotamia, by his army.

72. Flower has noted the extreme memory sanctions of the Severan period (2006: 281) and described their novelty more fully (2008).

73. D.C. 79.21.3; HA *Heliogab.* 17.5; *Epit. Caes.* 23.7. For a discussion, see Alföldy 1976.

middle of the first century CE and the start of the third: the act of Elagabalus' assassination was given no particular sanctity, either in its perpetration or in the memory of it. Assassination was becoming or had become a part of the political landscape of Rome, in tandem with the increased power of the army. Now, abuse of the corpse could simply degrade the deceased and, with it, the position of *princeps*.

Conclusion

Assassination developed in historical Rome out of some specific circumstances: inherent tensions in the constitution, the attitude toward murder, and traditions about the expulsion of Rome's legendary kings. Arguments in and over civic spaces resulted in the first murders. Scipio Nasica sought to contextualize his use of violence religiously, as did the later opponents of Gaius Gracchus constitutionally, followed by Marius and others. But in a classic illustration of the law of unintended consequences, these actions set precedents, with the result that assassination had become a part of political life by 100 BCE; it spread from the assemblies outward and became closely interwoven with full civil war in the 80s BCE, which undermined the traditional protection of citizens' lives against summary judgment. The assassins ended up assassinating the republic.

On the one hand, Caesar's murder can be seen as a point on this republican trend line; on the other hand, its perpetrators were (unlike, say, Cicero in 63) also reacting against this now well-developed tradition, trying—through the setting of their action, as well as their refusal to murder others—to distinguish themselves from earlier assassins and hark back more fully to the tyrant slayers of the legendary past of Greece and Rome. After the civil wars that followed the Ides of March, more horrible than those that came before, the principate was gradually established, and it managed to absorb a series of assassinations for several centuries. Assassination might then, in fact, be deemed necessary to end a failing reign, especially one such as Caligula's, which was considered an affront to the sanctity of gods and to the honor of men; memory of such assassination would be shaped to make it look justified and, thus, to protect the principate. The discourse of tyranny and assassination was a key part of imperial political culture. But once, by the age of Elagabalus, assassination became more commonplace, moving from the palace to the Praetorian Camp and beyond, political instability was concomitant. Now the assassins assassinated the principate.

Works Cited

Alföldy, G. 1976. "Zwei Schimpfnamen des Kaisers Elagabal: Tiberinus und Tractatitius." In J. Straub, ed., *Bonner Historia-Augusta-Coll. 1972–1974*, 11–21. Bonn.

Badian, E. 1984. "The Death of Saturninus: Studies in Chronology and Prosopography." *Chiron* 14: 101–47.

Badian, E. 2004. "The Pig and the Priest." In H. Heftner and K. Tomaschitz, eds., *Ad Fontes! Festschrift für Gerhard Dobesch*, 263–72. Vienna.

Barrett, A. 1989. *Caligula: The Corruption of Power*. London.

Barry, W. 2008. "Exposure, Mutilation, and Riot: Violence at the *Scalae Gemoniae* in Early Imperial Rome." *G&R* 55: 222–46.

Beness, J. 1991. "The Urban Unpopularity of Lucius Appuleius Saturninus." *Antichthon* 25: 33–62.

Beness, J. 2000. "The Punishment of the Gracchani and the Execution of C. Villius in 133/132." *Antichthon* 34: 1–17.

Broughton, T. 1951–52. *The Magistrates of the Roman Republic*. 2 vols. New York.

Campbell, J. 1984. *The Emperor and the Roman Army, 31 BC–AD 235*. Oxford.

Chassignet, M. 2001. "La 'construction' des aspirants à la tyrannie: Sp. Cassius, Sp. Maelius et Manlius Capitolinus." In M. Coudry and T. Späth, eds., *L'invention des grands hommes de la Rome antique*, 83–96. Paris.

Clark, A. 2007. "Nasica and *Fides*." *CQ* 57: 125–31.

Coarelli, F. 1969. "Le tyrannoctone du Capitole et la mort de Tibérius Gracchus." *MEFR* 81: 137–60.

Du châtiment dans la cité: Supplices corporels et peine de mort dans le monde antique. Table ronde organisée par l'Ecole française de Rome avec le concours du Centre national de la recherche scientifique (Rome 9–11 nomembre 1982). 1984. Collection de l'École française de Rome, Palais Farnèse. Rome: École française de Rome, Palais Farnèse.

Ehrenberg, V., and Jones, A. 1955. *Documents Illustrating the Reigns of Augustus and Tiberius*. 2nd ed. Oxford.

Fiori, R. 1996. *Homo sacer: Dinamica politico-costituzionale di una sanzione giuridoreligiosa*. Naples.

Flower, H. 2006. *The Art of Forgetting: Disgrace and Oblivion in Roman Political Culture*. Chapel Hill.

Flower, H. 2008. "Les Sévères et l'usage de la *memoria*: L'*arcus* du *Forum Boarium* à Rome." In S. Benoist and A. Daguet-Gagey, eds., *Un discours en images de la condamnation de mémoire*, 97–115. Metz.

Flower, H. 2010. *Roman Republics*. Princeton.

Ford, F. 1985. *Political Murder: From Tyrannicide to Terrorism*. Cambridge, MA.

Gaughan, J. 2010. *Murder Was Not a Crime: Homicide and Power in the Roman Republic*. Austin, TX.

Gelzer, M. 1968. *Caesar: Politician and Statesman*. Trans. P. Needham. Oxford.

Hinard, F. 1984. "La male mort: Exécutions et statut du corps au moment de la première proscription." In *Du châtiment dans la cité: supplices corporels et peine de mort dans le monde antique: table ronde*, 295–311. Rome.

Hinard, F. 1987. "Spectacle des exécutions et espace urbain." In *L'Urbs: Espace urbain et histoire (Ier siècle av. J.-C.- IIIè siècle ap. J.-C.)*, 111–25. Rome.

Horsfall, N. 1974. "The Ides of March: Some New Problems." *G&R* 21: 191–99.
Hurley, D. 1993. *An Historical and Historiographical Commentary on Suetonius' "Life of C. Caligula."* Atlanta.
Icks, M. 2011. *The Crimes of Elagabalus: The Life and Legacy of Rome's Decadent Boy Emperor*. Cambridge, MA.
Jardine, L. 2005. *The Awful End of Prince William the Silent: The First Assassination of a Head of State with a Handgun*. London.
Levick, B. 1999. *Vespasian*. London.
Linderski, J. 1984. "Rome, Aphrodisias, and the *Res gestae*: The *Genera Militia* and the Status of Octavian." *JRS* 74: 74–80.
Linderski, J. 1995. *Roman Questions: Selected Papers*. Stuttgart.
Linderski, J. 2002. "The Pontiff and the Tribune: The Death of Tiberius Gracchus." *Athenaeum* 90: 339–66.
Linderski, J. 2007. *Roman Questions*. Vol. 2, *Selected Papers*. Stuttgart.
Lintott, A. 1968. *Violence in Republican Rome*. Oxford.
Lintott, A. 1972. "*Provocatio* from the Struggle of the Orders to the Principate." *ANRW* I.2: 226–67.
Lintott, A. 1994. "Political History, 146–95 B.C." In J. Crook, A. Lintott, and E. Rawson, eds., *The Last Age of the Roman Republic, 146–43 B.C.*, 40–103. Cambridge.
Lintott, A. 1999. *The Constitution of the Roman Republic*. Oxford.
Lintott, A. 2009. "The Assassination." In M. Griffin, ed., *A Companion to Julius Caesar*, 72–82. Chichester.
Lowrie, M. 2010. "Spurius Maelius: Dictatorship and the *Homo Sacer*." In B. Breed, C. Damon, and A. Rossi, eds., *Citizens of Discord: Rome and Its Civil Wars*, 171–85. Oxford.
Mackay, C. 2009. *The Breakdown of the Roman Republic: From Oligarchy to Empire*. Cambridge.
Meijer, F. 2004. *Emperors Don't Die in Bed*. London.
Millar, F. 1977. *The Emperor in the Roman World: 31 BC–AD 337*. London.
Ober, J. 2003. "Tyrant Killing as Therapeutic *Stasis*: A Political Debate in Images and Texts." In K. Morgan, ed., *Popular Tyranny: Sovereignty and Its Discontents in Ancient Greece*, 215–50. Austin, TX.
Osgood, J. 2006. *Caesar's Legacy: Civil War and the Emergence of the Roman Empire*. Cambridge.
Packer, J. 2010. "Pompey's Theater and Tiberius' Temple to Concord: A Late Republican Primer for an Early Imperial Patron." In B. Ewald and C. Noreña, eds., *The Emperor and Rome: Space, Representation, and Ritual*, 135–68. Cambridge.
Pelling, C. 2011. *Plutarch, "Caesar."* Oxford.
Potter, D. 2004. *The Roman Empire at Bay: AD 180–395*. London.
Ramsey, J. 2008. "At What Hour Did the Murderers of Julius Caesar Gather on the Ides of March 44 B.C.?" In S. Heilen, ed., *In Pursuit of Wissenschaft: Festschrift für William M. Calder III zum 75. Geburtstag*, 351–63. Hildesheim.
Scheid, J. 1984. "La mort du tyran: Chronique de quelque morts programmées." *In Du châtiment dans la cité: Supplices corporels et peine de mort dans le monde antique; Table ronde*, 177–93. Rome.
Smith, C. 2006. "*Adfectatio regni* in the Roman Republic." In S. Lewis, ed., *Ancient Tyranny*, 49–64. Edinburgh.

Stewart, A. 1990. *Greek Sculpture: An Exploration*. New Haven.
Syme, R. 1939. *The Roman Revolution*. Oxford.
Talbert, R. 1984. *The Senate of Imperial Rome*. Princeton.
Taylor, L. 1966. *Roman Voting Assemblies*. Ann Arbor.
Várhelyi, Z. 2011. "Political Murder and Sacrifice: From Roman Republic to Empire." In J. Knust and Z. Várhelyi, eds., *Ancient Mediterranean Sacrifice*, 125–41. Oxford.
Whittaker, C. 1970. *Herodian, with an English Translation*. 2 vols. Cambridge, MA.
Winterling, A. 2011. *Caligula: A Biography*. Trans. D. Schneider, G. Most, and P. Psoinos. Berkeley.
Wiseman, T. 1991. *Flavius Josephus: Death of an Emperor*. Exeter.
Wiseman, T. 2009. *Remembering the Roman People: Essays on Late-Republican Politics and Literature*. Oxford.
Woolf, G. 2006. *Et tu, Brute? The Murder of Caesar and Political Assassination*. London.

NINE

Urban Violence

Street, Forum, Bath, Circus, and Theater

Garrett G. Fagan

Indications came early that all was not right with the new emperor Nero. Donning a wig and the clothing of a slave, the young ruler and his friends would prowl the streets of Rome at night, stealing goods from shops and attacking passersby. The prince's bruised face bore witness to these adventures. When word got out that Caesar was behind the attacks, copycats joined the fun and went unpunished, so that, in Tacitus' memorable phrase, nights in Rome "passed in the manner of a captured city" (*in modum captivitatis nox agebatur*). A senator who violently repulsed an imperial mugging was driven to suicide. Concerned by the prospect of stiffer resistance, Nero staffed his nocturnal escapades with soldiers and gladiators, who would allow a fight to develop only so far before intervening with their weapons. Corpses were stuffed into the sewers.[1] Nero's father was an ill-tempered man who once gouged out the eye of an equestrian in the forum during an argument (Suet. *Nero* 5.1). The ex-praetor Larcius Macedo was punched to the ground in a public bathhouse in Rome, and violence in the theater was so rampant that soldiers had to be placed on duty, especially during pantomimes.[2]

The impression we get from such anecdotes is that the public places of ancient Rome were not particularly safe. I have argued elsewhere that quantifying levels of violence in the Roman world is impossible, since the data are woefully insufficient to do so. Rather, the best we can hope for is to outline a

1. Tac. *Ann.* 13.25.1–3. Suetonius' account (*Nero* 26) varies slightly and adds the details about the wig and the sewers. See also Champlin 2003: 151–53.

2. Plin. *Ep.* 3.14.6–8 (Macedo). For trouble at the theater, see below.

Roman "etiquette of violence," a sense of who was doing violence to whom, under what circumstances, and for what reason.[3] In this essay, I extend this analysis by focusing on the matter of where violence took place. Consonant with the theme of this volume, can we say anything about how location lent violence a particular flavor or even a specific meaning? Or, to refine that question slightly, did location help render violence normative, transgressive, or egregious? In pursuit of these questions, I focus attention on five public spaces: street, forum, bath, circus, and theater.

In general, it seems inescapable that location shaded the meaning of violent incidents in Roman cities. The Romans, like modern urban populations, perceived their cityscapes partly in moral terms (at least, such is the case in our surviving literary sources, which are dominated by elite outlooks). Public buildings were monuments to be proud of, ornaments whose scale and beauty not only lent a city its dignity and grandeur but even established its very status as a city. So it is that Pausanias can deny polis status to the community of Panopeus in Phocis in Greece precisely because it lacked any significant public buildings, and this is why, conversely, the people of Orcistus in Phrygia, in petitioning the emperor Constantine to be recognized as a true city, point to their public buildings as a sign of their worthiness.[4] Other public regions of the city, in contrast, were held in low esteem, such as the taverns, cookshops (*popinae*), and brothels that crowded the backstreets. These were the haunts of the common mob—of drunks, prostitutes, actors, thieves, and gamblers.[5] Some impressive public spaces were sullied by the moral failings of the lowly as well, particularly buildings erected for leisure and entertainment pursuits, such as theaters, baths, or the circus. They were held to encourage bad habits and engender idleness.[6] From such outlooks as these, we can predict that violence in some public places, especially those deemed honorable, would automatically carry a very different moral complexion than that perpetrated in the less respectable urban regions.

3. Fagan 2011b. See also the survey in Africa 1971.

4. Paus. 10.4 (Panopeus); *CIL* III 352 = *CIL* III 7000 = *ILS* 6091 = *AE* 1981.779 (Orcistus). On the latter text, see Chastagnol 1981. For public buildings as ornaments of cities conferring *dignitas* and status, see Vitr. 1 *praef.* 1; Plin. *Ep.* 10.23.2; D. Chr. 40.10; *AE* 1921.45 = *ILAfr* 454a (Bulla Regia; the Baths of Julia Memmia "adorn her native town"). See also Laurence 1994: 20–37; Fagan 1999: 165–67.

5. See, e.g., Pl. *Trin.* 1021; Amm. Marc. 14.6.25; Hor. *Ep.* 1.4.21–26; Juv. 8.171–82; Sen. *Con.* 1.2.10.

6. E.g., Ammianus (loc. cit. in previous note) links the circus to the tavern, since the *vulgus* talk endlessly about their favorite charioteers while drinking in the taverns (see also Amm. Marc. 28.4.28–31), while theaters were thought to encourage the masses to sit around idling (Liv. *Per.* 48; Tac. *Ann.* 14.20.2). See also Coleman 2000; Dodge 2010.

Street

When Sextus Roscius, a man of rank in his hometown of Ameria but resident at Rome, was returning home from a dinner party in the city one night in 80 BCE, he was set upon and murdered in the vicinity of the Pallacine Baths. Cicero, contracted to defend Roscius' son and namesake on a charge of parricide, presents these facts without editorial comment. Such a thing was not unthinkable in Rome's dark streets (Cic. *S. Rosc.* 18). The Pallacine Baths cannot be located, but a Vicus Pallacinae is attested from a variety of sources, apparently near the Via delle Botteghe Oscure in the Campus Martius.[7] This was not the most respectable part of town, largely undeveloped in 80 BCE. Consonant with the stories about Nero's nocturnal depredations or the ancient law that deemed it legal to kill a thief at night but not in daylight unless he offered armed resistance (Twelve Tables 8.13–14), Rome appears to have been a treacherous place at night.

That impression is reinforced by the habit of people of substance only moving about at night when they had a retinue of retainers to secure their safety (Cic. *Mil.* 10). Juvenal parodies the drunken brawler who is unable to sleep without having first beaten someone up and who wanders the streets in search of victims but shies away from the man "whose scarlet cloak and long line of attendants, along with the torches and brass lamps, commands avoidance" (Juv. 3.282–85). While self-help was always a cornerstone of Roman criminal law, Augustus established three urban cohorts and seven cohorts of *vigiles*, whose duties included the maintenance of public order, though in a rather haphazard and ad hoc manner. These units did not constitute a police force in the modern sense, nor were they analogous even to the night watch or constables of medieval towns. However, should they have come upon a disturbance, they would certainly have intervened.[8] It is noteworthy that Augustus stationed extra guards around the city on days when spectacles were being staged, since the low density of residents on such days left the city open to "prowlers" (*grassatores*) who would get up to no good (Suet. *Aug.* 43.1). The assumption here is that, during the day just as at night, the emptier street is the natural habitat of the criminal.

Suetonius (*Aug.* 45.2) also reports that Augustus liked to watch boxers but preferred street brawlers of Latin birth, "the common townspeople who

7. *LTUR* 4.51–52, s.v. "Pallacinae" (Lega).

8. The role of the nine Praetorian cohorts in maintaining public order is, if anything, even more unclear. For recent discussions, see Nippel 1995: 85–100; Fuhrmann 2012: 113–20. On the urban cohorts and *vigiles* in particular, see Reynolds 1926; Freis 1967; Sablayrolles 1996.

fought roughly and without skill in the narrow alleyways of city neighborhoods" (*catervarios oppidanos inter angustias vicorum pugnantis temere ac sine arte*). Suetonius' wording may suggest not run-of-the-mill muggers or thugs but organized street fighting, possibly staged for spectators and enhanced with betting.[9] Whatever their precise nature, the setting for these fights was the "narrow alleyways" of the city. Study of the urban topography of Pompeii has revealed that brothels and bars—the archetypal venues for the masses to engage in their morally corrupt practices, at least as far as the elite was concerned—tended to cluster in the backstreets, even if they were architecturally associated with more respectable structures. Thus, the rear entrance of an elegant house might be flanked by prostitutes' cells, safely tucked away out of the gaze of the morally upright, who would use the main entrance that opened onto a fine thoroughfare.[10] Bars were places associated with drunkenness and fighting.[11] A series of graffiti from a bar wall in Pompeii famously documents the beginnings of a fight over a dice game: the customers argue over a throw, things get heated, and the taverner intervenes with "You're going outside. Enough ruckus!" (*CIL* IV 3494). The two then presumably take their fight out onto the street.

All in all, the streets of Rome were places where violence was not uncommon, particularly at night. This should not be surprising, as the same is true today, at least for some areas of modern cities, and was certainly true in many premodern urban contexts. Violence occurring in this context would be unremarkable, if not actually expected, especially in the more out-of-the way back alleys and lanes.

Forum

The forum was the display case of a Roman city's *dignitas*. Here Vitruvius recommends the placement of temples, colonnades, balconies, and basilicas, with the Senate House, Treasury, and prison nearby (Vitr. 5.1–2). Adding a personal note, he comments that he himself let out the contract for a basilica in the forum at Fanum Fortunae, a building of "no less dignity and elegance" (*non minus summam dignitatem et venustatem*) than the great

9. *Catervarius* can denote a troop or band, as well as that which is "common" by being related to the mob.

10. On prostitutes' cells on alleyways, see Laurence 1994: 70–87, 73–74.

11. On bars, see Kleberg 1957; Packer 1978; Hermansen 1981: 125–83; Toner 1995: 65–88. For the association of drinking, gambling, and fighting, see *Dig.* 11.5.1, 21.1.4.2.

basilicas of Rome. These were the qualities expected of the forum's environment, the quintessential public space of the Roman city. It was into the forum that fathers led their sons to mark their transition to manhood, and it was through the forum that elaborate aristocratic funeral processions or triumphs passed; the forum is where political rallies were held and where benefactors and eminent citizens were celebrated in bronze and stone likenesses and inscriptions. That is not to say that every occupant of the forum was a moral paragon. Plautus (*Cur.* 467–82) jokes how different parts of the Roman Forum attracted different types of people: wealthy gentlemen "at the lower end" (*forum infimum*), liars at the shrine of Venus Cloacina, pimps and whores at the basilica, slanderers at the Lacus Curtius, and swindlers around the Temple of Castor and Pollux. We cannot press the comedy too hard for evidence, of course, but it reflects the perceived reality that moral variegation mapped onto place, even within a single topographical context like the Roman Forum. This was a complicated space, so its moral landscape was correspondingly complex.

Violence perpetrated in the forum was bound to acquire a certain flavor. The most infamous incidents, of course, were cases of politically motivated violence. Among the quasi-legendary early examples stands the death of Sp. Maelius, a wealthy equestrian who, in 439 BCE, was murdered in the Forum on suspicion of aspiring to kingship (he had been distributing free grain to the people).[12] Stories like this are riddled with historical uncertainty and were certainly influenced by the widespread disturbances in the Forum at the end of the republic. Since the Forum was where the tribal assembly met and since the Senate also often convened there or nearby, it became obvious to ambitious and unscrupulous men of that era that physical control of the Forum effectively conferred control of state procedures.[13] Political violence was the result. Space precludes a survey of all the instances of such violence in the Forum, but some examples from the late republic and early empire may serve as an illustrative sample.[14]

In 100 BCE, L. Appuleius Saturninus, tribune of the plebs, worked in

12. Livy (4.15) names the killer as C. Servilius Ahala, then *magister equitum* for the dictator L. Quinctius Cincinnatus; D.H. (12.4.2–5) preserves a tradition that Ahala was a *privatus* when he murdered Maelius. The murder is explicitly set in the Forum at Liv. 4.15.1. For modern discussions, see Cornell 1986: 58–61; Garnsey 1988: 170–78; Forsythe 2005: 240–41.

13. Milar 1998: 112–14.

14. For a list of documented acts of violence (much of it political) from 287–44 BCE, see Lintott 1999: 209–16.

league with the praetor C. Servilius Glaucia to advance a radical populist agenda.[15] At the consular elections that year (which took place at a meeting of the *comitia centuriata* in the Campus Martius), Saturninus and Glaucia sent thugs to beat an opponent to death with clubs, and the election dissolved in chaos. The following day, in the Forum, a mob appeared looking to lynch Saturninus, but he had around him his own mob of supporters. The Senate called on the consul C. Marius, formerly a political ally of Saturninus, to "see to it that the republic come to no harm"— the apparent wording of an emergency decree, the *senatus consultum ultimum*—and Marius formed another armed gang to enforce the Senate's will. Saturninus and Glaucia were driven up onto the Capitoline Hill but forced down when the water supply was cut. As they descended, the mob attacked them, and they either sought refuge in the Senate House (the Curia Hostilia, located near the later Curia Julia, at the northwest end of the Forum) or, in some accounts, were received or shut in there by Marius, to be dealt with later. The crowd, however, broke in and murdered them—in some accounts (Florus) by bludgeoning them to death and then tearing them to pieces, in others (Appian, Pseudo-Victor) by tearing off roof tiles and stoning them to death. Other supporters died along with them.

When, early in 62 BCE, the tribune Q. Caecilius Metellus Nepos proposed that Pompey be allowed to return from Asia with his army intact, to assist in restoring order after the Catilinarian conspiracy, staunch opposition was aroused, on the suspicion that this was a thinly veiled attempt to allow Pompey to retain his army, with a view toward seizing control of the state.[16] The night before the meeting in the Forum at which the people were to vote on the proposal, Nepos occupied the space with thugs, gladiators, and armed partisans. He had support also from partisans of Caesar, who was then praetor. The following morning, Nepos' opponents, the tribunes M. Porcius Cato and Q. Minucius Thermus, approached the Temple of Castor in the Forum, where Nepos and Caesar were seated on the podium. Armed men surrounded the temple and blocked the stairs leading up to the podium. Undeterred, Cato and Thermus braved the guards and mounted the platform, and Cato forced himself into a seat between Nepos and Caesar. This show of defiance earned the admiration of some of the crowd, who shouted their support. As a clerk read out the law, Cato interceded his tribu-

15. For the main sources, see Cic. *Rab. post.*, esp. 20–23; App. *BC* 1.28–33; Liv. *Per.* 69; V. Max. 3.2.18; Flor. 2.4 (3.16); Oros. *Hist.* 5.17; Ps. Aur. Vict. *Vir. ill.* 73.

16. For this incident, see Cic. *Sest.* 62; D.C. 37.42–44; Plu. *Cat. Mi.* 26.1–29.2. C. Berns, and H. Ali Ekinci, "Gladiatorial Games in the Greek East: A Complex of Reliefs from Cibyra," *AnatStud* 65 (2015): 143–79.

nician veto, but Nepos took the document and continued reading it. Cato snatched it from his hands. Nepos continued, reciting the text from memory, so Thermus clapped his hand over Nepos' mouth. Chaos erupted, the crowd dispersed, and Cato, pelted with sticks and stones, was whisked away from the scene by allies. Seeing the podium empty, Nepos again attempted to enact the law, but Cato and his partisans advanced on the temple and drove him away. The podium of the Temple of Castor had long been used as a speaker's platform for the promulgation and passage of laws, so no particular religious meaning need be read into that location.[17] But the incident, along with that of Saturninus and Glaucia, shows that the corrupted politics of late republican Rome required the physical control of the traditional voting spaces in the Forum and that violence was the natural consequence when control was contested.

With the establishment of the principate under Augustus and the Julio-Claudian emperors, the primary locus of political violence moved from the Forum to the palace and the Praetorian Camp (see Osgood's contribution to this volume). An excellent illustration of this shift in the center of political gravity is provided by the events of 41 CE surrounding the transfer of power to Claudius on the night of January 24–25, after the murder of Gaius in the palace earlier that day.[18] With Gaius killed, the Senate met in the Capitolium [the temple of Rome's national god, Jupiter Optimus Maximus], overlooking the Forum, to discuss the future; the meeting was attended by Cassius Chaerea, the Praetorian guardsman who had done the killing.[19] The senators had command of three or four cohorts, who occupied the forum and the Capitol. Meanwhile the main body of Praetorians—some nine thousand men—had brought Gaius' lame uncle Claudius to their camp on the outskirts of the city, where they promptly proclaimed him emperor. Messages passed back and forth as the standoff stretched through the night and into the next morning. Since both sides had military support, a confrontation seemed inevitable. The turning point came when the troops backing the senators defected to Claudius—news of his granting a large donative to any troops who supported him was the probable stimulus.[20] The symbolism of

---

17. See Coarelli 1985: 156–66; *LTUR* 1.242–45, s.v. "Castor, Aedes, Templum" (Nielsen).

18. For the main sources, see Suet. *Cal.* 60; *Cl.* 10; D.C. 60.1; J. *AJ* 162–271; *BJ* 2.204–14. For discussions, see Levick 1990: 29–39; Osgood 2011: 29–32.

19. Suetonius (*Cal.* 60) and Dio (60.1.1) locate the meeting at the Capitol. Josephus (*AJ* 19.248) puts it in the Temple of Jupiter Victor, of uncertain location but perhaps at the base of the Palatine; see *LTUR* 3.161, s.v. "Iuppiter Victor, Templum" (Coarelli).

20. D.C. 60.1.4; J. *AJ* 19.259–60; *BJ* 2.211–12 (defection); *AJ* 2.247 (donative).

place is powerfully manifested in this episode. On the one hand, the Senate sought to control the traditional political spaces of the Forum and the Capitol and thus occupied those areas with troops. On the other, the new realities of imperial politics were reflected in where Claudius' regime was born—among soldiers in an armed camp.

The location of the Praetorian Camp at the periphery of the city reflected the wider imperial condition, whereby armies were stationed at the frontiers of the empire, with heavy troop concentrations on the Rhine-Danube and eastern frontiers and more legions stationed in Spain, Britain, and North Africa.[21] It was the rebellion of these provincial troops at the edge of empire that brought down the Julio-Claudian dynasty in June 68 CE and elevated the governor of Spain, Ser. Sulpicius Galba, to the purple. But by the following January, Galba's regime was floundering. Discontent among the troops led the German legions to renounce their allegiance to Galba on January 1. At Rome, M. Salvius Otho was actively undermining the regime from within by corrupting the Praetorians, in the hope of attaining power himself. Events moved quickly over the next two weeks, shifting rapidly between the palace, the Forum, and the Praetorian Camp.[22] On January 10, feeling the political ground shifting beneath his feet, Galba sought to shore up his tottering regime by adopting L. Calpurnius Piso Frugi Licinianus. Tellingly the adoption was first announced in the Praetorian Camp—after the Forum and Senate House had been considered and rejected as venues.[23]

Five days later, Otho moved. Slipping away as Galba sacrificed before the Temple of Apollo on the Palatine, Otho went down to the golden milestone in the Forum, where twenty-three *speculatores* (personal bodyguards) proclaimed him emperor. Appalled by their paltry number, Otho had them carry him to the Praetorian Camp, where confusion prevailed. Galba, informed of the threat, sent men around the city to gather various troops, who were scattered in detachments in different quarters, while the people flocked to the palace. There they called for the killing of Otho and his accomplices, "precisely as if they were demanding some show in the circus or theater," Tacitus acidly comments.[24] Galba donned a breastplate and was

21. See the famous passage in Tac. *Ann.* 4.5 for the disposition of the Roman army in 23 CE. See also Webster 1998: 28–95; Pollard and Berry 2012.

22. The primary source for these events is Tac. *Hist.* 1.12–49, backed by D.C. 63.4–6, Plu. *Galb.* 23–29, and Suet. *Gal.* 17–23. For a recent modern treatment, see Morgan 2006: 57–73.

23. Tac. *Hist.* 1.17.2; Plu. *Galb.* 23.2.

24. Tac. *Hist.* 1.32.1: *dissono clamore caedem Othonis et coniuratorum exitium poscentium*

carried off in a chair; Piso was dispatched to the camp to test the loyalty of the Praetorians. But they had gone over enthusiastically to Otho, and their shouts impelled Piso back to find Galba, who had by now descended into the Forum, which was packed with onlookers.

As Galba vacillated over his options—return the palace, advance to the Capitol, seize the rostra—cavalrymen from the Praetorian Camp burst into the Forum, scattering all before them. The troops accompanying Galba fled, while the crowds dispersed but did not leave the Forum. Instead, they took up stations in the surrounding buildings, as if viewing a spectacle (Plu. *Galb.* 26.4). Caught in the surge of people, the emperor was thrown from his chair and rolled on the ground near the Lacus Curtius. There he was butchered, decapitated, and mutilated. His advisor T. Vinius was chased down and transfixed in front of the temple of Divus Julius. Piso fled into the temple of Vesta and hid there, but he was soon discovered, dragged out, and cut down outside. At the Praetorian Camp, Otho rejoiced over the heads of his victims. His coup had been a success, and he was now emperor of the Roman world. He would rule three months and a day.

In his description of the irruption of the Othonian cavalry into the Forum, Tacitus' horror at the scene is unconcealed.

> Neither the sight of the Capitolium nor the holiness of the temples looming over them nor past or future emperors could frighten them away from committing the crime that would be avenged by whoever succeeded to the throne.[25]

What makes the crime so appalling, in Tacitus' view, is the location where it is about to be committed. Here was the religious and civic nerve center of the Roman world, a space overlooked by and packed with holy shrines and with statues and monuments of past and future emperors, and yet here Roman troops were bent on killing their own emperor, "an unarmed old man" (*inermem et senem trucidare*). Plutarch makes a similar observation

---

ut si in circo aut theatro ludicrum aliquod postularent.

25. Tac. *Hist.* 1.40.2: *nec illos Capitolii aspectus et immenentium templorum religio et priores et futuri principes terruere quo minus facerent scelus cuius ultor est quisquis successit.* Plutarch (*Galb.* 26.3) adds the details that the troops were both cavalry and infantry and that they charged through the Basilica Aemilia, almost adjacent to the Lacus Curtius, where Galba was located. Later, Otho was carried through the heaps of bodies in the forum, which was "still stained with blood" (*cruento adhuc foro,* Tac. *Hist.* 1.47.2), up to the Capitol and Palatine.

in his narrative. After Galba's murder, as headless corpses in consular robes lay outside in the Forum, the Senate convened to confer the imperial powers and titles on Otho (Plu. *Galb.* 28.1). Again, the hallowed context of the profane action lends the deed its peculiar atrocity. Had Galba been killed in a secluded palace corridor, as Gaius had been, the symbolic power of the murder and its aftermath would have been very different. The location of these crimes aggravated their heinousness.

There were other disturbances in the Forum, beyond the nakedly political. When the fleets of Sex. Pompeius interrupted the flow of grain to Rome in 39 BCE, the people attacked and stoned Octavian in the Forum, to the point that Mark Antony had to order in troops to disperse the crowd. Later, a hungry populace angered by a food shortage assailed the emperor Claudius in the Forum and pelted him with stale crusts until soldiers retrieved him and brought him to the palace.[26] These incidents were really a variation on the theme of political violence associated with the Forum, since the people were making an essentially political demand of their rulers, stimulated by an immediate complaint. But not all violence in the forum was automatically colored political by virtue of its location, though notices of what may be called "casual" violence there are scarce. Nero's father, Gnaeus, gouged out the eye of a Roman *eques* "in the middle of the forum" (*medio Foro*) because the *eques* had criticized him too freely. Suetonius notes this incident as an example of Gnaeus' "hatefulness in all aspects of life" (*omni parte vitae detestabilem*), and the outrage stems as much from the location of the crime as from the high social station of the victim.[27]

Bath

The bath was a locale of relaxation and camaraderie.[28] The ancient sources consistently associate baths and bathing with pleasure, socializing, and being at ease.[29] It was common, for instance, for hosts to meet their guests at the baths before adjourning to the dinner couch. Bathing features prominently in ancient aphorisms about the joys of life, such as "Hunting, bathing, gam-

26. On Octavian in 39 BCE, see App. *BC* 5.67–68. On Claudius in 51 CE, see Tac. *Ann.* 12.43; Suet. *Cl.* 18.

27. Suet. *Nero* 5.1.

28. For an excellent overview of Roman bathing culture, see Yegül 2010: 5–39. See also Yegül 1992: 30–47; Fagan 1999.

29. See, e.g., the material collected in Dunbabin 1989: 6–32.

bling, laughing—that's living!" or "Baths, wine, and sex ruin our bodies, but they make life worth living."[30] Even if the context of the baths was hardly "democratic" in its effects, the sociability expected there was clear to all and appeared to preclude the possibility of violence.[31]

And yet, the baths could be aggravating places. They were often crowded, so it was desirable to visit when the facility was less busy.[32] If the baths were busy, people would be jostled and harassed, and since drinking at the baths appears to have been not uncommon, the atmosphere might become fraught. For these reasons, some bathers could become a little tetchy. Pliny tells the story of Larcius Macedo, a senator of praetorian rank who was attacked and murdered by his slaves while using the private bath in his villa at Formiae. Baths, remarks Pliny, were inauspicious places for Macedo. Once, when bathing in public at Rome, one of Macedo's slaves had been seeking a way past an *eques* and had lightly touched the man, who had spun around and lashed out. The blow missed the slave but hit Macedo, who was almost punched to the ground. "In this way," writes Pliny, "the bath was for him by degrees first a place of insult and finally of death."[33] Galen tells the story of a young patient who overexerted himself. When he was at the gymnasium (*gymnasium* being the common Greek word for a Roman-style bath in this era), he was asked by another youth during his massage to move a little, and a quarrel broke out between them, "the kind that gymnastic types often fall into." As he was leaving the gymnasium, he came across some friends of his who were fighting, and he separated them.[34] Seneca compares the condition of life to the circumstances in the bath, the crowd, or the street: "Some things will be thrown at you; some will hit you."[35] These vignettes are instructive, as they suggest that crowding at the bath was the main source of aggression. The context of the bath does not appear to have lent acts of

---

30. *CIL* VII 17938 = *ILS* 8626f (an inscription from Timgad, possibly a gaming board: *venari lavari ludere ridere occ est vivere*); *CIL* VI 15258 = *ILS* 8157 (epitaph of Ti. Claudius Secundus, Rome: *balnea vina Venus corrumpunt corpora nostra set vitam faciunt*); Fagan 1999: 22–24 (dinner guests).

31. For my thoughts on the supposedly "democratizing" atmosphere at the baths, see Fagan 1999: 206–19, contra Yegül 2010: 34–39.

32. Anon. *Life of Aesop* 65–67: before venturing out himself, Xanthus sends his slave Aesop ahead to see if the baths are crowded. (The *Life of Aesop* is an anonymous composition of the first century CE, possibly from Egypt.)

33. Plin. *Ep.* 3.14.6–8. Note also Sen. *Dial.* 4.32.2, where Cato the Censor was accidentally hit at the baths and magnanimously did not retaliate.

34. Galen *Meth. med.* 10.2 = 10.672 K.

35. Sen. *Ep.* 107.2: *quaedam in te mittentur, quaedam incident.*

violence there any particular cultural coloring. They were just the products of frayed and harried nerves.

Circus and Theater

The circus, where chariot-racing spectacles were held, is one of the most infamous locations associated with large-scale outbreaks of violence in Roman cities. With chariot-racing fans divided into "factions" supporting different team colors—Blues, Greens, Whites, and Reds—enraged mobs of fans going on the rampage is imagined as part and parcel of these mass spectacles. In fact, the evidence for major disturbances is confined to the early Byzantine era, between ca. 450 and 610 CE, and to the cities of the eastern empire (the western empire having succumbed in 476 CE).[36] The locus classicus for circus violence is the Nika Riot in Constantinople that took place over the space of a week in January 532 CE. In the course of the mayhem, the regime of the emperor Justinian came close to collapse, the center of Constantinople was burned to the ground, and some thirty thousand people were killed. Rising tensions between the Blue and Green factions over imperial favoritism shown to the Blues, coupled with widespread discontent at Justinian's rule, fueled the chaos.[37]

Beyond vague allusions to rambunctious excitement and scattered fighting, no major riots are reported at circuses in the early and high empires.[38] Some argue that we should not take the silence of the sources in this regard at face value: "[it] does not mean we should assume that large groups of fans had rarely, if ever, been known to misbehave before."[39] Fanaticism in sup-

36. An exception is the massacre of seven thousand people at the circus in Thessalonica by Theodosius I in 390 CE. The spark, however, was not factional violence but popular unrest at a Gothic garrison recently installed in the city; see Theodoretus *Eccl. hist.* 5.17.

37. For the main ancient sources, see Procop. *Wars* 1.24; Malalas *Chron.* 18.71. For succinct modern accounts, see Meijer 2010: 5–21; Bell 2014.

38. Typical are Dio Chrysostom's notice of violence outside the hippodrome at Alexandria (*Or.* 32.42), Tertullian's description of the madness of the circus fans (*Spect.* 18), and Cassiodorus' damnation of the "futile struggles" of the circus fans (*Var.* 3.51.11–12). For a modern treatment of the earlier history of the factions, see Thuillier 2012.

39. Meijer 2010: 114. Meijer explains the silence of the sources on the basis of (a) the social circles the elite authors moved in, which looked down on the goings-on at the circus, and (b) a fear that reporting violence at circuses would make the emperor look bad. Neither argument is cogent, since the same authors report other incidents of mass disorder, such as food riots or disturbances at the theater (on which see below), neither of which redounded to the emperor's credit or were condoned by elite authors.

porting one's team—as evidenced by curse tablets invoking doom on rivals and by Juvenal's likening fans' distress at a loss to receiving the news of Cannae (*Sat.* 11.199–201)—suggest that sporting emotions ran high, which likely generated problems in the stands.

But curses and disappointment do not entail rioting. The crux of the matter surely lies in what motivated the disturbances. One view sees the rioters as ancient analogues of the soccer hooligans of more recent memory.[40] This view gives strength to the possibility that disturbances at the circus predate the late antique era but go unreported in the sources. Fans are fans, and when emotions burst their bounds, trouble ensues. A different proposition sees factional violence as venting the grievances of the underclasses against the background of a decline in traditional municipal institutions and politics.[41] Close analysis of seat and other inscriptions from Aphrodisias has shown that the two major factions, the Blues and Greens, appear to have consolidated their influence over a variety of public spectacles in the late empire and to have played a key role in the organized chants and acclamations that were part of city life in this era, thus generating sharp mutual rivalry and, with it, the potential for violence.[42] Proposals along these lines tie factional violence at the circus to conditions specific to the late antique era and would tend to validate the silence of early and high imperial authors about its relative absence in earlier epochs, since it was not a problem before the fourth century. All in all, this position appears sounder, as a conspiracy of silence among early and high imperial authors about large-scale, organized fighting at the circus is harder to swallow. That partisan emotions ran high at chariot races and that fights could break out seems entirely plausible—many sports can have that effect on people—but organized violence of the sort attested for late imperial hippodromes seems to have been absent.

The silence of early and high imperial authors with regard to circus violence is all the more striking in the face of the ample evidence provided by

40. This is the position of Cameron (1976: 271–96), who notes, "It may be that the soccer hooligan of today and the Blues and Greens of Byzantium can cast mutual illumination on each other" (271). For a concise overview of modern explanations, see Whitby 1999: esp. 229–33. See also Dagron 2011, on the hippodrome in Constantinople.

41. Liebeschuetz 2001: 203–21, 249–57. In Liebeschuetz's view, the traditional curial class, who had been visible to and elected by the populace, was replaced by individuals selected in less transparent ways, which forced the people to express themselves in mass demonstrations.

42. Roueché 1984, 1993. Whitby (1999) adds other factors: the politicization of factional support through open imperial favor or disfavor, the reliance of weak rulers on the popular support mobilized by the factions, and imperial tolerance of the factions' criminality.

the same authors for tumults at theaters, especially at pantomimes.[43] Pantomimes were a type of performance that particularly appealed to the emotions of spectators, as actors danced and mimed to musical accompaniment.[44] Ancient authors usually lay blame for unrest at theaters on the actors and their partisan supporters (*fautores histrionum*).[45] Whereas circus partisanship attached to the racing colors, we cannot clearly discern either the bases for fans' attachment to particular actors or the roots of their powerful animosity toward rivals.[46] We just know it was a reality. Tacitus specifically blames "the rivalry arising from the competition among actors" for disturbances at the Ludi Augustales in 14 CE.[47] Since the physical setting of the theater allowed the actors and their supporters to interact, it would be possible for actors to incite their partisans against rivals. The partisans were organized and had leaders. Collusion between actors and their supporters was therefore likely.[48] Politically charged allusions could also be made by actors (at least when they were not performing pantomimes), which might inflame the audience as well. For instance, soldiers attempted to intervene to prevent "abuse against magistrates" and "dissension among the mob" during disturbances in 14–15 CE.[49] While it is clear from seating inscriptions from the theater at Aphrodisias that groups of fellow workers, *collegia* brothers, and factional partisans sat together in late antique theaters, it is not obvious that this was the case in the early or high imperial eras.[50] The socially segregated seating rules,

43. For collections of the evidence, see Jory 1984; Slater 1994; Lim 2002.

44. On the nature of pantomime, especially its ability to arouse powerful emotional responses in the audience, see Lucian *Salt.* For modern overviews, see Balsdon 1969: 274–79; Beacham 1999: 141–46; Webb 2012: 222–35.

45. For blame on actors and fans, see, e.g., D.C. 57.14.10; Tac. *Ann.* 1.77.4, 13.25.4; Suet. *Tib.* 37.2. On the psychological factors involved, see Fagan 2011a: 147–54.

46. Pliny (*Nat.* 29.9) comments that actors and charioteers were followed about in public by large retinues of supporters—a physical manifestation of fans' devotion.

47. Tac. *Ann.* 1.54.3: *ludos Augustales . . . turbavit discordia ex certamine histrionum.* Cf. ibid., 14.21.4.

48. See, e.g., Suet. *Tib.* 37.2 (actors and leaders of factions exiled by Tiberius); Tac. *Ann.* 1.16.3 (Percennius, a ringleader of the Danubian mutiny in 14 CE, had been leader of a claque for pantomimes), 16.4.4 (people accustomed to rhythmic chants from theaters). Nero trained his own claque in the Alexandrian style; see Suet. *Nero* 20.3. See, further, Horsfall 2003: 39–42; Toner 2009.

49. Tact. *Ann.* 1.77.1: *probra in magistratus et dissensionem vulgi prohibent.* In a similar vein, Tacitus (*Ann.* 11.13.1) notes the crowd hurling abuse at the consular Pomponius Secundus, who wrote songs for the stage, and at eminent ladies. Elsewhere, the actors are accused of immodesty and indecency (*Ann.* 4.14.3).

50. Roueché 1993. The seating at arena and theater spectacles was regulated according to social class by Augustus empire-wide; see my discussion at Fagan 2011a: 96–120.

however, would have grouped partisans of the same rank together, though the precise details remain elusive.

The physical environment of the theater therefore assembled in a single place large numbers of emotionally charged spectators who harbored long-standing rivalries. As spectators were excited and aroused by the spectacle, organized into groups of claques, chanting slogans, and egged on by the performers and the counterchants of rival fans, it is hardly a wonder that these places generated disorder. The seating situation in the circus of the early and middle imperial eras is less clear to us. The same high-strung emotions were in play, but the fans, at least before the late empire, may not have been as well organized and dispersed throughout the crowd rather than concentrated in particular blocks of seats, and charioteers could not interact with their partisans during a race as readily as actors could during a performance. Changed social and political conditions in the late empire lent the circus factions greater prominence in various spheres of life, and this fed a more intense rivalry at chariot-racing events. The sorts of scattered fights or scuffles that were habitually generated by disagreements over spectacles morphed into large-scale and organized rampages.

Conclusion

This brief survey suggests that at least from the perspective of the Roman elite, violence that took place in the streets—especially at night—or in the circus or theater was considered habitual, if not expected. These were the domains of the common mob, the ruffians and scoundrels, who (as the elite imagined) made up the majority of the city's population. It may be assumed that the cramped living conditions and the prevailing squalor generated a certain trigger-happy tetchiness among the lower orders, in their teeming apartment blocks and narrow back alleys. Where they gathered in numbers, such as the theater or circus, trouble would be likely to follow.[51] But there is a whiff of classism about such suppositions, as they echo Roman aristocratic snobbery about the lower orders. Urban streets, particularly in their premodern, unlit nocturnal manifestation, are likely to have attracted an undesirable element, and we must not assume that these people somehow represented "the plebs." Violence at the circus, as we have seen, was a product not of the class of the fans gathered there but of sociopolitical conditions peculiar to late antique eastern cities. Trouble in the theaters was also partly

51. For the living conditions of the masses, see Yavetz 1958, 1965; Scobie 1986.

organized and encouraged by the intense rivalry of actors—and it does not appear to have been a universal problem, in any case. Certainly, in any age, sporting events can generate dissension that devolves into violence among spectators when conditions are right, but that does not mean that all circuses or theaters were inherently violent places—just that they could become so.

Works Cited

Africa, T. 1971. "Urban Violence in Imperial Rome." *Journal of Interdisciplinary History* 2: 3–21.

Baldson, J. 1969. *Life and Leisure in Ancient Rome*. London.

Beacham, R. 1999. *Spectacle Entertainments of Early Imperial Rome*. New Haven.

Bell, S. 2014. "Roman Chariot Racing: Charioteers, Factions, Spectators." In P. Christesen and D. G. Kyle, eds., *A Companion to Sport and Spectacle in Greek and Roman Antiquity*, 492–504. Malden.

Berns, C., and H. Ali Ekinci. "Gladiatorial Games in the Greek East: A Complex of Reliefs from Cibyra." *AnatStud* 65 (2015): 143–79.

Cameron, A. 1976. *Circus Factions: Blues and Greens at Rome and Byzantium*. Oxford.

Champlin, E. 2003. *Nero*. Cambridge, MA.

Chastagnol, A. 1981. "L'inscription constantinienne d'Orcistus." *MEFRA* 93: 381–416.

Coarelli, F. 1985. *Il foro romano: Periodo repubblicano e augusteo*. Rome.

Coleman, K. 2000. "Entertaining Rome." In J. Coulston and H. Dodge, eds., *Ancient Rome: The Archaeology of the Eternal City*, 210–58. Oxford.

Coleman, K., and Nelis-Clément, J., eds. 2012. *L'organisation des spectacles dans le monde romain*. Geneva.

Cornell, T. 1986. "The Value of the Literary Tradition concerning Early Rome." In K. Raaflaub, ed., *Social Struggles in Archaic Rome*, 52–76. Berkeley.

Dagron, G. 2011. *L'hippodrome de Constantinople: Jeux, peuple et politique*. Paris.

Dodge, H. 2010. "Amusing the Masses: Buildings for Entertainment and Leisure in the Roman World." In D. Potter and D. Mattingly, eds., *Life, Death, and Entertainment in the Roman Empire*, 229–79. 2nd ed. Ann Arbor,.

Dunbabin, K. 1989. "*Baiarum Grata Voluptas*: Pleasures and Dangers of the Baths." *PBSR* 57: 6–46.

Fagan, G. 1999. *Bathing in Public in the Roman World*. Ann Arbor.

Fagan, G. 2011a. *The Lure of the Arena: Social Psychology and the Crowd at the Roman Games*. Cambridge.

Fagan, G. 2011b. "Violence in Roman Social Relations." In M. Peachin, ed., *The Oxford Handbook of Social Relations in the Roman World*, 467–95. Oxford.

Forsythe, G. 2005. *A Critical History of Early Rome: From Prehistory to the First Punic War*. Berkeley.

Freis, H. 1967. *Die Cohortes Urbanae*. Cologne.

Fuhrmann, C. 2012. *Policing the Roman Empire: Soldiers, Administration, and Public Order*. Oxford.

Garnsey, P. 1988. *Famine and Food Supply in Graeco-Roman Antiquity*. Cambridge.

Hermansen, G. 1981. *Ostia: Aspects of Roman City Life*. Edmonton.
Horsfall, N. 2003. *The Culture of the Roman Plebs*. London.
Jory, E. 1984. "Early Pantomime Riots." In A. Moffat, ed., *Miastor: Classical, Byzantine, and Renaissance Studies for Robert Browning*, 57–66. Canberra.
Kleberg, T. 1957. *Hôtels, restaurants et cabarets dans l'antiquité romaine: Études historiques et philologiques*. Uppsala.
Laurence, R. 1994. *Roman Pompeii: Space and Society*. London.
Levick, B. 1990. *Claudius*. New Haven.
Liebeschuetz, J. H. W. G. 2001. *The Decline and Fall of the Roman City*. Oxford.
Lim, R. 2002. "The Roman Pantomime Riot of A.D. 509." In J.-M. Carrié and R. Lizzi, eds., *Humana Sapit: Études d'Antiquité Tardive offertes à Lellia Cracco Ruggini*, 35–42. Turnhout.
Lintott, A. 1999. *Violence in Republican Rome*. 2nd ed. Oxford.
Meijer, F. 2010. *Chariot Racing in the Roman Empire*. Baltimore.
Millar, F. 1998. *The Crowd in Rome in the Late Republic*. Ann Arbor.
Morgan, G. 2006. *69 A.D.: The Year of the Four Emperors*. Oxford.
Nippel, W. 1995. *Public Order in Ancient Rome*. Cambridge.
Osgood, J. 2011. *Claudius Caesar: Image and Power in the Early Roman Empire*. Cambridge.
Packer, J. 1978. "Inns at Pompeii: A Short Survey." *Cronache Pompeiane* 4: 5–53.
Pollard, N., and Berry, J. 2012. *The Complete Roman Legions*. London.
Reynolds, P. 1926. *The Vigiles of Imperial Rome*. Oxford.
Roueché, C. 1984. "Acclamations in the Later Rome Empire: New Evidence from Aphrodisias." *JRS* 74: 181–99.
Roueché, C. 1993. *Performers and Partisans at Aphrodisias*. London.
Sablayrolles, R. 1996. *Libertinus Miles: Les cohortes de vigiles*. Rome.
Scobie, A. 1986. "Slums, Sanitation, and Mortality in the Roman World." *Klio* 68: 399–433.
Slater, W. 1994. "Pantomime Riots." *ClAnt* 13: 120–44.
Thuillier, J.-P. 2012. "L'organisation des *ludi circenses*: Les quatre factions (République, Haut-Empire)." In K. Coleman and J. Nelis-Clément, eds,*L'organisation des spectacles dans le monde romain*,173–220. Geneva.
Toner, J. 1995. *Leisure and Ancient Rome*. Cambridge.
Toner, J. 2009. *Popular Culture in Ancient Rome*. Cambridge.
Webb, R. 2012. "The Nature and Representation of Competition in Pantomime and Mime." In K. Coleman and J. Nelis-Clément, eds., *L'organisation des spectacles dans le monde romain*, 221–60. Geneva.
Webster, G. 1998. *The Roman Imperial Army*. 3rd ed. Norman, OK.
Whitby, M. 1999. "The Violence of the Circus Factions." In K. Hopwood, ed., *Organised Crime in Antiquity*, 229–53. Swansea.
Yavetz, Z. 1958. "The Living Conditions of the Urban Plebs in Republican Rome." *Latomus* 17: 500–517.
Yavetz, Z. 1965. "Plebs Sordida." *Athenaeum* 43: 295–311.
Yegül, F. 1992. *Baths and Bathing in Classical Antiquity*. Cambridge, MA.
Yegül, F. 2010. *Bathing in the Roman World*. Cambridge.

TEN

Violence against Women in Ancient Rome

Ideology versus Reality

Serena S. Witzke

When, where, how, and who? These are the questions one must ask about gendered violence in Rome. There is no denying that it was dangerous to be a woman in Rome, given the prevalence of laws that allowed the beating or execution of women for minor offenses, the power that *manus* marriages gave to husbands over their wives, and the atmosphere created by the numerous historical tales about rape and murder of women. But to fully appreciate the nuances of the gendered atmosphere of violence in Rome, we must look more closely at the victims of violence and at where that violence occurred. Most students of Roman history would think of the raped Sabines or Lucretia and would generalize from their tales to citizen women generally. While citizen women were at risk of violence, the more common victims of gendered violence in Rome were noncitizens—slaves and free sex laborers[1]—overshadowed by the famous mythological stories in Livy. There was a culture of violence against women in ancient Rome, but we must carefully consider who was likely to suffer in it.

In an attempt to review many types of violence and victims in republi-

1. I prefer the more neutral term *sex laborer* to *prostitute* and have used the former throughout. I also put quotation marks around the term *girlfriend* when referring to the elegiac *puellae*. These women are paid for their services, and the men are their clients. They are "girlfriends" only from the perspective of men seeking to obscure the mercantile relationship in which they are participating. See Witzke 2015.

can Rome, I divide my examination here into two parts. Violence against women in Rome functioned in binaries: topographical zones (public/private), spheres of social class (citizen/noncitizen), and existential loci (ideology/reality). The first part of this essay explores public and ideological violence against citizen women in the mythohistories and law, while the second part surveys the private, common violence experienced by noncitizen slaves and free sex laborers in Rome. No overview of violence against women in Rome can adequately address one side of these binaries without examining the other. These types of violence and victims are two sides of the Janus face of gendered violence in Rome—brutal, institutional, and omnipresent, but very different in psychology and practice. I focus here primarily on the question of who was likely to suffer gendered violence in Rome in the late republic, the historical period most often focused on in books and courses on Roman social history and culture.[2] I have limited my scope this way for several reasons: (1) my findings apply to the imperial period, as the institutions and ideologies remain consistent throughout the high empire; (2) space limitations cannot accommodate a thousand years of Roman, pre-Christian history in all geographic areas; (3) focusing on Rome prevents problems of local legal variance in laws dealing with citizen women; (4) during the imperial period, many authors are focused on vilifying "evil" emperors rather than recording factual evidence, so it is very difficult to determine if the terrible violence inflicted on many women in this period is violence against women specifically or politically motivated violence (or trumped-up storytelling). There are a number of resources treating violence against women in the high empire, in Rome and in Roman territories, some of which I have referenced for the interested reader.[3]

I base my findings on a range of texts, from law to Livy to elegy to comedy, which I treat as sociohistorical texts (sources of historical informa-

2. My time line slightly expands the traditional dates of the late republic (133 BCE–27 BCE) to include the playwrights Plautus (d. ca. 180 BCE) and Terence (d. ca. 160 BCE) and extends through Augustus' reign (14 CE), as these periods include historical documents relevant to my argument.

3. Tacitus and Suetonius offer a large amount of anecdotal evidence for abuse of women by the imperial family, particularly Tiberius, Caligula, Messalina, and Nero. Rogers 1935 collects a number of cases involving Tiberius' politically motivated prosecution of women. Ash 2012 broadly discusses women in the empire, Clark 1999 investigates the late empire household of St. Augustine, Parca 2002 discusses violence against women in Ptolemaic and Roman Egypt, and Pomeroy 2007 offers a case study of the abuse and murder of an upper-class woman named Regilla (some later sources for domestic abuse may be found in Pomeroy's notes).

tion, not merely entertainment) and reflections of the reality they purport to portray. Slavery is realistically depicted in the comedies, and the lot of slaves does not change substantially in Roman law and practice until well into the Christian period.[4] The free *meretrix* of elegy stands for the purchasable woman in Roman culture generally and can therefore provide an exemplary view of noncitizen or lower-class women and the problems they encountered while trying to conduct their business. The use of fictional texts for historical evidence has been well established.[5] Garrett Fagan (2011: 469–70) explains, "Ancient anecdotes and fiction can act as mirrors that reflect social attitudes, assumptions, and realities, even if the immediate context is highly dubious or even fantastical. This is because in order to be effective, satires or novels have to present their audience with recognizable social paradigms." From these texts, we can extract much evidence about the lived realities of women in the ancient world.

Ideology—Women at Risk in Mythohistory, Marriage, and Law

Violence against Roman citizen women in the late republic was not systematic or quotidian; rather, it was (largely) ideological and often occurred in the public sphere. Laws punishing women had to be approved by the populace (a practice that put a check on violent husbands), virgin snatching was a foundational myth, and rape by tyrannical princes or public officials was improbable. Early Roman myths and law suggested a violent and deadly existence for the Roman citizen woman, but this situation was no longer a reality by the historical period, if it ever had been. Several factors, particularly political stability and the decline of *manus* marriages, explain this ideological shift. The stories of terrible violence against women in early Rome (Rhea Silvia, Sabine women, Tarpeia, Lucretia, Horatia, Verginia) are public, politically motivated, and largely symbolic. The laws (also part of the

4. The conditions of slavery are little different in the early second century BCE (per Plautus) from those in the late fourth century CE (per book 9 of Augustine's *Confessions*). Ovid's comments on the abuse of slave girls (*Ars* 3.235–44; *Am.* 1.14) are echoed in Juvenal's *Satire* 6 (487–95), and Apuleius' *Metamorphoses* is full of violence against slaves.

5. Livy based his work on many earlier historical sources (see Ogilvie's commentaries on Livy); the ancients considered comedy to be realistic and relevant to their lives (Feldherr 1998; Geffcken 1973; Leigh 2004; Richlin 2005); and elegy incorporates many historical references (Cairns 2006; Griffin 1985; Gurval 1995; Keith 2008; Syme 1978).

public sphere) that threatened women pertained to those under the *manus*, or marital power, of their husbands. Neither the literal level of the early mythohistorical narrative nor the prevalence of *manus* marriages depicted in it could reflect the reality of women in the late republican period.

Ideology links female sexual status to the male body politic of Rome from its inception, from the city's foundation by the children of the disinherited and raped Rhea Silvia to the rape of the Sabine women, violently snatched for the "proper" propagation of the city through their virgin bodies.[6] For men to be respectable, their women had to be pure; hence any threat to or compromise of female sexual status had to be met with male resistance and violence against the women themselves. Thus violence was the basis for Roman sexual and marital relations: Mars and Venus are more integrated into Roman psychology than simply as Rome's parent deities.[7] As we shall see, violence against citizen women overshadows Roman marriage, law, and mythohistory. But for the citizen woman of the late republic, the violent ideologies of Roman marriage and propagation were symbolic and not a frequent part of their day-to-day existence.[8]

Violence as Message: Livy's Raped and Murdered Women

Numerous stories in *Ab urbe condita* suggest a dangerous atmosphere for women in the early to middle republic. Rome was built on the raped and murdered bodies of women. One might easily assume that Roman citizen women lived under constant threat of violence. These episodes are cited often in articles and in classrooms focusing on the social status and lived reality of Roman women.[9] Violence against women is a stunningly repetitive structure throughout Livy's early history, in the stories of Rhea Silvia, the Sabine women, Horatia, Lucretia, and Verginia. These stories are always treated seriously, even when they seem far-fetched to the author himself.[10] But they do not accurately reflect the historical situation of citizen women

6. Miles 1995; Henry and James 2012.

7. Arieti 1997: 219–20.

8. Of course, as today, even women protected by the law and with the safeguard of an interested family were still at risk of violence on the streets or in the home. I contend merely that violence against citizen women was not the norm in Roman society.

9. Arieti 1997; Beard 1999; Brown 1995; Dougherty 1998; Feldherr 1998; Hemker 1985; Henry and James 2012; Joplin 1990; Joshel 1992; Miles 1995.

10. Livy (1.4) suggests that the tale that Romulus and Remus were nursed to health by a wolf (*lupa*) might be an aggrandizing gloss. "Lupa" may have been the moniker for the wife of the shepherd that took the boys in, marking her as a sex laborer.

in late republican Rome, Livy's own period. All the characters remain in the general realm of mythohistory, divided from Livy's reading audience by hundreds of years. They do not describe what we today consider typical violence against women (domestic violence, date rape, abuse in marriage). Instead, they describe horrific events that shaped and motivated political change within the Roman state, and they speak to ideological assumptions of male-female relations. They are dramas enacted on the public stage in public view, and the violence against women must be condoned by the social group as a whole or condemned and punished publicly.

The first of Livy's tales of gendered violence is the story of Rhea Silvia (1.4), mother of Romulus and Remus, future founders of Rome. So that she cannot continue her father Amulius' line, she is made a Vestal Virgin. She is raped (*vi compressa Vestalis*), claims the perpetrator was the god Mars, gives birth to Romulus and Remus, and is then imprisoned for having broken her vows of celibacy. She does not appear in the narrative thereafter, but her sons overthrow her enemies, specifically her persecuting uncle, when they come of age.

Next, most famously, is the rape of the Sabine women (1.9).[11] After Romulus founded Rome, he needed to populate it, but the neighboring states dishonored him by refusing intermarriage, a direct threat to Roman masculinity. To solve the shortage of women and redress the insult of his neighbors, Romulus conspired to snatch the daughters of the neighboring towns and force them into marriage. The girls, socially ruined by their seizure and captivity, had no choice but to submit to their abductors and become wives and mothers of Rome.[12] Romulus encouraged them to make the most of a bad situation and resign themselves to their lot (*mollirent modo iras et, quibus fors corpora dedisset, darent animos*, 1.9.15).

In the conflict that resulted from the abduction of these women, the Sabine commander Tatius bribed a young girl, Tarpeia, the daughter of the commander of the Roman citadel, to open Rome's gate. According to Livy (1.11.5–9), she desired the jeweled finery carried by the Sabines.[13] She

11. The story is told more salaciously in Ov. *Ars* 1.101–32. See Hemker 1985; Beard 1990.

12. Though the Sabines were "raped" (from the Latin verb *rapio*) in the sense of "abducted," their forced marriage to Roman soldiers for procreative purposes all but denotes rape in the modern sense of the word (forced sexual activity).

13. Propertius (4.4) says Tarpeia was motivated by love of the Sabine king Tatius, a love that permeated the physical boundary of the state through the betrayal of Tarpeia's sexual body. See Janan 2001: 70–84.

betrayed her father and people, opening the city to the enemy, but the Sabines crushed her to death with their shields for her treachery against her own people (*prodendi exempli causa, ne quid usquam fidum proditori esset*).

Later, during the war with Alba, the two armies decided to settle matters once and for all with a combat between two sets of brothers, Roman and enemy (Liv. 1.26). When a single Roman, Horatius, survived, his sister wept for one of the slain enemy, her fiancé. In a fit of anger, Horatius murdered her, calling her a traitor ("so perish any Roman woman who mourns the enemy"). The people were initially outraged at the violent murder, but her father's testimony swayed them—if he condoned her death, so should they (*moti homines sunt in eo iudicio maxime P. Horatio patre proclamante se filiam iure caesam iudicare; ni ita esset, patrio iure in filium animadversurum fuisse*).[14]

Next come the famous Lucretia (1.57–60) and Verginia (3.44–48). The prince Sextus Tarquinius desired the wife of Collatinus, Lucretia, because she was the only one of all the Roman princes' wives who was well behaved and chaste. After Tarquin had raped her, Lucretia reported his treachery and then stabbed herself, knowing that she was not guilty, but nevertheless unwilling to live unchaste. Brutus used this episode to motivate the people to eliminate monarchy at Rome (1.59). Finally, the wicked decemvir Appius, after working to establish the Twelve Tables to make public the rights of all Romans, was overcome with lust for a citizen girl, Verginia. He ordered his client to claim the girl as a slave and install her in his home so that Appius might rape her at his leisure (3.44). After Appius had fixed the trial over Verginia's freedom in his own favor, her father stabbed his daughter through the heart, saying that it was better for her to die with her chastity intact than live in dishonor (3.48).[15] His frenzied actions and appeals to the people led to the dismissal of the decemvirs and the reassertion of political order in Rome, with more power for the plebeian people (3.54).

These tales are vibrant and salient reminders of the violence faced by women in the ancient world. But although these stories display horrific violence, raped bodies, and murdered women, their point was not to threaten Roman women with terrible violence, rape, or murder. Once the women have served their purpose in motivating male action, they disappear from

14. Livy's story demonstrates that the cold-blooded murder of a sibling was not normative or condoned (the people objected) unless that killing was in pursuit of social change or commitment to the honor of one's house. This model of honor killing is repeated in the story of Verginia.

15. This model of honor killing is still observed in many cultures around the world, where the chastity of female family members is more important than their lives.

the narrative, because the stories were never really about them. Livy's aim is multilayered. On one level, he chronicles political change and the defeat of tyranny and opposes the situations under which violence against women and the family occur.[16] The underlying message regarding women is subtler. Because female sexual status is the civic status of the male body politic,[17] a violation of that status (symbolic or real) is a threat to the men of Rome. These tales warn women against betraying their family, their *pudicitia*, and their husbands' honor. But in the "civilized" world of Augustus' Rome, when Livy is writing, women who betray their home and family will be punished publicly and humanely by the law of the pater patriae, not bludgeoned to death by irate brothers. These stories portray public, ideological, and unrealistic violence that was far removed from the violence that was most likely to be suffered by actual women in Rome.

Violence as Statute: Marriage and Law

Early Rome's culture of violence toward women can also be seen in her laws. Early Roman law put women at the mercy of their husbands and at risk of violence or death for seemingly arbitrary offenses. Under closer examination, however, several patterns emerge: (1) the laws make violence against women public and subject to state approval, (2) the most violent punishments refer to the mythohistory of Rome, and (3) late republican law and marriage trends made it difficult for Roman husbands to harm their citizen wives with impunity.[18]

When the Twelve Tables, the first public inscription of collected laws, were erected in Rome (450–449 BCE), there were three types of marriage: *usus*, *confarreatio*, and *coemptio*.[19] All three were *manus* marriages, that is,

16. A number of studies (many noted in n. 9 above) examine the motive and message of Livy's tales of violence against women, focusing on the drama, the violence, the political change, the misogyny, and the symbolism. My aim here is not to delve deeply into Livy's motivations or message in these stories but, rather, to point out that the violence here is public, political, and ideological rather than personal and realistic in everyday Roman citizen lives.

17. Henry and James 2012.

18. One might consider the changing force of *patria potestas* as an analog here. Ostensibly, the paterfamilias had complete power of life and death over his children, but over time, this power weakened and was no longer enforced. By Hadrian's reign, a father who killed his son was stripped of citizenship and property and was exiled. See Frier and McGinn 2004: 193–211.

19. On *manus* marriage, see Gardner 1986: 11–14; Frier and MacGinn 2004: 89–94;

marriages under which the woman passed out of the *potestas* of her father and into the *manus* (hand, or power) of her husband. In a *manus* marriage, the husband had the power of life or death over his wife in limited circumstances. Divorce in early *manus* marriages was rare, and it was impossible for women to obtain. Women had to conform to husbands' wishes and had no recourse to their families for help.[20]

The laws for women under *manus* were draconian.[21] Supposedly established by Romulus himself, these laws made women subject to the power of their husbands and gave husbands the power to fatally punish their wives under socially condoned circumstances.[22] During this period, a husband could put his wife to death for drinking wine or committing adultery.[23] Made many years later, Cato's remarks on drinking and adultery indicate that this law extended through the middle republic to the beginning of the late republic.[24] Egnatius Metellus, we are told, beat his wife to death for drinking, and his act was approved by his neighbors and the state.[25] But as horrifying as this situation was, the scrutiny put on Egnatius Metellus for killing his wife tells us that uxoricide could not be committed with impunity. A wife's offense had to be acknowledged publicly, and her punishment was subject to the approval of society.

Hersch 2010: 23–26, 2014; Looper-Friedman 1987; Gaius *Inst.* 1.108–18, 136–37a. See Levick 2012 for women and law. Evans-Grubbs 2002 extends the survey to the late empire.

20. Gardner 1986: 83.

21. These laws reflect social ideals, not necessarily common function or practice. We may take away from them what early republican lawmakers wanted to be true about their society and the ideologies they adopted.

22. Socially condoned circumstances were always subject to change. Divorce was allowed to men for only a handful of reasons: if wives were using drugs, practicing magic, counterfeiting keys, or committing adultery (*FIRA*[2], vol. 1, p. 3, Tr. ARS, rev. L, in Lefkowitz and Fant 2005: 94–96). On divorce, see also Corbier 1999; Gardner 1986: 83–87; Treggiari 1991a.

23. To modern readers, the offense of wine drinking seems a light one to deserve a death penalty, but the Romans associated the wine drinking of women with immorality and promiscuity. A variety of stories in Livy exploit the "wine-drinking harlot" trope, particularly the tale of the Bacchanalia at Rome (Liv. 39.8–19), as well as his description of the other soldiers' wives carousing at home in the story of Lucretia (Liv. 1.57).

24. Gel. 10.23 notes that Cato said that a woman who was caught drinking wine was punished no less severely than one caught in adultery, by her husband, who acted as her judge.

25. V. Max. 6.3.9. Metellus was of Romulus' era, when such draconian laws were reported to have existed, preserving the dominant ideologies of the time: sobriety, utmost chastity in women, and complete power of husbands over wives.

The laws detrimental to women fell out of favor by the late republic, for two reasons: the social and moral legislation of Augustus and the decline of *manus* marriages.[26] After Cicero, *manus* marriage is almost never mentioned in the literature, and the practice of marrying *sine manu* was on the rise.[27] Under this type of marriage, a woman remained under the *potestas* of her paterfamilias or, if she were *sui iuris* (her paterfamilias dead), under the tutelage of a male relative appointed by her paterfamilias. She retained her property (or, rather, her natal family did), divorce was simpler, and she was not subject to her husband's control, remaining under the protection of her own family. Husbands now had to be concerned with how they treated their wives, and they had to have approval from their wives to use dotal funds. Abusing a wife resulted in a speedy divorce and removal of her property back to her family, so *sine manu* marriages may have kept husbands in line, as far as domestic violence was concerned.[28] By the empire, *manus* marriages disappeared entirely.[29]

Augustus' marriage legislation put an end to husbands' power to kill their wives for adultery, whether they were in *manus* marriages or not. The *lex Julia de maritandis* of 18 BCE and the *lex Julia de Adulteriis coercendis* of 17 BCE forbade husbands to kill adulterous wives. Instead, wives had to be divorced publicly, tried in court, and exiled if found guilty.[30] The power previously held by the paterfamilias was transferred to everyone's paterfamilias, Augustus, the pater patriae, making the private issue of adultery a public crime. Before the legislation, husbands could kill with impunity their wives (and their wives' lovers) whom they caught in the act of adultery, a law that

26. Further passages in V. Max. (6.3.10–12)—outlining the severe punishments (from Valerius Maximus' early imperial perspective) for women who went out of doors without a head covering (10), spoke to another woman in public (11), and attended the games without her husband's prior approval (12)—indicate changing ideologies in the midrepublic: the punishment prescribed is no longer death but divorce.

27. Looper-Friedman 1987: 281. Scholars are uncertain what motivated this shift. Looper-Friedman (296) speculates that "social and economic changes at this time did result in a new perception and definition of the family which was inconsistent with the tradition of *manus*, and which led to its eventual obsolescence."

28. As with any legal matter, the presence of a law did not equal adherence to the law, so domestic violence was, of course, still a possibility. Hesberg-Tonn (1983) contends that women married *sine manu* did not enjoy much more freedom than women married *cum manu*. I argue only that the law made it more difficult for men married *sine manu* to abuse their wives with impunity.

29. Looper-Friedman 1987: 281.

30. On the details of these laws, see Cohen 1991; Frank 1975; Galinsky 1981; Harries 2007: 95–101; Raditsa 1980; Treggiari 1994. See also Fantham 1991; Csillag 1976.

was likely abused previously as a means of eliminating inconvenient wives or personal enemies.[31] Husbands now could not kill adulterous wives, even upon catching them in the act.[32]

The law now made it complicated to kill an adulterous woman legally: caught in the act at her father's or husband's house,[33] she must be put to death immediately only by her father (not her father-in-law or husband).[34] This father must also be her paterfamilias (a man not under the *potestas* of another man) and her natural father (not a father by adoption).[35] Her execution could not be put off or take place anywhere else.[36] Furthermore, the adulterer had to be discovered physically penetrating the adulterous daughter, and the pair had to be killed in a single blow.[37] The difficulty in carrying out her punishment effectively eliminated the execution of adulterous women in Rome. In short, Augustus did not wish husbands to kill wives for the crime of adultery as they had been able to do with legal impunity prior to his law.[38] He desired, instead, a public court and public shame, to make a public example of errant women. Augustus' law took away male private rights over the female body.[39]

It is necessary to mention now the issue of domestic abuse. Thus far, we have been examining ideological, public, legally sanctioned violence against citizen women. When the law forbids certain practices, such as the abuse of

31. Cantarella 1991. Putting a captured adulterer to death or castrating him was allowed in Plautus' time (*Bac.* 859–60, 917–18; *Mil.* 1397–99). Citizen males were advised to stay away from married women, widows, virgins, youths, and freeborn boys (*Cur.* 33–38).

32. It was understood that husbands would be far more inclined to murder wives in the heat of the moment, whereas fathers would be more likely to spare a daughter (*Dig.* 48.5.23.4).

33. *Dig.* 48.5.24.2.

34. *Dig.* 48.5.24 pr.

35. *Dig.* 48.5.22.

36. *Dig.* 48.5.21–27. For a detailed examination of the right of the father to kill the adulterous daughter, see Treggiari 2002.

37. *Dig.* 48.5.24 [23] pr.; Ulp. *de adult.* Thus, only very specifically delineated "crimes of passion" were allowed in Augustan Rome, with the object of protecting the *dignitas* of a woman's natal family rather than punishing an adulterous wife. This is why such power is given only to a daughter's father rather than to her husband and why the specifications for legal murder are so narrow. See Treggiari 2002.

38. It is unknown how many men took advantage of the legality of killing a wife once divorce became common and thus offered a frequent solution to domestic problems.

39. Augustus did not exempt himself from this public justice: both his daughter and granddaughter Julia were tried and exiled for the crime of adultery (D.C. 55.10; Suet. *Aug.* 65).

wives, illegal activities are limited but not eliminated. They go underground, go unremarked upon in the historical sources, and are subject to speculation. No law in the late republic allowed a Roman man to discipline his wife physically,[40] and Cato the Elder informs us that it was reprehensible to beat one's wife or child,[41] but we should certainly assume that domestic abuse still occurred, though it seems that abuse of upper-class Roman women was unusual. Valerius Maximus (2.1.6) describes a tradition in which a quarreling husband and wife visit the temple of Viriplaca in the Palatine, talk out their problems, and return home untroubled (with violence successfully circumvented). Physical abuse of a person with high status (*dignitas*) was considered disrespectful: physical punishment was reserved for slaves, freed persons, or those of lower status.[42] Thus, if physical violence were perpetrated against citizen women within the home, it was shameful to speak of it in public. A few later authors make general comments: Quintilian (*Inst.* 7.8.2) creates a fictional case of a woman who was beaten by her husband, tries to sway him with a love potion, then divorces him when it fails; Augustine notes the faces of women scarred by husbands and intimates that his mother, Monica, was beaten by her husband; and Plutarch advises married women to have protectors aside from their husbands (one interpretation being that they needed protection from their husbands themselves).[43] In the Roman imperial household, violence against women was apparently common, but one must be cautious with Tacitus' and Suetonius' tales of "evil" emperors and their foul deeds.[44] In one notable case, in 160 CE, an upper-class woman named Regilla, married to a wealthy Greek named Herodes, was beaten to

40. Frier and McGinn 2004: 95. See Quint. *Inst.* 7.4.11; *CJ* 5.17.8.2; *P. Oxy* VI 903, L 3581 (cited in Fagan 2011). Physical abuse was clear grounds for unilateral divorce (Sen. *De ira* 3.5.4)

41. Plu. *Cat. Ma.* 20.2. On violence by the paterfamilias against children, see Saller 1991, who contends that while the paterfamilias legally had the power of life and death over his family members, he used it differently based on the status of the object. Children could be disinherited for disobedience, while slaves would be physically beaten. Saller does not discuss power over wives. See also Harris 1986.

42. See Saller 1991; Fagan 2011.

43. August. *Conf.* 9.9; Plut. *Quaest. rom.* 108. Both are cited in Pomeroy 2007: 121. One would think Juvenal, in his diatribe on women (*Satire* 6), would counsel the beating of annoying wives, but he never suggests violence for dealing with women: the husbands he describes are too dependent on their wives' dowries. On domestic abuse in Augustine's household, see Clark 1999. This material is problematic for demonstrating Roman attitudes, as Christian discourse on marriage (which used the language of slavery) was mingling with old Roman practices by this period.

44. Nero supposedly had his first wife, Octavia, and his mother, Agrippina Minor, murdered, and he is said to have kicked his pregnant wife Poppaea to death (Suet. *Nero* 34–35).

death by her husband's freedman, allegedly at Herodes' behest. It should be noted that Herodes had to remove Regilla from Rome and her family to Athens in order to isolate and harm her, as systematic abuse at Rome with a woman's family at hand would have been difficult, especially among the elite, and had Regilla suspected her husband's murderous intentions, she could have easily returned to her family. It took some time for information of her death to reach her family in Rome, at which point they charged Herodes for Regilla's murder.[45]

The literary evidence from the late republic is frustratingly quiet on this subject. Plautus' *Casina* contains a passage of domestic abuse in surrogate form (lines 404–8): when Cleostrata and Lysimachus tire of their verbal abuse, they instruct their personal slaves to hit each other. Either it was shameful to engage in domestic abuse, or it was inappropriate to portray it onstage. Domestic violence was not sanctioned by the state, so any illicit violence against citizen women necessarily took place indoors (or away from Rome altogether), away from the prying eyes of family, neighbors, friends, and colleagues. This hidden violence against citizen women stands in direct contrast to violence against noncitizen and slave women, which could legally happen anywhere. The extent to which domestic violence occurred is unknown,[46] but it may be safe to say that physical abuse was not a daily part of every citizen woman's life, and there was legal recourse for those who experienced it, especially for those women married *sine manu*. Husbands were accountable to wives' families in any case.[47]

Citizen women at the end of the late republic were almost exclusively married *sine manu*, and the imperator had taken over the role of the paterfamilias in the power of life or death over members of the *familia*, particularly over a wife. Generally speaking, Roman citizen women did not have to fear systematic abuse within the *domus* if they had a natal family to look after their interests. They were at less risk of punishment by suspicious husbands, so long as those husbands were law-abiding. Citizen women of the late republic lived in relative safety within their households, largely free from domestic violence or private persecution. Any punishment of the average citizen woman was supposed to come publicly from the state, in full view of the citizenry.[48]

45. Through the intercession of Emperor Marcus Aurelius, Herodes was acquitted (despite evidence against him), and the freedman took the full blame. See Pomeroy 2007: 123–29.

46. Treggiari 1991b: 430.

47. Pomeroy 1976.

48. As I have noted, I speak generally here. As today, even when legislation forbids abuse, violence can still occur.

Reality—Women at Risk (Noncitizen Slaves and Sex Laborers)

As we have seen, citizen women could experience violence in the public sphere, as the result of legal punishment or political upheaval, but there was generally less chance that the Roman citizen woman would be assaulted within the home, given law and custom by the late republic. Her slaves, however, experienced frequent violence and rape and lived with the constant expectation of violence within the home. Another class of women, the noncitizen sex laborers of Rome, also experienced frequent domestic violence. These two types of women, glimpsed through Roman comedy and elegy, most suffered the reality of violence in the Rome. The elegiac *meretrix* is representative of free purchasable women generally, and her experiences in elegy can offer evidence for the lived reality of the noncitizen sex laborer in Roman society.

The violence against enslaved and noncitizen women in Rome was quotidian and constant: it was publicly and legally approved, but it rarely took place in public; it was unrelated to preservation of the state or social change; it was not relegated to mythohistory; and it was unrelated to the male body politic. In short, it was divorced from the ideologies that interested the Roman historians; hence it was largely unremarkable to them. The violence against the citizen woman in Rome, while it might be initially conjectured from Livy to be constant and to take place in all spaces, was largely public and ideological. Abuse of female slaves and noncitizen women, which the law suggested was a public affair, was more prevalent in the home, the locus to which these women were largely confined. Looking at the experiences of slave women and noncitizen sex laborers, we see the reality of the topography of violence in the Roman state.[49]

Violence against Female Slaves

Slavery was a horrific institution in the ancient Roman world.[50] Slaves could be publicly beaten, tortured, and killed for any offense, great or minor, with

49. Violence was the slave's lot, regardless of gender, but women faced sexual violence more often than men did.

50. Unlike Greek slavery (for which see Hunt's contribution in this volume), which was unregulated and largely based on opportunity, Roman slavery was indeed an institution. Slaves were taken in vast quantities through conquest in war, slaves were owned by the state, the state regulated manumission, and laws to punish rebellious or murderous slaves were also created by the state. For statistics, see Scheidel 2005. I focus here on slave abuse in late republican sources. For a collection of sources on slave abuse in the empire, see Clark 1999: 122–25.

minimal governmental regulation or interference, and this violence could occur in the street in view of all.[51] Slave abuse was commonplace in the home as well, to discipline or make an example.[52] Sexual violence, a risk particularly to noncitizen women and slaves, typically took place in the home, not the street, in contrast to the public physical violence intended to make an example of recalcitrant slaves. Legally, "rape" did not exist concerning slaves: masters could do as they wished with their own property, and anyone else who violated a slave was guilty not of rape but of misusing the property of another citizen.[53] In the sexual availability of slaves, the lot of male and female slaves differed. While attractive male slaves might be forced to service the master sexually,[54] they did not suffer the risk of pregnancy. Male slaves also had a limited period of sexual attractiveness, according to Roman social conventions.[55] While male slaves were (generally speaking) desirable only as

51. Wiseman 1985: 1–10. Slaves could be killed on a grand scale, according to a law that dictated that all slaves in a household should be put to death if one slave killed his master (the justification being that the other slaves should have intervened; refusing to do so made them accessories to the murder). When an official, Lucius Pedanius Secundus, was murdered by his slave, Nero and the Senate decreed that all four hundred of his slaves should be crucified (Tac. *Ann.* 14.42–43). According to the *ius gentium*, slaves could be beaten or killed legally by their masters. Imperial laws limited this power to some extent: the early imperial *lex Petronia* prohibited death by beast fight; Claudius determined that a slave whose master abandoned him to die should be free and that a master who killed an infirm slave instead of abandoning him would be prosecuted for murder (Suet. *Cl.* 25). Much later, the constitution of Antoninus stipulated that if slaves were killed *sine causa*, the master faced the same penalties as a man who killed another man's slave (Gaius *Inst.* 1.52). Beatings, however, remained normative. Even freed slaves were subject to torture: Epicharis, a freedwoman involved in the Pisonian conspiracy under Nero, was taken and tortured to give up information about the conspirators (Tac. *Ann.* 15.57). In the empire, male freed slaves rose far higher socially than freedwomen. See Ash 2012: 449–51.

52. See Saller 1991; Lenski's contribution in the present volume.

53. Ancient Greek law preserves some of the laws on rape versus property crime in the Gortyn law code (*Inscr. Cret.* 4.72, cols. ii: 3–27) and the Athenian law code. On the question of whether we should use the term *rape* to describe sexual violence in the ancient world, see James 2013. On laws against sexual assault in ancient Greece, see Cole 1984; Omitowojo 2002. In Rome, rape of citizen women (provided the woman was not *infamis*) and of boys was prohibited by the *lex Julia de vi publica*; rape had no statute of limitations and could be prosecuted by a woman's father, her husband, or the general public. See Fantham 1991; Gardner 1986: 118–21; n. 63 below.

54. Olympio and Chalinus in Plautus' *Casina* likely did (see lines 450–62). On the abused *puer* from *Pseudolus*, see Jocelyn 2000; Kwintner 1992.

55. These conventions were ideological, however, and framed according to the norms of Roman male sexuality. While the poets and playwrights suggest that male desirability ended at puberty or shortly after, this standard was by no means absolutely representative of Roman sexual practices in reality. Enslaved males could be exploited sexually at any time

young men,[56] female slaves were considered sexual objects until they were worn out by old age, abuse, or overwork.[57] Female slaves were always available for their masters' pleasure, but they were also subject to abuse by male slaves within the household.[58] So common was the knowledge of slave rape by fellow slaves that Cato the Elder, with his keen eye for profit, segregated the male slaves from the female and then charged the male slaves for visits to the females, who served as sex slaves in addition to their regular duties (Plu. *Cat. Ma.* 21.1).[59]

The desirability of the slave girl is a common trope in ancient literature.[60] Female slaves were at risk not only of the dangers of pregnancy (potentially fatal in the premodern world) but of retribution from the master's wife should the master's sexual indiscretions be made known to her; the pregnancy of the slave girl itself could be a signal to the mistress of her husband's infidelity.[61] The female slave's lack of personal agency in her rape and pregnancy were of little concern to the vengeful mistress. Although neither male nor female slaves could reject the sexual advances of their masters, sexual abuse was an exception or a short-lived situation for male slaves but was the rule for female slaves, simply another aspect of the female slave experience.

---

and likely were. Since the scope of this article is limited to the abuse of women, I treat the vulnerability of male slaves only briefly.

56. Richlin 1992: 34–44; 1993; Williams 2010: 31–38.

57. See Marshall 2013 (on the sex slave in antiquity); Marshall 2015 (on exploited female slaves in Plautus' comedies); Rosivach 1998 (on exploited women in New Comedy).

58. So were attractive male slaves, if they did not have sufficient strength or authority to reject those advances.

59. The slaves of *lenones* (pimps) were even worse off: enslaved sex laborers, they were forced to have sex with many men and were threatened with beatings by their masters and customers. Ballio in Plautus' *Pseudolus* threatens his girls with beatings and worse unless they bring in lots of money and gifts (188–229). Antamoenides in *Poenulus* promises to beat his "girlfriend" black and blue because her pimp stuck him with the bill for lunch (1280–93).

60. Greek literature offers the examples of Agamemnon and Chryseis in Homer's *Iliad* (1.111–15) and Phoenix with Amyntor's concubine in the same work (9.447–454), as well as Laertes and Eurykleia in the *Odyssey* (1.429–33). The defendant in *On the Murder of Eratosthenes* (Lys. 1.12) was accused of having interfered with the slave girl; see also Dikaiopolis and Thratta in Aristophanes' *Acharnians* (lines 271–76). For examples in Latin literature, see Ov. *Ars* 1.382–98; *Am.* 2.7–8; Hor. *Odes* 2.4.

61. James 1997: 67. Sex with slaves was illegal for citizen women but legal for men, an inequity remarked on by Syra in Pl. *Mer.* 817–29. Nevertheless, as poetry and drama show, wives and *meretrices* were angered at finding out that their husbands and clients had strayed (e.g., Dorippa in Pl. *Mer.* 755–89, Matrona in *Men.* 559–61, and Artemona in *As.* 851–909, as well as Corinna in Ov. *Am.* 2.7–8).

In Livy's story of Verginia (3.47.7), the evil decemvir Appius must attempt to reclassify the girl as a slave before he can rape her.

Roman comedy (a genre that flourished in the second century BCE) offers an excellent source of social historical information about the life, status, and situation of the female slave girl. It has been well established in scholarship that despite the Greek origins and trappings of Roman comedy, Romans felt that the plays were mimetic of Roman life.[62] The social historical evidence in these plays must be carefully interpreted. References to the plight of slave women are not always immediately apparent but do, upon collection and reflection, throw light on the situation for slave women and noncitizen sex laborers. They thus provide examples of widespread and institutional violence against noncitizen women at Rome.[63]

In Plautus' *Casina*, the male slaves Olympio and Chalinus both seem to have been sexual subjects of the lascivious *senex* Lysidamus in their younger years (lines 460–66). But while they are no longer of interest to the *senex*,[64] the young maid Casina, now hitting puberty, becomes a sexual object for four of the men in the play: the master and his son, as well as their proxies Olympio and Chalinus. The play's entire plot is driven by the male desire for sexual possession of the slave maid Casina. Though Casina's mistress had raised her in the household as a daughter (45–46), her slave status is reasserted as soon as Casina is of age, and her mistress cannot prevent her husband from then claiming a sexual right to the girl. The play's humor rests on the myriad ways in which the wife Cleostrata thwarts her husband's sexual possession of Casina.[65]

---

62. For surveys of the scholarship on the mimetic qualities of Roman comedy and Roman attitudes toward the genre, see James 1998b: 3–5; Leigh 2004; Richlin 2005. For the influence of Roman comedy on Cicero's rhetoric and Livy's history, see Geffcken 1973; Feldherr 1998. See also Richlin, forthcoming; James, forthcoming.

63. Conversely, Roman comedy features a bizarrely high number of plays in which citizen girls are raped (Pl. *Aul.*, *Cist.*, *Epid.*, *Truc.*; Ter. *Ad.*, *An.*, *Eu.*, *Hec.*); these plots reflect a social anxiety about the sexual vulnerability of unmarried daughters but do not reflect reality. The *lex Julia de vi publica* outlawed the rape of women and boys (late republic), but there were earlier laws in place against rape (*Rhet. Her.* 4.8.12). See Fantham 1991; Gardner 1986: 118–21.

64. This is so except for a brief relapse by Lygdamus when he becomes overexcited at the prospect of Casina and molests Olympio in Casina's stead (lines 451–59).

65. In one scene, the maid Pardalisca, likely another of Lysidamus' sexual victims, imagines Casina's rebellion to the sexual threat. Telling Lysidamus that Casina has two swords she plans to use on him, Pardalisca enjoys Lysidamus' fear, perhaps as payback for her own past suffering. Later, Chalinus dresses up as "Casina" and beats both Lysidamus and Olympio when they try to sexually assault "her." See Andrews 2004.

In Terence's *Eunuchus*, a male citizen sees what he assumes is a slave girl being led into the house of a *meretrix*. The young man dresses up as a slave and enters the household, where he rapes the girl, who is actually a long-lost citizen. To highlight the horror experienced by the girl, Terence has another female slave maid, Pythias, describe aspects of the rape (643–67): shredded clothes, torn hair, and the house in an uproar. When the *meretrix* Thais accuses him of the rape, the young man Chaerea tries to justify his actions, impudently saying that he thought her a "fellow slave" (*conservam esse credidi*, 658). That he can make this argument highlights the plight of the female slave within any given *familia*: she is constantly at risk, both from her master and from the rest of the slave household.[66]

Roman comedy provides many examples of the vulnerability of slave girls in the houses of their masters. In addition to the threat of rape, slave maids could also be tortured by their households (or neighboring households) for testimony, for the suspicion of theft, or for being too beautiful.[67] The slave girls of Latin elegy are stabbed by mistresses irritated at mild hairdressing errors (*tuta sit ornatrix: odi, quae sauciat ora unguibus et rapta bracchia figit acu*, Ov. *Ars* 3.239–242; *Am.* 1.14.16), whipped and scarred on a regular basis (Ov. *Am.* 2.7–8), and tortured for speaking out of turn (Prop. 4.7.43–46).[68] While their female owners were generally safest at home, female slaves, because the locus of their work was located there, necessarily experienced torture, rape, and even death at home.[69]

---

66. James 1998a; Smith 1994.

67. For torture for testimony, see Pl. *Truc.* 775–882; Ter. *Hec.* 750–52, 756–60. For torture for theft, see Pl. *As.* 888–91. The *senex* Demipho argues that the family should sell the beautiful slave girl Pasicompsa because a housemaid must be worked hard (weaving, grinding, cutting wood, spinning wool, sweeping, and taking a beating), as well as that pretty slave girls will irritate their mistresses with the attention they get from other men (Pl. *Mer.* 395–411). The neighbor's wife Dorippa refuses to have a beautiful slave dressed as a *meretrix* introduced into her household (784–85), as she presumes that this girl is being installed as her husband's mistress.

68. Juvenal 6.475–93 mocks a woman for taking out her sexual frustrations on her maids.

69. An excellent example of the inviolability of the female citizen body and the institutional vulnerability of the slave woman is found in the celebration of the Matralia, a festival for Roman matrons to revere the goddess Mater Matuta on June 11. At this festival, women ritualistically beat a slave woman away and then embrace their nieces. The ritual represents citizen female solidarity and contempt for slave women, considered to be careless or dangerous to Roman children (Plu. *Cam.* 5.1–2).

Violence against the Puella*: The Fallacy of* Servitium Amoris

Officially, Roman marriages were business transactions, and Roman ideology dismissed the idea of "romance" in the married state.[70] Roman wives existed for procreation, not pleasure.[71] Sexual attraction, along with the violence that often attended it, was reserved for the large class of noncitizen, female sex laborers in Rome, who could expect violence and rape as workplace hazards.[72] Free noncitizen women were hardly safer from male sexual assault than were slave women. Ostensibly, they had ownership of their own bodies and the right to their own property, but these liminal persons in Rome had neither the same protections as citizens nor a wide-reaching family with the power to protect its members. Only by winning the protection of a powerful family (as do Bacchis in *Hecyra* [794–98] and Thais in *Eunuchus* [145–52, 864–71]) can these women hope for safety from violence, rape, or theft, as noncitizens had little recourse to the courts. Should they be assaulted, only a powerful protector could bring the case to court for them. Without the protection of a patron, noncitizen sex laborers had to rely on their customers to behave well, but there was little to force a customer to adhere to the rules

70. Roman comedy provides many examples of unhappy spouses utterly uninterested in any kind of passion with their marriage partner (Pl. *As.* [though the wife appears to be upset also that her husband has abandoned their marriage bed], *Cas.*, *Men.*, *Mer.*), in direct contrast to the young, unmarried men who have a strong desire for citizen girls who will become their wives (Pl. *Cas.*, *Cist.*, *Poen.*, *Rud.*, *Trin.*; Ter. *Ad.*, *An.*, *Ph.*, *Hau.*). On the late arrival of "love" to the institution of marriage, see Grimal 1967; James 1998a.

71. Demosthenes (*Against Neaira* 59.122) had made this distinction for the Greeks: "We have prostitutes for pleasure, . . . wives for the procreation of legitimate offspring." Wives were not supposed to be sexy or active in bed. Lucretius (4.1268–77) notes that wives should not move during intercourse, because they were there to get pregnant (immobility was considered necessary for conception)—sex laborers wiggled around because they were not there for procreation (see also Mart. 10.68.10; Plut. *Conjugal Precepts* 18). If a wife moved during sex, it proved that she had committed adultery (i.e., learned her moves elsewhere: Mart. 1.104, 7.18, Ov. *Am.* 1.10, 2.10.35; Tib. 1.9). See Parker 1997: 55. Even outward affection toward a wife was discouraged by some Roman men. Cato never embraced his wife unless it thundered, and he expelled a senator for embracing his wife in broad daylight (Plu. *Cat. Ma.* 17.7). Ovid's *praeceptor amoris* comments that wives are for arguing with (*Ars* 2.151–56) and that they are boring because they can be had anytime, whereas *meretrices* could ostensibly say no (*Ars* 3.585–86). When Cicero was accused of marrying Publilia for her pretty face, Tiro defends him, saying Cicero married not for love or sex but, rather, for money (Plu. *Cic.* 41.3; see also Treggiari 2007: 134).

72. This is still frequently the case in modern sex work: see Miller and Schwartz 1995.

of the business, and many men abused or raped sex laborers rather than pay their bills. These women could rely only on their wiles and strong doors to protect themselves from their own customers.[73]

Latin elegy most clearly betrays the gap between ideology and reality in the Roman topography of violence against women. It is important to remember here that though elegy is literary material, its *meretrices* are based on real, living sex laborers in Roman society, and much can be learned about their safety and status through the poetry. The locus of violence against the elegiac *puella* (the beloved of the poet-lover, a *meretrix*), like that of the slave girl, was necessarily within the home. The elegiac conceit dictated that the customers of the *meretrix* behave appropriately in public, giving no outward indication of the mercantile relationship between them and the *puella*.[74] This dissimulation resulted in a courteous, almost chivalrous demeanor by male customers in public spaces: the street was not the venue for impassioned violence or displays of dominance.

To gain physical access, the young men had to be admitted to the *meretrix*'s home. Propertius, Tibullus, and Ovid, Latin poets during the age of Augustus (31 BCE–14 CE), all write about passionate love affairs with their "girlfriends,"[75] emphasizing their eternal love and devotion in beautiful poetry that proclaims their own enslavement to their respective beloveds.[76] In several poems, the plaintive, shut-out lover bemoans his lack of access to the interior of the *puella*'s home.[77] The domicile of a *meretrix* was exclusive space, difficult to broach, and utterly private. The difficulty in gaining entry served two purposes: (1) to increase a customer's ardor by withholding access (and making the commodity all the more rare and thus more desired) and (2) to protect the *puella* from drunk, rowdy, and possibly violent young men who sought access to her.[78] Advisory *lenae* warned *meretrices* in training that men

73. On Roman sex labor generally, see McGinn 1998; 2004; James 2003a; Faraone and McClure 2006.

74. On the economics of the elegiac relationship, see James 2003b: 71–107.

75. Though elegy uses the language of legitimate marriage, these women are free *meretrices*, not Roman matrons. See James 2003b, 2012.

76. It is important to note that the characters Propertius, Tibullus, and Ovid in the poetry are not to be identified with the authors of the same names. The poets create personas and characters, but they do not write autobiographies.

77. The motif of the *exclusus amator* goes back to the paraclausithyron of Greek elegy. In Latin elegy, see Catul. 67; Tib. 1.2; Prop. 1.16; Ov. *Am.* 1.6. In Latin lyric, see Hor. *Odes* 3.10, 26. See also Copley 1956.

78. Even a strong door was not always sufficient protection: Tibullus (1.1.73–74) notes that youth is the time to break down doors (that prevent access to girlfriends), and Horace's

could get violent and that a girl should charge extra if her client got physical (*si tibi forte comas vexaverit, utilis ira: post modo mercata pace premendus erit,* Prop. 4.5.31–32). The passionate nature of the love affair between Roman citizen men and *meretrices* made that interior space dangerous for the *meretrix*: passion could quickly lead to jealousy, violence, and rape.

The poets portray this business relationship as a legitimate love affair, deemphasizing the economic aspects of the transaction and privileging the love. They profess to be so enamored that they will suffer all abuse with only a hope that their "girlfriends" will be faithful and loving in return, a conceit called *servitium amoris*, or the "slavery of love."[79] The women refuse the poets' advances, cheat on them, shut them out of the house, spurn their affections, and take contracts with other men, while the poets cling to their own constancy, true affection, and passivity. But despite the poets' claims to be the wronged parties, physically abused and broken by their girlfriends, the fantasy of female domination quickly breaks down, and the reality of male authority, physical abuse, and rape surfaces. Readers of Latin elegy (much like the viewers of Roman comedy) are given a glimpse of what must have been, in Roman life, common violence against noncitizen, unprotected women in a domestic space.

The Battered Puella*: Violence against the Noncitizen* Meretrix

The poets' disingenuous claims of slavery stand in flagrant opposition to the power relationship actually in place between themselves and their noncitizen, *meretrix* "girlfriends." The poets play at servitude, devotion, and love, but when the veneer cracks, the reader is reminded that these men are male citizens of Rome: they operate in a power dynamic, with their "girlfriends," that privileges male citizen authority. Though the poet-lovers condemn violence against their "girlfriends" and frequently promise not to do things other men have done, all acknowledge the possibility of violence against subaltern women.

Propertius' speaker (2.5.21–26) vows not to tear his girl's clothes, break

speaker (*Odes* 3.26) dedicates to a deity the crowbars that he used to break into the houses of *meretrices*. Tibullus (1.1) also approves of *rixae*, violent spats that result in sex with questionable consent. The old men in Plautus' *Bacchides* threaten Bacchis' door with axes (1118–19), and Micio in Terence's *Adelphoe* notes that it is not scandalous to break down doors or tear clothes (102–3, 120–21).

79. On *servitium amoris*, see Copley 1947; Fitzgerald 2000: 71–77; James 2003b: 145–50; Lyne 1979; McCarthy 1998; Murgatroyd 1981.

down her door, rip at her hair, or bruise her; Tibullus' speaker (1.6.73–74) swears that he would give up his hands rather than use them against his girl (*non ego te pulsare velim, sed venerit iste / si furor, optarim non habuisse manus*), and he scoffs at any man who would rip hair, tear clothes, or make a girl cry (1.10.59–66). Ovid's speaker similarly condemns violent behavior (*Am.* 1.7). Their common lists indicate that these were familiar acts of violence in the *puella*'s world. Despite their condemnations, all three poets threaten violence against their girls, should these women continue to spurn them or refuse free sex. Tibullus acknowledges his inclination toward violence (1.6), the Propertian speaker considers murder-suicide (2.8.25–28) and threatens to rip his girl's gown and bruise her arms if she tries to cover up when he wants sex (*quod si pertendens animo vestita cubaris, scissa veste meas experiere manus: / quin etiam, si me ulterius provexerit ira, / ostendes matri bracchia laesa tuae*, Prop. 2.15.17–20), and the emotion of Ovid's speaker urged him to tear hair, rake cheeks with his nails, and give free reign to anger, though he checked his rage before he got physical—that time anyway (*Am.* 2.5.30, 45–48). Threats eventually give way to actions. Tibullus' speaker (1.10) fantasizes about a backwoods soldier who bruised his girl, broke down her door, made her cry, and ripped her hair[80] (Propertius refers to Tibullus' fantasy when he condemns such behavior in 2.5). Ovid devotes an entire poem in his *Amores* (1.7) to describing a time when the speaker's anger prompted him to beat his girl.[81] Though he claims remorse in *Amores* 1.7, the lover lingers on the attractiveness of his pale, weeping, cringing girlfriend, and he ends not with apologies but with a command for his girl to rearrange her hair so as not to remind him of his violence.[82] Ovid's *praeceptor amoris* also warns his students in the *Ars amatoria* (2.169–74) not to give way to anger, as young men will then have to pay for broken doors and ripped dresses. His focus is not on the pain and suffering of the women but, rather, on the monetary repercussions for his students.

---

80. The *miles gloriosus* character is typically more prone to violence in ancient comedy and elegy: examples are Cleomachus in Plautus' *Bacchides*, Pyrgopolynices in Plautus' *Miles gloriosus*, and Thraso in Terence's *Eunuchus*.

81. For more detail on the violence of the elegiac speaker, see James 2003b: 184–97. On Propertius and Tibullus, see also Solmsen 1961.

82. The elegists, for all their condemnations of violence, fetishize the pale, weeping girl and are sexually aroused by proof of their violent power over these women. See James 2003a; Fredrick 1997.

In the Household of the Puella

In Roman comedy and elegy, we see the social reality that even nonslave free women and slaves within other low-status households are at risk; they can suffer rape, robbery, and torture from male citizens, and these women have no real recourse at law.[83] In theory, legal action could be taken against citizens who assault free women and their slaves; in practice, such legal recourse could be difficult to obtain without a citizen male patron to move the case along. A friendless foreign woman could expect little aid from the law. A free sex laborer's household, an extension of the vulnerable noncitizen *meretrix*, was at great risk from the men that patronized it. I observed above that slave maids in the household of the *puella* were at risk of sexual violence from the *meretrix*'s customers (Ov. *Am.* 2.7–8; *Ars* 1.382–98). As slaves, they would have had a difficult time refusing citizen males who pressed them, even though these men did not own them. Citizen male privilege effectively extended to the property of the women they paid for sex: in *Eunuchus*, Chaerea justifies raping Pamphila on the grounds that he is regaining some of his brother's investment in Thais' house. In another case, Syra, a slave in the household of the *meretrix* Phronesium in *Truculentus*, is taken by Callicles to be tortured for information about a client of her mistress. The fact that she is not Callicles' slave but the slave of the neighboring *meretrix* should not be underestimated. The noncitizen *meretrix* had little protection in Roman society, and her slaves had none at all.

Men in Roman comedy frequently use their position of citizen male privilege to threaten *meretrices* and their slave households, to vent their frustrations or achieve their goals. Diabolus, the rival of the *adulescens amator* Argyrippus in *Asinaria*, threatens the *lena* Cleareta and her daughter Philaenium with legal action, poverty, and hunger (127–50) should they not give in to his demands. In *Truculentus*, Astaphium, an enslaved sex laborer in Phronesium's household, gives a speech about the dangers of having lovers inside the house of a *meretrix*: they will steal and act as they wish once they are inside, to the detriment of the household (95–111). Laches makes vague threats against Bacchis in *Hecyra* when he thinks she may still be involved with his son Pamphilus (729–31, 761–67). Alcesimarchus snatches Selenium away by sword in *Cistellaria*, threatening to kill her and himself (519–27,

83. Smith 1994: 34 (nn. 19–20) lists the sources on punishments for hubris and rape in Athens and Rome.

640–50). Finally, in *Eunuchus*, Pythias thinks Chaerea stole from the house in addition to raping Pamphila (660–61). Though these *meretrices* are free women whose households belong to them, they are still at risk of violence or theft at the hands of the citizen male class if they do not acquire a citizen male patron to see to their interests. For this reason, some *meretrices* in Roman comedy seek the favor of citizen men when it is offered or possible (e.g., Bacchis in *Hecyra* [794–98] and Thais in *Eunuchus* [145–52, 864–71]).

Conclusions

The single most important determining factor in any woman's life in the ancient world was social status.[84] Status determined whom (or if) she could marry, where she could live, what she could do, and her safety while doing it. Status protected a woman from violence or ensured that she was susceptible to it. Violence faced by the Roman citizen woman of the late republic was largely ideological, carried out with transparency on the public stage. The violence one often thinks of in Livy, in mythohistorical tales where it motivated political change and the rehabilitation of the Roman family and state, should not be considered indicative of a culture of violence against citizen women in the late republic. Early Roman law allowed for terrible violence against Roman citizen women but made this violence a matter of public approval. In the late republic, the laws that had allowed men to punish their wives violently were subsumed by Augustus' social and moral legislation; this shift removed punitive power from the family and placed it in the public court. *Manus* marriages also disappeared, in a pattern that reduced or eliminated the *potestas* of husbands over wives and curtailed domestic violence by making a woman's natal family a powerful force in her marriage. Citizen women in the late Roman Republic had very little actual, physical violence to fear in their own homes, despite the culture of violence in which they lived.

Noncitizen and slave women, however, were institutionally subject to physical and sexual violence that occurred regularly and in private. The slave woman living in the same domestic setting that kept her mistress safe was susceptible to constant harassment and rape by other slaves and her master. She could be beaten because her mistress was in a fit of pique. Her daily

84. This statement is true of both men and women, but as I hope I have demonstrated above, women suffer the same physical violence as men, but with the added dimension of sexual, personal violence.

reality was one of constant violence or the threat of it. The noncitizen free woman was also limited by her status. The physical and financial safety of marriage was not open to her, and many noncitizen women resorted to sex labor to survive. This hand-to-mouth existence was made more dangerous by the nature of her job. She had to induce rivalries between clients, balance several men at once, and feign affection while also not neglecting the mercantile aspect of her trade. Her necessary self-interest led to anger and violence in clients, who could beat or rape noncitizen women with legal impunity. Because her work took place in a private, domestic setting, she was all the more vulnerable; she had to let men inside her home in order to do her work, and there was no guarantee her clients would behave peaceably once inside. The ancient world was a dangerous place for women, but while citizen women were subject to Rome's culture of gendered violence, noncitizen and slave women most commonly suffered it.[85]

Works Cited

Andrews, N. 2004. "Tragic Re-presentation and the Semantics of Space in Plautus' *Casina*." *Mnemosyne* 57: 445–64.

Arieti, J. 1997. "Rape and Livy's View of Roman History." In S. Deacy and K. Pierce, eds., *Rape in Antiquity*, 209–29. London.

Ash, R. 2012. "Women in Imperial Roman Literature." In S. James and S. Dillon, eds., *A Companion to Women in the Ancient World*, 442–52. Oxford.

Beard, M. 1999. "The Erotics of Rape: Livy, Ovid, and the Sabine Women." In P. Setälä and L. Savunen, eds., *Female Networks and the Public Sphere in Roman Society*, 1–10. Rome.

Brown, R. 1995. "Livy's Sabine Women and the Ideal of *Concordia*." *TAPhA* 125: 291–319.

Cairns, F. 2006. *Sextus Propertius: The Augustan Elegist*. New York.

Cantarella, E. 1991. "Homicides of Honor: The Development of Italian Adultery Law over Two Millennia." In D. Kertzer and R. Saller, eds., *The Family in Italy from Antiquity to Present*, 229–44. New Haven.

Clark, P. 1999. "Women, Slaves, and the Hierarchies of Domestic Violence: The Family of St. Augustine." In S. Joshel and S. Murnaghan, eds., *Women and Slaves in Greco-Roman Culture*, 109–29. New York.

Cohen, D. 1991. "The Augustan Law on Adultery: The Social and Cultural Context." In D. Kertzer and R. Saller, eds., *The Family in Italy from Antiquity to the Present*, 109–26. New Haven.

---

85. I thank Sharon James, who inspired my study of elegy and New Comedy and who has been with me through every draft of this essay from its inception. I also thank T. H. M. Gellar-Goad and Patrick Dombrowski for their numerous comments and suggestions.

Cole, S. 1984. "Greek Sanctions against Sexual Assault." *CP* 79 (2): 97–113.

Copley, F. 1947. "*Servitium Amoris* in the Roman Elegists." *TAPhA* 78: 285–300.

Copley, F. 1956. Exclusus Amator*: A Study in Latin Love Poetry*. Madison, WI.

Corbier, M. 1991. "Divorce and Adoption as Roman Familial Strategies." In B. Rawson, ed., *Marriage, Divorce, and Children in Ancient Rome*, 47–78. Oxford.

Csillag, P. 1976. *The Augustan Laws on Family Relations*. Budapest.

Dougherty, C. 1998. "Sowing the Seeds of Violence: Rape, Women, and the Land." In M. Wyke, ed., *Parchments of Gender: Deciphering the Bodies of Antiquity*, 267–84. Oxford.

Evans-Grubbs, J. 2002. *Women and the Law in Roman Egypt: A Sourcebook on Marriage, Divorce, and Widowhood.* New York.

Fagan, G. 2011. "Violence in Roman Social Relations." In M. Peachin, ed., *The Oxford Handbook of Social Relations in the Roman World*, 467–98. Oxford.

Fantham, E. 1991. "*Stuprum*: Public Attitudes and Penalties for Sexual Offenses in Republican Rome." *EMC* 35, n.s., 10: 267–91.

Faraone, C., and McClure, L., eds. 2006. *Prostitutes and Courtesans in the Ancient World.* Madison, WI.

Feldherr, A. 1998. *Spectacle and Society in Livy's "History."* Berkeley.

Fitzgerald, W. 2000. *Slavery and the Roman Literary Imagination.* Cambridge.

Frank, R. 1975. "Augustus' Legislation on Marriage and Children." *California Studies in Classical Antiquity* 8: 41–52.

Fredrick, D. 1997. "Reading Broken Skin: Violence in Roman Elegy." In J. Hallet and M. Skinner, eds., *Roman Sexualities*, 172–93. Princeton.

Frier, B., and MacGinn, T. 2004. *A Casebook of Roman Family Law.* Oxford.

Galinsky, K. 1981. "Augustus' Legislation on Morals and Marriage." *Philologus* 125: 126–44.

Gardner, J. 1986. *Women in Roman Law and Society.* Bloomington.

Geffcken, K. 1973. *Comedy in the "Pro Caelio."* Lugduni Batavorum.

Griffin, J. 1985. *Latin Poets and Roman Life.* Chapel Hill.

Grimal, P. 1967. *Love in Ancient Rome.* Trans. A. Train. New York.

Gurval, R. 1995. *Actium and Augustus: The Politics and Emotions of Civil War.* Ann Arbor.

Harries, J. 2007. *Law and Crime in the Roman World.* Cambridge.

Harris, W. 1986. "The Roman Father's Power of Life and Death." In R. Bagnall and W. Harris, eds., *Studies in Roman Law in Memory of A. Arthur Schiller*, . Leiden, 81–95.

Hemker, J. 1985. "Rape and the Founding of Rome." *Helios* 12: 41–47.

Henry, M., and James, S. 2012. "Woman, City, State: Theories, Ideologies, and Concepts in the Archaic and Classical Periods." In S. Dillon and S. James, eds., *A Companion to Women in the Ancient World*, 84–95. Malden, MA.

Hersch, K. 2010. *The Roman Wedding: Ritual and Meaning in Antiquity.* Cambridge.

Hersch, K. 2014. "Introduction to the Roman Wedding: Two Case Studies." *CJ* 109 (2): 223–32.

Hesberg-Tonn, B. 1983. *Coniunx Carissima.* Stuttgart.

James, S. 1997. "Slave-Rape and Female Silence in Ovid's Love Poetry." *Helios* 24: 60–76.

James, S. 1998a. "From Boys to Men: Rape and Developing Masculinity in Terence's *Hecyra* and *Eunuchus*." *Helios* 25: 31–47.

James, S. 1998b. "Introduction: Constructions of Gender and Genre in Roman Comedy and Elegy." *Helios* 25: 3–16.

James, S. 2003a. "Her Turn to Cry: The Politics of Weeping in Roman Love Elegy." *TAPhA* 133: 99–122.

James, S. 2003b. *Learned Girls and Male Persuasion: Gender and Reading in Roman Love Elegy*. Berkeley.

James, S. 2012. "Re-reading Propertius' Arethusa." *Mnemosyne* 65: 425–44.

James, S. 2013. "Reconsidering Rape in Menander's Comedy and Athenian Life: Modern Comparative Evidence." In A. H. Sommerstein, ed., *Menander in Contexts*, 24–39. New York,.

James, S. Forthcoming. *Women in New Comedy*.

Janan, M. 2001. *Politics of Desire*. Ewing, NJ.

Jocelyn, H. 2000. "The Unpretty Boy of Plautus' *Pseudolus*." In E. Stärk, ed., *Dramatische Wäldchen: Festschrift für Eckard Lefèvre zum 65. Geburtstag*, 431–60. Hildesheim.

Joplin, P. 1990. "Ritual Work on Human Flesh: Livy's Lucretia and the Rape of the Body Politic." *Helios* 17: 51–70.

Joshel, S. 1992. "The Body Female and the Body Politic: Livy's Lucretia and Verginia." In A. Richlin, ed., *Pornography and Representation in Greece and Rome*, 112–30. New York.

Keith, A. 2008. *Propertius: Poet of Love and Leisure*. London.

Kwintner, M. 1992. "Plautus *Pseudolus* 782: A Fullonious Assault." *CPh* 87: 232–33.

Lefkowitz, M., and Fant, M. 2005. *Women's Life in Greece and Rome: A Sourcebook in Translation*. 3rd ed. Baltimore.

Leigh, M. 2004. *Comedy and the Rise of Rome*. Oxford.

Levick, B. 2012. "Women and the Law." In S. Dillon and S. James, eds., *A Companion to Women in the Ancient World*, 96–106. Malden, MA.

Looper-Friedman, S. 1987. "The Decline of *Manus*-Marriage in Rome." *Tijdschrift voor Rechtsgeschiedenis* 55: 281–96.

Lyne, R. 1979. "*Servitium Amoris*." *CQ* 29: 117–30.

Marshall, C. 2013. "Sex Slavery in New Comedy." In B. Akrigg and R. Tordoff, eds., *Slaves and Slavery in Ancient Greek Comic Drama*, 173–96. Cambridge.

Marshall, C. 2015. "Domestic Sexual Labor in Plautus." *Helios* 42: 123–41.

McCarthy, K. 1998. "*Servitium Amoris: Amor Servitii*." In S. Joshel and S. Murnaghan, eds., *Women and Slaves in Greco-Roman Culture: Differential Equations*, 174–92. New York.

McGinn, T. 1998. *Prostitution, Sexuality, and the Law in Ancient Rome*. Oxford.

McGinn, T. 2004. *The Economy of Prostitution in the Roman World: A Study of Social History and the Brothel*. Ann Arbor.

Miles, G. 1995. *Livy: Reconstructing Early Rome*. Ithaca.

Miller, J., and Schwartz, M. 1995. "Rape Myths and Violence against Street Prostitutes." *Deviant Behavior* 16: 1–23.

Murgatroyd, P. 1981. "*Servitium Amoris* and the Roman Elegists." *Latomus* 40: 589–606.

Omitowojo, R. 2002. *Rape and the Politics of Consent in Classical Athens*. Cambridge.

Parca, M. 2002. "Violence by and against Women in Documentary Papyri from Ptolemaic and Roman Egypt." In H. Melaerts and L. Mooren, eds., *Le rôle et le statut de la femme en Égypte Hellénistique, Romaine et Byzantine*, 283–96. Paris.

Parker, H. 1997. "The Teratogenic Grid." In J. Hallet and M. Skinner, eds., *Roman Sexualities*, 47–65. Princeton.

Pomeroy, S. 1976. "The Relationship of the Married Woman to Her Blood Relatives in Rome." *AncSoc* 7: 215–27.

Pomeroy, S. 2007. *The Murder of Regilla: A Case of Domestic Violence in Antiquity*. Cambridge.

Raditsa, L. 1980. "Augustus' Legislation concerning Marriage, Procreation, Love Affairs, and Adultery." *ANRW* II.13: 278–339.

Richlin, A. 1992. *The Garden of Priapus*. New York.

Richlin, A. 1993. "Not before Homosexuality: The Materiality of the *Cinaedus* and the Roman Law against Love between Men." *JHSex* 3: 523–73.

Richlin, A. 2005. *Rome and the Mysterious Orient: Three Plays by Plautus*. Los Angeles.

Richlin, A. Forthcoming. *Plautine Comedy as Slave Theater*.

Rogers, R. 1935. *Criminal Trials and Criminal Legislation under Tiberius*. Middleton.

Rosivach, V. 1998. *When a Young Man Falls in Love: The Sexual Exploitation of Women in New Comedy*. New York.

Saller, R. 1991. "Corporal Punishment, Authority, and Obedience in the Roman Household." In B. Rawson, ed., *Marriage, Divorce, and Children in Ancient Rome*, 144–65. Oxford.

Scheidel, W. 2005. "Human Mobility in Roman Italy." Part 2, "The Slave Population." *JRS* 95: 64–79.

Smith, L. 1994. "Audience Response to Rape: Chaerea in Terence's *Eunuchus*." *Helios* 21: 21–38.

Solmsen, F. 1961. "Propertius and His Literary Relations with Tibullus and Virgil." *Philologus* 105: 273–89.

Syme, R. 1978. *History in Ovid*. New York.

Treggiari, S. 1979. "Sentiment and Property: Some Roman Attitudes." In A. Parel and T. Flanagan, eds., *Theories of Property: Aristotle to the Present*, 53–85. Waterloo, Ontario.

Treggiari, S. 1991a. "Divorce Roman Style: How Easy and How Frequent Was It?" In B. Rawson, ed., *Marriage, Divorce, and Children in Ancient Rome*, 31–46. Oxford.

Treggiari, S. 1991b. *Roman Marriage:* Iusti Coniuges *from the Time of Cicero to the Time of Ulpian*. Oxford.

Treggiari, S. 1994. "*Leges Sine Moribus*." *AHB* 8: 86–98.

Treggiari, S. 2002. "Caught in the Act: *In Filia Deprehendere* in the *Lex Iulia de Adulteriis*." In J. Miller, C. Damon, and K. Myers, eds., Vertis in Usum*: Studies in Honor of Edward Courtney*, 243–49. Munich.

Treggiari, S. 2007. *Terentia, Tullia, Publilia: The Women of Cicero's Family*. London.

Williams, C. 2010. *Homosexuality*. 2nd ed. Oxford.

Wiseman, T. 1985. *Catullus and His World: A Reappraisal*. New York.

Witzke, S. 2015. "Harlots, Tarts, and Hussies? A Problem of Terminology for Sex Labor in Roman Comedy." *Helios* 42: 7–27.

ELEVEN

Violence and the Roman Slave

Noel Lenski

It is arguable that, in its purest essence, slavery represents the continuous and excruciatingly drawn out application of violence by one human being over another. In slave systems, the master's right to coerce and abuse his or her slaves is generally absolute. Even at times when the master chooses not to exercise that right—which is most of the time—violence subtends his power both to command action from the slave and to treat the slave as property. Roman jurists' awareness of this harsh reality is reflected in their derivation of the etymology of the word *servus* (slave) from the Latin *servare* (to save). Justinian explains, "Slaves [*servi*], however, are called this because generals order the sale of captives and because of this they tend to be saved [*servare*] and not killed."[1] To the Roman lawyer, slavery was thus a perpetual extension of the moment of imminent death over a defeated foe.

The same idea subtends one of the most influential definitions of slavery current in contemporary scholarship. In his widely read cross-cultural investigation of slavery, Orlando Patterson defines slavery as "the permanent, violent domination of natally alienated and generally dishonored persons."[2] By "permanent," Patterson means "enduring" rather than never-ending, for slaves can and do come free from bondage through flight or manumission—although they cease to be slaves in so doing. By "natally alienated," in turn, he refers to the condition of exclusion from the community of rights derived

1. Just. *Inst.* 1.3.3: *Servi autem ex eo appellati sunt, quod imperatores captivos vendere iubent ac per hoc servare nec occidere solent*; cf. *D.* 1.5.4. This etymology also enjoyed currency outside the specialist world of juristic literature. Cf. Aug. *CD* 19.15; Cass. *Exp. Ps.* 118.122 (*CCSL* 98.1113).

2. Patterson 1982: 13.

from attachment to a family, clan, tribe, polity, or state. For Patterson, referring to these persons as "generally dishonored" does not deny that some slaves in some societies—including Roman society—attain considerable prestige; it asserts only that the condition of slavery is dishonorable in and of itself. While each of the parts of this definition plays a role in describing the slave condition, Patterson foregrounds "permanent violent domination" as the first element in his scheme, because, like the Roman jurists, he understands violence—both actual and potential—as foundational to the slave-master relationship.

Some have rejected Patterson's definition in favor of formulas that privilege property relations. These scholars might prefer the definition still used in international law today from the Slavery Convention adopted by the League of Nations in 1926: "Slavery is the status or condition of a person over whom any or all the powers attaching to the right of ownership are exercised."[3] There is, by all means, merit to this simpler criterion, yet it, too, assumes a baseline in violence, for as Western sociology has recognized since Marx, all property relations are, at root, relations of power that are necessarily subtended by violence. This basic idea can also be found in Roman law, which uses only a single word to denote both "owner" and "master," the Latin *dominus*, from which we derive the English verb *dominate*. There is, in other words, no way to extricate the notion of slavery from violence; at its very roots, slavery assumes one person's compulsion to submit to another under the enduring threat—actual or potential—of violence.

In light of this inescapable reality, this essay examines Roman slavery as a violence-based institution that kept open a space for the ongoing exercise of violent force by masters but also encouraged the enactment of violence by slaves. The examination begins by showing how both the induction of humans into slavery and their maintenance as slaves entailed violence. It then turns to the ways in which the contradictions inherent in systems of slavery fed a heightened level of violence unique to systems of slavery. Finally, it examines the ways in which the violence so integral to slaveholding often spilled over into the lives of free individuals as well. We will ultimately see, in other words, how slaves internalized the violence of the system responsible for their suppression and sometimes projected it back through their own violent acts.

---

3. http://www.ohchr.org/EN/ProfessionalInterest/Pages/SlaveryConvention.aspx, accessed January 30, 2014. This definition and the historical background to its generation occasioned book-length discussion and debate at Allain 2012. See also Zeuske 2013: 97–128.

Violence in the Making of Slaves

For many slaves, induction into servitude involved the direct application of violence through forced capture. As the passage quoted above from Justinian reveals, the Romans conceived of the whole institution of slavery as rooted in captivity. Lists of the number of prisoners taken in war over the course of Roman history have been cataloged elsewhere.[4] For purposes of this discussion, a few instances can suffice to convey the scale that these mass enslavements could attain: after the defeat of the Macedonians at the battle of Pydna in 167 BCE, the Romans took seventy Greek cities and some 150,000 prisoners;[5] the victories of C. Marius against the Cimbri and Tuetones in 101 are also said to have yielded 150,000 slaves;[6] the capture of Jerusalem in 70 CE generated 97,000;[7] and over the course of his decade-long war in Gaul, Julius Caesar is said to have transferred one million captives into the hands of Roman slaveholders.[8] Most mass enslavements were considerably smaller in scale,[9] but the regular infusion of new slaves via violent capture both bolstered the overall supply of slaves and undergirded a system founded on the exercise of violence.

The Romans did not need to rely on their own conquests to supply captives, for the peoples beyond frontiers yielded captives into Rome's empire. Certain peoples, such as the nomadic Saracens of Rome's eastern frontier or the Garamantes of the African Fazzān, seem to have specialized in this sort of human trafficking.[10] The kidnapping of free citizens for resale elsewhere in the empire was also a common—though never legally sanctioned—method of generating slaves, particularly as Rome's political superstructure began to crumble in the later empire. Writing in the late fourth-century, John Chrysostom informs us of slave catchers who used sweet cakes to lure children into their clutches, and only a few decades later, Augustine reports a massive slaving raid in the territory surrounding

4. Welwei 2000: esp. 159–60; Thompson 2003: 14–29; Scheidel 2011.

5. Liv. 45.34; Polyb. 30.16; Str. 7.322.

6. Liv. *Per.* 68.

7. Joseph. *BJ* 6.416.

8. App. *Celt.* 1.6; Plut. *Caes.* 15.3. Cf. Vell. 2.47.1.

9. Welwei 2000: 149–50 catalogs attested numbers that amount to 84,000 captives from the twenty-three years of the First Punic War and 160,000 from the seventeen years of the second, for annual averages of 3,652 and 9,412, respectively.

10. On the Saracens, see Lenski 2011. On the Garamantes, see Fentress 2011; Harper 2011: 87–88.

his homeland in North Africa by Galatian slavers intent on carrying off captives in their cargo holds.[11]

To be sure, the Roman slave supply was highly diversified. In addition to the sources mentioned above, slaves were generated from natural reproduction by enslaved mothers (always the most significant source), the enslavement of exposed newborns, self-sale (especially in the early republic), the sale of one's children (especially in the later empire), and judicial condemnation.[12] At all periods, however—particularly in the middle and high republic and the later empire, periods when Rome was regularly engaged in successful foreign warfare—violent capture represented a major source in what Augustine calls "a sort of never-ending stream" of slaves.[13] The importance of captivity rested in no small part on the fact that it best generated slaves whose "natal alienation"—that is, whose cultural and political otherness—was obvious and beyond question. Unsurprisingly, captive takers tended to favor women and children as their victims, for two reasons: adult male enemies were much more likely to die fighting than suffer enslavement, and women and children tended to be more docile and, thus, better suited to assimilation within the dominant system as permanently disadvantaged subalterns.[14] Nevertheless, the Romans had no exclusive preference for women and children slaves, as some other slaveholding cultures have tended to show, and their insistence that the offspring of female slaves remain in slavery will have normalized sex ratios among captive populations within a couple generations of their capture. Violence was, in other words, very much at the heart of the subjection of a significant proportion of slaves in Roman society.

Violence in the Keeping of Slaves

To draw captives into slavery and retain them in bondage while compelling obedience and extracting forced labor from them, various means of violent restraint were deployed. The most basic and common was the chain. Slavery and bondage in iron have been considered all but synonymous across cultures, and the Romans were no exception. Indeed, the use of such devices

11. On child catchers, see Joh. Chrys. *Adv. Iud.* 1.1 (*PG* 48.855); *De statuis* 16.2 (*PG* 49.164). Cf. Jul. *Ep.* 89b (305C). On Galatian slave raiders, see Aug. *Ep.* 10* (*CSEL* 88.46–51).

12. For more, see Scheidel 1997, 2011; Harris 1999; Harper 2011: 67–99.

13. Aug. *Ep.* 10*.5.1 (*CSEL* 88.49): *perpetuo quasi fluuio.*

14. Gaca 2010.

was so common in the territories of the Roman Empire that it has left a lasting mark in the archaeological record. Shackles, manacles, and coffle chains have been found from Syria to Gaul, with predictable concentrations in territories known to have been particularly reliant on slave labor.[15] The practice of binding captives is well attested in the high empire (e.g., Josephus reports that Flavian-era legionaries each carried a chain with which to bind prisoners of war) and continued into the late empire (e.g., a large band of Huns and Sciri captured in 409 CE was marched from the Danube to Constantinople in chains).[16] Chains were also used as a means to control those already held in slavery, by preventing flight, restraining aggression, and compelling labor. The most brutal example of this is the chain gang—groups of slaves shackled together by iron ankle bands that bit into the flesh as they restricted independent movement, so as to regiment action into a macabre parade of agony. References to chain gangs are particularly common in the first centuries BCE and CE, although they were surely used in other periods of Roman history as well, particularly in circumstances where low master-slave ratios rendered unbound slaves uncooperative, if not downright dangerous.[17] Similar concerns surely influenced the rise of slave prisons (*ergastula*), where thralls were kept in unhealthy subterranean barracks to minimize their chances of flight and revolt. This method of violent domination, too, is best attested in the late republican and early imperial periods, when its unchecked excesses forced the emperors to impose restrictions.[18]

Restraint alone often did not suffice to compel obedience, coerce labor, and prevent flight or rebellion. In instances requiring additional effort, the master had a variety of methods for abusing and torturing slaves at his disposal. These included burning, beating, caning, and, above all, whipping. Indeed, the whip constituted the symbol par excellence of masterly authority, standing in as a veritable metonym for the right of a master to punish or simply abuse his property. Numerous sources attest to the readiness of the master to resort to such beating. Juvenal, for example, describes a master

15. For catalogs of shackles and chains, see Henning 1992; Thompson 1993.

16. Joseph. *BJ* 3.95; Soz. 9.5.5. Cf. *CTh* 5.6.3.

17. Cato *Ag.* 57; Colum. 1.9.4; Plin. *Ep.* 3.19.7. Masters often felt entirely justified in condemning their slaves to chains: see Juv. 14.23; *CJ* 3.36.5 (a. 222–35); Joh. Chrys. *Gen. hom.* 39.4 (*PG* 53.366). Thompson 2003: 217–21 offers full literary references on the use of shackles.

18. Colum. 1.6.3; Plin. *NH* 18.36; Sen. *Ira* 3.32.1; Petron. *Sat.* 105.11–106.1; Juv. 14.24. Tiberius (under Augustus) and Hadrian both attempted to limit the abuse of *ergastula*. See Suet. *Aug.* 32.1; *Tib.* 8.1; SHA *Hadr.* 18.10.

threatening to pummel his slaves if they fail to clean his house adequately for dinner parties, and Ammianus Marcellinus reports that late imperial masters in Rome struck their slaves with as many as three hundred lashes even for petty offenses.[19] A fascinating inscription of the early first century CE from Puteoli (Pozzuoli) in southern Italy demonstrates that masters could also spare themselves the hassle of torturing and even killing their slaves—a messy and sometimes risky affair—by resorting to the local society of undertakers, who would take care of the matter for a small fee.

> Whoever wishes to exact a punishment from a slave-man or slave-woman privately, let that person exact said punishment thus: if he wishes to have the slave crucified on a beam, let the contractor and floggers provide the poles, the shackles, the ropes for the floggers; and whoever exacts this punishment must pay four sesterces each to the individual laborers who bring the crossbeam and to the floggers, as well as the executioner.[20]

The same system that trafficked in human bodies could, in other words, be activated to occasion their abuse and even destruction.

Such calculating and systematic violence was also deployed by the state, which employed the same private operation for the dirty work of torturing and killing criminals—slave and free—but also required the torture of slaves in any instance where their testimony was needed in court. Because slaves lacked all legal capacity, it was understood that their testimony could only be validated if it were extracted under torture.[21] The appalling contradictions to which this situation led are well illustrated in the instance of slaves whose masters were themselves accused of crimes, for slaves were also forbidden to testify against their owners—except in cases of incest. To escape this double bind, the slaves of a master accused in high-profile cases of the early empire were purchased by the state before the torture began.[22]

While the abuse of slaves could be carefully calculated and highly orchestrated, it was much more random and unpredictable in most instances, representing a master's excessive display of authority or simply the indis-

19. Juv. 14.59–69; Amm. 28.4.16. Cf. Lib. *Or.* 49.24, 56.6; Salvian. *Gub.* 4.3.13–16 (*CSEL* 8.67–69). For more on the abuse of slaves, see Bradley 1987: 113–37.

20. *AE* 1971, no. 88, sec. II, lines 8–10, with Bodel 2004.

21. *D.* 48.18, with Watson 1987: 84–89. For sources on the enactment of this policy in practice, see Bradley 1987: 118–23; 1994: 165–67.

22. Tac. *An.* 2.30; cf. Robinson 1981: 235–40.

criminate expression of surplus anger and aggression.[23] This sort of behavior depended heavily on the nature and comportment of the individual master or mistress, whose self-control or lack thereof could spell agony and even mortal danger for the slave. Preaching from his own experience of daily life in late Roman Antioch, John Chrysostom reports,

> When women are angry with their maidservants, they fill the whole house with their screams. Often, if the house happens to be built on an alleyway, all the passersby hear her yelling and the maidservant wailing. . . . Straightaway all the women stoop to peep in and ask, "What's going on," then say, "So and so is beating her slave girl . . ." And the most outrageous thing is they are savage and fierce enough to whip the girl so much that the markings do not disappear by day's end, for they strip them and call in their husbands to do the job, and often bind the slave to her pallet.[24]

Following a long ancient tradition rooted in Stoic ethics, Chrysostom is here not so much reprimanding the mistress for beating her slave as counseling against doing it in such a shamefully unrestrained fashion.[25] This behavior thus represented a natural outgrowth of the master's unrestricted rights over the slave's body. It was bound to occur from time to time with nearly every master, extending up the social ladder as high as the emperor himself. The physician Galen reports that Hadrian, in a fit of rage, struck one of his slaves in the eye with a writing stylus and blinded him permanently in that eye.[26] Although he later regretted his outburst, his behavior occasioned no consequence, nor would it likely have done so had he been a mere commoner.

Slaves were also targets for sexual abuse. The economy of sexual morality in Rome, as in most societies, was based in honor. As "generally dishonored persons," slaves obviously stood outside the protections of laws governing sexual violence and could thus be raped and forced to all manner of sexual

23. Harris 2001: 317–36.

24. Joh. Chrys. *Eph. hom.* 15.3–4 (*PG* 62.109–10). For women beating their slaves or having them beaten, see also Cic. *Cluent.* 175–77; Juv. 6.475–93; Aristaenetus *Ep.* 2.15 (Vieillefond 74–76). Cf. *Coll.* 3.3.4.

25. For similar rebukes, see Sen. *Ira* 3.32.1–2; Joh. Chrys. *Gen. hom.* 9.5, 37.5 (*PG* 53.80, 350–51); Aug. *Serm. nov.* 21.159A.4 (Dolbeau pp. 281–83).

26. Galen *De propriorum animi curatio* 4 (Kühn 5.17). In the same treatise (Kühn 5.40–41), Galen also reports that his own mother went so far as to bite her slaves. For examples of slaves and freedmen murdered in impetuous fits of rage, see Suet. *Nero* 5.1; SHA *Tyr. trig.* 22.3; Severianus Gabalensis *De tribus pueris* 2 (*PG* 56.596).

acts by their masters with utter impunity. In fact, the sexual abuse of slaves was so common that it goes largely unremarked before the later empire, when Christian ethical standards led clerical leaders to insist that sexual congress with slaves was just as sinful as any other form of adulterous sex.[27] Insofar as sexual abuse provoked remarks from earlier Roman commentators, it was often in the manner of satirists like Martial, whose epigrams are filled with titillating wisecracks aimed at embarrassing randy masters and mistresses with allusions to the sexual excesses they permitted themselves with their slaves.[28] Again, the emperor was emblematic of the extremes this behavior could reach; for example, Nero paid a handsome purse to have the freedman Sporus converted into a girl by a forced sex-change operation, whereupon he "married" his hapless charge in a sham wedding ceremony.[29]

As the incident of Sporus confirms, the Roman sexual aesthetic sanctioned not just heterosexual but also homosexual sex between master and slave, provided the slave was the pathic partner. Seneca's criticism of masterly excesses in his famous *Epistle* 47 thus extends to those who forced ephebic males to struggle against the onset of puberty by depilating their bodies in preparation for nude service at dinner parties.[30] The most obvious solution to this problem was, of course, to castrate young male slaves—as Nero had done with Sporus—although this was an extremely risky, often deadly operation in antiquity. Aware of this cruel fact, several emperors—Titus, Domitian, Hadrian, Severus Alexander, Diocletian, Constantine I, Leo I, and Justinian—attempted to set restrictions on surgical emasculation and the trade in eunuchs.[31] Nevertheless, the slave market's insatiable appetite for eunuchs rendered such laws difficult to enforce and did little to prevent the importation from outside the empire of boys forced to undergo this painful and humiliating procedure.[32] Sexual violence was thus part and parcel of a larger system rooted in the forceful domination of the slave's body.

27. Harper 2013: chap. 3.

28. Mart. *Epig.* 3.33, 12.96.

29. Suet. *Nero* 28; Dio Cass. 62.28.2–3, 63.12.2–13, with Champlin 2003: 145–50.

30. Sen. *Ep.* 47.7; cf. Lenski 2013. At the other extreme, Cato is said to have permitted his male slaves to enjoy sexual relations with the females only in exchange for a price (Plut. *Cato* 21.2; cf. SHA *Aurel.* 49.3–4).

31. Titus: Dio Cass. 67.2.3. Domitian: Suet. *Dom.* 7.1; *D.* 48.8.6; Dio Cass. 67.2.3, 68.2.3; Mart. *Epig.* 2.60, 9.5(6). Hadrian: *D.* 48.8.4.2; Paul. *Sent.* 5.23.13. Severus Alexander: SHA *Alex.* 23.3–4. Diocletian: Amm. 18.4.5. Constantine: *CJ* 4.42.1 (a. 337). Leo I: *CJ* 4.42.2 (a. 457/465). Justinian: *Nov. Just.* 142 (a. 558); Procop. *Bell.* 8.3.15–19; Evag. Schol. *HE* 4.22.

32. For more on eunuchs, see Hopkins 1978: 172–96. Cf. Ringrose 2003; Tougher 2008.

Extreme violence against Roman slaves was sometimes so calculating that it can only be characterized as sadistic. Here again, the emperor's behavior charts the contours of the possible. Caligula, an emperor not noted for his self-restraint, notoriously punished one of his slaves for thievery by having the man's hands cut off and hung around his neck; the mutilated slave, wearing a placard advertising his misdeeds, was then ostentatiously paraded among the emperor's dinner guests.[33] Yet it was not mad emperors alone who failed to check their own vindictiveness. The wealthy upstart Vedius Pollio—himself the son of a freedman—was notorious for having kept a pool of bloodthirsty lampreys, into which he had misbehaving slaves tossed to serve as an example to their peers and as food for his fish. When Augustus witnessed Pollio preparing to employ this bizarre instrument of torture against a table servant who had broken a valuable crystal vase, the emperor demonstrated his own authority—and the limits of Roman tolerance for masterly cruelty—by ordering that the slave be pardoned and that Pollio's entire collection of vases be smashed.[34]

Such wanton destruction of slaves represented an extravagant waste of capital resources, for an average slave was sold for something on the order of five years' worth of wages for the average laborer.[35] This meant that most masters checked their anger far short of torturing slaves to death. Often, abuse was meted out in mundane and blasé fashion, calibrated to exploit the labor of the slave while slowly grinding his or her body into oblivion. Such was the fate of slaves condemned to mining. Diodorus Siculus describes the labor of such slaves in the mines of Spain, who

> produce incomes unbelievable to most but wear down their bodies in trenches under the earth all day and all night, and many die because of their excessive abuse. They enjoy no relief or pause in their labors, but their overseers compel them with blows to endure the most horrific tortures, and they throw away their lives miserably.[36]

A similar fate was endured by those relegated to bakeries, where slaves and asses worked interchangeably at pushing the unwieldy millstones in use in classical antiquity. Relegation to the bakery was a fate regularly threatened

33. Suet. *Cal.* 32.2.

34. Dio Cass. 54.23.1–4; Sen. *Ira* 3.40.2–5.

35. On slave prices, see Drexhage and Ruffing 2008; Harper 2010.

36. Diod. Sic. 5.38.1; cf. Str. 3.2.10 = Polyb. 34.9.9.

as a punishment against unruly slaves in Roman comedy,[37] and its effects are vividly illustrated in a scene from Apuleius' novel *Metamorphoses.*

> Good gods, these emaciated men were covered with purple welts all over their bodies, and their whipped backs were draped, or rather shaded, with ripped rags; some were covered only lightly across their loins with a tiny drapery, but all were clothed in such a way that you could see their bodies through the tatters; their foreheads were tattooed, their hair shaved, and their feet shackled. They were hideous with jaundice, and their eyelids were so gnawed away by the dark smoke of the humid blackness that they could hardly see. Like a boxer who covers himself with dirt before a fight, they were whitened by a filthy powder of flour.[38]

These slaves were, in other words, treated like animals, human engines fated to turn a mill wheel in sickly squalor unto death. Indeed, in some ways, the prevalence of slave labor in antiquity discouraged the development of technologies like the water mill, which became common only in the fourth century CE; forced drudgery was not so much the only option available for heavy tasks as the best method for controlling the labor output of otherwise ungovernable slaves.[39]

The Contradictions Inherent in Slavery Foment Violence

At this point, it is appropriate to step back from this catalog of callousness and abuse and ask how the Romans could treat their fellow humans with such appalling violence. Such a question can only arise in a context assuming that the notions "human" and "violence" are fixed and universal categories rather than contingent and complex. In keeping with the theme of this volume, it is important to point out that violence, like any other human action, is a discursive practice that can only be identified with reference to the status and interests of the parties involved. Calling persons or their

37. Plaut. *Bacch.* 781; *Most.* 17; *Ps.* 494; Ter. *And.* 199.

38. Apul. *Met.* 9.12. For more on tattooing, see Jones 1987; Gustafson 1997.

39. On the rise of water mills in the fourth century, see Ritti, Grewe, and Kessener 2007, with bibliography. It is interesting that Libanius, writing late in the fourth century, still conceived of relegation to human-powered mills as a fitting punishment for unruly slaves (*Dec.* 1.41, 33.33–34).

deeds "violent" makes a claim that is automatically negative, for it assumes, first, that the level of force used by an individual exceeds due measure and, second, that the motives of that person lack proper justification. In most cases, however, what one person calls "violence," another might term "self-defense," "reasonable force," "justifiable punishment," or "necessary compulsion." The dichotomous and contested nature of the distinction between force and violence is well illustrated in contemporary situations of political protest. When police or military forces clash with political dissidents, both sides—and their supporters—charge that they are using "force" to defend what is "right" against the "violence" of their "lawless" or "unruly" opponents. A similar distinction can be found in ancient contexts, where force (*bia* in Greek, *vis* in Latin) could be contrasted with violence (*hybris*, *iniuria*) in legal petitions and official pronouncements, depending on the point of view of the parties involved.[40]

In addition to these distinctions in the categorization of action—ultimately differences of perspective—distinctions of person also mattered greatly. Social norms excluded entire categories of people from redress for grievances concerning violence, including enemy combatants, convicted criminals, and, above all, slaves. Thus, from the perspective of the Roman citizen—certainly of the Roman slaveholder—few, if any, of the horrific acts cataloged in the preceding discussion counted as violence: the use of force to punish wrongdoing or coerce action was not termed "violence," nor was the slave legally capacitated in any way that would have permitted redress. The legal personlessness of the slave, however distasteful to modern sensibilities, seemed perfectly natural to the Roman mind and obviously had important consequences for the treatment of individuals whose bodies were open and available to the master for coercion, abuse, sexual assault, starvation, and elimination free of moral or legal consequence.[41]

This same exclusion from the social community also necessitated the transfer of legal action for redress of violence done to the body of a slave from that slave to his or her master. Compensation for a slave's death or for mutilation by third parties was to be paid not to the victim but to the master. This was provided under the *lex Aquilia*, which categorized slaves as property, alongside domesticated animals, and thus prescribed measures

40. See esp. Bryen 2013: 51–85; cf. 117–20, 135–36, for the firm distinction between free and slave in Egyptian court actions charging violence.

41. This conclusion should be tempered by occasional glimpses into ancient views of slavery that emphasized the humanity of the slave, such as Plutarch's critique of Cato for callously selling off older slaves (*Cato* 4.4–5.6). Cf. Garnsey 1996.

for reparations to be paid by the perpetrator to the owner.[42] The same was true of violent actions that did no permanent damage to the slave. Such offenses were also actionable, but only by the master, who retained the right to redress under the law of *iniuria*.[43]

The most obvious example of the utter evacuation of the slave's personhood came in the instance of his or her murder. The master enjoyed a nearly unchecked right of life and death over his slaves.[44] To be sure, the wanton or angry murder of a slave occasioned reproof from contemporaries, and beginning in the first century CE, the law gradually forced masters to bring their slaves to trial in front of a magistrate before killing them. Nevertheless, the master retained the right to execute his slaves down to the early fourth century, and even beyond that time the master could not be prosecuted if he happened to kill the slave unintentionally while inflicting corporal punishment.[45]

One of the most common methods for the execution of slaves was crucifixion, a punishment we witnessed above in the instance of the Puteolan undertakers. In fact, crucifixion was so commonly associated with slaves that the phrase "Go hang on a cross" (*i in malam crucem*) and the slur "crossbearer" (*furcifer*) are a stock threat and a regular insult, respectively, against slaves in Roman comedy.[46] Slave owners would have laughed wryly at such mockery, for it was just as amusing to them as it was instructive to their slaves. They also would have felt reassured at Augustus' insouciance when Fannius Caepio had a slave of his son's publicly crucified in the Forum for having refused to flee Italy with his master when the young man was under investigation for conspiracy against the emperor himself.[47] When it came to protecting the right to life and death over slaves, the ruler of Rome thus put the master's interests above his own.

The flip side of this supreme masterly authority over the life of the slave was the slave's unconditional responsibility for the life of the master. This

42. *D.* 9.2; Just. *Inst.* 4.3.4–11, with Watson 1987: 54–58. Note that the same law was applied in the instances of a virgin slave who was raped by a third party, thus decreasing her value; cf. *D.* 47.10.25.

43. *D.* 47.10.15.34–49; Just. *Inst.* 4.4.3–7, with Watson 1987: 61–63.

44. See Watson 1987: 115–20.

45. See n. 59 below.

46. See, e.g., Plaut. *Cas.* 641; *Poen.* 347; *Ps.* 335; *As.* 484; *Rud.* 717; *Most.* 69, 1172. On slaves in Roman comedy, see McCarthy 2000; Fitzgerald 2000: esp. 32–41 (on punishment).

47. Dio Cass. 54.3.7. Cf. SHA *Pert.* 9.10. On executions as public spectacles in a cross-cultural context, see Fagan 2011: 49–70.

protection was afforded under the terms of the *Senatus Consultum Silanianum* of 10 CE, a law providing that if a master was killed in his or her own home, all the slaves on the premises at the time who had not attempted to save the master were to be executed.[48] The theory was that a master's slaves were all equally responsible for protecting his life. In practice, of course, this ruling put impossible burdens on slaves, particularly in larger households. This is illustrated in spectacular fashion by an incident that occurred in 61 CE when the urban prefect of Rome, Pedanius Secundus, was killed in his own home by his own slave, either for refusing to honor an agreement to manumit the slave or because both were rivals for the amorous attentions of another male slave. Pedanius Secundus was so fabulously wealthy that he had over four hundred slaves in his mansion at the time of his murder. When the authorities began to take steps to execute them all in keeping with the *SC Silanianum*, the sheer inhumanity of the matter brought the people of Rome to the brink of riots, but the Senate held firm and approved their death sentence. As the senator C. Cassius argued, "Who shall find help in his domestics, when even fear for themselves cannot make them note our dangers?"[49] The complete negation of the slave's personhood meant that his or her life became forfeit upon the violent death of the master. For purposes of the law, then, the slave's identity was entirely subsumed by that of his owner. This normative situation was, in turn, reflexive of a broader mentalité that conceived of the slave as incapable of social existence and, thus, far removed from claims to immunity from violence.

State Limitations on the Exercise of Violence

The unease of the urban masses at the execution of Pedanius Secundus' slaves demonstrates that at least some Romans understood the contradictions inherent in slavery and were not entirely comfortable with them. Evidence for the recognition of the basic humanity of the slave can be found already in the earliest sources for Rome's history, and they begin to be articulated more clearly in the first century CE. Among the most eloquent defenders of this

---

48. The provisions of the law are laid out at *D.* 29.5.1–27; cf. 48.19.28.11, which recommends that slaves who actively plotted against their master be burned alive. For more on the *SC Silanianum*, see Buckland 1908: 94–97; Robinson 1981: 233–35; Watson 1987: 134–38.

49. Tac. *An.* 14.42–45. Contrast *CJ* 1.19.1 and 7.13.1 (a. 290), rescripts granting freedom to a slave woman for having avenged the murder of her master; cf. Grubbs 2000.

notion were Stoics like Seneca the Younger, who admonished slaveholders that their chattels were no less human than they and that moderation was in order for this reason, as well as because fortune could just as easily turn against the masters and render them slaves.[50]

With this same underlying notion in mind, Roman emperors gradually introduced a series of regulations that hemmed in the authority of masters to mistreat their slaves. None of these regulations had the effect of eliminating violence against slaves, but they did apparently tamp down some of the most egregious abuses. Already in the forties BCE, the Senate granted all persons—regardless of status—the right to take asylum at the temple of the deified Julius Caesar in Rome, a right extended to the temples and statues of the emperor in the provinces under Tiberius in the twenties CE.[51] This blanket amnesty included slaves and freedmen, who could demand a temporary reprieve from punishment by their masters or patrons until either a magistrate or (in the later empire) a bishop could intervene to adjudicate.

Gradually, more specific limits were also extended over the abuse of slaves. The emperor Claudius decreed that all slaves who had been exposed to die by masters unwilling to pay a doctor to cure them were to be summarily freed if they survived.[52] The first-century CE *lex Petronia* forbade masters from turning over their slaves for mauling by wild beasts in the arena without a magistrate's approval, a ruling reaffirmed by Marcus Aurelius and Lucius Verus in the second century.[53] This proscription was then extended by Hadrian, who ordered that all slave executions needed prior approval by a magistrate and who restricted the sale of slaves to pimps and gladiator trainers.[54] Antoninus Pius further restricted slave killing and even provided that a master who abused his or her slaves excessively could be forced to sell them to another owner.[55] We have seen already that Domitian and emperors following him attempted to curb the practice of castrating slaves, with limited success. The imperial period thus witnessed the gradual—if

50. Sen. *Ep.* 47; *Clem.* 1.18.1–3. See Garnsey 1996 for a broader spectrum of attitudes toward slavery, many of them critical.

51. For the early development of asylum in the Roman context, see Dio Cass. 47.19.2; Tac. *An.* 3.36.1–3, 60.1. Asylum eventually became the province of the Christian church: see, e.g., Greg. Mag. *Ep.* 3.1 (*CCSL* 140.146–47); Venant. Fort. *VGerm. Paris.* 10 (*MGH SRM* 7.379). See also Derlien 2003; Ducloux 1994.

52. Suet. *Claud.* 25.2; *D.* 40.8.2. Cf. *CJ* 7.6.1.3. For more on laws limiting the power of the master, see Buckland 1908: 36–38; Watson 1987: 120–33.

53. *D.* 18.1.42, 48.8.11.1–2.

54. SHA *Hadr.* 18.7–8.

55. Gaius *Inst.* 1.53; Just. *Inst.* 1.8.2; *D.* 1.6.2; *Coll.* 3.3.1.

circumscribed—introduction of limitations on the master's right to inflict or impose physical violence on the slave.

Constantine continued this trend toward the recognition of the humanity of the slave but based his new strictures on a moral code rooted in Judeo-Christian religion. For one thing, he forbade crucifixion, a means of punishment that still endured for a brief period in the fourth century but then died out.[56] He also forbade masters to tattoo the faces of their slaves, with the explicit rationale that "the face, which is formed in the likeness of heavenly beauty, should not be marred."[57] The likelihood that this provision had at least some effect on slaveholders is reflected in the fact that, beginning precisely in this period, they seem to have turned instead to the use of metal collars to track runaways.[58] Most important of all, Constantine issued a law forbidding the deliberate murder of slaves, whose text reveals much about continuities and changes in the treatment of slaves in late antiquity.

> The master shall not use his own right immoderately, but he shall be guilty of homicide if he should kill [a slave] willingly by hitting him with clubs or stones, or certainly if he inflicts a mortal wound using a spear, or hangs him from a noose, or by giving a wicked order that he should be cast off a cliff or poisoned or that his body should be torn to shreds in a public punishment, or by clawing off their sides with metal tracks, or burning their limbs with fire should compel them to depart life through torture with the savageness of evil barbarians even as their limbs grow weak and flowing with blackened blood mixed with gore.[59]

This catalog of cruelty offers a window into the limitlessness of the violent imagination of the Roman master, but its horrors should not obscure the central point here, which was precisely to forbid the deliberate murder of the slave as an act of homicide. The modes of execution it lists should thus be viewed as methods heretofore employed to kill slaves but hereinafter forbidden. The root of this prohibition is, without doubt, the Mosaic law

56. Aur. Vict. *Caes.* 41.4–5; Soz. 1.8.12–13, with Cook 2012.

57. *CTh* 9.40.2 = *CJ* 9.47.17.

58. Almost all collars cataloged thus far are late antique; cf. Bellen 1971: 27–29.

59. *CTh* 9.12.1 = *CJ* 9.14.1 (May 11, 319). At *CTh* 9.12.2 (April 18, 329), Constantine clarified the law with a rescript guaranteeing amnesty to those who accidentally killed their slaves in the course of punishment, arguably a serious impediment to legal action against murderous masters.

punishing the killing of slaves, found first in Exodus and upheld by the Christian Council of Elvira of ca. 306, the same year Constantine came to power.[60] In the Christian moral economy, the slave—for all that he was socially subordinate—had a soul just like that of his master. In the eyes of the Christian God, then, killing that slave was like killing any other human and was thus forbidden by the fifth commandment. This does not mean, of course, that masters ceased to kill their slaves, but it did seem to have a measurable effect on the purposeful murder of slaves for the remainder of Roman antiquity.[61]

The Slave as an Instrument of Violence

The Romans never succeeded in fully suppressing an innate understanding of the humanity and subjectivity of the slave. Such a failure is true of all slave societies, for try as the master class does to objectify the slave as market commodity, living tool, or violently dominated other, it never manages fully to efface the indelible personhood of the bondsman. Slaveholders would never truly wish to do so, for it is precisely the slave's humanity—the slave's human brain, her human form, his human spirit—that renders him or her so valuable. This reality applied in the realm of violence as well, for slaves were just as capable of violent action as were their masters, a fact that made slaves simultaneously extremely useful and extremely dangerous.

Slaves could be and were employed quite regularly by their masters as instruments of brute force. The most obvious example of this is gladiation, for slaves were regularly used in the arena, where they likely constituted a majority of combatants in the republican period but were increasingly supplanted by freeborn and freed fighters under the empire.[62] Owning gladiator slaves was an obvious advantage to masters, as these could garner a tremendous amount of revenue from their earnings. Slaves trained in combat were also useful in that they could be deployed as bodyguards or used to threaten and even assault rivals and enemies. This type of behavior became especially common in periods of political instability like the late republic and later empire, when the rise of personal armies and the deployment of political violence by private individuals became commonplace in the face of a weak

60. Ex. 21.20–21; *Conc. Eliberitanum can.* 5 (Mansi 2.6 = Hefele 1.138).

61. Eus. *Praep. ev.* 13.21.2–13; *Syro Roman Lawbook* 56c (Selb and Kaufhold 76); Agath. *Hist.* 2.7.1–5; *Ecloga* 17.49 (a. 741).

62. Wiedemann 1992: 102–27.

state.[63] The late republic in particular is notorious for figures like P. Clodius Pulcher and T. Annius Milo, both of whom played a key role in the civil warfare of the fifties BCE and intimidated their respective opponents using bands of armed slaves, especially slave gladiators. Their two factions eventually met in 52 on the Via Appia at Bovillae, where Clodius was stabbed to death, an incident that led to Milo's exile and the passage of laws designed to curb election violence.[64] The related *lex Julia de vi* of 19/16 BCE provided that slaves who had been deployed by their masters as assassins were to be condemned to hard labor in the mines, while the masters themselves were to be branded with *infamia*.[65] The very fact that such a law was necessary is a clear indication of the degree to which slaves were used as agents of violence for the master.

The deployment of slaves as perpetrators of violence was not confined to the political arena. Masters also regularly used their slaves to commit violent crimes for personal or economic benefit or to aid and abet the master in his own wrongdoing. Slave murderers and assassins are attested throughout Roman antiquity, stretching from the midrepublic, when Gaius Gracchus and three thousand members of his faction were assassinated by a band of armed senators, each accompanied by two slave attendants;[66] to the late republic, when Cicero attempted to recover damages for a certain M. Tullius of Thurii for the murder of a number of his slaves by those of his neighbor P. Fabius in a land dispute;[67] to the high empire, when Tiberius notoriously used his hulking freedman to assassinate quack astrologers by throwing them off the cliffs of Capri;[68] and even into the later empire, when an opponent of the Constantinopolitan bishop John Chrysostom attempted to have him knifed by a slave acting as a hit man.[69] Slaves were also useful perpetrators

63. On the use of private militias consisting of gladiators, see Sall. *Cat.* 30.6–7; Cic. *Att.* 7.14.1–2; Caes. *BC* 1.14.4–5; Tac. *An.* 1.23, 3.43. On the use of private armies of slaves, see Welwei 1988: 113–66; cf. Lenski 2009.

64. For the incident, see Tatum 1999: 214–40. On both sides' use of slave gladiators, see esp. Cic. *Quint. frat.* 2.4.5; *Vat.* 40; *Off.* 2.58; *Sest.* 95; Caes. *BC* 3.21; Ascon. 31C–32C; App. *BC* 2.21; Dio 39.7–8. Cf. Lintott 1999: 83–85.

65. *D.* 48.6.3, 7.3, with *CTh* 9.10.4 = *CJ* 9.12.8 (a. 390). Cf. Crawford et al. 1996: 2.789–92 (no. 62). On the enforcement of the law in late antiquity, see Joh. Chrys. *Exp. in Ps.* 49.8 (*PG* 55.253).

66. Plut. *Grac.* 35.4.

67. Cic. *Tull.*

68. Tac. *An.* 6.21; cf. 2.68.

69. Soz. 8.21.6–8; Pallad. *Dial.* 20.93–99 (*SCh* 341.403). See also the fictional story of a slave assassin at *Hist. Apollonii* 31–32.

of thievery and mugging, as revealed in a fourth-century CE trial transcript from Hermopolis describing how a slave owner named Sergius used a group of slaves to mug and rob a local town councillor with whom he had a legal dispute.[70]

Slaves were sometimes used to aid with the commission of violent sex crimes. The notoriously corrupt governor C. Verres arranged for his slaves and those of an associate to help him abduct an aristocratic girl from Lampsacus with whom Verres had become infatuated. The plan met with resistance from her father (who used his own slaves to mount a defense) and eventually resulted in the death of one of Verres' bodyguards and the execution of his associate.[71] Similar stories can be repeated going all the way down to late antiquity, when, for example, a tax collector named Lucianus ordered his slaves to tie down a chaste peasant girl so that he could rape her.[72]

At other times, slave force was deployed toward much less salacious ends. Slaves were, for example, regularly used to intimidate neighboring landowners or take over parcels of their land.[73] In the instance of slave shepherds, who were generally armed for defense against bandits and beasts, violence was likely an everyday occurrence on the open range, and the fighting skills they developed could be cross applied to theft, brigandage, and even murder.[74] The ancient slave was thus a tool for violence, every bit as useful to the master for his ability to intimidate, threaten, strong-arm, and even murder as he was for his strengths as a field hand, herder, craftsman, or arena fighter.

The Slave as Agent of Violence

The slave was not always willing to subject his capacity as a perpetrator of violence to the will of his master. Slaves are regularly attested as agents of violent actions performed on their own behalf or at least with their full control. The ultimate act of violent self-assertion, suicide, is well attested among ancient slaves, especially those whose lives were most miserable due to the drudgery of their existence or the cruelty of their masters.[75] Nero's eunuch

70. *P. Lips.* 1.40 = *ChLA* 12.518.

71. Cic. *Ver.* 1.67. See the similar story at Tac. *An.* 13.44.

72. Lib. *Ep.* 636. See a similar incident at Theod. *HR* 9.12 (*SCh* 234.426–30).

73. Cic. *Mil.* 26; Symm. *Ep.* 1.74. Cf. Plut. *Grac.* 35.4.

74. Liv. 39.29.8–9, 39.41.6–7, 40.19.9–10.

75. For comparison with modern slave societies, see Genovese 1974: 639–40; Karasch 1987: 316–20.

Sporus, mentioned earlier, took his own life when, after Nero's death, he was to be forced to play on stage the role of Proserpine being ravaged by Pluto—self-destruction was the only avenue open to rescue what remained of his honor or at least to avoid further degradation.[76] The problem was not limited to high-profile figures. The jurist Ulpian from the early third century CE devoted part of his treatise on the Aedile's Edict—warranting purchases of slaves—to the question of slaves who killed themselves after purchase by hanging, poisoning, jumping off precipices, and so on.[77] This sort of problem continued into the fourth century CE, when St. Martin of Tour saw fit to revive the young slave of a Gallic nobleman who had hung himself, and even into the fifth century, when the Council of Arles conceded that the masters of slaves who committed suicide despite them were not to be held spiritually liable.[78] Particularly well attested are the suicides of captive slaves condemned to fight in the arena—a frightful fate by any standards. Seneca catalogs several gruesome stories: a captive gladiator stabbed himself with a spear in combat; another suffocated himself with a toilet sponge; and a third deliberately allowed his neck to be broken in the spokes of the cart carrying him to the arena.[79] A similar tale is told three centuries later by the Roman senator Symmachus, whose feathers were irremediably ruffled when he learned that twenty-nine captive Saxons he had acquired to serve as gladiators in games he planned to host had killed themselves prematurely.[80] Suicide clearly represented the internalization of the fear, loathing, and hatred of the slave condition that characterizes slavery and its excess across cultures.

Suicide was not, however, the only violent response available to victims of the slave condition. As we might expect both from common sense and from comparative studies, slaves also externalized their anger, revulsion, and violent urges by attacking and even killing their masters.[81] Among the best-attested instances of this behavior in Roman antiquity were the slaves of Larcius Macedo, a senator and ex-praetor who was himself the son of a freedman. Precisely this, Pliny tells us, made him an especially cruel master, so cruel that a group of his slaves literally beat him to death in his own

76. Dio Cass. 65.10.1.

77. *D.* 21.1.17.4–6, 21.1.23.3, 21.1.43.4; cf. Sen. *Ep.* 4.1.

78. Sulp. Sev. *VMart.* 8.1–3 (*SCh* 133.270); *Conc. Arelatense* II (442–506) *can.* 53 (*CCSL* 148.124).

79. Sen. *Ep.* 70.20–26.

80. Symm. *Ep.* 2.46.

81. For comparative examples, see Genovese 1972: 616–17; Rasmussen 2011.

bath chamber.[82] The proximity to their masters that slaves and freedmen enjoyed—and the trust this proximity engendered—also furnished slaves with the opportunity to become embroiled in other people's plots to murder their masters. Such a conspiracy ensnared, for example, Drusus, the son of the emperor Tiberius, and nearly the emperor Galba as well.[83] Unsurprisingly, this sort of violence against the master also extended down the social ladder to the lowest rungs, as in the instance of a certain Iucundus, a shepherd freedman whose epitaph in Mainz reveals that he was murdered by his slave, who then drowned himself in the river Moenus.[84] It also continued through late antiquity, when, for instance, Gregory of Tours reports the story of a merchant named Christopher, a cruel and avaricious master who was stabbed, robbed, and decapitated by two of his slaves during a business journey in 585 CE.[85] Given the constant propinquity and, indeed, intimacy of masters and slaves, it should come as no surprise that the former was victimized by the latter with some regularity, for, as a famous proverb quoted by Seneca aphorized, "You have as many enemies as you have slaves."[86]

Slaves could and did sometimes band together in uprisings much larger in scale, aimed not just at punishing their masters but also at attacking the broader Roman community that had conspired in their domination. Slave uprisings are attested in nearly every century of Roman history from the sixth century BCE onward. Some revolts never progressed beyond their nascent stages, as when a group of about five hundred captive and slave Carthaginians attempted, in 198 BCE, to take over the town of Setia, sixty-five kilometers south of Rome, and had to be suppressed by the praetor L. Cornelius Lentulus.[87] Similar small-scale uprisings occurred deep into late antiquity, often in the wake of local military or political unrest.[88] Rebel slaves were sometimes able to carve out maroon communities, semiautonomous polities that took refuge in wastelands bordering established cities and that survived by predatory banditry. The best attestation of this in antiquity comes from the second-century writer Athenaeus, who reports that a com-

82. Plin. *Ep.* 3.14; cf. 8.14. For further literary examples of slaves killing their masters, see Sen. *Nat. quaest.* 1.16; Lib. *Prog.* 9.7.9–11.

83. Tac. *An.* 4.10.1–3; Suet. *Galba* 10.

84. *CIL* XIII 7070 = *CLE* 1007 = *ILS* 8511.

85. Greg. Tur. *HF* 7.46 (*MGH SRM* 1.1.365).

86. Sen. *Ep.* 47.5: *proverbium iactatur, totidem hostes esse quot servos.*

87. Liv. 32.26.4–18.

88. 419 BCE: Liv. 39.29.8–10; Dion. Hal. 12 fr. 6.6. 259 BCE: Oros. 4.7.11. 24 CE: Tac. *An.* 4.27.1–2, with *CIL* IX 2335 = *ILS* 961. 64 CE: Tac. *An.* 15.46.1. 69 CE: Tac. *Hist.* 2.8.1–2. 260s CE: SHA *Gall.* 4.9. 280s CE: Zos. 1.71.3. 400 CE: Zos. 5.13.3–4. 414 CE: Paul. Pell. *Euch.* 328–37. 509/11 CE: Cass. *Var.* 4.43 (*CCSL* 96.171–72).

munity of bandit slaves formed by the fugitive Drimakos on the island of Chios negotiated a long-term peace with the island's Greek inhabitants that endured until the end of Drimakos' life.[89]

Much more threatening was a series of three large-scale rebellions that plagued the late second and early first centuries BCE, arguably the height of Rome's slave society. Two of these occurred on the island of Sicily, where extraordinarily high concentrations of slaves took control of much of the island from 135 to 132 and from 104 to 100, before being suppressed with great difficulty.[90] Even more spectacularly, as well as more dangerous for Rome, was the uprising led by the Thracian gladiator slave Spartacus, which generated a force reported to have been as high as seventy thousand slave rebels, capable of marching up and down the Italian Peninsula for three years before being suppressed by consular forces in 71 BCE.[91] Unsurprisingly, each of these revolts is attested as resulting from the excessive cruelty of masters, and each resulted in an orgy of violence directed against the master class. More difficult to comprehend (for moderns, at least), none of these revolts appears to have striven for the abolition of slavery. Rather, in the brief period when they held sway in Sicily and southern Italy, these rebel groups appear to have been content simply to overturn the prevailing order—former slaves became masters, and their ex-masters became slaves. No other slave revolts ever reached the scale or intensity of these three in Roman antiquity or any period before the slave uprising in Saint-Domingue (Haiti) in 1791. Surely this explosive concatenation of three massive revolts within sixty years of each other is a reflection of the scale and brutality of Roman slaveholding in this period. Action caused reaction, making it all but inevitable that the bloated slave culture of the late republic—obscene in its dimensions and ferocity—would occasion violent rebellions that threatened the very existence of Roman rule in Sicily and Italy.

Conclusion

At its very roots, slavery is a system conceived in violence. As symbol and lived reality, it embodies the subjugation of one person to another using all

89. Athen. 265d–266d; cf. Bradley 1989: 38–41.

90. The sources, especially Diod. Sic. 34/35.2.1–3.11 (for the first Sicilian revolt) and 36.1.1–10.2 (for the second), are conveniently assembled in translation in Shaw 2001: 79–129. For more on ancient slave revolts, see Bradley 1989; Urbainczyk 2008.

91. For the sources in translation, especially Plut. *Crass.* 8–11 and App. *BC* 1.116–21, see Shaw 2001: 130–65.

the tools of domination available in the human repertoire: capture, force, intimidation, psychology, legal restrictions, physical restraints, sexual abuse, torture, and execution. This reality governed an existence for slaves that was totalizing in its violent impact. Sometimes the effect was that desired by the master class—obedience and submissiveness on the part of the slave. In fact, the massive scale of the Roman slave system and its endurance for at least a millennium, from the fifth century BCE through the fifth century CE, give solid testimony that, to a very large extent, the violence in slavery at Rome remained primarily unidirectional and proved highly efficacious; the violence of the master largely succeeded in dominating the slave and permitting his or her exploitation. However, the all-encompassing nature of slave violence sometimes crossed over into the control of the slave, who could act as the agent of violence, whether on behalf of the master or very much to the master's disadvantage. The slave serving as assassin or thug at the behest of his master was able to participate in a broader system of violence in an active way, but his actions were clearly still circumscribed by the interests of his owner. Those slaves who murdered their masters or even rose up in rebellion took violence into their own hands, assuming the role of subject and enacting the anger and hatred engendered in them by the cruelty and inhumanity of their domination. That such outbursts occurred should come as no surprise in a system as violent as was Rome's slave society. That none succeeded to the extent that slaves could ultimately benefit from their violent actions by gaining legally recognized freedom or long-term domination over the master class confirms that Roman slaveholders succeeded in maintaining their monopoly on the use of violent force from the beginning of antiquity to the end.

Works Cited

Allain, J., ed.. 2012. *The Legal Understanding of Slavery: From the Historical to the Contemporary*. Oxford.

Bellen, H. 1971. *Studien Zur Sklavenflucht Im Römischen Kaiserreich*. Wiesbaden.

Bodel, J. 2004. "The Organization of the Funerary Trade at Puteoli and Cumae." In S. Panciera, ed., *Libitina e dintorni*, 149–70. Rome.

Bradley, K. 1987. *Slaves and Masters in the Roman Empire: A Study in Social Control.* New York.

Bradley, K. 1989. *Slavery and Rebellion in the Roman World, 140 B.C.–70 B.C.* Bloomington.

Bryen, A. 2013. *Violence in Roman Egypt: A Study in Legal Interpretation*. Philadelphia.

Buckland, W. 1908. *The Roman Law of Slavery: The Condition of the Slave in Private Law from Augustus to Justinian*. Cambridge.

Champlin, E. 2003. *Nero*. Cambridge, MA.

Cook, J. 2012. "Crucifixion in the West: From Constantine to Recceswinth." *ZAC* 16: 226–46.

Crawford, M., et al. 1996. *Roman Statutes*. 2 vols. London.

Derlien, J. 2003. *Asyl: Die Religiöse und rechtliche Begründung der Flucht zu sakralen Orten in der griechisch-römischen Antike*. Marburg.

Drexhage, H.-J., and Ruffing, K. 2008. "Antke Sklavenpreise." In *Antike Lebenswelten: Konstanz—Wandel—Wirkungsmacht: Festschrift für Ingomar Weiler zum 70. Geburtstag*, 321–51. Wiesbaden.

Ducloux, A. 1994. *Ad Ecclesiam Confugere: Naissance du droit d'asile dans les églises (IVᵉ-milieu du Vᵉ S.)*. Paris.

Fagan, G. 2011. *The Lure of the Arena: Social Psychology and the Crowd at the Roman Games*. Cambridge.

Fentress, E. 2011. "Slavers on Chariots." In A. Dowler and E. Galvin, eds., *Money, Trade, and Trade Routes in Pre-Islamic North Africa*, 65–71. London.

Fitzgerald, W. 2000. *Slavery and the Roman Literary Imagination*. Cambridge.

Gaca, K. 2010. "The Andrapodizing of War Captives in Greek Historical Memory." *TAPhA* 140: 117–61.

Garnsey, P. 1996. *Ideas of Slavery from Aristotle to Augustine*. Cambridge.

Genovese, E. 1974. *Roll, Jordan, Roll: The World the Slaves Made*. New York.

Grubbs, J. 2000. "The Slave Who Avenged Her Master's Death: *Codex Justinianus* 1.19.1 and 7.13.1." *AHB* 14: 81–88.

Gustafson, M. 1997. "*Inscripta in Fronte*: Penal Tattooing in Late Antiquity." *Classical Antiquity* 16: 421–33.

Harper, K. 2010. "Slave Prices in Late Antiquity (and in the Very Long Term)." *Historia* 59: 206–38.

Harper, K. 2011. *Slavery in the Late Roman World, AD 275–425: An Economic, Social, and Institutional Study*. Cambridge.

Harper, K. 2013. *From Shame to Sin: The Christian Transformation of Sexual Morality in Late Antiquity*. Cambridge, MA.

Harris, W. 1999. "Demography, Geography, and the Sources of Roman Slaves." *JRS* 89: 62–75.

Harris, W. 2001. *Restraining Rage: The Ideology of Anger Control in Classical Antiquity*. Cambridge, MA.

Henning, J. 1992. "Gefangenenfesseln im slawischen Siedlungsraum und der europäische Sklavenhandel im 6. bis 12. Jahrhundert." *Germania* 70: 403–26.

Hopkins, K. 1978. *Conquerors and Slaves*. Cambridge.

Jones, C. 1987. "Stigma: Tattooing and Branding in Graeco-Roman Antiquity." *JRS* 77: 139–55.

Karasch, M. 1987. *Slave Life in Rio de Janeiro, 1808–1850*. Princeton.

Lenski, N. 2009. "Schiavi armati e formazione di eserciti privati nel mondo tardoantico." In G. Urso, ed., *Ordine e sovversione nel mondo greco e romano: Atti del Convegno Internazionale, Cividale del Friuli, 25–27 settembre 2008*, 145–75. Pisa.

Lenski, N. 2011. "Captivity and Slavery among the Saracens in Late Antiquity (ca. 250–630 CE)." *AnTard* 19: 237–66.
Lenski, N. 2013. "Working Models: Functional Art and Roman Conceptions of Slavery." In M. George, ed., *Roman Slavery and Roman Material Culture*, 129–57, with figs. 5.1–14. Toronto.
Lintott, A. 1999. *Violence in Republican Rome*. 2nd ed. Oxford.
McCarthy, K. 2000. *Slaves, Masters, and the Art of Authority in Plautine Comedy*. Princeton.
Patterson, O. 1982. *Slavery and Social Death: A Comparative Study*. Cambridge, MA.
Rasmussen, D. 2011. *American Uprising: The Untold Story of America's Largest Slave Revolt*. New York.
Ringrose, K. 2003. *The Perfect Servant: Eunuchs and the Social Construction of Gender in Byzantium*. Chicago.
Ritti, T., Grewe, K., and Kessener, P. 2007. "A Relief of a Water-Powered Stone Saw Mill on a Sarcophagus at Hierapolis and Its Implications." *JRA* 20: 139–63.
Robinson, O. 1981. "Slaves and the Criminal Law." *ZRG* 98: 213–54.
Scheidel, W. 1997. "Quantifying the Sources of Slaves in the Early Roman Empire." *JRS* 87: 157–69.
Scheidel, W. 2011. "The Roman Slave Supply." In K. Bradley and P. Cartledge, eds., *The Cambridge World History of Slavery*, vol. 1, *The Ancient Mediterranean World*, 287–310. Cambridge.
Shaw, B. 2001. *Spartacus and the Slave Wars: A Brief History with Documents*. Boston.
Tatum, W. 1999. *The Patrician Tribune: Publius Clodius Pulcher*. Chapel Hill.
Thompson, F. 1993. "Iron Age and Roman Slave-Shackles." *Archaeological Journal* 150: 57–168.
Thompson, F. 2003. *The Archaeology of Greek and Roman Slavery*. London.
Tougher, S. 2008. *The Eunuch in Byzantine History and Society*. London.
Urbainczyk, T. 2008. *Slave Revolts in Antiquity*. Stocksfield.
Watson, A. 1987. *Roman Slave Law*. Baltimore.
Welwei, K.-W. 1988. *Unfreie im antiken Kriegsdienst*. Vol. 3. Wiesbaden.
Welwei, K.-W. 2000. *Sub corona vendere: Quellenkritische Studien zu Kriegsgefangenschaft und Sklaverei in Rom bis zum Ende des Hannibalkrieges*. Stuttgart.
Wiedemann, T. 1992. *Emperors and Gladiators*. London.
Zeuske, M. 2013. *Handbuch Geschichte der Sklaverei: Eine Globalgeschichte von den Anfängen bis zur Gegenwart*. Berlin.

TWELVE

The Roman Battlefield

Individual Exploits in Warfare of the Roman Republic

Graeme Ward

During the early stages of the Second Macedonian War (200–197 BCE), Roman and Macedonian cavalry forces met and briefly skirmished in eastern Illyria. Livy halts his narrative of the war to describe how Macedonian soldiers under King Philip V reacted to the site of battle.

> [Philip's soldiers], who had been used to fighting with Greeks and Illyrians, had seen wounds inflicted by pikes, by arrows, and, in rare cases, by lances. But after seeing corpses mutilated by the Spanish sword [*gladius*], arms hewn from the shoulder, heads entirely cut off from the neck, bowels exposed, and other hideous wounds, the multitude realized with terror the sort of weapons and men against whom they had to fight.[1]

Livy's description of their reaction leaves us, too, with a startling image of the effect of Roman arms. While brutal, lethal violence existed in many spatial and cultural contexts in the Roman world—the arena, the forum, and the *domus*—none was more visceral and shocking in scale than the battlefield. In this passage, moreover, Livy theorizes a particularly Roman way of waging war during the republic, stressing the Roman preference for the cut and thrust of the *gladius* in contrast to the fixed Macedonian pike (*sarissa*),

1. Liv. 31.34.4–5.

for the aggressive charges of individual Roman legionaries and cavalrymen compared with the disciplined march of the Macedonian phalanx.

This interest in Roman warfare is as old as the history of Rome itself, and our own perceptions of it have changed significantly in recent years. Earlier military theorists focused on tactics and the structure of legionary ranks, portraying Roman soldiers waging war with machinelike precision. This image was challenged, however, by studies that reinterpreted the evidence in light of psychology and personal experiences of soldiers in combat.[2] More recently, a wealth of scholarship has examined the textual evidence of Roman warfare from a cultural perspective, paying particular attention to behavior associated with the Roman idea of *virtus* during the republic. Treated as more complex and fluid than in its usual English translations as "courage" or "valor," *virtus* is now usually taken to describe a behavior on the battlefield that is far more aggressive, individualistic, and, above all, competitive.[3] A more common image of the Roman soldier today is one of a "fierce wolf" (*vehemens lupus*), exceptionally aggressive and full of an anger (*ira*) that was foolhardy and even dangerous to his comrades.[4]

This newer image of Roman behavior on the battlefield reflects, in part, both ancient and modern attention given to "individual exploits" by Roman soldiers, which ranged from dramatic duels against enemy champions to aggressive skirmishing and suicidal charges beyond one's line of battle. These individual actions in particular were glorified by all levels of Roman society and received the greatest attention in ancient accounts of Roman battle. Individual exploits during the republic were often portrayed as a sort of *spectaculum*, a performance whose civic audience would later discuss, praise, and commemorate it at Rome.[5] Understanding the development of this tradition of praise for individual exploits, however, requires greater focus

2. For seminal works on tactics and organization, see Domaszewski (1908) 1967; Delbrück 1975; Kromayer and Veith 1928; Fuller 1965. On the "experience" of battle, see esp. Keegan 1976; Goldsworthy 1996.

3. On *virtus* generally, see McDonnell 2006. On the competitive aspects of *virtus* and its opposition to *disciplina* and the collective, see Dumézil 1942: 11–33; Neraudeau 1979: 249–58; Oakley 1985: 404–7; Phang 2008: 73. This phenomenon is most comprehensively and effectively argued by Lendon (2005: 173–232).

4. For *vehemens lupus*, see Hor. *Ep.* 2.2.28; for *ira*, Cic. *Tusc.* 4.25. The modern interpretation is based primarily on Polybius' description (6.52.7) of the Romans' "rage" (*orgē*). On the violence of Roman warfare, see Harris 1979: 53; 2006: 304–8, 316–17; Keegan 1993: 265–66. James (2011: 53–59) sees a difference in degree rather than kind. See also Rich 1993.

5. Feldherr 1998: 82–111.

on their effect on their "immediate audience" in battle, including nearby comrades, superiors, and enemy soldiers. In addition to the soldier who inflicted the violence and the victim who suffered it, the reactions of nearby observers—Roman and foreign—were crucial to how such acts were later interpreted and judged.[6] This was especially true in instances when Roman soldiers appeared to have succumbed to fear (*timor*) and become panic-stricken (*pavidi*).

To reassess how individual, martial exploits became meaningful in Roman society, this study focuses not just on an exploit itself but also on the immediate context in which it occurred—the circumstances of battle and condition of the Roman soldiers who were fighting, the emotions and intentions ascribed to the individual perpetrator, and the reactions of those who witnessed the act. The scope of the study is limited to evidence of exploits during the republic (ca. 509–27 BCE), particularly those described by Polybius, Caesar, and Livy. As always, caution is needed when interpreting battle from this period, since some of these historical accounts were written secondhand and long after the battles they describe.[7] The historical tradition of individual deeds in warfare of the republic, however, was durable and widely disseminated; it was a touchstone in Roman society and provided both positive and negative exempla for future Roman soldiers, officers, and commanders to praise or condemn. It also featured prominently in Roman literature, a legacy to which later historians and poets of the principate referred. This remained true even as large-scale campaigns became less frequent and as the legions were increasingly employed in functions other than out-and-out warfare.[8]

I argue two points in this analysis. Principally, a closer examination of many individual exploits demonstrates that the varying circumstances in which one was performed were crucial to how it was judged in Roman society; there are subcontexts to consider in understanding how individual performances shaped Roman expectations of behavior on the battlefield and whether or not certain acts of violence were "appropriate." More broadly, while Roman society glorified individuals who rushed past the line and engaged enemies on the battlefield, textual accounts of them suggest that

6. On the so-called triangle of violence, see Whitehead 2004: 3–24.

7. This is particularly true with Livy, who was centuries removed from the battles of early Rome that he describes. See Walsh 1961: 110–64, esp. 157–63; Roth 2006: 49–55.

8. On the legacy of Rome's past, see Lendon 2005: esp. 261–309. On Rome's changing military role, see MacMullen 1963; Isaac 1992: 101–60, 269–310; Alston 1995; Speidel 2009; Fuhrmann 2012: 123–46, 201–38.

the most important aspect of such seemingly individualistic actions was the effect on one's immediate audience—the collective. The most praiseworthy individuals were those who were judged to have performed not merely in front of but on behalf of the legion, so that the battlefield became a space for promoting cooperation as well as competition between members of the Roman community.

The Importance of Being Seen

The lethal and destructive violence of war was not only acceptable but also praiseworthy and desirable in many ancient Mediterranean societies, where demonstrations of physical strength and martial prowess on the battlefield were important to defining social status, masculinity, and bravery in one's household and community.[9] Warfare seems to have been especially integral to Roman society during the republic. Men of Rome's ruling class who died on the battlefield were not mourned solemnly in private but celebrated with pomp in public. Funeral processions, eulogies, and internments of military heroes were performed in full view of the civic community, and all observers were to mourn the dead and celebrate his deeds as if he were family.[10] The height of this public glorification of warfare was the triumph. In a procession, at once solemn and rowdy, from outside the walls of Rome to the Capitoline Hill, a commander rode into the city accompanied by his soldiers and officers, while enslaved prisoners bore spoils taken during the campaign. Such spectacles were not to be missed.[11] Public monuments that glorified the violence inflicted against enemies in war were ubiquitous at Rome and were meant to stir, rather than curb, the next generation's desire for war.[12]

For members of Rome's republican nobility, personal status (*dignitas*) was largely constructed from the glory (*gloria*), praise (*laus*), and renown (*fama*) acquired through deeds and victories on the battlefield. A lengthy

9. For Ancient Greece, see Lendon 2005: 45–47, 103–5, 127–28. More broadly, see Gat 2006: 215–17; Raaflaub and Rosenstein 2009.

10. Plb. 6.53–54.3. See James 2013: 101–6.

11. E.g., Liv. 10.46.5, 14; Plu. *Pomp.* 45. Florus (*Epit.* 1.13.26–27) similarly imagines such a spectacle. They appear to have been granted according to varying criteria. See Beard 2009: 187–219; Rosenstein 2007: 142–43.

12. On pervasiveness of warfare and images of martial violence at Rome, see Harris 1979; Flower 2009: 65–76; Gilliver 2007: 1–3; James 2011: 24–28, 163–66, 198–204.

period of military service was necessary for a public career, and showing scars from battle helped an aspirant to political office to claim greater authority.[13] By tradition, older generals and younger military tribunes had sought combat and bloody victories in pursuit of the *gloria* that was expected of their class. Although barred from the political aspirations of the elite, the mass of Roman male citizens were also crucial partners in warfare and imperial expansion during the republic and were often encouraged by the hope for material rewards of battle, such as new land, spoils, and slaves.[14] In the earliest recorded incidents of Roman warfare, aristocratic warlords had fought battles against rival families or clans (gentes) by forming war bands from their large retinue of followers.[15] Following the broader military and political developments that later Roman authors attributed to reforms by Servius Tullius during the sixth century BCE, male Roman citizens became organized by census into military-political classes according to wealth and were levied en masse through the *dilectus* for annual campaigning against their neighbors.[16]

A critical feature of Roman warfare during the republic was visibility. It was important not simply to perform certain acts on the battlefield but to be seen doing so. Individual exploits had no intrinsic value in and of themselves and required an audience of one's comrades and superiors to acquire any reward or commemoration. The greatest and rarest of military honors, for example, were the *spolia opima*, given only to a Roman commander who sought out, killed, and despoiled an enemy commander before the eyes of his army. Once seized, the armor would be dedicated for all to see at the Temple of Jupiter Feretrius.[17] Ordinary Roman soldiers (*milites*) were encouraged to display spoils of war in visible spaces in their homes, where guests and relatives could view (and hopefully ask questions about) them. Conspicuous action on the battlefield was the name of the game, and

13. According to Polybius (6.19.4), aristocrats were required to have participated in at least ten campaigns before beginning a political career. On scars, see Liv. 45.39.16–17. Cf. McCall 2002: 91–95; Rosenstein 2007: 132–47.

14. Harris 1979: 9–68, 75–104; Oakley 1993: 18–22.

15. See Cornell 1995: 130–45, 216–18; Connolly 1998: 87–128; Rich 2007: 11–16.

16. Liv. 1.42–43; D.H. 4.13–23.

17. Only three winners are recorded: Romulus (Liv. 1.10.4–6), A. Cornelius Cossus (Liv. 4.19.5–7), and M. Claudius Marcellus (Plu. *Marc.* 6–7). M. Licinius Crassus may also have applied for the *spolia opima* after killing a king of the Bastarnae in 27 BCE but was blocked by Augustus (D.C. 51.23–27). On this incident and *spolia opima* generally, see Rich 1996: 85–127.

those whose deeds were witnessed could hope to be praised by their city and gens, as well as to become positive exempla of Roman martial traditions that would be emulated by future generations.[18]

The flip side of the coin were military punishments. Desertion, lying under oath, cowardice witnessed in battle, and disobedience against a commanding consul or dictator were punishable by death—by collective stoning and cudgeling (*fustuarium*) or by scourging and beheading in a formal ceremony in front of the entire legion. After eyewitness testimony of the transgression was acquired, the punishment was administered publicly and collectively, with one's comrades acting as either witnesses or active participants. Ancient authors who record these ceremonies seem most interested in describing the emotions and opinions among spectators who watched the punishment rather than in representing the suffering of the victims.[19] The goal of the punishment was not so much to reform the individual transgressor as to shame and make an example of him in front of his entire military and civic community.[20] Whether in rewarding acts of valor or in punishing acts of disobedience, the focus was on the community at least as much as the individual.

Martial exploits were performed first and foremost in battle, and it was here that an exploit was first witnessed and its effect most keenly felt. Roman authors consistently described the important role of spectators in interpreting an individual's actions in battle. The nearby presence of one's comrades or superiors would have affected soldiers' behavior in several significant ways. Through the physical excitement produced by nearby shouting and clamor, a large crowd can often encourage and contribute to the intensity of violence inflicted by a perpetrator on a victim.[21] Those Roman soldiers who observed an exploit, moreover, were witnesses rather than mere bystanders, and their presence was required either to validate and acclaim a man for praiseworthy deeds or to goad and shame him for blameworthy ones.

18. Plb. 6.39.9–11; Liv. 26.48. On the requirement of witnesses, see Caes. *Gal.* 1.52; Liv. 26.48. On displaying spoils, see Rawson 1991: 583–98. On emulation by Roman soldiers in war, see Feldherr 1998: 104–5; Marincola 2009: 11–20; Roller 2009: 214–30.

19. Significantly, Polybius (6.36.6–38.4) directly relates punishments to rewards in discussing Roman discipline. For witness and spectatorship of punishment, see Flor. *Epit.* 1.3.5; Liv. 3.36.3–5, 8.7.16, 9.24.15, 24.20.6; Cic. *Ver.* 5.161; Frontin. *Str.* 4.1.16, 20, 35.

20. On military punishments generally, see Brand 1968; Lintott 1999: 41–43; Phang 2008: 116–39; Brice 2011: 39–41.

21. This is one effect of a broader phenomenon that Collins (2009: 128–31) describes as the "crowd multiplier," in which a crowd amplifies an individual's emotions and tension that have been building over time.

The deployment of Roman legions during the republic may have contributed to the visibility of individual deeds on the battlefield. Unfortunately, the evidence for the tactics of the legions of the middle republic is often frustratingly unclear, and detailed accounts of their organization and development from the early to the late republic is well beyond the scope of this study.[22] However, a singular point regarding the flexibility of Roman legions can be addressed here. Although the Romans themselves believed that they initially fought battles in the style of a Greek phalanx,[23] it is clear that this configuration was no longer favored by the third century BCE at the latest, and the legions were increasingly deployed in far more fluid formations over the next few centuries.

Rome conquered most of the Mediterranean with legions deployed in maniples. While the exact workings of this formation on the battlefield are obscure, Polybius reports that a legion's forty-two hundred soldiers were first assigned to four different classes according to ascending ages.[24] The bulk of soldiers fought in a very loose formation, among three lines (*hastati*, *principes*, and *triarii*) arrayed in depth. Every line comprised ten maniples, or "handfuls," of soldiers, nominally of 60 to 120 men, each led by two junior officers (centurions). They were all equipped with the *gladius* and ovular shield (*scutum*). The *hastati* and *principes* also bore the Roman javelins (*pila*), while *triarii* apparently retained the older, thrusting spears (*hastae*). Roman soldiers during the early to middle republic equipped themselves at their own expense, and armor seems to have varied a bit more then according to rank and wealth, ranging, over time, from bronze corselets to iron mail, as well as helmets and greaves. The youngest and poorest class of soldiers, the *velites* (fast men), had no immediate officers and fought as skirmishers in front of the maniples. They wore cloaks or wolf skins in battle and bore javelins.[25] Roman cavalrymen (*equites*), who comprised the wealthiest segment of Rome's citizenry, operated loosely in squadrons (*turmae*) around an opposing army's flanks, skirmishing with enemy cavalry and pursuing fleeing soldiers. The open nature of such skirmishing gave its aristocratic

22. For detailed analysis, see Delbrück 1975: 272–96; Kromayer and Veith 1928: 251–469; Keppie 1984; Goldsworthy 1996: 12–38; Sabin 2000: 1–17; Zhmodikov 2000.

23. On the Roman phalanx, see Wheeler 1979: 303–18; Keppie 1984: 14–23; Rosenstein 2010: 289–303.

24. Distinctions in wealth may also have remained relevant. See Kromayer and Veith 1928: 288–373; Wheeler 1979: 303–18; 2001: 169–84; Keppie 1984: 33–40.

25. Plb. 6.19.1–24; Liv. 8.8. On the *velites*, see Liv. 26.4, 30.33. Cf. Gilliver 2007: 3–6; James 2011: 25 n. 51.

membership many opportunities for displays of prowess, and some apparently used to fight with bare torsos in order to present a frightening form and be noticed by peers and superiors.[26]

Over the course of the middle to late republic, however, the favored formation for the legion changed once again. Its thirty maniples were increasingly deployed within ten larger, tactical units: the cohorts.[27] These cohorts still often fought three lines deep (in the so-called *triplex acies*), but distinctions in arms and formation were reduced. Roman citizens were no longer used as *velites*, and all legionaries were now equipped by the state as heavy infantry.[28] Rome now also drew cavalry and light infantry more and more from non-Italians, with the result that its wealthiest class now served primarily as military tribunes and officers of cavalry squadrons.[29]

Whether deployed in maniples or cohorts, the legions typically decided matters in large, set-piece battles fought at close quarters. Ancient accounts of battle during the republic often describe fighting that was fluid and sporadic, particularly at the outset, when Roman soldiers threw their *pila* before engaging with their *gladii* or *hastae*. Depending on numbers and the size of the battlefield, the range of Roman weapons sometimes allowed only segments of the legion to engage with an opposing army at the same time, so that skirmishes between separate units or even individuals often took place between the larger collisions of the two armies.[30] The openness of this fighting offered individuals in the Roman legion many opportunities to acquire *gloria* for themselves in front of their peers, and Polybius specifies these voluntary, individual actions as praised and rewarded in Roman society.[31] This open type of fighting also produced circumstances in which an individual's action greatly affected those around him, for good or ill. With this in mind, we need to consider what ancient authors thought about Roman soldiers' emotions and what we today would call "morale."

26. On the cavalry, see Plb. 2.24.14–16, 6.25.3–4. See also Keppie 1984: 33–35, 66–67; McCall 2002: 26–30, 78–99, 100–136.

27. Polybius mentions cohorts during the Second Punic War (218–201 BCE), but their use as the Romans' favored tactical unit is traditionally credited to Marius. On cohorts in the republic, see Bell 1965: 404–22; bibliography in Lendon 2005: 427–28.

28. Keppie 1984: 63–67; Isaac 1998: 388–402; Goldsworthy 1996: esp. 12–28, 131–40. On the problematic image of homogeneity of Roman arms, however, see Bishop and Coulston 1993.

29. See Keppie 1984: 21–23, 79; McCall 2002: 100–113; Harris 2006: 308.

30. E.g., Liv. 5.19.9; 8.8; Caes. *Gal.* 2.25. On the sporadic nature of Roman warfare, see Goldsworthy 1996: 248, 257; Sabin 2000: 1–17.

31. Plb. 5.39.4.

The Roman Fear of Battle

While ancient sources do not offer sophisticated psychological analysis of soldiers in battle, some Roman authors refer to something resembling a "fighting spirit." Caesar sometimes described it as *animus* or *impetus*, a behavior on the battlefield comprising a combination of anger, enthusiasm, and confidence.[32] Caesar's descriptions of battle suggest that it was highly unstable and quick to turn from victory to defeat—and to turn its combatants from confidence to despair—in a single moment. When Caesar criticizes the overconfidence of Pompey's legions following Caesar's defeat at Dyrrachium, he explains how "insignificant causes, either from false rumors, sudden terror, or religious scruples, have often caused great defeats."[33] Despite the modern perception of the ferocity of Roman soldiers and their glorification of combat during the republic, Caesar's opinion regarding the delicacy of *animus* is supported by other accounts of battle in which Roman soldiers succumbed to fear and panic. Livy consistently describes incidents in which Roman soldiers, though judged to be morally and tactically superior to their adversaries, nonetheless abandoned their positions and legionary insignia in the face of a fierce enemy. In other cases, Livy asserts that the spirit of the Roman legion was the only difference between victory and defeat.[34]

Fear has consistently been cited by military historians as a major influence on soldiers' behavior in battles of all times and places; military units are, in essence, organizations designed to prevent soldiers from fleeing and to urge them to continue to face mortal danger.[35] While the Roman cohort arguably promoted greater *disciplina* and offered commanders superior control over their soldiers in comparison to the looser maniples, the newer unit might have derived its name from the Latin verb *cohortari*, meaning "to exhort, encourage, or rouse," not "to restrain or control." This suggests, at the very least, that Roman soldiers were increasingly deployed in the larger cohort in order to curb fear more than aggression.[36]

32. See Lendon 1999: 286–87, 290–99, 304; Harris 2006: 300–304; Phang 2008: 37; James 2011: 14–37, 39–41.

33. Caes. *Civ.* 3.72. Cf. *Civ.* 3.92; *Gal.* 1.39, 1.52, 2.24, 4.12, 4.24, 5.15.

34. For panic at Sentinum, see Liv. 10.28.11; at Lake Trasimene, Liv. 22.6.4–5; during the Second Macedonian War, Liv. 42.60.6, 61.6, 65.6. On the distinction between victory and defeat, see Liv. 3.60.3, 10.41.1. Cf. Eckstein 1995: 170–71; Oakley 1998: 120; Sabin 2000: 13–14; James 2011: 24.

35. Du Picq 1921; Marshall 1947; Lynn 1984, esp. 182; Holmes 1985: 236–37. On organizations and fear, see Collins 2009: 1–35.

36. The exact derivation of the term is unclear, since it might also be related to *hortus* and

Even Caesar's cohorts, arguably the best in their day for maintaining their nerve and executing complex movements under pressure, sometimes chafed at waiting for the signal to advance or even raced forward from their line before Caesar could communicate an order to commence battle. At Thapsus in 46 BCE, for example, the constant movement of the forces of Cato and Scipio in front of Caesar's legions made his soldiers increasingly edgy, until they finally rushed forward, despite the attempts of the centurions to restrain them.[37] Caesar disguises his soldiers' behavior as the result of an overzealous desire for *gloria* rather than fear, yet such incidents seem more likely to reflect the desire of soldiers to "get it over with," because of strained nerves and the anxiety that typically preceded battle.[38] This seems all the more likely since such prolonged tension and frayed nerves often leads to a rush of aggression and relentless violence in the pursuit of a defeated or defenseless foe—a phenomenon that happened with Caesar's troops in their victory at Thapsus and is common to ancient warfare generally.[39]

In light of this awareness of the delicate nature of Roman soldiers' spirits, the importance of individual exploits on the battlefield becomes more apparent: the performance occurred in front of soldiers whose emotions were changing rapidly between fear, anger, and elation during extremely intense periods of violence.[40] The relative fluidity of the Roman maniple and cohort encouraged individuals to seek *laus* in front their peers and superiors, but it also created an environment in which an individual's action (or inaction) was expected to have a profound impact on the emotions of those around them and, therefore, on the outcome of the battle. Over time, Roman attitudes regarding the appropriateness of individual exploits seem

so have a sense of "enclosure." On the cohort as a possible means to curb aggressive *virtus*, see Lendon 2005: 222–32.

37. *B. Afr.* 82–83.

38. This occurred also at Heraclea during the Second Punic War (Liv. 25.21.1). Cf. Goldsworthy 1996: 191–94. For this concern in Greek warfare, see Hanson 1989: 96–104, 139–47; Lazenby 1991: 90–91. Collins (2009: 83–112) calls this phenomenon "forward panic" and discusses its impact on warfare at length. Du Picq (1921: esp. 149–56) referred to accounts of Roman battles to articulate this phenomenon as "flight to the front." Cf. Keegan 1976: 88–89, 94, 99–101; Holmes 1985: 139–47, 229–31.

39. *B. Afr.* 85. See also Caes. *Civ.* 3.93; Plu. *Aem.* 22.4. The phenomenon has been discussed in varying terms in other studies of warfare: see Keegan 1976: 82–114, 150–51; Holmes 1985: 381–88; Hanson 1989: 182; Goldsworthy 1996: 223–24; Sabin 2000: 15. Caesar generally contrasts the fear of his opponents in contrast to the confidence of his own soldiers (see, e.g., Caes. *Gal.* 7.52; *B. Hisp.* 30).

40. Cf. Rosenstein 1990: 95–96.

to have taken account of this concern for the fears or spirit of their soldiers. The advisability of commanders seeking individual *gloria* in single combat, for example, was decidedly mixed during the republic, since a commander's death or rumor of it could spread panic.[41] One of Rome's greatest military heroes, P. Cornelius Scipio Africanus, famously avoided such risky attempts at *laus* and reportedly claimed, "My mother bore me as a general, not a warrior." C. Marius, one of the preeminent generals of the late republic, was later claimed to have turned down and made light of a challenge to duel.[42] This sentiment predictably reflected a recorded decline in the frequency of Roman commanders and aristocrats engaging in hand-to-hand combat. There were always exceptions, but the scattered accounts of them in the textual record highlight their rarity.[43] Polybius suggested that even junior officers like centurions should place the responsibilities of the unit above their own desire for individual *gloria*.[44]

Although one's rank and file became the more appropriate space for demonstrating courage, opposition was not raised against all forms of individual exploit, since exceptions were made for certain circumstances. Livy, who describes the voluntary oath that Roman legionaries traditionally took before a battle, suggests the criteria by which such circumstances were appropriate: the soldiers swore "that they were not to desert for fear or flight and that they would not quit the ranks except to pick up or retrieve a weapon, to strike at an enemy, or to save a comrade."[45] This pledge was considered authoritative enough that it was later integrated into the formal military oaths (*sacramenta*) that were sworn before the military tribunes at the outset of a new campaign.[46] The three exceptions to the rule of not abandoning one's unit, moreover, identify the primary motives ascribed to individual exploits: the desires to avoid shame, to acquire *gloria* by killing

41. Liv. 10.29.1. This is later also cautioned by Onasander (32.1–3, 33.1–6). Cf. A. Lee 1996: 211; Lendon 2005: 259–60, with n. 46; McDonnell 2006: 241, 247, 293–319.

42. On Scipio, see Plb. 10.13.1–5. Scipio is quoted at Frontin. *Str.* 4.7.4. On Marius, see Plu. *Mar.* 25.2; Frontin. *Str.* 4.7.5.

43. See the list of duels in Oakley 1985: 393–97. For decline in hand-to-hand combat, see Goldsworthy 1996: 150–63; Lendon 1999: 273–329; 2005: 212–22.

44. Plb. 6.24.9.

45. Liv. 22.38.2–5: *fugae atque formidinis ergo non abituros neque ex ordine recessuros nisi teli sumendi aut aptandi et aut hostis feriendi aut civis servandi causa.* Cf. Plb. 6.21.2; D.H. 10.18, 11.43.

46. According to Plutarch (*Sull.* 27. 4), the later stipulation "to follow the commander wherever he may lead" was added by Sulla. For general discussion of the *sacramentum*, see Smith 1958: 31–33; Phang 2008: 115–19.

an opponent, and to save one's comrades. These three actions, as we shall see, were not mutually exclusive, and they collectively illustrate the primary concern in Roman thinking for both the observance and the performance of individual acts on the battlefield.

"To Retrieve a Weapon"

The fear of shame or public dishonor (*pudor*) affected the behavior of Roman soldiers and commanders alike and could be expected to spur one to perform exploits beyond the line of battle, particularly when one was not entirely inclined to do so.[47] One of the most basic forms of shame resulted from being visibly without a weapon, particularly one's *gladius*. The *gladius* symbolized the Roman soldier more than any other equipment and connoted aggression, manliness, and courage. Losing it was not only inadvisable in military practice but also tantamount to losing one's masculinity, which stood at the core of one's *virtus*. A lost weapon compelled both Roman officers and soldiers to hurl themselves into the midst of an enemy and, if necessary, kill scores of them in frantic attempts to retrieve it.[48]

The idea of leaving one's comrades in order to retrieve a weapon epitomizes a broader spectrum of individual actions attributed to the desire to avoid *pudor* in the eyes of others, including one of the most dramatic of exploits: the suicidal charge into an enemy's ranks. When his prior actions have doomed his soldiers to destruction, for example, a legionary commander could redeem his honor (*honos*) by killing as many enemy soldiers as possible before succumbing to his wounds. Near the end of the disaster at Cannae, one of the two commanding consuls, L. Aemilius Paulus, refused to save himself when a military tribune offered him a horse to escape. He rejected the offer, claiming that he would rather die now with his soldiers than later defend his actions or blame his colleague.[49]

No formal expectation existed that a Roman commander should die with his troops. Indeed, the Roman Senate rarely punished generals for military incompetence, and military defeat did not necessarily derail one's political career.[50] Yet Livy commends Paulus' desire to die with his troops and avoid

47. On the powerful influence of *pudor*, see the speech by Curio in Caes. *Civ.* 2.31.

48. E.g., Plu. *Cat. Ma.* 20.7–8. Cf. Rosenstein 2007: 134. On this characteristic of Roman warfare, see Liv. 31.34.4. On the symbolic importance of the sword, see James 2011: 16–21.

49. Liv. 22.49.11.

50. Varro, the consul most responsible for the disaster at Cannae, was thanked for "not

facing the shame of the defeat at home, and other defeated commanders were likewise praised.[51] While the fear of bringing shame to one's ancestors and gens was particularly acute for Rome's competitive nobility, Livy ascribes similar motives to lower officers as well. One example is M. Centenius Paenula, a centurion who led a small, ill-prepared legion against Hannibal following the defeat at Cannae. When the defeat of his outmatched soldiers was assured, he threw himself into the enemy's spears, in the fear that he would be considered shameful (*dedecus*) if he were to be seen alive after the disaster.[52]

Caesar interpreted such exploits in death similarly, although he attributed the motive to his legion and himself rather than to the desire to avoid bringing shame to one's gens or *patria*. This attitude is apparent in Caesar's account of the death of his friend, C. Scribonius Curio, who led an army to destruction in Numidia in 49 BCE against the forces of King Juba. While Caesar plainly considers Curio's defeat the result of his fervent character, he nonetheless praises the young man's desire to avoid the shame of appearing before Caesar in defeat. If aggressive acts of *virtus* could enhance the *fama* of commanders and soldiers in victory, similar acts of aggression could restore it in defeat.[53]

While Roman commanders might have been commended for risking or giving up their lives to avoid personal shame before their senatorial peers at Rome, greater praise was reserved for military tribunes, centurions, and other officers who, in a more productive way, manipulated the fear of *pudor* of nearby soldiers who were observing them. The paradigmatic expression of this was the legendary exploit of Horatius Cocles, an idealized Roman officer who, in the nascent republic, single-handedly defended the Pons Sublicius from Etruscan warriors until it could be destroyed. While Horatius' willingness to defend the bridge by himself demonstrated his *virtus*, he did so, according to Livy, in order to goad the nearby watching soldiers not to retreat. Having already appealed to their sense of *honos* to protect their city, his defense of the bridge apparently checked the retreat of two men, who returned to help him.[54]

According to Polybius, this great desire to protect the *patria* was the

---

having despaired of the republic" (Liv. 22.61.14). Cf. Rosenstein 1990: 9–53; Lendon 2005: 202–3; Rich 2012: 83–111.

51. Liv. 22.50.6–7. Other examples include Flaminius (Liv. 22.6.1–3), Cn. and P. Scipio (Liv. 26.2.13), and Catiline (Sal. *Cat.* 61).

52. Liv. 25.19.16. See also Liv. 25.14.

53. Caes. *Civ.* 2.31. Cf. 3.73; *Gal.* 1.39, 7.50.

54. Liv. 2.10.3–4. It was a moderately successful return, although no Etruscan accepted his challenge for a duel. Cf. D.H. 5.23–24. In Polybius' version (6.55.1–4), Horatius drowns and receives no honors. See Ogilvie 1970: 258–61.

source of Roman soldiers' vaunted "rage" (*orgē*) in warfare and was a major factor behind Roman victories.[55] Polybius' attribution of this civic patriotism to his own period is problematic, to say the least, since Roman legions during the second century BCE successfully fought battles far away from their ancestral *patria* and against those who themselves were defending hearth and home. Many of the soldiers in the "Roman" army during Polybius' time, moreover, were not Roman citizens, and some were not even drawn from Italy.[56] Yet the expectation to fight and not shame oneself before one's comrades nonetheless appealed to a developing sense of military, if not civic, community. As military obligations during the republic increasingly drew the legions farther from Rome for longer periods of time, soldiers who served together over many years began to adopt collective nicknames, and legions began to acquire their own identities, including fixed designations, insignia, and proclaimed loyalty to specific commanders. All of this helped to foster in soldiers a sense of pride and identity beyond the walls of Rome.[57]

This emerging sense of community was physically represented during the middle to late republic by the manipular standards (*signa*) and legionary eagle (*aquila*). Losing these was shameful to oneself and the legion and motivated Roman soldiers and officers to hurl themselves against enemy lines to protect or retrieve them. In Caesar's invasion of Britain in 55 BCE, when his soldiers who had landed on the shores hesitated to disembark, an eagle-bearer (*aquilifer*) goaded them to push onward.

> "Jump down, comrades, unless you wish to hand over the eagle to the enemy. At least I shall perform my duty [*officium*] to the republic and my general." When he had said this with a loud voice, he hurled himself from the ship and began to carry the eagle toward the enemy. Then our men, exhorting one another that so great a shame [*dedecus*] not be permitted, all leaped together from the ship.[58]

---

55. Plb. 6.52.7. See n. 4 above.

56. See n. 29 above.

57. Later authors attributed these developments to Marius (see, e.g., Sal. *Jug.* 86.2; Plin. *Nat.* 10.5; Plu. *Mar.* 25.1–2; Veg. *Mil.* 2.6.2), but they probably developed over a longer period of time. See Keppie 1984: 57–78. Nicknames were typically drawn from service under a specific commander, as in the cases of the Valeriani (App. *Mith.* 59) and the Sullani (Sal. *Cat.* 16.28).

58. Caes. *Gal.* 4.25. For similar speeches, see Caes. *Gal.* 5.37; *Civ.* 3.64, 91; Liv. 25.14.6–7, 26.5.15; D.H. 10.36.5.

This behavior was taken to an extreme when, during particularly difficult phases of some battles, Roman officers threw their unit's standards into the midst of an enemy line in order to drive their soldiers forward to retrieve them. Being seen hesitant to reacquire them brought great shame to Roman soldiers, and throwing them among opposing forces in this way became a common tactic during the republic.[59]

The spectatorship of one's comrades and officers placed great pressure on individuals to perform exploits, and few wished to be witnessed failing in their test of *virtus*, whether by losing their weapons, their standards, or, in the case of commanders, the battle itself. Especially praiseworthy were those men, particularly officers, who not only avoided shame in others' eyes but also used the fear of it to spur watchers to fight. Such action was seen to benefit the entire group. By the same token, an observing crowd of soldiers and superiors actively encouraged and praised those who were seen advancing beyond their lines to attack opposing soldiers in pursuit of *gloria*.

"To Strike at an Enemy"

In contrasting Rome's glorious past with its perceived decline during the late republic, Sallust eulogized the competitive desire of Roman men to seek conspicuous combat on the battlefield.

> But among [young men], the great contest was for *gloria*, and each sought to strike an enemy, to scale a wall, and to be seen while performing such deeds. This they regarded as wealth, great *fama*, and nobility.[60]

Members of Rome's aristocracy who pursued *gloria* on the battlefield were given heroic, even mythic status. Probably the most famous was the young military tribune T. Manlius Torquatus, who accepted the challenge to duel with another Gallic chieftain and fought him as both the Roman and Gallic soldiers watched.

59. Liv. 34.46.11–13: "a method often attempted in desperate battles, after snatching the standards from the standard-bearers, they threw them among the enemy" (*rem in asperis proeliis saepe temptatam, signa adempta signiferis in hostes iniecerunt*). For other examples, see Liv. 4.29.3; Caes. *Gal.* 1.40.15; Plu. *Aem.* 20; App. *BC* 2.60.249; Frontin. *Str.* 2.8.1–5.

60. Sal. *Cat.* 7.4–6.

> They withdrew to their positions, and the two armed men were left alone between them, more in the manner of a *spectaculum* than of a war. . . . With no chanting, no exultation, no pointless flaunting of weapons, but with his heart filled with *animus* and quiet rage, Manlius kept all his ferocity for the critical moment of contest itself. . . . He despoiled nothing from the corpse of his fallen enemy except for his necklace, which, although it was spotted with blood, he drew around his own neck. The Gauls were struck motionless with panic and amazement, while the fervent Romans advanced from their position to meet their own soldier and, while rejoicing and praising him, they conducted him to the dictator.[61]

Formal duels of this sort captured the imagination of ancient authors. Livy notes the archaic theatricality of the incident by describing the manner in which the two men faced one another in front of their armies as resembling a spectacle more than a war, yet he cannot resist describing the dramatic fight and its effect on those observing it. Such stories are common in a Roman literary tradition and broader society that glorified individual demonstrations of martial prowess.[62] While Caesar had little interest in describing the martial achievements of his aristocratic rivals, he nonetheless commemorated similar exploits for *gloria* performed by those who fought under his own name and imperium.[63] In recalling the siege of a Roman camp by the Nervii in 54 BCE, for example, Caesar describes at length the heroics of two centurions, T. Pullo and L. Vorenus, who had long competed with one another to determine who possessed greater *virtus* and greater merit for promotion to the highest level of the centurionate.

> While the fight proceeded fiercely before the fortifications, one of them, Pullo, said, "What are you waiting for, Vorenus? What better place for showing your *virtus* do you want? This day will decide our contests." After he said this, he advanced beyond the fortifications, and rushed against the part of the enemy forces that appeared dens-

61. Liv. 7.10.6–12. See also Gel. 9.13.

62. Examples are the stories of Horatius Cocles (Liv. 2.10) and M. Valerius Corvus (Liv. 7.26; D.H. 15.1; Gel. 9.11.5). Polybius (6.54.4) considered single combat a defining characteristic of Roman warfare. On single combat generally, see Oakley 1985: 394, 404–7; Rosenstein 1990: 117–21; Wiedemann 1996: 91–103; Feldherr 1998: 94–111; Stoll 2001: 108–29; Lendon 2005: 174–76.

63. Caes. *Gal.* 2.22–25, 5.35. 6.38–40, 7.47; *Civ.* 91, 99; *B. Hisp.* 23. Cf. Lendon 2005: 212–22.

> est. Nor did Vorenus keep himself within the rampart, but, in fear of everyone's opinion, he followed.

The two centurions fought hand to hand with countless warriors, and one actively helped the other when in trouble. They were both cheered on by their soldiers watching from behind the rampart.

> And after both had killed a great number [of the enemy], they retreated within the fortifications to the greatest applause. Fortune thus dealt with both in this rivalry and competition, that one rival was an aid and a safeguard to the other, and it could not be determined which of the two seemed greater in *virtus*.[64]

For *milites*, being seen slaying multiple enemy soldiers in a single action could be rewarded with a greater share of spoils or with promotion to the rank of centurion.[65] Rewards of less commercial value but arguably greater social importance were military decorations (*dona militaria*). Conferred by a commander with imperium, they were for not simply "bravery" but conspicuous, voluntary actions beyond one's ranks. Lesser decorations included discs (*phalerae*), armbands (*armillae*), and necklaces (*torques*). The oldest and most prestigious *dona* were crowns (*coronae*), which, during the republic at least, seem to have been awarded according to specific actions regardless of one's rank or social status. The golden crown (*corona aurea*) was the lowest order and was given for general acts of individual prowess. The rampart crown (*vallaris*) was awarded to the first soldier to storm an enemy encampment, while the wall crown (*muralis*) went to the first man to scale a fortress or town wall.[66] The visibility of one's exploit was all the more critical since one required witnesses to confirm it in order to receive any decorations.[67]

Praise for such competitive displays was hardly guaranteed. While Tor-

64. Caes. *Gal.* 5.44. For commentary and bibliography on this famous passage, see the excellent account in Brown 2004: 292–308.

65. On spoils, see Harris 1979: 9–68. On promotion, see D.H. 9.39; Plb. 6.19.1—24; Caes. *Gal.* 6.40; *Civ.* 3.53. Centurions received higher pay during the midrepublic (Plb. 6.39.12), and Caesar doubled their pay during the civil wars (Suet. *Jul.* 26).

66. This is partly described in Plb. 6.39.1–6. See Domaszewski (1908) 1967: 68–70, 109–11, 137–39, 184–85; Maxfield 1981: esp. 67–95.

67. This rule persists with modern military decorations. For examples at the siege of Carthago Nova in 209 BCE, see Liv. 26.48. Caesar (*Gal.* 1.52) assigned officers specifically for this reason: "Caesar appointed legates and quaestors for every legion, so that each of them would have eyewitnesses to record their *virtus*" (*Caesar singulis legionibus singulos legatos et quaestorem praefecit, uti eos testes suae quisque virtutis haberet*).

quatus became famous for his duel with the Gaul, he later became infamous as the commander in charge of a campaign against the Latin League in 340 BCE. His son, a young *eques*, had disobeyed the consuls' command to maintain his position, when he dueled against an Italian warrior. Although the son had matched his father's earlier success and proudly carried his enemy's spoils back to the legion, Manlius ordered him to be tortured and executed for his defiance of the consul's authority and for violation of military discipline.[68] Caesar, too, disapproved of certain individuals pursuing personal fame, as he did of one centurion, Lucius Fabius, at Gergovia. Refusing to allow anyone else to acquire glory before him, Fabius scaled the Gallic town's wall in front of his soldiers. If the siege had been successful, Caesar might well have praised this exploit. As it happened, it was a failure, and when Fabius and his soldiers were cut off and killed inside the walls, Caesar interpreted the centurion's behavior as an overzealous, reckless display.[69]

These incidents do not illustrate Roman opposition to the individual pursuit of glory per se. Although sanctioned by his imperium and the unwritten rules regarding military discipline, the elder Torquatus' decision regarding his son was thought, by present observers and by later generations, to have shown excessive harshness (*severitas*) rather than *disciplina*, and his precedent was promptly challenged.[70] The distinction that Livy himself draws between praise and condemnation for such individual exploits seems to have been based on their perceived effect on nearby spectators. The elder Torquatus had acquired permission from the consul and performed his duel in front of his fellow soldiers. He had, essentially, become the legion's surrogate, and his duel determined the outcome of the battle. His son, in contrast, had performed an equally brilliant exploit but without the consul's permission, out of sight of and without benefit to the legion. His exploit had no effect on the battle's outcome. As his father tells him, he acquired not true *gloria* but a false image (*vana imago*) of it.[71] Similarly, Caesar did not criticize all aggressive assaults of his centurions, even when many could

68. Liv. 8.7.1–8.2. The evidence is unclear whether a would-be duelist was required first to acquire permission of his commanding officer (see, e.g., Liv. 7.10. 2–4, 7.26.2). See Oakley 1998: 436–51; Feldherr 1998: 92.

69. Caes. *Gal.* 7.47–50.

70. On the reaction, see Liv. 8.7.20–22; on the challenge, Liv. 8.30–36. Feldherr (1998: 110–11) does not see criticism implied against the elder Manlius here, but the consul's legacy is hardly positive in later references and even taints his descendants. Cf. Liv. 22.60; Sal. *Cat.* 56. Vergil (*A.* 825) associates him only with the axe (*securis*) of execution.

71. On dueling as representative of battle, see Fries 1985: 88–105, 154–65; Feldherr 1998: 93–108.

hardly have acquired his prior approval or were in keeping with Roman notions of *disciplina*.[72] His criticism was reserved for centurions, like Fabius, whose individual pursuit of *gloria* brought no apparent benefit to observing soldiers or their commander.

Upon closer examination, most praiseworthy duels and aggressive charges are depicted in specific circumstances when their perpetrators' actions were seen to have a positive effect on observing Roman soldiers. Torquatus' successful duel, for example, had a critical effect on those around him: the Gauls were rendered motionless, while the Roman soldiers became eager (*alacres*). The visible, contrasting effects of individual exploits on friend and foe is stressed repeatedly in the textual record, and their benefit to Roman soldiers' spirits was often presented as having been calculated by the perpetrator—the Roman officer's equivalent of a "morale booster."[73] Polybius asserts that Romans engaged in single combat specifically to decide a battle.[74] Conversely, the failure of a commander or officer to accept a challenge or be willing to skirmish beyond his line when his troops were failing was thought to have a damaging effect on his soldiers.[75] As portrayed in our ancient sources, leaving one's position to "strike at an enemy" was praiseworthy inasmuch as it had a positive, visible effect on the legion. Spectators were needed to grant a man the *laus* that he desired for his own prestige, promotion, or spoils, but the ideal exploit, particularly for Roman officers, was visibly performed on behalf of the soldiers as well.

"To Save a Comrade"

A third form of individual exploit that was explicit in its benefit to the collective was that which saved or avenged another Roman citizen. Friendship (*amicitia*) and dutifulness (*pietas*) between comrades were idealized by Roman authors. Vergil projected these martial virtues back to Rome's mythic origins in the *Aeneid*, when describing Nisus' actions after the death of his friend, Euryalus. After expressing shame at failing to protect his younger companion, Nisus avenged him by single-handedly attacking his many kill-

72. See, e.g., Caes. *Gal.* 5.44, 6.38; *Civ.* 3.91; *B. Hisp.* 23.

73. On Torquatus, see Liv. 7.10.12. For similar cases, see Liv. 2.10, 7.26, 25.18.4–15; Caes. *Gal.* 5.44, 6.38, 8.48.1–7; *B. Hisp.* 23; App. *BC* 1.50. On Livy's focus on the effect on spectators, see Oakley 1998: 119–20.

74. Polybius (6.54.4–55) cites Horatius Cocles' deed as an example.

75. See, e.g., Plu. *Sert.* 13.3–4; Caes. *Gal.* 6.40.

ers, until he himself fell beside his friend, so that they were inseparable even at death.[76]

During the late republic, it is possible that such attitudes reflected a nostalgic feeling that the recent civil wars had broken traditional, civic bonds and ideas of obligation.[77] More broadly, however, they illustrated a growing sense of identity within certain legions during the period. Caesar, the majority of whose soldiers fought together for well over a decade, actively encouraged bonds of friendship and loyalty (*officium*) within his legions and praised those who aggressively fought beyond their unit in order to protect or avenge comrades and superior officers. Although Caesar blamed his failed siege at Gergovia in 52 BCE on the overzealous desire for *gloria* and plunder of his soldiers and centurions, he withholds criticism for M. Petreius, a centurion who bought time for his soldiers' escape by sacrificing himself.[78] Not only did Petreius avoid the shame of having to face Caesar after disobeying his orders, but the centurion acquired *laus* for saving his comrades in the process. For Caesar, such actions guaranteed that the death of officers spurred their soldiers to avenge them.[79]

The praiseworthiness of actions intended to save a comrade is again reflected in *dona militaria*, among which the most valued crowns were awarded to those whose exploits were seen to benefit the collective. The civic crown (*civica*) was awarded to someone who was witnessed saving the life of a fellow Roman citizen, whether a comrade or superior. According to Pliny the Elder, it was "the most glorious award that can be bestowed for military *virtus*."[80] In describing two legendary soldiers of the Roman republic, Siccius Dentatus and Spurius Ligustinus, Livy highlights their winning of fourteen and six civic crowns, respectively.[81] Although the civic crown is sometimes compared with the Victoria Cross of the British Army, the criteria for winning it also required an accompanying act of aggression. One had to be seen not only saving a comrade in distress but also killing an enemy, at the same time and in the same space.[82] To praise violence against a foe and com-

76. Verg. *A.* 9.367–449.

77. On breaking of civic bonds, see Meban 2009: 239–59.

78. Caes. *Gal.* 7.50.

79. *B. Hisp.* 24.

80. Plin. *Nat.* 16.3: *militum virtutis insigne clarissimum.* For general accounts of *coronae*, see *Nat.* 16.3, passim; Plb. 6.39; D.H. 10.37; Gel. 6.5.13–17; Maxfield 1981: 67–81.

81. On Ligustinus, see Liv. 42.32–35. On Siccius Dentatus, see D.H. 10.36.3–37.5; Val. Max. 3.2.24; Plin. *Nat.* 7.101–3; Gel. 2.11.1–4.

82. Plin. *Nat.* 16.5; Gel. 6.5.13. Cf. Rosenstein 2007: 134. For comparisons to the Victoria Cross, see Parker 1928: 228–29.

passion toward a comrade simultaneously was not contradictory in Roman attitudes toward warfare.

The rarest military decoration was the "grass crown" (*corona graminea/obsidionalis*). Granted only through acclamation by all the legion's soldiers who witnessed the action, this crown was given to those credited with saving the entire legion. It rewarded the ultimate expression of the individual's action on behalf of the community and was given almost exclusively to Rome's most famous military heroes.[83] One particular recipient was also the perpetrator of perhaps the most extreme of recorded exploits, the *devotio*, a ritual in which a Roman consul was consecrated and, having made a formal prayer to offer his life and that of his enemies to the gods of the underworld in exchange for his army's victory, charged into the midst of an enemy army and, by killing himself also, doomed them to destruction. Only three occurrences of *devotio* are recorded, all apparently performed by members of the Decius Mus family.[84]

The ritualistic aspect of the *devotio* is beset with historical difficulties, yet the circumstances of battle in which each instance occurs are noteworthy. In each case, the spirit of the legions is breaking, and the commander has thus far failed to spur his soldiers through verbal exhortation; both to avoid the shame of failure and to obtain a Roman victory, the commander charges at the enemy soldiers, who are struck with terror. The act instills eagerness in the Roman soldiers who see it and determines the outcome of the battle in their favor.[85] In the two cases that Livy records, he dwells less on the religious meaning of the commander's action than on the dramatic effect of self-sacrifice on its spectators—friend and foe alike. Other ancient authors recall the *devotio* when describing suicidal charges in different circumstances, and they, too, interpret such suicides as a calculated decision by Roman centurions or tribunes to spur the observing soldiers behind them.[86]

Although one was praised for being seen to kill other men in order to save a comrade, the reverse was also true, as demonstrated by Cn. Petreius

83. Plin. *Nat.* 22.5–6. Recipients mentioned by Pliny include L. Siccius Dentatus, Q. Fabius Maximus, Scipio Aemilianus, L. Cornelius Sulla, and Augustus, who seems to have been the final recipient. See Maxfield 1981: 67–69.

84. The action occurred at Veseris (Liv. 8.9.12–14) and at Sentinum (Liv. 10.28–29). For possible but conflicting reports of a grandson performing it at Ausculum, see Cic. *Fin.* 2.61; Enn. *Ann.* 191–94. On historical problems regarding literary accounts of *devotio*, see Oakley 1998: 477–86; Feldherr 1998: 99; James 2011: 46.

85. Liv. 8.9.10, 12–14; 10.29.1–3.

86. See, e.g., Plu. *Pomp.* 71.2–3 (cf. Caes. *Civ.* 3.91, 99); Amm. Marc. 15.4.10–12. See Oakley 1998: 483–84.

Atinas, the only centurion recorded to have received the grass crown. In 102 BCE, many Roman soldiers under the command of Q. Lutatius Catulus were cut off from retreat by marauding Cimbri, and the incompetence of the unit's military tribune in command was causing panic. Atinas responded by killing the military tribune in front of the army, taking command himself, and then single-handedly leading the soldiers to safety. Rather than being punished by Catulus for murdering his superior officer, Atinas was praised by the legion and awarded Rome's greatest military decoration.[87] While the tribune's ineptness was blameworthy, the idea that Atinas could be decorated for "fragging" a superior officer would strike modern military authorities as absurd, and it certainly seems far from the exemplum of obedience and military hierarchy set earlier by Manlius Torquatus. But to Atinas' legion (and, presumably, to later generations of Romans), this individual's violation of discipline was nonetheless considered exceptional and praiseworthy, an individual exploit performed on behalf of his legion.

Conclusion

To understand the relationship between the performer and the audience of an individual exploit in Roman warfare, it is perhaps best to reflect again on the account of T. Pullo and L. Vorenus. Caesar's description of their feat recalls phrases of Homer's *Iliad* in which Greek heroes exhort those around them to fight and compete for greater renown (*klēos*), and the scene has been taken to illustrate the individualistic motives and behavior of Roman soldiers par excellence. This aggressive, competitive spirit is certainly prominent here, but a closer look at the context of their actions demonstrates that there is more to Caesar's praise than that. Vorenus was responding to his comrade's criticism, goaded into battle to avoid the *pudor* of appearing hesitant in the eyes of the soldiers behind them. As Caesar emphasizes, moreover, these competitors were compelled, by chance, to protect one another, and each of them performed this task admirably. The desires to avoid shame, to kill enemies in pursuit of *gloria*, and to protect fellow citizens—the motives Livy attributed to earlier generations of soldiers through their voluntary oath—are all exhibited here.

These actions, however, were praiseworthy for being performed not in isolation but in full view of one's legion. A Roman soldier or officer required

87. Plin. *Nat.* 22.11.

witnesses so that his exploit could be given meaning, judged praiseworthy, and subsequently commemorated by his gens and community. This "need for an audience," however, always carried with it great social pressure and, as we saw in several cases, the danger that one's actions would be questioned or condemned outright, producing exempla to be avoided rather than emulated.[88] Crucial to this determination was not simply the nature of the act itself but its effect on the immediate audience who witnessed it. It should be no surprise that Caesar places the tale of Pullo and Vorenus in the midst of his account of the desperate situation that his besieged legion was facing and highlights how these exploits served not only to glorify the two centurions but, apparently, to boost the spirits of those soldiers who observed them.[89]

All of this evidence argues that the perceived motives of Romans who performed individual exploits was relevant to how they were judged both on the battlefield and off it. Early heroes among Rome's nobility were expected to surpass their ancestors' achievements by competing for individual *gloria*, though within accepted boundaries of behavior that benefited the *senatus populusque Romanus*. Caesar's officers were similarly praised for individual actions beyond their line, but only inasmuch as they also brought greater glory to their legion and, of course, its most illustrious commander. In other words, the needs of the individual and the collective were complementary concerns (rather than contradictory ones) in how these deeds were commemorated. The Roman battlefield provided a context in which individual actions could be promoted (or disguised) as being undertaken in service of the larger Roman community.

Works Cited

Alston, R. 1995. *Soldier and Society in Roman Egypt*. London.
Beard, M. 2007. *The Roman Triumph*. Cambridge.
Bell, M. 1965. "Tactical Reform in the Roman Republican Army." *Historia* 14: 404–22.
Bishop, M., and Coulston, J. 2006. *Roman Military Equipment from the Punic Wars to the Fall of Rome*. 2nd ed. Oxford.

88. See Stewart and Strathern 2002: 3.

89. Since Caesar does not state explicitly that their assault altered the military situation, Brown (2004: 293–94, 301) doubts its consequentiality. However, fighting before one's fellow soldiers need not change the final outcome of the battle to be deemed consequential. While Caesar alone could save the day, the besieged soldiers' praise for both centurions punctuates the otherwise desperate situation. As Brown himself admits (303), such displays were considered glorious and inspirational.

Brand, C. 1968. *Roman Military Law*. Austin.

Brice, L. 2011. "Disciplining Octavian: A Case Study of Roman Military Culture, 44–30 BCE." In W. Lee, ed., *Warfare and Culture in World History*, 35–59. New York.

Brown, R. 2004. "*Virtus Consili Expers*: An Interpretation of the Centurions' Contest in Caesar, *De bello Gallico* 5, 44." *Hermes* 132 (3): 292–308.

Collins, R. 2008. *Violence: A Micro-sociological Theory*. Princeton.

Cornell, T. 1995. *The Beginnings of Rome: Italy and Rome from the Bronze Age to the Punic Wars (c. 1000–264 BC)*. London.

Delbrück, H. 1975. *History of the Art of War within the Framework of Political History, Vol I, Warfare in Antiquity*. Trans. W. Renfroe Jr. Westport. Originally published as *Geschichte der Kriegskunst im Rahmen der politischen Geschichte, I, das Alterthum* (Berlin, 1900).

Domaszewski, A. von. (1908) 1967. *Die Rangordnung des römischen Heeres*. Ed. B. Dobson. 2nd ed. Cologne.

Dumézil, G. 1942. *Horace et les Curiaces*. Paris.

Du Picq, A. 1921. *Battle Studies: Ancient and Modern Battle*. Trans. J. Greely and R. Cotton. New York. Originally published as *Études sur le combat* (Paris, 1880).

Eckstein, A. 1995. *Moral Vision in the Histories of Polybius*. Berkeley.

Feldherr, A. 1998. *Spectacle and Society in Livy's "History."* Berkeley.

Flower, H. 2009. "Alternatives to Written History in Republican Rome." In A. Feldherr, ed., *The Cambridge Companion to Roman Historians*, 65–76. Cambridge.

Fries, J. 1985. *Der Zweikampf: Historische und literarische Aspekte seiner Darstellung bei T. Livius*. Königstein.

Fuller, J. 1965. *Julius Caesar: Man, Soldier, and Tyrant*. London.

Fuhrmann, C. 2012. *Policing the Roman Empire: Soldiers, Administration, and Public Order*. Oxford.

Gat, A. 2006. *War in Human Civilization*. Oxford.

Gilliver, K. 1996. "The Roman Army and Morality in War." In A. Lloyd, ed., *Battle in Antiquity*, 219–38. London.

Gilliver, K. 2007. "Display in Roman Warfare: The Appearance of Armies and Individuals on the Battlefield." *War in History* 14 (1): 1–21.

Goldsworthy, A. 1996. *The Roman Army at War: 100 BC–AD 200*. Oxford.

Hanson, V. 1989. *The Western Way of War: Infantry Battle in Classical Greece*. New York.

Harris, W. 1979. *War and Imperialism in Republican Rome, 327–70 B.C.* Oxford.

Harris, W. 2006. "Readings in the Narrative Literature of Roman Courage." In S. Dillon and K. Welch, eds., *Representations of War in Ancient Rome*, 300–320. Cambridge.

Holmes, R. 1985. *Firing Line*. London.

Isaac, B. 1992. *The Limits of Empire: The Roman Army in the East*. Oxford.

Isaac, B. 1998. "Hierarchy and Command Structure in the Roman Army." In *The Near East under Roman Rule: Selected Papers*, 388–402. Leiden.

James, S. 2011. *Rome and the Sword: How Warriors and Weapons Shaped Roman History*. London.

James, S. 2013. "Facing the Sword: Confronting the Realities of Martial Violence and Other Mayhem, Present and Past." In S. Ralph, ed., *The Archaeology of Violence: Interdisciplinary Approaches*, 98–115. Albany.

Keegan, J. 1976. *The Face of Battle*. New York.
Keegan, J. 1993. *A History of Warfare*. New York.
Keppie, L. 1984. *The Making of the Roman Army*. Norman.
Kromayer, J., and Veith, G. 1928. *Heerwesen und Kriegführung der Griechen und Römer*. Munich.
Lazenby, J. 1991. "The Killing Zone." In V. Hanson, ed., *Hoplites: The Classical Greek Battle Experience*, 87–109. London.
Lee, A. 1996. "Morale and the Roman Experience of Battle." In A. Lloyd, ed., *Battle in Antiquity*, 199–218. London.
Lee, W. 2011. "Warfare and Culture." In W. Lee, ed., *Warfare and Culture in World History*, 1–11. New York.
Lendon, J. 1999. "The Rhetoric of Combat: Greek Military Theory and Roman Culture in Julius Caesar's Battle Descriptions." *ClAnt* 18: 273–329.
Lendon, J. 2005. *Soldiers and Ghosts: A History of Battle in Classical Antiquity*. New Haven.
Lintott, A. 1999. *Violence in Republican Rome*. 2nd ed. Oxford.
Lynn, J. 1984. *The Bayonets of the Republic: Motivation and Tactics in the Army of Revolutionary France, 1791–1794*. Boulder.
MacMullen, R. 1963. *Soldier and Civilian in the Later Roman Empire*. Cambridge.
Marincola, J. 2009. "Ancient Audiences and Expectations." In A. Feldherr, ed., *The Cambridge Companion to Roman Historians*, 11–23. Cambridge.
Marshall, S. 1947. *Men against Fire*. New York.
Mattern, S. 1999. *Rome and the Enemy: Imperial Strategy in the Principate*. Berkeley.
Maxfield, V. 1981. *The Military Decorations of the Roman Army*. Berkeley.
McCall, J. 2002. *The Cavalry of the Roman Republic: Cavalry Combat and Elite Reputations in the Middle and Late Republic*. London.
McDonnell, M. 2006. *Roman Manliness:* Virtus *and the Roman Republic*. Cambridge.
Meban, D. 2009. "The Nisus and Euryalus Episode and Roman Friendship." *Phoenix* 63: 239–59.
Néraudeau, J. 1976. "L'Exploit de Titus Manlius Torquatus." In A. Balland, ed., *Mélanges offerts à Jacques Heurgon*, vol. 2, *L'Italie préromaine et la Rome républicaine*, 685–94. Rome.
Oakley, S. 1985. "Single Combat and the Roman Army." *CQ* 35: 392–410.
Oakley, S. 1998. *A Commentary on Livy, Books VI–X*. Vol. 2. Oxford.
Ogilvie, R. 1970. *A Commentary on Livy, Books 1–5*. Oxford.
Parker, H. 1928. *The Roman Legions*. Oxford.
Phang, S. 2008. *Roman Military Service: Ideologies of Discipline in the Late Republic and Early Principate*. Cambridge.
Raaflaub, K., and Rosenstein, N., eds. 2009. *War and Society in the Ancient and Medieval World*. Cambridge.
Rawson, E. 1990. "The Antiquarian Tradition: Spoils and Representations of Foreign Armour." In W. Eder, ed., *Staat und Staatlichkeit in der frühen römischen Republik: Akten eines Symposiums, 12–15 Juli 1988, Freie Universität Berlin*, 158–73. Stuttgart.
Rich, J. 1993. "Fear, Greed, and Glory: The Causes of War-Making in the Middle Republic." In J. Rich and G. Shipley, eds., *War and Society in the Roman World*, 38–68. London.

Rich, J. 1996. "Augustus and the *Spolia Opima*." *Chiron* 26: 85–127.

Rich, J. 2007. "Warfare and the Army in Early Rome." In P. Erdkamp, ed., *A Companion to the Roman Army*, 7–23. Malden.

Rich, J. 2012. "Roman Attitudes to Defeat in Battle under the Republic." In F. Simón, F. Pina Polo, and J. Rodríguez, eds., *Vae Victis! Perdedores en el mundo antiguo*. Barcelona.

Richlin, A. 1992. *The Garden of Priapus: Sexuality and Aggression in Roman Humour*. 2nd ed. New York.

Roller, M. 2009. "The Exemplary Past in Roman Historiography and Culture." In A. Feldherr, ed., *The Cambridge Companion to Roman Historians*, 214–30. Cambridge.

Rosenstein, N. 1990. Imperatores Victi: *Military Defeat and Aristocratic Competition in the Middle and Late Republic*. Berkeley.

Rosenstein, N. 2007. "Military Command, Political Power, and the Republican Elite." In P. Erdkamp, ed., *A Companion to the Roman Army*, 132–47. Malden.

Rosenstein, N. 2010. "Phalanges in Rome?" In G. Fagan and M. Trundle, eds., *New Perspectives on Ancient Warfare*, 289–304. Leiden.

Roth, J. 2006. "Siege Narrative in Livy." In S. Dillon and K. Welch, eds., *Representations of War in Ancient Rome*, 49–67. Cambridge.

Sabin, P. 2000. "The Face of Roman Battle." *JRS* 90: 1–17.

Smith, R. 1958. *Service in the Post-Marian Roman Army*. Manchester.

Speidel, M. 2009. *Heer und Herrschaft im Römischen Reich der Hohen Kaiserzeit*. Stuttgart.

Stewart, P., and Strathern, A. 2002. *Violence: Theory and Ethnography*. London.

Stoll, O. 2001. *Römisches Heer und Gesellschaft: Gesammelte Beiträge, 1991–1999*. Stuttgart.

Walsh, P. 1961. *Livy: His Historical Aims and Methods*. Cambridge.

Watson, G. 1969. *The Roman Soldier*. Ithaca.

Wheeler, E. 1979. "The Legion as Phalanx." *Chiron* 9: 303–18.

Whitehead, N., ed. 2004. *Violence*. Oxford.

Wiedemann, T. 1996. "Single Combat and Being Roman." *AncSoc* 27: 91–103.

Wieviorka, M. 2009. *Violence: A New Approach*. Trans. D. Macey. London.

Zhmodikov, A. 2000. "Roman Republican Heavy Infantrymen in Battle (IV–II Centuries B.C.)." *Historia* 49: 67–78.

THIRTEEN

War as Theater, from Tacitus to Dexippus

David Potter

What has Tacitus to do with Dexippus? Such a question might seem to invite the same response as Tertullian's inquiry about the relevance of Athens to Jerusalem. Tertullian's denunciation of the relevance of classical philosophy to Christianity was, of course, wishful thinking (and concealed links that were far more important in his own time than he would allow). The link between Tacitus and Dexippus is far less close than the one that would develop between Athens and Jerusalem, and that is the point. These historians represent different phases of historiographic battle descriptions, one that mirrors the transformation of Rome's own fortunes between the age of Trajan and that of Aurelian. For Tacitus, military voyeurism was emblematic of the power of Rome. For Dexippus, who was writing against the background of defeat and ruin in the mid-third century, the ability to deploy cultural commonplaces in the description of battle is no less significant. For Dexippus the commonplace explicates the horrific. In his handling of material, Dexippus could not rely on the reportage of events at Rome, as did two earlier third-century historians, Cassius Dio and Herodian. War is theater insofar as battle descriptions enact the historian's capacity to reinterpret material that already exists in the minds of readers and to imbue it with meaning.

The concept of theater—in both ancient and modern terms—is not unproblematic. In this essay, I use the term *theater* to represent the mimesis through which an audience is invited to participate in an event beyond itself. This audience is intended to experience something of the emotions experienced by the original participants, though not their entirety. The historian cannot re-create the earlier event, because the audience approaches what happened with hindsight. The classical historian, like the producer of classic theater, must pick the themes from earlier work that he wishes to stress for the new audience; he cannot simply repeat an earlier account, any more than a theatrical producer can simply reproduce an earlier production. To a greater or lesser degree, a producer can select and rearrange elements from earlier productions to draw attention to themes that he or she thinks especially important. The image of history as something that one could "see" was deeply ingrained within the tradition well before the imperial period (Livy had written of his history as something to be gazed on), and the problem of "tragic" history—at least in Polybius' terms—had arisen because of the perceived similarities between rhetorically sophisticated historical works and drama. The issue was complicated by the fact that history was meant to be read aloud, historians describe their audiences as "auditors" rather than as "readers."[1]

The historian writing in the second and third centuries AD depended, to some degree, on the audience's sense of the earlier "performance history" of a given scene. The ideal audience member should be able to appreciate what he was doing with the material—whether that was changing a received account with new details that he had somehow uncovered or simply reproduced inherited moments in pithier or more memorable ways. Tacitus did not come up with the notion that Galba was a man whom everyone agreed was capable of ruling if only he had never done so (*omnium consensu capax imperii nisi imperasset*); he just put the idea more memorably.[2] The value of conventional or well-known material was that the audience could appreciate his skill in manipulating it all the more readily. As a point of comparison, Shakespeare does not indicate who the speakers are in the crowd that assembles to listen to Mark Antony's funeral oration in *Julius Caesar*. If those responding are simply members of the crowd, the audience will appreciate

1. Livy praef. 10, with Feldherr 1998: 1–19; Jaeger 1997: 1–29. For tragedy and history, see Walbank 1960 (= Walbank 1985: 224–42); Fornara 1983: 25–34; Marincola 2003: 285–315; Rutherford 2007: 504–14. The notion of the historian's "gaze" is derived from Davidson 1991; for recent stress on the performance of historical works see Wiseman 2015: 98–102. For Tertullian, see *De praescriptione haereticorum* 7.9: *Quid ergo Athenis et Hierosolymis? quid academiae et ecclesiae? quid haereticis et christianis?*

2. Tac. *Hist.* 1.49.4, with Plut. *Galba* 29.2; Damon 2003: 200–201.

the significance of Antony's demagoguery. If, however, the lines demanding riot in response to Caesar's death are spoken by the ghost of Caesar himself (as was the case in the production that the Royal Shakespeare Company brought to Ann Arbor, Michigan, in 2006), the audience will appreciate the mystical role of Caesar in driving the action. Shakespeare himself evidently enjoyed this sort of production trick, as he is said to have liked playing the role of the ghost of Hamlet's father. Audiences also seem to have liked the joke when the playwright (by then thoroughly recognizable) started shouting directions to his players as he descended into the ghost hole.[3] In their choices of the way that they will present the thoroughly conventional, historians establish their own personae for audiences. The analogy that I wish to draw with theater is thus not with specific actions that took place on the ancient stage but, rather, in the mimetic process that linked (and links) the practicing historian with the impresario.

Cassius Dio on War

In describing the three great set pieces of the civil wars—the battles of Pharsalus, Philippi, and Actium—Dio deploys all the rhetorical equipment he inherited from the long tradition of battle narratives. Before recounting the battle of Pharsalus, he stresses the fame of the combatants and how they were fighting for the domination of the Roman state; his narrative of the battle itself, once it gets started, is not recognizably the contest described by Caesar in the third book of the *Bellum Civile*. Pompey's order that his army not advance is left out altogether or, on a more generous interpretation, reinterpreted as a statement that the battle began with auxiliaries because the Romans were unwilling to fight each other.[4] The final victory follows from not the defeat of Pompey's cavalry but, rather, the poor quality of the "Asiatic" troops in his army, and Dio points out, at the end, that there had been portents predicting the outcome. In describing the first battle of Philippi, Dio opens with a meditation on the importance of the end of the republic, stating that while other battles were concerned with who would lead the empire, this was a battle between the forces favoring *dynasteia* and those

3. W. Shakespeare, *The Tragedy of Julius Caesar*, act 3, scene 2 (the various speakers are identified as four plebeians); for Shakespeare's playing of the ghost in Hamlet, see Greenblatt 2004: 322.

4. Dio 48.51.3; Caes. *BC* 3.92.2 for Pompey's instructions. See also Lintott 1997: 2501–2; Kemezis 2014: 117–18.

favoring *autonomia*. As a result of the battle, the *demos* would never again attain the *parrhesia* that it once enjoyed, and the democratic element in the state had weakened itself through its quarrels, strengthening the monarchical.[5] There follows a suitable array of portents, summaries of speeches that officers on either side might have given. The battle then begins, with men fighting at first cautiously, then ever more fiercely. The first day ends with Brutus defeating Octavian (solely because the latter was weakened by disease), while Antony defeats Cassius, because the former is a far better soldier. Cassius then commits suicide, as he does in other versions, because he cannot recognize Brutus' messengers. The second battle of Philippi does not require the elaborate buildup of the first or even the elaborate narrative, as Brutus' army follows the eagle that represented its fortunes in an ominous prebattle portent into flight.[6] Once the scene is set at Actium, after Antony decides that he must fight, there are the necessary portents to convince Cleopatra that she should convince Antony to flee, then two enormously long speeches from Antony and Octavian.[7] The subsequent battle does live up to the prebattle rhetoric (at least in terms of action), as Dio stresses the differences between the ships on both sides, as well as the difficulty that Octavian encounters until he decides to burn Antony's fleet. That decision, taken long after Antony's flight, wins the day.

The description of the battle of Actium is more expansive than that of other battles and more visual, as befits an event that Dio says was the turning point in Roman history.[8] We see Octavian's smaller ships moving in to ram Antony's larger vessels. Missiles of all sorts fill the air, and ships fall foul of each other. We see Cleopatra waiting anxiously behind the main fleet, in agonized suspense. Suddenly, she raises her sails to take flight; we see Antony deciding to follow her squadron. Antony's ships appear as fortified cities, their crews defending the walls against Octavian's men who are climbing over the side. Finally, Octavian sends for fire from the camp, seeing that he could not win in any other way, and the fires spread through Antony's fleet.[9] The description looks as if it might be taken from a series of paintings; at this point, Dio's writing recalls Plutarch's dictum that the effective historian makes his work like a painting.[10]

---

5. Dio 47.39, with Kemezis 2014: 119. For Dio's understanding of the monarchy as the savior of the empire, see Ameling 1997: 2480–82; Kemezis 2014: 129–39.

6. On this description, see esp. Gowing 1992: 218.

7. Dio 50.16–22 (Antony's speech), 50.24–30 (Octavian's speech).

8. Millar 1964: 44.

9. Dio 50.32–35, esp. 50.32 (initial conflict), 33.1–3 (Cleopatra), 34.1–5 (fire).

10. Plut. *De glor. Ath.* 347, with Marincola 2003: 293.

Fig. 13.1. Soldiers disembarking from boat; image from Trajan's Column, Rome, 113 CE. (Picture by David S. Potter, used by permission.)

A historian who wrote in a vivid, "pictorial" fashion did not necessarily have to be looking at pictures, but the overlap between the increasingly realistic depictions of combat in imperial art and Dio's narrative are striking. Both rely on such stock scenes as imperial *adlocutiones* to soldiers, the receipt of embassies, depictions of multiple troop types and tactical formations, siege operations, and other feats of engineering. In this sense, visual media would appear to be at least one source (if not directly, then indirectly) for Dio's narrative of the decisive battle in Severus' war with Pescennius Niger.

There were certain things Dio appears to have expected to have happened. He evidently preferred that important battles should be hard fought and should be won only after a sudden change of fortune, hence his stress on the meteorological phenomenon that enabled Niger's defeat at the passage of the Taurus. In this case, the battle narrative once again offers several pictorial panels. Dio begins with a description of the way the two armies were arrayed (legionaries in front, missile troops behind), then describes the terrain and Severus' maneuvers. The next apparent panel depicts Severus' attack on Niger's lines, his men forming into a *testudo*, and, finally, the repulse of the attack until a great storm blew up in the faces of Niger's troops, who then broke in flight.[11] It is also striking that Dio has the wrong place for the decisive battle. Severus' final victory took place on the plain of Issus, which is not at all near the Cilician Gates, where Dio locates the action, in

11. Dio 74.7.1–8; see also Birley 1988: 112–13, for a rational reconstruction of the campaign (and see also n. 18 below).

what may be a conflation of events or images. Dio did know the area, having accompanied his father when the latter was governor of Cilicia under Commodus,[12] which makes the error more puzzling than it would be if Dio was dealing with some other part of the empire.

Dio's description of the battle of Lyons in 197, at which Severus defeated Clodius Albinus, is quite different (and better). In this case, he refers to an account written by Severus and implies that he thought it was false. Instead of being presented with clear tableaux depicting the course of action over time, we are told that Laetus defeated Albinus' army on one wing and that the wing under Severus' command was lured into a trap. Severus had to join in the fighting, but even he could not turn the tide of battle in his own favor. Only when Laetus arrived, at the head of his cavalry, was the victory assured. This description has some visual elements (the reader is asked to visualize Severus' men falling into ditches, as well as Severus moving among his men), but it does not break down as clearly into parts as does the description of the battle of Issus. The difference between the two descriptions suggests a substantial difference in Dio's source material: in the case of the battle of Lyons, he seems to have relied on living informants and documents. Given that Dio knew many who suffered as the result of their support for Albinus' cause, the truth about what happened might have been especially important to him, as would have been the fate of Laetus, who appears to have been executed within the year.[13] In terms of the topographies of violence, Dio establishes the locus of information in the reader's own mind in the case of the battle of Lyons; he seems to have extracted a narrative from some sort of public monument and translated it into a new form in the case of the battle of Issus.

In his account of the sieges of Hatra (problematic in that there was only one siege, in the wake of the capture of Ctesiphon in 198), Dio appears to adapt material from a variety of sources, including painting. The image of Severus observing the siege from a high tribunal looks like a description of a standard scene in second-century AD imperial "war art," and also here are the elements of siege warfare that appear on Severus' arch in the Roman Forum—war engines and diverse troops attacking the walls of a city depicted with some major buildings (in the case of the siege of Hatra, it is the sun god's temple).[14] Although the elements of such art are present, the

12. Dio 72.7.2, with Millar 1964: 15.

13. Dio 76.6 (Lyons), 75.10.2–3 (death of Laetus).

14. Dio 75.10–12; for the representations on the arch of Severus, see Lusnia 2006: 244–71(see also works cited in n. 19 below, on the use of pictures).

description as a whole is probably not influenced by an actual picture of the event; rather, it is a pastiche made up from pictures with which Dio enfolds the story of an embarrassing setback. In this respect, his technique is one that will have been employed by Herodian in the same case, but with some very different results.

Herodian's Vision of War

Herodian's historiographic personality is that of the outsider. He says nothing directly about himself, and it is easy to overinterpret his statement that tax collectors under Maximian were not as rapacious as those of later times.[15] He was privy to the counsel of no one and presents the Romans to his audience as if they are a people about which he has had to learn (which is surely one actually believable thing about his persona). While Dio presents himself as the conscience of the senatorial class, Herodian presents himself as a man who can derive significance from the observable and obvious.[16] He tells people what they may see for themselves, but he provides the context they may lack. His use of paintings and other battle monuments offers his readers a direct confrontation between the verbal and visual record of events.

Although Herodian has earned a fair measure of the scorn he received in earlier generations of scholarship, simple rejection of what he has to say is unjustified.[17] He is very uneven. On the positive side, he gives more good

15. For the notion that Herodian was a freedman from western Asia Minor, see Alföldy 1971: 263–69 (= Alföldy 1989: 227–33), noting especially that Herodian has a very solid knowledge of Rome's topography, which suggests that he lived there. Kemezis (2014: 304–8) shows how anonymity was a critical aspect of Herodian's authorial persona. H. Sidebottom's view that Herodian represents the view of the elite of the eastern empire is not thereby rendered impossible but is insufficiently nuanced to do credit to the complex notion that a long-term resident of Rome whose social standing depended on his connection with the imperial court saw himself as the voice of the provincial elite (Sidebottom 1998: 2822–26). For a sensible summary, see De Blois 2003: 148–51, pointing out that Herodian is, like Dio, a strong advocate of a monarchical system (150–51). See also the subtle discussion in Kemezis 2014: 265–72.

16. For this view of Dio, see Kemezis 2012: 413–14.

17. The crucial positive discussion of Herodian's abilities, especially his ability to properly record generally available material, is Bowersock 1975: 229–36. The issue of Herodian's sources is complex and is complicated by the view that he must have used Dio's history. For the extreme version of that view, see Kolb 1972: 159–62, summarizing the argument, which is essentially that Herodian is the funnel for Dio's views into the Latin tradition; Sidebottom (1998: 2780–92), who argues that Herodian knew Dio's work but that it was

detail than Dio about, for instance, Elagabalus (god and man) at Rome. But Herodian is also differently observant in his narrative of Severus' war with Niger. Dio's version conflates two battles—it does seem that there were two battles—so that the decisive encounter is at a place called Issus near the so-called gates, a place he appears to have made up. Conversely, although Herodian shares a number of elements with Dio, Herodian has two battles—one in the mountains, the other at Issus. He shares with Dio the story of the decisive storm, of which there was presumably but one in the original tale (miracles being, by definition, rare events).[18] In describing the battle of Lyons, Herodian and Dio seem to be following the same account with roughly similar accuracy: Severus only wins the battle when Laetus is able to intervene. The story of the Parthian expedition is another matter. Here, despite the reference to the pictures that Herodian says Severus had distributed of the campaign, Herodian is plainly not describing a picture.[19] Like Dio, he is using a pastiche of pictorial elements and showing such ignorance of geography as to exclude the possibility that he himself could have come from the easternmost parts of the empire. According to Herodian, Severus' army proceeds from Adiabene to Arabia Felix and thence to Hatra, after which it floats downstream to capture Ctesiphon, none of which is possible (see fig. 13.1). Still he has the image of a big walled city, soldiers attacking a city in various ways, and archers defending the walls, which does look like it is inspired by images such as those on Severus' arch.[20] Between his account and Dio's, we are perhaps left with the further conclusion that while an attack on Hatra was mentioned in some sort of public way, details of its capture were never released (for the obvious reason that it was never captured). Failure was perhaps even more interesting than success, and if one was to believe that the elements of imperial art offered the building blocks on which to construct the picture of a campaign, it would be to the well-known elements that an author looking to play up such a failure could turn.

In the post-Severan sections of his book, Herodian makes use of pictorial

not his chief source, makes a very good case that Herodian had no need of Dio whatsoever, but he offers a very weak case for any sort of direct reference (2780–82). For the (correct) view that there was no direct contact, see Rubin 1980: 130–31.

18. Dio 74.7.1 (on the location), 6–7 (on the storm); Herod. 3.3.1–2 (on the first battle), 3.4.2–3 (on the location), 3.4.4–9 (for the battle). On the propagandistic elements, see Rubin 1980: 66–68 (on Dio), 118–20 (on Herodian).

19. For Herodian and imperial art, see Picard 1962: 13; Brilliant 1967: 172–4; Rubin 1975: 428–30.

20. Herod. 3.9.3–11.

elements in two other significant locations, accounts of Caracalla's murder and Maximinus' German war. In the case of Caracalla's death, the narrative is filled with specific visual elements. Dio, whose complete text is preserved at this point, tells us merely that when Caracalla had dismounted to relieve himself, the assassin Martialis approached with a small dagger and killed him. Martialis is then killed by one of Caracalla's guards (this guardsman was himself later killed by Martialis' employers). In Herodian, the emperor, suffering from a stomach ailment, withdraws with a single retainer; everyone else turns away out of respect for the emperor's dignity; Martialis approaches, pretending that the emperor had summoned him with a nod, and kills him while he is pulling down his clothes. The fatal blow strikes Caracalla near the shoulder. The next scene shows Macrinus weeping over the body, then the funeral.[21] There is a lot here not to like if one is trying to write the political history of the period, but Herodian, who was plainly in Rome at this point, was in no position to learn the specific details of a high-level coup d'état, and he does not seem to have been the least bit interested in reading histories by people like Dio or collective biographies by people like Marius Maximus (the *Historia Augusta*'s life of Caracalla, deriving from Marius, gives many of the same details). Details of Macrinus' role in the murder would have been made public after Macrinus' death. Herodian's refusal to adjust his narrative accordingly is perhaps a statement of what he thought about this "new information."

In the case of Maximinus, Herodian says that the emperor, who could not be bothered to come to Rome in person, sent paintings of his battles in Germany, which were set up outside the Curia in Rome. Herodian's description of the campaigns focuses on four tableaux: the crossing of a river (by this point, presumably de rigueur for depictions of imperial campaigns in the north), different troop types, the destruction of German villages and fields, and the bravery of the emperor (especially in a battle in a swamp).[22] Perhaps most striking here is the absence of any discussion of the ballistae that we now know to have been employed with considerable vigor in Maximinus' army.[23]

The contrast in the handling of Maximinus' German campaigns, with the description of his siege of Aquileia, might, at first glance, be striking in quantity of detail, some of which seems actually to be true. For instance, local detail about the planting of vines among groves of trees is accurate, and

21. Herod. 4.13.3–8, with Dio 78.5.3–6; HA *V. Car.* 6.6–7.

22. Herod. 7.2.1–8; the pictorial aspect is discussed in Whittaker 1969–70: 167 n. 1.

23. Pöppelmann, Deppmeyer, and Steinmetz 2013: 272–84, 368–74.

there is a nearly accurate reference to the local cult of Belinus. There are also some sentiments that might well have been lifted straight from a published account of the victory.[24] No one, so we are told, was so young or old that they could not play a useful role in the defense of the fatherland, and the discussion of Belinus' support for the city's defenders, which included the story that Maximinus' soldiers claimed to witness epiphanies of the god, is held believable since it is unusual. As the siege goes on, the besiegers even become besieged: supplies run short, while the defenders are especially good with fiery projectiles.[25]

Perhaps most revealing are the accounts that Dio and Herodian provide of Macrinus' battle against the Parthians. For Herodian, the battle opened with a disorderly attack on the ordered Roman lines; on the wings were the light infantry and the Moorish cavalry, who appear to have fascinated him. The Persian arrow storm caused the Romans heavy casualties, as did the attack from the Persians' heavy cavalry (including some soldiers on camels). When the Romans had taken all the casualties they could stand, they withdrew, dropping caltrops behind them, which disabled their enemy's mounts. Eastern barbarians, Herodian reminds his audience, fight bravely when mounted but surrender when dismounted. The battle lasted two days in this fashion. On the third day, the Parthians made use of their vastly superior numbers to try and encircle the Romans, who responded by extending their line. There was great slaughter on the field (especially of camels). At the end of the day, Macrinus realized that the only reason the Persians were fighting so hard was that they believed they were fighting Caracalla. When the Persian king Artabanus learned from Macrinus that Caracalla was dead, he was happy enough to make peace and go home, knowing that Caracalla, the violator of treaties, had met a just end.[26]

For Dio, Artabanus is also very mad, but the battle, fought at Nisibis, begins quite differently, after a fight for control of a water hole. The Persians nearly take the Roman camp, being driven off only by armor bearers and baggage carriers. At this point, there is a lacuna, though we do get reference to a night. At the end of the lacuna, Macrinus appears to have run away, an event that leaves his troops dejected (and foreshadows his conduct with Elagabalus). For Dio, the important point is that Macrinus is a lousy soldier,

24. For Beles/Belinus, see Herod. 8.3.8–9, with *ILS* 4867–74; Whittaker 1969–70: ad loc. For the vines, see Herod. 8.4.5, with Strabo 5.1.8; Whittaker 1969–70 ad loc.

25. For defense of the fatherland, see Herod. 8.4.7; for the besiegers becoming besieged, see Herod. 8.5.5, with discussion in Stein 1957: 139.

26. Herod. 4.15.

and the narrative is clearly intended to bring this out—how else could one explain his failure against Elagabalus?[27] Neither Dio nor Herodian appears to have had access to an official account, which is perhaps a sign that things really did not go all that well. If there was no victory, there was really no need for Macrinus to talk about what happened.

Taken together, Dio and Herodian reveal considerable range in the construction of battle narratives. In some cases, it appears that some sort of imperial bulletin could be rewritten to suit the author's purposes, a process not all that dissimilar from Dio's rewriting of the battle of Pharsalus to make a point he thought important (that good Romans did not like killing each other). It seems that both authors were willing to incorporate elements from visual media elsewhere in their narratives—either by describing an actual monument (which seems to be the case with their treatments of the battle of Issus) or by using pastiches of themes from imperial art to fill in gaps in their information. Each technique could resonate with audiences exposed to actual war from a distance. These accounts are a literary equivalent of depictions on articles made for domestic consumption that made it possible to bring home scenes based on public art—as in the case of the Boscoreale cups—or to recollect great moments on the stage or amphitheater.[28] The result is the domestication of the distant, making it comprehensible, which appears to have been a cause that Dio and Herodian regarded as more important than attempting to render such events with literal accuracy—they are interested in showing readers the way they think the world works, and appeal to stock scenes and themes is part of the process.[29] Dio noted that the transition from republic to monarchy had made it impossible to find out what was actually happening at any distance from where one lived.[30] Under such circumstances, the verbal theatricality of these historians' narratives allows readers to encounter a kind of imitation truth—just the sort of truth they would encounter when going to the theater.

Dexippus and Warfare

War had a different meaning for Publius Herennius Dexippus. Now that it has been shown, beyond any reasonable doubt, that Dexippus was the

27. Dio 78.6.5–8.

28. Kuttner 1995: 199–206 and passim. See Rowell 1958, on gladiatorial souvenirs.

29. On formulaic aspects of Herodian's narrative, see Sidebottom 1998: 2815–17.

30. Dio 53.19.

speaker of the speech that he wrote for the leader of the Athenians after the Herulians had captured their city in 268, it is possible to say that, unlike Dio or Herodian, he had actually seen a battle.[31] For Dexippus, war involved the joint effort of imperial government and local communities to resist the forces of barbarism. He himself drew attention to the fact that a Roman fleet was in the offing, as he was rallying the Athenians after the Herulian raiders had occupied their city, evidently through a surprise attack.[32] A recently published Dexippan passage, from a palimpsest of a twelfth-century Antiochene religious text, gives us a portion of a speech that a Roman governor named Marianus gave to Greeks assembled at Thermopylae to resist a Gothic invasion (the date of which might be around either 253 or 259). Marianus reminds his men, many of them recently drawn from civilian life and armed with the most rudimentary of weapons, of the glories that Greeks had won in the past on the very spot. Among them was the triumph over "the dynast from Asia" Antiochus III.[33] Other surviving quotations from the history of Dexippus include three siege narratives, two long accounts of Aurelian's dealing with tribes he had defeated (in the west), and the enormously long letter Dexippus invented as correspondence between Decius and the city of Philoppopolis—evidently intended to show that Decius did not know his business, as Decius denies a role to local forces in defense of

31. For Dexippus' Athenian background, see Martin 2006: 14–41; Mecella 2013: 1–14. For the issue of Dexippus' role at the time of the Herulian attack, see esp. Mecella 2006, along with Martin 2006: 37–40, 185–87.

32. There are now four numbering systems for the fragments of Dexippus, that of Müller 1849 (a work that still repays attention), Jacoby's in *FGrH* (retained by MacInerney in the *Brills' New Jacoby* edition), and the systems in Martin 2006 and Mecella 2013. Unless indicated otherwise, my citations give Mecella's fragment number first, followed by Martin's, Jacoby's, and Müller's—in this case, fr. 31/25/28a/21.

33. Martin and Gusková 2014a: 107–9 and now Mallin and Davenport 2015: 205–6. In my view, the invasion under discussion here is that mentioned in Sync. *Chron.* p. 318c, which I take as being linked in time to Valerian's capture, as the passage reads, οἱ δὲ Σκύθοι μετὰ πολλῶν λαφύρων ἐς τὰ ἴδια ἦλθον. ἐπὶ τούτοις Σαπώρης ὁ τῶν Περῶν βασιλεὺς καταδραμὼν Συρίην ἦλθεν. . . . κτλ. For this reason I do not find the argument in Mallin and Davenport 2015: 215–20 that this fragment deals with an invasion in 262 compelling; it is one thing to regard Syncellus as slipshod (he is), it is another to suggest that he gets things out of order (which he does not); while I agree that Marianus and Marcianus are, as they suggest, two different people (210–12) and that there may be good reason not to accept the standard emendation of HA *Gall.* 6.1, but HA *Gall.* 5 offers a summary of the disasters of the reign (note, e.g., reference to Aureolus at HA *Gall.* 5.6), which means that this reference cannot be attached to the consulship of Gallienus and Faustianus.

their homeland.[34] Without the evidence of Dexippus' own speech, it would be very difficult, despite Dexippus' actual experience of battle, to maintain that his contact with battle was anything but a vicarious experience channeled through the text of Thucydides.

There are three extant Dexippan battles, all sieges—two in 251, the third probably in 269. In the first, that of Marcianopolis, the barbarians arrive and gather stones from around the city to use as projectiles. The people of Marcianopolis are advised by Maximus, a man of philosophic inclination as well as a descendent of ancient Thracian kings, that they should endure any initial bombardment from their attackers without responding.[35] The barbarians duly launch an intense bombardment—a virtual hailstorm of missiles—to no effect. They then withdraw for a few days, but when they attack again, more carelessly than before, the Marcianopolitanians, following Maximus' advice, respond, doing significant damage and discouraging the barbarians, who withdraw—or at least we think they do. It is quite possible that the excerptor who preserves this extract left out the next phase, as we now know that he did in the case of the second siege, that of Philippopolis. The end of the siege of Marcianopolis was apparently not quite so pleasant as it seems from Dexippus' account, for we are elsewhere told that the barbarians received a substantial payment from the city before finally leaving.[36] The siege of Philippopolis, the longest surviving siege, also ends well in the surviving excerpt but ended very badly in fact. Another newly discovered passage reveals that the barbarians did not withdraw far from the city and very soon found that there were traitors willing to betray the place. The fragment breaks off as the "Skythian" leader, Cniva, is sending men to

34. Dexippus fr. 34/28/6/24 (Aurelian and the Juthungi); 36/30/7/24 (Aurelian and the Vandals); 29/23/26/19 (letter of Decius). On the letter of Decius see also Davenport and Mallin 2013.

35. For the date, see Potter 2014: 242; for doubts and other options, Mecella 2013: 315–16. For the identity of Maximus, see Mecella 2006: 246–49.

36. Jordanes *Get.* 92. It is not impossible that section 93, describing the city's particular charms and the connection with Trajan, is based on Dexippus; section 101 picks up from the narrative abandoned for a digression on the origins of the Visigoths and Ostrogoths, which cannot be earlier than the late fifth century (at which point there was a group self-identifying as Ostrogothic). On these issues, see esp. Heather 1989; Goffart 2006: 56–72. The appearance of Cniva in the new fragment should confirm that the Cniva sections of Jordanes have their origin in the *Skythika*. Barbarian chieftains are very rarely named in classical sources, and given that Jordanes is the source of Dexippus fr. 35/29/30/25, economy of hypothesis dictates that his narrative is behind the narrative involving the campaign of 251; no other extant source names Cniva.

negotiate with these traitors.[37] He promises to reward them in "darics," presumably because that is what Dexippus decided barbarians should use (in a related fragment, he uses another archaism, *harmost*, to describe the Roman governor).[38] The siege itself is a pastiche of moments largely borrowed from Thucydides' account of the siege of Plataea and attributes remarkable skill in building advanced siege machinery to the "Skythians." With the aid of the recently published fragment, which would suggest very strongly that Dexippus went on to describe the city's sack, we can now see that the choice of Plataea was even more deliberate than had previously been thought, for both cities would fall, as would the city of Naissus when Attila attacked it much later, an event Priscus described with ample Thucydidean detail. From these references, we may see that the siege of Plataea was adapted not simply because it was a siege but, rather, because it was a successful siege.[39] In the final Dexippan siege narrative, that of Side, the barbarians once again show up and find a well-prepared city waiting for them. When their elaborate siege machines are foiled by the defenders' countermeasures, they leave. The story of the attack on Side, stressing (as was also true in the case of Marcianapolis) the preparation of the defenders, contrasts with what we can see the story to have been at Athens, which the Herulians appear to have taken by surprise.[40]

Dexippus was not lacking in subtlety. The vastly long letter that he provides from Decius to the people of Philoppopolis undercuts itself repeatedly. Decius tells the people of the city that they should not seek to fight the invaders in the field, because he is afraid that they will rebel against him if they win. The real problem that the people faced—as Dexippus' original audience knew—was that once Decius failed to relieve the city (the "Skythians" destroyed his army), it was betrayed from within, and the governor himself appears to have played a significant role in the act of betrayal.[41] The

37. See Grusková 2010: 39–40. See also Grusková 2012; Dexippus fr. 14 (Mecella); Martin and Gusková 2014b: 737.

38. For the darics, see Dexippus fr. 14 Mecella; for the *harmost*, fr. 29.2/23.2/26.2 (not read by Müller).

39. See Stein 1957: 61, noting that the allusions to Thucydides are far more prevalent in this fragment than in the other two siege narratives. See also Blockley 1972; Thompson 1945; Blockley 1981: 54.

40. Dexippus fr. 28.1–2/22.1–2/25.1–2/18.1–3 (Marcianopolis); 33.1/27.1/29.1/23.1 (Side); 31.5/25.5/28a.5/21 (Athens).

41. Bleckmann1992: 161–67 reviews the sources for these events; see also Potter 2014: 242. See Martin and Gusková 2014b and Gusková and Martin 2014 for new fragments relating to the fall of Philippopolis and the battle in which Decius was defeated before the

negotiations between Aurelian and the defeated tribes in the *Skythika*'s last surviving fragments serve to incorporate the Balkan emperor within the cultural world of Dexippus' audience, while simultaneously seeming to reflect Aurelian's message of the empire's renewal.[42] The siege narratives are similarly pointed. Dexippus had played a role in some sort of successful military action against the Herulians at Athens yet did not seek to provide accounts that were more literally correct, which suggests that he knew that no one who had participated in a battle was in a very good position to describe more than a small part of it. His references to Thucydides are not direct efforts at copying but, rather, references that assert a common cultural heritage with his predecessor, just as are his other odd archaisms (e.g., Cniva's darics or the Roman *harmost*). Dexippus' battle narratives eschew the visual elements of Herodian (a near contemporary) and Dio to make a more specific point: that the current struggle was part of the grand narrative of human history that set civilization at odds with barbarism. This is not a history that stresses the war simply between Greeks and barbarians; the incorporation of Aurelian's victories over tribes that were invading Italy shows that Dexippus' vision included the imperial authorities, when functional, and should be seen as part of a struggle to preserve a world built on shared cultural values.[43]

The literary purpose of Dexippus' battle description, quite different from the more confident pastiches of imperial propaganda or political theory produced by Dio and Herodian, resonate outside the Greek imperial tradition, with a historian working in a very different time and place. Given that Dexippus' gaze appears to be shaped entirely within the Greek tradition, there is no need to postulate that he had ever read or even ever heard of Cornelius Tacitus. The point of contact between the two is, rather, a shared interest in how battle descriptions might serve the purpose of informing an audience of the historian's broader intellectual purpose. Dexippus does so by withdrawing his descriptions from the visual realm. Tacitus will, in several notable cases, place his descriptions in explicitly visual contexts, as a way of inviting

---

battle at Abrittus, as well as for important new information on the identity of the Gothic leaders (including Ostrogotha, on whom see Gusková and Martin 2014: 40–42) and on command structure.

42. Potter 2011: 336; Martin 2006: 203–9. For an analysis that is somewhat different but correctly stresses the importance of Aurelian's victories being in the west, see Mecella 2013: 96–112. The discussion of authorial perspective is generally shaped by Millar 1969 (= Millar 2004: 265–97); the point is also made in Mallin and Davenport 2015: 222.

43. Mecella 2013: 105; see also the speech of the Roman governor Marianus cited in n. 33 above.

the people in his audience to consider who they are. In so doing, he is willing to address the possibility that in the eyes of civilians, war might not be so much a horror as an entertainment.

Tacitus' Visions of Warfare

The sense of tradition that variously manifests itself in the three Greek historians of the third century is evident in Lucian's earlier critique of the historians' art. Historians, as Lucian makes clear, are supposed to be both stylish and able to tell fact from fiction. The persona of the historian in the Greek tradition remained that of a person who could cast independent judgment on events through the construction of a narrative. The addition of new media to the historiographic palette might not have enhanced literal accuracy, but it did enable historians to continue in the development of a culturally relevant product. In an age where spectacle—especially as performed in the imperial capital—was a crucial medium for the assertion of core cultural values, the introduction of spectacular or theatrical elements into the rhetoric of descriptive narrative was a statement of relevance. For a provincial writer such as Dexippus, the vast Roman spectacle of imperial power was distant; he could use an older rhetoric more closely attuned to his own and his audiences' aesthetic senses. The same had not been true of historical writing in Latin, which, appears to have become so intertwined with panegyric as to be irrelevant by the third century. A critic of Dio's age—most obviously Marius Maximus—would write imperial biography rather than narrative history. In the work of the last great narrative historian of the tradition, it is possible to see a tendency to incorporate the meaning of spectacle into historical idiom. Tacitus' explorations of spectacular violence reflect a consciousness of the generation of theoretical realities through public display, as well as an ability to adapt theatrical elements that had long been a feature of the Roman historiographic tradition. However, unlike Livy, who used such elements to bring his readers into the story, Tacitus tended to use the observation of others viewing spectacle as a way of distancing his audience from public entertainment culture.[44] Whatever role actual theater had in shaping the Romans concept of their early history (a role likely unknown and unknowable by Tacitus' time), Tacitus commented on the phenomena absorbed by Herodian and Dio. He was not ready to accept the visual as

44. For the visual in Livy, see the works cited in n. 1 above.

truthful, though he was willing to admit that historians needed to address the theatricality of the world in which they lived.

Early in his career as a historian, Tacitus drew explicit connections between war, drama, and historical accuracy. Such connections are made during his discussion of events in AD 69, with the clearest linkage between war and spectacle occurring as Vespasian's army is fighting its way into Rome during December of that year.

> The population of the city was present as an audience, as at a public entertainment [*ludicro certamine*], favoring the one side, then the other, with applause and cheering. As often as one side or the other turned in flight, if they were escaping, hidden in shops or some house, demanding that they be taken out and killed, the people took over the bulk of the spoils, for the soldiers, turned to fighting and slaughter, left the plunder to the crowd.[45]

Tacitus' terminology here is vague—*ludicrum* is Tacitus' word for a public spectacle of any sort. The generalization of the audience's behavior continues as Tacitus distinguishes the current events from battle that had happened in the streets before.

> Then there was no less cruelty, but now inhumane security and pleasures, only interrupted for the briefest of times, added joy just as on holidays: they cheered and enjoyed themselves with no care for either side, happy in public distress.[46]

45. Tac. *Hist.* 3.83.1: *Aderat pugnantibus spectator populus ut que in ludicro certamine, hos, rursus illos clamore et plausu fovebat.* For Tacitus' use of *ludicrum*, cf. *Ann.* 1.54.2: *ludos Augustales tunc primum coeptos turbavit discordia ex certamine histrionum. indulserat ei ludicro Augustus, dum Maecenati obtemperat effuso in amorem Bathylli; neque ipse abhorrebat talibus studiis, et civile rebatur misceri voluptatibus vulgi*; 12.41.2: *et ludicro circensium, quod adquirendis vulgi studiis edebatur, Britannicus in praetexta, Nero triumphali veste travecti sunt: spectaret populus hunc decore imperatorio, illum puerili habitu, ac perinde fortunam utriusque praesumeret*; 16.21.2: *quod que Iuvenalium ludicro parum [et] spectabilem operam praebuerat; ea que offensio altius penetrabat, quia idem Thrasea Patavi, unde ortus erat, ludis cetastis a Troiano Antenore institutis habitu tragico cecinerat*; *Hist.* 2.68.1: *Et <victas> quidem partes modeste distraxerat: apud victores orta seditio, ludicro initio, <ni> numerus caesorum invidiam Vitellio auxisset*; 3.62.2: *Et <victas> quidem partes modeste distraxerat: apud victores orta seditio, ludicro initio, <ni> numerus caesorum invidiam Vitellio auxisset.*

46. Tac. *Hist.* 3.83.3: *nec tunc minus crudelitatis: nunc inhumana securitas et ne minimo quidem temporis voluptates intermissae: velut festis diebus id quoque gaudium accederet, exultabant, fruebantur, nulla partium cura, malis publicis laeti.*

Not only here does Tacitus remark on the way the people of whom he wrote could treat war and disaster as a form of spectator sport or tourist attraction. He reports that when Germanicus was at the gulf of Actium, "made famous by victory," the general had "approached victory monuments dedicated by Augustus and the camp of Antony with memory of his own ancestors."[47] Previously, Tacitus—quite probably following an earlier account, as battlefield visits for emotional effect were hardly new in his lifetime—had used Germanicus' visit to the sight of Varus' defeat as a vehicle for describing the disaster itself.[48] Germanicus saw not only the whitening bones of the dead but the original camp, then the final fortifications that had been broken down by the enemy, the signs of rout on the field, and the sites where tribunes and senior centurions had been sacrificed. Survivors showed him where legates had died, where eagles had been snatched, and where Varus suffered his first wound and where he had taken his own life. Compressed in a few lines, then, is the vision of a battle fought over a wide area and many days. Somewhat differently, in AD 69, Vitellius would visit the battlefield at Bedriacum to see the traces "of the recent victory with his eyes." Here, unlike in Teutoberger, where age had cleansed the field, there were swelling bodies, and the ground was soaked with blood, as the people of Cremona offered sacrifice along the way, while Valens and Caecina pointed out the spots where the battle had turned. Officers sung their own praises; regular soldiers shouted with joy when they recognized important places in the fight, and they gazed on the piles of the slain and heaps of arms. Vitellius expressed no surprise or shock at the sight of so many bodies deprived of proper burial; he could not foresee how similar would be his own fate. There is some irony, too, in the delight that Vitellius' soldiers took in visiting the spot where Galba had been murdered. These people met history quite literally on the spot.[49]

47. Tac. *Ann.* 2.53.2.

48. Tac. *Ann.* 1.61.1–62.2. For discussion of the significance for Tacitus, see O'Gorman 2000: 49–56. Suet. *Cal.* 3.2 shows that a description of Germanicus' actions at the site appeared in another source, despite Woodman (1979: 152 = 1998: 80), who simply obfuscates an issue otherwise difficult for his argument. For Tacitus and his sources, see Devillers 2003. Rutland (1987: 158 n. 15) rightly calls attention to *cupido invasit Caesarem* as the motivation for the visit (the language of the *pothos* theme in Alexander historians). For an earlier battlefield visitation, see Sall. *Cat.* 61.8, with Marincola 2003: 313; note also Tac. *Hist.* 3.51, on conventional aspects of battle description (killings of close kin), one of which occurs at *Hist.* 3.25 (see also Ash 1999: 64).

49. For Vitellius' visit, see Tac. *Hist.* 2.70. Note, though, that Tacitus appears to have toned things down, omitting a line that Dio (65.1.3) picked up about Vitellius' attendance

In the cases of Vitellius' victory at Bedriacum and the visits to the place where Galba died, Tacitus has a point to make about the different ways in which people might understand what they were seeing. With Vitellius' exploration of the past, Tacitus looks to the future, underscoring the lack of decency on Vitellius' side; whereas Germanicus might feel emotion at the sight of old disasters, Vitellius cannot display any appropriate emotion. Vitellius' response was that of the crowd watching the destruction of his last supporters in the streets of Rome. The point here is not simply to suggest that what goes around comes around (though there is an element of this) but also to invite readers to think about what spectacle teaches the astute viewer. Germanicus' introspection offers an important clue. Although the Tacitean Germanicus is a subtly drawn character not lacking in fault, his behavior at Teutoberger and Actium models that of the ideal aristocrat who knows to look behind the surface to discern the meaning of spectacle.[50] Tacitus' contemporary, Juvenal, took that point as a theme in *Satire* 10, alluding to Tacitus' own image of a man deluded by overly optimistic assessment of his own power. The scholiast on line 63 of *Satire* 10 directs our attention, accidentally or otherwise, to Juvenal's probable intertext in his description of Sejanus' career, ending with details drawn from Tacitus' description of Sejanus' daughter's execution.[51] Those who do not understand and who look at the surface—the common folk who once ruled the world—are dominated by the externals of spectacle and pass over their influence through addiction to spectacle and free food. At the very opening of the *Annals*, while describing Augustus' funeral, Tacitus drew attention to the significance of spectacle, noting that unlike Caesar, Augustus, after all his years in power, had a mili-

at a gladiatorial exhibition, as if the piles of dead bodies were not enough; cf. also Suet. *Vit.* 10.3 on Vitellius' statement that nothing smells better than a dead citizen. On the theme of unburied bodies in the *Historiae*, see Ash 1999: 61; see also Tac. *Hist.* 2.88.3, with Haynes 2003: 104.

50. Ross1973 remains fundamental. See also Rutland 1987; Pelling 1993.

51. Schol. ad Juv. 10.63: *Seianus fuit Tiberio usque adeo carus amicus, ut nihil esset quod ei a Tiberio petenti negaretur; usque adeo <autem ingratus, ut> etiam de eo cogitaverit necem, ut dispositis coniurationis sociis occiso Tiberio ipse regnaret. Cum hoc cognovisset Tiberius, super eius nomine epistolam ad senatum misit, et sic per consules damnatus est cum omni progenie sua usque adeo, ut filiam eius viginem iubaret senatus a carnifice stuprari et sic occidit, ut iure vdeatur fuisse occisa.* Cf. Tac. *Ann.* 5.9.2: *tradunt temporis eius auctores, quia triumvirali supplicio adfici virginem inauditum habebatur, a carnifice laqueum iuxtra compressam*; Dio 58.11.5. Dio 58.10.6–8 gives the leading role to Memmius Regulus (one of the consuls; the other, Fulcinius Trio, was thought to be a partisan of Sejanus, on which see Tac. *Ann.* 6.38.2–3). For Juvenal's reading of Tacitus, see Keane 2012: 421–23.

tary escort to his funeral pyre. Was this because his power was founded on the army or simply because there was some reason to think people hated him?[52] In modeling the ideal response to spectacle, Tacitus simply raises a question about what it all means.

Vitellius' battlefield visit is not just a (somewhat heavy-handed) thematic moment; it is also a methodological exposition. The tradition of battle description was one that Tacitus generally deplored. Although he would follow a tradition if he wished—for instance, noting the eagles flying off in the direction of the forest before the battle of Idistaviso—he is elsewhere more openly suspicious. He was willing to believe that the victory over Boudicca was on a par with the greatest victories of the past (his father-in-law was there), but he questioned whether eighty thousand people were killed. There were those who said so,[53] but Tacitus need not avow belief. Mass murder on that scale was the stuff of the epic battle description. He knew better than to take such things on faith. Vitellius' visit to the battlefield tracks the original battle narrative in significant detail, which is significant because participants would later deny that they knew what actually happened.[54] Even without the denials, that would have been hard to know without going over the scene again; Tacitus is clear on this point in his account of the Second Bedriacum, where soldiers are locked in their private conflicts, unable to see the bigger picture.[55] Only the winning general could see that and, as did Caesar, create the image of his own foresight to guide his forces to the inevitable victory.[56] There was no place in Caesarian narrative style for the workings of chance and luck—the very factors that were crucial in both of the great battles of AD 69. The story of Vitellius' autopsy reminded Tacitus' readers that some things could be known about what happened despite deliberate obfuscation in some quarters, given that some wished to cloud the truth in ways that were totally self-serving.

Tacitus was not the most unmilitary of historians, but he is among the most implicitly critical of the tropes with which the superstructure of military history tended to be constructed.[57] The avoidance of rhetorical battle descriptions is part of his greater plan. So he says in book 4. Big battles

52. Tac. *Ann.* 1.8.6.

53. Tac. *Ann.* 2.7.2 (eagles at Idistaviso), 14.37.2 (Boudicca).

54. Plut. *Otho* 14, with Syme 1958: 172; see also Tac. *Hist.* 2.60.

55. Tac. *Hist.* 3.16–25, with Ash 1999:61–64.

56. Goldsworthy 1998.

57. Syme 1958:157.

are the thing of bygone days.[58] To repeat the style is to surrender judgment to tradition or the victor's authorized edition. On this point at least, Tacitus, Dio, and Herodian might agree. More generally, however, in rhetorical theory, *historia* and *dramatikê* were meant to describe quite distinct forms of mimesis—to distinguish a narrative that was about things that happened from a narrative that was like things that happened—though the dividing line between the two was sufficiently imprecise that it lent tension to the discourse on historiographic accuracy.[59] For historians of the empire, familiar though they were with the theory, the distinction was not unproblematic, for to practice *historia*, the historian had to engage with realities generated through other art forms. *Historia* needed to be able to encompass *dramatikê*, not avoid it, and the dividing line between the two was individually determined as a spot on the continuum of representational practice, rather than some metaphoric wall of Hadrian dividing the two into different realms.

Bibliography

Alföldy, G. 1971. "Herodians Person." *Ancient Society* 2: 204–33.

Alföldy, G. 1989. *Die Krise des Römischen Reiches: Geschichte, Geschichtsschreibung und Geschichtsbetrachtung.* Stuttgart.

Ameling, W. 1997. "Griechische Intellektuelle und das Imperium Romanum: Das Beispeil Cassius Dio." *ANRW* 34.3: 2472–96.

Ash, R. 1999. *Ordering Anarchy: Armies and Leaders in Tacitus' "Histories."* Ann Arbor.

Birley, A. 1988. *Septimius Severus: The African Emperor.* London.

Bleckmann, B. 1992. *Die Reichskrise des III. Jahrhunderts in der spätantiken und byzantinischen Geschichtsschreibung: Untersuchungen zu den nachdionischen Quellen der Chronik des Johannes Zonaras.* Munich.

Blockley R. 1972. "Dexippus and Priscus and the Thucydidean Account of the Siege of Plataea." *Phoenix* 26: 18–27.

Blockley, R. 1981. *The Fragmentary Classicizing Historians of Late Antiquity.* Vol. 1. Trowbridge.

Bowersock, G. 1975. "Herodian and Elagabalus." *YCS* 24: 229–36.

Brilliant, R. 1967. *The Arch of Septimius Severus in the Roman Forum.* Rome.

Damon, C. 2003. *Tacitus, "Histories," Book 1.* Cambridge.

Davidson, J. 1991. "The Gaze in Polybius' Histories." *JRS* 81: 10–24.

Davenport, C., and Mallin, C. 2013. "Dexippus' Letter of Decius: Context and Interpretation," *Museum Helveticum* 70: 57–73.

De Blois, L. 2003. "The Perception of Roman Imperial Authority in Herodian's Work." In L. De Blois, P. Erdkamp, O. Hekster, G. de Kleijn, and S. Mols, eds., *The Repre-*

58. Tac. *Ann.* 4.32.

59. Potter 2003: 12–18.

sentation and Perception of Roman Imperial Power: Proceedings of the Third Workshop of the International Network Impact of Empire (Roman Empire, c. 200 B.C.–A.D. 476), 148–56. Amsterdam.

Devillers, O. 2003. *Tacite et les sources des Annales: Ênquetes sur la méthode historique*. Louvain.

Feldherr, A. 1998. *Spectacle and Society in Livy's History*. Berkeley.

Fornara, C. 1983. *The Nature of History in Ancient Greece and Rome*. Berkeley.

Goffart, W. 2006. *Barbarian Tides: The Migration Age and the Later Roman Empire*. Philadelphia.

Goldsworthy, A. 1998. "'Instinctive Genius': The Depiction of Caesar the General." In K. Welch and A. Powell, eds., *Julius Caesar as Artful Reporter*, 193–219. Swansea.

Gowing, A. 1992. *The Triumviral Narratives of Appian and Cassius Dio*. Ann Arbor.

Greenblatt, S. 2004. *Will in the World: How Shakespeare became Shakespeare*. New York.

Grusková, J. 2010. *Untersuchungen zu den griechischen Palimpsesten der Österreichischen Nationalbibliothek. Codices Historici Codices Philosophici et Philogici Codices Iuridici. Denkschriften der philosophisch-historischen Klasse 401*. Vienna.

Grusková, J. 2012. "Further Steps in Revealing, Editing, and Analysing Important Greek and Byzantine Texts Hidden in Palimpsests." *Zborník Filozofickej Fakuly Univerzity Komenského Rocník XXXIII–XXXIV Graecolatina et Orientalia*, 69–82.

Grusková, J., and G. Martin, 2014. "Neue Textstücke aus den 'Scythica Vindobonensia' zu den Ereignissen mach der Eroberung von Philoppopolis." *Tyche* 29: 29–44.

Haynes, H. 2003. *The History of Make-Believe: Tacitus on Imperial Rome*. Berkeley.

Heather, P. 1989. "Cassiodorus and the Rise of the Amals: Genealogy and the Goths under Hun Domination." *JRS* 79: 103–28.

Jaeger, M. 1997. *Livy's Written Rome*. Ann Arbor.

Keane, C. 2012. "The Historian and the Satirist: Tacitus and Juvenal." In V. Pagán, ed., *A Companion to Tacitus*, 403–28. Oxford.

Kemezis, A. 2012. "Commemoration of the Antonine Aristocracy in Cassius Dio and the *Historia Augusta*." *CQ* 62: 387–414.

Kemezis, A. 2014. *Greek Narratives of the Roman Empire under the Severans: Cassius Dio, Philostratus, and Herodian*. Cambridge,

Kolb, F. 1972. *Literarische Beziehungen zwischen Cassius Dio, Herodian und der Historia Augusta*. Bonn.

Kuttner, A. 1995. *Dynasty and Empire in the Age of Augustus: The Case of the Boscoreale Cups*. Berkeley.

Lintott, A. 1997. "Dio and the History of the Late Roman Republic." *ANRW* 34.3: 2497–2523.

Lusnia, S. 2006. "Battle Imagery and Politics on the Severan Arch in the Roman Forum." In S. Dillon and K. Welch, eds., *Representations of War in Ancient Rome*, 244–71. Cambridge.

Mallin, C., and Davenport, C. 2015. "Dexippus and the Gothic Invasions: Interpreting the new Vienna Fragment (Codex Vindobonensis Hist. gr. 73, ff. 192v–1923r). *JRS* 105: 203–26.

Marincola, J. 2003. "Beyond Pity and Fear: The Emotions of History." *Ancient Society* 33: 285–315.

Martin, G. 2006. *Dexipp von Athen: Edition, Übersetzung und begleitende Studien.* Tübingen.

Martin, G., and Grusková, J. 2014a. "'Dexippus Vindobonensis' (?): Ein neues Handschriftenfragment zum sog. Herulereinfall der Jahre 267/268." *WS* 127: 101–20.

Martin, G., and Grusková, J. 2014b."'Scythica Vindobonensia' by Dexippus: New Fragments on Decius' Gothic Wars." *GRBS* 54: 728–54.

Mecella, L. 2006. "πάντα μὲν ἦν ἄναρχά τε καὶ ἀβοήθητα: Le città dell'Oriente romano e le invasioni barbariche del III secolo d.c." *Mediterraneo Antico: Economie Società Culture* 9: 241–66.

Mecella, L. 2013. *Dexippo di Atene: Testimonianze e frammenti.* Rome.

Millar, F. 1964. *A Study of Cassius Dio.* Oxford.

Millar, F. 1969. "P. Herennius Dexippus: The Greek World and the Third-Century Invasions." *JRS* 59: 12–27.

Millar, F. 2004. *Government, Society, and Culture in the Roman World.* Ed. H. M. Cotton and G. M. Rogers. Chapel Hill.

Müller K. 1849. *Fragmenta Historicorum Graecorum.* Vol. 4. Paris.

O'Gorman, E. 2000. *Irony and Misreading in the "Annals" of Tacitus.* Cambridge.

Pelling, C. 1993. "Tacitus and Germanicus." In T. Luce and A. Woodman, eds., *Tacitus and the Tacitean Tradition*, 59–85. Princeton.

Picard, G. 1962. "Les reliefs de l'arc de Septime Sévère au Forum Romain." *CRAI*, 7–17.

Pöppelmann, H., Deppmeyer, K., and Steinmetz, W.-D., eds. 2013. *Roms vergessener Feldzug: Die Schlacht am Harzhorn.* Stuttgart.

Potter, D. 2003. *Literary Texts and the Roman Historian.* Rev. ed. London.

Potter, D. 2011. "The Greek Historians of Imperial Rome." In A. Feldherr and G. Hardy, eds., *The Oxford History of Historical Writing*, vol. 1, *Beginnings to AD 600*, 316–45. Oxford.

Potter, D. 2014. *The Roman Empire at Bay, AD 180–395.* 2nd ed. London.

Ross, D. 1973. "The Tacitean Germanicus." *YCS* 23: 209–27.

Rowell, H. 1958. "The Gladiator Petraites and the Date of the *Satyricon*." *TAPA* 89: 14–24.

Rubin, Z. 1975. "Dio, Herodian, and Severus' Second Parthian War." *Chiron* 5: 419–41.

Rubin, Z. 1980. *Civil War Propaganda and Historiography.* Brussels.

Rutherford, R. 2007. "Tragedy and History." In J. Marincola, ed., *A Companion to Greek and Roman Historiography*, 504–14. Oxford.

Rutland, L. 1987. "The Tacitean Germanicus: Suggestions for a Re-evaluation." *RhM* 130: 153–64.

Sidebottom, H. 1998. "Herodian's Historical Methods and Understanding of History." *ANRW* 34.4: 2776–2836.

Stein, F. 1957. *Dexippus et Herodianus rerum scriptores quatenus Thucydidem secuti sint.* Bonn.

Syme, R. 1958 *Tacitus.* Oxford.

Thompson, E. 1945. Priscus of Panium, Fragment 1b. *CQ* 39: 92–94.

Walbank, F. 1960. "History and Tragedy." *Historia* 9: 216–34

Walbank, F. 1985. *Selected Papers: Studies in Greek and Roman History and Historiography.* Cambridge.

Whittaker, C. R. 1969–70: *Herodian*. 2 vols. Loeb Classical Library, vols 454–55. Cambridge, MA.

Wiseman, T. P. 2015. *The Roman Audience: Classical Literature and Social History*. Oxford.

Woodman, A. 1979. "Self-Imitation and the Substance of History: Tacitus, *Annals* 1.61–5 and *Histories* 2.70, 5.14–15." In D. West and A. Woodman, eds., *Creative Imitation in Latin Literature*, 143–57. Cambridge.

Woodman, A. 1998. *Tacitus Reviewed*. Oxford.

FOURTEEN

Manipulating Space at the Roman Arena

Garrett G. Fagan

Arena Theatricality

The spectators at a Roman gladiatorial spectacle (*munus gladiatorum*) were confronted with many indicators of the theatrical and artificial nature of what they were witnessing, even if the violence meted out during the event—whether to animals, execution victims, or defeated gladiators—was all too real. The whole show was kicked off by a procession (the *pompa*) across the arena floor, in which the sponsor (*munerarius/editor*) led a parade of the combatants, their gear, and the prizes on offer.[1] Before the fights started, the weapons were publicly inspected, and the gladiators "warmed up."[2] Mock fighters (*paegniarii*) could open the show or amuse the crowd between bouts.[3] Trumpet blasts announced the start of each fight, and music appears to have been playing as the combat progressed.[4] Umpires were present on

1. E.g., Tert. *Spect.* 7.2–3; [Quint.] *Decl.* 9.6; *CIL* IV 3883; *AE* 1947.53. A relief from a tomb outside Pompeii, now in Naples, depicts the opening *pompa*, with local officials leading the way, then attendants holding placards and palm fronds of victory, and the *editor* followed by figures (the gladiators themselves?) carrying helmets and shields; see Jacobelli 2003: 95–97 (fig. 77).

2. Dio 68.3.2; Suet. *Titus* 9.2 (inspection); Cic. *De orat.* 2.235, 316 (warm-up).

3. Suet. *Cal.* 26.5. A *paegniarius* also appears among the arena performers and staff initiated into the cult of Silvanus Aurelianus, see *CIL* VI 631 = *ILS* 5084 = *EAOR* 1.45. See also n. 27 below.

4. [Quint.] *Decl.* 9.6, Petron. *Sat.* 36.6; *CIL* X 4915 = *ILS* 5150, *SgO* 07/05/01. The famous Zliten mosaic includes two fight scenes in which a band is playing (three horns

the sand, equipped with rods to enforce the rules of combat at a safe distance from the action.[5] The performers themselves wore costumes. Huntsmen, who participated in the morning show, donned elaborately embroidered outfits or, in at least one instance attested in a mosaic, stalked their quarry on stilts.[6] Other performers leaped or pole-vaulted over wild animals, rode rodeo on bulls, or interacted with animals in other interesting ways, using special equipment. Alternatively, specially trained animals performed surprising tricks.[7] Executions could be prosaic or highly dramatic, such as the "fatal charades" whereby motifs from mythology informed modes of execution—an "Orpheus" failing to soothe the bear that kills him, an "Attis" castrated.[8]

When the main attraction, the gladiators themselves, took to the sand, they looked like no warriors from any ancient battlefield. Many dozens of gladiator types can be identified from the literary, artistic, and epigraphic sources.[9] The *retiarius* (netter) was unhelmeted and largely unarmored and carried a net, trident, and dagger as offensive weapons. His left (net) arm was padded with a *manica*, and on his leading shoulder sat a device, the *galerus*, that shielded his neck and face as he moved forward in attack. His opponent, the *secutor* (follower), wore a visored helmet, a *manica*, and shin pads and carried a large shield and short stabbing sword. Another gladiator, the *Thraex* (Thracian), wore a wide-brimmed, visored and elaborately plumed helmet, carried a small shield, and wielded a bent sword, while his opponent, the *murmillo* (fish man), wore a similar helmet, decorated with an eponymous fish motif, and carried a large shield and short sword. Both had padding on their legs and sword arm. The extraordinary device wielded by the *scissor*

---

and a water organ); see Aurigemma 1926: 149 (with figs. 87–89). On arena music, see Simpson 2000.

5. On umpires—termed *summa rudis* (supreme stick), *secunda rudis* (second stick), and so on—see Ville 1981: 367–72. See also Carter 2007, 2011. The umpires are shown in many images of gladiatorial fights, dressed in striped tunics and wielding their eponymous sticks.

6. For images of arena huntsmen in fancy tunics and other costumes, see Augenti 2001: 50–52 (nos. 20–21), 54–57 (nos. 23–24). The famous Magerius Mosaic from Smirat in Tunisia (third century CE) shows a hunter on stilts: see Beschouach 1966; Bomgardner 2007.

7. See Cassiod. *Var.* 5.42 and below, for more on animal shows. Note Martial's tame lion (*Ep.* 1.6, 14, 22, 44, 48, 51, 60, 104) and elephants trained to kneel before the emperor (*Spect.* 20, 22) or dance (*Ep.* 1.104).

8. Coleman 1990.

9. For types of gladiators and their equipment, see Junkelmann 2008: 43–128; Ville 1981: 306–11.

(carver) deserves special notice. On his left arm, he wore a cuff that reached to his elbow and ended in a vicious crescent-shaped blade that looked like a cobbler's tool, which appears to have given the performer his Greek name, *arbelas* (cobbler).[10] There were also very dramatic types: the *essedarius* either fought out of a chariot or, more likely, entered the arena in one and then disembarked to fight; the *eques* rode out in horseback and engaged in some lance-play with his opponent before dismounting and fighting on foot. Most gladiatorial armatures protected the extremities—head, arms, legs—while leaving the torso exposed, encouraging aggressive combat while leaving the door open for a killing blow to end the bout. In effect, the armatures constitute a type of costume, instantly recognizable to the knowledgeable spectator. The weapons were specifically fashioned to meet the demands of the spectacle and also designed to generate interesting encounters: the more exposed *retiarius* tried to fend off his opponent with the longer reach of his trident and the threat of his net, while the more armored *secutor* sought to evade these obstacles to bring his short sword to bear.

In addition to their costumes, masks (in the form of visored helmets), and specialized equipment, slave gladiators used stage names that were often descriptive, erotic, or ironic, such as Ferox (Fierce), Pugnax (Fighter), Scorpio (Stinger), Cupido (Lusty), Clemens (Gentle), Murranus (Perfume Boy), or Hilarus (The Joker).[11] Stage names are part and parcel of showmanship, and that gladiators used them is therefore revealing. Freeborn or freed gladiators are usually listed under their regular names, such as M. Attilius, L. Raecius Felix, or P. Ostorius. But even this practice was part of the show, since it advertised their special status as volunteer fighters under contract (*auctorati*).[12] This fact apparently mattered to spectators, as one of the freedmen in Petronius' *Satyricon* (45.4) makes plain: "We're going to have a great show during the three-day festival; no *lanista*-trained troupe, but lots of freedmen." Because they were participating by choice, perhaps the contract fighters were more enthusiastic or more skillful than the unwilling, slave fighters. They put on a good show and, for that reason, were appreciated by the crowd.

Indeed, putting on a good show was a matter of life and death for gladia-

10. See Carter 2001; Ritti and Yilmaz 1998: 469–79.

11. For a list of documented gladiator names, see Junkelmann 2008: 267–68; see also Ville 1981: 306–10. More mundane names are also attested (e.g., Cic. *Tusc.* 4.48), as are gladiators named after gods (e.g., Hermes) or heroes (e.g., Hector or Achilles).

12. For Attilius and Raecius, see *CIL* IV 10236, 10238; for Ostorius, *CIL* IV 3884 = *ILS* 5145. On *auctorati*, see Fagan 2011: 212–13.

tors. If one fell or was injured or disarmed, he would raise a finger to appeal to the games' sponsor, at which point the fighter had lost the bout. Whether the defeated gladiator lived or died depended on a decision based on his performance in the contest. Technically, the sponsor made this decision, but the crowd expressed its views on the matter vocally by shouting "Iugula! Iugula!" (Cut his throat!) or "Missus! Missus!" (Dismissal!) and gesticulating with their thumbs (in a way that remains obscure to us).[13] Since sponsors had spent a lot of money on the spectacle precisely to gain popular favor, it was in their interest to agree with the spectators' judgment, and they made the call accordingly. The combats had rules and regulations, umpires were on hand to see them enforced, and the crowd was knowledgeable about gladiatorial combat moves to the point of being able to assess performances in making their life-or-death judgments. One of Petronius' freedmen (*Sat.* 45.12) complains about a recent disastrous show of cheap and decrepit gladiators in which even the one fighter who showed any spirit fought "by the book" (*ad dictata*). "In short," he continues, "they all had their throats cut afterward, for they'd had shouts of 'Get stuck in' from the large crowd." Tertullian goes further and reports (*Ad Mart.* 1.2) that spectators would shout out combat tips to the fighters as they engaged. Cicero (*Att.* 4.8.2 = SB 79.2) writes to Atticus, "You might write to me about your gladiators [Atticus had contracted some for a show], but only if they acquit themselves well. If not, I'm not interested." Martial (*Ep.* 5.24.7) praises the gladiator Hermes for, among other things, being trained to win without harming, and Nero once staged a gladiatorial show in which no one was killed (Suet. *Nero* 12.1). Notices and comments like this make it clear that arena spectators were there to watch a performance. To be sure, it was a violent, potentially lethal performance, but it was a show, an exhibition. Gladiators and their trainers—often themselves retired gladiators—must have known this and acted accordingly. Cicero says that gladiators sought to please the crowd above all else, while Seneca comments that they were believed to plan out their fights on the sand by subtly indicating to each other where the next blow will fall.[14] Gladiators were, above all else, showmen.

---

13. For the calls, see *CIL* IX 1671 = *EAOR* 3.72 (relief from Beneventum, now lost). For the thumb signal (*pollice verso*), see Juv. 3.36–37; Prudent. *C. Symm.* 2.1099. The gravestone of the Pergamene gladiator Chresteinos, found in Thessaly, may show a hand in the thumbs-up position, although the image is hard to read, see Toynbee 1948: 34. The crowd could also flap handkerchiefs or parts of their clothing (Mart. *Ep.* 12.28.8).

14. Cic. *Tusc.* 2.41 (pleasing the crowd); Sen. *Ep.* 22.1 (choreography). Note also Sen. *Dial.* 1.3.4, where it is considered ignoble by gladiators to win without risk—that is, without putting on a good show.

Moments of showmanship might be identified in arena scenes. In a third-century mosaic from Zliten in Libya, an umpire has to physically restrain a victorious gladiator from delivering a killing blow while an appeal is being decided (fig. 14.1, at left). In the same mosaic, an umpire intercedes his cane between the fighters as the loser appeals, and the winner adopts a quasi-heroic statuesque stance to await the result (fig. 14.2).[15] In recently discovered reliefs from Kibyra in Asia Minor, we see the victor exulting over his defeated opponent (fig. 14.3).[16]

Also revealing are gladiatorial epitaphs such as the following: "Flamma [The Flame], *secutor*, lived thirty years. He fought thirty-four bouts, won twenty-one, drew nine, lost four. Syrian by birth. Delicatus [Pet] made [this tomb] for this worthy comrade in arms."[17] The inclusion of bouts that Flamma lost but from which he earned dismissal on appeal obliquely reflects skill in showmanship and, indeed, expresses a certain pride in it. He had lost but put on a good enough performance to be sent from the arena alive.[18]

Finally, fights began with trumpet blasts, and music may have been playing as the combats progressed or at least at key moments, such as when an appeal was being adjudicated.[19] The music and all of the aforementioned features of gladiatorial spectacles demonstrate that a high degree of theatricality marked the shows. The primary focus of this essay is the most striking element of this aspect of the games, arena stagecraft, particularly the way space was manipulated to meet the requirements of the show.

Manipulating Space

A basic observation is that gladiatorial games took place in their own, dedicated space. The amphitheater was a form of building specifically developed for the requirements of such spectacles. Other venues that could be utilized include theaters, the circus (normally reserved for chariot racing), or sta-

15. Umpires having to restrain a victor from killing his opponent appear in other gladiatorial art; for similar scenes, see, e.g., Augenti 2001: 97 (no. 54), 122–23 (no. 74). It may have been a standard "move" in the show.

16. This, too, is a familiar scene in gladiatorial art; see, e.g., Augenti 2001: 78–79 (no. 42), 96 (no. 54), 98–99 (no. 55), 136–37 (no. 83).

17. *CIL* X 7297 = *ILS* 5113 = *EAOR* 3.70.

18. For more on gladiatorial epitaphs, see Hope 2000.

19. [Quint.] *Decl.* 9.6 (opening trumpet blast). See also fig. 14.2, for an arena band; n. 4 above, for more sources on amphitheatrical music.

Fig. 14.1. Arena mosaic, Zliten, Libya. Mixed scene showing a bust on a plinth, a band, a *libitina*, an appeal in progress, and gladiators engaging. (Art Resource 416019, with permission.)

Fig. 14.2. Arena mosaic, Zliten, Libya. Detail of gladiatorial combats with an appeal in progress. (Art Resource 416021, with permission.)

Fig. 14.3. Kibyra reliefs, Burdur Museum, Turkey. A *retiarius* defeats a *secutor* and exults over his fallen body. (Photo: G. Fagan, used with permission of the Burdur Museum.)

dia.[20] But in those cases, the space was modified to accommodate arena events: seats close to the orchestra in theaters were filled in to accommodate podium walls that more sharply separated the seating from the performance space, sockets for netting to protect the audience from beasts are sometimes identifiable, and the rounded ends of stadia could be walled off to create a mini-arena. Just as is the case for modern sporting events, space was tailored to the needs of the gladiatorial show.

Even more striking than the physical context of the arena was the intricacy and extravagance of stage sets deployed to enhance gladiatorial displays. A considerable body of evidence—literary, epigraphic, and archaeological—attests to the complexity of arena stagecraft. Stage sets and the manipulation of space had, of course, long been a part of theatrical shows (*ludi scaenici*)—think of Socrates hanging in a basket in Aristophanes' *The Clouds*. But they were now adopted by and adapted for use in arena spectacles.

As in a theater, the arena could be pre-equipped with sets and other enhancements for the show. Pliny tells how amber was used to adorn the nets used to keep the animals away from the podium in the wooden amphitheater that Nero built in the Campus Martius in 57 CE: "the weapons, the biers [*libitina*], and the equipment used in one day were fitted with amber."[21] Titus staged set-piece battles around a wall and a landscaped island erected in the grove of Gaius and Lucius, where the sea-battle arena (*naumachia*) was located (Dio 66.25.3–4). Probus planted an entire forest in the Circus Maximus as the setting for a spectacle.[22] Strabo (6.2.6) reports,

> Recently, in my own time, a certain Selurus, dubbed "son of Aetna," was sent up to Rome, since he had led an army, and, for a long time, had overrun the vicinity of Mount Aetna with frequent raids. I saw him torn to pieces by beasts in a scheduled gladiatorial spectacle in the Forum. He was put on a high stage set [*pegma*]—as if he was on Aetna—that disintegrated and collapsed, and he fell down with it into animal cages, constructed to be fragile beneath the stage set.

Similarly, Septimius Severus staged a hunt that began with a huge stage set (in the form of a ship) that broke apart and released four hundred animals at

20. On amphitheaters, see Golvin 1988; Bomgardner 2000; Welch 2007. On the use of other venues, see Welch 1998, 1999.

21. Pliny *NH* 37.45; cf. Calp. Sic. *Ecl.* 7.47–56, on that arena's fine appointments.

22. HA *Probus* 19.2–4. For more on landscaping the arena, see Tuck 2007; Carter 2014. (I came across this latter article only as this chapter was going to press; Carter reviews much the same body of evidence as I do here.)

Fig. 14.4. Relief, Sofia, Bulgaria (fourth century CE). Animal show scene. (Photo: Krassimir Georgiev, used with permission of the Stone Monuments Collection of the National Institute of Archaeology with Museum at the Bulgarian Academy of Science, Sofia, Bulgaria.)

once (Dio 76[77].1.4–5), and Apuleius describes a moveable house built by the very prisoners who were to be exposed to the beasts it was likely intended to house (*Met.* 4.13).

Better evidence is found in ancient art. The podium walls of arenas were often painted with animals and plants, evoking the flora and fauna put on display.[23] A relief of the fourth century CE from Naulochus in Bulgaria, now in the museum in Sofia (fig. 14.4), shows an animal hunt, which opened the day's proceedings in the full gladiatorial spectacle (called a *munus iustum et legitimum*).[24] In the Sofia relief, several bears, a lion, a crocodile, and a bull are recognizable as performers, as are various people, including a chap who

23. Examples are the walls of the amphitheaters at Eleutheropolis or Scythopolis and the hippo-stadium at Caesarea; see Weiss 2014: 163–64, esp. fig. 3.9 on 164. Similar painted panels (long lost) once adorned the podium walls of Pompeii's amphitheater; see Carter 2014: 5–6.

24. For the "typical" daily format of a spectacle, see Dio 72(73).19.1–2; Suet. *Claud.* 21.1 and 21.4 (for *munus iustum atque legitmum*); Luc. *Tox.* 59. See also Futrell 2006: 84–103; Kyle 1998: 34–127.

Fig. 14.5. Consular diptych of Flavius Anastasius. Animal show scene. (Art Resource 43001, with permission.)

boxes bears for a living (at upper center). We know from epigraphic evidence that such bear baiters were called *ursarii*, "bear men," and a relief from Istanbul shows them in action boxing and wrestling bears.[25]

More informative are the stage sets and other devices depicted in the relief. At left is an arrangement in three parts, featuring two figures in compartments above and two people below. The two figures, who are female, are most likely deities. The central one is enthroned, holds a staff in her left hand, and extends a *patera* in her right. Given the animal sitting to her right, this figure is likely Cybele. In that case, the two figures below are corybants, the orgiastic devotees of Cybele, beating shields. The topmost figure is bare-breasted and gazes into a mirror. This is likely Venus.[26] If so,

25. See *CIL* XII 533.10 = *EAOR* 5.31; *CIL* XIII 5703 = *EAOR* 5.51; *CIL* XIII 5243 = *ILS* 3267 = *EAOR* 5.52; *CIL* XIII 8639 = *EAOR* 5.50. For the Istanbul relief, see Augenti 2001: 47 (no. 18).

26. On corybants, see Dodds 1951: 64–101. I thank R. J. A. Wilson for help in identifying these figures.

this is a shrine, possibly set up in the arena, featuring the deities in whose honor the *venatio* was being staged, with their worshippers below. A parallel is found in the Zliten mosaic, where a bust is displayed on a plinth with a shield resting against it (fig. 14.1, at left). This is likely an image of the ancestor honored by the show. Two other elements in the Sofia relief (fig. 14.4) warrant closer inspection. At center bottom is a garlanded stage on which performers dressed as apes, possibly children or dwarves, act out parodies of arena events: at right, one "hunts" a domesticated animal (a dog? a bear cub?) that sits compliantly on a chair; at left, ape versions of a *retiarius* and a *secutor* engage. Between them, another ape man seems to be mimicking blacksmithing. To their right, a horseman also sports a simian mask. As we saw above, such mountebanks were called *paegniarii* and entertained the crowd as a warm-up act or in the intervals between main events. They were regularly costumed: an inscription from the Ludus Magnus in Rome commemorates a *paegniarius* who appears to have dressed as a fly or a gnat.[27]

Even more curious is an image at the center right of the Sofia relief (fig. 14.4), where a bear baiter dodges his bear by means of a latticed panel fixed in the ground by a pole. Such devices are also depicted on late antique consular diptychs, such as that of Flavius Anastasius from 517 CE, which shows two of these same contraptions in action, with the beasts prowling around one side as the performers leap and evade on the other (fig. 14.5). The contemporary writer Flavius Cassiodorus, commenting on animal shows put on in the age of Theodoric (454–526 CE), explains what we are looking at: "One performer puts his trust in angled screens fitted into the ground in a four-part rotating device. He flees by not retreating; he retreats by not moving far off. He follows the beast who follows him, coming close with his knees to escape the bear's maw" (Cassiod. *Var.* 5.42.7). In the diptych, three figures at the left and top of the arena peek out from behind stage doors, the use of which Cassiodorus also illuminates.

> Other performers dare to provoke the rage prepared against them by using a set up, so to speak, of three little doors. In the open arena, they hide behind latticed doors, showing now their faces, now their

27. A *p(a)egniarius in culice* once lived in the Ludus Magnus; see *CIL* VI 10168 = *ILS* 5126 = *EAOR* 1.79. See n. 3 above, on these performers. Toynbee (1973: 97–98) interprets the ape figures in the Sofia relief as either performers wearing dog masks or trained baboons dressed like people, but surely neither suggestion is correct. The masks have distinctly simian features, and beyond the fact that the figures are in human proportions, it seems a stretch that baboons could be trained to wield the sword and trident or work the hammer and anvil.

> backs, so that it is a wonder they escape, as you watch them fly among the teeth and claws of the lions. (Cassiod. *Var.* 5.42.9)

These late imperial events were a sort of cross between gymnastic displays and the traditional *venationes* in which the animals were usually slaughtered. Later, as the expense of shows had increased significantly, the animals were given a chance to win, and the performers, human bait, sought to avoid them.[28] There can be no doubt that these shows were bloody, even fatal. In the Sofia relief (fig. 14.4), one man is brought down by a bear at top left, and in the diptych (fig. 14.5), a performer's leg is mauled at bottom right. It is no wonder, then, that Cassiodorus broadly condemns the whole exercise (*Var.* 5.42.4): "this cruel game, this bloody pleasure, impious cult, and, as it were, human bestiality."[29]

Other temporary sets and devices are on record, such as the stakes set into racing chariots so that execution victims could be tied to them and then pushed toward beasts, as shown in the Zliten mosaic (fig. 14.6). Elsewhere in the same mosaic, we see a band playing (fig. 14.1). Behind the band is what looks like a large rectangular crate or cabinet. The best interpretation is that it is a *libitina*, the bier on which fallen gladiators were carried out of the arena (Pliny *HN* 37.45). Other gladiatorial scenes depict them,[30] and one might be tentatively identified in an image from the Kibyra reliefs (fig. 14.3), where a *retiarius* pushes his opponent against a stage set of some sort—possibly a *libitina*, although it has a stool with drapery over it at the front—so that he loses his balance and the *retiarius* wins.

The reliefs from Kibyra were discovered in 2009 and are on display in the Burdur Museum. They appear to have formed a balustrade (fig. 14.7) surrounding a cemetery for arena performers and are dated to the third century CE. As well as gladiatorial combats, the reliefs depict animal shows, of a sort reminiscent of Cassiodorus' late antique animal gymnasts. We see performers pole-vaulting over beasts (fig. 14.8, at right), an event also described by

28. Exhibitions of animals, including nonlethal human interactions with them, had always been a part of arena spectacles; see n. 7 above and p. 376 below (an inscription from Pompeii that mentions bulls and bullfighters). In late antiquity, the form of animal show depicted in figs. 14.4 and 14.5 appears to dominate over the traditional mass slaughters that had characterized the earlier *venationes*.

29. Cassiodorus' disapproval and the artistic images tend to undermine Jennison's judgment about these shows: "Danger is not eliminated, . . . but the risk of death has almost gone" (Jennison 1937:180).

30. See, e.g., Augenti 2001: 100–101 (nos. 57–58).

Fig. 14.6. Arena mosaic, Zliten, Libya. Execution by exposure to beasts. (Art Resource 416053, with permission.)

Fig. 14.7. Kibyra reliefs, Burdur Museum, Turkey. (Photo: G. Fagan, used with permission of the Burdur Museum.)

Fig. 14.8. Kibyra reliefs, Burdur Museum, Turkey. A performer pole-vaults over an animal; an elaborate stage set sits at left. (Photo: G. Fagan, used with permission of the Burdur Museum.)

Fig. 14.9. Kibyra reliefs, Burdur Museum, Turkey. A performer rides rodeo on a bull. (Photo: G. Fagan, used with permission of the Burdur Museum.)

Fig. 14.10. Kibyra reliefs, Burdur Museum, Turkey. Elaborate stage set. (Photo: G. Fagan, used with permission of the Burdur Museum.)

Cassiodorus (*Var.* 5.42.6). One performer rides rodeo on a bull and another summersaults over a wild beast (fig. 14.9). Other figures, some carrying whips, dodge and avoid animals or leap over them (fig. 14.11). One animal is released from a crate, which has an operator on top, hauling the gate open (fig. 14.8, at center). Most intriguing is the elaborate device depicted to the left of the crate (figs. 14.8 and 14.10). It is a complicated stage set in four registers. At the top are a series of narrow and wider compartments in alternating sequence, with arches over the wider ones. A raking element underneath ends with a series of curved features adjacent to these compartments, and a figure (a live person? a statue?) rests on (or manipulates?) these curved features. Below are three pairs of compartments with triangular elements over them that appear to be linked to the raking feature by an arch-like attachment at far left. Finally, at bottom, is a base with decorative motifs. The

Fig. 14.11. Kibyra reliefs, Burdur Museum, Turkey. Elaborate stage set. (Photo: G. Fagan, used with permission of the Burdur Museum.)

whole set seems firmly planted on the ground. The central compartments each have five notches on their left-hand side, which look similar to those on the animal cage immediately to the right (fig. 14.8). These are probably animal cages, opened in pairs by means of pulleys and ropes, represented by the triangular features over the compartments and the raking element, all of which are operated by the figure at the top.

Animal cages are certainly represented by another extraordinary structure from these same reliefs (fig. 14.11), where we see a performer leaping over a beast in front of an elaborate stage set. This set features a recurved element at the top, more curved elements over four compartments below that, and what look like rollers or wheels at the bottom, although they cannot be either, since the front of the whole set is fixed in the ground. The same arrangement of five notches is visible on the edges of the compartments, which are here definitively revealed as animal cages, because we see a beast emerging from the rightmost one. This was a set designed to allow the safe and simultaneous release of animals into the arena. A mosaic from Thysdrus (El Djem) in Tunisia shows an animal exhibition with executions in progress. In the center of the arena is a rectangular structure, apparently made of blocks (or painted to look like it is made of blocks), with an opening at one end and with four military trophies on posts at the corners. Presumably, the cats had come out of the opening. Another relief, from Miletus, shows a complicated set with multiple beams, what appear to be placards, several bears (one emerging from a crate at left), and a wheel (fig. 14.12). These images are all visual representations of the sorts of animal-releasing sets mentioned in the literary sources, such as Septimius Severus' ship or the set mentioned in Apuleius, the house-like shape of which is echoed by the Miletus device.

Like the animal hunts and mock fights, the gladiatorial combats featured masks, costumes, stage sets, and specially designed devices. One format of fight involved a raised platform with ramps on one or both sides. A *retiarius* would be set on the platform and have to fend off attackers from one or both sides, as shown in one of the Kibyra reliefs (fig. 14.13), where the platform only has one ramp, at left, but two gladiators take on the *retiarius* on top. The right-hand *secutor* has grabbed the trident and is trying to wrest it from the grasp of his opposing *retiarius*; the *secutor*'s colleague approaches menacingly up the ramp behind the distracted *retiarius*. A relief from Trieste shows the same format, with a *retiarius* named Kritos taking on the *secutor* Mariskos.[31]

The wheel on the Miletus relief (fig. 14.12) demonstrates that the set depicted there could be rolled into and out of the arena as needed, but we cannot readily say whether it was common for sets to be fixed, prefabricated features erected in the arena for the duration of the show or temporary devices constructed as needed and then taken down again. It probably varied from show to show, and well-trained stagehands could rapidly change sets in the intervals between events, when the sand was raked and the next spectacle readied.[32] But where the infrastructure existed, more dynamic options were available.

In his *Epistle* 88, Seneca comments on Posidonius' classification of the arts. "Amusements" (*ludicrae*) are those activities that give pleasure to the eyes and ears.

31. For this relief, see Augenti 2001: 98–99 (no. 55).

32. Suet. *Claud.* 34.2; *Nero* 12.1.

Fig. 14.12. Relief, Miletus, Turkey. Complicated stage set with a wheel, cages, and multiple beams. (Art Resource ALB 1753170, with permission.)

Fig. 14.13. Kibyra reliefs, Burdur Museum, Turkey. *Pontarii* engage. (Photo: G. Fagan, used with permission of the Burdur Museum.)

> Among these you may count the machine operators [*machinatores*], who contrive stage sets [*pegmata*] that ascend on their own account or platforms [*tabulata*] that rise silently into the air and the other varieties of surprising device: things that were conjoined disintegrating, or things that were separate coming together of their own accord, or things that stood tall gradually collapsing in on themselves. Such contraptions strike the eye of the inexperienced, who marvel at everything that happens without warning, since they do not know their causes. (Sen. *Ep.* 88.22)

Seneca is talking about stagecraft in general, in both the theater and amphitheater, but examples of the sorts of devices he has in mind are on record for gladiatorial shows. At Claudius' *naumachia* that preceded the draining of the Fucine Lake in 52 CE, a silver Triton rose mechanically (*per machinam*) from the middle of the lake and blew a trumpet to announce the start of the show (Suet. *Claud.* 21.6). Apuleius (*Met.* 10.34) describes an artificial Mount

Ida—complete with plants, running water, and goats—that rose from the arena floor and then sank back down again. A related set of devices allowed animals to emerge from trapdoors in the ground, as described by Calpurnius Siculus.

> Oh how we trembled, whenever we saw the soil upturned as the arena split apart and beasts emerged from the chasm torn in the earth; and often from those same caverns golden trees grew, with a sudden spray [of perfume].[33]

Similarly, Martial (*Spect.* 24.3; cf. HA *Probus* 19.3) comments how "cliffs crawled and a forest ran forward—a wonder to behold; the wood of the Hesperides is thought to have been like that." These are poetic allusions to scenery sliding into place at arena events. Some of this scenery comprised three-dimensional objects, but others must have been painted flats that could be unfurled and refolded for rapid deployment and removal.

Along with sets that rose and sank from the arena floor, Seneca mentions devices that make things ascend into the air (*pegmata*). Suetonius (*Nero* 12.2) describes a person dressed as Icarus who seems to have "flown" mechanically in the arena before falling close to Nero and spattering the emperor with blood. Phaedrus (5.7) mentions a flute player who fell from a *pegma* and broke his leg, Martial (*Spect.* 18, 19) refers to a bull snatched from the midst of the arena and carried off into the air, and Juvenal (*Sat.* 4.121–22) tells of boys "snatched up to the awning" by a *pegma*. The remains of a machine used in such stagecraft—beams, mortise joints, rusted iron elements, and stone and iron counterweights—were found in the central underground trench of the amphitheater at Xanten (Colonia Ulpia Traiana).[34]

The complicated infrastructure demanded by dynamic stagecraft like this is best exemplified by the *hypogeum* of the Colosseum, viewed by millions of tourists every year.[35] Over the five hundred years of the Colosseum's operation, the *hypogeum* underwent various renovations and alterations that

33. Calp. Sic. *Ecl.* 7.69–72. The date of Calpurnius is generally agreed to be Neronian, though some want to ascribe him to the third century: see, e.g., Champlin 1978 (advocating a Severan date); Townend 1980 (supporting a Neronian date).

34. See Golvin 1988: 331, where other vestiges of machines and their emplacements are documented for other amphitheaters, such as those at Nîmes, Trier, or Lambaesis.

35. On the Colosseum's *hypogeum* and the arena floors, see Beste 1999, 2000, 2001. On *hypogea*, see Golvin 1988: 330–33; Welch 2007: 38–42 (also describing the *hypogea* in the Roman Forum).

present the modern visitor with a two-story, dazzlingly complex labyrinth of walls, cells, and passages (fig. 14.14). Fourteen corridors, seven on each side, symmetrically flank a wider, central passageway that leads to two larger arrangements of chambers at the east and west end of the arena. Raking features can be identified in the walls of these corridors. They worked in tandem with a system of winches and lifting devices worked by two-story capstans operated by four men on each level, the emplacements for which are still visible in the *hypogeum* today. Some sixty capstans have been identified in the Colosseum. The winches raised caged animals to the level immediately below the floor, from which trapdoors slid downward (hence the raking features) to form a ramp affording access to the arena above. Other winches raised scenery or performers directly into the arena through simple trapdoors in the arena floor. The Colosseum is, of course, uniquely complex in its subterranean apparatus. Other arenas, such as those at Puzzuoli (Puteoli) and Capua in Italy, Augusta Emerita (Merida) in Spain, or Thysdrus (El Djem) in Tunisia, have simpler underground arrangements.[36] At Thysdrus, for instance, there is a single corridor with two trapdoors on either side. As surmised above, practiced stagehands could impress the crowd with their expertise even in the absence of *hypogea*. Inscriptions boast of games that were held in places where the arenas had no underground structures but that were nonetheless staged "with fine equipment" (*splendido apparatu*) or "with fantastic equipment" (*apparatu magnifico*).[37]

Finally, there were ancillary attractions, such *missilia* or *sparsiones*, prizes thrown to the crowd or perfume sprinkled over the spectators, such as Calig-

36. Golvin (1988: 332, table 42) tabulates the known *hypogea*, which he classifies as central corridors (thirteen examples), cruciform corridors (six examples), or elaborate multichamber arrangements (five examples, four of which are in Italy).

37. See, respectively, *CIL* IX 4208 = *EAOR* 3.13 (from Amiternum); *CIL* IX 2237 = *ILS* 5060 = *EAOR* 3.28 (from Telesia, where the amphitheater has no basement; see Welch 2007: 226–30). To be sure, *apparatus* is a vague term that can denote any and all sorts of gear, such as royal paraphernalia or a lavish display in general (see *OLD*, s.v.), so it could conceivably denote the gladiators' armor and weapons or any sort of careful preparation for the exhibition. Pliny (*NH* 33.53) notes that Caesar, as aedile, was the first to use all-silver gear (*apparatus argenteus*) in his games, which seems unlikely to denote stage sets at first glance, until we note that Pliny goes on to say that C. Antonius and L. Murena presented plays on silver stages. So when we read, in another inscription, of *honestissimus apparatus instructus* (*CIL* X 7295 = *ILS* 5055 = *EAOR* 3.53), it is hard not to conclude that the phrase covers constructed sets for the games. The same inscription, by the way, honors the benefactor for *epulum instructum amplissimo apparatu* for all the citizens of his town, which must include the setting out of tables, chairs, triclinia, bunting, and so on—the stage sets, if you will, of public feasting.

Fig. 14.14. Colosseum, Rome. The underground structures (*hypogea*). (Photo: G. Fagan.)

ula liked to have done at his shows.[38] Nero, being Nero, took matters to the extreme at games he gave in 59 CE called the "Greatest Games." These took place over several days in five or six venues around the city and included gladiatorial shows. At them, Nero had various items thrown to the crowd—birds, food, and prize tickets for grain, clothes, gems, pearls, gold and silver, slaves, paintings, draft animals, ships, apartment blocks, and farms.[39] But not just emperors did this: an advertisement for games at Pompeii reads, "There will be a hunt, athletes, the awning, and *sparsiones*."[40]

The foregoing demonstrates clearly that the audience at Roman arena games was everywhere confronted by theatricality and artificiality, from the strange gear the gladiators wore and wielded, to the particular physical setting of the shows, to the stage sets and dynamic machinery deployed to

38. Sen. *Nat.* 2.9.2; Suet. *Cal.* 18.2.

39. Suet. *Nero* 11.2; Dio 62[61].17.2–5

40. *CIL* IV 1177 = Sabbatini Tumolesi 1980: 38 (no. 11): *venatio, athletae, sparsiones, vela erunt.*

enhance the spectacle, to the prizes and food tossed into the crowd. The stage sets were an integral part of the show. Some arenas were fitted with underground chambers to accommodate them, and specialist staff were on hand to service them. Claudius, Suetonius tells us, would throw the *fabri* and *ministri* (artisans and servants) into the arena if any of their devices failed.[41] Conversely, inscriptions show that grateful spectators praised sponsors for successful use of lavish apparatuses. What are we to make of all this?

Making Sense of It All

Prior scholarly assessments of arena stagecraft have taken two main lines of analysis. The first links the development and use of elaborate sets and other gear to the documented quest for novelty in Roman spectacle. Suetonius (*Claud.* 21.2) reports that heralds would announce the staging of games with the formula that they offered sights "no one has seen or ever would see again." This set the bar rather high for sponsors. It was imperative to stage something new and unique. The quest for novelty and ever-increasing scale has been well documented by scholars of the arena, with more and more pairs of gladiators put to the sand; new and exotic animals sought out, captured, and exhibited in the arena; and novel and inventive ways of execution devised and staged.[42] The elaboration of stage sets fits neatly into this pattern.

The desire to show something new was further fueled by the competitive ethos among the oligarchs who funded the games in the republican era or among the later emperors, as sponsors tried to outdo their predecessors. This imperative, coupled with high expectations of lavish spectacle among the people, can be traced even at the municipal level. It stands, in part, behind the famous decree of 177/8 CE by which the Senate imposed empire-wide limits on how much such shows could cost.[43] It is even more strikingly echoed in the Magerius Mosaic from Smirat in Tunisia, showing an animal hunt in which the crowd cries out to Magerius, the sponsor,

> By your example, let future generations learn of the show and how it was staged! Let your predecessors [in office?] hear about it! Where did

41. Suet. *Claud.* 34.2; cf. *Nero* 12.1, for *varia harenae ministeria.*

42. On the growth of the games over the course of the republic and early empire, see Hopkins 1983: 3–14; Kyle 1998: 43–52; Ville 1981: 57–127; Wiedemann 1992: 5–14.

43. *CIL* II 6278 = *ILS* 5163. On this text, see Carter 2003; Potter 2010: 363–71.

> such a show come from? When was one like it put on? As an example to the quaestors, you will put on a spectacle! You will put it on at your own expense! This is your day![44]

The acclamation states explicitly that, in putting on the show, Magerius is both outdoing his predecessors and setting a new standard for future sponsors, in that the show stands as an example to the town's quaestors, the junior officials who would one day rise to the higher offices requiring them to stage a *munus*. In this competitive dynamic, then, the pressure to find something new and interesting to exhibit drove the technical evolution of the stage sets designed to enhance the spectacle.

The second line of analysis focuses on the social, cultural, and political messages implicit in the spectacles. With respect to the stage sets in particular, Kathleen Coleman, for instance, has argued that they assured the audience of the Roman capacity to control natural forces and of the emperor in particular to make the unreal become real.[45] Richard Beacham likens Roman stagecraft to a fascist aesthetic manipulating the emotions of spectators with images and rituals of power and so generating in them feelings of "exaltation, celebration, and awe."[46] Recently, Dean Hammer has suggested that Roman spectacles and their stage apparatus—what he calls "the technology of reality"—were a kind of ancient reality TV where the spectators were led to believe they were watching reality unfold unfiltered and unscripted before their eyes. As a result, they enjoyed an "illusion of proximity to power," because the spectacle cast "both nature and humanity as fundamentally equal by making them appear transitory, reproducible, and conformable to human desire."[47]

These are all useful and illuminating perspectives, but even more fundamental forces were at work. The theatricality of arena spectacles hedged the violence of the shows with an air of artificiality, making all the more palatable the very real violence these spectacles entailed. Some psychological studies have shown that people, when confronted with raw images of violence—such as epicures eating freshly extracted monkey brains or scenes from an abattoir—are repulsed. But when that violence is given an artificial context, related as part of dramatic narrative or staged as part of a spec-

44. On this mosaic, see n. 6 above. For the text of the inscriptions, see *AE* 1967.549.

45. Coleman 1990: 71. See also Fagan 2011: 17–22, for a summary of prior approaches to interpreting the games.

46. Beacham 1999: 240.

47. Hammer 2010: 67.

tacular event, people readily consume it.[48] A modern combat sport, such as ultimate fighting, can be hideously violent and bloody, but the packaging and the context of the action render acceptable to the spectators a degree of violence that, in an ordinary context, would involve calling the police. As should be clear by now, the very real violence of the Roman games was artificially packaged and presented to the audience in a manner analogous to the way it is in modern films or in some live events, particularly combat sports. In films, the violence is often set to music, sped up or slowed down for effect, and carefully choreographed for maximum visual impact. Gladiatorial combats, too, were packaged in all sorts of ways, could be accompanied by music, and may have been choreographed to a degree. Music is a feature of live combative sports events also, and the setting of the fight ring, the gear the combatants wear, and the overall pizzazz of the presentation serve an important function: they tell the audience that what they are witnessing is not real in any quotidian sense but taking place in an artificial landscape that gives psychological cover for them to consume and enjoy violence, no matter how graphically portrayed or even real that violence is.[49] This psychological mechanism has proven efficacy, and there is no reason to assume that it applied to Roman conditions any less than to our own. Indeed, Tertullian expressly makes this very point.

> The one who subdues a disagreement in the streets as it comes to blows or who expresses detestation of it, will in the stadium approve of far more serious fights, or the one who is appalled by the cadaver of a person who died according to the shared human condition will in the amphitheater stare down from above with the most tolerant eye on bodies chewed and ripped apart, caked with their own blood. (*Spect.* 21.2–22.4)

A recent media phenomenon points to yet another layer in what is going on when people consume violence.[50] In what has been dubbed "Internet body horror" (IBH), some websites devote themselves to offering up precisely the sort of decontextualized atrocious imagery supposedly repulsive to most people. Sites such as Ogrish.com or LiveLeak.com assemble images

48. McCauley 1998.

49. Performance theorists like Richard Schechner have long noted that the artificiality of context serves this critical function; see Schechner 1981.

50. For what follows, see White 2006; Tait 2008. I thank Kyle Gervais for bringing this material to my attention.

and videos of real-life death and suffering (e.g., war carnage, the aftermath of car crashes, suicides caught on tape) and violence done to animals. Most (in)famous are the videos of beheadings posted by Muslim extremists, notably the decapitation of the journalist Daniel Pearl (in 2002) and the contractor Nick Berg (in 2004). Recently, such videos have made a comeback under the aegis of ISIS. Following the interpretation offered above, are we simply to think of the people who watch these sorts of things as being deviants, sadists, or somehow mentally disturbed?[51] This is a pat answer, it seems to me, and hardly explains the phenomenon.[52] One way the reality-gore sites have been explained and/or justified is that they offer a chance to "bear witness" to body horror in a fashion eschewed by the mainstream media out of a misconceived sense of "taste and decency." The argument is that the sites allow people to witness the raw reality of something like war in order to cause people to be alert to its actual consequences and perhaps to help prevent it in the future, whereas the mainstream media's sanitized version of war conceals those same consequences and, thus, indirectly promotes war.[53]

Is this what the visitors to the body horror sites are thinking as they click the download button? Do they desire to "bear witness" to atrocity in order to prevent future outrages? It is difficult to see how watching a suicide, for instance, has much to say about learning anything from consequences. Vital here is that the message boards and forums attached to the sites allow spectators to post their personal reactions to what they are watching, to offer justifications for their spectatorship, and to interact with other spectators. These posts are unsolicited and voluntary, so they are unlikely to be disingenuous, since someone who wants to watch anonymously can do so easily enough.[54] Posters report that they watch out of sheer titillation and

51. The video showing the killing of Nick Berg—whose head was sawn off with a large knife—was downloaded fifteen million times in the year after it was posted on Ogrish.com, and the site has received as many as sixty thousand hits an hour when a new beheading video became available for viewing; see Tait 2008: 92. At time of writing, viewing figures were not yet available for the more recent ISIS videos.

52. I personally know several perfectly normal, well-educated, and psychologically stable people who watched the beheading videos out of a kind of curiosity, one with the sound turned off. Tait (2008) is critical of decrying these sites as a form of "pornography," a category so broad as to have virtually no explanatory power.

53. This, indeed, is how the owners of Ogrish.com came to justify the site's existence after some changes in its format in 2006. The site's tagline, for instance, changed from the machismo challenge "Can you handle life?" to the more public-service sounding "Uncover reality" (currently, in its new guise as LiveLeak.com, the tagline is "Refreshing the media").

54. See Tait 2008: 101–7.

to be entertained; that they experience repulsion and even physical illness at what they are seeing, but a repulsion from which they simultaneously derive pleasure and displeasure; that they want to see the world as it "really is," unfiltered by the media; or that they are preparing themselves for actual combat or for careers in journalism or medicine. We find echoes of precisely these same justifications/lures in the ancient evidence. Some arena spectators were doubtless simply titillated and entertained by it all.[55] As a child, Caracalla cried at the sight of arena executions and turned away, a reaction that suggests a strong physical repulsion.[56] The closest we come to a justification for the whole phenomenon of arena violence in the ancient sources are comments by elite writers that the games provided a robust lesson in how to endure pain and death. This may constitute a variation on the "bearing witness" motive, though one suspects it is an intellectualization of a crasser experience.[57] In any case, the degree to which it motivated attendance by the average spectator cannot be assessed.[58] These, of course, are but scattered snapshots from different times and places and from people of different temperaments. Although they intersect strikingly with IBH evidence, the precise content of these claims is less significant than their variety. Watching violence, it turns out, is a dynamic psychological experience.

It is particularly instructive that the Romans bracketed lethal combats with nonviolent forms of spectacle. Apuleius (*Met.* 10.34), as we have seen, describes the elaborate (nonviolent) pantomime of Mount Ida that preceded the scheduled execution, by donkey rape, of a multiple murderess in the

55. Examples are the emperor Claudius, who was addicted to the games (Suet. *Claud.* 34); the "very many people" whom Seneca says preferred the straight butchery of the executions to the gladiatorial combats (Sen. *Ep.* 7.4); and Augustine's friend Alypius upon attending the Colosseum at Rome (Aug. *Conf.* 6.13). The latter case is particularly instructive. Augustine presents Alypius as being opposed to arena violence until dragged along by his friends to watch a show. After sneaking a peak, he becomes instantly enthralled and returns again and again. Cf. this anecdote with a comment from a poster on the Ogrish.com forum: "The first time I found a site like this, I spent 8 hours straight, couldn't log off" (quoted in Tait 2008: 103).

56. HA *M. Ant.* 1.5 (the crowd, interestingly, found this reaction endearing). Note also the observation in Pseudo-Quintillian (*Decl.* 9.16) that there are people who grow pale at the sight of blood and weep over the misfortunes of complete strangers. Such delicate types most likely stayed away from the arena altogether.

57. A poster on the Ogrish.com forum commented, "[I]t has been said that this site is an independent news site or some shit, that's just an excuse for people who feel guilty looking at it. Let's look at it for what it is, senseless violence, death, and gore for our entertainment" (quoted in Tait 2008: 101).

58. See Cic. *Tusc.* 2.41; Pliny *Pan.* 33.1. See, further, Wistrand 1992: 55–80.

arena. Philo (*In Flacc.* 84–5) reports a spectacle put on in the theater at Alexandria that opened with a morning show of Jews scourged, stretched, bound to wheels, and beaten before being led off for crucifixion; this display was followed by dancers, mimes, flute players, and plays. An inscription from Pompeii commemorates a spectacle staged in the forum that featured a wide variety of performers.

> Aulus Clodius Flaccus, son of Aulus, of the voting tribe Menenia. Three times *duovir* with judicial power, five-yearly *duovir*, [made] military tribune by the people. In his first duumvirate, at the Games of Apollo, in the forum, [he gave] a procession, bulls, bullfighters, fast runners, three pairs of bridge fighters, group boxers and Greek boxers, and games with every sort of clown, pantomime, and Pylades, and [he gave] ten thousand *sesterces* to the public for his duumvirate. In his second duumvirate, the five-yearly one, at the Games of Apollo, in the forum, [he gave] a procession, bulls, bullfighters, fast runners, group boxers; on the next day, on his own account in the amphitheater, [he gave] thirty pairs of athletes and five pairs of gladiators and, along with his colleague, thirty-five pairs of gladiators and a hunt, bulls, bullfighters, boars, bears, and the other varied kind of hunt. In his third duumvirate, [he gave] games along with his colleague featuring a troupe of the first rank, with clowns added.[59]

The staging of these shows in conjunction, violent and nonviolent alike, tells us that, to the Roman mind, they were all of a type, simply *spectacula*, "things worth watching."

The evidence suggests a spectrum of potential psychological lures to watching real brutality, even in our age when it is culturally taboo to do so. There are indications that a similar range of attitudes and responses prevailed among Roman arena spectators. Watching was and is a psychologically stimulating and alluring prospect. But crucial to both circumstances is the detachment of the watcher from the victim, mediated, in one instance, by the computer screen or, in the other, by the physical setting, theatricality and artificiality, and stage sets of the show. The manipulation of space in the arena was integral to the manipulation of audience responses in the stands. Relevant also are those facets of the Romans' historical moment that molded their expectations of and attitudes toward what confronted them in

59. *CIL* IX 1074d = Sabbatini Tumolesi 1980: 18–21 (no. 1).

the arena: ubiquitous slavery that regarded whole swaths of the population as instruments, the hierarchical cast of Roman social thought that calibrated individual worth against group membership and regarded many groups as worthless and expendable, the celebration of violence and war as the cardinal virtues of an imperial people, and the absence of ready access to palliatives and the close proximity of death.[60] Life experienced in contexts like this is likely, at the very least, to have made the typical Roman more callous about the pain and suffering of others. Their cultural norms when it came to violence were far removed from ours.[61] Nevertheless, perhaps the powerful overlap in the way theatricality and artificiality functioned at the Roman games and in modern forms of watching violence makes the Roman arena spectator a little like us—a fact that should cause some deep reflection.

Works Cited

Augenti, D. 2001. *Spettacoli del Colosseo nelle cronache degli antichi*. Rome.

Aurigemma, S. 1926. *I mosaici di Zliten*. Rome.

Beacham, R. C. 1999. *Spectacle Entertainments of Early Imperial Rome*. New Haven.

Beschouach, A. 1966. "La mosaique de chase à l'amphithéâtre découverte à Smirat en Tunisie." *CRAI*, 134–57.

Beste, H.-J. 1999. "Neue Forschungsergebnisse zu einem Aufzugssystem im Untergeschoss des Kolosseums." *RM* 106: 249–76.

Beste, H.-J. 2000. "The Construction and Phases of Development of the Wooden Arena Flooring of the Colosseum." *JRA* 13: 79–92.

Beste, H.-J. 2001. "I sotterranei del Colosseo: Impianto, transformazioni e funzionamento." In A. La Regina, ed., *Sangue e Arena*, 277–99. Rome.

Bomgardner, D. 2000. *The Story of the Roman Amphitheatre*. London.

Bomgardner, D. 2007. "The Magerius Mosaic: Putting on a Show in the Amphitheatre." *Current World Archaeology* 3: 12–21.

Carter, M. 2001. "Artimedorus and the Arbelas Gladiator." *ZPE* 124: 109–15.

Carter, M. 2003. "Gladiatorial Ranking and the *SC de Pretiis Gladiatorium Minuendis* (*CIL* II 6278 = *ILS* 5163)." *Phoenix* 57: 83–114.

Carter, M. 2007 "Gladiatorial Combat: The Rules of Engagement." *CJ* 102: 97–113.

Carter, M. 2011. "Blown Call? Diodorus and the Treacherous *Summa Rudis*." *ZPE* 177: 63–69.

Carter, M. 2014. "Landscaping the Roman Arena." *Studies in the History of Gardens and Designed Landscapes: An International Quarterly* 10: 1–9. Accessed March 30, 2015. http://dx.doi.org/10.1080/14601176.2014.940176.

Champlin, E. 1978. "The Life and Times of Calpurnius Siculus." *JRS* 68: 95–110.

60. For my further thoughts on this point, see Fagan 2011: 22–38.

61. See Pinker 2011 (note esp. pp. 12–17, on the Roman world).

Coleman, K. 1990. "Fatal Charades: Roman Executions Staged as Mythological Enactments." *JRS* 80: 44–73.

Dodds, E. 1951. *The Greeks and the Irrational.* Berkeley.

Fagan, G. 2011. *The Lure of the Arena: Social Psychology and the Crowd at the Roman Games.* Cambridge.

Fagan, G. 2014. "Gladiatorial Combat as Alluring Spectacle." In P. Christesen and D. Kyle, eds., *A Companion to Sport and Spectacle in Greek and Roman Antiquity*, 465–77. Malden.

Futrell, A. 2006. *The Roman Games: A Sourcebook.* Malden.

Golvin, J.-C. 1988. *L'Amphithéâtre romain: Essai sur la théorisation de sa forme et de ses fonctions.* 2 vols. Paris.

Hammer, D. 2010. "Roman Spectacle Entertainments and the Technology of Reality." *Arethusa* 43: 63–86.

Hope, V. 2000. "Fighting for Identity: The Funerary Commemoration of Italian Gladiators." In A. Cooley, ed., *The Epigraphic Landscape of Roman Italy*, 93–113. London.

Hopkins, K. 1983. *Death and Renewal.* Sociological Studies in Roman History 2. Cambridge.

Jacobelli, L. 2003. *Gladiators at Pompeii.* Los Angeles.

Jennison, G. 1937. *Animals for Show and Pleasure in Ancient Rome.* Manchester. Reprint, Philadelphia, 2005.

Junkelmann, M. 2008. *Gladiatoren: Das Spiel mit dem Tod.* Mainz. 2nd ed.

Kyle, D. 1998. *Spectacles of Death in Ancient Rome.* London.

McCauley, K. 1998. "When Screen Violence Is Not Attractive." In J. Goldstein, ed., *Why We Watch: The Attractions of Violent Entertainment*, 144–62. Oxford.

Pinker, S. 2011. *The Better Angels of Our Nature: Why Violence Has Declined.* New York.

Potter, D. 2010. "Appendix: Two Documents Illustrating Imperial Control of Public Entertainment." In D. Potter and D. Mattingly, eds., *Life, Death, and Entertainment in the Roman Empire*, 351–71. Ann Arbor. 2nd ed.

Ritti, T., and Yilmaz, S. 1998. *Gladiatori e venationes a Hierapolis di Frigia.* Rome.

Sabbatini Tumolesi, P. 1980. *Gladiatorum Paria: Annunci di spettacoli gladiatorii a Pompei.* Rome.

Schnecher, R. 1981. "Performers and Spectators Transported and Transformed." *Kenyon Review* 3: 83–113.

Simpson, C. 2000. "Musicians and the Arena: Dancers and the Hippodrome." *Latomus* 59: 633–39.

Tait, S. 2008. "Pornographies of Violence? Internet Spectatorship and Body Horror." *Critical Studies in Media Communication* 25: 91–111.

Townend, G. 1980. "Calpurnius Siculus and the *Munus Neronis*." *JRS* 70: 166–74.

Toynbee, J. 1948. "Beasts and their Names in the Roman Empire." *PBSR* 16: 24–37.

Toynbee, J. 1973. *Animals in Roman Life and Art.* London. Reprint, Baltimore, 1996.

Tuck, S. 2007. "Spectacle and Ideology in the Relief Decorations of the *Anfiteatro Campano* at Capua." *JRA* 20: 255–72.

Ville, G. 1981. *La gladiature en Occident des origines à la Mort de Domitien.* Rome.

Weiss, Z. 2014. *Public Spectacles in Roman and Late Antique Palestine.* Cambridge, MA.

Welch, K. 1998. "Greek Stadia and Roman Spectacles: Asia, Athens, and the Tomb of Herodes Atticus." *JRA* 11: 117–45.

Welch, K. 1999. "Negotiating Roman Spectacle Architecture in the Greek World: Athens and Corinth." In B. Bergmann and C. Kondoleon, eds., *The Art of Ancient Spectacle*, 125–45. New Haven.

Welch, K. 2007. *The Roman Amphitheater from Its Origins to the Colosseum*. Cambridge.

White, M. 2006. *The Body and the Screen: Theories of Internet Spectatorship*. Cambridge, MA.

Wiedemann, T. 1992. *Emperors and Gladiators*. London.

Wistrand, M. 1992. *Entertainment and Violence in Ancient Rome: The Attitudes of Roman Writers of the First Century AD*. Göteborg.

FIFTEEN

Party Hard

Violence in the Context of Roman Cenae

John Donahue

Better is a dry morsel with quiet than a houseful of feasting with strife.
—Proverbs 17:1 (English Standard Version)

This simple quote from the Old Testament neatly summarizes much of the complexity attached to eating and drinking in antiquity. It calls for moderation and self-control, conduct in the Roman world that was especially embraced by the likes of Stoics and Christians. At the same time, this proverb confirms a second reality: as essentially social activities, eating and drinking were always susceptible to discord and violence. This concept was not entirely new, of course. The Greek symposium and the *komos*, while essential to the identity of the ancient polis, were never entirely free from violence, especially since much of this activity featured heavy wine drinking by the male participants. The Greeks, therefore, were well aware of the close relationship between alcohol consumption and violence and of the need to control the consumption of alcohol through ritualization.[1] Similarly, the Romans were no less immune to violence at the dining table. Indeed, the space of the *cena* helped the Romans to charge violent acts with specific meanings, which included the violence associated with war, political assassinations through poisonings, and remarkable displays of cruelty and humiliation by festal hosts, from the republic into the imperial period.

Before we assess this evidence in greater detail, several preliminary points

1. See Murray's contribution in this volume.

need to be made. First, in talking about violence, I will be adopting the definition most recently advanced by the World Health Organization (WHO), which characterizes violence as the

> intentional use of physical force or power, threatened or actual, against oneself, another person, or against a group or community, that either results in, or has the high likelihood of resulting in injury, death, psychological harm, maldevelopment or deprivation.[2]

The WHO is far removed from the Roman world, and there is little evidence in the ancient medical literature that the Greeks and Romans even had a concept of "public health." Nevertheless, this definition is especially appropriate because it views violence as an essentially physical act committed against an assortment of victims and with a range of outcomes. As we shall see, this description meshes neatly with much of the Roman evidence at our disposal.

Second, the definition of violence recently put forth by Randall Collins will also be essential.[3] He embeds violence in a process of social interaction, an approach that has special application in the context of the Roman *cena*, where social mixing was a prominent feature. Furthermore, he argues that violent people are successful at circumventing confrontational tension/fear by turning a situation to their own advantage and to the disadvantage of their opponent.[4] In a Roman context, the emperor especially fit this description as the one person with the stature and autocratic power to act in this way. He exerted more control than anybody else over the emotional tenor of the gatherings he sponsored, and their success or failure rested solely on him. As we shall see, however, this analysis cuts both ways. The emperor's character was also revealed by the tenor of his dinners, as Pliny remarked in his praise of the emperor Trajan: "Our leisure gives us away."[5]

Third, beyond issues of terminology, any study of this topic must also confront the reality that violence ran counter to the values of the Roman dining experience, at least as conceived by Roman elites, who provide the bulk of the evidence. Here, as John D'Arms has noted, the emphases were on equality, friendship, and the lowering of social barriers, but only in the most attenuated sense, as Roman notions of status and hierarchy were never

2. Tyner 2012: 5–6.
3. Collins 2008.
4. Collins ibid., 19–20.
5. Plin. *Pan.* 82.9.

far from the festal surface.[6] A similar ethos applied to festal entertainment, which was geared toward reinforcing the influence of the powerful host as magnificent spectacle maker.[7] It is clear that violence in this setting was not at all the norm; in fact, such occurrences were all the more disturbing given that the banquet, especially among the elite, was supposed to be a place of conviviality, good cheer, and entertainment, forming, in effect, a deliberate "assault upon the senses."[8] We must consider, then, how we are to make sense of these conflicting objectives, as well as what might they tell us about Roman social relations.

Finally, these interpretative challenges are compounded by the reality that the Romans never specifically set out to discuss violent feasting in their treatment of food and drink in general. Instead, the topic appears in the background, whether as part of a larger biographical assessment of a particular emperor, as one of the regulations governing a particular association (*collegium*), or as found in the imaginative literature of the period, such as epic poetry, which typically does not treat violence at the table but, rather, utilizes the festal setting for the "telling" of such violence. The point in all of this is that we are unable to quantify and document this topic through the modern social scientist's method of producing statistical data or examining evidence by time period or region. Consequently, as Garrett Fagan has recently argued, the best we can hope for is to arrive at a certain "etiquette of violence" at the Roman table, an approach whereby "we can glimpse the sort of violence that was done, by whom and to whom, and under what circumstances."[9] While the sources are less than what we might hope for, this approach will still allow us to survey this overlooked topic by type and context and, ultimately, to set it in its proper place within a topographical interpretation of violence in ancient Roman society.

Festal Violence in Epic and the Novel

As always, any attempt to tease out the real world from imaginative literature must be careful to avoid the distortion and sensationalism that frequently characterizes such source material. At the same time, these sources are worthy of examination because, in order to be effective, their authors

6. D'Arms 1984, 1990.
7. D'Arms 1999.
8. Ibid., 303.
9. Fagan 2011b: 469.

were compelled to portray social institutions and situations with which their readers could readily identify. In other words, if it was to be successful, fiction had to be based, at least in part, on reality.[10] Two genres especially well suited to portraying the *Realien* of feasting and violence in antiquity were epic poetry and the novel, as a brief examination of each genre will confirm.

Vergil's *Aeneid* is our iconic Roman source for epic. Here the poet skillfully relies on the banquet table as a setting not directly for violence but for meals of welcoming where narratives of violence can be dramatically retold for larger thematic purposes. The Homeric antecedent is crucial here. According to the oral theory of Homeric origins, banquets were a likely setting in which classical epic arose, as itinerant bards sang tales of military valor to Dark Age warlords amid feasting on roasted meats and wine.[11] In the context of ancient Greek epic, we are especially reminded of the three tales sung by the blind poet Demodocus while Odysseus is entertained by the Phaeacians in book 8 of Homer's *Odyssey*. The three tales that he sings,[12] all of which feature violence as a theme, culminate in the sack of Troy, a painful reminder of loss that brings Odysseus to tears. Vergil skillfully adopts, for his own purposes, this device of violence embedded within the larger framework of the feast. In the first occurrence, Dido, the Carthaginian queen, welcomes Aeneas and his men with a generous feast amid blazing torches, glittering gold, free-flowing wine, and the music of the lyre.[13] Amid the luxury and high culture of Dido's court, the tale that Aeneas subsequently tells is one of war, violence, loss, and displacement, as he recounts his escape from the smoldering ruins of Troy in order to seek a new destiny in a new land. Dido's banquet, then, is not in itself a venue for violence but, rather, one that facilitates the memory of violence, with the setting of the banquet hall and the horror of war further meant to evoke for Vergil's audience both contemporary dining practices and the recent destruction of the Italian civil wars.

No less evocative is a second welcoming scene, in book 7, where Latinus, king of the Latins, receives the Trojans at their sacred temple, which Vergil describes as a locus for religious feasts—a place where rams are slaughtered and where the elders sit at long tables to feast. This scene is followed by a description of the carved statues of the Latins' foremost ancestors, among them Sabinus, planter of vines (*vitisator*), who guards the curved pruning

10. Ibid., 469–71; Saller 1980.

11. Sherratt 2004.

12. Hom. *Od.* 8.62–95, 266–369, 482–534.

13. Verg. *Aen.* 695–756; Perkell 1999: 46–49.

hook.[14] Equally prominent are many implements of war hung on the temple doors—captured chariots, curved axes, crests of helmets, great bolts from the gates of cities, spears, shields, and beaks wrenched from ships.[15] Again, we find a dining hall that is conceived not as a place for actual violence but as a setting appropriate for considering this problematic behavior. Sabinus, the symbol of viticulture, is thus juxtaposed with weaponry and warfare in order to remind the reader that the prosperity and peace of the civilized world—the world of settled agriculture as symbolized by the grape—were never far removed from violence and destruction. Motifs of dining and food thus continue to serve as powerful symbols in the poet's treatment of violence.

The final welcoming feast occurs in book 8, when Evander, king of the Arcadians, offers the Trojans meat, bread, and wine in response to Aeneas' request that the Arcadians assist the Trojans in the war against the Latins.[16] Interestingly, the feast that Evander offers the Trojans is part of an annual religious celebration dedicated to Hercules, a rite meant to recall the sacrifice made to the god each August at the Great Altar, or Ara Maxima, in the Roman Forum Boarium in the time of Augustus. This fusion of Roman political and religious institutions with Arcadian values occurs later in this same scene, when Evander discusses at length Hercules' triumph over the monstrous Cacus.[17] This story, which involves the use of violence to remove moral evil and danger and to protect the established community, prefigures Augustus' victory over the monstrous gods of the East and foreshadows Aeneas' killing of Mezentius.[18] Clearly, as with the two earlier welcoming feasts, the Arcadian banquet provides an entry point that allows the poet and, by extension, his readers to consider the problematic issue of violence in the Roman world. Once again, the shared meal is a particularly effective device in this regard because it allows for the dramatic juxtaposition of commensality and good cheer with the isolation and violence of war.

When we turn to the ancient novel, we find a somewhat different situation, as the *cena* is indeed a place of violence, although things are not always what they appear to be. Petronius' *Satyricon* provides the best example. In its Latin form, the ancient novel parodied the faithful young lovers of the Greek novel by emphasizing sex, humor, and low-life sensibilities. All of these features are present in Petronius' work, most notably in the over-the-

14. Verg. *Aen.* 7.178–79.
15. Verg. *Aen.* 7.183–86.
16. Verg. *Aen.* 8.175–83.
17. Verg. *Aen.* 8.184–279.
18. Boyle 1999: 149–54.

top dinner offered by the wealthy ex-slave Trimalchio (*cena Trimalchionis*) to a group of adventurers making their way through southern Italy. Meant to show wit and learning, the dinner and conversation reveal instead the pretentiousness and ignorance of the bombastic host as well his penchant for violence, an impulse that always lurks just beneath the surface of Petronius' account.

Two episodes are illustrative. The first involves the main course, when Trimalchio threatens to strip and execute a cook for failing to cook the dinner pig—or so the reader is led to believe—until a clever trick is revealed when the cook slits the stomach of the pig, allowing sausages and black pudding to flow out. After receiving acclaim from the household slaves for this generous and clever dish, Trimalchio then rewards the once-suspected cook with money and a drink.[19] In the second episode, a young male acrobat accidentally crashes into Trimalchio during a performance. Although the host is not seriously injured, the dinner guests are immediately suspicious of the punishment that Trimalchio will inflict on the luckless lad.[20] As with the cook, Trimalchio lets the boy off, stating, in this instance, that it would be beneath his dignity for such a great man to be injured by a mere slave.

The two episodes differ in that the first one is staged whereas the second is not. Consistent in both cases, however, is the theme of violence done to or threatened against slaves. That Trimalchio turns the tables on his guests and punishes neither transgressor provides for much drama and comic entertainment, but it also reveals several dark truths: that violence blighted the slave's life in general, no matter what the context of interactions with the owner; that violence, whether staged or real, was endemic to the dining hall; and that the severity of the punishment typically depended on nothing more than the whims of the host. As we shall see, certain Roman emperors were to provide proof of these realities with punishments that would far exceed those imposed by our bombastic freedman and that would extend well beyond the abuse of slaves. Even so, the ancient novel remains a valuable source for helping us to appreciate these kinds of social realities, which presumably would have resonated deeply among Petronius' audience of first-century Italy.

Beyond its appearance in ancient literature, feasting and drinking was popular among the Romans because it was a useful way to maintain or to dissolve political and social bonds. Ideally, the feast allowed the host to

19. Petron. *Sat.* 49.

20. Petron. *Sat.* 53–54.

advertise his political power and social standing while encouraging loyalty through his own generosity. As we might expect, when such bonds were challenged or simply fell apart, violence was often the result. The Roman evidence for these kinds of meals, scattered but revealing, tends to cluster in three areas: in the political maneuverings of dynasts during the late republic; among ordinary citizens, in the food and drink of the tavern (*popina*) and of various associations (*collegia*); and in feasts provided by the emperor, especially during the first century, when uncertainty about imperial succession could result in the elimination of rivals, whether real or imagined, at the dining table.

Political Violence and the Republican *Cena*

During the republic, one of our earliest and most dramatic references to political violence at a meal concerns the heroic suicide of Vidacilius, one of the rebelling Italici during the Social War of the early first century BCE. Appian records that the rebel commander, whose native Asculum had been attacked by the forces of Cn. Pompeius Strabo, forced his way into the town, reproached the citizenry for their cowardice, and put to death his political enemies. He then erected a funeral pyre in the temple, placed a couch on it, and proceeded to hold a feast with his friends. Perhaps realizing the futility of his situation, he consumed a poison draft at the height of a drinking bout and ordered his friends to set the pyre on fire.[21] We know of no additional details, but the account provides an early instance of the ritual of the "suicide dinner," the most famous of which was Tacitus' account of the demise of the Stoic philosopher Seneca during the reign of the emperor Nero.[22] As Paul Plass has noted, unlike the *munera* meant for mass entertainment, this kind of festal violence occurred on a much smaller scale and was "controlled by loose conventions to accommodate the flexibility required for political action."[23] That the dining table was a useful setting for such political action is clear enough from evidence of this sort. Furthermore, as long as power among competitors remained more or less in balance, as in Vidacilius' world of the republic, suicide fell beyond, rather than within, the political system; once the emperor achieved a position of superiority, however, this type of

21. App. *BCiv.* 1.6.48.
22. Tac. *Ann.* 15.60–63.
23. Plass 1995: 135–36.

suicide was established as a (quasi-)routine alternative, as Seneca's death dramatically demonstrates.[24]

A different kind of festal violence, that involving murder instead of suicide, is also notable during the republic. Of particular interest are the proscriptions of the later republic, which, once recognized as an intentional policy of sanctioned violence, often gave rise to acts of grotesque butchery and mayhem. For example, Marc Antony ordered that the head and hands of Cicero be cut off and is said to have kept the severed head within view of his dining table.[25] While this gesture may be attributable to the Italian practice of featuring gladiatorial matches as entertainment at banquets,[26] the connection here between eating and violence is unmistakable. In another instance, we find the tribune Salvius identified as a political enemy by the triumvirs Lepidus, Antony, and Octavian and brutally slain by a centurion, who bursts in on a feast, cuts off the victim's head, and threatens to do the same to the guests should they move from their places.[27] Noteworthy too are the feasts that Sextus Pompey, Antony, and Octavian provided to each other in 39 BCE to mark the Pact of Misenum. The account is filled with tension, as the participants take all kinds of precautions: ships are moored alongside the mole where the men are dining, guards are stationed at the ready, and the trio is armed with concealed daggers.[28] The drama intensifies as Pompey receives a message that he should overtake the other two men to avenge past wrongs, but he declines the opportunity.[29]

Actions of this sort were meant to induce horror. Indeed, tales of murder, concealed weaponry, and armed guards clearly breached the ethos of conviviality normally expected at the dinner table (see D'Arms, cited at n. 6 above). Furthermore, violence of this sort had to be seen in order to send a message, and the act had to be "conspicuous and incongruous in its excessiveness"[30] if that message was to be understood. The *cena* was particularly well suited to such objectives.

---

24. Ibid., 136.
25. App. *BCiv.* 4.4.20; cf. Sen. *Ep.* 83.25.
26. Plass 1995: 144.
27. App. *BCiv.* 4.4.17.
28. App. *BCiv.* 5.8.73.
29. App. *BCiv.* 5.8.73; Plut. *Ant.* 32.
30. Plass 1995: 146.

Festal Violence during the Empire

In turning from the republic to the imperial period, it is useful to consider first our evidence for violent meals among the lower orders. While the testimony is generally thin, both *collegia* (associations) and *popinae* (taverns) provide helpful insight.

As organized societies within the larger Roman community, *collegia* were especially popular among workmen and worshippers of various sorts during the principate.[31] The nature and objectives of these groups have always been a source of debate, yet two features of them are clear: such associations undertook a broad range of commensality at various times and places;[32] and sociability—that is, the opportunity for men who shared a common occupation or religious cult to have a good time through eating and drinking together—was always a strong, if not a defining, principle.[33] The latter feature is particularly well known from the regulations and calendars of various groups, where there is much emphasis on feasting throughout the year. Given this evidence, it is not surprising to find officials of private associations going to great lengths to enforce codes of conduct and to publicize this fact in their inscriptions. Of interest here is the most familiar of all collegial inscriptions, that of the college of Diana and Antinous (*cultores Dianae et Antinoi*) at Lanuvium in the second century, where fines were imposed for rowdiness at meetings.

> It was resolved that if any member moves from his place to another place in order to create a disturbance, he should be fined HS 4. If any member insults another or becomes rowdy, he should be fined HS 12. If any member becomes insulting or abusive to the president at feasts, he should be fined HS 20.[34]

These behavioral regulations can be viewed as evidence of the group's willingness, at least in public, to accept civic values. At the same time, however, the very need for such regulations suggests that propriety was a challenge to maintain and that members were not always successful in identifying with these values. Contributing to this situation was the intensely hierarchical nature of these organizations, each of which had ruling mag-

31. Perry 2011.
32. Ascough 2008.
33. MacMullen 1974; Alföldy 2011.
34. *CIL* XIV 2112.

istrates who could exert some measure of control over their association by distributing food and drink on the basis of one's rank within the group.[35] Indeed, van Nijf has argued that brawls during these banquets seem to have been precisely about the places of individuals within this hierarchical model and not about the existence of the hierarchical model itself.[36] This may well be true, but it was violence nonetheless and surely contributed to the image of the *collegium* as being potentially disruptive to the political order of the city.[37] As we shall see next, these types of behaviors were reproduced at the feasts of the emperors, but on a more lavish scale and often amid unspeakable cruelty and humiliation.

The *popina*, a bar that sold drinks and hot food, was a fixture of the urban landscape. While elites held these establishments in low regard, *popinae* were vital to the lower orders as a source of food, drink, and leisure.[38] The favorite activities here, drinking and gambling, often led to violence, as found in a well-known wall painting from Pompeii now in the Naples Museum;[39] its accompanying inscription captures an argument over a game of dice (*alea*) and the landlord's threat to toss the rowdy gamers out on the street.[40] The legal sources provide additional insight, as evident in a number of laws that ceased to apply in the *popina*, including those having to do with rape, adultery, assault, and theft—although the gamblers themselves could bring action for assault and theft in order to gain legal redress.[41] Such restrictions on the application of the law were clearly aimed at changing the culture of the tavern by discouraging gambling and trying to disincentivize women from working there, yet there is little evidence to suggest that such measures were effective in eradicating violence within the *popina*.[42]

Elites and the Emperor

When we turn to feasts provided by imperial elites, the evidence clusters around violence inflicted on dining room slaves by their elite masters and

35. Donahue 2004: 84–89.
36. van Nijf 1997: 110 n. 183.
37. Nippel 1995: 70–84; Lintott 1972: 77–83.
38. Broekaert and Zuiderhoek 2013: 330–31.
39. Museo Archeologico Nazionale di Napoli 111482.
40. *CIL* IV 3494; Beard 2010: 229–30.
41. *Dig.* 11.5.1 at Laurence 2007:100.
42. Laurence 2007: 100–101.

around those dinners provided by the emperor at which violence occurred. Concerning slaves, we have already witnessed the violence, however much staged, in Petronius' *Satyricon*. The additional evidence is similar in its cruelty. Here we find slaves being punished for a host of transgressions, including the theft of food or dinner items, inadequate table service, and improperly prepared food. Punishments range from blows, lashes, and beatings to scalding with a burning iron and torture, with slaves even committing suicide to avoid the punishments of a displeased master.[43] Missing is any suggestion of elite-on-elite dinnertime violence, a circumstance that supports the prevailing ethos of conviviality among social equals. Slavery was a different story, however; indeed, domestic service on the household staffs of elites was no guarantee of an easier life for slaves, who continued as easy targets of derision and abuse in the dining rooms of the wealthy.[44]

Turning to dinners provided by the emperor, the situation is both the same as and different from those banquets provided by earlier republican dynasts—the same because fears about political instability were often the driving force behind such meals, but different because it was now the emperor who maintained sole authority, a reality that allowed him to behave in any way that he saw fit, no matter how hideously. This kind of behavior had a long history in the Greco-Roman world. The meals of Greek tyrants combined luxury with the humiliation of guests in order to secure the position of the festal dynast, and among the Macedonians, the feasts of Alexander the Great featured excessive consumption amid an atmosphere of subordination and fear. Indeed, these same values of luxury and social distancing achieved through fear and humiliation found their way into the dinners of Roman republican dynasts and, subsequently, of the emperors.[45] The evidence tends to fall into two categories: meals sponsored for a specific violent purpose, especially the removal of a rival through poisoning; and those that do not seem to have been organized with violence in mind but that nonetheless descended into violence, usually through the dangerous combination of moral depravity and heavy drinking. Both categories present interpretative challenges that make it difficult to judge the validity of these stories.

Among poisonings, two incidents are best known, though poorly understood: those involving the emperor Claudius and his son, the young Britannicus. The poisoning of Claudius is variously reported. Tacitus attributes the act to the physician Xenophon, who, recruited by Agrippina, carried

43. D'Arms 1990: 175–76.

44. Ibid., 179.

45. Vössing 2004.

out the deed by plunging a feather dipped in poison down the throat of the emperor, supposedly to induce vomiting after heavy eating and drinking.[46] Dio follows the more popular story at the time, that the emperor was the victim of a poison mushroom administered by the infamous poisoner Locusta, who was able to mask the immediate effects of the poison because of the emperor's heavy drinking that night.[47] Suetonius is more reluctant to assess blame, claiming that some accused Halotus, the eunuch and official taster for the emperor, while others pointed to Agrippina. He offers two possible settings for the deed, a meal with the priests in the Citadel and a family banquet where Agrippina administered the mushrooms herself.[48] The poisoning of Britannicus is more consistently reported, as the accounts of Suetonius and Tacitus share several common elements: Nero as instigator, Locusta as provider, trial poisonings of animals to strengthen the dose, and Britannicus' sudden demise at an imperial dinner. Tacitus provides an additional colorful detail: in order to allay suspicion, a drink that had been previously tasted was provided to Britannicus when it was too hot, and after he rejected it for that reason, it was infused with cold water containing the lethal dose of poison.[49]

What are we to make of these accounts? For starters, the divergence in the sources suggests that we cannot know what happened behind the closed doors of the palace. Rumors surely must have circulated at the time of these deaths, but the facts simply cannot be confirmed.[50] That having been said, two features are worth bearing in mind. First, on a larger political scale, incidents such as these must be placed within the wider context of concerns over imperial succession, a reality especially apparent within the Julio-Claudian family, where an "eccentric stability" was indeed established for the regime,[51] but where suspicions and insecurities persisted. It is no surprise, then, to find that conspirators wanted to kill Caligula at a dinner but waited for five days and killed him in a passageway of the palace;[52] nor is it surprising that Claudius always attended the banquets of the early days of his reign with an escort of javelin-bearing guards and was waited on there by soldiers who per-

46. Tac. *Ann.* 12.67.
47. Dio 61.34; Grimm-Samuel 1991.
48. Suet. *Claud.* 44.
49. Suet. *Nero* 33; Tac. *Ann.* 13.15–16.
50. Osgood 2011: 245.
51. Potter 2009: 180–94.
52. Dio 59.29.

formed the duties of dinner servants.[53] It is more than ironic that Claudius' attention to the dangers of feasting could not prevent his putative poisoning at the banquet table. The same situation arose after Nero's death, when succession again became an issue during the year of the four emperors, in 69 CE. Tacitus reminds us of this in his report that soldiers who feared a plot against the emperor Otho wounded a tribune and a prefect after bursting in on a banquet provided by the emperor to the men and women of nobility. The soldiers withdrew only when Otho himself stood on a banquet couch and staved off the attackers with appeals and tears.[54]

Second, it is clear that the imperial banquet retained its attractiveness as a means to effect this kind of political change. It is difficult to determine what really happened in these cases. Even so, the popularity of the poison feast suggests that a powerful and reliable modus operandi was in play here, one that drew on a stock set of characters, including female poisoners, tasters, and ruthlessly paranoid instigators. In the absence of more sophisticated means of eliminating a rival, this method retained a special appeal as a convenient and effective solution to political problems. Finally, it is no coincidence that stories of this sort tend to disappear from the sources once the issue of imperial succession was more securely established in the later first century. Indeed, our narrative sources become quite thin after the early imperial period, and what does survive, such as the problematic *Historia Augusta*, tends to focus not on violence at the table but on fantastical accounts of festal extravagance.[55]

Concerning violent meals of the emperors that did not involve poisoning, the evidence tends to cluster around rulers whom the sources typically treat with hostility. At a dinner hosted by the gluttonous Vitellius amid the tumult of the civil war of 69, soldiers burst in and demanded the death of his dinner guest, the ex-consul Verginius.[56] Once, the guests of Elagabalus were smothered to death by an excess of decorative flowers.[57] Especially prominent, however, are Caligula's violent feasts, notorious for their cruelty and excess. At a public dinner in the city, he reportedly ordered executioners to cut off the hands of a slave who had stolen a piece of silver, to tie the slave's hands to his chest, and to parade him around the dinner with a placard

53. Suet. *Claud.* 35.
54. Tac. *Hist.* 1.81–82.
55. SHA *Heliogab.* 19.
56. Tac. *Ann.* 2.68.
57. SHA *Heliogab.* 21.

explaining his punishment.[58] Furthermore, we are told that he used to take the attractive wives of his dinner guests to bed during the meal, then return and report in detail on their sexual performance.[59] Finally, there is the story of the bridge at Baiae,[60] which is difficult both to interpret and to date.[61] Here, in perhaps his greatest display of megalomania, Caligula attempted to build a bridge across the Bay of Baie off the coast of Italy by fastening ships together. Once completed, he celebrated an undeserved triumph, gave out cash to friends and soldiers gathered for the occasion, and feasted with them for the rest of the day and night—he on the bridge, the rest on boats anchored in the vicinity. The event exploded into violence, however, when the drunken emperor threw many of his guests to their death from the bridge and killed many others by attacking them with beaked ships.[62]

The bias of the sources presents significant interpretative challenges. In the case of Caligula, stories of this sort have traditionally compelled scholars to characterize him as "mad, bad, ill, or all three,"[63] although the focus now is on concentrating as much as possible on the events of his reign while remaining skeptical of the interpretation of these events.[64] As in the instances of imperial poisonings, it is difficult to know what is really going on here. Even so, despite the hostility of our sources, it can be argued that festal violence served an important function by providing a convenient measure by which to judge imperial behavior. Indeed, we can gain some additional perspective in this regard by recognizing the philosophical reaction to violence at the table. The Stoic philosopher Seneca, cited at the beginning of this essay, claimed that it was madness to be incensed over warm wine or an out-of-place couch cushion at a feast[65] or to whip a slave for talking at dinner, because there was not "the silence of the desert in a room that could hold a crowd as large as a mass meeting."[66] Such evidence suggests that the violent feast became something of a topos in the philosophical literature, indicating that these abuses were both common and a convenient way to cite objectionable behavior. At the same time, much like the complaints of

58. Suet. *Cal.* 32; on humiliation in general, see Miller 1993.

59. Suet. *Cal.* 36.

60. Suet. *Cal.* 19; Jos. *AJ* 19.5–6. For the most sensationalist account, see Dio 59.17.

61. On the interpretation of this incident as a deliberate and extreme break from Roman traditions, see Winterling 2011: 126–31. See also Malloch 2001; Kleijwegt 1994.

62. Donahue 2011: 99–100.

63. Massaro and Montgomery 1978.

64. Wilkinson 2005: 83.

65. Sen. *De ira* 2.25.1.

66. Sen. *De ira* 3.35.2.

Christians against the idolatry they witnessed in the arena,[67] these charges were not enough to change behaviors in any significant way. We might do well, however, to ask why all of this violence still persisted, which is the focus of this essay's final section.

Interpretative Challenges

Clearly, it is difficult to come to terms with much of the evidence for violence at dinners. Often gruesome and sensationalist in nature, the ancient testimony begs for some kind of causal explanation. There are clearly limitations to what we can know. As A. Lynn Martin has argued in the case of traditional Europe, this kind of drunken disorder is difficult to separate from what the authors considered to be orderly and disorderly, because they simply do not provide the kind of data that would allow us to make such a judgment. Adding to our difficulties is the challenge of determining what really happened, especially given that our sources are often separated in time from the incidents on which they are reporting.[68] We are on similar ground with the Roman evidence, although we can at least read between the lines to infer an ethos of shared fellowship at the *cena*, and that violence seems to violate that ethos, at least among the upper classes. While these challenges are significant, it is still useful to explore very briefly some potential reasons for violent behavior at dinner parties, especially if it can bring us to a better understanding of the role of festal violence in the larger sphere of Roman social relations.

One approach, traditional in its interpretation, focuses on the character of the violent offender. Timonen has argued that the immediate cause of festal violence of this sort is to be found in the nature and background of the ruler himself, a perspective that allowed ancient writers to "exaggerate, generalise, mythicise, and dramatise" these acts of violence.[69] As we have seen, this was especially the case in ancient biography, where "bad emperors" tended to embrace transgressive feasting in a way that was consistent with an overall negative assessment of their personality and character. While this may be true enough, modern theory allows us to advance a bit further.

Collins argues that one way to perpetuate violence in the context of fun

67. Wiedemann 1994: 146–64.

68. Martin 2009: 110–11.

69. Timonen 2000: 216.

and entertainment is to attack a weak victim,[70] something we certainly see in the singling out of slaves for harsh treatment and of women for sexual abuse by the likes of Caligula at feasts. A second way is to confine violence in a protected enclave, that is, to stage and organize it so that violence was limited or at least predictably shaped.[71] In other words, staging an event in a space that could be easily controlled contributes to the unleashing of violence. One can argue that this process was already underway during the reign of the Julio-Claudians, as is evident in the case of Tiberius' retreat on Capri, where the emperor could control space for his own lascivious pursuits.[72] We see this motive especially in play, however, under the Flavian emperors, who redefined space from the outside to the inside. Domitian's elaborate dining room (*triclinium*) on the Palatine, soaring in its marble magnificence, stands as the most prominent example of this new attitude toward space. This emphasis helps, in turn, to explain evidence like Domitian's wildly inventive but ghoulish feast in which his invited guests dined in a blackened dining room meant to prompt fears of death.[73] Here, as David Fredrick has noted, the violence was not physical but purely psychological, with the *cena* becoming an "apparatus of torture,"[74] a condition that was not relieved until the dinner slaves delivered gifts to the attendees at their homes at the end of the evening. We should realize here, too, that the juxtaposition of death and having fun was common to Roman festal ideology, a mind-set seen in the appearance of the silver skeleton to serve as a "reminder of death" (*memento mori*) in Petronius' *Satyricon*, where Trimalchio himself reminds his guests "to live while it goes well with us."[75] Even so, the encroachment of imperial surveillance into the private social and emotional space of the upper class was notable under Domitian, who cleverly utilized the most essential of elite domestic rituals—the dinner party—to keep an eye on the group he most mistrusted.[76]

Finally, Collins points to considerable evidence that while drunkenness can indeed lead to violence, the vast majority of drunken experiences do not

70. Collins 2008: 242.

71. Ibid.

72. Champlin 2011.

73. Dio 67.8–9.

74. Fredrick 2003: 212–13.

75. Petron. *Sat.* 34.

76. Fredrick 2003: 214.

do so.[77] This is an important point to keep in mind concerning the ancient evidence as well. Not surprisingly, the most egregious examples of festal cruelty are the ones that we hear about, precisely because they were so lurid and sensational. But many *cenae* did not end in this way. Augustus, for example, was known for his genial and moderate banquets.[78] As Collins argues, it took someone who could dominate an entire space to steer it in a particular direction, whether good or bad. Again, in a Roman context, the emperor was best qualified to act in this way. These perspectives are most useful as points of contact between the ancient evidence and a theory of violence that is more complex than we can fully treat here. Even so, it is easy to see the value of modern approaches in helping us to sort out problematic behaviors that the ancients often merely reported without analysis.

Conclusion

I close here with an attempt to gain additional perspectives on the violence of the *cena* by briefly considering comparison with the Mafia, where, for generations, members of crime families have been routinely murdered or "whacked" by rivals for various transgressions, whether real or imagined. These executions have typically occurred at meals, and we must ask why. As Martin Parker has reminded us, men who eat and drink together form a very particular kind of community, one characterized by a strong sense of belonging.[79] In Mafia circumstances, the solidarity in the sharing of food becomes even more attractive and intense because it is in such close proximity to its absolute other—violent hostility.[80] In one of the most famous of the execution incidents, the New York gangster Joe "Crazy Joe" Gallo was gunned down by rivals while he enjoyed a late-night birthday meal with his family and friends at Umberto's Clam House in the Little Italy neighborhood of New York City in April 1972. Gallo, seated at a butcher-block table in the back of the restaurant, was shot five times before he staggered out to the street and died.[81] Umberto's Clam House, once known for its calamari, scungili, and mussels, thus came to be forever associated with one of the

77. Collins 2008: 263. For modern studies on drunkenness and violence, see Giancola 2013; Heath 2000; Parker and Rebhun 1995; Room 1998, 2001; Room and Rossow 2001.

78. Suet. *Aug.* 74.

79. Parker 2008: 990.

80. Ibid., 1003.

81. *New York Times*, May 3, 1972, 1.

more sensational Mafia murders in New York City history, while the image of the bloodied tablecloth was to become a powerful reminder of the proximity of commensality and raw violence.

Gangsters who are involved in a criminal enterprise and eat together present a set of initial circumstances different from Roman senators at the dining table. Even so, like the Mafiosi who were compelled to eliminate rival threats to power over a plate of spaghetti, Romans animated by concerns with rank, status, and political prestige also relied on the shared meal to sort out social and political complexities through violence. In the end, Roman festal conviviality was surely present, but, given the delicate boundaries between inclusion and exclusion and between fellowship and violence, it was fragile and could never be fully guaranteed. Seneca once famously remarked that "to eat without a friend was to live like a lion or a wolf."[82] But the irony was that the lion or the wolf might also be a poisoner or a political rival who could strike quickly and with deadly force precisely because the dining table was destined to remain a place of bloody violence and not just one of good cheer.

Works Cited

Alföldy, G. 2011. *Römische Sozialgeschichte*. 4th ed. Stuttgart.

Ascough, R. 2008. "Forms of Commensality in Greco-Roman Associations." *CW* 102: 33–45.

Beard, M. 2010. *The Fires of Vesuvius: Pompeii Lost and Found*. Cambridge, MA.

Bergmark, K., and Kuendig, H. 2008. "Pleasures of Drinking: A Cross-Cultural Perspective." *Journal of Ethnicity in Substance Abuse* 7: 131–53.

Boyle, A. "*Aeneid* 8: Images of Rome." In C. Perkell, ed., *Reading Vergil's "Aeneid": An Interpretive Guide*, 148–61. Norman, OK.

Broekaert, W., and Zuiderhoek, A. 2013. "Industries and Services." In P. Erdkamp, ed., *The Cambridge Companion to Ancient Rome*, 317–35. Cambridge.

Bryen, A. 2008. "Visibility and Violence in Petitions from Roman Egypt." *GRBS* 48: 181–200.

Champlin, E. 2011. "Sex on Capri." *TAPA* 141: 315–32.

Collins, R. 2008. *Violence: A Micro-sociological Theory*. Princeton.

Cresswell, T. 2004. *Place: A Short Introduction*. Malden.

Cunliffe, B. 1988. *Greeks, Romans, and Barbarians: Spheres of Interaction*. Swindon.

D'Arms, J. 1984. "Control, Companionship, and *Clientela*: Some Social Functions of the Roman Communal Meal." *EMC* 28: 327–48.

D'Arms, J. 1990. "The Roman *Convivium* and the Idea of Equality." In O. Murray, ed., Sympotica*: A Symposium on the* Symposion, 308–20. Oxford.

82. Sen. *Ep.* 1.19.

D'Arms, J. 1991. "Slaves at Roman *Convivia*." In W. Slater, ed., *Dining in a Classical Context*, 171–83. Ann Arbor.

D'Arms, J. 1995. "Heavy Drinking and Drunkenness in the Roman World: Four Questions for Historians." In O. Murray and M. Tecusan, eds., *In Vino Veritas*, 304–17. Rome.

D'Arms, J. 1999. "Performing Culture: Roman Spectacle and the Banquets of the Powerful." In B. Bergmann and C. Kondoleon, eds., *The Art of Ancient Spectacle*, 301–19. Studies in the History of Art 56. Washington, DC.

Dietler, M. 2006. "Alcohol: Anthropological/Archaeological Perspectives." *Annual Review of Anthropology* 35: 229–49.

Donahue, J. 2004. *The Roman Community at Table during the Principate*. Ann Arbor.

Donahue, J. 2011. "The Floating Feasts of Ancient Rome." In M. McWilliams, ed., *Celebrations: Proceedings of the Oxford Symposium on Food and Cookery*, 95–104. Devon.

Douglas, M., ed. 1987. *Constructive Drinking: Perspectives on Drink from Anthropology*. Cambridge.

Dunbabin, K. 1996. "Convivial Spaces: Dining and Entertainment in the Roman Villa." *JRA* 9: 66–80.

Dunbabin, K. 2003. *The Roman Banquet: Images of Conviviality*. Cambridge.

Elsner, J. 1994. "Constructing Decadence: The Representation of Nero as Imperial Builder." In J. Elsner and J. Masters, eds., *Reflections of Nero: Culture, History, and Representation*, 112–27. Chapel Hill.

Engs, R. 1995. "Do Traditional Western European Drinking Practices Have Origins in Antiquity?" *Addiction Research* 2: 227–39.

Fagan, G. 2011a. *The Lure of the Arena: Social Psychology and the Crowd at the Roman Games*. Cambridge.

Fagan G. 2011b. "Violence in Roman Social Relations." In M. Peachin, ed., *The Oxford Handbook of Social Relations in the Roman World*, 467–95. Oxford.

Fisher, N. 1992. Hybris*: A Study in the Values of Honour and Shame in Ancient Greece*. Warminster.

Fox, A. 2011. "The Origins of Drunkenness." In A. Fox and M. MacAvoy, eds., *Expressions of Drunkenness (Four Hundred Rabbits)*, 53–119. London.

Fredrick, D. 2003. "Architecture and Surveillance in Flavian Rome." In A. Boyle and W. Dominik, eds., *Flavian Rome: Culture, Image, Text*, 199–227. Leiden.

Gage, N. 1972. "Story of Joe Gallo's Murder." *New York Times*, May 3, 1.

Garnsey, P. 1970. *Social Status and Legal Privilege in the Roman Empire*. Oxford.

Giancola, P. 2013. "Alcohol and Aggression: Theories and Mechanisms." In M. McMurrin, ed., *Alcohol-Related Violence: Prevention and Treatment*, 39–59. Malden.

Gordon, R., Heim, D., and MacAskill, S. 2012. "Rethinking Drinking Cultures: A Review of Drinking Cultures and a Reconstructed Dimensional Approach." *Public Health* 126: 3–11.

Grimm-Samuel, V. 1991. "On the Mushroom That Deified the Emperor Claudius." *CQ* 41: 178–82.

Harries, J. 2007. *Law and Crime in the Roman World*. Cambridge.

Harris, W. 2001. *Restraining Rage: The Ideology of Anger Control in Classical Antiquity*. Cambridge, MA.

Heath, D. 2000. *Drinking Occasions: Comparative Perspectives on Alcohol and Culture*. Philadelphia.

Holloway, L., and Hubbard, P. 2000. *People and Place: The Extraordinary Geographies of Everyday Life*. New Jersey.

Hopkins, K. 1983. *Death and Renewal: Sociological Studies in Roman History*. Cambridge.

Horsfall, N. 2003. *The Culture of the Roman Plebs*. London.

Jayne, M., Valentine, G., and Holloway, S. 2011. *Alcohol, Drinking, Drunkenness: (Dis) orderly Spaces*. Surrey, UK.

Kaster, R. 2005. *Emotion, Restraint, and Community in Ancient Rome*. Oxford.

Kleijwegt, M. 1994. "Caligula's Triumph at Baiae." *Mnemosyne* 47: 652–71.

LaCombe, M. 2012. *Political Gastronomy: Food and Authority in the English Atlantic World*. Philadelphia.

Laurence, R. 2007. *Roman Pompeii: Space and Society*. 2nd ed. New York.

Lintott, A. 1999. *Violence in Republican Rome*. 2nd ed. Oxford.

MacAndrew, C., and Edgerton, R. 1969. *Drunken Comportment: A Social Explanation*. Chicago.

MacMullen, R. 1974. *Roman Social Relations, 50 BC to AD 284*. New Haven.

Malloch, S. 2001. "Gaius' Bridge at Baiae and Alexander-*imitatio*." *CQ* 51: 206–17.

Martin, A. 2009. *Alcohol, Violence, and Disorder in Traditional Europe*. Kirksville, MO.

Massaro, V., and Montgomery, A. 1978. "Caligula: Mad, Bad, Ill, or All Three?" *Latomus* 37: 894–909.

McGovern, P. 2009. *Uncorking the Past: The Quest for Wine, Beer, and Other Alcoholic Beverages*. Berkeley.

Miller, W. 1993. *Humiliation*. Ithaca, NY.

Murray, O., ed. 1990. Sympotica*: A Symposium on the* Symposion. Oxford.

Nippel, W. 1995. *Public Order in Ancient Rome*. Cambridge.

Osgood, J. 2011. *Claudius Caesar: Image and Power in the Early Roman Empire*. Cambridge.

Parker, M. 2008. "Eating with the Mafia: Belonging and Violence." *Human Relations* 61: 989–1006.

Parker, R., and Rebhun, L. 1995. *Alcohol and Homicide: A Deadly Combination of Two American Traditions*. Albany, NY.

Patterson, J. 2006. *Landscapes and Cities: Rural Settlement and Civic Transformation in Early Imperial Italy*. Oxford.

Perkell, C. 1999. "*Aeneid* 1: An Epic Programme." In C. Perkell, ed., *Reading Vergil's "Aeneid": An Interpretive Guide*, 29–49. Norman, OK.

Perry, J. 2011. "Organized Societies: *Collegia*." In M. Peachin, ed., *The Oxford Handbook of Social Relations in the Roman World*, 499–515. Oxford.

Plass, P. 1995. *The Game of Death in Ancient Rome: Arena Sport and Political Suicide*. Madison, WI.

Potter, D. 2009. *Ancient Rome: A New History*. New York.

Room, R. 1998. "Drinking Patterns and Alcohol-Related Social Problems: Frameworks for Analysis in Developing Societies." *Drug and Alcohol Review* 17: 389–98.

Room, R. 2001. "Intoxication and Bad Behaviour: Understanding Cultural Differences in the Link." *Social Science and Medicine* 53: 189–98.

Room, R., and Mäkelä, K. 2000. "Typologies of the Cultural Position of Drinking." *Journal of Studies on Alcohol* 61: 475–83.

Room, R., and Rossow, I. 2001. "The Share of Violence Attributable to Drinking: What Do We Need To Know and What Research Is Needed?" *Journal of Substance Abuse* 6: 218–28.

Saller, R. 1980. "Anecdotes as Historical Evidence for the Principate." *G&R* 27: 69–83.

Sherratt, E. 2004. "Feasting in Homeric Epic." *Hesperia* 73: 301–37.

Timonen, A. 1993. "The *Historia Augusta*: Two Faces of Violence." *Eos* 81: 83–92.

Timonen, A. 2000. *Cruelty and Death: Roman Historians' Scenes of Imperial Violence from Commodus to Phillipus Arabs*. Turku.

Tyner, J. 2012. *Space, Place, and Violence: Violence and the Embodied Geographies of Race, Sex, and Gender*. London.

Ulrich, K. 2007. "Food Fights." *History of Religions* 46: 228–61.

Unwin, T. 1991. *Wine and the Vine: An Historical Geography of Viticulture and the Wine Trade*. London.

van Nijf, O. 1997. *The Civic World of Professional Associations in the Roman East*. Amsterdam.

Vössing, C. 2004. *Mensa regia: Das Bankett beim hellenistischen König und beim römischen Kaiser*. Munich.

Wiedemann, T. 1992. *Emperors and Gladiators*. London.

Wilkinson, S. 2005. *Caligula*. London.

Wilson, T. 2005. *Drinking Cultures: Alcohol and Identity*. Oxford.

Winterling, A. 2011. *Caligula: A Biography*. Trans. D. Schneider, G. Most, and P. Psoinos. Berkeley.

Contributors

John Donahue is an associate professor and the chair of the Department of Classical Studies at the College of William and Mary in Virginia. His books, articles, and reviews deal with aspects of Roman social history, especially ancient health, diet, and dining practices. His most recent book is *Food and Drink in Antiquity: A Sourcebook of Readings from the Greco-Roman World* (2015).

Garrett G. Fagan is a professor of ancient history at Penn State University. He is the author of two monographs—*Bathing in Public in the Roman World* (1999) and *The Lure of the Arena: Social Psychology and the Crowd at the Roman Games* (2011)—and of numerous scholarly papers. His current project is a book on the political purge.

Peter Hunt is a professor of classics at the University of Colorado at Boulder. His publications include *Slaves, Warfare, and Ideology in the Greek Historians* (1998) and *War, Peace, and Alliance in Demosthenes' Athens* (2010). He is currently working on a college textbook on Greek and Roman slavery and a monograph on cultural and economic interactions between Athens and Thrace.

Noel Lenski is a professor of classics and history at Yale University. His publications include *Failure of Empire: Valens and the Roman State in the Fourth Century AD* (2002), *The Cambridge Companion to the Age of Constantine* (2006), and *Constantine and the Cities* (forthcoming).

Ellen Millender is a professor of classics and humanities at Reed College and specializes in archaic and classical Sparta. She has published articles on various aspects of Spartan society, including literacy, kingship, military organization, and women. Her recent work includes chapters on Spartan women and kingship for the forthcoming *Blackwell Companion to Sparta*. She is also working on a monograph entitled *The Strangest of the Greeks: The Spartans in the Democratic Athenian Imagination*.

Oswyn Murray is an emeritus fellow of Balliol College, Oxford, where he taught from 1968 to 2004, a fellow of the Royal Danish Academy, and the Scuola Normale di Pisa. He is the author of *Early Greece* (1980; 2nd ed., 1993) and studies of Hellenistic Greek political thought, the Greek *symposion*, and the history of classical scholarship from 1700 to the present day. He is an editor of numerous books, including *The Oxford History of the Classical World* (1986), *Sympotica* (1990), *The Greek City* (1990), and an edition of books 1–4 of Herodotus (2007).

Rosanna Omitowoju is a fellow of King's College, where she is currently an admissions tutor and director of studies in classics. She also runs all the language programs in the Faculty of Classics at Cambridge. She has published on women and law in Athens and on Greek drama, particularly Menander, though her most recent work has been a student reader for book 4 of Ovid's *Metamorphoses*.

Josiah Osgood is a professor of classics at Georgetown University. He is the author of *Caesar's Legacy: Civil War and the Emergence of the Roman Empire* (2006) and *Claudius Caesar: Image and Power in the Early Roman Empire* (2011).

David D. Phillips is an associate professor of history at the University of California, Los Angeles, with a research specialty in ancient Greek (primarily, but not exclusively, Athenian) law. His books include *Avengers of Blood: Homicide in Athenian Law and Custom from Draco to Demosthenes* (2008) and *The Law of Ancient Athens* (2013).

David Potter is a Francis W. Kelsey Collegiate Professor of Greek and Roman History, an Arthur F. Thurnau Professor of Greek and Latin, and the director of the Interdepartmental Program in Greek and Roman History at the University of Michigan at Ann Arbor. He got his AB at Harvard University and his DPhil from Oxford. His fields of study are Greek and Roman

Asia Minor, Greek and Latin historiography and epigraphy, Roman public entertainment, and warfare.

Werner Riess is a professor of Ancient History at the University of Hamburg, Germany. He is the author of *Apuleius und die Räuber: Ein Beitrag zur historischen Kriminalitätsforschung* (2001) and *Performing Interpersonal Violence: Court, Curse, and Comedy in Fourth-Century BCE Athens* (2012).

Matthew Trundle is a professor and the chair of the Department of Classics and Ancient History at the University of Auckland, New Zealand. His research interests are primarily in ancient Greek history, and his publications focus on the military, social, and economic aspects of the classical Greek world. He is the author of *Greek Mercenaries from the Late Archaic Period to Alexander* (2004) and has edited volumes entitled *New Perspectives on Ancient Warfare*, with Garrett G. Fagan (2010), and *Beyond the Gates of Fire: New Perspectives on the Battle of Thermopylae*, with Christopher Matthew (2013).

Graeme Ward currently teaches at McMaster University in Hamilton, Ontario. He received his PhD from the University of North Carolina at Chapel Hill in 2012. His research examines how violence and representations of authority shaped Roman military and social practices. He is working on a book based on his dissertation, "Centurions: The Practice of Roman Officership," which offers the first comprehensive study of Roman legionary centurions. His most recent article, in *Phoenix* (2013) and coauthored with Claude Eilers, examines the Caesarean administration of political and military rights and privileges in ancient Judaea.

Serena S. Witzke received her PhD from the University of North Carolina at Chapel Hill. She is currently a Visiting Assistant Professor in the Department of Classical Languages at Wake Forest University. She is interested in Greek and Roman New Comedy, women in antiquity, and classical reception. Her recent publications include "An Ideal Reception: Oscar Wilde, Menander's Comedy, and the Context of Victorian Classical Studies" (in Alan Sommerstein, ed., *Menander in Contexts* [2013]) and "Harlots, Tarts, and Hussies? A Problem of Terminology for Sex Labor in Roman Comedy" (*Helios* 42 [2015]).

Index

Terms with nearly synonymous meanings, which are categorized under one entry, are separated by a slash (e.g., wife/spouse). Morphologically related words are separated by a comma (e.g., senate, senator). Cross references are introduced by a period and *See also* (e.g., adultery. *See also* seduction). Entries are not provided for broad categories covered in designated sections of chapters (such as "baths").